To
Rev Dr. Leonard Kennedy CSB
Director
Center for Thomistic
Studies

— with kindest
personal regards

Francis J. Lescoe

I-MAN:
AN OUTLINE OF
PHILOSOPHICAL ANTHROPOLOGY

I-MAN:
AN OUTLINE OF
PHILOSOPHICAL ANTHROPOLOGY

by

Mieczysław A. Krąpiec, O.P., Ph.D., D.D.
President-Rector, University of Lublin

Translated by

Marie Lescoe, Andrew Woznicki, Theresa Sandok et al.

MARIEL PUBLICATIONS

New Britain   Connecticut

Library of Congress Catalog Card No. 83-60961

Krąpiec, Mieczysław A., *I-Man: An Outline of Philosophical Anthropology,* trans. by Marie Lescoe, Andrew Woznicki, Theresa Sandok et al.

ISBN 0-910919-01-1

I-Man: An Outline of Philosophical Anthropology is a translation by M. Lescoe, A. Woznicki, T. Sandok et al. of *Ja-Człowiek. Zarys antropologii filozoficznej* by M. A. Krąpiec, Lublin: Towarzystwo Naukowe Katolickiego Uniwersytetu Lubelskiego, 1979.

Acknowledgements
Grateful acknowledgment is made to the following publishers for permission to quote from copyrighted material: René Descartes, *Discourse on Method* and *Meditations.* Indianapolis, 1960 © by The Liberal Arts Press; Etienne Gilson, *Elements of Christian Philosophy.* Garden City, New York, 1960, © by Doubleday and Co.; *Works of C. G. Jung.* London, 1953 © by Routledge and Kegan Paul; C. Lévi-Strauss, *The Savage Mind.* Chicago, 1968, © by University of Chicago Press; Plato: *The Collected Dialogues,* ed. E. Hamilton and H. Cairns. Princeton, 1961 © by Princeton University Press; P. Teilhard de Chardin, "The Phenomenon of Spirituality," *Human Energy.* London, 1969 © by Collins Ltd.; C. Thompson, *Psychoanalysis' Evolution and Development.* New York, 1950 © by Thomas Nelson and Sons. Paul-Louis Landsberg, *The Experience of Death,* trans. Cynthia Rowland. New York, 1953 © by Philosophical Library Inc.

1 2 3 4 5 6 7 8 9 (Current Printing: first digit.)

Distributed by:
MARIEL PUBLICATIONS
196 Eddy Glover Boulevard
New Britain, CT 06053

TRANSLATORS' FOREWORD

About thirty years ago, a group of Polish philosophers at the University of Lublin, undertook to formulate a system of thought which would incorporate the best of the *nova et vetera*. The resulting philosophy is referred to as *Lublin Thomism, Lublin Existentialism* or *Lublin Existential Personalism*. Lublinism is a striking synthesis of two disparate components: (1) Thomistic realist metaphysics, as interpreted by Etienne Gilson and Jacques Maritain and (2) the best insights of contemporary phenomenological existentialism and hermeneutics.

This new Existential Personalism was established as the basis for the philosophical curricula in all diocesan seminaries in Poland. The Polish hierarchy, under the late Stefan Cardinal Wyszyński, was so convinced of the crucial role that the new philosophy should play in the education of its future priests, that it mandated that all candidates for the priesthood should earn forty-eight credits (the American equivalent of a major and minor) in Lublin existentialism.

The decision of the Polish bishops is bearing fruit today. The clergy are incorporating this Lublin Thomistic philosophy into their preaching and catechesis of the people; they are translating philosophical principles into everyday practical application. As a result, Poland has a cadre of superiorly trained spiritual leaders. Its seminaries are filled to capacity (in stark contrast to the bleak American scene). Last year, Poland ordained more priests than all the other Western European countries combined. It is now "exporting" priests to the Third World countries, as well as to such "missionary" lands as the United States and Canada.

Because this new philosophy still remains in its original Polish (about 15 lengthy volumes), only a handful of English speaking scholars have been aware of this vibrant system of thought forged behind the cultural Iron Curtain in Lublin.

In the 1978 Spring issue of the journal of the American Catholic

Philosophical Association (*New Scholasticism*), there appeared an article entitled, "Dialogistic Thomism and Dialectical Marxism" by a Lublin alumnus, Rev. Andrew N. Woznicki, currently Professor of Philosophy at the University of San Franscisco. To our knowledge, this article marks the first time that English speaking scholars as a group, became aware of the new Lublin philosophy. A short time later, a joint meeting of the Catholic Philosophical Societies and Polish Catholic Philosophers, which convened in Kraków under the auspices of the American Catholic Philosophical Association and the then Cardinal of Kraków, Karol Wojtyła (Pope John Paul II) initiated a very small number of scholars into the basic tenets of Lublinism. Pope John Paul II's *The Acting Person* appeared in translation the following year.

The reaction to Dr. Woznicki's article was both positive and enthusiastic. For several years, seminary leaders from throughout the country had been holding Workshops under the leadership of Fr. Ronald D. Lawler, O.F.M. Cap., Ph.D., Director of the Institute for Advanced Studies in Christian Doctrine at St. John's University, New York, in order to diagnose the malaise of our American seminary system. The meetings, which had been held at St. Louis, Toronto, Washington and Houston, agreed on two pivotal points: (1) Seminary theological education is in disarray. (2) The failure in theology is due to a dismantling of the seminary philosophical curriculum. The recommendation was unequivocal: We must begin with a reorganization of the philosophical component of the seminarian's education if we wish to improve his theological training.

Fr. Woznicki's article, which pointed to the strengths of the Lublin philosophy and its role in developing a vigorous and vibrant Catholicism, seemed to be a providential answer to the beleaguered American seminary leaders. The direct result of the article was the establishment of the *International Center for Lublin (KUL) Translations*. Its aim was to inaugurate the translation of the Lublin philosophy texts and to adapt them for use in our American and Canadian seminary curricula.

TRANSLATION PROJECT

The first work which the Editorial Board selected for translation was the present volume, *Ja-Człowiek. Zarys antropologii filozoficznej (I-Man. An Outline of Philosophical Anthropology)*, a Philosophy of Man text by Mieczysław A. Krąpiec (Crúmp-yes), President-Rector of the University of Lublin since 1970. Fr. Krąpiec is the founder and leader of the so-called Lublin School of Philosophy which includes such original thinkers as Kalinowski, Kaminski, Swiezawski, and Karol Wojtyła (Pope John Paul II).

I-Man was selected because there have been recurring demands for a suitable Philosophy of Man text for use in our American and Canadian seminaries. (Dr. Krąpiec has also authored a highly significant *Metaphysics* (550 pp.), in addition to 10 other volumes in Philosophy). Four other Lublin works are in the process of translation. They include: *Człowiek i religia (Man and Religion)* by Dr. Zofia Zdybicka. (The first draft of the entire translation has been completed by Dr. Theresa Sandok.) Two other works in Ethics, i.e., *Etyka niezależna? (An Independent Ethics?)* and *ABC etyki (The ABC's of Ethics)* by Dr. Tadeusz Styczeń, who succeeded Pope John Paul II to the Chair of Ethics at Lublin University. The fourth book is *Metafizyka. Zarys teorii bytu (Metaphysics. An Outline of the Theory of Being)* by Mieczysław A. Krąpiec.

In order to expedite the translation of the first volume, the Board decided to "team-translate" the work, since almost all of the volunteer scholars were engaged in full time teaching.

In a comparatively short time, the translators found the author's style extremely difficult to render into "readable" English. Several factors were responsible. First, not unlike German periodic sentences, Krąpiec's philosophical Polish abounds in sentences which are 10 to 12 lines of print in length. Many of these defy a "re-casting" into three or four short sentences in English. Secondly, the author uses a large number of philosophical terms strongly reminiscent of Heideggerian hyphenated neologisms (the longest extending to full four lines of type). Again, the shortage and even complete lack of appropriate words in the English language made the rendition of metaphysical nuances and precisions extremely difficult.

To cite a case in point: Polish, Greek, Latin and German denote being as the "act of to be" respectively as *bytowość, ἔιναι, esse,* and *Sein.* There is another set of terms which indicate being, understood substantively: they are *byt, τὸ ὄν, ens, Seiende.* The English language, on the other hand, is very impoverished in this respect. It has only one word "being" to indicate both the substantive and the "act of to be." After much consultation with the author, the Board decided to resort to Etienne Gilson's use of the term "be-ing" for *bytowość, ἔιναι, esse, Sein.* It was decided to use "being" for the translation of *byt, τὸ ὄν, ens, Seiende.*

The English language is similarly deficient in the translation of *człowiek, ἄνθρωπος, homo, der Mensch,* on the one hand, and *mężczyzna, ἄνηρ, vir, der Mann,* on the other. English is limited to the use of one word "man" to indicate both a member of the human race without regard to gender and to the male of the human species. Philosophically *osoba* (person) cannot be substituted for *człowiek* (man). This is why the title of the present work reads *I-Man.*

The final difficulty encountered by the translators was a number of completely new Polish words, which the author had coined from the Greek. Since no Polish lexicon contained these terms and because of the complexity of philosophical terminology used by Fr. Krąpiec, Dr. Andrew Woznicki undertook a trip to the University of Lublin, where he spent more than a month consulting with the author. The result of these consultations was the establishment of a *Glossary* and the Board is reasonably confident that they have not become *translatores traductores*.

NOTANDUM

The reader will note that this volume departs somewhat from the customary single bibliography which includes all titles cited in a book. The author of *I-Man* has furnished us with twelve specialized bibliographies, one for each chapter, in addition to a short general listing. Titles which have been cited in footnotes do not, as a rule, appear again in the bibliographies. In all, this *Outline* of Philosophical Anthropology contains approximately 1,000 titles in eight languages.

ACKNOWLEDGMENTS

The present volume is truly a *labor amoris* on the part of the translators who so generously gave their services *gratis* to this undertaking. The Board hereby acknowledges its debt of gratitude to these dedicated scholars. In particular, the Board is indebted for special services rendered by the following:

ANDREW WOZNICKI. The Board is immeasurably indebted to Dr. Andrew N. Woznicki, without whose efforts, Lublin Existentialism would still remain unknown, for the greater part, to the English speaking world. As we have indicated, his article, "Dialogistic Thomism and Dialectical Marxism" first alerted the English academic community to this new Christian philosophy. The present translation of *I-Man* owes its existence almost totally to his indefatigable efforts. He has personally read and checked for philosophical accuracy the entire text as well as all the footnotes of the translation. The crucially important *Glossary* is the result of his efforts. He has even assisted the Board in coining several English words to express difficult metaphysical nuances in the Polish text. His monograph, *A Christian Humanism: Karol Wojtyla's Existential Personalism* is, without question, the best exposition in the English language of his former teacher's Lublinism. Both the University of Lublin and the entire English speaking community of scholars are in debt to this self-effacing philosopher. His total dedication to the Translation Project has been a source of inspiration to the entire Board.

ZOFIA ZDYBICKA. To Dr. Zofia Zdybicka, Professor of Philosophy of Religion at the University of Lublin, the Board owes a debt of gratitude not only for the masterful presentation, *Man and Religion*, but also for assistance in up-dating all the bibliographies of *I-Man*.

BOLESŁAW KUMOR. The Board expresses its deep appreciation to Rev. Dr. Bolesław Kumor, Professor of History at the University of Lublin and author of the definitive four volume *History of the Catholic Church in Poland*. During his annual visits to the United States, Dr. Kumor has given the Board invaluable advice, encouragement and assistance.

WŁADYSŁAW STRÓŻEWSKI. Dr. Władysáw Stróżewski, Professor of Philosophy at the Jagellonian University, and former student of the Polish phenomenologist, Roman Ingarden, has rendered our translators incalculable service in connection with the rendition of passages from his teacher's *Spór o istnienie świata*. The Board gratefully acknowledges this kindness.

DAVID LIPTAK. Rev. Dr. David Q. Liptak, Chairman of the Theology Department at Holy Apostles Seminary, Cromwell, Connecticut, Consulting Editor of *The Catholic Transcript* and nationally known homilist has done the editorial work for the entire book. Since the translation is a "composite" of a number of different styles, Dr. Liptak read and revised the entire manuscript for stylistic uniformity. The Board is deeply grateful to Fr. Liptak for this contribution.

WILLIAM HART and ROGER DUNCAN. The Board wishes to thank Rev. Dr. William Hart, Professor of English at St. Joseph College, West Hartford, Connecticut and Dr. Roger Duncan, Professor of Philosophy at the University of Connecticut in West Hartford for their invaluable insights and suggestions concerning the translation of certain difficult metaphysical terms, used by the author of *I-Man*.

Many other individuals have aided, in various ways, in making this translation a reality and the Board wishes to express its gratitude to the following: His Eminence Władysław Cardinal Rubin, Cardinal Prefect of the Sacred Congregation for the Oriental Churches; Most Reverend John F. Whealon,

Sedes Sapientiae Institute, Rome; Rev. Edward Gicewicz, C.M., Brooklyn, New York; Dr. James Byrne, Chairman, Philosophy Department, St. John's University, Jamaica, New York; Marie Mulcahy, Barry Bostedor, and Kathy King, Marketing Executive, Account Specialist, and Coordinator respectively of BookCrafters, Chelsea, Michigan.

Rev. Francis J. Lescoe, Ph.D.
Director

THE EDITORIAL BOARD IS PREPARING AN ABRIDGED EDITION (app. 200 pp) of *I-MAN* FOR USE AS A STUDENT TEXTBOOK.

*The Editorial Board wishes to express its gratitude
to the Reverend Leo J. Kinsella
of Our Lady of the Snows, Chicago, Illinois
for financial assistance in the printing of this volume.*

CONTENTS

CHAPTER I—AT THE ORIGINS OF THE THEORY OF MAN

CHAPTER II—THE HUMAN FACT

CHAPTER III—ATTEMPTS TO INTERPRET THE HUMAN FACT

CHAPTER XI—THE PERSON AN EGO OF A RATIONAL NATURE

CHAPTER XII—THE HUMAN BEING IN THE PERSPECTIVE OF DEATH

APPENDIX—NOTES ON THE METAPHILOSOPHY OF MAN
by Stanisław Kamiński

M. A. KRĄPIEC

Mieczysław Albert KRĄPIEC, (Cruḿp-yes) O.P., Ph.D., D.D., was born May 25, 1921 in Berezòwice Mała near Zbaraz and Tarnopol (Podole—now in the Soviet Union). After receiving a classical education in Tarnopol, he entered the Dominican Order in 1939. In 1946, he became Professor of Philosophy at the Philosophical Institute of the Dominican Province in Kraków. Five years later (1951), he was appointed Professor of Philosophy at the Catholic University of Lublin. He served three terms as Dean of the School of Philosophy and in 1970, he was elected President Rector of the University of Lublin, the only Catholic university in the entire Soviet bloc.

Fr. Krąpiec's area of specialization is in metaphysics and philosophical anthropology. For nearly forty years, he has lectured and written widely on the entire range of the theory of real and analogical being.

He has explained the human phenomenon with deep acumen, by drawing on the rich anthropological material contained in the general theory of being. Pivotal to this analysis is the experience of the "I" as subject of one's actions and in which the "I" is simultaneously immanent and transcendent. Such a position, to which Thomas Aquinas had already alluded in his *Summa Theologiae* I, q. 75, a. 1–2), enables us to go beyond a one-sided conception of man. In this way, Fr. Krąpiec has succeeded in constructing a theory of being which is thoroughly classical in content, yet modern in its formulation.

The author has been acclaimed as the organizer and undisputed head of the so-called Lublin School of Philosophy. Together with Jerzy Kalinowski, Stefan Świeżawski, Stanisław Kamiński and Cardinal Karol Wojtyła (Pope John Paul II), he has published a series of studies in philosophy which view contemporary problems in their historical perspective. Chief among these is a genuine Christian humanism which recognizes man's proper place in reality and insures his basic human rights.

Fr. Krąpiec's work has provided an impetus to studies in classical philosophy which are, at once, new and attractive in content and formulation. As such, they provide a most effective antidote to the numerous scientisms and ecclecticisms which pose as genuine philosophical systems of thought.

Dr. Krąpiec is the author of 13 volumes in philosophy and of more than 150 articles and monographs in various Polish and foreign journals.

MAJOR PUBLICATIONS

Realizm ludzkiego poznania (The Realism of Human Knowledge). Poznań, 1959, Pp. 652.

Teoria analogii bytu (Theory of the Analogy of Being). Lublin, Pp. 415.

Dlaczego zło? (Why Evil? Philosophical Reflections), Kraków, 1962. Pp. 190; French translation, *Pourqui le mal?*, Paris, 1967. Pp. 227.

Co-author: *Z teorii i metodologii metafizyki (Selected Problems in the Theory and Methodology of Metaphysics*. Lublin, 1962. Pp. 412.

Struktura bytu. Charakterystyczne elementy systemu Arystotelesa i Tomasza z Akwinu (The Structure of Being. Characteristic Elements of the Systems of Aristotle and Thomas Aquinas). Lublin, 1963. Pp. 361.

Co-author: *Arsitotelesowska koncepcja substancji (The Aristotelian Conception of Substance)*. Lublin, 1966. Pp. 214.

Metafizyka. Wybór podstawowych zagadnień (Metaphysics. A Selection of Fundamental Problems). Poznań, 1966. Pp. 558.

Tomasz z Akwinu. De ente et essentia. Przekład-komentarz-studia (Thomas Aquinas. De ente et essentia. Translation-Commentary-Study), Lublin, 1981. Pp. 164.

Człowiek—kultura—uniwersytet (Man-Culture-University). Lublin, 1982. Pp. 450.

Język i rzeczywistość (Language and Reality). In preparation.

Człowiek i prawo naturalne (Man and Natural Law), Lublin, 1975. Pp. 259.

Metafizyka. Zarys teorii bytu (Metaphysics. An Outline of the Theory of Being. Lublin, 1978. Pp. 549.

THE TRANSLATORS

Marie E. Lescoe, Ph.D. (Fordham University). Professor Emerita, Central Connecticut State University, New Britain, Connecticut.

Rev. Andrew N. Woznicki, Ph.D. (University of Toronto). Professor of Philosophy, University of San Francisco, California.

Theresa H. Sandok, O.S.M., Ph.D. (University of Notre Dame). Professor of Philosophy, Bellarmine College, Louisville, Kentucky.

Rev. Stephen Minkiel, C.M., Ph.D. (Angelicum). Chairman, Philosophy Department, Gannon University, Erie, Pennsylvania.

Frances Tuszynska, Ph.D. (University of Toronto). Los Angeles, California.

Richard J. Fafara, Ph.D. (University of Toronto). Washington, D.C.

Joseph Koterski, Ph.D. (St. Louis University). Professor of Philosophy, University of St. Thomas, Houston, Texas.

Rev. Janusz Ihnatowicz, S.T.L., Th.M. (University of Ottawa). Professor of Theology, University of St. Thomas, Houston, Texas.

Sr. M. Consolata, C.S.S.F., M.A. (Jagellonian University) Enfield, Connecticut.

Rev. Stephen Ptaszynski, M. Div. Terryville, Connecticut.

Stella Kornacki, M.A. Terryville, Connecticut.

Rev. Francis J. Lescoe, Ph.D. (University of Toronto). Chairman, Philosophy Department, Holy Apostles Seminary for Adult Vocations, Cromwell, Connecticut. Director of Lublin Project.

LIST OF ABBREVIATIONS

CWJ—*Collected Works of C. G. Jung*. London: Routledge and Kegan Paul, 1953.

KUL—Katolicki Uniwersytet Lubelski

NECW—Karl Marx/Friedrich Engels, *Collected Works*. New York: International Publishers, 1975.

PG—*Patrologiae Cursus Completus*. Accurante J. P. Migne; *Series Graeca*. Parisiis apud Garnier et Migne, 1886. 162 volumes.

PL—*Patrologiae Cursus Completus*. Accurante J. P. Migne; *Series Latina*. Parisiis apud Garnier et Migne, 1878. 221 volumes.

SCG—*Sancti Thomae de Aquino Doctoris Angelici Summa Contra Gentiles*. Editio Leonina Manualis. Romae, 1934.

ST—*Sancti Thomae de Aquino Summa Theologiae*. Textus editionis Leoninae cum adnotationibus fontium . . . ex editione altera Canadiensi Ottawa 1953. Romae: Alba, Editiones Paulinae, 1962.

SECPWSF—*The Standard Edition of the Complete Psychological Works of Sigmund Freud*. London: Hogarth Press, 1955.

GLOSSARY OF TERMS

act, spontaneous—*akt wyłoniony (actus elicitus)*; demanded act—*akt nakazany* (actus imperatus) as an act that is "demanded."

agent—*czynnik* as factor, element or constituent feature, never as cause.

be-ing—*bytowość* referring to the "beingness" of a thing; its act of "to be," *esse, Sein.*

being—contingent—*byt przygodny;* in the order of being—*na polu bytu.*

cause, efficient—*przyczyna sprawszcza (causa efficiens).*

cognition—*poznanie,* indicating relation to object, hence spontaneous; whereas knowledge (*wiedza*) involving both object and subject—more generic and result of reflection.

community—*spólnota; społeczeństwo*—society (more political); *społeczność*—society as a natural group.

content—*treść;* _____, of a thing — *treść rzeczy;* also as sense and essence.

concept—*pojęcie* (sometimes rendered also as "notion."

creation—*stworzenie* as God's creation "*ex nihilo*"; *tworzenie*—an artist's creation (from previously existing matter).

designation—*oznaczenie;* whereas *znaczenie*—signification.

dynamization (dynamic)—*spotencjalizowanie*—referring to the process of actualizing one's potentialities; cf. K. Wojtyla, *The Acting, Person,* pp. 60–101.

ego (sometimes "I")—*jaźn*—used in the sense of traditional and classical philosophy as "the complete man, body and soul, the conscious and permanent subject of one's own psychical actions and experiences."

experience—*przeżycie*

expression—*wyraz, wyrażenie* (as against *wypowiedź*—utterance).

general—*ogólność;* generality—*powszechność,* also universality.

impression—*wrażenie* (as in D. Hume).

individuality—*twarz*

justification—*uzasadnienie*

knowledge—*wiedza*—more generic and applying to both object and subject; (cognition—*poznanie* as applying to object and spontaneous in character.

meaning—*sens o ile umyśle.*

—*treść*—in Husserl, equivalent to *Inhalt,* sometimes *Materie.*

moral rectitude—*prawe pożądanie.*

non-contradictable—*uniesprzeczniający.*

notional—*treściowy,* referring to cognitive contents.

"objectivistically"—*rzeczowo* (not objectively).

phronetic—*fronetyczny*—Polish neologism from Greek φρόνησις, closest English rendering "prudential."

poietic—*pojetyczny,* Polish neologism from Greek ποιείν; closest English rendering, "productive."

production—*wytworzenie*

psychic—*psychiczny,* from Greek ψυχή in the sense of belonging to the soul (not in the sense of "a psychic.")

purpose (end)—*cel* as goal, aim, intent.

reason of being—*racja bytu (raison d'être).*

reason, theoretical and practical—*sąd teoretyczny i sąd praktyczny.*

relation (coordination, correspondence)—*przyporządkowanie* when taken in general (*ogólne*); sometimes "subordination," depending on context.

representation (in knowledge)—*przedstawienie* which can be *wyobraźenie* as "*imago*" or *pojęcie* as "concept" and sometimes as "notion."

self-cognition—*samowiedza;* A. Woznicki, *A Christian Humanism. Karol Wojtyła's Existential Personalism,* pp. 12–15; 17 ff. K. Wojtyła, *The Acting Person,* pp. 35 ff.

signification—*znaczenie,* whereas *oznaczenie*—designation.

society—*społeczeństwo* (more political); *społeczność*—society as natural group; *spólnota*—community.

subjectivity, subjectivization—*podmiotowanie*

subsistence—*samoistność,* as against *samodziałność*—self-independence.

utterance—*wypowiedź,* as against *wyraz, wyraźenie*—expression.

CHAPTER I

AT THE ORIGINS OF THE THEORY OF MAN*

Different intellectual interests dominated different periods of history. Antiquity and the Mediaeval Ages were periods of development in philosophical and theological concepts. The Renaissance favored the development of *belles-lettres*. The present age prefers technological studies. For other natural sciences, like physico-chemistry and biology—as well as humanistic studies, especially sociology and psychology—are also, to a great extent ancillary to technocracy. For the conditions of contemporary life, e.g., the population explosion, the shrinking of the world resulting from the new means of communication, force man to apply—to the highest degree—his study toward the organization of the most complicated demands of human life. Hence, it is no surprise that today, those studies are valued most which show themselves to be most directly useful for human living in an urban civilization, which is the most typical human environment.

The preference of studies that have an immediate practical application and which are understood from a completely technocratic and sociological point of view cannot, however, deny the value of other areas of knowledge. For man works and thinks, not merely so that his life might become more comfortable and useful since—beyond usefulness, comfort and functionalization—there exist other never-aging values, whose object is man himself. And the noblest human action—knowledge as such, love and creativity—are those essentially human values which cannot be treated from a purely pragmatic point of view. Further, the highest expression of the human per-

---

*Translator's Note: "man" is the English equivalent of the Polish *człowiek*, which is synonymous with ἄνθρωπος, *homo, der Mensch*. As such, it includes all human beings, both masculine and feminine genders.

1

son: contemplation of truth and beauty, along with the attainment of the good has always been recognized as the most eminent goal of man's life.

Those studies whose subject of investigation is man himself and his cultural creations (therefore humanistic studies), cannot become outmoded. For man in himself, in his most human activities and happenings, is an interesting and most significant subject matter of knowledge. We do not know ourselves directly; we do not have a direct intuition of our nature; but we can get to know ourselves through our activities and creativity. An indirect way of getting to know man through his activities and creativity can show us who man is, what the meaning of his life is, what his essential functions and the conditions for their attainment are, and what man's destiny is. This will be the chief subject of our considerations in this book. First, however, we must review the sources of the various concepts of man which have arisen in Western European cultural circles.

I. RELIGIOUS ORIGINS OF THE THEORY OF MAN

The first indications of a concept of man, in Western European culture, appeared against the background of religious beliefs and experiences.

Above all, Sacred Scripture—both the Old Testament and New Testament—constitutes a doctrinal source on views concerning man. According to the Biblical conception, man is a special product of God's creativity. It is around man that the world-drama is enacted—a drama in which God takes part and, even further, that he became Incarnate, in order to give the utimate "meaning" to human life. This life is completely meaningless if it is separated from God.

From the very beginning of the Bible, we learn that man was created "to the image and likeness of God," and that man's lot was completely linked to God in all its essentially human aspects. The foundation for this bond between man's lot and God is man's "soul," which God himself breathed directly into a form of the body ("from the slime of the earth"). Man's soul is indeed that abode, where the inner communion with God takes place. Naturally, the concept of "soul" and of human being undergoes a fuller clarification in subsequent pages of the Old and New Testament.[1]

First, from a general understanding of the term RUAH as a soul which is a supersubjective reality (almost a divine soul), develops a concept of NEPHESZ, as an individual, immortal soul which is joined to BASAR. As a result, man now appears as an ontic unity.[2] But under the influence of Hellenic thought, there appears an idea of a kind of anthropological dualism: "Bloody political upheavals of the Second and First Centuries B.C. had discredited earthly reward as the purpose of a religious-ethical life. Hope for a happy life beyond the grave found justification in a dualistic Hellenic anthropology. And so, the authors of the Books of *Maccabees* and of *Wisdom* use a traditionally anthropological terminology when they express, at the same time, a hope in the resurrection of the body, a happy life for the soul, or when they oppose bodily sufferings with the happiness of the soul. (II *Macc*. 6, 30)"[3]

The question of man and his soul is further developed in the New Testament. From the concept of NEPHESZ (PSYCHE) as a biological element, the emphasis on man is transferred to RUAH (PNEUMA), as a spiritual element, directing man from within to supernatural ends. The New Testament describes the soul as *anima spiritualis,* the object of divine intervention and divine destiny. The PNEUMA, thus understood, is completely bound, according to St. Paul, with the life and works of Christ.[4]

A second set of sources of anthropology in the Western European cultural milieu are Orphic beliefs which replaced—or even transformed—the earlier Shamanistic folk beliefs of the Greeks.[5] We find traces of them in Homer's period. Homer's man is subjected to stormy experiences, hypostasized in the form of the two deities THYMOS, which expresses drives and feelings, and NOUS, expressing intelligence. Man possesses a soul *(psyche)* which is the element of life. (Homer generally identifies life with *psyche.)* Man lives only on this earth. After death, his "shade" enters the netherworld, where it loses consciousness. (It can regain it when the shade "drinks" sacrificial blood, whence shades have need of sacrifices.) Homer also knows the concept of *pneuma,* which man loses with the last breath of life.[6]

According to Orphic tradition, the soul enters man's body by breaking away from the divine cosmos, borne on the wings of the winds and it dwells in man for a short period of life. After that, it returns to its cosmic source, to "TOTALITY" with which it merges upon its return. In Orphic language, the soul comes from Zeus and it returns to Zeus. The body is understood as a prison of the soul—its temporary tomb—from which it wants to free itself by means of ascetics and ethical ritual observances.[7] The Orphics are the first of the Greek world to be representatives of a dualism: (i.e.,) body-soul, in that by "psyche" they understand not only biological life but also a psychical one, in a sense which is very close to our contemporary meaning.[8]

In Orphic circles, there also arose a belief—perhaps under the influence of Eastern thought—in the transmigration of souls. And because the soul is a part of the cosmic god (it came from him and will return to him), it possesses a life which does not belong to the body. The soul only passes through the body; it is not an entity which is bound to the body. The soul has a different origin—a divine one. (In tombs of the Pythagorean era—the

Pythagoreans had accepted and formed the Orphic religion—there have been discovered gold utensils with inscriptions professing the belief, "I am of divine origin").[9]

A certain relationship can be detected between the Orphic religion and the Platonic and Aristotelian notions of the soul. In the Ionic School, i.e., in the case of Anaximenes, Orphic religious thought is combined with philosophical reasoning. Orphic religious thought linked man with God, i.e., with Zeus. The philosophical reasoning of this thought indicated that Zeus is, indeed, the entire universe and that the human soul is only one part of this cosmic, pantheistic God. As we well know, this school was investigating the nature of the cosmos, of which man became aware during this era. And while the whole universe appeared to Anaximander to be emerging from the APEIRON, as its limited manifestation, which is also divine, Anaximenes called attention to the fact that life is precisely the divine element of the APEIRON. Just as the soul animates man (a fact that is evident in breathing), so the element of the APEIRON is "life," i.e., the soul which is symbolized by air. Heraclitus will advance one step further, when he will make this cosmic god "Logos" *the self-conscious law,* which directs the course of the entire universe and of all men.[10]

With Anaximenes, there appeared in Greek philosophy the notion of a very intimate connection between the inner man—his psyche—and "all the rest," i.e., the cosmic god. Hence, this inner life of the self, this self-witness of the soul about itself, and the uniform motion of the heavenly bodies are —according to Aristotle's later pronouncements—the ultimate source of our knowledge about God.[11]

The concept of the soul was further developed in the area of philosophy: among the Pythagoreans, who understood the soul as ARYTHMOS —number, a perfect proportion which was the source of motion from within. It was developed further with Heraclitus, who joined the LOGOS of the microcosm with the LOGOS of the macrocosm. The concept of the soul was also developed, finally, with Anaxagoras, who identified the NOUS, which is one and the same for all, with the human *psyche.*[12]

II. THE PLATONIC CONCEPT OF MAN

Along with the development of Orphism and Pythagoreanism, there is also the Platonic concept of man as one who exemplifies and represents, in the most general outlines, the structure of the entire cosmos. If we observe in the cosmos a changeless reality in itself—the Ideas—and, at the same time, a changeable, material world, man is likewise a reflection of this cosmic dualism. Man is a union of body and soul. The human soul is tripartite: intellectual, spirited and vegetative.[13] Animals possess a sensible-spirited soul and plants possess a vegetative soul. The essential element that differentiates man from all living things is his intellectual soul.

Plato's tripartite division of the soul was connected with his concept of the State and the three basic classes: the wise men, who were capable of governing, the military class who was charged with the protection of the State, and the artisans and peasants, whose obligation it was to support the higher classes.[14] The intellectual soul is not the exclusive possession of man, since the daemonia and heavenly bodies also possess intellectual souls. The essential function of the soul is to animate the body. Plato accepted this concept of the soul as agent of life, from the earlier Ionic philosophers. Besides the function of life, which is auto-kinesis or the immanent ability to put oneself into motion, Plato designated a strictly immaterial function of the soul, namely knowing the world of Ideas. He writes that the soul does not have a distinct organ of knowledge but, through and by itself, it sees the common properties of all things. It is not the body that knows but, rather, the soul ". . . that while we are in the body and while our soul is infected with the evils of the body, our desire will never be satisfied. And our desire is the truth. For the body is a source of endless troubles to us. . . . It has been proved to us by experience that if we would have pure knowledge of anything, we must be quit of the body—the soul in herself must behold things in themselves . . . for if while in company with the body, the soul cannot have pure knowledge, one of two things follows—either knowledge is not to be attained at all, or, if at all, after death. For then, and not until then, the soul will be parted from the body and exist in herself alone."[15] Neither the body nor any other organ is capable of understanding the immaterial, necessary, universal and immutable Ideas. Plato thus united the concept of the soul with the entire realm of knowing the Ideas, and thus he took a new and essential step in the understanding of man.

In addition, Plato accepted Orphic, religious, personal conceptions. Hence, the soul is a being which existed previously without the body. The soul was weighed down by some sin or transgression and hence, it was sent to the body to be liberated. (There is present here an important ethical moment in the area of redemption.) When the sin is atoned for, the soul becomes free. Plato describes endless activities of the soul, its various incarnations, judgment after death, change of bodies etc. To make all this understandable, he accepted the immateriality of the soul and its fundamental opposition to the body, its independence of the body and its simplicity— when we speak of the sublimest aspect of the soul—whether it be intelligence or its immortality. In a word, man is a soul governing the body like a sailor in a ship or a rider on a horse.[16]

As a result of his views concerning the soul, Plato's theory of man must be described as a dualism which found its expression in its ontological and epistemological positions.

III. ARISTOTLE'S THEORY OF MAN

In Cicero's *Tusculanae Disputationes,* I, 10, 22, we find mention that, in the first period of his life, Aristotle was under the obvious influence of Plato in the area of the problematics of anthropology. Specifically, he accepted the existence of the soul as an eternal source of motion and he called such a soul ENTELECHEIA. *"Quintum genus (Aristoteles) adhibens vocans nomine et sic ipsum animum entelecheiam appellat novo nomine quasi quandam continuatam motionem et perennem."* (After having accepted the fifth category, Aristotle termed the soul "entelechy" and he recognized it as the eternal and never-ending source of motion.) Once he began to direct his own thinking, Aristotle also changed his notion of the soul.

In discussing Platonism, as we know, Aristotle attacked, above all else, in his *Metaphysics,* the theory of Ideas as the prototypes and as both the objects of intellectual knowledge, as well as the reason for this knowledge. By showing that the theory of Ideas is completely superfluous and also erroneous, he was forced to change the concept of the soul as one which contemplates the Ideas through itself. In Platonism, there existed a certain symmetry between the eternal and immaterial Ideas and the soul, which is likewise eternal, simple and immaterial. Now, if the concept of the Ideas, which Plato advanced is false so too is the concept of the soul. There are no universal Ideas, nor is there any ideal being, conceived as the soul. Only concrete, sensibly-known entities exist: TODE TI.[17]

Aristotle found it necessary to oppose, on the one hand, Platonic spiritualism and, on the other, Democritean materialism, which held that the soul was only a composite of well-fitted atoms. Against the Platonic notion of the soul, Aristotle advanced the argument that the human soul needs bodily organs in order to perform its essential functions. On the other hand, he asserted, against Democritus, that these organs are only instruments of psychical being and are not its essence. And just as, on the one hand, a soul cannot exist without the body so, on the other hand, the soul is not just a body. Rather, it is the principle of life and of sensible and intellectual knowledge; in a word, it is the form—EIDOS—which performs its functions by means of bodily organs. To a certain extent, he already presupposes a constituted body. But a body without a soul is lifeless, just as a soul without bodily organs does not manifest any of its essential functions. For this reason, the soul may be defined as the first act of the physical, organic body which potentially has life—*"actus primus corporis physici, potentia vitam habentis."*[18] And it is exactly in this sense that Aristotle agrees that the soul is the "act-form" of a physical body and not something or other which is endowed with eternal motion and which does not belong to the body. Aristotle therefore breaks with his former views and, by the same token, with Platonic-Pythagorean positions, according to which the soul is, above all, AUTOKINETOS—i.e., a being which is in motion.

Hence the soul, which is joined to the body as its living act, is prior to the body not really but only conceptually. The soul did not exist prior to the body. Neither are there more "soul-acts" in the body as the Platonic position maintained. Rather, it is only one "soul-act," just as there is only one human life. But the one soul has its own various functions, namely three, for which Plato posited a separate soul. Hence the one intellectual soul performs the functions of the vegetative soul in its relation to the vegetative functions of the body. It fulfills the sensible functions in relation to sensible knowledge, in addition to the intellectual, cognitive functions.[19]

It is at this point, however, that Aristotle encountered a great difficulty because, by subscribing to the position of man's conceptual and intellectual knowledge, he was forced to accept an intellect which could understand or could make possible—in some effective way—a knowledge of universal, intelligible substances. Aristotle held the position that the NOUS POIETIKOS (agent intellect) is of divine origin, separate from the body, without sensation, simple and it is act from its own being.[20] This intellect participates in the life of God—in NOESIS NOESEOS.[21] There is, however, a difficulty with another power of the soul, i.e., with the possible intellect, which is a "something" of the soul,[22] while the agent intellect is something divine and immortal. But man is not immortal and the human soul, which is essentially joined to the body, is not a substance separated from the body—this is why it dies along with the body. For the soul is not a substance; it is only the function[23] and act of the body.

Aristotle's followers (Aristosenos and Dicearchos) understood the soul as a harmony of the four fundamental elements.[24] The Aristotelians separated the agent intellect from the soul. The agent intellect itself was thus supposed to be something divine and immortal—whereas the individual soul, which fulfilled the biological and sensible functions—shared the destiny of the body.[25]

For other reasons and causes, Aristotle's materialism was continued, to a certain degree, by the Epicureans and Stoics. Epicureanism, which accepted the Democritean notion of being, also accepted, to a large extent, the Democritean notion of the soul as something which was composed of atoms.[26]

A similar situation exists in Stoicism, which recognizes only a corporeal soul. Obviously, the soul has many functions which the Stoics number in different ways. Nevertheless, the soul always remains only a function of a living human being. They also called the soul and life "Zeus' spark" as if it were his light. When we observe that according to the Stoics, Zeus is also the universal material cosmos, then the soul as Zeus' spark must be equally understood as such in this system. For this reason, the soul loses its individuality upon death and is dispersed through-out the universe.[27]

In summary, the Greek tradition has left us two (*resp. 3*) powerful elements of thought namely, the Platonic, Orphic-religious current—wherein man is a soul and a god who can liberate himself through philosophy—and a second current, that agrees with the entire philosophical current which is a rationalization of mythology. According to this tradition, the soul is a function of man but man himself is either a higher animal, who participates for a moment in divine life, or only a pantheistic moment or a panentheistic "universum."

IV. PATRISTIC MODIFICATIONS OF THE CONCEPT OF MAN

Patristic thought, which interpreted Christian revelation, arrived at the following fundamental principles on the question of the soul:

1. The human soul comes directly from God by virtue of the act of creation (according to *Gen.* II, 7).

2. Nature—(a) the soul differs essentially from the body; (b) the soul is imparted to the body, which lives through it.

3. Each individual soul is immortal—after death, comes judgment of man's actions.

4. Man bears original sin, from which Christ frees him. Our union with Christ is accomplished through Baptism.

The above propositions give a sharply different outlook on man, in the light of Christian revelation, than the one which Greek tradition set forth. As we have seen above, the Greeks transmitted to the Christians three concepts of the soul and, by the same token, three concepts of man:

(a) Aristotelian—biological.

(b) Stoic—according to which man is an element of the cosmos and the human soul is only a momentary "light" and manifestation of a cosmic divinity.

(c) The human soul is a god—one of the cosmic gods.

The soul became man and it clothed itself with a human body, as the result of some sin (perhaps some unexplained original sin?), and for this reason, it needs "redemption." Redemption can come from the soul itself, to the degree that it testifies to its divine dignity and it despises matter—in a word, to the degree that the soul, which lives in man becomes a philosopher.

In Greek tradition, the "soul-man" needed neither grace nor redemption from someone outside himself. To the Greek way of thinking, the kind of redemption which Christianity proposed was something degrading to the soul. This is so because, the soul which of course is itself a god, has an eternal intellectual capability and hence a necessary and true knowledge. Accordingly, Christian theologians found it necessary to make fundamental changes in the Greek concepts of man, so that they could be used for a Christian interpretation of Revelation. Augustine was the first to accomplish this most comprehensively. Up until this time, there were only certain suggestions in this area.

In the thought of Irenaeus of Lyons, the image of God appears in man's soul. Man is comprised of body, soul and spirit. The three elements constitute a complete man and they show the manner of his existence. For there are people who guide themselves by their body (hylotheics—"the material ones"); and those who are directed by their soul (psychics—"the besouled ones"); and those who are directed by the spirit (pneumatolytics—"the spiritual ones.")[28] Obviously, the Christians must belong to the last group. Because of the influence of the Stoics, Irenaeus understands the soul as something material, which evidently, in his way of thinking, means "created." The soul extends through-out and animates the entire body. It is an image of Christians who are in the whole world and who must fulfill a role analogical to the one which the soul performs in the human body.[29]

It is obvious that the tripartite division of the human soul into body, soul and spirit—even if it did come from the Gnostics—does not necessarily indicate the ontic status of man. It can be an expression of the threefold aspirations of man, which were very frequently expressed in the form of a triad. The remainder is due to the influence of Platonic thought.

In the opinion of some apologists, Arnobius for example, the soul's immortality is God's gift to those who believe in Christ.[30] Beyond that, it is difficult to say how Arnobius himself understood the immortality and mortality of the soul. Contemporary theologians who comment on Arnobius' statements caution us that, by "death of the soul," he meant loss of redemption. Not all texts, however, agree: "The souls which are reduced to nothingness disappear, when they are consumed by eternal annihilation . . . their death is unavoidable when the frightful fire burns them in endless time."[31] With Lactantius, we immediately find a decidedly orthodox understanding of man's destiny, the personal immortality of the soul and a proportionate repayment for one's life. His notion of the soul, however, still betrays traces of Stoic-Neoplatonic influences.[32]

Although Tertullian was a Christian—in his understanding of the soul—he was under the influence of the Stoics and, probably, of the medical doctor, Soranos of Ephesus.[33] He wrote two books on the soul: *De Anima* and *De Sensu Animae,* in which he debates with contemporary gnostics and philosophers, i.e., Hermogenes. In the end, he acknowledged that the soul comes from God. He also acknowledged the soul's immortality, its corporeity, understanding, freedom and ability to improve itself. He expressed all these points in his famous definition of the soul: *"Definimus animam Dei flatu natam immortalem, corporalem, liberam arbitrii, accidentis obnoxiam, per ingenia mutabilem, rationalem, dominatricem, ex una redundantem."*[34] After death, all souls—with the exception of those of the martyrs—await in Hades the resurrection of bodies and the coming of Christ. Tertullian accepts all the elements of Christian faith but, because he is equally under the influence of Stoic thought, he emphasizes corporeity. (This corporeity can be here understood in the sense of "dependency on God.")[35]

In the Alexandrian School (Origen and Clement of Alexandria), Platonism held complete sway: The soul was understood as a substance, *rationabiliter sensibilis et mobilis.*

According to Origen, man is only a fallen pure spirit. In his justice, God created all spirits equal. Some of the spirits acknowledged God and remained as angel-spirits. Others, however, turned in upon themselves. They fell and were deprived of the spiritual state. Man is also a fallen spirit who, in future ages, will return to his original dignity. "Also known are those (spirits) who were removed from the state of original happiness but not forever, because they were handed over to the direction and governance by those blessed spirits about whom we wrote above. And when they have been renewed through their help, governance and salvific discipline, they can return and reclaim their state of happiness. And as I judge—insofar as I can judge in these matters—from these fallen spirits, comes the state of human nature. In a future age or in a distant future era—when there will be a new heaven and earth—this human nature will also return to its original unity."[36]

"Everyone who falls to the earth in accordance with his/her merits, (faults) and the place which he/she originally held, is born on earth and carries with him an earthly lot or condition. This condition reflects the locale, country, customs, sicknesses of religious or irreligious parents."[37]

In connection with such an understanding of man's condition Origen accepted—what his contemporaries viewed as blasphemous—that Christ's soul existed before He became man.[38]

For Clement of Alexandria, the body was the tomb of the soul. The soul by itself is a rational spirit. It is called spirit, since it comes from the Holy Spirit. It receives, however, another bodily spirit, i.e., an irrational soul. The latter soul is born concomitantly with the body. The rational soul, which stands in opposition to the body was probably created.[39] Man, however, receives immortality through grace. "Hence it is evident that the soul is incorruptible, not because of its nature but through the grace of God, it becomes incorruptible through faith, justice and undertstanding."[40]

Towards the end of the fourth century, in a letter to Marcellinus, St. Jerome enumerated previous opinions concerning the soul, according to five categories: "I remember your questions regarding the origin of the soul, which is an important question for the Church:

1. Whether it fell from the heavens as the philosopher Pythagoras and all the Platonists and Origen thought.

2. Whether it is a substance emanating from God as the Stoics, Manicheans and the Spanish Priscillian heresy maintained.

3. Whether the souls are found as formerly created in a divine "treasury" as some churchmen held in their stupidity.

4. Whether God is constantly creating them and sending them into bodies, according to what we find in the Gospel: 'My Father always does and I also do.'

5. Whether they come into existence through inheritance as Tertullian, Apollinaris and the greater part of the West do not hesitate to assert—that just as a body is from a body, so soul is born, in like manner, from soul. In this respect, it has being in common with animals."[41]

In the last category (#5), St. Jerome, who does not recall St. Augustine correctly mentions his position and immediately rejects it. He cautions that the acceptance of such a position would make man participate in the condition of animals.

St. Augustine's theory, however, was not as clear-cut as St. Jerome formulated it. As we have already pointed out, Christians found it difficult to reconcile the Gospel with Greek philosophy, especially in the area of understanding the human soul. For if we were to admit the human soul's ability to know eternal truth, then, as a consequence, we would be forced to agree that man is a god, since his human activity is, in its character, essentially timeless because he knows necessary, permanent and changeless truths. Such a condition, according to Greek tradition is a divine prerogative. According to this position, the human soul as god would need no other redemption except through philosophy. This was the position of Platonism.

Because St. Augustine was aware of this dilemma, he preferred to deny the possibility of authentic intellectual knowledge, i.e., he held that by itself, the human soul was incapable of knowing the truth. Rather than diminishing Christ's redemptive role, he accepted the concept of illumination so that, in this setting he could establish in some way the truth of faith which holds the necessity of man's redemption by Christ.

According to St. Augustine, man is composed of body and soul so that man *is* both body and soul *". . . neque sine corpore neque sine anima esse posse hominem; quisquis a natura humana corpus alienare vult desipit."*[42] Naturally, the soul is a more important element than the body. *"Ego sum qui memini—ego animus"* (I am he who remembers . . . I the spirit). The soul is designated to rule the body: *"Nam mihi videtur (animus) esse substantia ratione particeps, regendo corpori accommodata."*[43] St. Augustine's problem is not so much the soul's substantiality as its spirituality.

As a former Manichean materialist, in his *opusculum, De Quantitate Animae,* St. Augustine is careful to say that the soul is neither a body nor can it have spatial dimensions. It is not designated by any corporeal attributes. Augustine sees in this fact a negative proof for the spirituality of the soul. Positively, however, he argues for its spirituality by appealing to what is obvious. The soul is conscious of itself as a spirit who understands, recalls, and possesses a will. The soul knows what it is and what it is not.[44]

Augustine has no clear opinion concerning the origin of the soul. He knows that it does not come from God's substance because it is a creature and, hence, distinct from God. It did not evolve from matter nor from an animal soul. No soul existed before the body; neither was it imprisoned in a body as punishment. It was not formed from some kind of immaterial substance which was to have been created at the beginning of the world. There are four possibilities left for Augustine:

(a) Souls are derived from the souls of parents but there remains the difficulty of preserving the reality of man's person.

(b) Souls are created directly by God at the moment they are joined with the body. But then, there is the difficulty of the inheritance of original sin.

(c) Souls were created by God at the beginning of creation. God unites them later on, one by one with the body.

(d) Souls unite themselves with bodies. But in the last two instances, it is difficult to understand the reason for the union of body and soul. Finally, in the *Retractationes,* he cannot decide between traducianism and creationism.[45]

Augustine declares himself in favor of the immortality of the soul. God, who is the Truth, is the life of the soul. The soul is a mirror, which reflects eternal truth and this guarantees its immortality. These are, therefore, arguments from Plato's *Phaedo*, which have been adapted and studied more thoroughly. The soul is in the body; it imparts life to the body. It is completely in the body and complete and whole in every part of the body. It itself is not subordinate to the body. Since the soul exceeds the body many times in its spirituality, it is thus joined to the material parts through the most delicate and, as if, the most spiritual parts. Finally, the union of the body and soul is a mystery: "The manner in which the soul is joined to the body and how it causes life is completely a mystery, which man cannot understand—that is, man himself."[46]

The reason for the union of body and soul is the role of the soul as a mediator, with regard to the body, to which it shows the contemplated divine ideas. Between the self-evident ideas and the body and its potentiality to uniting with these ideas, the soul is an absolute necessity. The be-ing of the body exhausts itself in the organization of the whole from its parts, according to numerical laws. The soul, however, imparts all of this to the body. The soul must, therefore, govern the body through this governing of the body, the soul must ultimately submit the body and itself to God, through interior acts of the soul—especially through love.[47] The activities of man-soul are inwardly bound with the activities of all humanity, of redemption, inner organization, spiritual community—the divine state—experiencing the drama of evil, which was permitted in order to attain a greater good which would be accomplished.[48]

In addition to St. Augustine and Avicenna, the principal source of anthropology for later scholasticism (of Albert and Thomas) was Nemesius of Emesa—sometimes confused in theological thought with Gregory of Nyssa. Nemesius' work, *On Nature of Man* was known to mediaeval scholastics and his positions were also known as presented by John of Damascene. According to Gilson,[49] Nemesius' concepts are directed to an emphasis on and, sometimes, a presentation of proofs of the development of the following important anthropological issues:

1. Considerations about man are, at the same time, a study of the entire universe, since man is a microcosm.[50]

2. Man is a being who is composed in a completely unique way, so that the Greek thinkers were fundamentally wrong in their explanation of this problem.

3. The foundation for human dignity is man's soul, which is incorporeal, substantial and not reincarnated.

4. The soul's presence in the body is all its own, comparable to a radiation in the atmosphere as two people in love.

5. The soul's origin could have taken place on the first day of creation.

6. The soul is immortal (a distinctly Platonic element).

7. The soul is endowed with knowledge, free will and freedom of choice.

8. The body is destined for resurrection.

The "Last Roman" and Roman philosopher who had a profound influence on the Middle Ages was Manlius Boethius who was executed in Pavio in 525. His fundamentally Platonic notion of man transmitted to the Middle Ages, the theory of the pre-existence of the soul—in agreement with Plato's doctrine—along with a modification of the theory of reincarnation in the moral sense. Specifically, if man is evil, he slowly bestializes himself, i.e., he becomes a beast, "it comes about that those who reject uprightness— cease being people, since they cannot become divine—(they) are changed into animals."[51] ("Upright people resemble God but the evil ones are like animals. Hence, already in their life, the greedy individual is a wolf; the crafty one, a fox; the lazy, an ass and the lustful man—a pig.").

In the West, the last witness to the tradition of Origen and Dionysius, the Pseudo-Areopagite was John Scotus Eriugena (born c. 800 in Ireland.) He lived in the convent of St. Denys in Paris and died after the year 875. He knew Greek and effected a metaphysical synthesis of Christianity with Neoplatonism.

According to Eriugena, man was a spirit but his body was just as spiritual as the ideas of God are spiritual. The body, however, becomes material through its union with invisible principles, namely substance and accidents but it is capable of "respiritualizing" itself.

Man was created to the image and likeness of God but he sinned and fell into difficulties—the effects of sin:

(a) A separation from the Ideas and a division of bodily nature into ideal and real, for the original bodily nature was only in the intellect. And because God foresaw man's fall, He created beforehand, for man, an earth as a place of punishment and exile for fallen nature.

(b) A second effect of sin is a division into sex. Originally, man was sex- less and he was to multiply in a sexless manner.´After man's sin, God had to add something to this nature: *supermachinatus est*—i.e., reproduction in the manner of animals.

(c) Differentiation of mankind according to place, hierarchy and time.

All these things are not acts of revenge but only a necessary effect of sin. There is a possibility of returning to the original status by way of (a) death (b) resurrection of bodies (c) return of the body to the soul (since there is nothing within us which would not be intelligible, hence the body can be- come this kind).

(d) Return of the spirit to a divine nature by means of contemplation.

(e) Return of all nature: of man, of the idea of divine nature—divinizing without the destruction of individuality. Theophany finds its limit with di- vinizing, i.e., a divinizing of saints and of the whole nature in heaven which, however, does not establish any identity with God.[52]

In the same way, neither the Western Fathers nor the Greek Eastern Fathers limited themselves, in their study of man, to a mere repetition of the content of revelation or to an explanation of Greek philosophy. The notion of man which was developed in the first centuries of Christianity was a u-nique and original notion. This concept takes into account given Christian revelation, which the Fathers took pains to render in Greek philosophical ter-minology, but usually they were not aware of the systematic meaning of the terminology which they used. The result is that the thought of the Fathers concerning the question of man and the soul is more Greek than Christian. This was all the more significant, especially in the case of St. Augustine, be-cause care was taken to make supposedly Platonic concepts express the same truths which revelation contains.

V. THE ANTHROPOLOGICAL OPINIONS OF AVICENNA

Avicenna's anthropological opinions exerted a fundamental influence in the Middle Ages, especially in the case of Albertus Magnus and Thomas Aquinas, on the formation of a classical theory of man. This theory is still valuable in its fundamental schema for present-day thought. The Arabian philosopher's treatise, *On the Soul* was translated into Latin in Toledo, after the year 1150 by Gundissalinus. From that time on, it became an important source of a modified understanding of Aristotle, in the philosophical thought of Western Europe.[53]

As G. Verbeke observes—to whose study on Avicenna's theory of man I refer briefly[54]—although Ibn Sina named his treatise *De Anima,* in agree-ment with the rest of Aristotelian tradition, he nevertheless assembled, in a very remarkable way, not only psychological subject matter in the ancient sense but also anthropological data. The questions which Avicenna asks at the beginning of the treatise about man have a completely contemporary sound.

In the manner of certain contemporary formulations, Avicenna begins his treatise on man in the manner of a phenomenological work. He emphasizes the uniqueness of human reality and its distinct reality in the world, espe-cially in comparison with animals. Keeping in mind that discussions about man formed an integral part, in the classical current of philosophy of the philosophy of nature, Avicenna has a right to inquire about the characteristic traits of man's transcendence in relation to nature. Above all, he sees them as emphasizing characteristic traits of human nature:

(a) Man is a social being.[55] Isolated from society, he is not able to develop and to fulfill his human task. An animal is self-sufficient and, by nature, possesses all the equipment which enables it to lead a normal life. Man's existence, on the other hand, is existence in society.

(b) Man is a being who creates culture since he is both a' discoverer and user of many fine arts, as well as practical ones.[56] As contemporary anthropologists express it, man therefore lives not only in a world of nature but also in a world which he has fashioned artistically in a cultural environment. Of course, animals also build "homes" for themselves—nests, etc., but their activity is instinctive and always the same, while man's activity is the result of reflection and creative invention.

(c) Man uses language.[57] It is true that animals also make sounds but animal "language" cannot be compared with that of man. Animal language is "natural" and non-articulated. Animals invent no new, particular sounds; neither do they impose a significative sense to naturally expressed sounds. By contrast, human language is a collection of sounds which are freely chosen, selected and established by man. The result is, that with the aid of such an articulated and fashioned language, everything can be expressed. Language reveals itself as a recognized sign of man's transcendence with respect to his surroundings.

(d) Man differs from animals by living in accordance with morality, especially by recognizing and living according to what is appropriate and what is inappropriate.[58] From childhood, man is inclined to recognize matters and things which are permitted and those which are forbidden (the feeling of shame) and to recognize moral values whose particular nature depends on one's upbringing. Feelings of moral values are totally alien to animals, since they are directed only by instinct.

(e) Since man looks to the future, he plans his life accordingly. On the other hand, the animal is completely absorbed by the here and now.[59]

(f) Since man is an individualized specific being whose soul is *substantia solitaria*,[60] he is an entity separate from the world, different from everything that can be called the environment. Man's improvement takes place through the soul which is the inner center of activity.

As a *substantia solitaria,* the soul is the immaterial principle, which is the source of activity, of the organization of the body and of expressing itself, as through an instrument, by means of the body. The thesis about the necessity of the bodily organism for the expression of the soul, as also that the soul should know itself with the help of the body, was accepted, developed, and made more precise by St. Thomas Aquinas. Avicenna calls attention to the superiority of the intellect to the senses and their organs which are necessary for the process of intellectual cognition.[61]

The problem which was particularly developed by Avicenna was the spirituality (immateriality), as well as the immortality (pre-existence) of the soul.[62] The first and fundamental question for the Arabian philosopher is connected with an Aristotelian understanding of this problem and the method which Aristotle proposed to solve it: i.e., an analysis of human actions which reveal the nature of being. This method which was accepted by the Aristotelians was instrumental in leading one group to a materialistic position: Alexander of Aphrodisias and later, in the Renaissance, Peter Pomponazzi). Another group, e.g., Thomas Aquinas, followed a moderate spiritualist position.

According to Avicenna's opinion, the human soul exists in man as a spiritual (i.e., immaterial) principle (*principium*), which is united to the body and which uses the body. In Avicenna's understanding, the basic argument for the spirituality of the soul is its "self-cognition," which excludes the possibility of using a bodily organ. For if the soul would know with the help of a corporeal instrument, i.e., an organ, it would not be able to know itself; it could not know its own organ nor the fact that it knows intellectually. The Latin translation of Avicenna's argument is stated succinctly: *Si intelligeret (anima) instrumento corporali, oporteret ut non intelligeret seipsam, nec intelligeret instrumentum suum, nec intelligeret se intelligere."* *(De Anima,* V, 2, p. 93, 60) . . . *sensus non sentit nisi aliquid extrinsecum nec sentit seipsum nec instrumentum suum, nec quod sentiat."(Ibid.,* p. 96, 5) Avicenna even goes on to claim that the soul would know itself, even if separated from any sensible knowledge. For this reason, the soul is a self-subsisting spiritual substance and its existence does not depend on the body.

Concerning his second question, i.e., the immortality and pre-existence of the soul—Greek philosophy customarily treated these two questions together—the soul can be immortal only when it exists eternally, i.e., when it "pre-exists" with relation to its presence in the body. For if it does not exist previously to its union with the body, then it is not immortal. Avicenna's statement, however, is interesting, inasmuch as he rejects the pre-existence of the soul but retains, at the same time, its immortality. He thereby breaks with the position according to which the very beginning of a being which begins to be is inescapably also bound with its termination. For Avicenna, the reason for rejecting the soul's pre-existence is its probable distinctness and separateness with relation to other souls. For the only reason for the separateness of souls is the union of soul with body as the principle of individuation. Hence, unless there is a union with the body, the very basis for the separateness of different souls is destroyed. As the result of a possible pre-existence of souls, there would be nothing whereby souls could be different from one another, which is an equal proof of their sameness. As a result, one soul would exist which, because it is spiritual or indivisible, could not divide itself and become many. Having acquired its individuality by its relationship to matter, the soul can live on as a separate entity after man's death.

The reason for the immortality of the soul is the fact that it does not originate from the body. If the soul were to acquire its being as an effect of the body's activity and as a result of its activity, then its existence would be bound with the body's destiny.

Avicenna stands firm on the position that, in no way, can the body be considered to be an efficient cause of the soul. This being so, the soul was created as a pure and simple form and, for this reason, it is immune to death, since it cannot be divided into simpler composing elements. It is not subject to metempsychosis, i.e., of passing from one body to another because in such a case, it would be created anew. The spirituality and simplicity of the soul are so strongly emphasized in Avicenna that he does not hesitate to acknowledge that the soul is its own being in itself. Further, since the soul is a being in itself, it can even know without the activity of the senses of the body, which Avicenna compares to clothing that covers an interior self-knowing ego.

Against this background is traced the Arabian philosopher's view on the question of the soul's relation to the body. In this respect, Avicenna occupies a Platonic and Neoplatonic position, i.e., I am a soul: *"cum enim intelligo quod ipsa anima est principium motuum et apprehensionum, habeo et finis earum ex his omnibus, cognosco, quod aut ipsa verissime est ego, aut quod ipsa est ergo regens hoc corpus"* (De Anima, V, 7, p. 164, 85). The soul, however, is created by some higher immaterial substance[63], as if in commensuration with "this particular" body, which is an instrument of the soul and its realm. The fitting and commensuration of the body to the soul are expressed in the proper mixture of bodily and material elements for each individual.

The various arrangements, however, are only accidental and not essential, since the soul is a singular (individual) substance (*substantia solitaria*). Since the body is intimately united with the soul, it even helps the soul in knowing; but intellectual knowledge itself does not belong to the body: *"Anima humana juvatur a corpore ad acquirenda principia illa consentiendi et intelligendi; deinde cum acquiesierit, redibit ad seipsam."* (Ibid., V, 3, p. 104, 22.) These views concerning the relation of soul to body are reminiscent of Platonic views with, however, the following difference: with respect to the origin and the creation of the soul and its first period of inhabiting the body, Avicenna emphasizes the role of the body alone. In proportion, however, as the soul develops (as well as the potential development through the body), the role of the body becomes increasingly weaker, since the soul is increasingly present in itself as a perfect substance.

Specifically, the Avicennian problem is a question of the agent intellect.[64] This question is also basically connected with the historical interpretation of Aristotle's theory of the intellect which likewise constitutes a purely theoretical problem for Avicenna. For the Stagirite was seeking an explanation: How is it possible that in the end result of the action of material forms on our sense organs, there appear abstract, immaterial, intellectual essences? For, if all knowing has its beginning in a sensible perception of the material world, then there must arise, at some moment in the knowing process, the intervention of a mutually indifferent—i.e., indifferent to intellectual and immaterial essences—a power which is called the "agent intellect." According to Aristotle's opinion, the agent intellect must act within the soul but it is, at the same time, separate from the body, since of its nature, it is constantly in act.

In the eyes of many commentators, such an assertion was synonymous with an affirmation of the transcendent character of the agent intellect, with respect to a knower. According to Alexander of Aphrodisias, Aristotle's opinion could even mean the immediate activity of the "First Mover" himself as "Pure Thought," i.e., Aristotle's God. Other commentators held completely different opinions. According to Avicenna, however, we must distinguish between two agent (active) intellects: one is the soul itself as a substance which receives intellectual forms; and the second is a substance which imparts these forms to the soul.

To this extent, Avicenna is in agreement with his theory of the soul as existing independently and as not accepting any intellectually-knowing forms from matter and the body. According to him, intellectual cognition does not take place in the basis of empirico-sensible data. Rather, it comes fundamentally from the agent intellect, with which there will be an ultimate union after a liberation from the body takes place. "When the soul is freed from the body and from corporeal accidents, only then will the soul be able to join with the agent intellect and then, it will discover in it, an intellectual beauty and eternal joy."[65]

The elements of anthropological thought which first made their appearance in the ancient period and were expanded in mediaeval times, reached a flowering in the thirteenth century, when Thomas Aquinas [66] made his great philosophical synthesis. This also includes the question concerning man. The problematic of man did not appear as something separate and distinct from the other philosophical issues. On the contrary, it was most intimately connected with it. For this reason, the theory of man which St.

Thomas developed is part of the general metaphysical theory of reality. In agreement with the nature of classical philosophy, Thomas treated anthropological problems in an intimate connection (close conjunction) with the theory of analogically conceived being and all the basic elements of reality. After these were developed, they became the basis for the theory of God, the theory of the material world, etc. This work presents the Thomistic notions of human reality, viewed in the light of contemporary philosophical trends and the advances of the history of philosophy.

René Descartes, however, treated the matter quite differently. He began the great current of the "philosophy of the subject," by making man the focal point of all pre-occupations and, at the same time, the point of departure in thought and the foundation for theoretical developments.

VI. CARTESIAN CONCEPT OF MAN

Descartes' concept of man is closely connected with his philosophical reform and his starting point in philosophical thought. By accepting the universal doubt (as a result of sense deceptions for lack of a clear distinction between conscious states and dreams and the possibility of our being deceived by a more powerful being), Descartes found in it, a point of departure for philosophy and a foundation for certitude. If I doubt, I am thinking. Thought exists, even though I am dreaming or if an evil demon would lead me into error.[67] Even though what I think may be a dream, the fact that I do think cannot be doubted. Likewise, I can even be mistaken in my thinking, but I can be mistaken only while I am thinking. Hence, the foundations of knowledge should be sought not in the object but in the subject and in the conscious spirit.

"From the very fact that I know with certainty that I exist, and that I find that absolutely nothing else belongs / necessarily / to my nature or essence except that I am a thinking being, I readily conclude that my essence consists solely in being a body which thinks / or a substance whose whole essence or nature is only to think /. And although perhaps, or rather certainly, as I will soon show, I have a body with which I am very closely united, nevertheless, since on the one hand I have a clear and distinct idea of myself insofar as I am only a thinking and not an extended being, and since on the other hand, I have a distinct idea of body insofar as it is only an extended being which does not think."[68]

From Descartes' time, there occurs a fundamental division of objects which constitute the world. In ancient and mediaeval times, two divisions of beings were recognized: living and non-living. Descartes introduces a division of beings into conscious and unconscious. For ancient thinkers, everything which was living possessed a soul as the first principle of life. From Descartes, arose the theory that consciousness is something distinct from matter. Life was now understood as a purely material process and because the soul lost its union with life, it also lost, at the same time, its union with the body. The soul became a thinking thing—*res cogitans*. Hence we have a clear-cut dualism and all the more distinct, because the body as a *res extensa* was completely subject to mechanistic laws. For the body can have only "passive" properties, i.e., a three-dimensional extension; but dynamic qualities like motion come from God who, once at the beginning, freed the world from passivity. From that time on, the sum total of motion has remained invariable. As a result, there are two substances in the world—a thinking substance and an extended substance—soul and body. There are two separate worlds which have no contact with each other. Not only inorganic bodies but even animals have no souls because they lack consciousness.

There is only one exception where the soul and body are in contact, i.e.,—man. "First, there is no doubt but that all that nature teaches me contains some truth. For by nature, considered in general, I now understand nothing else but God himself, or else the / order and / system that God has established for created things; and by my nature in particular, I understand nothing else but the arrangement / or assemblage / of all that God has given me.

"Now there is nothing that this nature teaches me more expressly / or more obviously / than that I have a body which is in poor condition when I feel pain, which needs food or drink when I have the feelings of hunger or thirst, and so on. And therefore I ought to have no doubt that in this there is some truth.

"Nature also teaches me by these feelings of pain, hunger, thirst, and so on that I am not only residing in my body, as a pilot in his ship, but furthermore, that I am intimately connected with it, and that / the mixture is / so blended / as it were /, that / something like / a single whole is produced. For if that were not the case, when my body is wounded I would not therefore feel pain. I, who am only a thinking being; but I would perceive that wound by the understanding alone, as a pilot perceives by sight if something in his vessel is broken. And when my body needs food or drink, I would simply know the fact itself, instead of / receiving notice of it by / having confused feelings of hunger and thirst. For actually all these feelings of hunger, thirst, pain, and so on are nothing else but certain confused modes of thinking, which have their origin in / and depend upon / the union and apparent fusion of the mind with the body."[69]

Descartes did not explain this union of the body and soul. He advances the possibility that the soul unites with the body in the function of the brain: "I also take notice that the mind does not receive impressions from all parts of the body directly, but only from the brain, or perhaps even from one of its smallest parts—the one, namely, where the senses in common have their seat. This makes the mind feel the same thing whenever it is in the same condition, even though the other parts of the body can be differently arranged, as is proved by an infinity of experiments which it is not necessary to describe here."[70]

Sensible impressions are useful for living but not for the attainment of truth. They are communicated to the intellect in the same manner that feelings are communicated, but only in order to indicate what is suitable for man and what is harmful, though not for the demonstration of truth. Sensations have only a practical meaning and they do not constitute the beginning of knowledge. They only provide the occasion for informing themselves, through the intellect, of innate ideas (a link with the Platonic concept and Augustinian illumination).

Error is an act of the will and not of the intellect, since judgment belongs to the will. Descartes has no notion of a soul, constituted of powers; the soul alone, insofar as it performs various functions bears different names.

There are also data which are intellectual representations. These representations are of two kinds: those which the spirit refers to external sources and those which it derives from itself (passions). Affections are produced by external powers and directly only through "living powers" which are in the blood. These powers vary and they form the basis for a theory of temperaments. Affections awaken the soul to action (e.g., fright is an urging to escape). The direction of these affections for the usefulness of the spirit constitutes the object of ethics.[71]

The soul as a spirit, which is distinct from the body is subject to the laws of the spirit: "I first take notice here that there is a great difference between the mind and the body, in that the body, from its nature, is always divisible and the mind is completely indivisible. For in reality, when I consider the mind—that is, when I consider myself insofar as I am only a thinking being—I cannot distinguish any parts, but I / recognize and / conceive / very clearly / that I am a thing which is / absolutely / unitary and entire. And although the whole mind seems to be united to the whole body, nevertheless when a foot or an arm or some other part / of the body / is amputated, I recognize quite well that nothing has been lost to my mind on that account. Nor can the faculties of willing, perceiving, understanding, and so forth be / any more properly / called parts of the mind, for it is / one and / the same mind which / as a complete unit / wills, perceives, and understands, / and so forth/. But just the contrary is the case with corporeal or extended objects, for I cannot imagine any, / however small they might be /, which my mind does not very easily divide into / several / parts, and I consequently recognize these objects to be divisible. This / alone / would suffice to show me that the mind / or soul of man / is altogether different from the body."[72]

Concerning the soul's immortality, the first edition of the *Meditations* bore the title, *Meditationes de prima Philosophia in qua Dei existentia et animae immortalitas demonstratur.* Later, after the objections of Fr. Mersenne, Descartes published his *Meditations* (in Amsterdam—1642), under a different title: *Meditationes de prima Philosophia in quibus Dei existentia et animae humanae a corpore distinctio demonstratur.* In his answer to the Second Objection, he writes, ". . . *that the immortality of the soul does not follow from its distinctness from the body, because that does not prevent its being said that God in creating it has given the soul a nature such that its period of existence must terminate simultaneously with that of the corporeal life.* For I do not presume so far as to attempt to settle by the power of human reason any of the questions that depend on the free-will of God. Natural knowledge shows that the mind is different from the body, and that it is likewise a substance; but that the human body, insofar as it differs from other bodies, is constituted entirely by the configuration of its parts and other similar accidents, and finally that the death of the body depends wholly on some division or change of figure. But we know no argument or example such as to convince us that the death or the annihilation of a substance such as the mind is, should follow from so light a cause as is a change in figure, which is no more than a mode, and indeed not a mode of mind but of body that is really distinct from mind, Nor indeed is there any argument or example calculated to convince us that any substance can perish. . . . But if the question, which asks whether human souls cease to exist at the same time as the bodies which God has united to them are destroyed, is one affecting the Divine Power, it is for God alone to reply. And since He has revealed to us that this will not happen, there should be not even the slightest doubt remaining."[73]

VII. FORMATION OF THE PHILOSOPHICAL NOTION OF SUBJECT

The ensemble of questions concerning the philosophical reasoning about man shared the vicissitudes of philosophy itself. For man, his vital structure, his essential character of activity, his origins and destiny, were always of interest to philosophy. And from the time of Socrates, there was no period in the history of philosophical reflection, in which the problematic of man in philosophical systems was not further developed. And even in the original

Pre-Socratic period of philosophy—when the special object of interest was the discovery of the cosmos—the spontaneous religious thinking of man reacted in creating for itself an image of the cosmos as a living and all-embracing divinity.

In the history of philosophy, we can discern without any great difficulty two different approaches to the philosophical analyses relating to man. The terminal point here is the system of R. Descartes. Obviously, the designation of the person and system of Descartes is, in great measure somewhat arbitrary, since the ideas which he taught were already known in the history of philosophical thought. Nonetheless, it was Descartes who exerted the greatest influence on the subsequent history of philosophy, and with respect to the over-all influence of Cartesian thought, its originator can be considered as a "boundary figure" between the ancient-mediaeval and the modern-contemporary approach to anthropological questions.

The ancient and mediaeval periods presented philosophical anthropology as being interconnected with a general theory of reality. In such a reality, man occupied a very important, although not the *most* important place. He was the object of revealing analyses in the light of a previously constructed system and in the light of "first principles." In the eyes of ancient and mediaeval classical thinkers, man was, very simply, a spiritual being who, however, had his predetermined place in the total picture of reality. In this picture, which was common to all men of that time, there were combined such important components as the general structure of the universe and the world, the hierarchical arrangement of communities, and the hierarchical arrangement of beings—among whom God occupied the highest position, then the angels and below them, man, then animals, plants and, finally, the inanimate world.

Against the background of a general picture of the world as given by a pre-scientific conviction and one which was accepted by philosophy and theology, man was shown as occupying a special place, joining together the world of matter with the world of the spirit. Hence, an understanding of man presupposed, at least some understanding of beings, both higher and lower in the hierarchy. Such a philosophical interpretation of man constantly required more direct and less complicated structures of reality as being "above" and "below" man. This enabled man to be seen, or otherwise understood, as a synthesis of spirit and matter, like a microcosm.

The situation was diametrically changed when an analytical way of thinking about man became the point of departure for a coherent construction, in imitation of mathematics, of a closed philosophical system. In Descartes' philosophical thought, the primary "given" is no longer the world and its pre-philosophical image, but human thought—not every thought but only a clear and distinct one. In a word, a subjective idea. Henceforth, the analysis of a clear and distinct idea became—in Descartes' system, as well as in post-Cartesian rationalism and even in English empiricism—the Archemedian supporting fulcrum and final state of judging the truth and accuracy of solutions.

The subjective idea of man as the ultimate agent who judged the value of philosophical thought, fulfilled, willy-nilly, the old sophistical postulate of Protagoras: ANTHROPOS METROS TON PANTON. Henceforth, philosophy follows slowly, but all the more constantly, a path of philosophy of the human subject. Philosophy becomes, more properly, an anthropology. For if man, his recognition, his psychic reactions and his cognitive situation become the one "bridge," which unites him with the rest of the world—and if it is solely and exclusively in recognition of and in psychic reactions that the "meeting" of man with the world takes place—then, in fact, human cognitions and the mental reactions joined to them become the first object of analysis. The analysis of man and the disclosure of his cognitive structures which condition the possibility of a (valid) knowing become the principal efforts of philosophers of the same ilk as Kant. On the other hand, with the passage of time, the objective world—the non-human world which does not belong to a thinking subject—is given over, among the German transcendental idealists, to doubt, to such a degree that it appears as a function of the subject.

And even if Hegel's subjective philosophy takes on a seeming appearance of a strongly objective philosophical system—which only *pretends* to uncover the ultimate governing laws (these become, in the dialectic of evolution, the absolutely real Idea)—nevertheless, the logic of the system is nothing more than the logic of the human subject. Even in Hegel, we are dealing with an extrapolating human thinking about the world, which becomes "obedient" to the dialectic that it has uncovered.

The reaction to this fictitious, idealistic objectivism becomes S. Kierkegaard's philosophy of the human subject or of human existence. At the same time, the influence of other idealistic objectivist sources of philosophy, chiefly Neo-Kantian and Hegelian, is decisive on the philosophical thought of the 19th and 20th century. All the philosophical currents of the 19th century, with the exception of Marxism are philosophies of the subject; they are, precisely, philosophical anthropologies. The starting point of these philosophies is human cognition, expressed either in its function or in the a priori conditions, which make possible the functioning of this kind of cognition. This course of events is by no means ended. It is still continuing in existentialist, Kantian and transcendental directions. In such a state of affairs, the whole of philosophy resolves itself, almost totally, into an anthropology, a theory of man.

And once man was able to break away from the objectively real world, and the only data for philosophical analysis were those things which first appeared in the human, and later on in some closer (intentional) indefinite knowledge, the enlightening sense of philosophy disappeared. There was nothing to elucidate if elucidation was to take place by a rejection of a real and objective world. Philosophy began to elucidate only that which was given to man—either in his point of departure or in an indefinite consciousness. Finally, under the Neo-Kantian influence, particularly Cassirer's formulation of it, philosophy became the expression of what man, who was cast and drowned in existence, was living out. Anthropology itself was reduced to analyses of the relation of consciousness, to its appearing contents which appeared or were produced by it. Everything, whether conscious or subconscious, became the domain of inner depth. As a result, conscious facts or contents began to be explained by an appeal to pre-conscious states, especially when the conscious states revealed some abnormal characteristics. The appeal to preconscious states—which potentially contained in themselves, everything which later transpires as conscious activity of man— proved to be something very significant and positive in psycho-neurotic therapy. However, it was worse when an attempt was made to build an ontic theory of personality by basing it on either a method of healing or of experimentation: For the results that were sometimes achieved denied the person as the subject of actions and an attempt was made to lead to a "pre-personal" (sometimes purely mechanistic) interplay of those powers, which would later present themselves as the components of this very personhood itself. In this way, a self-subsistent subject was denied and, in its place, mutually conflicting powers were affirmed, whose result would be a psychism. All of this was presented as a philosophizing, but it was irresponsible, unverifiable and even harmful.

Within existentialism, philosophical anthropology was led basically to a dismantling of the very act of transcendence and of everything else which consciously revealed itself in a transcendent survival. Along with this, ordinarily use was made of this or that kind of understood phenomenological description which has been applied to the data of consciousness, requesting such a kind of model of man that would agree with selectively accepted phenomenological moments revealing descriptions.

An emphasis and, sometimes, an over-emphasis of the subject's role became, if not the reason, then at least, a convenient occasion for the construction of an anti-subjective picture of reality. This reality was one which resolved itself into STRUCTURE (resp. the arrangement of structure), examined purely objectively through a logical analysis of cultural facts, especially language as the principal structure, which explains the pseudo-subjectivity of man. Structuralist anthropology, which is a purely objective methodology, destroyed the human subject, leading him "rationally" to an interiorization of language. The course of the history of philosophy completed a full circle. Philosophical thought, which emerged in the 7th century B.C. from a pre-personal, hazy but also rational "UNLIMITED", arrived at the "disclosure" of a fundamental, infinite structure of a collection of accidents, which is supposed to be the total reality.

*   *   *

The vagaries of human thought which we have sketched above, the various, proposed solutions which were presented on the subject of man, prompt us to present "the human fact" and to propose—against its background—the kind of anthropological theory that will consider in great measure—not only the achievements of the history of philosophy—but it will likewise show the fundamentally essential structure of man, his characteristic traits, as well as the basic context of human rational life.

CHAPTER II

THE HUMAN FACT

I. THE PROBLEM OF DETERMINING THE FACT

In any genuine science, we must distinguish two stages in the theoretical procedure: 1. establishment and description of facts 2. demonstration of their interpretation, as well as their explanation. In philosophical anthropology, as well as in the theory of man, we must indicate the fact which is assigned us for explanation. We must likewise outline the manner in which the explanation of the data will take place. The given fact which is to be explained is man himself, understood in his ontic and essential properties.

The first concern, then, is the philosophical determination of the so-called "human fact." In accomplishing this, however, we encounter a difficulty. First of all, it is not easy to separate a description of the human fact from a theoretical interpretation. The reason is that there are no "bare facts" which are not interconnected with some kind of cognitive experience, determining and directing a recognition of the fact itself. Next, it is frequently stipulated that the "human fact," for the theory of philosophical anthropology, should be an image of man that is given us by the specialized sciences. Philosophy should reflect on man only when science has given its judgment. The assertion is made that only then we shall be dealing with the human fact, which has been rationally and properly established.

But the matter is not as simple as it appears to proponents of such a position. The image of man which is given by the specialized sciences is only seemingly uniform. In reality, it is differentiated with respect to the different aspects of the objects of particular, specialized sciences. The result of the investigations of a particular science—as well as the ultimately general picture of a set of specialized sciences—is completely bound up with the particular

29

aspects and methods of specialized sciences. For it is evident that the very selection of aspects and the employed method of research already imply a specific cognitive position of knowledge which is bound up with a philosophical trend and a theory of knowledge that follows a certain philosophical direction. Understood in a classical sense, philosophy arises from a pre-scientific knowledge, and, from data of this knowledge, it elaborates on it in its own manner, for philosophy is an independent cognitive area of knowledge whose outcomes do not belong to the specialized sciences. There is, in fact, a different concept which is based on the specialized sciences. The methodological status of such a philosophy, however, is not clearly delineated beyond certain general postulates. In practice, it appears that the realization of such a kind of philosophy ultimately leads to its destruction.

Hence, at the very starting point of philosophy, we can accept, in principle, a pre-scientific description of the human "fact." In this description, we emphasize those elements which were already emphasized in universal consciousness, along with the influence of current up-bringing as well as the history of human thought. In addition, we can reach—in a pre-scientific description of the human "fact"—even such attempts of the description of this fact which exerted a special influence on the history of human culture. Hence statements of this kind already became a common "good" in the pre-scientific understanding of man.

For in the general consciousness of educated people, man—the creator of technology, of science and of individual and social culture—still remains in himself, in his ontic structure, a mystery to himself. It is true that contemporary psychology has been able to explain much, e.g., how man responds to various stimuli and what are the laws of his actions. The natural sciences, like physics, chemistry, and biology, have given much information about his material structure and the various vegetative and organic functions. The economic and sociological sciences have brought to light a whole range of complexities in the area of social life. Nevertheless, man as man, still remains, as A. Carrell has expressed it, "an unknown being."

And precisely what does "man" mean? Every answer or attempt to qualify and, even more so, any effort to explain, at once becomes involved in some philosophical system. This neither threatens nor makes knowledge impossible, since systems have a tendency to develop usually on the confines of pre-scientific knowledge. And even if knowledge of this kind is, in no way, superior to philosophical knowledge, nevertheless, it is available to all. In addition, it provides a kind of common, practical wisdom which exercises a negative control over often-times extravagant philosophical speculations.[1]

It is precisely in the pre-scientific, so-called "common sense" knowledge, that man shows himself to be a highly developed vertebrate animal (a mammal) who, thanks to his intellect, is transcending the whole nature and the animal world. Such an understanding would agree with the definition of man which is accepted in some philosophical circles, i.e., "rational animal," *animal rationale,* ZOON LOGIKON.[2]

When, however, we look at the "animal" side of ourselves, we immediately perceive our shortcomings. We recall the investigations of Arnold Gehlen,[3] which call attention to the fact that man, precisely as an "animal," is characterized by inadequacies rather than by a perfection of "natural equipment." In comparison with other animals, who are so admirably adapted to nature, man is in large measure like an intruder, who is not suited to the environment. He does not possess a hair-covering suitable to the climate which would protect him from changing temperatures and inclement weather. Nor does he have any developed organs for struggle, enabling him to capture his prey. Nor does he possess naturally formed organs for self-protection. In comparison with other animals, his senses of smell, sight and hearing are weak and he is in constant danger of losing his life. Because of his many enemies, as a species of animal, he should have disappeared long ago from the face of the earth.

Yet it is man alone, who has remarkably survived the difficult eras of struggling with nature. He has developed and conquered the earth. He has decimated and destroyed many species of animals stronger than himself. He has changed the face of the earth. . . . Although our planet is generally shaped today the same as it was several hundred thousand years ago, nevertheless, it would look totally different to one today than if the same individual had observed it years ago. The reason is because man has changed nature so markedly. He has made it to suit his own needs because from his very birth, he was never completely adjusted to it. Therefore, he fashioned for himself an artificial niche, in the form of homes, estates, cities and everything which is associated with urban culture. He compensated for his deficiencies linked with his biological equipment. Mindful of this, we can assert somewhat paradoxically that, man as animal—precisely because he is not suited to his natural surroundings since nature did not endow him with ready-made specialized organs that would help him to survive and to conquer nature—was forced to treat his deficiency of natural specialization as a "raw material" of his new nature, which was built as the result of his many-sided activities.[4]

Everything which is understood by the term "culture" was achieved by man's reason. As a matter of fact, in a certain sense, many animals have intelligence. This is evident in the purposeful adjustment of the animal species to its environment. The more "intelligent" an animal is, the better it can adapt itself to the changing conditions of its habitat. Considered from this point of view, man is incomparably more intelligent than any kind of animal. This is so because he is able to fashion for himself artificial (cultural) conditions which are necessary for subsistence and development. At the same time, he is better able to take advantage of the forces of nature and better able to arrange them in every respect with his objectives.

But man's intelligence is something essentially different from that of animals. For man manifests a way of knowing which is completely different from that of the animal and which lies at the basis of all human accomplishment and constant progress. All areas of man's life, as specifically human, are inextricably bound up with rational knowing. The areas of technology, as well as of science, of human decision, the formation of moral attitudes— as well as those of social living and, finally, those of art and religion—are manifestations of specifically human life, which is directly connected with intellectual knowing. Obviously, it is difficult to discuss in detail all the individually mentioned, specific aspects of man. Further sections of this book will formulate and develop some of these apsects. But the general observations, which do not go beyond the purely common sense knowledge seem to be necessary for exactly this purpose, i.e., so that the importance of philosophical considerations about man's reality will be realized.

The fundamental property which differentiates man from other creatures of nature is his ability to know rationally. In agreement with philosophical tradition, extending all the way back to Socrates and Plato,[5] it was customary to point, above all, to concepts as man's specifically fundamental elements of a rationally-knowing structure. Early in the history of human thought, there appeared, along with Socratic rationalism, a theory of concepts fundamentally different from concrete, singular images that are changeable and subject to the fluctuation of time. In contrast to sensible knowledge, concepts had shown themselves reflecting human thought, as universal, necessary and stable elements on which a genuine human knowledge can be built. Judgments, as a further manifestation of rational thought were observed most often, in principle, only as an activity for concepts.[6] And even though later on, D. Hume—who repeated, in this case, the old mediaeval position of the nominalists—denied a difference between sensible and conceptual (intellectual) knowledge,[7] by identifying concepts with the so-called "ideas" that were the result of a concrete abstraction—according to him, the human knowing faculty ignores or neglects certain non-essential notes included in the knowledge of an object—it was later on, along the lines of psychological introspection that the Würzburg School of Kulpe, Acha, as well as the researches of Benet showed that imagination alone, even understood as typical, is not sufficient to explain what we call "thought," which fundamentally transcends the sensible character of knowledge peculiar to animals.[8] The transcendence of man's thought independently of an interpretation of its ontical character, is something which is not subject to discussion, i.e., that the universal understanding of man as *animal rationale* is confirmed, at the very outset, in a superficial realization of the contents of this definition.

II. RATIONAL ANIMAL—THE CONTENT OF THE HUMAN FACT

The "human fact," symbolized by the expression "rational animal" attains its characteristic expression by calling attention to those traits which most differentiate man from the whole ensemble of nature. Let us turn our attention to some of those that are easily perceived with respect to their general character.[9]

Human, rational activity found its most characteristic expression in the area of technics (skills), whose reality amounts to this, that man is able to use tools which are his own creation. It is true that some animals, e.g., monkeys can sometimes make use of those tools to secure food, but they never created instruments and, in fact, they do not need these tools to assure their life. It is man who, from his first appearance on the surface of the earth is using tools as a kind of embodiment of his thought, and not only as an extension of some organ. He is constantly improving these tools so that by means of the creations of his thought, he has dominated the world. He has multiplied his powers and he has assured himself the conditions of life on the level of his rational needs. It is a long way from a plain, ordinary stick, fire and wheel to contemporary computers that direct factory operations and cosmic flights. Nevertheless, it is the way of never-changing human thought, that transcends nature.

And we are no more human today, when we are "promenading" on the moon, than we were yesterday when we were still worshipping the moon as a deity which intrudes in human life. And even if we are able today to use tools infinitely more perfectly, nevertheless the tools we create are only an expression of thinking, an embodiment of thought for the needs of human life. And yet, thought taken by itself, in its ontical structure, is the same today as it was yesterday. Technology is only a distinct expression of the specificity of human thought, its transcendence in the presence of animal knowing and in the presence of all nature.

Obviously, such a development of thought connected with technics could never be possible if man were not a social being. And we do not mean the kind of community of which an analogue can be observed, e.g., among bees, ants or termites—a community operating by instinct and without free will. We mean, rather, a human community of rational and free beings, a community which is an expression of a rational and free human nature. For a human community is a community of persons, and therefore, of people who are striving to develop and improve their knowledge and various intellectual endeavors.

Through tradition, community makes possible a growth of human culture. And tradition is not something inborn in the human being as, for example, "community" instincts are inborn in ants, termites and bees. Ultimately, man must learn tradition by accepting freely its obvious values which have been achieved by humanity in bygone ages and by rejecting seeming or outmoded values.

The assimilation of human tradition which appropriates all the achievements of the labors of former generations is made possible through language which is a system of constantly developing and evolving signs. The system of language signs which differs in different community groups—which serves as a means of communication among people and which is, ultimately, freely accepted by men, for each language sign can be changed for another—enables man to develop his personality. This is so because it unites him in the streams of tradition with its rational achievements. It enables people to open up to each other and with whom they can further develop and deepen the already acquired cultural values. The very fact of a cultural tradition which is accepted with the help of a conventional language and culture and which is constantly developing with the support of language and hence, the fact of community progress, is an eloquent expression of man's transcendence with respect to nature and the various phenomena of non-human life. And, although, from the biological point of view, man is the same today as he was in the time of Alexander the Great, from the point of view of cultural progress (technics, science and social organizations), he has developed immensely.

Man's ability to abstract and to create ideas stands at the basis of science as an organized, methodical and fundamental rational knowledge. Scientific knowledge, especially today, has become a highly esteemed sign of the presence and dignity of man. For in its essence, it is always disinterested knowledge, even though its results are most practical and serve the interest of various groups of people. Disinterested, scientific knowledge which has as its aim, knowledge of reality (however it be understood) i.e., having as its aim truth understood as a conscious agreement with its object of knowledge, is testimony of a humanity understood in the most sublime manner. The phenomenon of science is something undeniably connected with the "human" and which never occurs in nature. If animals "know" how they should behave in the presence of certain objects with which they are in contact, their knowledge bears always the stamp of gaining some concrete benefit which the animal nature tends to achieve but which comes from an inherited or concretely acquired knowledge on the part of the particular animal. Only man acquires knowledge for itself, even if he does not see any immediate advantage for his nature. And science, strictly understood, is indeed the attainment or transmission of knowledge in its disinterested form.

Artistic, aesthetic and religious human activites show, perhaps, an even more disinterested type of knowledge. For side by side with creative moments, stands pure contemplation, which is not ordained to any other end than acts of contemplation itself. The perception of musical compositions, the creative or aesthetic vision of some kind of work of art are ends in themselves, in the same way as religious contemplation is its own end. Magnificent temples of various religions on different continents, religious rites, pilgrimages conducted in Christian, Buddhist and Islamic religions, prayers and liturgical rites are not oriented to achieve any concrete advantage or practical interest. In other words, such activities are testimony to the transcendent human spirit not confined to the area of material gain and natural interests, as we notice in the case of animal behavior and reactions.

And finally man alone—among all the other living creatures of nature— *reflects on the fact of his own death*. In relation to this fact which, with its brutal eloquence breaks out as of prime importance among all the human facts of life, man adopts an attitude of reflective stance, so that his human life becomes a life in the perspective of death. This fact makes itself known at various moments of human existence. As human beings, we ask questions concerning the fact of death: whether death will totally annihilate us? Whether there is some essential "I" which survives this death? We ask ourselves these questions a great number of times in a theoretical way. But we all articulate them more frequently through our actions, our works and creations, through which we hope to endure and to extend our own short biological lives. Man's spiritual creativity, his works, his love, his studies and acts of intellectual contemplation, which transcend fleeting time and space, are also these real questions under the heading of the fact of death. In the area of philosophy and religious experiences, these questions take on the form of clearly articulated questions. The very fact of man's religiousness can be recognized as a desire to survive death, a desire for a life under changed conditions, beyond death.[10]

And independently of the manner in which these very existential questions are resolved (concerning our existence after death), the very fact of their constant presentation, in a practical and theoretical form, is something completely unique in the realm of living creatures. For we do not observe, even in the highest animals, a fear before approaching death. We do no observe an attitude of entering into death as any kind of final end, of any kind of eventual, possible chance of another life. The animal locates itself totally in transient time and in its own environment. It does not exhibit, in its actions, any transcendence in relation to a time-space *continuum*.

Hence, the fact of the problematic of death which presents itself in "the human race," and which is met nowhere else is proof that there exists in man a real foundation for the appearance of such questions. This is so because where, in general, there are no such existentialist questions, there are likewise no real foundations for the presentations of such questions. And independently of a theoretical development of this problematic, whether in a negative or positive sense, this fact cannot be denied. Besides, it is precisely these existential questions about our further existence after death, about the sense of death, which become the object of philosophical and religious interpretation and, hence, a large area of man's cultural creativity.

And because man is, at the same time, an animal and hence a creature of nature, he constantly expresses himself as man in a varied transcendence, thanks to which, he can make the whole world the object of his activities. In this same transcendence, he can likewise make himself, by means of reflection, the object of cognitional, creative and volitional activity. Man's many-sided transcendence, which finds its expression in human activities and creations is the foundation for human cultural activities. And if we were to understand culture as a world of symbols produced by man, and this same man as the producer of symbols, which are the manifestation of his spiritual life, we could call him, with E. Cassirer, *"animal symbolicum."* [11]

Having given this cursory description of man, insofar as it discloses our pre-scientific and common sense thinking, this description explains nothing as yet about the ontological structure of man, his destiny and his essential functions. It merely focuses attention on man as a marvelous and unique being, emerging from nature and being a part of that nature—but, at the same time, as variously transcending that nature, having as the purpose of its activities, not nature but man himself, as he dominates, transforms and organizes nature for a purpose which is beyond space and time. Such an incomprehensible phenomenon as "the fact of man" needs better organized interpretations and explanations.

Attempts explaining "the human fact" appeared more than once in the history of human thought. There were a great number of them which were formulated on the canvas of philosophy, religion, scientific studies etc. Let us examine, however briefly, some of them which have a connection with the subject of the considerations we have presented. In this way, we shall be able to account, in a more critical way, for the foundation of those solutions that touch on man's behavior with respect to himself and others.

And to make this survey more coherent, let us first observe those explanatory attempts which emphasize the biological side of man, standing—in its own proper way—on the position that ultimately, the "human fact" can be reduced to a system of materially biological powers, since man is, in a way, the product of nature. To this group we can add the attempts of the interpretation of man formulated by J. Huxley, Teilhard de Chardin, the Marxist notion of man, Freud's depth-psychology, along with the structuralist implications in anthropology.

At the same time, we should point to another source which emphasizes the spiritual side of man and which transcends the biological aspects. The sources of the contemporary understanding of man as a manifestation of the spirit reach all the way back to Descartes' concept. For this reason, we must give the general outlines of the theory of man in Hegel (against the background of the forerunners of his thought), so that we can present the theories of the existentialists. These latter theories are reactions to the extreme systematism of Hegel and Max Scheler, who are regarded as classical in their anthropological concept of philosophy. The aim of a general examination of anthropology is to acquaint the reader with the problems of reality which we must now present, more systematically, step by step, in our philosophical examination.

CHAPTER III

ATTEMPTS TO INTERPRET
THE HUMAN FACT

I. CONCEPTIONS OF MAN AS A CREATURE OF NATURE

A. BIOLOGICO-EVOLUTIONARY INTERPRETATION

Against the background of the natural sciences—as their particular generalization—a conception of man developed which treated him as the most perfect stage in the evolution of nature. Understood in this way, man is explained ultimately by an appeal to the laws of nature and to their development. Let us glance at some evolutionary solutions.

1. Naturalistic Evolutionism

A typical example of a purely biological evolutionism is J. Huxley's conception of man which, in acknowledging the uniqueness of the "human fact," attempts to show that the origin, development and structure of man are the necessary result of an evolutionary process. His reasoning, which is somewhat reminiscent of "science fiction," became classical in many circles and found its repercussions even in philosophical literature.[1] He writes

> The course followed by evolution appears to have been broadly as follows. From a generalised early type, various lines radiate out, exploiting the environment in various ways. Some of these comparatively soon reach a limit to their evolution, at least as regards major alteration. Thereafter they are limited to minor changes such as the formation of new genera and species. Others, on the other hand, are so constructed that they can continue their career, generating new types which are successful in the struggle for existence because of their greater control over the environment and their greater independence of it. Such changes are legitimately called "progressive."

39

The new type repeats the process. It radiates out into a number of lines, each specialising in a particular direction. The great majority of these come up against dead ends and can advance no further, specialisation is a one-sided process . . .

Sometimes all the branches of a given stock have come up against their limit, and then either have become extinct or have persisted without major change . . .

In other cases, all but one or two of the lines suffer this fate, while the rest repeat the process. All reptilian lines were blind alleys save two—one which was transformed into the birds, and another which became the mammals. Of the bird stock, all lines came to a dead end; of the mammals, all but one—the one which became man.[2]

According to Huxley, the result is that

Evolution is . . . seen as an enormous number of blind alleys, with a very occasional path of progress. It is like a maze in which almost all turnings are wrong turnings. The goal of the evolutionary maze, however, is not a central chamber, but a road which will lead indefinitely onwards.[3]

There are many reasons which impede the evolutionary development of various creatures of nature, as, for example, the necessary proportion of the volume of the body to its surface, which cannot be ignored. Only vertebrates and, among them, only those living gregariously in trees, could become the subject of evolution in the direction of man. In this connection Huxley writes

We are now in a position to define the uniqueness of human evolution. The essential character of man as a dominant organism is conceptual thought. And conceptual thought could have arisen only in a multicellular animal, an animal with bilateral symmetry, head and blood system, a vertebrate as against a mollusc or an arthropod, a land vertebrate among vertebrates, a mammal among land vertebrates. Finally, it could have arisen only in a mammalian line which was gregarious, which produced one young at a birth instead of several, and which had recently become terrestrial after a long period of arboreal life.

There is only one group of animals which fulfills these conditions—a terrestrial offshoot of the higher Primates. Thus not merely has conceptual thought been evolved only in man; it could not have been evolved except in man. There is but one path of unlimited progress through the evolutionary maze. The course of human evolution is as unique as its result. . . . Conceptual thought on this planet is inevitably associated with a particular type of Primate body and Primate brain.[4]

Before man's existence,

> Progress has hitherto been a rare and fitful by-product of evolution. Man
> has the possibility of making it the main feature of his own future evolution
> and of guiding its course in relation to a deliberate aim.[5]

We can quote with profit a somewhat humorous treatment by Mascall of
this concept of man,

> . . . the picture of man which science puts before us would seem to be
> simply the picture of the successful cosmic bandit, the character who, by
> a happy combination of good fortune and adroitness, has carved out for
> himself in the universe a position of prominence and affluence for which
> he can plead no official authorization or backing, and whose ultimate fate
> is a matter of complete indifference to the supreme administrative author-
> ity, if indeed any such authority exists. In fact, one of the tragedies of sci-
> entific humanism is the implicit or explicit philosophy of most educated
> Anglo-Saxons which sees man as occupying a position of unprecedented
> achievement and at the same time as having no guarantee for his future,
> either here or beyond the grave.[6]

2. Directed Naturalistic Evolutionism (Vision of Teilhard de Chardin)

Similar to Huxley's conception, P. Teilhard de Chardin[7] presents, in his
many writings, a vision of human evolution, its exceptional character and
consequently the exceptional status of the human creature in the midst of all
creatures of nature. Obviously Teilhard de Chardin's conception is different
from the previously mentioned one because it is influenced by elements of
Christian Revelation. This conception is well known today and hence we
shall limit ourselves here to an outline of its more characteristic moments of
a view of the universe and, against this background, of man's role and
human life in it.

It is difficult to give a concise presentation of Teilhard's conception because the author uses threads of thought drawn from all kinds of areas of
knowledge. In addition, his explication of the "human fact" has traits of
prophetic-predication because it is connected with a religious vision. Besides, he himself writes that his doctrine is

> rather a sort of empirical and pragmatic explanation of the universe, con-
> ceived in my mind from the need to reconcile in a solidly coherent system
> scientific views on evolution (accepted as, in their essence, definitively es-
> tablished) with the innate urge that has impelled me to look for the Divine
> not in a cleavage with the physical world but through matter, and, in some
> sort of way, in union with matter.[8]

Hence man appeared against the background of the evolution of the cosmos which always existed and was always created, if by creation we understand the "unification" of scattered elements and powers. (Understood in this way, creation presupposes a henological conception of being, the kind that existed in early Greek philosophy.) About the evolving cosmos, he writes,

> However far back we look into the past, we see the waves of the Multiple breaking into foam as though they emerged from a negative pole of being. The fringes of our universe, we have seen, are lost in material and unconscious plurality. To our experience this ocean is as boundless as the material space that surrounds us. We often hear the expression, 'the first moment of the world'—it is a very mistaken way of putting it, and to look for such a thing would be a waste of time. The creative act is not interpolated in the chain of antecedents. It is imposed upon the universe taken in its full extension and full duration. It is impossible, therefore, for the elements of the world to emerge from the world, to reach even a lower limit of the world. . . . All around us, until it is lost to sight, radiates the net of spatial and temporal series, endless and untearable, so closely woven into one piece that there is not one single knot in it that does not depend upon the whole fabric. God did not will individually (nor could he have constructed as though they were separate bits), the sun, the earth, planets, or Man. He willed his Christ;—and in order to have his Christ, he had to create the spiritual world, and man in particular, upon which Christ might germinate;—and to have man, he had to launch the vast process of organic life (which, accordingly, is not a superfluity but an essential organ of the world);—and the birth of that organic life called for the entire cosmic turbulence.
>
> At the beginning of the perceptible world what existed was the Multiple; and that Multiple was already rising up, like one indissociable whole, towards spirit under the magnetic influence of the universal Christ who was being engendered in it.
>
> This ascent was slow and painful; for from that moment the Multiple was, through something in itself, evil.[9]

Continuing and emphasizing his thought in the *Phenomenon of the Spirit,* (Does he by such a title deliberately refer to Hegel?), Teilhard de Chardin undertakes the question of the appearance and exactly the presence of the spirit in the cosmos. On this theme of its history he writes

> Certain minds may still hesitate before the notion of a biosphere. No one can any longer doubt that insofar as it exists, it is rooted over its whole surface in the abyss of past centuries. Spirituality is not a recent accident, arbitrarily or fortuitously imposed on the edifice of the world around us; it is a deeply rooted phenomenon, the traces of which we can follow with certainty backwards as far as the eye can reach, in the wake of the move-

ment that is drawing us forward. As far back as we can recognize a surface of the earth, that surface is inhabited. . . . The consciousness that we see filling the avenues of the past, does not flow simply like a river which carries an unchanging water past ever changing banks. It transforms itself in the course of its journey; it evolves; life has a movement *of its own*. If we follow it backwards in time, we see it reducing the organic complexity of its forms and the range of its spontaneity. Nervous systems become increasingly rudimentary. And to judge from the present survivors of these ancient stages, the animate world disappears at the farthest end into a swarm of living particles that are hardly separate from molecular energies. Inversely, in the direction of the arrow of time, cellular constructions are formed and, step by step with a growth in complexity, consciousness increases its powers of internal clairvoyance and interconnexion until, at the level of man, reflective thought bursts forth.[10]

Looking at the course of evolution in creatures with sensory perception, we can observe, according to Teilhard, a necessity in the entire process:

All the metamorphosis leading up to man reduces, from the organic standpoint, to the question of producing a better brain. But how could this perfecting of the brain have been produced, how could it have taken place, unless a whole series of other conditions had been realised all together and at once? If the being which issued in man had not been a biped, his hands would not have found themselves free to take over the prehensile functions from the jaws, and so the thick bundle of maxillary muscles which constricted the skull would not have been relaxed. It is thanks to the liberation of the hands through the adoption of biped movement that the brain has been able to grow, and also that the eyes have been able to draw together, across the narrowed face, and so to converge and 'fix' whatever the hands may have grasped, brought near and, in every sense of the word, *presented;* the very outward gesture of reflection.[11]

The moment when the spirit in man has freed itself through reflection, the "noosphere" begins to surround the Earth:

Because we are individuals ourselves, life around us affects us principally on the individual scale. Atoms ourselves, we at first see only other atoms. But it does not require much reflection to discover that animate bodies are not as separate from one another as they appear. Nor only are they all, by the mechanism of reproduction, related by birth. But by the very process of their development, a network of living connexions (psychological, economic, social, etc.) never for a moment ceases to hold them in a single tissue, which becomes more complicated and tenacious the further they evolve. . . .To the extent that it is subject to experiment, the phenomenon of spirit is not a divided mass; it displays a general manner of being, a collective state peculiar to our world. In other words, scientifically speaking,

> there are no *spirits* in nature. But there is a *spirit,* physically defined by a certain tension of consciousness on the surface of the earth. This animate covering of our planet may with advantage be called the biosphere—or more precisely (if we are only considering its thinking fringe) the noosphere.[12]

Understood in such a way, the noosphere is a layer of the spirit which reveals itself on the Earth's surface. This spiritual layer, however, is nothing foreign to the world; it is only a different state of matter:

> Hence our evidence that, from a purely scientific and empirical standpoint, the true name for 'spirit' is 'spiritualization.' Taken as a whole, in its temporal and spatial totality, life represents the goal of a *transformation* of great breadth, in the course of which what we call 'matter' (in the most comprehensive sense of the word), turns about, furls in on itself, *interiorizes,* the operation covering, so far as we are concerned, the whole history of the earth. The phenomenon of spirit is not therefore a sort of brief flash in the night; it reveals a gradual and systematic passage from the unconscious to the conscious, and from the conscious to the self-conscious. It is a cosmic *change of state*.
>
> This irrefutably explains the links and also the contradictions between spirit and matter. And in a sense they are both fundamentally the same thing, as the neo-materialists allege; but between them lies also a point of deflection which makes them in some way the opposite of one another, as the ancient spiritualists maintained. All antimony between souls and bodies disappears in the hypothesis of a movement that has reached its 'critical point.'[13]

The moment that the spirit understood in this way manifested itself, there follow its intensifications about an irresistible, unavoidable and irreversible character.[14]

> Considered in its broadest dimensions and its most distant future, the phenomenon of spirit therefore ultimately represents the certain and definite appearance of a cosmic quantum of consciousness: that is to say in fact (since the two terms are identical) a quantum of personality.[15]

As soon as personality arises, there follows a further, almost cosmic process of joining together with consciousness:

> When we imagine that 'persons' cannot totalize (because their totalization would abolish the personalities that it set out to 'add to one another') we are instinctively thinking of rivers flowing into the sea, of salt dissolving in the ocean, of matter breaking down into cosmic energy. But these are deceptive analogies drawn from cases in which the unitive medium is indefinitely widespread: 'centrifugal' union by common relaxation or dis-

solution in an imagined homogeneous unconsciousness. In fact, in the case of the spirit, by virtue of the 'centripetal' movement of the spheres of consciousness (as we have accepted it) the phenomenon tends towards an exactly opposite result. In this convergent universe, all the lower centres unite, but by inclusion in a more powerful centre. Therefore they are all preserved and completed by joining together.[16]

With the appearance and concentration of a personalistic *centrum,* there follows also a change in morality, from a static morality based on an observance of prohibitions (being a system for the protection of the individual and society), to a dynamic morality which is no longer a limitation of energy, but rather its development. Dynamic morality brings about a cultivation of progress in the direction of spiritual good.

A morality of balance can be constructed and subsist closed in on itself. Since it sets out only to adjust associated elements to one another, it is sufficiently determined and sustained by a mutual agreement of the parties it reconciles. A minimum of internal frictions in a regulated state is both the ideal to which it tends and a sign that it has reached it.[17] . . . A morality of movement necessarily inclines towards the future, in pursuit of a God.[18]

He advances the postulate then that God should be

. . . a God of cosmic synthesis in whom we can be conscious of advancing and joining together by spiritual transformation of all the powers of matter . . . , that this same God shall act in the course of this synthesis as a first nucleus of independent consciousness: a supremely personal God, from whom we are the more indistinguishable the more we lose ourselves in him. The time had passed in which God could simply impose himself on us from without, as master and owner of the estate. Henceforth the world will only kneel before the organic centre of its evolution.[19]

Hitherto, a God of cosmos (that is, a creator of the 'efficient' type) was apparently all that was needed for our emotional and intellectual satisfaction. Henceforth (and it is here without a doubt that we should look for the underlying source of the modern religious uneasiness of mind) nothing but a God of cosmogenesis—that is a creator of the 'animating' type can come up to the full measure of our capacity for worship.

We must, of course, in the first place and as a matter of cosmic necessity, at all costs retain the primordial transcendence of this new *evolutive God,* who rises up at the heart of the old maker-God; for, if he had not pre-emerged from the world, how could he be for the world an issue and a consummation lying ahead? It is, nevertheless, equally important to look more deeply into his immanent character, to appreciate it with wonder and delight—or even more important, since it is precisely in this immanence that the new vision of God we look for consists.

In a system of convergent cosmogenesis, to create is for God *to unite*. To unite, to form one with something, is to be immersed in it; but to be immersed (in the plural) is to become a particle within it. And to become a particle in a world whose arrangement statistically entails disorder (and mechanically calls for effort) is to plunge into error and suffering, in order to overcome them.

And thus it is that there gradually emerges a remarkable and fruitful connexion between theology and Christology.[20] God cannot appear as a prime mover (ahead) without first becoming incarnate and without redeeming— in other words *without our seeing that he becomes Christified;* and in which, by way of complement, Christ can no longer 'justify' man except by that same act super-creating the entire universe. In consequence, if Christ is (in the words of St. Paul) 'to incorporate all things in himself and then to return to himself,' it is not enough (as, maybe, we used to think it was) that he supernaturally sanctify a harvest of souls—he must do more, and in that same movement, he must creatively carry the noogenesis of the cosmos to the natural term of its maturity.

Thus we witness the gradual emergence of the astonishing notion and vision of a certain universal *Christic energy, at once super-naturalizing and ultra-humanizing,* in which it is at the same time materialized and personalized the field of convergence that is necessary to explain and ensure the general and global involution of the cosmos in itself.[21] The Cosmic Christ is the *Centrum,* the Omega of the cosmos, a *Centrum* which constantly directs evolution and unfailingly brings it to completion. Christ's resurrection . . . marks Christ's effective assumption of his function as the universal centre. . . . Now he radiates over the whole universe as a consciousness and activity fully in control of themselves.[22] The world is the final, and the real, Host into which Christ gradually descends, until his time is fulfilled. Since all time a single word and a single act have been filling the universality of things: *Hoc est corpus meum.*[23]

Teilhard de Chardin's vision is fascinating and, to a great degree it satisfies the yearnings of contemporary man who seeks to reconcile science with religion. Teilhard de Chardin seems to show how these two aspects of human life not only mutually complement each other but, even more so, mutually postulate each other creating, it would seem, a perfect synthesis. Meanwhile, in order to evaluate the cognitive worth of this vision, we must look at the entire problem from the side of the applied methods of cognition. For the value of the results of cognition is closely connected with the character of cognition applied in a given area of science. And it is precisely in the vision that is presented here that we notice very serious omissions.

And so the "human fact" or the "human phenomenon" as interpreted by Teilhard de Chardin is drawn not from pre-scientific cognition but, on the one hand, from natural science, and, on the other hand, Christian religion.

If man appears against the background of nature as the result of evolution understood in a very wide sense, then such a determination of the "human fact" immediately implies a philosophical solution that concerns the ontic structure of man. "Scientific man" is not already something given to be explained but he is a "fact partially explained," and the character of this explanation is completely of the same order as the general character of a given science. Hence, man, who is presented against the background of nature, appears as the final member of the evolution of the material world. From a philosophical point of view, this is subject to doubt because the conception of evolution is a theory of nature that performs a similar role—from the point of view of a unifying cognition—in the area of natural science, just as the theory of analogy performs it in the area of classical philosophy, with the restriction that the theory of analogy is verifiable from the point of view of the system, while the theory of evolution is not a fully verifiable theory according to methods applied in the natural sciences. Furthermore, the necessary hypothetical conditions of an accepted evolution are either designated or presumed by a philosophical type of reasoning.

Concerning the second matter, namely, the fact of man seen with the eyes of revelation, we stand not so much on a cognitive and autonomous position, as rather on a believing one, where the will plays the deciding role by persuading reason by an act of faith. For faith is not an informing, verifiable cognition that directs itself by a single criterion of truth. Rather it is a complicated human act that equally involves the intellect as well as the will.[24] Hence, insofar as the human phenomenon appears in Revelation, it cannot be taken as some kind of scientific fact that is given further explication in philosophy. Illumined by faith, man is already interpreted ultimately (as the human fact) in a trans-scientific way. There is no further appeal from such an interpretation because the intellect is unable to verify what is given by faith.

If then in interpreting the human phenomenon, Teilhard de Chardin begins with both a natural interpretation, as well as one based on faith, and he builds against this background, his fascinating vision of man, that synthesizes science and religion, then such a vision is only a vision of a prophet and not a scientific vision, verifiable and capable of being proved in some way. It can be accepted only as a personal statement but not as an intersubjective, reasonable theory.

In addition we can detect many methodological errors in the Teilhardian vision, of which the basic one is a too daring extrapolation of the concept of evolution. For if palaeo-anthropological facts allow us to construct a parabola symbolizing man's evolution, this curve, however, partially shown on the canvas of facts investigated by palaeo-anthropology, was extended by

Teilhard de Chardin into infinity in both directions. As a result, we have received an impressive but non-verifiable vision.

From a purely philosophical point of view we can charge Teilhard with a henological conception of being which is experienced along with Neo-platonism. For to be a being does not mean to unite, but to exist. Teilhard achieves a determination of the spirit in a naturalistic-physical terminology (even though the description concerns fundamental structural-ontic discussions of man) in a way that recalls the pronouncements of the Pre-Socratics (Anaxagoras), and it makes no use of analyses of the problem made by mediaeval and contemporary thinkers.[25] I am not entering into a discussion of the relationship between the natural and the supernatural, because this would demand a further critique from another point of view.

B. MARXIST CONCEPTION OF MAN

It has become a truism that the present Marxist conception of man which is enriched in many ways is different from that of Marx himself. Marx[26] belonged to the Hegelian Left Wing, and after taking from his master the concept of the dialectic, he joined it not with the evolution of the Absolute Spirit or "Idea," but with matter. He took the concept of matter and materialism from Feuerbach, but along with Engels, his life-long friend, he gave to Feuerbachian materialism a different, precisely a "dialectical," character.

Concerning man himself, Marx pointed to his deformation that came from defective economico-social relations; man became a servant and slave of these relations which, of course, are his own creation. The alienation of man became the fundamental object of statements that constituted the basis for Marx's revolution. By his work, his creation, his government, his beliefs, man alienated himself so profoundly that he is individually incapable of returning by himself to a normal condition. For this reason, he is compelled to appeal to a basic, and as yet uncorrupted class, the proletariat, in order to create a classless society, which will enable man "to recover himself" anew and to cease being a "servant" and hence a slave of human productions. For Marx, the problem of alienation flows fundamentally from the problem of religious alienation,[27] but it is not exclusively limited to it. It affects the entire formation of social relations. "The criticism of religion ends with the teaching that *man is the highest being for man* and hence with the *categorical imperative to overthrow all relations* in which man is a debased, enslaved, forsaken, despicable being."[28]

Hence the securing by force and grounding of new economico-social relations in which man could develop all his abilities in which he feels himself a free co-creator of human culture and in which man will be respected and not thwarted: this is Marx's vision of a communistic community that would constitute the human environment. Of course Marx not only spread his "vision," but in his principal work, *Das Kapital,* he subjected to penetrating analysis and profound critique, capitalistic relations as a basis for contemporary conditions and commonly known historical data.

In contemporary times, Marxism[29] treats the problem of man in its descriptive aspect which concerns man's ontological and axiological status, as it is also connected with the concept of law. The following statements concern man's ontological structure:

(A) Man is a being of nature.[30] The materialistic and evolutionistic elements of the Marxist conception of man have as their object only the emphasizing of the genetic sameness of man with the surrounding world of matter: for in man's structure, material elements are only the foundation on which the edifice arises—in which are emphasized the essential or "qualitative" differences of man and of other creatures of nature.

(B) Qualitative traits that differentiate man from other creatures of nature seem to reduce themselves to three basics: consciousness, work, and social relations.

(1) Man's consciousness is different from that of animals. Man possesses self-consciousness. The animal in its consciousness, however, is directed to the world and its surroundings and by means of its instinct, it is bound to a particular segment of nature. On the other hand, man's consciousness is richer. Man "exists-for-himself," and thanks to this fact, he is independent of nature: he even dominates it. Human consciousness is reflective, universal and even free (in the Marxist interpretation).

(2) The phenomenon of work is the component or trait that distinguishes the human race from the other "remaining creatures of nature." The world of work is a specifically human world. Work is the consequence of the fact that, on the one hand, man is a being of nature; and on the other hand, he is a conscious being who dominates the world. The conscious character of work means that it is purposeful. When man undertakes work, he already has a prepared model in his mind of work and the various activities are arranged for the purpose of realizing this model. As a result of man's work, objective reality becomes a "human-world," a world of civilization and culture. "And in transforming the objective reality—nature and society—man transforms the conditions of his own existence, and consequently himself, too, as a species. In this way, the human process of *creation* is, from man's point of view, a process of *self-creation.*"[31]

(3) The third specific element of man's ontic structure is his social condition. This means that man lives in union with other people and this union is necessary for the preservation of being and the creation of conditions for

man's further development. Marx writes: "The essence of man is no abstraction inherent in each single individual. In its reality it is the ensemble of the social relations."[31a] (*Theses on Feuerbach*) Hence man possesses nothing that he has not drawn from society, and not only is he incapable of existing outside society but he cannot even be thought of independently of society. Above all, this is represented today as a class. For this reason man is a "class" being. Work and consciousness are derivative elements in relation to the social constitution of man; and, therefore, "personhood" in the Marxist sense is a function of social relations. This means that the spiritual personality of the human individual is changeable, even if nothing stands in the way of its being acknowledged as an individual and unrepeatable ontic exemplar. On the other hand, in the spirit of dialectical materialism, man cannot be understood as a spiritual being, because this would lead to the fallacy of an idealistic understanding of man. A human individual, however, possesses his own personality, and in relation to the community, according to the thought of some Marxist theoreticians, develops a correlation, which leads to a "dialectical oneness" that unites the community with the individual. In this way, it creates such a field of tensions, which do not permit the reduction of the individual to society nor of society to an aggregate of human individuals.[32]

However, in spite of these general precisions, man possesses nothing independently and beforehand which is "his own," nothing "independently" nor "personally." "Prior" to society, man of himself is like a *tabula rasa*. It is true that society itself is understood as a system of inter-related individuals; but even in relation with individuals, society is first: "It constitutes man's particular individuality and designates his manner of conduct in real social circumstances."

Any attempt to evaluate the Marxist conception of man presupposes a more or less critical reference to many components of this theory, i.e., to Hegel's philosophical system, to Feuerbach's materialism, to economic and social conditions of the nineteenth-century science itself (philosophy of science) which is at the basis of this philosophical interpretation.

However, independently of taking under consideration these very important and patently fundamental components, we can observe that this theory is not an explanation of the human fact which is given us in prescientific common sense cognition. Rather it presupposes an already constituted image of the human phenomenon that is given us against the background not only of various specific science, but in the light of an already interpreted complex of economico-social relations.

C. PSYCHOANALYTICAL INTERPRETATION OF MAN

The expression "psychoanalysis" is generally used to mean[33]

(a) empirical observations of such psychical determinants of personality that do not permit themselves to be uncovered by an analysis of rational motivations, e.g., by way of introspection.

(b) methods or a complex of activities directed toward the disclosure and examination of unconscious psychical activities for the purpose of psychical therapeutics by removing disorders caused by these unconscious factors.

(c) A theoretical anthropological system which would already be a theoretical conception truly rooted in empirical observations but modelled on a hypothetically deductive theory.

A theoretical psychoanalytical, anthropological system would perform the role of a source and model, which would permit an easier and more suitable application of therapeutic psychoanalytic treatments. A psychoanalytical model of man is already a theoretical interpretation of the "human fact," understood in some of his important aspects of illness, i.e., the neurotic "I." The workability of this model is not in fact necessarily linked with therapeutic treatments themselves. It can however help or make the diagnosis itself more difficult. It is important to examine the proposed model of man since "Freud attempted to formulate a theory which would explain the entire man, all his experiences and manifold directions of all his activity. We can judge that Freud was perhaps the last psychologist who understood the great calling of psychology as the science of man. And we can judge that he was the first modern psychologist who understood that there is needed, above all, a new science of man, a complete philosophical anthropology."[34]

The psychoanalytical direction would differ from the former direction of a psychology of consciousness with respect to the following moments:[35]

1. The principle of absolute determination of psychic phenomena; for each psychic phenomenon possesses a determinate cause, one or many, most often unknown to consciouness and which can be discovered and rationally explained with the help of analysis.

2. That of which we are unconscious (*das Unbewusste* which already appears in Hegel, Schopenhauer, Nietzsche, Hartmann and James) became understood as a power resulting from suppressed desires and which played a dominant role in the psyche.

3. The principle of motivation and purposefulness of psychic phenomena. The conscious psychic life is motivated by the unconscious and it strives to realize suppressed desires.

4. An evolutionary historical approach to psychic phenomena. They are processes and actualizations of personal traits which germinally appear in childhood.

5. A biologically sexual orientation in agreement with which personality is treated as having been determined by biological-sexual causes and the entire life is explained with the help of this principle.

6. An individualistic principle according to whose thinking social life is explained by laws which govern the individual. Society considers itself as the means of satisfying or restraining biological-sexual needs.

The Libido Theory is linked (in its beginnings) with an attempt to explain psychic disturbances which Freud had observed. Freud judged that in this kind of illnesses, the suppressed sexual energy is seeking substitute outlets. For the conscious "ego" censors certain thoughts that are connected with sexual experiences as if they were not to be accepted. The troublesome sexual drives leave traces and a permanent impress on the psyche:

> In the case of hysteria the unbearable idea was said to be made innocuous by the 'transmutation' into some bodily form of expression of this quantity of excitation which had been attached to the idea, a process which was called *conversion*. This conversion may be either partial or total and may 'proceed' along motor or sensory paths of innervation.[36]

Freud himself discusses the problem as follows:

> In the case of anyone who is predisposed to hysteria, the onset of his illness is precipitated when, either as a result of his own progressive maturity or of the external circumstances of his life, he finds himself faced by the demands of a real sexual situation. Between the pressure of the instinct and his antagonism to sexuality, illness offers him a way of escape. It does not solve his conflict, but seeks to evade it by transforming his libidinal impulses into symptoms.[37]

Further on, however, Freud observes:

> It is by no means only at the cost of the so-called *normal* sexual instinct that these symptoms originate—at any rate such is not exclusively or mainly the case; they also give expression (by conversion) to instincts which would be described as *perverse* in the widest sense of the word if they could be expressed directly in phantasy and action without being diverted from consciousness.[38]

Such neuroses as hysteria, neurasthenia, anxiety and depression have as their immediate cause specific "disturbances of a neurological economy" and as their common source, sexual disturbances. In the case of neurasthenia and anxiety neuroses, these disturbances refer only to an actual sex life; other neuroses are caused by past occurrences. The sex drive, *libido,* appeared to Freud as the principal driving force of the entire human life. When objections were raised from various quarters that he uses the term "sexual" to determine too wide an area of desires, he wrote in his work, *Massenpsychologie und Ich-Analyse:*

> Anyone who considers sex as something mortifying and humiliating to human nature is at liberty to make use of the more genteel expressions 'Eros' and 'erotic.' I might have done so myself from the first and thus have spared myself much opposition. But I did not want to, for I like to avoid concessions to faintheartedness. One can never tell where that road may lead; one gives way first in words, and then little by little to substance too.[39]

The Libido Theory which had such an essential influence on the general conception of man appears especially prominent in the so-called First Theory of Instincts. This theory appears explicitly in Freud's work around the year 1900. But he had already affirmed the libido much earlier as a vital force of neurosis. Now he incorporated the conception of the libido into the outlined theory of instincts, and assigned it one of the fundamental drives in life. They are the sexual drive as a drive to pleasure, and the drive to self-preservation. Contrary to the drive of self-preservation, *libido* does not subordinate itself easily to the "principle of reality." On the other hand, the instinct of self-preservation which recognizes this principle and defends itself against pain, can oppose libido so as not to expose itself to an even greater pain. Hence the principle of reality performs a very essential role in the formation of man's personality.

Both drives, and especially the sexual drive, are chiefly characterized by the fact that their impulses arise from the same human organism; and consequently the drive is at the same time a physiological drive and its mental representation. And because it has its source in the organism, it acts as a continuous power from which there is no escape. These drives express definite needs, and these can be removed only by their satisfaction:

> Each drive has its own *end*—the removal of the physiological irritation—as well as its *object*—the means of achieving satisfaction; the drive directs itself toward some *object* when this latter drive is particularly suited to its satisfaction. The object of a drive may be subject to change—then we are dealing with a so-called *transformation of a drive*. . . . A drive can also be subject to a so-called sublimation. *Sublimation* is a process in which the goal of a direct gratification, for example, of a sexual drive becomes abandoned as the result of the activity of a so-called suppression. In its place there appears a new goal, although it is connected with the original goal and the object of the drive has been changed.[40]

The very essence of suppression depends on the negation of the sexual drive and not admitting it into consciousness.

Freud was especially interested in the succession of vicissitudes of libido and especially in the influence of the instinct of self-preservation on the different forms of its activity. The dialectical tension between the sexual drive and that of self-preservation passes through different phases: unconscious, pre-conscious and conscious. Between the particular phases (understood in a topographical sense—as a region of the psyche and in the sense of explaining the phases), are so-called "censors" that control the transformation of the context from the unconscious to the conscious. This censoring is the activity of the *ego drive* of self-preservation, but the transformation from the unconscious to the conscious is the dialectical movement of the psychic contents and the moments of this movement are the psychic states as the results of the conflicting instincts: libido and ego.

The development of the libido, and the simultaneous activity of the moral-aesthetic censors from the side of the ego, take on many different forms of expression, among which dreams and mistakes can be recognized as factors that can help in deciphering the proper content which reaches consciousness in a camouflaged state. Above all however, man must be regarded as a historical creature in whom sexuality develops from childhood and assumes many different forms of expression, which are not unimportant for understanding psychoneurosis in adulthood. Sexuality and neuroses of adulthood which are linked with it should be explained not only by repression and displacement, but also by sexual experience in childhood in which the libido's activity moves from the oral to the anal and genital spheres:

> Freud suggested that three orifices of the body, the mouth, anus and genitals were especially endowed with libido, and he noted that there seemed to be a uniform order of development of interest and satisfaction in these three parts. The first organ of interest for the child is the mouth. For the newborn infant this is the all-absorbing organ of pleasure. Through it he makes contact with the first object of libido, the mother's breast. In the absence of the breast he hallucinates contact with it by sucking his thumb. Freud likened the infant's bliss after nursing to the relaxation after orgasm. This was seen as the first pre-genital stage of development characterized by sucking pleasure and the latter by biting pleasure.
>
> According to Freud, towards the end of the first year of life the center of libidinal interest begins to shift to the anal region, and the infant's chief source of erotic pleasure becomes connected with retention and expulsion of feces. This, he noted also, is related to the parents in terms of defiance and submission and has much to do with a developing feeling of power. The child discovers that the retention and expulsion of feces excites great interest in those who care for him. By prolonged withholding he can reduce

the parent at times to distraction, or by choosing his own ways of expulsion he can arouse feelings of annoyance and exasperation in those responsible for his care, and he presently learns that submitting to the parents' wishes gains approbation. The tendency to have an active or passive attitude towards life first becomes apparent at this time. It is evident that in describing this stage Freud is, in fact if not in intention, describing much more than the possible erotic pleasures connected with the anal zone. He is describing also a complex interpersonal situation.

The next place the libido has as its object of interest is the penis, ushering in the phallic stage, which is the third pregenital stage of libidinal development.[41]

It is at this stage that the oedipus and castration complex appear. Meanwhile the awakening psychic powers of the ego repress the sexual drive which enters into a latent state until the period of puberty, when the increased activity of the sexual glands causes a new awakening in sexual interests in the genital period.

Freud's second theory of instincts is connected with World War I happenings, as well as with certain phenomena (of aggression) of psychic life, which could not be explained any more through the activity of the libido. In observing soldiers who had been stricken with traumatic neuroses, Freud noticed a tendency to repeat past, even unpleasant situations. This tendency acts as a compulsion—an automatic repetition independently of actual requirements of a situation—which might be an attempt to neutralize the trauma either by returning to the state prior to the shock or by subduing them due to repetition. If, then, the soldiers were not able to recall the suppressed experiences but they reactivated them as actual experiences along with the compulsive tendency of repeating such experiences, this would be contradictory to the general psychoanalytical principles, where the drive to pleasure constituted the foundation for interpretation.

In view of this it was necessary to change the psychoanalytical foundations by accepting in the human "personality" the existence of two contradictory drives that mutually condition each other: EROS the instinct of life and THANATOS the instinct of death. EROS is not a new invention since it includes the previous LIBIDO as well as a portion of the instinct of self-preservation, i.e., EGO. Not abandoning his fundamentally biological interpretation, he emphasizes the instinct of death which is the foundation for explaining the phenomena of aggression and certain neuroses. The instinct of death would be the drive of organic life to return to the inorganic state from which it arose.

The energy of this instinct is definitely not libido but destructiveness or aggression directed primarily towards the self. It is the force within us which is working towards death. This death instinct Freud now conceived as playing fully as important a part in human life as the libido. The repetition compulsion theoretically is related to the death instinct. It is an expression of the tendency of life to return to earlier states. In the last analysis, this is the tendency of organic life to return to the inorganic.

Sadism must be fitted into this picture. Sadism is produced by combining some of the forces of the death instinct with the libido. This Freud saw as an attempt at self-preservation. By erotizing some of the destructive forces they become less dangerous to life. The life force tends to neutralize some of their power.

In order to be consistent with the theory of a death instinct, it was necessary to assume that the destructive drive was directed primarily against oneself and was only secondarily turned outward in aggression towards others. This meant revising his earlier conception of sadism and masochism. He now thought of masochism as the most direct type of union between libido and destructiveness, and sadism as a secondary development, whereas his early idea had been that sadism was primary and masochism was the result of turning sadism against the self.

The problem of life as he now saw it was to keep the self-destructive drive within bounds. This was done either by erotizing it (combining it with libido to form masochism or sadism) or by turning it outwards towards others in aggression. This death instinct turned outwards supplied the drive producing wars. A nation which does not fight, he thought, must destroy itself. Therefore a war is a nation's attempt at self-preservation. Suicide is seen as evidence of failure to turn the death instinct outward; so are expressions of masochism.

According to the new theory, there are two reasons why we manage to live for many years in spite of our death instinct. One is our ability to turn the energy outward and attack others, and our second protection is the tendency of the life instinct to combine with the death instinct to form masochism. It was assumed that in the combination, the two forces tend to neutralize each other, and the destructive drive, for a time at least, becomes less harmful. But it eventually succeeds in 'doing' the individual to death.[42]

In this second version of psychoanalysis, we have dealt with three areas of human life: ID—it; EGO—self; and SUPEREGO—superself.

The functions of unconsciousness, pre-consciousness and consciousness can be connected with each of the three regions:

Id (unconscious system) which is lined to somatic processes, is a great reservoir of the libido and the death drive. Irrational by its nature and alien to the Ego and its values, the Id, as if insensible to the passage of time is, in this sense, immortal. *Ego* is a a coherent organization of psychic processes; it represents reason and health. At the same time, it exercises a control over consciousness both during waking moments as well as in sleep (censors) and it is responsible for repressions. Essentially, however, ego is a part of id which is formed by its relation to the external world and it draws its energy from the id; on the other hand, ego controls id's blind impulses; it saves it from self-destruction. *Super-ego* is a function of the ego which arises as the result of ego's ability to treat itself as an object. Not only does it possess a great independence with respect to the ego but it even dominates and controls it with complete severity. Superego represents moral and social demands. It is the source of so-called moral conscience, "feelings of guilt," etc. Children have no inner inhibitions about seeking pleasure: the impulses of the id, which cause their conduct, direct themselves only to the selection of an object which will give them satisfaction (*cathexis*). In the process of education, these impulses are restrained by the ego and superego powers of the parents, who counteract the cathexis drives of the id (*anticathexis*). Gradually the child accepts as its own (introspection) the moral and customary commands and prohibitions of the parents and in this way, it educates its own superego. The superego's development is fundamentally a process of *identification* of the child's ego with the ego or, more precisely, the superego of the parents (chiefly of the father), next with that of teachers, of educators and of other social authorities. Thus the educational process guarantees the continuity of tradition and it 'inserts' the individual into the stream of a given social and cultural life.[43]

Against the background of the general outline of human personality which we have presented, we can notice delineated a theory of neurosis composed of various experiences: "fixation," which takes place when parts of the libido restrain themselves in the earlier development or earlier object of *cathexis;* "regression," when parts of the libido regress to a lower level; regression is the result of "frustration," i.e., repression of the drive and the impossibility of its satisfaction by the superego.

Conflict is the product of the libido's frustration by the superego. When the repressing power is stronger, libido withdraws to an earlier stage of development and the ego loses its control over it and neurosis erupts. We must distinguish perversion from neurosis when we are dealing with a fixation of the libido which is sanctioned by the ego. In neurosis, the stifled libido finds an outlet in fantasies and "symptoms" that are the deformed expression of unconscious drives and the disguised repetition of infantile sexual experiments. Fantasies and symptoms are a "psychic reality" for the neurotic. Even for healthy people they can become a substitute for pleasures which were not realized in reality.[44]

Freud's psychoanalytic theory of personality was constructed in order to explain many facts of human life. But these facts can be explained in a different way than that which Freud postulated. In actuality, after Freud there appeared a whole series of psychoanalytical schools which explained these very facts differently than what the creator of depth psychology suggests. As an example, it will suffice to quote the judgment of C. Thompson, who observes:

> Freud's errors in theory were of two general types. He often mistook cultural phenomena for biological instinctual phenomena. Some of the stages of development are definitely products of this culture. Even when it is pretty clear that there are strong biological elements, these are not always sexual in nature. Freud placed all the emphasis on the erotization of a situation when it may have been purely developmental; that is, a stage in the process of growing appearing when the nerve paths are adequately developed. For instance, to be consistent with Freud's theory, a child learns to stand upright and learns to take his first steps because of the erotic pleasures from such use of his muscles. It seems much more likely that it happens because nerve pathways and muscles are sufficiently developed for the next stage in growth.
>
> When we consider the stages in Freud's scheme in the light of these criticisms, it will be found that the general order of development in our society has been accurately observed by him and that the stages may be re-evaluated in the light of other data. The oral stage seems to be chiefly determined by biological development. The newborn infant is chiefly a mouth. The most developed part of the cortex at birth is that which governs the oral zone. We are justified in assuming that the infant contacts the world and comprehends it in the beginning primarily in terms of mouth. We, however, question whether the erotic satisfaction obtained is the determining factor. It seems more likely that he contacts the world by mouth because it is his most adequate organ.[45]

As a result, while the author acknowledges Freud's contributions, the same facts can be interpreted differently in the light of cultural experiences. Besides, Freud very quickly encountered dissidents within his own circle; namely, Adler and Jung.

The unusually serious matter of a psychoanalytical model of man which Freud proposed appears as a background and, at the same time, a direction of therapy. This model is fundamentally wrong. For Freud denies the one, subsistent, substantially-personal subject of activity, who is man. Man and his consciousness would be something secondary, something that has arisen from the dialectical (and sometimes mechanical), a combination of superpersonal forces, sometimes of purely mechanical ones. These forces called instinct are, in their primordial phase, unconscious. Consciousness in man would be something merely historical. It is true that historically consciousness does appear in a circumscribed state of biological development, but its recognition as something secondary in man—as something which must be explained by appealing to instinctive and prepersonal powers and their natural mechanism of activity—cannot be accepted if we admit from another source the acknowledged ontic unity of man. In Freud's theoretical conception, man appears as a mish-mash of rather haphazard impersonal forces. In addition it is most evident that along with the conception of unconsciousness, struggle and accumulation of impersonal forces, Freud used the old Hegelian conception of dialectical evolution from thesis through antithesis to synthesis and although imprecisely, nevertheless there can be recognized the foundation for the evolution of the ID as a power of the inorganic state which is fundamentally common to the entire universe. Man would appear as a particular place for the struggles of various powers, but precisely as such he would have to be only a "moment," a "reflection" of the whole, which is the power of the inorganic state. This is the position formulated by Hegel. The denial of the subjective-ontic personality makes it impossible to accept the model of personality proposed by Freud as the model for the universal understanding of man.

This does not mean, however, that the Freudian model is useless and that his investigations are useless for science. It only means that this model is inadequate in relation to the "human fact," which appears richer than the one drawn from it, and selected (usually a priori) elements that were subject to individual interpretation—thanks to which the model of man is oriented practically; it allows for the achievement of certain therapeutic actions and shows itself to be restricted and incorrect because it omits the essential trait of man's subjectivity.

Beginning with the analyses of neurosis as described by Freud, Adler denies the foundations of their explanation. "My critical remarks," writes Adler in *Über den nervösen charakter,*

> permit us to surmise the kind of answer to the questions which can present themselves in connection with neuroses. How do manifestations of neuroses appear? Why is the patient striving to be a complete man and why is he constantly seeking to give proof of his own superiority? Whence arises in him the strong need to foster feelings of his own personality? Why does he seek certain ways and not others? Why does he seek to assure for himself feelings of security? To our mind, all these facts can be explained very directly: the starting point of the evolution of neuroses is a threatening feeling of uncertainty and inferiority, a feeling which begets a compulsive need to find some kind of purpose which would make life bearable, would give it some kind of direction, would be the source of peace and security. To our mind, the essence of neuroses is due to the constant and exaggerated use of psychic media on the subject. These psychic media are to a great extent auxiliary and conventional constructs that are furnished by thought, will and action. It is evident that a psyche which finds itself in

such a state of pressure, a subject which is trying so hard to elevate the value of its own personality, does not bend easily to the structure and demands of social life and so, independently of this or that kind of apparently banal and commonplace neurotic phenomena, a neurotic is subject to such a degree to an obsessive consciousness of that which is a weak point so that without realizing it, he directs all his powers to the creation of an ideal and imagined superstructure from which he expects help and protection.[46]

Jung explains neuroses in yet another way and he thereby modifies the psychoanalytic model of man. In *Über die Psychologie des Unbewusten*, he writes:

Both are obviously working with the same material; but because of personal peculiarities that each see things from a different angle, and thus they evolve fundamentally different views and theories. Adler sees how a subject who feels suppressed and inferior tries to secure an illusory superiority by means of 'protests,' 'arrangements,' and other appropriate devices directed equally against parents, teachers, regulations, authorities, situations, institutions and such. Even sexuality may figure among these devices. This view lays undue emphasis upon the subject, before which the idiosyncrasy and significance of objects entirely vanishes. Objects are regarded at best as vehicles of suppressive tendencies. I shall probably not be wrong in assuming that the love relation and other desires ~~directed against objects~~ exist equally in Adler as essential factors; yet in his theory of neurosis they do not play the principal role assigned them by Freud.

Freud sees his patient in perpetual dependence on, and in relation to, significant objects. Father and mother play large parts here; whatever other significant influences or conditions enter into the life of the patient go back in a direct line of causality to these prime factors. The *pièce de résistance* of his theory is the concept of transference, i.e., the patient's relation to the doctor. Always a specifically qualified object is either desired or met with resistance, and this reaction always follows the pattern established in the earliest childhood through the relation to father and mother. What comes from the subject is essentially a blind striving after pleasure; but this striving always acquires its quality from specific objects. With Freud objects are of the greatest significance and possess almost exclusively the determining power, while the subject remains remarkably insignificant and is really nothing more than the source of desire for pleasure and a 'seat of anxiety.' As already pointed out, Freud recognizes ego-instincts, but this term alone is enough to show that his conception of the subject differs *toto coelo* from Adler's where the subject figures as the determining factor.

Certainly both investigators see the subject in relation to the object; but how differently this relation is seen! With Adler the emphasis is placed on a subject who, no matter what the object, seeks his own security and supremacy; with Freud the emphasis is placed wholly upon objects which, according to their specific character, either promote or hinder the subject's desire for pleasure.

~~The~~ *this* difference can hardly be anything else but a difference of temperament, a contrast between two types of human mentality, one of which finds the determining agency pre-eminently in the subject, the other in the object. A middle view, it may be that of common sense, would suppose that human behavior is conditioned as much by the subject as by the object. The two investigators would probably assert, on the other hand, that their theory does not envisage a psychological explanation of the normal man, but *is* a theory of neurosis. But in that case Freud would have to explain and treat some of his patients along Adlerian lines and Adler condescend to give earnest consideration in certain instances to his former teacher's point of view—which has occurred neither on the one side nor on the other.

The spectacle of this dilemma made me ponder the question: are there at least two different types, one of them more interested in the object, the other more interested in himself? And does that explain why the one sees only the one and the other only the other, and thus each arrives at totally different conclusions? As we have said, it was hardly to be supposed that fate selected the patients so meticulously that a definite group invariably reached a definite doctor. For some time it had struck me, in connection both with myself and with my colleagues, that there are some cases which make a distinct appeal, while others somehow refuse to 'click.' It is of crucial importance for the treatment whether a good relationship between doctor and patient is possible or not. If some measure of natural confidence does not develop within a short period, then the patient will do better to choose another doctor. I myself have never shrunk from recommending to a colleague a patient whose peculiarities were not in my line or were unsympathetic to me and indeed this is in the patient's own interests. I am positive that in such a case I would not do good work. Everyone has his personal limitations and the psychotherapist in particular is well advised never to disregard them. Excessive personal differences and incompatibilities cause resistances that are disproportionate and out of place, though they are not altogether unjustified. The Freud-Adler controversy is simply a paradigm and one single instance among many possible attitude-types.

I have long busied myself with this question and have finally, on the basis of numerous observations and experiences, come to postulate two fundamental attitudes, namely introversion and extr*a*version.[47]

In addition, in *Das Unbewusste im normalen und kranken Seelenleben*, Jung tried to define the concept of non-consciousness by distinguishing between individual and collective consciousness:

The fact of this inheritance explains the truly amazing phenomenon that certain motifs from myths and legends repeat themselves the world over in identical forms. It also explains why it is that our mental patients can reproduce exactly the same images and associations that are known to us from the old texts. I give some examples of this in my book *Symbols of Transformation*. In doing so I do not by any means assert the inheritance of ideas but only of the possibility of such ideas, which is something very different.

In this further stage of treatment, then, when fantasies are produced which no longer rest on personal memories, we have to do with the manifestations of a deeper layer of the unconscious where the primordial images common to humanity lie sleeping. I have called these images or motifs 'archetypes,' also 'dominants' of the unconscious. For a further elucidation of the idea, I must refer the reader to the relevant literature.

This discovery means another step forward in our understanding; the recognition, that is, of two layers in the unconscious. We have to distinguish between a personal unconscious and an impersonal or transpersonal unconscious. We speak of the latter also as the collective unconscious, because it is detached from anything personal and is entirely universal, and because its contents can be found everywhere, which is naturally not the case with the personal contents.[48]

Karen Horney, the German psychoanalyst who lived in the United States, sees the problem of neuroses which were described by Freud, Adler and Jung in still another way. According to her, neurosis arises from social frustration: a neurotic personality is the product of our times. It is the product of urban civilization, of competition and anxiety which are caused by certain forms of social life. She broke completely with Freud's biological view: "In the last analysis, the advances of neurosis in particular individuals have their source in feelings of isolation, hostility, fear and lessened faith in oneself."[49]

Other models for the explanation of neurosis were given by E. Fromm and H. S. Sullivan who analyze man against the background of interpersonal relationships. Fromm sees the problem of man as a specific kind of relation of the individual to the world and to himself.

. . . man gets into neurotic difficulties as a result of the new needs created in him by his culture as well as because of deprivations and frustrations of his potentialities forced upon him by it. Man's lust for power and his yearning for submission, for example, are not basic biological needs but attitudes developed out of the raw material of human nature by a specific culture. When predominating trends in the culture are destructive, the individual in it becomes frustrated and also destructive of himself and others. So man's most compelling problems have to do with the needs his society has created in him. These, not sex or aggression as such, create his greatest difficulties. Today man has finally become aware of himself as a separate entity.

With the growing realization of separateness there comes a sense of isolation and a longing to return to the earlier feeling of solidarity with others. But man cannot return to his original state. On the other hand, he has gained 'freedom from' but often he has acquired 'freedom to' develop as an individual. So he uses certain irrational methods of relating back to the group: sado-masochism, destructiveness, automaton conformity. These Fromm calls mechanism of escape.[50]

Sullivan calls his conception the theory of interpersonal relationships:

I add that, given a biological substrate, the human is the product of interaction with other human beings, that it is out of the personal and social forces acting upon one from the day of birth that the personality emerges. The human being is concerned with two inclusive goals, the pursuit of satisfaction and the pursuit of security. The pursuit of satisfaction chiefly deals with biological needs, but pursuit of security is primarily concerned with and is a result of the cultural process. The two are intertwined.[51]

The outlined general conceptions of man appearing against the background of psychoanalysis show that the theoretical model of man can be changed, depending on the emphasis of certain facts or aspects in psychoanalytical research. These theories present a certain conception of man. Their common danger is to conceive man as a set of relations of certain powers or drives, chiefly biological and sometimes social or cultural. Doubtless such matters are properly analyzed. However they can fulfill their role of a useful model only when the outlined conception of man appears with the use of a strictly philosophical method. The conception of man that appears in the light of such an applied method will show us a subsistent, personal being who is the bearer of the most diverse powers and tendencies — who, however, is not only the sum of these powers but a person who directs more or less consciously his psychic activity. In man's life, however, there are also such elements or moments which, isolated from context and correspondingly interpreted, give as a result a psychoanalytical picture which is sometimes useful for understanding certain human conditions.

D. PHILOSOPHICAL IMPLICATIONS OF STRUCTURALISM IN THE AREA OF ANTHROPOLOGY

Structuralism does not present any one concise conception of thought but it is rather a general direction in which there appear and develop various currents of a scientific interpretation of all kinds of areas of human life.[52] And for this reason the philosophical aspects of structuralism are connected more with epistemological consequences of methods proposed by some authors than directly with affirmations or propositions of leading thinkers of this trend.[53] This does not mean, however, that such propositions—at least in the case of some authors—are lacking or that they are something entirely marginal and not connected with a pursued method of investigation. On the contrary they are, so it seems, very essential affirmations whose understanding and acceptance make known a minute method of describing cultural phenomena, especially in the field of ethnology, which is perhaps most intimately connected with the understanding of man.[54] But structuralism also finds its expression in psychoanalysis, sociology and linguistics.

Linguistics has become perhaps one of the most rewarding areas of analysis for structuralists. More strictly speaking, it was the structuralists who sought to contact linguists of the caliber of G. F. de Saussure, his historic work, *Cours de la linguistique générale* (Ed. in 1916 but known earlier through his lectures), as well as the Russian linguists, R. Jacobson, S. Karczewski and N. Trubecki. By observing that there is no necessary connection between concepts and their material significants—even though within the framework of a language they are not a merely arbitrary arrangement, the differentiation between language and speech which a human individual uses and who includes himself through his speech in the objective structure of the language and finally, the investigation of these structures of language, both in neopositivistic circles as well as from another aspect, with the Kazan (Russian) School—became to some degree, a premise for the affirmation of an objective structure of the human language and its function in the formation of the psyche of man.[55]

Claude Lévi-Strauss, one of the originators, and at the same time most representative structuralist thinkers, expresses his conviction that objective human language contains within itself everything which *de facto* was expressed and became a cultural property of mankind, as well as everything that can be expressed by man. Hence language is a structure which embraces all spiritual possibilities of man or otherwise: the spiritual possibilities of man and their limits are conditioned and circumscribed by the objective function of language:

> For language does not consist in the analytical reason of old-style grammarians nor in the dialectic constituted by structural linguistics nor in the constitutive dialectic of individual *praxis* facing the practico-inert, since all three presuppose it. Linguistic thus presents us with a dialectical and totalizing entity but one outside (or beneath) consciousness and will. Language, an unreflecting totalization, is human reason which has its reasons and of which man knows nothing. And if it is objected that it is so only for a subject who internalizes it on the basis of linguistic theory, my reply is that this way out must be refused, for this subject is one who *speaks:* for

the same light which reveals the nature of language to him also reveals to him that it was so when he did not know it, for he already made himself understood, and that it will remain so tomorrow without his being aware of it, since his discourse never was and never will be the result of a conscious totalization of linguistic laws.[56]

The difference between reflexive or rational and spontaneous and uncontrolled thought loses its ontic reason since in both forms of thinking, the sense comes from an objective system of signs, which is expressed by man who speaks independently of the kind of *stadium* of historical development in which man finds himself.

> The idea that the universe of primitives (or supposedly such) consists principally in messages is not new. . . . Physical science had to discover that a semantic universe possesses all the characteristics of an object in its own right for it to be recognized, that the manner in which primitive peoples conceptualize their world is not merely coherent but the very one demanded in the case of an object whose elementary structure presents the picture of a discontinuous complexity.
>
> The false antinomy between logical and prelogical mentality was surmounted at the same time. The savage mind is logical in the same sense and the same fashion as ours, though as our own is only when it is applied to knowledge of a universe in which it recognizes physical and semantic properties simultaneously.[57]

Objective language permeates the whole of human life which is above all a social life. It is bound up with all kinds of symbols, since even such a fundamental prohibition as that of incest in various cultures is not the direct result of nature but of culture which evidences itself in the form of functioning of suitable symbols. The problem therefore depends on this: that with the help of sufficiently advanced analyses of various phenomena of social life (or human life in general) we should find a suitable structure in which are expressed (or eventually it will be possible to express) all forms of symbols that appear in social life. Such a structure is language whose analysis can make possible an understanding of other symbolic functions of social life which are realized on the basis of logic bound with the very function of language. Hence anthropology as the most general theory of relation (perhaps fundamentally interhuman) would be understandable only through an analysis of linguistic structure.[58]

Clearly such a "structural" vision stands fundamentally in opposition to a historical understanding of man.

> In fact history is tied neither to man nor to any particular object. It consists wholly in its method which experience proves to be indispensable for

cataloguing the elements of any structure whatever, human or non-human, in their entirety. It is therefore far from being the case that the search for intelligibility comes to an end in history as though this were its terminus. Rather, it is a history that serves as a point of departure in any quest for intelligibility. As we say of certain careers, history may lead to anything, provided you get out of it.[59]

Truly human thought, even when uncontrolled, is deeply rooted in historical thinking, nevertheless, "the characteristic feature of the savage mind is its timelessness; its object is to grasp the world as both a synchronic and a diachronic totality and the knowledge which it draws therefrom is like that afforded of a room by mirrors fixed on opposite walls, which reflect each other (as well as objects in the intervening space) although without being strictly parallel."[60]

A complete understanding of diachrony is attained only with synchrony but, on the other hand, the attainment of the deepest unconscious structures is accomplished only by appealing to diachrony.

If, as we believe to be the case, the unconscious activity of the mind consists in imposing forms upon content, and if these forms are fundamentally the same for all minds—ancient and modern, primitive and civilized, (as the study of the symbolic function, expressed in language, so strikingly indicates)—it is necessary and sufficient to grasp the unconscious structure underlying each institution and each custom, in order to obtain a principle of each institution and other customs, provided of course that the analysis is carried far enough.

How are we to apprehend this unconscious structure? Here anthropological method and historical method converge. It is unnecessary to refer here to the problem of diachronic structures, for which historical knowledge is naturally indispensable. Certain developments of social life no doubt require a diachronic structure. But the example of phonemics teaches anthropologists that this study is more complex and presents other problems than the study of synchronic structures, which they are only beginning to consider. Even the analysis of synchronic structures, however, requires the constant recourse to history. By showing institutions in the process of transformation, history alone makes it possible to abstract the structure which underlies the many manifestations and remains permanent throughout a succession of events.[61]

Synchrony and diachrony which mutually condition and interpenetrate each other, reveal the fundamental unconscious anthropological structures. But ultimately how is man to be understood against the background of such an outlined anthropology? Who is he? Is he the subject of an objective language? Probably not. On the basis of structuralism, subjectivity is radically denied. "There would be plenty to say about this supposed totalizing continuity of the self which seems to be an illusion sustained by the demands of social life—and consequently a reflection of the external on the internal—rather than the object of an apodictic experience."[62]

Western European civilization is under the powerful influence of philosophers who affirm that the human subject is the focal point for the understanding of the world. A philosophy of subjectivity begun by Descartes and developed by Kant and Hegel undoubtedly influenced the thinking of contemporary existentialists. "Descartes, who wanted to found a physics, separated Man from Society. Sartre, who claims to found an anthropology, separates his own society from others. A Cogito—which strives to be ingenuous and raw—retreats into individualism and empiricism and is lost in the blind alleys of social psychology."[63] Besides, these are communities by accident, as a strike, a boxing match, football game, waiting in line at a bus stop. They are secondary incidents of social life and hence do not lend themselves to the discovery of its foundations. Man can be understood only on the basis of ethnology. "I regard anthropology as the principle of all research, while for Sartre it raises a problem in the shape of a constraint to overcome or a resistance to reduce."[64] In order to investigate man, we must learn—as Rousseau has already postulated—to look afar and it is not enough to limit ourselves even to some investigation of natural groups of humanity. For

each of the tens or hundreds of thousands of societies which have existed side by side in the world or succeeded one another since man's first appearance, has claimed that it contains the essence of all the meaning and dignity of which human society is capable, and, reduced though it may have been to a small nomad band or a hamlet lost in the depths of the forest, its claim has its own eyes rested on a moral certainty comparable to that which we can invoke in our own case. But whether in their case or our own, a good deal of egocentricity and naivety is necessary to believe that man has taken refuge in a single one of the historical or geographical modes of his existence, when the truth about man resides in the system of their differences and common properties.[65]

Keeping in mind the necessity of a widest, objective (because ethnological view of man), C. Lévi-Strauss disqualifies methods of analysis of our own "I" which, besides, does not exist because it is only an interiorization of objective language. Besides, "he who begins by steeping himself in the allegedly self-evident truths of introspection never emerges from them. Knowledge of men sometimes seems easier to those who allow themselves to be caught up in the snare of personal identity. But they thus shut the door on knowledge of man."[66]

Hence the widest view of man which ethnology furnishes, enables us to recognize the importance of objective linguistic structure which expresses everything that culture contributes. For objective language is the bearer at the same time of what is called in Freud's psychoanalysis, the "Super-ego." J. Lacan called attention to the fact that the Super-ego conveyed through the language of a maturing man, gives content to the human psyche. It is grafted on language; along with language, it is the objective structure. Hence man's subjectivity disappears. We can no longer speak about a talking subject, about the fact that "I" am speaking but only about the fact that "one speaks," *"ça parle."*[67]

Linguistic structure, however, reveals other, perhaps more fundamental structures, which are at the same time more understandable. "Scientific explanation consists not in moving from the complex to the simple but in the replacement of a less intelligible complexity by one which is more so."[68] For it turned out that man as a speaking subject—seemingly self-knowable, according to Lévi-Strauss' statement; in reality, however, finding his understanding in a linguistic totality (of which the supposedly evident "I" is only an interiorization)—is only the beginning of a process in reduction. "But if, as a speaking subject, man can find his apodictic experience in an *other* totalization, there seems no longer any reason why, as a living subject, he should not have access to the same experience in other, not necessarily human, but living beings."[69] Hence we must achieve a reduction based on a defined method which Lévi-Strauss calls a doubly progressive-regressive ethnological method:

> In the first stage we observe the datum of experience, analyse it in the present, try to grasp its historical antecedents as far as we can delve into the past, and bring all these facts back to the light of day to incorporate them into a meaningful totality. The second stage, which repeats the first on a different plane and at a different level, then begins. This internalized human thing which we have sought to provide with all its wealth and originality, only fixes the distance analytical reason must cover, the leap it must make, to close the gap between the ever unforeseen complexity of this new object and the intellectual means at its disposal.[70]

Lévi-Strauss realizes that by achieving this reduction and by broadening the structures, he exposes himself to so-called "lessening of sensibility" and because of it, the loss of gains for some kind of trace of intelligibility. Nevertheless he expresses the conviction that the real problem is not to know—whether in hastening to understand, we transmit the sense or lose it—but rather, whether the preserved sense is more valuable than that which we have relinquished. Because, and this is an extremely important matter:

All meaning is answerable to a lesser meaning, which gives it its highest meaning, and if this regression finally ends in recognizing a 'contingent law of which one can only say: *it is thus,* and not otherwise', this prospect is not alarming to those whose thought is not tormented by transcendence even in a latent form. For man will have gained all he can reasonably hope for if, on the sole condition of bowing to this contingent law, he succeeds in determining his form of conduct and in placing all else in the realm of the intelligible.[71]

What, however, is this sphere of intelligibility? Perhaps we are dealing with an intelligibility understood incorrectly. Let us turn our attention to the sequence of thought explained by C. Lévi-Strauss. First of all, we are searching for the general, insofar as possible for the most universal structures which will explain the general human relations which ethnology reveals. General, human, social relations which constitute the area of anthropology are understood and explained through objective linguistic structure that is capable of explaining even the feeling of the ego, since at the foundation of things, it is only an appearance and interiorization of language. But the structure of language, even if it is mutually extended in relation to culture and even if the limits of language are the limits of thinking and of culture, nevertheless it is not the only structure because there appear in it such aspects that testify about the existence of more fundamental structures which must be shown in the application of a progressive-regressive ethnological method, since, in the case of an analysis of an exotic society,

. . . it would merely confront us, in a more general manner than others, with an unconscious teleology which, although historical, completely eludes human history: that of which certain aspects are revealed by linguistics and psycho-analysis and which rests on the interplay of biological mechanisms (structure of the brain, lesions, internal secretions) and psychological ones. This, it seems to me, is "the bone" (to borrow a phrase from Sartre) which his critique does not manage to break, and moreover cares nothing about, which is the most serious charge one could level at it.[72]

The revealed and increasingly more basic structures, linguistic, psychoanalytical and biological, are only stages of a reduction for the disclosure of the ultimate and most fundamental structures which are inert matter and the law of accidentality that governs it.

Secondly, one must be ready to accept, as a consequence of each reduction, the total overturning of any preconceived idea concerning the level, whichever it may be, one is striving to attain. The idea of some general humanity to which ethnographic reduction leads, will bear no relation to any one may have formed in advance. And when we do finally succeed in understanding life as a function of inert matter, it will be to discover that the latter has properties very different from those previously attributed to it.[73]

Indeed, Lévi-Strauss holds the position that the new appearance of a property does not imply the destruction of the structure or of a prior totality. It only makes possible a better understanding of it, just as the dissolution of a stable body changes the arrangement of its particles but at the same time is an effective way of preserving a better examination of their property. Nevertheless he believes that "the ultimate goal of the human sciences is not to constitute, but to dissolve man. The preeminent value of anthropology is that it represents the first step in a procedure which involves others. Ethnographic analysis tries to arrive at invariants beyond the empirical diversity of human societies; and, as the present work shows, these are sometimes to be found at the most unforeseen points."[74] And perhaps the most unexpected point is the already mentioned assertion,

> Every sense can be explained by a lesser one and if this regress ends in recognizing the 'law of accidentality' which can only state that it is thus and not otherwise—then such a perspective contains nothing alarming to the mind which is not disturbed by transcendence, even if it is in a larval form. For man obtains everything which he could reasonably desire if, on the condition of inclining to this law, he is fortunate to determine his practice and to locate all the rest in a sphere of intelligibility.[75]

The combination of Lévi-Strauss' texts indicates those philosophical consequences which flow in the area of understanding from the application of the ethnological progressive-regressive method. Leví-Strauss himself does not hesitate to point to the ultimate consequence of his position, namely, the negation of transcendence even in the larval form. If transcendence based on human consciousness was still preserved in existentialism—the kind that has a place in K. Jaspers' thought—then structuralism which denies the existence of the human subject, which is the interiorization of objective language, both cancels out and deletes the final place for transcendence. The human subject is ultimately cancelled out because it is objectively reducible (and exclusively understood) to the structure of language. This structure reveals in itself other structures which can be reduced to even more intelligible structures, less and less linked with transcendence. And everything was already accomplished in the first approach to an explanation of man, i.e.,— the movement of the point of gravity from consciousness to non-conscious structures. The model of intelligibility for man is not conscious being but an unconscious structure. Everything else is a more and more logically developed consequence of this first step.

No wonder, then, that where consciousness is denied so radically, there is also a denial of history, which can be reduced only to objective structures, to "mytho-logy." Christianity, in particular as history *sui generis* (more strictly of the past) of redemption, becomes an a priori mythology.[76]

Ultimately an objective linguistic analysis is reduced not so much to an analysis of sense, but rather to an analysis of the very structures of language, its syntactic aspect independently of sense. It is a gigantic, all-embracing structure of nonsense, which finds its ultimate "justification" in acknowledging the law of accidentality as the ultimate model of intelligibility, in which transcendence is denied, even in its larval form; only agnosticism remains.[77]

II. CONCEPTION OF MAN AS A SUBJECT MANIFESTING A SPIRIT

A. POST-CARTESIAN HERITAGE

From the time of Descartes, as we have already mentioned in Chapter I, a fundamentally different division of objects takes place than formerly. If in ancient and mediaeval times two groups of beings were recognized, i.e., living and non-living, Descartes introduces a distinction of objects into conscious and non-conscious beings. For the ancients, everything which lives possesses a soul as the first source of life. For Descartes, the fundamental element differentiating being from matter is consciousness. Life became viewed as a purely material process; and the soul, which had lost its union with life also lost its union with the body. The soul became a "thinking thing." Hence a sharp dualism was defined, and all the sharper since the body as *res extensa* is completely subject to mechanistic laws.

The Cartesian self-conscious spirit-substance was denied in the analyses of D. Hume.[78] As we know, he also began with an analysis of the idea but he understood this idea in a different way, and hence he arrived at different conclusions than those of Descartes. Specifically he denied the intelligibility of the human soul's existence (perhaps even its existence). He substituted the "self" for the Cartesian conception of the spirit, and this "self" henceforth became the functional element which connected impressions—if in general it exists and does something.[79] Beginning with an analysis of our representations of things, Hume recognized the representations as primary, and he called them "impressions" or those which come from the primaries, and these he called "ideas." And because ideas are derived from impressions, only impressions are the ultimate verification of cognition.

On the question of ideas he investigated the relations of ideas as, for example, mathematics does and matters of fact which do not exhibit the kind of precision that relations between ideas do.

In asking the question what experience contains beyond a statement of facts, he criticized the Principle of Causality as a principle of a necessary connection, as well as the idea of substance. He arrived at the conclusion that its function is analogous to that of the Principle of Causality and it gives rise to uniting facts into a one. Causality connects facts which follow one another, while substance joins facts that are contemporaneous. We refer to the same substance the impressions given us by the different senses; for example, of this particular flower whose color I observe with my sight, its scent with the sense of smell, etc. This explains our acceptance of a "self" as a permanent spiritual substance which is the unifying foundation of changing impressions.[80]

By doing this, however, we exceed facts becasue it is justified neither *a priori,* i.e., by an analysis of concepts and their mutual relations nor *a posteriori,* since it is not ascertained by facts. It is the imagination and instinct which are acting here, and not the intellect. For if it seems to us that we have a "self," and that it perseveres independently of our perceptions and feelings, we succumb to an illusion. "When I analyze more thoroughly that which I call the self, I always stumble on one or other particular perception and I never observe anything else but perceptions."[81]

This somewhat paradoxical position (to which psychology will refer a half century later) was completed and interrelated by I. Kant. The starting point in understanding Kant's theory of the self is his peculiar (unique) theory of cognition. According to Kant, human cognition is enclosed within the limits of activity of two faculties of cognition: sensory cognition which takes place within the framework of the a priori categories of space and time, as well as rational cognition, which enables us to create concepts on the basis of experience shown us in the framework of the categories of space and time. And this is the sound function of reason which fashions a valid knowledge that does not transcend the data of experience. Naturally judgment classifies and unites the data of experience by using the a priori categories, of which those of causality and substance are especially important for science. These very categories show that causality and substantiality are necessary modes of our thinking. This does not mean in any way that they are categories of being itself which in itself is unknowable to our judgment and valid knowledge—analytical knowledge.

As a subject, man is the condition of the object. Judgment has the ability to unite what is a reflection of the unity of the very self. The unification does not lie in objects and it cannot be grasped through perception. Rather it is the function of judgment alone which is nothing more than the ability to unite a priori. For even in the simplest perceptive statement (I feel warm), or one based on experience (The sun gives heat), both subject and judgment are involved if we feel that the impressions come from the same object. For the very creation of the "object" is an activity of the understanding: object is that in whose conception the variety of a given experience is united.

Hence in this case a subject's valid cognitive function was understood as the ability of uniting a priori given experiences. And only such a valid knowledge can say something about "self." But the activity of the understanding *(Verstand)*—transcendental analytic—demands its completion by reason *(Vernunft)* of the dialectic because what we know on the basis of understanding is only fragmentary and it does not go beyond the framework of experience and this is only a fragment of being in itself. As A. Wawrzyniak[82] correctly observes, "A scientific view of the world according to Kant is the result of cooperation on the part of various a priori subjective forms, which organizes the chaotic matter of sensibility. This does not mean however that the cognizing subject should experience this kind of his own creative ability. Empirical consciousness is presented with an object of consciousness that is organized and transcendent in relation to it. But we need determined cognitive operations to disclose a so-called transcendental consciousness which performs a creative and at the same time unifying role in relation to phenomenal reality. The transcendental subject (consciousness) is moreover reasoned out like a priori forms." Then reason integrates and concludes the limited, fragmentary results of understanding, referring them to absolute and infinite objects. These pure concepts of reason Kant called the Ideas. There are three ideas brought into being by reason, i.e., of the soul, the universe, and God. By means of the idea of the soul, the thinking subject attempts to encompass the whole of internal experience; by means of the idea of the universe, the whole of exterior experience and in the idea of God, he looks for a foundation of all experience.

From internal experience we know only particular experiences but reason attempts to establish on their foundation the existence of the soul. But the idea of soul is given us as an a priori idea which can never be verified, and neither can we ever be freed from it. The same applies to the idea of God.[83] That which is useful in the area of science—is "I"—but it is only a form of unifying images a priori. Meanwhile as Hume had already observed, we have no image of the soul and hence we apprehend it only as a function and not as a substance.

Kant's philosophy of the subject found its continuators in Fichte, Schelling and Hegel. Fichte began the conception of the Hegelian dialectic. He attempted to reduce the whole world-outlook to some principal foundation.

If Kant located the subject in the middle of the world, then Fichte in like manner affirmed the "I." But this affirmation of the self is fruitful and experienced only when we simultaneously apprehend it along with the affirmation "non-I"—when I understand and affirm my "I," I assure myself that being "I," I am different from "non-I." In a word, the affirmation of self postulates the antithesis "non-self." Fichte turns to the strongest emphasis of the thesis and antithesis: the dualism of self and non-self, of the subject and that which is not a subject.[84]

The emphasis of bipolarity is accepted by Schelling in whose thought there clearly appears a reduplication of subject and object, spirit and nature. The polarity appears not only in human experience but likewise in nature as magnetic and electrical phenomena prove.

Both of these philosophers try to overcome this bipolarity in the direction of a monism. This is the way in which G. Hegel understood them, for very early in his treatise, *Differenz des Fichtschen und Schellingschen Systems,* he wrote that the first (Fichte) is a subjective idealist for his starting point was the affirmation of the "I." The second, Schelling, by observing the identity in polarity (Schelling's philosophy of Identity) of the conscious and unconscious spirit itself, is an objective idealist. On the other hand, Hegel attempts to achieve a synthesis of these positions—as an absolute idealist because beyond the subjective and objective spirit, there stands the absolute Spirit. It is precisely this absolute Spirit which manifests itself in man.[85]

Essential to Hegel's philosophy is also the departure from conscious data and revealing in the human spirit (thinking) the opposition of thesis and antithesis which Hegel levels in a higher manifestation of thought, i.e., synthesis. The synthesis in turn is the thesis of a further antithesis and even a higher synthesis. Most peculiar to Hegel as a philosopher was the position that the dialectic of thinking is only a logical form but, at the same time, it was something objective, ontological or a form of being. Moreover for Hegel, thought and being are the same. The entire evolutionary process which we observe in the world is only an introductory dialectical evolution of the spirit. And the task of philosophy is to uncover and deal with this process as far as possible in full consciousness.

And hence the evolutionary process of the spirit moves dialectically according to the well known forms of the Hegelian triad.

In the first stage, the "objective spirit" finds itself in a situation of "being-in-itself" (*An-sich-sein*), and the philosophical discipline answering to this objective state of the spirit is logic.

In the second stage the spirit finds itself in a state of alienation (*Anders-sein*) the spirit is distinguishing from itself as its own antithesis takes on the form of nature which is clothed in the form of space and time. To this evolutionary stage of the spirit which is already alienated corresponds the philosophy of nature.

In the third and final stage of synthesis, the spirit returns to itself and finds itself in a situation in which it is "in-itself-and-for-itself" (*An-und-für-sich-sein*). To this third and principal member of the dialectical evolution, to this fundamental member corresponds to the philosophy of the spirit.

This final stage of the spirit's evolution passes through its own further dialectical triad: from the subjective spirit through the objective spirit up to the ultimate synthesis of the Absolute Spirit.

The science about the subjective spirit is a science about the life of an individual man.[86] For the first time, the spirit in man becomes aware (this does not take place in animals) of its consciousness, and precisely of its self-consciousness. In this stage the spirit passes from the stage of "being-beyond-itself" to the stage of "being-for-itself." However, it is not "for-it-self" in complete fullness because man is an exemplar of a species; and by the same fact, he is also "for" the species, since he belongs to a definite nature. In its lowest stage, the subjective spirit is still on the confines of NATURE. He is a natural soul who possesses within himself, in his "immateriality" as an echo, the whole life of nature. In this state, the soul revives itself, grows old the same as the body. In this period the soul expresses itself in the form of sense life: *Empfindung,* which is a "deaf activity of the spirit in its individualization of a non-conscious and non-intelligent spirit."[87]

To sensibility thus understood there opposes itself *Gefühl,* which leads itself to an inner feeling of the soul as an "indefinite self"—*Selbtichkeit* where self-consciouness and the intelligent pole of consciousness have not as yet formed themselves. The feeling of self—*Selbtichkeit*—is not as yet something personal. We meet it in a child or in somnambulist states. This type of feeling within the soul—*Gefühl*—passes slowly into feeling itself—*Selbstgefühl*—as yet not uniting man with the external world which, when it becomes known, will become "my" world.

The soul which makes effective its feelings frees itself from them and slowly establishes conscious contact with the external world. Sentient life, a self-feeling and its effectiveness—these are the first three dialectical manifestations of the bodily spirit which can be called in general "non-consciousness."

Our consciousness awakens itself along with a sensible certitude. It "enters into a sensible certitude as a pure 'I.' To put it in another way, 'I' am in the area of a sensible certitude—only THIS HERE I (*reiner Dieser*) and the object is only THIS HERE OBJECT (*reines Dieses*) 'I,' this I. I am positive of this thing not because I as consciousness passed through this certain kind of evolutionary process and I made use of my thoughts in diverse ways. . . . I do not enter here as a many-sided representation or thinking, a thing as a multitude of miscellaneous traits but a thing EXISTS and it EXISTS because it EXISTS. A thing EXISTS—this is what is essential for sensible knowledge. And precisely this pure BEING, this straight directness constitutes TRUTH of the thing. . . . Consciousness is *'I'* and nothing more; it is only this 'I!'"[88]

The further essential stage of the spirit's self-manifestation is "perception" as a direct grasping of a thing: "This thing becomes established in perception as NOT THIS ONE or as nihilated but as a result of it; it does not become anything but a determined nothingness or a nothingness of a certain content, namely of THIS THING. The sensible moment still appears here but not as if it were to appear in a sensible certitude as an individual thing of our opinion but as something general or as something which will later define itself as a certain property."[89] At this point of consciousness the self (ego) comes out of itself and grasps things in itself. It conforms itself to things and becomes objective truth. "Hence with perception, there also takes place what took place in sensible certitude, namely a thrust of consciousness with a return to itself but not in the manner that it was then, so called not in the sense that the perceived truth would come from consciousness. On the contrary consciousness rather sees that the UNTRUTH appearing in perception comes from it. Thanks to this, it is able at the same time to lead to annihilation of this UNTRUTH, for it distinguishes its grasping of the truth from untruth of the perception. It corrects this untruth insofar as it itself undertakes this correction. Truth as PERCEIVED truth comes FROM IT."[90]

Hence consciousness passes through the stage of perception which the sensible data grasp in unity (which is experience in Kantian understanding) and it come to UNDERSTANDING (*Verstand*) which grasps the necessary law in the changing data of experience. Further, on a higher level of evolution, consciousness reflects on itself. The I is the subject of this reflection but it is also the undetermined object. It is not as yet an object in the full sense because it does not differ from the subject. The spirit overcomes the egoism of the subject in a sharp battle in the family, friendship and above all in governmental relations. It permits itself to be assimilated by the egoistic self and to liberate REASON (*Vernunft*) from the spirit which shows that determinations of self are just as objective as determinations of the essences of things. The spirit therefore manifests itself objectively in human creations: in writing, artifacts, of some kind of theory so that we can speak about the spirit of some group of people or even of the spirit of a nation. A special area, i.e., ethics, devotes itself to deliberations of problems of the objective spirit. In particular, the area of history is one in which the objective spirit and its laws manifest themselves.

The absolute spirit in turn rises above the subjective and objective spirit. In the order of alienation which expressed itself in the area of the objective spirit, it returns to itself—from *Andersein* it passes to *"An-und-für-sich-sein"* —to a "being-in-itself-and-for-itself."

Hence the spirit is the certainty of itself and of truth. Its development is accomplished simultaneously through interiorization and exteriorization by means of theory and practice. The highest form of interiorization is the liberation of oneself from intuition and images. It is the beginning of the use of an objective language which permits thinking and hence knowing that what is thought exists and that which exists is being thought at the same time. Practice, on the other hand which arises from subjective tendencies is entangled in conflicts, contradictions, in dialectical tensions and it remains overcome by justice and universal good. Theory and practice unite in a free spirit which is able to become aware of itself as an absolute spirit whose domain are art, religion and philosophy. The last, i.e., philosophy "constitutes a larger state in the development of the absolute spirit, its self-knowledge as a subject-substance of the whole reality."[91]

Hegel's anthropology is nothing else than the application of the general conception of dialectics to psychology. Understood in this way, psychology is to reveal to man the "self" as a spirit whose passing through dialectical differentiation is the "very heart" of the totality.

B. SOME EXISTENTIALIST CONCEPTIONS OF MAN

Just as Marxism is bound up with Hegelian conceptions so the sources of existentialism are to be looked for in a reaction to an extreme system-thing treatment of the human subject in the Hegelian school, namely in a student of Hegel, the Danish pastor Søren Kierkegaard.[92]

If the alienation of man by contemporary culture and society was shown in Hegel as a moment and an aspect of the dialectical development of the idea, this "gain" of man was already achieved differently according to Hegel's pupils. Marx sees the liberation of oneself from alienation by means of the proletariat class and revolution which will lead to a classless society, but Kierkegaard sees it through the experience of his own existence on the boundary of nihilism and Christianity. In man's concrete human existence or in his conscious human life, he has been abandoned, condemned to nothingness. From nothingness it is only one step to "regaining" oneself through faith in Christ. In human consciousness Christianity borders on nihilism. A limit situation is basic for man. Man's fundamental trait is his *temporality*, which cannot be grasped in a formula because it is constantly developing itself. Only thought, and not existence, can be grasped in a system. "Man is the synthesis of finitude and infinitude, of temporality and eternity, of necessity and freedom," whence come the antinomies and sufferings in human life. There is no escaping them because the border situation between nothingness and God is man's condition. In his transitory existence man is constantly yearning for eternity, a fact which expresses itself in religion. In this "yearning," however man feels his own helplessness; he experiences fear and dread. Fear and dread are the leitmotif of human life. Besides, religion itself and its experience fills a man with dread, from which he wants to free himself; and which, at the same time, he desires. Religion which leads man into "eternity" fills him with dread; it demands everything; it gives "nothing" in exchange which might have a temporal value.

The experiencing of border-situations was undertaken by other existentialists who concentrated on an explanation of man. And even if the anthropological conceptions of existentialists are chronologically closest to us, nevertheless in order to complete the picture of thought which arose as a reaction to the systematic of Hegel, we should examine Heidegger's conception of man.[93]

Heidegger's conception of man was influenced not only by Kierkegaard's position but also by that of Nietzsche and Dilthey. Nietzsche's thoughts on man who finds himself in his aspirations "beyond good and evil," whose existence is meaningless, whose questions about truth are meaningless and whose morality founded on these questions is a slave morality, whose meaning—if we can speak in general about the meaning of man—is the emphasizing of such an individual existence which is the existence of a "Superman"—these ideas had an influence on Heidegger's attitude in his investigations.

Dilthey's conceptions determined Heidegger's outlook on two points:

a) The first was the overcoming of a mechanistic way of thinking by a clarifying psychological thinking. For in a mechanistic way of thinking we have a kind of "objective" picture of psychic life which is to be composed of psychic "atoms." Dilthey opposed such a vision by taking into consideration the concrete in real experience. For this reason his historical investigations are also investigations of an essential manifestation of the soul. By analyzing particular individuals in their historical conditions, man is investigated in the context of a totality, in his "totalizing" mutual conditions. Hence if Dilthey took the historical man under consideration, it was in the moment of reflecting on the meaning of such a man that there appears a place where M. Heidegger could enter with his analysis of human existence.[94]

b) A second point which coincided with Dilthey was Heidegger's critique of Dilthey's historical reason as a theory of cognition. In his analysis Heidegger took under consideration man's time and he even raised the "time aspect" to one of the principal moments of human existence. He simultaneously advanced an esentially different aspect of concerns. As an ontologist, Heidegger is interested not only in the historicity of the concrete man, but "man in general," whose form of existing is specific and in time.[95]

In the period of creating a philosophical anthropology presented in his work *Sein und Zeit,* Heidegger's ontological problems are focused on man. The essential problem for philosophy is the question about the meaning of being: *Philosophie als die Frage nach dem Sinn von Sein.* It is precisely the concrete, historical man "now constituting himself," *"Dasein,"* who is the one revealing the meaning of being. This kind of man precisely as *Dasein* is the catalyst ("pole," "agent") in whom *Sein*—being—manifests itself and is given us in *"Seiende"* or a limited form of being. In the historical process of creating ourselves it is we who in every stage are the first *Seiende* of a determined form of being which is given us, which is the basis for our ability to ask ourselves questions about the "sense of being." *"Diese Seiende das wir je selbst sind und das unter anderen die Seinsmöglichkeit des Fragens hat, fassen wir terminologisch als Dasein."*[96]

Heidegger likewise explains that this "I" (obviously "I" is this "I" who consciously thrusts himself into the world and hence "I" is consciousness) is existence, of which *Seiende* are the existential and ontic forms of both manifesting and understanding being—*Sein.*

Within the range of *Sein und Zeit* the entire problematic of *"Dasein"* is pivotal according to Heidegger. *Dasein* is a concrete, historical existence (or human consciousness) in which *Sein* manifests itself and becomes easily legible to man as *Seiende,* all the more since man himself who is constituting himself historically, is a certain *Seiende,* given to us as a first for a rational treatment for understanding. To understand in the Dilthean sense is LEGEIN TA PHAINOMENA and hence through a concrete analysis of a concrete human historical appearance. The fundamental concepts in Heidegger are SEIN, whose sense we must "read" and which normally manifests itself as a SEIENDE and in a human, concrete historical DASEIN, which is precisely a historical existence forming itself in the world. The task of metaphysics is to attain the SEIN of being by means of a phenomenological analysis of SEIENDE.

The reading of the sense of being (*Sein*) in a human and by means of a human *Dasein* shows that for us to be is, before all else, "to-be-in-the-world," (*"In-der-Welt-sein"*). Man perceives above all that "to be" for him is to find himself in the surrounding of what exists as *Seiende*. "That which exists," *Seiende*, falls into two groups: the historical man himself, *Dasein*, who is the concrete, historical modification of existence; and secondly, existing objects, *Seiende* which constitute the huge range of *Zuhandesein* or objects that are objects "for something," objects of which man makes use and which "are-at-hand."

For Heidegger, the world is a collection not only of "objects" of cognition but rather of "objects-for-use." We discover the world not in cognition but in use. Man is interested in existing objects as serving for something (*"etwas-um-zu"*). Every man constructs for himself a hierarchy of objects which are of value to him with respect to "that for which," whence there appears in Heidegger a pyramid of usefulness "um-zu-Pyramide." Heidegger overcomes Kant's question about *"Ding-an-sich"* by accepting the fact that man finds himself in the world (*"in-der-Welt-sein"*), and he knows the world not only theoretically but through *besorgen*.[97]

Along with the "at-hand" objects with which a relation is expressed in *besorgen*, we must meet other existing objects: other people along with whom man "exists together" (*"mit-sein"*), and a relation with them is expressed in the forms of *Fürsorge*, which leads to an existential understanding of another man's fate.

But the most important way of existential be-ing is the manner of human conscious being in oneself, in one's own DASEIN. And here the essential manifestation is precisely SORGE—a concern about one's own DASEIN, and for this reason it takes on the form of dread (ANGST). For even as man uses the world by having dominion over things (*besorgt*) and even if he "empathizes" (*für-sorgt*) with other human beings, he does not feel at home in the world. He is "homeless" in the world. He is "thrown," "immersed" in an alien world of existing objects. For this reason man's essential *"modus"* of existence is GEWORFENHEIT. This "thrownness" and immersion in the world of objects reveals "nothingness" to man and places man in dread in the presence of nothingness. It is not a nothingness which stands before man only in the future; it stands before man now as his real inner possibility.

Hence man is a "being-toward-death" (*Dasein ist ein sein-zum-Tode*). But death itself cannot be experienced. We know only an "animal" death, but we do not experience our own death in its fulfillment. However, the presence of death stands before us in the existential experience of dread. For death which we will ultimately experience "individualizes" man. It is something most individual and individually experienced "bestowing on man his ultimate personality." In death there manifests itself the passage from *Seiende* to *Nichts*. For the essence of the human *Dasein* is his historicity and along with it its termination: *"Das eigentliche sein-zum-Tode d.h. die die End-*

lichkeit der Zeitlichkeit, ist der verborgene Grund der Geschichlichkeit des Dasein.[98]

Heidegger's conceptions can be criticized on many points. But an undoubtedly interesting and very creative moment of his speculations is the calling of attention to the fact that man as a concrete conscious being, who is involved in the world and in human history and hence human existence, cannot base himself on the traditional Aristotelian model of substance which of itself is "atemporal," and it is only through its activity that it is joined with time which, after all does not bring anything very new to the structure of being.[98a]

Another especially important moment in the Heideggerian conception of man is the emphasis on man's death, which is linked with the temporality of human experiences. And it is connected not only as the termination of the temporal human existence, but as an inner, constantly menacing real potentiality which manifests itself in all human experiences, more so as a kind of "tension-towards-death."

An existentialist who shows new aspects in the anthropological conception is Karl Jaspers.[99] The starting point in his analysis of man is existence itself. "As a being, I am fundamentally different from the be-ing of all things because only I can say: I am."[100] For "my" situation as a being is unique since I understand myself as existing. It is a glance at the "ego" from within. For I cannot of myself cause an object to become in the act of affirming the ego. In the moment of objectifying myself, we create only an object of inquiries of scientific psychology because everything that is an object is one of the objects of the world. My existence—in auto-affirmation—can never become authentically objectivated. It is original: it transcends objects; it "makes" contents and even objects themselves on the pattern of consciousness and it "leads" to the grasping of a "pure consciousness" which postulates the existence of an absolute consciousness. The moments of the transcendence of consciousness are seen best in border situations as for example, death, suffering, guilt, war. To experience border situations is the same as "to exist." The transcending consciousness reads the world like a cyphered absolute spirit and metaphysics is the reading of the "cyphers of the world." For everything that is finite is only a symbol of infinity. In philosophy it is a question of establishing "what" is a cypher and "what sense this cypher possesses."[101] This history of man is a basic cypher in the foundation of things and the sense of the symbol opens "the doors of faith."

Between Jaspers and Heidegger there is this fundamental difference that Jaspers is more closely allied with Kierkegaard's concept, the concept of human consciousness in which is played the "drama of existence" and it asks less about the essential sense of the human conscious existence. For Jaspers, existence is above all something non-factual, even non-objectivated, and all objectivation of a conscious existence is, at the same time, its falsification. Man appears essentially as transcendence.

C. MAX SCHELER'S VISION OF MAN—THE REVERSE OF POWER AND VALUE

In his youth, Max Scheler (1873–1928), a pupil of Eucken, was under the influence of the idealists. Later he was influenced by Husserl's philosophy, and he was impressed by the ideas of the phenomenologists. After his conversion to Catholicism, he "colored" them with an Augustinian tinge, especially in the concept of an ethics of value. This period of his life ends in 1919 when, as a professor of philosophy and sociology in Cologne, he moved on to a position of his own metaphysics which, in its content argues against the formerly accepted Catholic world-outlook (*Weltanschauung*).

Two periods of his scientific activity are most interesting: the Munich period when he found himself under the influence of a Catholic world-outlook, and the last period in which he proposed an entirely original conception of man as a manifestation of a "powerless spirit."[102]

In the second period of activity he published the work, *Zur Phänomenologie und Theorie der Sympathiegefühle* (Halle, 1913), in which he presents the relation of man to the problem of cognition. He offers a thesis (already known to St. Augustine and Goethe) that we can know truly only that which was previously embraced in an act of love. Before man became an *ens cogitans* or an *ens volens*, he was already an *ens amans,* for the order of love precedes the order of cognition. Man's special status in the world depends above all on his ability to love, for man is truly a part of nature, and he stands in the midst of all nature, which fundamentally explains man. Nevertheless, through his ability to love, man creates a bridge between his nature and a new world, a world of value, and through it, of new possibilities, It is only through love that man can become a perfect being, a "completed" being, and can escape the "blind alley" of his own nature. Fundamentally, love distinguishes man from animals. Animals, in relation to the environment and their instincts, are always without reflection, and they completely respond spontaneously. They always fulfill and affirm their instincts toward individual life and that of the species. Man, however, through a love which is freed from desire, is capable of transcending the contents of a desired thing. He can arrive at a kingdom of the spirit. He can protest against his impulse. Such a situation reflects on his acts of cognition: since he is a person-spirit, man can relate himself to a purpose-good which, at the same time, is being in itself.

The anthropological interests that Scheler experienced in the period of his affirmation of a Christian world-view continued during his later years, when he understood man's role in the world in a different way. He was always aware of the unique situation of man, and especially in the problematics of questions related with man. He wrote, "We are from about the 10,000th year of the history of the first epoch, during which man became completely and without the rest 'problematical,' an epoch during which man still does not know truly who he is but at the same time knows that he does not know."[103] Scheler thereby postulates that the problem of man should be examined in a more organized manner. It is precisely for this purpose that he devoted his deliberations in the work, *Die Stellung des Menschen im Kosmos*,[104] in which he attempts to overcome the one-sided approach of naturalistic and historical anthropology.

He observes that man's development can and should be understood as the self-development of God. "The fundamental connection between man and the world is based on the fact that it expresses itself at the same time in man in the form of a spirit as well as of life. And man is precisely this *centrum* of that Spirit and Power that is through itself. . . . Man is that unique place in which God realizes himself but, at the same time, this same man is a part of this transcendental process."[105] Hence "man" manifests himself as the last instant that can provide foundations for giving answer to all the questions accumulated by the various sciences.

Scheler did not bring his analyses to completion because they were interrupted by his untimely death. However he did make many interesting observations concerning man's role in the cosmos. Hence by relying above all on the works of contemporary naturalists and zoopsychologists, he calls attention to the fact that man and animal differ in the order of practical intelligence and not only in the degree of development.

A very important question arises here: Is man merely a more highly organized animal? From the point of view of practical intelligence, it is impossible to give a satisfactory answer.

Fundamentally there could be a truly enormous difference in development between a chimpanzee and Thomas Alva Edison but it would be only one of degree. There is another dimension in man which fundamentally differentiates him from animal and that is the spirit.

The spirit is found external to everything that can be called biological life. The spirit cannot be reduced to various systems of biological life.[106] In face of this, what is the spirit? Scheler developed his new metaphysics around this question. According to him, the spirit is a state which is independent of all physiological processes. For man can go against his physiological and animal drives, which the animal can never do. Man experiences the "objectivity" of things, their "essence," and he forms the "personality" of his spirit which is apprehended as an "object." On the other hand, the animal experiences itself only as the source of impulses "to" or "from"; and for this reason, it can never grasp and present itself "objectively." The animal is only a *centrum* of drives in relation to its surroundings. Hence its behavior is in respect to this environment—*Umwelt*—and never to a "world of objects." It can be called purely "ecstatic" even in cases of the practical intellect's activity. In opposition to plants, the animal obviously possesses "consciousness," but it does not have self-consciousness; the animal does not "possess itself" cognitively. On the other hand, man possesses self-consciousness and the ability to think objectively. As a result he can oppose himself not only to the world of external objects, but he can also grasp himself as an object, and he can oppose himself to himself. Only man has the ability to choose suicide. He can "objectivize" his life and throw it away. The animal can never do this.

For there exists in man a *centrum* of activity (which Scheler calls "person"), and which creates itself through the opposition of man's organism and the surroundings. And in this *centrum* is found the spirit and its will understood as an enduring, as a *"continuum"* which transcends the changes of animal drives. Hence man is a being who transcends both himself and the world of objects. Thanks to this, he can "outdistance" himself in relation to himself. An examination of such an outdistancing of oneself from oneself, and of a transcendence in relation to oneself, is "auto-irony" and genuine humor. This is an outstanding trait of the spirit alone.

But what *is* this spirit in itself which inhabits the *centrum* of human personal activity? Is it some kind of subjective being? Scheler's answer, which in this respect refers to Kant, is negative. The spirit is this unique "something" which of itself cannot "subjectivate" itself; it cannot become "that which is." The spirit can only be pure actuality, a fulfillment of act and not "that which" is some kind of subject.

In addition, the spirit is subject to "ideazation." The problem of ideazation is the activity of an intelligence other than a merely technical one, and of another act which hypostasizes experienced states. If for example, I experience pain in some part of my body, I usually consult a physician who examines the functions of particular organs and determines the character of the pain as a specific sign of an organic function. But I can also "ideazate" the experience of pain. I can hypostasize the pain as a certain combination of experienced and felt content and I can think, for example, that the world is a pain, an evil. Then I will be asking, "What is pain?" "Is it evil in itself, detached from the fact that I had experienced or am experiencing definite states of evil?" A characteristic example of such an "ideazation" of pain is the experience and conversion of Buddha who, in the fact of suffering and death, reached such an advanced ideazation that he understood the desire to live as the primary desire from which we should free ourselves. Buddha succeeded in opposing the desire to live; he succeeded in saying "no" to a fundamental drive. According to Scheler, this act of Buddha is the highest manifestation of the spirit, and the highest expression of a human world-outlook in relation to suffering. If the animal is a creature which always says "yes" in relation to life and even in suffering, even if its very life is escaping it, man is the one who can say "no." Man is the one who eternally "protests" in the presence of reality because between his drive and action there lies a large "hiatus." For this reason, too, he can expend the energy of his drive to the building of an ideal kingdom of thought, and on it depends chiefly the sublimation of biologico-animal drives.[107]

Freud has already observed that a drive constitutes the essence of life. The energy of the drive is the fundamental mover of psychic vitality and all spiritual experiences are only sublimation of a drive. Scheler differs from Freud by observing that the spirit manifests itself through *ascesis,* by suppression and sublimation, at the same time by the ability to say "no" in relation to the reality of drives. The sublimated energy of the drive becomes by that very fact the nourisher of the soul.

According to Scheler, however, the spirit itself is that kind of potentiality of being which is given to man, with whose help man is capable of transcendence. He had already emphasized this latter point in his Catholic faith period by constructing a theory of love that draws man out of himself.

As we had already said, the human spirit cannot become some kind of "subject"; it cannot be "substantialized" and for this reason it can be grasped as actualizing itself as a function. The spirit does not possess its ontic base and therefore of itself it is powerless. It acquires power only because of the ability of saying "no," thanks to *ascesis,* thanks to sublimation.[108]

According to Scheler's opinion, the ancient Greeks had already made a grave error by observing that the order of function postulates the order of substance which would have been the source of this function, and therefore it was asserted that the higher the manifestation of the spirit, the more powerful the substance as the source of spiritual functions; whereas the matter is completely otherwise. There exists an inverse proportion of value and power. The higher the value, the less power it possesses. Therefore the lowest values, like material values (purely material ones), possess the greatest power. The higher values live at the expense of the power of the lower ones. As the highest value, the spirit is of itself completely powerless, and if it does have power, it derives it only by a sublimation of greater powers from lower values.

It was already observed long ago that the highest spirit, the kind that God is supposed to be, is omnipotent while a pure spirit can be only completely powerless. Scheler is a theoretician of a powerless spirit, and of an inverse proportion of power and value. The lowest drives, almost purely material ones, possess the greatest powers which must be used in order to nourish the higher values. In this conception Max Scheler approaches N. Hartmann, who proclaimed that "the higher categories of being and value are by their nature weaker." Scheler affirmed similarly, *"Mächtig ist ursprünglich das Niedrige, ohnmächtig das Höchste. Jede höhere Seinsform ist im Verhältnis zu der Niedrigeren relativ kraftlos, und sie verwirklicht sich nicht durch ihre eigene Kräfte, sondern durch die Kräfte der Niedrigeren."* [109] In this instance, Scheler uses Freud's theory, but he also refers to Marx's conception, especially to his conception of a base and superstructure. Every superstructure lives only on its base. The base is the fundamental power, but the superstructure, whether all political, social and cultural manifestations of life, is only something derivative that draws its fundamental power from the material base, which is an aggregate of economic conditions.

The spirit in man builds its own pyramid of value, which, the higher it rises, the more noble and more valuable it is, but at the same time it becomes weaker. This is evident for example in the order of cognition where the fundamental cognitive layer is the so-called *Leistungswissen,* a "layer of productive thinking," a "layer of work," a "layer of technical knowledge," whose aim is nature itself, its transformation and its domination by subordinating the world. A higher cognitive layer but at the same time weaker is *Wesenswissen,* a sphere of "theoretical cognition." If the first layer is based on the apprehension and adaptation of nature itself, then this layer extends as far as "pure matter" from which arise creatures of nature, all beings and necessary internal and inter-ontic relations. And above it, there still is the layer of metaphysical cognition, which is a manifestation of wisdom that leads to an apprehension of holiness and a cognitive realization of the highest cognitive value, which is the layer of "redemptive" or religious cognition. [110] Scheler was already developing these thoughts in the earlier period of his life, but their full actualization took place only in the last period.

On some points, Scheler's conceptions from the last period of his life remind us, generally speaking, of the doctrine of the ideas of Jacob Böhme, Spinoza, Schelling and even Hegel. On the question of the ontic structure of the spirit, they call to mind the ideas of Freud and Klages. (According to the latter, the spirit does not belong to the order of the world. For Scheler, the spirit and the world are mutually subordinated in a sublimating ascent.) Finally Scheler's conceptions can be recognized as his own anthropologico-cosmic pantheism. [111]

Although Max Scheler's anthropological ideas undoubtedly explain in a very interesting manner the specificity of the spiritual and, therefore, man's distinctiveness in relation to the world of nature, nevertheless they cannot be accepted basically because of their contradiction in relation to man's fundamental, direct, self-conscious experience. For we affirm ourselves as subjects in the act of subjectivation.[112] Furthermore, an analysis of the "ego" as an agent of my acts shows the character and nature of man. Above all, however, a description of the process of the spirit's manifestation against the background of a denial of biological drives cannot be treated—without falling into a clear contradiction—as the birth of a spirit from matter. Neither can it be treated as the genesis of an immaterial spirit and hence as the kind of being (whose subjectivity is given directly—hence its be-ing is affirmed primordially) which does not possess traits that are indigenous to matter.

CHAPTER IV

THE ONTICAL STRUCTURE OF MAN

I. ANALYSIS OF THE POINT OF DEPARTURE

In the tradition of classical philosophy man was conceived as a microcosm.[1] In a somewhat different sense theologians of the Middle Ages, particularly Thomas Aquinas, also understood man in this manner.

As a point who synthesizes the whole cosmos in his nature, man has always appeared to be the most difficult object for a definitive explanation of philosophical investigations.[2] Consequently, the matter was simplified, separately analyzing the spiritual side of man based on theological speculation about "pure spirits," and separately considering human nature as common with animals.[3] The simplified and deforming vision of man was most often the foundation of moral didactics and preaching.[4]

The point of departure of the analysis of the nature of man in realistic philosophy are certain data obtained in the immediate experience of the human subject,[5] wherein I distinguish in myself all that which is "mine" from that which constitutes my very self, that which is the "I." For, as we already mentioned, the original human situation in which we are conscious of ourselves, in which we feel precisely as human beings, performing "our" acts—is immediately given to us in the knowledge of self-cognition that I exist as "myself" who am the subject (in acts of subjectivization, i.e., of realization!) of all that which is "mine." This originally human situation is like a field of human self-cognition, the poles of which are the "Self" on the one side and "mine" on the other.[6]

Of course, the problematic of "I-the-Self," connected with the theory of person, is more complicated and demands a more detailed discussion; and it is not possible to do this without a prior analysis of that which is "mine."

Hence, one ought at least very generally to consider the "content" of that which I call "mine" and its original relationship to the "I" as subject.[7]

A) Most often we speak of "mine" when we have in mind some results of our work broadly understood, of our immanent activity, remaining within "me" and transcending beyond "me"—to a thing. "Mine," therefore, in the broadest sense, appears as a designation of the external objects of our productive activity, work, or other appropriations. "Mine," in this broadest, purely external sense, is all that which, both in the philosophical category as well as in ordinary language, is called "possessions." In this sense a house, field, forest, money, clothes, all objects of external use, can be "mine."

When, with respect to all of these objects of use, even if they were the products of our work, we say "mine"—we have in mind the connection or relation of the belonging of these objects to "me," i.e., to that which I can call "I." That relation of belonging is in this case purely external. It sometimes "comes" to "me" as an already constituted being. It does not "construct" my be-ing. One can break off this relationship in various ways and not thereby diminish one's be-ing. The external relation of the belonging of "my" objects is in fact "mine" only denominatively, but nevertheless with a foundation as such.[8] This foundation, i.e., the reason of denomination, is the same as that which was the cause of the coming-into-being of that relation. These are, therefore, either functions, or processes, or any kind of connections between the external object and all that which I call "I-myself."

The "I," however, understood in this way (a correlate of possessions), can be rightly identified with the phenomenological "I," i.e., with the dispositional center (the psychic center) of external things. This "I" arises, is formed in man in early childhood, grows, reaches a peak in the prime of life; and then decreases, dwindles, and at times greatly "withers," together with a loss of the desire to live. For man, in relation to the world of external things, is their disposing "possessor." Things constitute for him a certain—as M. Heidegger said—"pyramid of value;" they are useful (*um-zu-sein*) and subject to man. Hence, there must arise within man in relation to the world of things—into which world man was "passively thrown" (*Geworfenheit*)—one dispositional center, a single center that does not permit man to become lost in this world, but to use it for himself. That center disposing the world of things is this phenomenological "I," different from the "I" as the subject subjectivizing "my" acts and not the external world.

The "I" is opposed, therefore, to all that which is called "mine." In the elements seen more closely, the correlates of this relation (usually) appear as external "objects" of some sort, with an existence of their own—and we conceive the "I" also as an individual "object," subject to time and a definite place in space. The "I" occurring here, we take basically externally, as indeed living and conscious, but only an object—some "James X," being the "center" disposing possessions. Consequently, "mine" and "I" are understood basically purely externally, as two "objects," one of which is a "subject"—but not in an act of subjectivization—and the other only an "object" of law. Of course, the matter of the subjectivity of law already presupposes an adequately understood conception of person.[9]

B) In addition to "mine" understood externally as belonging to "me," though not bearing witness to the ontical structure of my "I," we should distinguish the other types of that which we call "mine," and which is connected with the act of the subjectivization of the "I" broadly understood.[10]

Above all, we should distinguish here "my" physiological functions from "my" psychic functions, and among these latter, the more concrete functions "fused" with organic changes, such as sensory cognition and emotions, from the higher, more spiritual, psychic functions, and these both in the area of cognition as well as desire.

Let us first consider physiological functions, such as eating, breathing, muscular activity, moving, sleeping, etc. Having these functions in mind, we say: "I am breathing," "I am eating dinner," "I am going for a walk," "My head aches," "My leg hurts," etc. In the statements just cited, we notice above all a direction of this type of function to a single "center," to the same subject of the functions, which subject is also the performer of those functions: "I am eating," "I am breathing." That subject and performer of the physiological functions, called the "I," occurs here as an "I" in a different sense than that which occurred in the first instance, when to my "Self" was opposed "mine," understood in the sense of "possessions," i.e., in the sense of the ownership of external objects, ordinarily ontically independent: "my horse," "my field," etc. And so "I" refers to a physical, material object, definite in itself, such as some "James X." On the other hand, the "I," which appears as the subject and performer of physiological functions, no longer appears as an externally defined object, but as a conceptually indefinite physical-bodily "center," and as a kind of focal point with which all functions are connected: either somehow radiated by this center, or radiated and performed at the same time.[11] And here the physiological functions together with their organs are called "mine;" it is "my" head which aches, it is "my" stomach which digests, it is "my" legs which carry me, etc. Hence, "mine" is distinguished from "me," i.e., from that which we call "I." But at the same time, it is "I" who am breathing, "I" who am digesting, etc. And so "I" am the subject and performer of these functions. They are "mine." This "mine" is inseparable[12] from "me," since the cessation of "my" functions annihilates "me" through death and therefore, "mine" thus understood is able to bear witness to, and does bear witness to, the "Self." Since, however, "mine" manifests itself as a definite physiological, material function and since it is connected with the structure and function of some material organ of "my" body, and this organ and its functions can be and are precisely described, the "Self" too, understood as a subject of physiological functions, is commensurate in its ontical structure with these functions; this "I" is in some sense material.[13]

The "I," however, is not identified with any organ, since I can say of each organ that it is "my" organ, and I can also say of every function of any given organ that it is "my" function, i.e., in one sense or another, a function connected ontically with the "I." Furthermore, I can dispose of some of my organs, sometimes even of very important ones, considered to be an essential part of my "I," comprehensively understood, and yet the "I" continues to remain the same subject of "my" physiological functions. The "I" as subject and performer of those functions is also the same "I" that thinks, wants, hates.

Here the question arises: how is the ego "to be conceived," if it is a subject of material functions? It is, after all, in some sense something material, although it is not identified either with any material function or with any material organ that is "my" organ, and which ultimately can be disposed of in a definite manner, or replaced, as has recently become feasible in connection with transplants of the heart and other important organs of our body. As yet, therefore, it is some cognitively indefinite and undoubtedly material "I."

But is it only material? If the "I" existed as a material subject, if there were not in man other functions beyond purely material functions, then there would really be no grounds for raising the problem of the ontical dichotomy of the "I" and "mine."[14]

We perceive, however, occurring in ourselves also such functions, recognized as "mine," which definitely are not a function, or at least are not an exclusive function, of bodily organs. These are the cognitive and appetitive functions. For the sake of precision, however, it is necessary here to distinguish the cognitive functions more closely connected with the activity of a material organ by reason of the content character of cognition. For we differentiate sensory cognition in man from so-called mental cognition.[15] Sensory cognition of such types as the sight of colors, the hearing of sound, the sensation of impressions of scent, taste, touch, impression of warmth and cold, of weight, etc., is closely connected with a definite sensory organ, e.g., the eye, ear, taste buds, etc. Impressions, of this kind, recognized as "mine," are in a different degree directed toward some "center," more closely cognitively indefinite: toward that "I," which is in equal measure the subject and performer of these very cognitive impressions, as purely physiological functions. In equal measure, I feel that I am "myself," i.e., essentially the same subject "I," who "eats," who "breathes," as well as the same one who "sees," "hears," and moreover—who "thinks," who "loves," who "hates."

For I can also take as the subject of my cognitive attentions the functions of thought, manifesting themselves in both abstract conceptual and "judgmental" cognition as well as in reasoning. For whenever I think, i.e., perform some cognitive operation upon ideas and am cognitively engaged, I constantly perceive that I am the same subject, the same "Self," which is also the subject of both physiological functions as well as sensory-cognitive functions. "My" most sublime cognitive functions, moments of some intellectual ecstasy, contemplation, understanding of some law, moments of creativity in which I actively intervene in the existing course of events, all the moments of human "spiritual" life recognized as "mine" are also performed through that same, identical "I," which digests, breathes, feels pain. And I do not feel more "myself" when I think than when I eat, when I go for a walk, when I breathe. Furthermore, it is sometimes precisely "my" physiological functions that allow me to become more conscious of "myself," of my "I" and its character, than the lofty acts of contemplation. Only let my head or my heart begin to ache and I distinctly feel the threat to "myself" and the ontical contingency of that which I call "I."

But in all of "my" acts, both material, performed through "my" various bodily organs, as well as purely spiritual acts, intellectual cognition, creativity, decision, etc., I notice without great difficulty that they are directed toward the same "center," toward the same "subject," of which we are conscious as the "ego," as the "I." And this "I" is also the same subject and performer of "my" vegetative, animal, or typically—as will be later shown—human functions, such as, for example, acts of intellectual cognition.[16] The "Self," therefore, as "center" and performer of "my" functions stands before us as something that at the same time can be both material and immaterial. Above all, however, the "Self" appears as the subject in acts of the subjectivization of all those functions that I see as "mine." This course of thought, and, more precisely, description of the fundamental human situation, found its place in the *Summa Theologiae* of St. Thomas Aquinas. In an article entitled "Whether the Intellectual Principle is United to the Body as Its Form?"—Thomas expresses himself very typically: "We must assert that the intellect which is the principle of intellectual operation is the form of the human body. For that whereby primarily anything acts is a form of the thing to which the act is to be attributed." After a systemic justification that activity is act and so act is also a principle of this activity, and act in the Aristotelian system is called (is also!) form—he expresses himself characteristically: . . . *ipse idem homo est qui percipit se et intelligere et sentire: sentire autem non est sine corpore* ("it is the same identical man who perceives both that he understands intellectually and feels sensorially, but sensory feeling does not occur without a body").[17] Hence, Thomas appeals to the inner experience in which we perceive the IDENTITY OF MAN —THE EGO, which is immanent both in acts of intellectual cognition as well as in sensory cognition occurring with the help of a bodily organ.

II. THE "SELF"—A SUBSISTENT SUBJECT

If the data of immediate experience continually make known the ego as the subject, performer, and unique "center" of "my" functions—vegetative, animal, as well as spiritual-cognitive, such as intellectual cognition and wanting—then they thereby point to a single subject: "me." The "I" as the center from which all my functions flow and toward which they are directed is spontaneously recognized and continuously confirmed as the permanent subject of those same functions. Only through a demonstration resting also upon the immediacy of inner experience would it be possible to try to dismiss the permanency and identity of the subject, co-experienced in all the functions of man as performing functions. If, on the other hand, the possible proof were to rest on some general-systemic premises, then that kind of reasoning, attempting to show the non-identity of the subject or the non-existence of a subject actuating and performing the functions of man, would be a faulty argument. For the immediate data of experience can be refuted only through data immediately attained in other experience relating to the same subject.

Meanwhile, the negation of the original experience of the "I" as co-appearing in all conscious psychic experiences is not possible, since this is something that is manifested in our psychic life as original and which is also generally recognized as a preliminary condition of psychic and conscious life. For if someone does not have "consciousness of oneself," if someone is not *compos sui,* he is not recognized as a human being performing his acts, and even in legal behavior he is regarded as irresponsible. Hence, to be "conscious of oneself" is considered to be a preliminary stage of the normal psychic life of man and a fundamental human situation. There is really no difference between "consciousness of oneself" and the ascertainment of the factual existence of the "I" as subject. "Consciousness of oneself," i.e., self-cognition, is, after all, nothing other than the cognition of the existence of the "I," appearing as the subject and performer of physiological and psychic functions.

The immediate experience of one's "I," i.e., the concrete affirmation of its existence as a subject—performing functions recognized as "mine"—can also be confirmed by an indirect, systemic way of causal, philosophical explanation. For, starting from the fact of the existence of somatic-psychic functions in man, it is necessary ultimately to explain them. Therefore, either "my" functions of this kind are subsistent beings (and are not subjectivized, but are ontically independent and autonomous), or they are dependent, subjectivized beings, ultimately existing through the existence of a subject. Only the second alternative is conceivable, namely: the functions recognized as "mine" are not independently existing beings, but are only emanations of the "I;" i.e., they are beings indicating a subject, and their existence without the subsistent subject would be contradictory.

For if we accept the hypothesis, to some extent suggested by Bergson in *Creative Evolution,* and also appearing in the works of Freud and the so-called "actualistic" trends of psychology, that our functions, especially the higher, psychic ones, are only a so-called "stream of consciousness" (I emphasize: *are*), and not merely in the investigations of psychology appear as a stream of consciousness, as a film thrown on a screen (all comparative hypotheses are permissible, since they clarify understanding; here, however the concern is not with the comparison and the use of a model, but with the claim of an authentic type)—then, meanwhile, it must be understood that each act of consciousness, each act of will, or any unsubjectivized act of operation whatsoever, is an autonomous being, incommunicable to another being, i.e., it is that which classical philosophy calls a "substance." That which is called "to be a man," would be—in this case—only an accidental unity of some kind, in which various and independent acts that exist independently, converge by themselves. Each of these acts would be a separate being. The essentially single human being would disappear. And there would be as many subjects and separate beings as there are separate acts of consciousness and psychosomatic acts of man.

Such a state of affairs, however, is contrary to the facts immediately accessible to us in inner experience, specifically that "I" feel and constantly co-ascertain in inner experience that I am a single being whose acts are "mine." Next, in order to understand the allegation concerning the autonomy and "subjectivelessness" of human acts, one would have to emphasize a whole range of obvious consequences. And so, one should not regard an individual as responsible for his acts; one would have to deny the individual as the subject of laws and as a member of society.

In addition, it would still be possible here, to devise the hypothesis that one act could be a subject for other acts—and so on to infinity: but even such a possible understanding would ultimately confirm the necessary existence of the subject, the "I," as a being in itself,[18] ontically noncontradicting the existence of variable acts and the continuous conscious conviction concerning the identity of the subject, the "I", as performing acts and being the subject of those same acts of man.

Therefore, both immediate experience, conditioning man's intellectual consciousness and systemic reasoning, as well as external consequences point in a convincing way to the real existence of a single "center," a single "I," as the unsubjectivized subject of acts and the somatic as well as the psychic activity of man.

A particular confirmation of the subsistence of the ego, accentuated by Karl Jaspers, is the affirmation of personal existence in the judgment: "I am." He noted that man alone in the whole of nature can say: "I am," i.e., he has consciousness of the existence of himself—an ego. The cognitive grasp of one's "I" occurs as though "from within," since it occurs from the side of the very act of being, i.e., from the side of existence, if the existing ego subjectivizes "my" acts. For when I affirm that "I am," then that judgmental affirmation is an act of the intellect, an act not representing "contents," i.e., not any set or some definite "bundle" of attributes, in contrast to the content of each cognitive act that refers to the cognition of that which is recognized as "mine." For everything that is "mine" represents a definite content, able to be expressed in the form of an enumeration of the appropriate "attributes" of things, i.e., it is qualified with respect to content; it is "characterized." On the other hand, the affirmation "I am" does not represent any definite concept, any determinate qualification, any definite collection of attributes, but it is the primary, "pure" affirmation of one's autonomous existence, nonobjectivized in other "things-objects." Everything that appears "in me" as "thing-subject" is established in the "I," whose authenticity of subsistence we affirm immediately in the judgment: "I am."[19]

The impossibility of a cognitive grasp of the "attributes" of our "I" became the reason for the negation of a subsistent "I" by Hume. That which fundamentally is most immediately given, as a result of Hume's faulty theory of cognition, as a result of empirical nominalism, reducing the cognizability of real objects to an enumeration of concrete, sensorially given attributes—became the reason of the negation of the ego. Hume's reasoning is as follows: "Unluckily all these positive assertions are contrary to that very experience, which is pleaded for them, nor have we any idea of *self,* after the manner it is here explained. For from what impression cou'd this idea be deriv'd? This question 'tis impossible to answer without a manifest contradiction and absurdity; and yet 'tis a question, which must necessarily be answer'd, if we wou'd have the idea of self pass for clear and intelligible. It must be some one impression, that gives rise to every real idea. But self or person is not any one impression, but that to which our several impressions and ideas are suppos'd to have a reference. If any impression gives rise to the idea of self, that impression must continue invariably the same, thro' the whole course of our lives; since self is suppos'd to exist after that manner. But there is no impression constant and invariable. Pain and pleasure, grief and joy, passions and sensations succeed each other, and never all exist at the same time. It cannot, therefore, be from any of these impressions, or from any other, that the idea of self is deriv'd; and consequently there is no such idea."[20] Granted! There is no idea of the "I," if by this idea we were to understand a definite group of attributes. But we ascertain the "I" not through an impression and idea, but in the existential judgment: "I am"—"I exist." And all possible "ideas" referring to "me" are ideas of my psychic or psycho-somatic acts. These acts, however, are only emanations of the "self-existing I," whereas the judgment, "I am," is a confirmation "from within" of one's self-existence, i.e., a confirmation of that which is called "substance." If, on the other hand, we cognize the be-ing of another being— also human—then we do this above all through the indication of its content. Our cognitive attention rests mainly on the content of the particular being, for only through the enumeration of the attributes constituting or characterizing the content can we specifically define the really existing being.

On the other hand, if it is a question of the cognitive confirmation of the existence of ourselves, then, expressing the judgment "I am," we observe at once that I, the "existing Self," am not the same as any of the contents of "my" acts in which my existence, my ego, is manifested. Granted, both psychic as well as physiological acts are "mine," and we can more or less exactly specify the content of these acts, but they are not "I."

The "Self" always appears as a "contentless" performer and an existing, precisely self-existing, subject, while the acts are acts-emanations of this contentlessly and immediately ascertained "I."

This kind of accentuation of the subject's own existence coincides with suggestions proposed by various transcendentalizing philosophers, found in the circle of the so-called "philosophy of subject," that the affirmation of one's ego be recognized as the sole and indubitable point of departure in the metaphysical intuition of being. For although a man entertained doubts about the possibility of the cognition of transcendental being, yet he does not entertain doubts about his ego's existence. In the opinion of many philosophers, the fact of the consciousness of one's existence, the confirmation that I am *compos sui*, constitutes the point of departure in the confirmation of the fact of existence in general. If I could not affirm the being of my own "Self," I would not have a point of departure for metaphysics. There exist broad philosophical circles that regard the ego as an *a priori* condition of the cognizability of the world. Clearly the error of such a position, however, does not rule out the consciousness of the cognitive self-affirmation of one's own ego. It can even serve as an illustration of the kind of position in which the "I," as an individual subsistent subject, is a condition of the rational cognition of being itself.

Undoubtedly, however, the analysis of the "I" and of that which is "mine," as well as general philosophical premises, and finally the experience of subsistence, testify that this "center" and subject of all "my" acts subsists. Hence, the ego as subject is a subsistent being, or a substance.

For many, however, the substantiality of the ego is likely to be associated with the Aristotelian schematism, with his theory of categories, according to which the highest expression of being was to have been substance itself, and everything else to which the name "being" can be assigned is only a property of substance or its modifications, understood in one way or another. This is just what concerned Heidegger, who questioned the meaning of terminology expressing the substantiality of the human ego, since it "exists" differently than what is suggested to us in the substantial model. The human ego is a "here - now - happening - in - time - something - that - exists - toward - death - as - passively - thrown - into - the - world - of - objects - useful - in - one - way - or - another - together - with - other - human - beings - about - whom - together - we - care - fashioning - for - ourselves - ultimately - a - face - through - the - act - of - death." Thus understood, the ego would be something far from the ideal of Aristotelian substance, always the same, unchanging, necessary.

It is true that the model of Aristotelian substance, understood statically and unequivocally transferred to man, would be something artificial. And yet the intuition of Aristotle on his essential moments would be closer to the truth than the phenomenological description of human "fate-destiny," having somehow to constitute the "meaning of the being" (since this is what was always of concern to Heidegger)—of man. For in the conception of substance, in application to man, it is not all a matter of some "reification" or "objectification" of the vital human ego. And the model of substance is false to that extent in which it suggests such "reification" or some sort of "objectification" of man. There is, however, something exceptionally valuable in the concept of substance, namely the expression of the possibility of self-existence, the possibility of such a (more closely unknown to us) being, which already subsists, which no longer is an attribute of something, whose existence is an original act constituting that something as a real being, the bearer of many attributes. Precisely as an indication of the real identity of a human being, despite his many-sided variability, we call man a subsisting being, a "substance." This in no way means that man does not change, even in the structure of his substantial qualities. For through his acts man can so rationally and freely modify his qualitatively substantial endowment, that they attain their precisely substantial-personal, unrepeatable expression.[21] To be such a subsistent subject existing in oneself and for oneself is "to be man."

III. SOUL ORGANIZING MATTER (THE FORM OF THE BODY)

In previous considerations we arrived at the conviction that there exists (subsists) an ego understood as the "center," as the "subject," of physiological as well as of psychic acts. For both physiological acts as well as psychospiritual acts (of the same order as intellectual knowledge and intellectual desire) are truly "mine," are therefore an emanation of a single "center." And so this "center," which we call the "I" or the "ego," manifests itself at once both as (somehow) material and as spiritual, if there must be commensurability and proportionality of act and potentiality,[22] as well as of the source from which a given act flows. At the same time, taking stock of "my" particular material organs, and even of "my" whole body, one cannot say that it is really the "I" in the strict sense, because every organ of my body, even the most important, is "mine," and indeed my whole body is "mine." Consequently, a difficulty arises: how is the "materiality" of the ego to be understood so as at the same time not to deny its spirituality as the bearer of specifically spiritual acts, i.e., of intellectual-cognitive acts?

The fact of this kind of material as well as spiritual aspect of the ego has long fascinated philosophers, and for a long time—since from the days of Aristotle—the theory was constantly improved whereby one could, from one side, explain the subsistence of the human ego and, from another, indicate its immaterial and material side, although in an imprecise way.[23]

But what is the relationship of the "I" to the human soul? By any chance, do we not in the analysis (having the inner experience of the ego referring to a "whole" and expressing that "whole" of man as the subject in the act of subjectivization) make a subtle leap from the "I" to the "soul," which is said to be the essential, fundamental, and most important "part" of that "I?" Undoubtedly the problem is difficult, complicated, and also subtle, since this subjective "I," speaking *grosso modo* and having in mind the later results of systemic philosophical analysis, is also the soul which, subsisting, is the essence, the core, the formal agent (in the Aristotelian sense) of the immediately appearing "I." But without making clarifying reservations, one cannot say that the soul is the ego, except perhaps in a presupposition defined by a philosophical system. For, first of all, we do not experience the soul as soul (in its classical understanding: the form of body and the source of intellectual functions), but we experience the "I" in each human act.

Consequently, where and how does the problem of the soul appear? We arrive at the notion of soul solely as a result of systemic philosophical analysis and philosophical explanation of our "I." In the immediate cognitive experience, the ego is given to us from the existential side, insofar as it is the subject in acts of subjectivizing that which is "mine." The ego thus given to us, as has been already frequently mentioned, refers to the "whole" of our human being, i.e., to the fact that we exist and are the way we are, and that we express ourselves in "my" material and immaterial acts.

The ego thus given to us, however, is subject to systemic philosophical interpretation, just as all facts given to us immediately in cognition. The philosophical interpretation relies above all on the manifestation of those ontical functions that do not contradict the ontical fact originally given to us for explanation. Therefore, it is necessary to indicate those functions that do not contradict the ontical fact originally given us in experience, namely the "I" subjectivizing acts of material and immaterial content, and above all the immanence of the "I" in my acts, with the preservation of the unity and identity of the "I," despite the continually changing multiplicity of my acts. Hence, the first matter that demands philosophical explanation is the non-contradictoriness of the being that appears as essentially one (the experience of the identity of the "I" in "my" variable and multiple acts of various contents) and also "composed" of many factors (of acts that admittedly do not integrate, since I do not experience this, but in which the immanent "I" becomes present).

Hence, the relation of multiplicity to unity in our experience is very specific: we have a feeling of the identity of the "I," of its fundamental, essential unity (in general, we construct the concept of ontical unity after the model of the unity of ourselves), which expresses itself in the multiplicity of "my" elements-acts, maintained by that single "I." The essential unity in multiplicity is noncontradictory only when it is connected in the relations of act to potency, when a single act has the potentiality of being expressed in multiple "structures," actualized finally by a single act.

Consequently, the inner experience of one's ego as subjectivizing "my" contents is noncontradictory when, among these elements of experience, there is a unification expressing itself in the categories of act and potency.

The relations of act and potency—as is clear from the analysis of general metaphysics—can take place in the existential-ontical order as well as in the order of content, presupposing, however, the first order, since real contents are only in real (existentially given) beings. And precisely the first relations, existential-ontical, are nothing other than the experience and expression of personal beings; whereas the relations of act to potency taking place in the order of content, of essence (manifested through the content of all that is "mine"), are precisely the relations of form to matter, i.e., in our human condition: of soul to body.

For we observe that our ego, performing acts of both material and immaterial content, is somehow "composed" (the essential composition is noncontradictory only when it is a composition of act and potency). If it is composed, however, then there exist ontical foundations noncontradicting just such a composition, actually manifesting themselves in "my" acts of both material and immaterial content. The composition justifying such diametrically different contents is a composition in the order of content—of a being where the act is form (in the human instance called soul) and the potency is matter, organized by the soul to be the body.

The concept of the human soul, appearing against the background of a philosophical, systemic analysis of originally human experience, appears as act organizing matter to be a human body in the fundamental sense, and moreover as the kind of act that self-exists, that is, as a content act,i.e., form, to which the act of existence belongs immediately, by reason of itself. On the strength of this act of existence, the soul is a self-existing subject and in a limited sense can therefore be called an "I"—although the ontical "I" is the human person. The "I" of the human soul, however, is manifested not directly—but indirectly—through a systemic, noncontradicting analysis. In spite of this indirectness of cognition (of the systemic explanation), the "ego" of the soul is the ultimate foundation (in the order of content and nature) of the ontical identity of man.

If be-ing basically assumes the form of substance, as the Stagirite rightly affirmed, then one can likewise righty speak about the soul, inasmuch as it is a content act, as about a substantial form. Such a conception of soul (as substantial form) already appeared in Aristotle against the background of an analysis of the structure of material beings, which arise and perish, are changeable and multiple. And so in metaphysics the fact of substantial coming-into-being as well as the fact of change is explained only through the composition of matter and form.[24]

Obviously the composition of matter and form is particularly suitable for the philosophical interpretation of essential changes of living beings, i.e., plants, animals, and humans. In Aristotle's system, changeable beings appear as composed of two factors: matter and form; with the qualification that form alone is "act," i.e., is the factor constituting the being, since it is the factor organizing and determining the being. In this system, however, each form—apart from the forms of heavenly bodies—had to be completely material, and so a separate form could not be an independent being.[25] For Aristotle did not find in man such functions that would be the work of only form-soul alone. Indeed, he discovered a special function, which is intellectual cognition, but he associated a function of this kind not so much with the activity of the form-soul, but more with the activity of the "active intellect," which was supposed to be something different from the soul, since it, i.e., the active intellect, alone is "uncompounded" and "active."[26] Those who made essential corrections in, and gave precision to, the Aristotelian model of man were Avicenna and Thomas.

Nemesius of Emesa had already warned Christians against the Aristotelian conception of the soul as the form of the body, since such a definition jeopardized belief in immortality.[27] For all that is form perishes together with the dissolution of the whole being. This is also the reason why many Christian thinkers thought it was necessary, on the one hand, to accept Aristotle's definition and regard the soul as form, and on the other, that it was necessary to accept Plato's definition and regard the soul as a spirit.[28] Thomas Aquinas found the right way out by conceiving the soul primarily as a subsistent substance, as a subsistent being.[29]

In normal ontical circumstances the act of existence belongs to the whole being composed of matter and form, and not to the form separately. But in the case of man—due to the fact that he possesses intellectual cognition and desire, which in their ontical structure and manner of activity (full reflection, cognitive transcendence and immanence) appear immaterial and are the emanation of an immaterial base—the act of existence does not belong to man as already composed of matter and form and as a result of this composition, but existence is the "act" of the rational soul and through "actualization"— the realization and calling-into-being of the soul—as the act of the soul and through the soul belongs to the whole man, and thus also to his body.[30] For because of its natural immateriality, the human soul is a subsistent form, i.e., a form absolute in its be-ing, not mixed with matter. For this reason, too, the soul—in the opinion of Thomas Aquinas—possesses its own act of existence and imparts this existence to the body, if it alone is the form of the body that it organizes for itself.[31]

Hence, if the composition of matter and form appears in all material substance, then this composition also appears in man as well, and in just such a composition the soul is the "form" of the body, together with which it constitutes one substantial being. And where there is one being, there is only one existence. Consequently, man as one being possesses one existence. There is, however, a fundamental difference between man and all other material substance (beings) insofar as the act of existence-life which man has, he receives not as an already constituted being, by reason of the composition of matter and form, but he receives existence through the soul as an immaterial form organizing and animating the body. The soul subsisting (of course, not prior to the body and apart from the body; the concern is with ontical grounds), imparts its very same existence to the whole body.

There is, therefore, only a single existence of man, but man has this existence not because it is a result and consequence of material organization, but because it belongs to the soul, which, being subsistent on the strength of the existence belonging to itself, likewise is also the form of the body, to which it imparts its existence. If it were otherwise, man could not explain his acts, which, psychic, intellectual and bodily alike, are acts of man radiating from one center as from a single subject.

Why has only such a solution appeared as solely possible? Perhaps this will become clearer against the background of the relationship of Aristotle's and Plato's solutions as well as a comparison of their position with the immediate data of human self-cognition (inner experience).

A proposition such as Aristotle presented agrees perfectly with the general conception of a changeable world. For if things are truly changeable, then they are changeable from within, entirely, which, after all, is given to us in everyday experience where we observe the corruption and generation of new beings. Man, therefore, being also a changeable being, coming into existence and perishing, is inwardly composed. But being inwardly composed of non-independent material and formal factors—in this case, of body and soul—he exists as a consequence, as a result, of this composition. Existing by reason of the composition, however, he does not have any functions independent of this composition, and consequently he does not have self-cognition, the experience of his own "I" as transcending the functions. For the possible experience of the ego would be a consequence of the functions, but the ego would not transcend these functions since, existing as a result of the organization of content, man would first have consciousness of the content, and only as a result of content cognition—the cognition of what was called "mine"—would he arrive at self-cognition, at the cognition of the existence of the "Self," which would (and this is important!) not transcend the content of "my" acts; it would appear as their consequence (if it would appear at all—in the case of animals, self cognition would be impossible). And meanwhile we have perfect self-cognition of the fact that I cause, I perform, my acts; I transcend them, since I know that I cause them, that I am not wholly expressed in my acts, that I can substitute them for others. In a word, the moment of transcendence of the ego over the content of what is "mine" is self-evident in inner, original, and immediate experience. Therefore, Aristotle's theory cannot be correct, that man is, exists, as a result of the composition of non-independent factors: soul and body. Self-cognition contradicts this.

The Platonic model of man is suitable to the extent that it emphasizes the moment of the transcendence of the ego over all that is "mine." For if man is a spirit (a god) residing in the body and using the body like a tool, then the moment of self-recognition and the transcendence of the "Self" over all acts, especially the material, is well emphasized. But this model too is faulty because in original, inner experience I well know that "I" am the cause of "my" acts, both spiritual and material. Material acts are not any less "my" activity than purely intellectual activity is. If, therefore, I am conscious of this and experience myself as the cause and subject of "my" material acts, then the Platonic conception of man is faulty, inasmuch as it does not agree with the experience immediately given to me of my own "inwardness." And in this regard Aristotle's theory better explains this original fact.

The middle way out, finally proposed by St. Thomas, seems to be the most sensible and agreeable with original experience. Moreover, the denial of such a solution is also denial of this very experience immediately given to me.

In this formulation, the soul is the real form of the human body, in agreement with Aristotle's conception. The body is a real co-factor of man, and not just a place where the drama of consciousness is performed. Ontical existence, however, is bound to the soul immediately; this means that the act of existence actualizes the soul in the ontical order, and the subsisting soul organizes (forms) for itself the body needed by it so it can act, so that it can express itself and attain full development using its powers of activity. For the body, to exist means to be organized; the moment of the disorganization of the body is the moment of the cessation of the existence of a human body and a return to the state of non-human matter. The body is the first "mine" of a special order, which is formed and organized by the soul, in which the soul is expressed for the first time and through which it comes in contact with the external world and has the possibility of the self-cognition of itself. The body, therefore, is an actual co-element of man, although not existing in any way independently from the organization of it by the soul.

As a result, it is possible for man, in the inner, immediate experience of himself, to possess the cognition of the characteristic transcendence of the "I" over all that is "mine," since in the ontical order the soul also transcends the body, possessing its own existence belonging to it by reason of itself. It is also possible to possess consciousness of "my" material acts too, since being the form or organizer of the body, the soul is truly the cause and per-former likewise of my acts with material content. The denial of any element of the explanation results in the denial of original experience. The solution proposed by Thomas, and read in our day, seems to solve the main problem of man: his ontical structure.

And so R. Le Troquer fittingly writes:[32] "This union of soul and body is experienced by us in all our conscious activities, and our experience tells us that their subject is ourselves and not part of ourselves. The body is the sole vehicle of both thought and love. Hence, when absorbed in these activities, we are aware, no doubt in a very general way, that it engages the whole of our personality, our feelings, our intellect and our will, which knows and loves. Further in all our actions, insofar as they express ourselves to ourselves or to others, there are two dimensions, one corporeal, the other spiritual, from whose union these actions derive their meaning. From the circumstances that our concrete actions take place in time and space they are transitory and material events; but at the same time the spirit is present at the centre of these actions, and were this not the case they would be devoid of all meaning. It is strictly true that the value of a human act, which as such takes place in a historical context, depends on its bond with the spirit, with the spirit as incarnate, which communicates to it all its own human fullness and unitive power. Consequently, whether I consider my act at its source or as a fact, I shall always find in it these two dimensions and their unity; time and eternity, matter and spirit, body and soul. The pairs of terms seem indeed to prove the texture of all our thoughts and actions."

The soul, therefore, is in certain aspects "material"—insofar as form animates matter and together with it constitutes a single corporeal human being; on the other hand, however, as (taken in this aspect) the subject of purely spiritual acts (which will be discussed below), in itself, due to its be-ing, the soul is a spiritual being, because it is ontically subsistent. The same soul is also the form of the body, performing all those functions that—according to Aristotle's system—form performs in relation to matter in living beings. Therefore, in its inner ontical structure the soul is "incomplete,"[33] because it exists in a conformity with matter, and we feel like "someone" bound to matter, despite the fact the "I" cannot be identified with any material organ or even with my whole body. This "materiality" of our ego flows from the essential conformity with the subsisting soul to matter. Nevertheless, a conformity, even essential, is not the same as "to be matter," and therefore, although the testimony of our consciousness is correct, according to which we feel like a material being, our feeling of ascendancy over matter is also correct, because we do not identify with any definite material organ nor even with the whole materiality of our body, of which we know and also are aware that it is "mine"[34]—"mine" even in the first and foremost sense: and it is in large measure the reason for the "mine" that we feel in the variety of our psychosomatic experiences. If we were to agree that our soul exists by itself and in itself, and the body exists only through the soul organizing it (as "this here" body of mine), then in such a case the manner of existence of our body would not be its own existence (as in the case of the soul), but the first manner of a "possession" of that which originally is "mine" and which precisely is our bodily organism, organized and existing by the existence of the "ego-soul," which "increases" and as though from within "weaves" for itself an organism through which it can externally "express" itself. And furthermore: through the body organized and "woven" for itself it can become aware of itself.

In the reality of our body and through it we first of all feel our real existence and we experience in it our presence in the world as well as the presence of the world in us. "The emergence of self-consciousness," observes Le Troquer,[35] "requires the impact of the external world, but we apprehend this world in the first place through our body, which appears to be the point at which consciousness of the world and of self will begin. The child, while still an infant, is entirely subject to his 'organo-affective' occupations, consisting of alternate sleeping and waking, the rhythm of breathing, vague gesticulations which have no purpose as far as the world outside of him is concerned and indicate a state of initial lack of differentiation of his motor activities and through the operation of his senses, which, as they are awakened, seem daily to enlarge his space and to locate him more and more within it. Exploration of his body reveals to him that it is his own. Sight and hearing gradually differentiate him from his surroundings. We are well aware of the way in which self-consciousness is increased during infancy and childhood by the handling of objects and the mastering of the physical world through action and play. The soul has been defined as a spirit which acquires its consciousness of self as it builds up its body by relating it to the world. Our presence to the world by means of our body is a factor of our presence to ourselves and a guarantee of the forward movement of our thought. . . . Our presence to the world . . . is to begin with a physical presence. . . . Through our bodies we are located in space and time, in an environment, that is in a network of relations, and consequently of discriminations or connections, according to circumstances. This situation makes us part of that universe, a unique point included in that immense network of cosmic forces and movement. As such, we are subject to the cosmic laws, we are no more than a fragile unity which tends by its own weight to relapse into multiplicity. Yet man, who is at the same time both spirit and matter, 'lives' in this situation, this physical presence to the world. Hence man, passing beyond the level of absorption in the universe, inseparable from bodily existence, will become present by his spirit to this universe . . . "

The essential unity of man, with the "two-sided" ontical dimension of spirit and body, becomes more intelligible in the light of an interpretation of a philosophical system employing the theory of act and potentiality. The "composition" of soul and body as one of matter and form or, expressing it still more generally, as one of potency and act, is—in the thought of this theory—the only possible and noncontradictory "composition" of human nature. Nevertheless, we feel like a single being and we know that if ontical unity exists anywhere in the world, then it is realized above all in our very selves—in human beings, beings essentially one, beings not divisible—as not only our consciousness testifies, but also the observation and analysis of the observable data of human activity, both physiological as well as psychic. For all the activities of man are a manifestation of an essential ontical unity.[36]

Together with the unity, however, we experience that we are divided, that we are composed of milliards of parts of matter. The composition from numerous parts, however conceived,[37] is only then noncontradictory, given the maintenance of the essential unity of the composed being, if this composition is conceived as precisely one of potency and act.

For if there were more actual "parts," and they are to remain "acts," i.e., independently existing parts, after the composition, there would no longer be an essentially single being. There would have to be as many beings as ontical acts. If, on the other hand, all the "parts" were something only potential, then there would be no being at all. And if there exists an essentially single being-man, then his "composition" from spirit and body is possible only when there is a single act constituting be-ing: the act of existence being a property and belonging to the soul-ego as to form. And we are conscious of the unity of this act of existence-life as our ontical act.[38]

The question yet arises, having its source in Plato, whether there is a possible greater number of "forms-souls" in man.[39] In principle that would be noncontradictory, given the assumption of a certain conception of being, which is unacceptable for other reasons. For if a particular being is supposed to be an essentially single being, and if we do not agree with ontical monism, then in an essentially single being there can only be its one essential form. In man this form, constituting human nature, can only be spiritual form, as the subject of spiritual functions. Nevertheless, it is not contradictory that one existing (subsisting) spiritual form would be the form of matter as well, and would for itself also organize material life: vegetative and sensory. And a single noncontradictory state of this sort should be accepted in the case of man as a being that is a "composition" of potential factors, which in various orders (integrating, with respect to perfection, essential) is more, whereas it is a single act in the ontical order: one human existence-life, subjectivized only in a subsistent spiritual form, if man has spiritual functions, such as intellectual cognition and volitive desire.[40]

Hence, man in his deepest "I" is a subsistent being, i.e., substance that subsists because it is spirit. Matter, neither in any of its parts nor in the whole, identifies with the spirit subsisting and acting in it. The personal "I" embraces both spirit and matter; it becomes comprehensible ultimately through an appeal to the subsisting spirit, called soul.

Thus appears the solution of the paradox of our consciousness, according to which we feel as a "Self" different from everything that is "mine," even though this "mine" is the whole body; according to which we feel like one being: material and at the same time transcending matter, present in the world and present to ourselves.

It is necessary to add, however, as E. Gilson rightly observes in *Elements of Christian Philosophy,* that within the sphere of the metaphysical structure of a complete being, it is true that the soul shares with its body the same act of being that it received from God. Man, as an ontological monolith, is truly one, owing to the unity of the existential act of being: "For indeed, it is not unfitting that the act of be-ing (*esse*) in which the composite subsists should be the same act of being in which the form itself subsists, since the composite exists only through the form, and neither one exists apart from the other."* [Footnote added by translator] Hence, participating in the very being of the soul, the body does not become the soul but, as something that receives the soul in the character of a subject, is raised to the level of an act of being that has soul as the principle and cause of the body. The whole universe, in the understanding of Thomas, constitutes a hierarchy of higher and lower forms, in which, so to say, the lower ascend beyond their levels by reason of the perfection of the higher. One of the consequences of this state of things is a certain kind of continuity of order imposed on the lack of continuity in the degrees of being, in agreement with the opinion of Dionysius, that the highest degree of a lower order always adjoins the lower degree of the immediately higher one. The often quoted observation of Thomas himself, that the rational soul is similar to a horizontal or border line between noncorporeal and corporeal substances, finds its justification here. Why? Because, says Thomas, "The human soul is a noncorporeal substance, and at the same time the form of the body."

IV. IMMATERIALITY OF MAN'S SOUL

The general problem of immateriality is bound up with the concept of matter itself. For the concept of immateriality is negative in relation to the concept of matter and from the concept of the one we form the concept of the other. On the topic of matter, however, there exists a whole series of works presenting the various and divergent concepts of matter. Some sort of general systematization of views on the topic of matter seems possible only through the relation of them with a more general theory, against the background of which the problem of matter was set,[41] appearing always in the context of some conception of science (*resp.* rational cognition).[42]

Taking under consideration investigations conducted in the area of the history of philosophy, one can put forth the thesis that there are actually two different concepts of matter known to us: philosophical, related basically to Aristotle's conception of science (and also in a certain sense to Kant's conception of science), as well as scientific, related to that conception of science represented by positivism and neopositivism. Expressing the matter differently, matter investigated by various thinkers appears to us either as some "factor," "element," "constituent part," or "moment" of being, or else it is that which is the subject of empirical investigations usually conducted by various measuring methods. Hence, matter in the second instance is the most general object of scientific, empirical investigations. This object appears first of all to our sensory cognition, to our cognitive, perceptual apparatuses; we can sharpen this perception with the help of ever more perfect cognitive instruments.[43] This second formulation is connected with the concept of rational cognition presented by Kant and Comte.

In the first sense, matter is an element of being, of its constituent factors, elements, perceived solely intellectually against the background of the conducted analysis of being as changeable. Such a conception of matter appeared in a moderate way in Plato and Aristotle. Other philosophical systems presented merely a modification of it. Matter thus conceived was an individuating agent, a multiplying principle, a potential, unknowable factor, a nonperfected factor.[44] Matter, however, did not reveal itself in immediate cognition. What appears in original cognition, is a changeable, multiple, and consequently, strange being, a being arousing wonder, a being as an object given to philosophical clarification. The concept of matter originated as a theoretical justification explaining the changeable and multiple being originally given to us in cognitive intuition. In this sense, too, matter presented as a factor actually "justifying" change, is at the same time the factor impeding the cognizability of the object. From the time of Plato, the conviction was generally accepted that this very matter impedes cognition and at times renders it impossible, whereas the withdrawal from matter, i.e., some form of "immateriality," is the foundation of worthwhile, scientific cognizability, if such cognition is characterized by necessity, universality, and immutability.[45]

Matter in the second interpretation is an object of empirical, chiefly sensory, cognition, In this sense matter is all that is cognized in a measurable way. Therefore, it is some kind of "temporal-spatial continuum," being precisely the object of the physical science, in the broad understanding, insofar as these sciences in the process of their cognition make use of sensory cognitive data, as well as of data obtained by means of various measuring apparatuses, and finally, of the intellectual "processing" of measurable data.

The history of science knows no other conceptions of matter fundamentally different than the two here presented. Granted, in the compass of the one or the other conception of matter, related to the conception of rational cognition, there are different variations of them,[46] but these are contained either within the compass of the concept of matter as an element or constituent of the potential character of being, or matter as a measurable object of cognition.

After having outlined these conceptions of matter, we are now able to construct, on their basis, a conception of immateriality, i.e., of "spirituality," since immateriality is the negation of materiality. In the first case, then, we call the "formal" element in being immaterial if we accept the conception of being in which compositions of matter and form appear. Aristotle, and also in large measure Plato understood immateriality in just such a manner. Immateriality thus will be: a) either that side of being that is the ground of the ontical identity, the immutabilty, and also even the universality—if we connect the concept of immateriality with abstractive cognition (since precisely universality appeared as an attribute of abstractive-conceptual cognition)—of the only valuable human cognition; b) or being itself, which, speaking in Aristotelian terms, is "pure form" or, using Platonic terms, is "idea." It was just such a conception of immaterial being that had already appeared in antiquity.

If we wanted to create an idea of immateriality bound up with the second conception of matter, then we would construct an idea of the kind of being that is neither an object of sensory cognition nor even an object of any measurable cognition. It would be difficult to know anything about such a possible being on the basis of pure empiricism. For, on the basis of empirical cognition, one could only speak of the possibility of the existence of the kind of being that is neither an object of empirical cognition nor of any cognition of the measurable type. Nevertheless, one could not speak of the fact of existence.[47]

One can speak of the fact of the existence of an immaterial being in this second sense, however, given a somewhat modified first type of immateriality. For if we were to accept Aristotle's intuition as correct in a general sense, then—according to the terminology of Thomas Aquinas—the "immaterial" side of being is not so much "form," as the identifying element, as it is existence realizing being. For existence is the act of being, just as the act of being (in the Aristotelian sense) is form. Form, however, is act in the essential order only, and not in the real-ontical order. For it is not due to form that a being is truly something real, but it is due to the act of existence. If existence is an act of a simple substance, i.e., is an act of a self-existing form, then we can speak of the essential immateriality of being; then the whole being is truly immaterial. And in precisely this sense one can speak of the immateriality of the human soul. For the soul is a form (substantial) that exists on the strength of the fact that it is a spirit and, therefore, is an immaterial being: it is not just that it has immaterial sides.

But what are the arguments in favor of the immateriality of our soul?

Relying on the ascertainment that the "ego" manifests itself as the subject and performer of psychic functions, one finds that it is necessary to analyze these functions themselves, see whether they are material or immaterial in the manner of their very activity as well as in the structure of their products, and then having ascertained the possible immateriality of the psychic-cognitive products as well as of the manner of their performance, one is able to arrive at a conclusion concerning the ontical structure of the subject commensurate with these products of the functions [and] of their very manner of activity. In sum, if it is ascertained that some psychic functions are performed in an immaterial manner and the products of the higher psychic functions are immaterial in their structure, then there exists a foundation for putting forth the conclusion that the immaterial functions, emanated from the subject, are not the function of a material being, if the principle of contradiction holds: being does not come from non-being, spirit does not come from non-spirit.

It is also necessary to give careful attention to the fact that the characteristic functional connection with matter remains in agreement with the concept of immateriality. What is at issue here is the ascertainment of the existence of immaterial structures, and not the negation of their connection with matter.

First we should inquire about the possibility of thinking matter in general. Locke (who admittedly does not deny the spirituality of the human soul) had already judged that one cannot justify spirituality from the fact of intellectual thought, since no one knows whether God in his omnipotence would not be able to make thinking matter. Our ignorance, both in regard to the potentiality of matter as well as the omnipotence of God, was to serve as justification of such a hypothesis.

In response to Locke it was observed that indeed we do not know the omnipotence of God and its limits in a positive sense but, given the assumption of the rationality of the principles of cognition, one can assert the so-called "limits" of God's omnipotence negatively, and they are these: being and non-being. This means that with the preservation of the minimal principles of rationality, non-being is not being; hence, that which is being cannot at the same time and in the same respect be non-being and *vice versa*. This refers equally to the so-called "potentiality of matter"—matter in the same aspects cannot be non-matter. Consequently, being and non-being are limits both of the potentiality of matter as well as the power of God, although we take the one and the other "potentiality" (of God and of matter) in different suppositions. Granted, we cannot define the limits of God's omnipotence, but we know that contradiction (annihilating itself, the poles of its opposition: being—non-being) cannot be the object of God's activity. The object of such activity can only be being. Since, however, contradiction is the cancellation of being, it would at the same time be the cancellation of God's activity. Similarly, if matter cannot be at the same time non-matter, then it cannot think. For matter cannot be non-concrete, non-individual, non-empirical (this refers to the concept of matter both in the context of Aristotle's science, as well as in the context of contemporary science, of which more will be said later). The thinking of man through general ideas is precisely connected with non-individuality, with universality. Because of this, it is not possible to accept the hypothesis that matter would be able to think. For the essential attributes of thought and the essential attributes of matter are to one another as being and non-being.[48] In order, therefore, to show the contradiction of matter thinking intellectually, it is not necessary to know all the powers of matter, but it suffices to take under consideration some of its essential attributes which stand in contradiction to some attributes of intellectual cognition, just as it is not necessary to know all the properties of a triangle in order to show that a square triangle is contradictory. In this case of matter and intellectual cognition, a contradiction arises because conceptual, intellectual cognition is universal, necessary, ontical, while matter—given to us in sensory empiricism—is always individual, concrete, changeable, and temporal.[49]

If, approaching the problem more concretely, we were to take under consideration the concept of immateriality related to the Aristotelian concept of matter, then we would call "immaterial" that side of being which is not potential and changeable from within, which is not the reason of the alteration of being. In man there exists such a side, since the fact of consciousness speaks to us of the identity of our very selves. The denial of the identity of ourselves is not rational. Hence, besides alterable matter, there is in us something that is the reason of this ontical identity in the course of the whole of human life. The real "reason" of identity is self-conscious, for we well know that precisely I myself am what I was several years before, and that I myself, as the same being, am continually the same center toward which I refer all my changeable, physiological acts, as well as purely psychic acts.

I feel like the same being, and I have self-consciousness of my identity. In addition to the changeable element, there is in me a self-conscious element, being the reason of identity and immutability, that very element that in the self-conscious "Self" constitutes the ultimate ontical ground of identity. Therefore, if in the "ego" we discover the human soul through philosophical explanation, then precisely the human soul as the ground of identity is the ground of the self-consciousness of the "Self." And it is not something ontically changeable nor the ground of alteration, but on the contrary, being the ground of self-conscious identity, it is thus the "immaterial" side of man.

If, on the other hand, we were to take the contemporary concept of matter under consideration and, in relation to it, create a concept of immateriality (a concept of immateriality which completes "immateriality" in the Aristotelian understanding), then we call "immaterial" such a being that is not a temporal-spatial measurable continuum. If, then, in the activity of our ego, we perceive the presence of such acts and of such a manner of activity, which precisely are not temporal-spatial, nor are they changeable either, then we will have the right to speak of the presence in us of acts immaterial in their content. In consequence, both the source of these acts as well as their subject, is immaterial.[50] The analyses of this problem can be conducted through an examination of the acts of intellectual cognition and, subsequently, of volitive activity.

And so acts of conceptual intellectual cognition (concepts taken in their structure) present a cognitive content detached from all the attributes of matter—both in the Aristotelian understanding of matter as well as in the contemporary—as a temporal-spatial continuum. For we form concepts distinct from impressions,[51] concepts abstracted from matter and materializing conditions, general, necessary, universal concepts. And although these concepts refer to material objects, such as "man," for example, yet in their content there are no changeable potential, spatial, temporally conditioned attributes. For in the concept "man" none of the attributes described in scientific or prescientific cognition is measurable, because none is concrete, individual.

When, however, we consider that we have ideas such as these that are immaterial, then the immateriality of the ego is shown even more conclusively. For if there existed in man only a material subject of cognition, then such a subject could cognize only what is material, what acts on it as a stimulus. Meanwhile, we understand such objects as "unity," "good," "beauty," "being," "cause," "relation," "science," etc. We express judgments about these matters. All objects of this kind do not constitute anything in their structure that would be some sort of temporal-spatial continuum quantitatively measurable in any manner whatsoever. The objects, being in themselves immaterial, do not constitute a material stimulus for cognition; and yet they are cognitive, they awaken discussion, etc. Hence, the subject cognizing them is commensurate with objects of this type, so in itself, in its structure, there is no matter.[52]

The immateriality of cognition comes still more to light in the structure of judgments that are an intellectual affirmation of certain attributes in the subject. There takes place in judgment a total and simultaneous grasp of the parts and the whole, and there also appears the necessary perception of the belonging, or not, of the parts to the whole. The total, simultaneous grasp of both the parts as well as the whole is a grasp not in spite of the "parts," not by contact with the parts, but totally—that transcends the purely external activity of matter, in spite of the point of contact with the limits of extension.

On the other hand, existential judgments in which we affirm existence are an indicator that we are capable of grasping what in its nature is not matter. "Intelligence is at rock bottom a readiness to make contact with being which it consequently seeks to appropriate. Intelligence, in fact, strives to obtain a truer and more faithful idea of what is. It seeks a clearer understanding of reality, to lay bare its pattern of relations, its whys and wherefores, with the ultimate object of reaching the unity which underlies and envelops diversity: herein resides the meaning of all scientific activity at whatever level. It therefore seems that intelligence, in pursuit of this aim, must transcend the phenomena of space and time. For beneath the particular, and the specific here and now, intelligence discovers the universal, the principle of unification, and expresses it in the form of a personal judgment. . . . From this readiness to make contact with the whole of reality . . . a number of consequences may be immediately drawn. If it is to have any scope, it means in the first place that the being who is its subject is able to distinguish the self from the non-self. In fact, to be ready to make contact is to be able to encounter and to welcome. Before we can welcome anything we must first withdraw into ourselves: that is, we must simultaneously possess ourselves and distinguish ourselves from that toward which we are moving, and this leads us back to a certain state of inwardness, which must be an awareness of and a presence to the self. It is precisely this which testifies to the immaterial nature of the mind. Ready as he is to make contact, the knowing subject is not enclosed within himself, since he is capable of possessing being and of summing it up in himself in all its universality. Yet this capacity is linked to a deliverance from everything material, to the mind's situation beyond space and time.

"The fact that we are capable of contact with the totality of being, that we are able to reach it beyond its spatial and temporal aspects, and identify ourselves with it in a living relationship, not only reveals an immaterial and spiritual principle, but also necessitates, at the very source of this intellectual activity, an actual concrete subject, a reality which exists in the spiritual order, since there is a necessary correspondence between the mode of action and the mode of being. It is, in fact, by reflection that we discover ourselves as existing subjects and in our highest mode of being, that of the spirit. We experience ourselves as inward, as the source of our intellectual acts; we realize experimentally that we are 'mind' present *within* and through all the activities in which we engage. This existence within oneself, unlike that of matter whose every part is external to every other part, is the privilege of the spirit, which is the subject of existence. To be within oneself, to be present to oneself, therefore necessarily implies a spiritually subsisting subject which is the source of all our intellectual acts, and for that very reason manifests itself as always present and disclosing itself everywhere."[53]

The volitive experiences of man, love and whatever conditions it and is its necessary consequence, are another sign of the immateriality of the human soul.

Ordinarily, in a philosophical analysis of the act of love as a product of the human will, i.e., of rational desire, there are distinguished the objects of this love, the act of love itself, and the manner of its performance. An analysis of these very moments of the act of love indicates a transcendence over matter and the presence of spirit as a main factor of love.

Let us consider, now only in a most cursory fashion, some aspects of this problem, subjecting to analysis the universal desire for happiness and the concrete desire of good and love.

Thomas Aquinas[54] and, recently, M. Blondel paid close attention to a characteristic division in this sphere. The latter noted that the human will is always disposed toward something more than it wants concretely. No concrete wanting equals the constantly energetic capacity of the will, which is disposed toward infinity (in Thomas Aquinas that division of the will was called *"appetitus naturalis"* — natural desire of the will, and *"appetitus elicitus"* — desire concretely brought forth in relation to a concrete good). At the same time, he observed that no concrete good constituting the object of acts of will fills, appeases, human desire, which on the strength of natural desire (on the strength of its structure) is directed toward universal good. That direction toward universal good is the natural desire for happiness, being the driving force of all concrete desires and at the same time concurrent with every emergent act of desire; the natural and never extinguishing desire for the Absolute-God. And although man does not always become aware of this concretely, and even if he became aware of his insatiable desire and, being an atheist, wanted to resign from that "desire for more," from the desire for infinity, yet this would not be possible for him. On the contrary, the richer man is in knowledge, the richer in material resources, the richer in love of others, the more often does the conviction accompany him that he has not possessed happiness, that the something that could satisfy him is always beyond him.

This division of the will into the desire for ultimate happiness and the desire for concrete goods, although it can be explained in philosophy by considering the derivation of infinite desire from the cognitive, intellectual grasp of analogously general being (in which, as it is explained elsewhere, there is also an obscure grasp of God as the reason of being), yet, as the natural desire for "something more," testifies that the subject itself (man, soul) is in its nature infinitely receptive and constantly reveals this in every manifestation of wanting, of desire. The desire, unceasingly flowing from us, for an infinite happiness transcending all partial goods, indicates the source-subject, which must likewise transcend in existence material conditions amid which it finds itself. This source is also immaterial, since its functions also greatly transcend the condition of the activity of matter.

Still another sign of the immateriality of the essential part of our "I" is the possibility of our self-mastery. Only a spiritual and immaterial power can say "no" in relation to itself and master its inclinations, because such mastery presupposes full reflection over oneself, and, simultaneously, the grasp of oneself and the object of one's aspirations. That self-mastery, flowing from thoughtful consideration, was always acknowledged as an essential manifestation of the spirituality of man, for acts of reflective self-mastery, in the full sense of the term, cannot be observed anywhere in nature apart from man.

Hence, the fact of the immateriality of our ego-soul appears to be rationally justified. For it is possible to devise further, more particular, reflections relating to the concrete ways of man's activity, as Marcel does in his works, for example, and show the unceasing transcendence of the human spirit over matter, but the signs shown here of man's transcendence and of the immateriality of his ego-soul are sufficient in order to maintain the justified conviction that I am someone, subsistent, a subject, and not just "something" that is the result of the organization of material relations.

V. THE ASPECT OF IMMORTALITY

Linked with the analyses conducted here is another essential human aspect, extremely important for man: immortality.[55] For, keeping in mind the fact of the ontical subsistence of the human "soul" and also its immateriality, one can perceive the real ontical foundations of the immortality of the human soul, of the ego.

For if the soul possesses its own existence—experienced in the subjectivizing "I"—[if] it is a subsistent being (which expresses itself continually in the judgments, "I am") organizing the body for itself, which exists by the existence of the soul, then in the moment of the disintegration of the body, the subsisting and immaterial soul, as the subject of acts immaterial in their structure, cannot cease to exist. It would perish only if its existence were the result of the bodily organization. But in such case the absurd would follow: being would come from non-being; the body which is not spirit would organize itself in the form of non-body, i.e., it would "create" spirit, as appears in all of human cognition and wanting. The essential ground underlying the immortality of the human soul is its subsistence, i.e., expressing it in the language of the philosophical tradition: the fact that existence (ascertained in the judgment, "I am") belongs immediately to the soul, which at the same time is the form of the body.

If existence belongs immediately to the soul, and to the body only and exclusively through the soul, then the destruction of the body does not entail the destruction of the subsisting substance that is the human soul-ego. Thomas briefly notes: "That which has existence through itself cannot either come into being or undergo destruction, except through itself. For this reason, too, the soul cannot come into being by way of generation, i.e., material alterations, since it has an immaterial existence; and likewise it cannot cease to exist by way of natural destruction."[56] There would have to occur a special intervention of the Absolute, who would annihilate the soul, since the soul in itself, being in its essence an uncomposed spirit, cannot forfeit existence. Only the Absolute, therefore, is the essential reason for the existence of the soul, and only he—obviously acting contrary to the natural order—could annihilate it. Consequently, the context of the existence of the soul is not nature, which the soul transcends through its cognition and love, but the context of its existence is Absolute Being alone, God as the person with whom the human spirit, coming to know or contemplating nature, carries on a dialogue ascending unceasingly beyond nature. There exists, then, as Gilson observes, "a necessary connection between the notion of 'the act of being' (*esse*) and the demonstrability of the immortality of the soul. But the notion of the human soul conceived as an intellectual substance is the very core of the Thomistic notion of man."[57]

Jaspers clarified this problem from another point of view by accenting the role of the immediate, intellectual, cognitive grasp of our own existence in the privileged judgment, "I exist," in which we affirm our ego not from the side of its content qualification, but from the side of the act of existence penetrating all "my" activities that color, with respect to content, and qualify my own "ego."

We daily encounter the problem of immortality and thereby its germinal solution in the repeatedly posed questions: "Will we continue to exist after death?" "Is there immortality of our ego?" These questions are raised not only directly in the form of questioning sentences, but also equivalently in one way or another; questions such as these make up the whole of human activity, i.e., rational activity. The very character of our cognition, the use of necessary, universal concepts, the character of our judgments in one way or another affirming be-ing; the simplest acts and declarations of love, manifesting themselves externally with the help of the quantifiers "forever," "never;" the whole of creative and cultural work, attempting in the course of changeable and transitory matter to leave behind a lasting trace of our thought; in sum: all that is somehow a rational expression of man, is an expression of transcendence beyond changeable matter, is at least the really posed question: "Will we continue to exist when the changeable state of matter, entering into our ontical structure, undergoes still further, still more radical alterations, called death?"

The very raising of the question and the attempt toward its resolution were not always correct and well-aimed, even in authors associated with the thought of St. Thomas. An example—how especially instructive in this issue—is the dispute about the immortality of the soul at the beginning of the sixteenth century at the Fifth Lateran Council, where Cajetan, the foremost commentator on St. Thomas, declared himself against the possibility of a demonstration of immortality. But this matter already belongs to history: so let this general reminder of it suffice.[58]

CHAPTER V

MAN AND KNOWLEDGE

The primary and distinctive moment in which man fulfills himself precisely as man is his cognition. This affirmation, however, is very general and has little precision, because immediately there arises the question, "What is cognition?" Usually in attempting to give an answer, we appeal to our inner experience which is available to everyone. At the same time, it is a preliminary condition for every interpersonal communication. Hence cognition is something very primary and undefinable. Such a state of affairs, however, does not prevent a broader and more profound answer which is connected with a system and, in the first contact with the problematic, is somewhat unclear. This kind of answer, however, is necessary. It will constitute the contents of the entire chapter in which, after an introductory description of the fact itself of cognition, we shall analyze its many-sided non-contradictability.

One view of cognition, however, which is very common is, at the same time, highly deceiving: namely, the attempt to explain and to elucidate cognition by appealing to consciousness: to know—is to locate something (or it manifests itself) in the field of consciousness. This attempt is connected with the Cartesian position where the primary and inital situation in philosophical thinking resolved itself into consciousness and its clear and distinct idea. That which appeared clearly and distinctly to consciousness was at the same time, in the primary datum and something to which one could appeal ultimately in the process of justification. Cognition—or rather thinking—as the fundamental act of the spirit is accomplished in its "interior" and not in the line of the relation and contact of the spirit with the material world.

Meanwhile in cognition—as we shall speak about it later—there appears

119

a system of signs: (a) speech-gestures-writings (b) concepts, fostered by the mind of the meanings of our speech or writing (c) the designated things, material objects.

Before all else, we come to know a concrete material thing (usually!), e.g., this running dog. This concrete dog is ultimately the known thing, which remains grasped (always in an aspective way!) as an abstract content, as "dog" which is the meaning of general terms, such as the expression "dog." All three elements constitute a single cognitive process. Speech or writing is a system of symbols or conventional signs: meanings fostered in the spirit are also signs—not conventional but necessary, formal and "transparent" signs of the designated thing. These very meanings as known things are, in Descartes' system, ideas manifesting themselves in consciousness. At the same time, meanings constitute signs of the thing itself—of that particular individual dog who is running down the street. The concrete dog—as the foundation of a system of signs appearing in cognition—cannot be separated from the cognitive process.

Cognition, therefore, is not a meaning which appears in consciousness but it is the understanding of a concrete thing under the aspect of a grasped meaning. The meaning which presents itself in consciousness is also a sign subordinated to the thing. Between the existing thing and man (through his cognitive apparatus, chiefly the intellect), a specific bond called cognition is effected.

I. THE FACT OF HUMAN COGNITION

In man's cognition, we meet two almost mutually-occurring aspects of the cognitive act: (a) external utterance (understood in a wide sense) and (b) an understanding of the sense of this utterance.

Obviously, understanding the sense is commonly considered as the essential factor of cognition itself but the peculiarity and specificity of man's cognition accentuates at the moment we look more closely at the character of the utterance itself as well as the structure, or at least a description of the sense itself, which is marked with a given utterance.

External cognitive utterances vary greatly: in speech, writing, art and whatever conventional sign. When, for example, I stand on the street and notice a colored spot moving and making a characteristic sound, I say "dog." "The man and the dog," writes E. Gilson "are concrete individual beings, they are even bodies; that is, visible and tangible things whose actual existence can be verified by sense perception and, in case of doubt, can be checked by a comparison of the sense perception of several perceiving subjects. But the very word spoken by any one of those observers is also a concrete, particular, and material thing whose existence can be checked by a similar test. As a thing, a word exhibits all the characteristics common to material objects. As the nominalists of the Middle Ages used to say, a word is a *flatus vocis,* a vocal utterance. As such, it is a sound produced by the vibration of the vocal chords as air coming from the lungs is forced through them; such a biological and physical phenomenon can be observed, recorded, and measured."[1]

Likewise, just as the sound of the voice is something material, spatio-temporal and measurable with the aid of physical instruments, so too the inscriptions which are left on paper, clay, stone or wood are something material. Certain of these inscriptions as, for example, Etruscan writing, the rope writings of the Incas, or the wooden tablets of the rongo-rongo from the Easter Islands, are unintelligible to us: they are not read and they constitute (up until the time of their reading) only a material thing. However, in the normal course of external utterances which are disclosed through speech, writing or gesture are only the external, material sign of something else—of an experienced, inner, cognizing subject of some kind of meaning of this utterance, of understanding its sense.

The sense of various utterances is as if their animating soul. The understanding of the sense of the utterance (viewed in the widest sense) is synonymous with human cognition. If we should return again to the mentioned utterance, and if we were to consider the Polish word *pies,* we shall see without any difficulty that this word sounds completely different in the Latin language: *"canis,"* different in the German language *"der Hund,"* different in English: *"the dog,"* still different in Russian: *"sobaka"* and in other languages; but the meaning or sense of this expression in the various languages is the same. The articulations in the different languages are only vocal signals: they constitute the sign of the same indicated content about which we are fundamentally concerned in the cognitive act. For when we use various vocal signals as signs, it is always a question of communicating to someone a determined cognitive content which we have experienced cognitively, or of a definite meaning, of a determined sense. "'Meaning' or 'signification,'" writes E. Gilson, "is not a word, it is not the voice of the speaker, nor is it in any sense of the term a thing. It has no materiality; so much so, that it cannot even be an object of sense perception. For we can hear a spoken word, but we do not 'hear' its meaning, we 'understand it.'"[2]

The understanding of the meaning of articulations, grasped in a wide sense—is a specifically human trait. Everything, whatever man has accomplished in nature within the limits of his existence, is the result of understanding the sense of his utterance or, precisely the result of human cognition—which awakened, from the beginning of the sensation of a perceived particular object; but it is nevertheless a particular representation of a thing. Even so-called "typical representations" of Galton[4] or "schematic representations" portray fundamentally individual traits of one individual object that is similar to many individuals. Besides, a kind of blurring of particular traits is not as yet a general sense but an indistinct presentation of one object. The case of a schematic representation is similar to a picture of a man which is sketched by a child. This picture differs from a picture of an animal or a flower, but it can represent equally a man as well as a woman, an elderly person as well as a child. "A schematic representation is, as it were, general," writes Chojnacki,[5] "not because it does not supposedly possess the traits of concreteness, as Locke erroneously imagined, but because it does not represent any particular object which is determined in time and space; and because it has a meagre and incomplete content, it can represent many objects. The schematic representation itself is concrete. Owing to a meagre content, it possesses a greater range of association and a greater potentiality of assimilation; hence we speak of its generality."

In the meantime, we are conscious within ourselves of a cognitive experience of such contents (being the sense of general expressions), which are really general and which do not contain within themselves particular, concrete, spatio-temporal traits. The clearest example of such precisely general, necessary and "atimely" concepts (or understood meanings) is the content of a mathematical definition. If, for example, I know that the *definitum* of points of a given surface is equidistant from one point of a given area such an aggregate is called a circle. I can be convinced at each moment that such a formulated concept of a circle is not a presentation only of some particular circle, but it presents every circle. And such a concept of a circle is equipped to predicate about every concrete circle: (a) in a univocal sense (b) separately and (c) identically. This characteristic is true not ony of mathematical concepts but of all others as well.

Further, since representations constitute fundamentally a depicting of only one concrete thing, they do not lend themselves to a univocal, distributive, and identical predication about individual objects. For I cannot say that every existing rose is precisely pictured as "this particular" red rose growing in my garden in June 1981. Other roses can be similar to it; whereas the concept of a rose or the understood meaning of the expression "rose" is the same and identical with every rose which existed, exists, or will exist at some time. Thus understood, the immaterial sense of our general expression can be understood only from a certain aspect which is an identical relation between the elements of a thing, a relation that realizes itself in many objects.[6]

It is difficult to expatiate more fully on the theme of the meaning of general expressions, or that which we usually call universals.[7] But, in order to complete the general outlined picture, it would be proper to assert that this identical relation between the elements of things is realized in many objects; it can concern either an autonomous being called substance, or also a non-autonomous being called some sort of accident. If an identical relation concerns the elements that constitute substance (an autonomous being), then, in the thought of Aristotelian tradition, we shall call it "second substance"—if, however, so-called "accidental" traits of a first substance, we simply call it a "universal." In this case, we acquire universals of such a kind as "color," "white," "black" and the like. Both one and the other type of universals (pertaining to both substance and its property) are cognitively grasped in a determined aspect of an identical relation between the traits of a substance or its property.

Such a universal, however, can never be real, i.e., a really and individually existing subject, despite the fact that in a sentence construction it appears as a subject. Thomas Aquinas already called close attention to this in *S.T.I.,* q. 13, a. 12; that in every affirmative proposition (and the same applies to negative sentences), the subject and predicate are only symbols (*significant*) of this same thing (*secundum rem*), but something different with respect to an apprehended attribute (*secundum rationem*). In other words, subject and predicate refer to the same but they mean something else. For example, in the sentence, "man is white," the expressions "man" and "white" are referring to the same real being, but one expression means in the same subject-being the mark (*resp.* combination of traits) which constitutes humanity and the other, its "whiteness." Hence the sentence, "man is white" is an abbreviation of the sentence "that which is man is the same which is white." Hence general propositions can be expressed in the formula: "every thing that possesses feature 'x', possesses also feature 'y.'"

Keeping in mind the qualification made concerning the use of universals, we can perceive that conceptual knowledge, which presents itself in the form of universals, concerns being and not only some sensible impressions. In his conceptual knowledge, man is completely turned to and bound with being and, ultimately, this explains to us why conceptual knowledge is necessary and changeless. The manner of grasping—namely that we humans (people) know—is expressed in the universality of these concepts. If, therefore, it was observed in the Platonic Academy that all conceptual knowledge is stable (changeless, eternal), necessary and universal, then, man's transcendence in relation to nature and his essential superiority to animals was perceived and sometimes affirmed. If universals which embrace the aspective identity of relation appear in many individuals, they concern being in which this identity is grasped by our intellect. We must also add that we do not grasp it directly and positively but, rather, negatively: as an "area of disturbance" whose negation would make being itself unintelligible. For it is evident that every particular being is unrepeatable and the aspective grasping of the identity of relation is accomplished through the schematizing intellect (unable to understand the original grasping of an individual) with the foundations in a thing. The foundations in a thing—as a content-ontic necessity—unites with the general schematizing way of grasping and it brings about the permanence and changelessness of conceptual contents. Thus, necessity (of the thing), generality (manner of intellectual apprehension) and the resulting changelessness (of the content): these are the three traditionally convertible traits of universals.

But not only general conceptual knowledge, which weighed heavily in the history of culture and European science, concerns being. This is evident to an even greater degree in judgmental knowledge and by directing attention to the specific character of our judgments. As the mediaeval philosophers used to say, the expression "is" constitutes the "soul" of the judgment. In predicative sentences, it performs the function of a copula in it, and it usually expresses a truth because it concerns being; whereas in existential judgments, it actually affirms the existence of being. For our knowledge expressed in judgments is a specific, psychical grasping of objective, real, ontical states and not an optional construct. Above all, a factual ontic state exists really. We ascertain this in very direct and primary and, as yet, pre-reflective judgments of the type: "John exists," "my thinking exists" etc. Such a type of knowledge expressesd in existential judgments is a cognitive grasping of a being immediately, spontaneously and primarily. In addition, I also know what a thing is. I already perceive that the concrete thing which I know "is" or "exists." This primary human knowledge which affirms being (as yet very imperfectly) is so natural and spontaneous that usually we pay no attention to it. Rather, we concentrate on the cognitive grasping of the very contents of the thing.

A fuller cognitive grasping of the content of a thing is achieved in a predicative judgment of the type: "Peter is a man," "man is a mammal." In such judgments, there appears anew the expression "is" as their core and the element distinguishing them, from merely the concepts themselves, which indicates or designates being, whose meaning symbolized by universals is aspectively identical, inter-relational "between notes." (*miedzycechowy*)

For if universals and judgments concern being, this points, in man, to the existence of a special cognitive power that is higher than the senses and representations which cannot affirm being but only something sensible. Furthermore, if universals are the aspective identity of inter-relational relations of different things, then, this type of identity of relations can be the object of only a rational, essentially higher knowledge than that of the senses. For we are not dealing here with any sensible or representational things. It is for this reason that every thing is capable of being understood, to the degree that its component elements are not mutually exclusive in contradictory relations. It is precisely this internal construction which excludes contradiction and determines the possibility of an object's existence, that is usually called, in the most general way, the essence of a thing.

For the sense of a man's cognitive expressions and, at the same time, an understanding of this sense or the use of universal concepts and judgments, indicates the existence of reason (intellect) as the source of these concepts and judgments. For whatever came into existence—which previously did not exist—has its own commensurate cause, which does not contradict the fact of the rising and coming into existence of a new being.

And since we are constantly aware of the formation of concepts and judgments within us, for which we take a cognitive responsibility—we feel ourselves to be their creators (authors)—there exists, therefore, an undeniable cause of these concepts and judgments. And this cause cannot be only an organic, sensible apparatus if the sense of our statements is actually spiritual and immaterial in its ontic structure and manner of functioning. Hence there exists a suprasensible, non-organic source—even if we do not exclude certain aspects which demand a cooperative function of the organ of the brain—which, in philosophical tradition, is usually called, in a most general way, reason or intellect.

The existence of a reason, which is different from the senses, as the source and commensurate cause of our intellectual knowledge, can be further established be appealing to an analysis of more specialized manners of cognition, for example, of conscience, self-cognition and the like, but not all are based on the fact of understanding the sense of generally-cognitive expressions.[8] For the understanding of the sense of generally-cognitive expressions—whether conceptual or judgmental—is the acceptance "for ownership" or as something *my own* of a content "which is not mine." Here occurs the paradox of identifying that which is"mine"—because the cognitive processes are indubitably my processes, for which I take "responsibility"— with the content "not mine," which intrudes from the outside (even though this content concerns me myself). This content finds itself in a state of constantly "attacking" me, with cognitive power (*est in statu obiectali*). The entire be-ing and reality of knowledge is built on my cognitive acts but the sense, the content which thrusts itself on me, is foreign to me. It is something other than myself.[9] This unique manner of "suspending" an alien content on my real acts of the intellect is an intentional being—peculiar and existing only through "my" existence—a content which is "objective." This, essentially, is the mystery of the act of cognition.

On its periphery, in its aspective vision there appear derivative properties or particularizations which presuppose the act of cognition. And so: "consciousness" is nothing else than continuous, reflected, cognitive acts which join together two opposites: object and subject. Consciousness is this cognitive "area" which is constituted through cognitive acts between "I" and "not-I." Understood in this way, consciousness can be intensified, increased, or diminished in its dependence on accomplished acts of cognition. As a glow above the conflagration, so consciousness rises above cognitive acts. And if we reflect the object of cognition on our "I," there comes into being self-cognition, in which we must carefully distinguish the content-side, which is marked by our physiological-psychical acts, from the non-content side, from the side of grasping the existence of our "I." This grasping from one side is something which is given us directly and, from another side, it is given us embryonically, in every judgment and, specifically, in the personal affirmation of truth expressed by the copula of the sentence "is," for which I take responsibility. Kant and the Post-Kantian transcendental school (e.g., Rahner), perceive this and they consider that anthropology is the *a priori* knowledge (as self-cognition) of every kind of cognition. This is a classical confusion of a real function of cognitive affirmation in judgments connected with "I," transcending reality, with an idealistic apriorism, which is completely unnecessary and harmful and which deforms the essential sense of cognition.

II. OBJECTIVE NON-CONTRADICTABILITY OF COGNITION

We had already mentioned—in connection with the analysis of the sense of general statements—about the ontic objectivizing of our intellectual cognition. It is nevertheless proper to devote more attention to this question and its understanding, with respect to the significant implications of this fact. If being presents itself as an object of our intellectual cognition, it remains an open question how, precisely, this "being-object" of human cognition should be understood. For being can be variously understood. The entire history of philosophy is an example of a very varied understanding of being; and being which is understood in one way or another, as the object of intellectual cognition, in one stroke, properly "sets up" the extent and the manner of cognition. Therefore, we must first see in what way the objectivity of being is proved in intellectual cognition.

During the time of the Golden Middle Ages, when the question of man's intellectual cognition was investigated against the background of his ontological structure—his soul finding itself, as if midway, in the hierarchy of being, between pure spirits and animals (man as a microcosm)—very proper distinctions were made which, independently of man's eventual central place in the nature of universal beings, prove themselves true in the analysis of our cognition. For it was observed that animals know as well as people and, also, so-called pure spirits whom theology calls angels.

Every level of being, however, had its own appropriate manner of cognition. Animals cognize only sensible properties, insofar as they are connected, to some extent, with the demands of an individual or species of their nature. Animal cognition does not go beyond the limits of matter, which is understood as a potential element of being, as a singular, changeable and temporal element. Animal souls are forms totally immersed in matter because they are the result of the organizing of matter and its influence on other material beings. They "feed" exclusively on forms which are completely bound with matter and its own characteristic temporal-individual manner of activity.

On the opposite end of the hierarchy, stand angels, as pure spirits who know with the help of cognitive, intellectual forms, that have been received directly from God, or they "see" what they wish in their own immaterial nature. Their nature can serve as a cognitive form. For this reason, too, their vision is clear, without error, without reasoning, without drawing conclusions and the whole logical apparatus. For spirits possess only an intellect and a purely intellectual, intuitive manner of cognition.

Man, who finds himself midway in this hierarchy, "participates" in something from the animals and in something from the spirits. Less precisely, man's intellect as a spiritual and immaterial form of the human body (more precisely: the first power of this form), benefits from sensible knowledge which is the sole ontic source of intellectual concepts, formed through abstraction from sensibly-expressed data. But because it is at the same time an immaterial form, it produces these concepts as immaterial beings. These are deciphered in sensible data as necessary, permanent and ontic; and because they are formed by the human intellect, they are at the same time general.[10]

In connection with just such a status of man, it is customary to say that the proper object of his intellectual cognition are neither the data of sensible perception nor the cognitive forms of a purely spiritual, intellectual intuition: but rather the contents given in intellectually-cognitive forms and which are attained via abstraction from sensible perception, that are called the sensibly cognized essences of things.

The matter, however, is sometimes understood erroneously and, for this reason, we must make traditional, but always valuable, distinctions concerning the question of the object of cogniton. Usually, a distinction is made between a so-called "material object" and a "formal object." The first—whatever thing, with its entire ontic endowment—is simply any thing whatsoever, with all the traits that it possesses; for example, an apple, along with its weight, smell, taste, color, etc. However, this same material object can represent a collection of various formal objects. In the case, e.g., of an apple, its taste is the formal object of the human sense of taste and color, of sight. And hence, since the apple is in itself a material object, it comes into contact with man through the "formal object," which is an aspect, thanks to which, by using the cognitive power or suitable methods, man encounters the material object itself. Thus, the formal object distinguishes the appropriate powers of man (e.g., colors., sounds, and the like testify to distinct senses), or appropriate cognitive disciplines as, for example, biology, anatomy, physiology and the like, which investigate nature from a specified aspect. Hence nature as material being (*resp.* an aggregate of material beings), presents a large mosaic of formal objects which are distinguished through manifold scientific-cognitive endeavors. Obviously, this mosaic is constantly growing larger, along with the development of sciences. This enables us to understand better these same material objects, in the midst of which we live and which we use.

In the case of a formal object of man's intellectual cognition, the question is somewhat complex, since the analysis of the character of our cognition shows that one formal object of intellectual cognition (it is being—about which we shall be speaking later) possesses two dimensions: the first, "the how," and the second, "the what." It appears to us as "clothed" in the attire of the essences of things which are sensibly cognizable. In connection with such a situation, a distinction was made in the tradition of classical philosophy (within the area of the so-called formal object of intellectual cognition), into a so-called "proper object", and an "adequate object," or "what" we know in an intellectual perception and "how" we know.

That which we know, or the adequate formal object is being; on the other hand, *"how"* we know—the proper object—is the so-called essences of things that are sensibly cognizable.[11] For man "feels himself" certain only when he grasps intellectual cognitive perceptions in the form of a definition, in the form of such a content which finds its foundation in sensible perceptions. The intellectual understanding of the nature of things which are sensibly cognizable or the essence of a material thing expressed in a definition discloses the human tendency, about which E. Gilson[12] writes: "Intellectual knowledge naturally tends to assume the form of an apprehension of abstract essences, or "quiddities," tied together by the discursive operation of reasoning. In saying that the proper object of the intellect is that which the thing is (*proprium obiectum intellectus est quod quid est*), Thomas has provided a simple and exhaustive explanation for the tendency, so obvious in the human mind, to turn all its objects into abstract essences. Since these essences themselves are reducible to their definitions, and therefore to mere quiddities, the complex structure of reality finds itself represented by a pattern of abstract notions, To conceive such notions, to define them, to combine them to separate them by his judgments, such seems to be the habitual and normal form of the intellectual activity of man."

The history of philosophy seems to substantiate this fact amply. Philosophy has always been connected with analysis, description and classification of separate entities, sometimes called ideas, sometimes a third nature and sometimes pure possibility. From the time of Plato until the present, the pivotal theory about reality (whether it is called ontology, metaphysics, logic or even dialectics) is basically an activity about ideas which become better understood when they are set forth in a surrounding of represented sensible perceptions.

These facts testify that our mind is at ease when it acts on concepts and when, in an intersubjective sensible cognition, it uses univocal symbols of these concepts. For, "nothing is more fit to be taught than a set of abstract notions, all of them accurately defined and woven together by the rules of syllogistic reasoning. Essentially it consists of definitions and demonstrations, as if the ideal approach to metaphysical problems were through a sort of mathematics of concepts. . . . Reduced to its essentials, this method coincides with what is often called the 'method of exposition' as distinct from, and sometimes contrary to, the 'method of discovery' or invention. And, indeed, after completing all the intellectual operations required for the solution of a problem, we feel the need to present a discussion of it under a clearer and more ordered form, free of the many hesitations, corrections and unnecessary complications usually attending the first attempts to solve problems. But the chief difference lies in this, that we usually solve problems by proceeding upward from the data of sense experience until we reach the general notion or principles, in whose light those data can be understood; on the other hand, following the method of exposition, we go down from the principles to the concrete data we want to understand."[13] Thus, the proper conception of the object of intellectual cognition would recall the method of an exposition, since it leads to the apprehension of a thing's essence in the surroundings of sensible data.

Keeping in mind "how" we basically know intellectually, we cannot, at the same time, lose sight of the "what" we know. For, if Thomas Aquinas asserted that the proper object of intellectual cognition is the essence of things which fall within the range of sensible cognition, this does not mean at all that he asserted that we are incapable of grasping anything else than only the essences of sensible things, or, that there would be nothing more in being itself, than only that essence, i.e., that being reduces itself to essence alone. It only means that by knowing every being intellectually, we are, above all else, disposed to grasp that being in its essential aspect (and of such an essence that is subordinated to a representational clarification), but other aspects or sides of being are intelligible to us when we present them to ourselves on the model of sensibly knowable essences. Thomas himself frequently called attention to the fact that essence is not the most important element of being, that the "be-ing" of being does not lead exclusively to essence, that even the essence of things understood by our mind separately can, in the thing itself, identify ontically with itself. In a word, essence is not identical with being in the strict sense of the word.[14]

Considering the matter very briefly—the character of our cognitive acts shows that the proper object or "how" we understand rationally is precisely the essence of things which is sensibly cognizable. For our first judgments about reality concern material things: our terms and words which are used to indicate whether a supernatural reality or supernatural intellectual "creations" (e.g., God, soul, theory), always come from such terms which originally were used to designate material objects that were grasped sensibly. In addition, we observe that we do not have any proper concepts of such objects which we would never experience sensibly. And we construct for ourselves some kind of analogical concepts which are always improper symbols of reality, which they render in some kind of approximation. For when we want to understand something better or to explain something more clearly, we resort to examples and pictorial representations. For this reason, too, representations always accompany our thought and, to a great extent, constitute the basis for the understanding of things.[15]

Above all, man's very structure is eloquent testimony to the fact that our intellectually-rational cognition is accomplished in the context of the material thing. Since man is a psychophysical, ontic individual, he is not a kind of "pure spirit," but he is joined with matter in an essential manner. And hence, the activity of such a thing, especially activity which is most intimately connected with the structure of such an understood being, bears with itself the stamp of its inner structure, of an essential connection with matter and with material conditions. For the very act of cognition likewise is accomplished in agreement with the essential conditions of human existence.[16] Hence it is not surprising that the proper object of human intellectual cognition or—"how" we know—is the essence of a thing given us in sensible experience. The spirit of abstraction is this proper climate in which man is constantly developing. Abstract concepts, in their most proper understanding (in separation from sensible data) and the abstract subordination of given essences of things are something necessary in the intellectual life of man. Without the ability for abstraction there is no intellectual creativity.

But all this does not mean that the abstraction of a thing's essence from sensibly cognizable data and the coordination of abstractly apprehended essences constitute the ultimate purpose of human intellectual life. As a matter of fact, in the history of philosophy and science, there were tendencies that regarded the purpose of science as the creation of abstract concepts and their coordination. To a great extent, the Aristotelian conception of science is a witness to this position—but this "spirit of abstraction" also became the dread of man's intellectual life.

"It would be a fruitful subject of reflection," writes E. Gilson,[17] "to consider the dreadful consequences of what might be called "the spirit of abstraction." In speculative matters, it invites the substitution of the definition for the defined, which is a sure way to render definitions sterile. It also invites the illusion that one can increase knowledge by merely deducing consequences from already coined definitions, instead of frequently returning to the very things from which essences and definitions were first abstracted. In the practical order the spirit of abstraction probably is the greatest single source of political and social disorders, of intolerance and of fanaticism. Nothing is more uncompromising than an essence, its quiddity and its definition.

"The reason for this fact lies in a characteristic common to all abstract notions . . . namely, that the characteristics of the abstract are exactly opposed to those of the concrete. Now reality is concrete, and this is the reason that abstract descriptions of it are liable to deform it.

"Abstractions are mutually exclusive, because 'to abstract' is 'to set apart.' The definition of an abstract notion expresses its very essence such as it is in itself. This is to say that the definition of an abstract notion posits it as 'other than' any other notion. In the words of Thomas Aquinas, of anything whatever considered abstractly, it is true to say that it contains nothing foreign to its essence: *non habet in se aliquid extraneum, quod scilicet sit praeter essentiam suam.* If I say 'humanity' I mean just that, and I do not mean 'whiteness' because humanity is solely that whereby some being is a man, just as in saying 'whiteness' I point out only that whereby something is white. Now a thing formally is a man by that which belongs to the notion of humanity, just as a thing formally is white in virtue of that which belongs to the notion of whiteness. In other words, a man is not man *qua* white, nor is a man white *qua* man.

"Now the very reverse is true in concrete reality. Humanity cannot be whiteness, but a man can be white. Precisely, a man is that which has humanity, and there is nothing to prevent that which has humanity from also having whiteness. Generally speaking, there is nothing to prevent any concrete being from having anything that is not contradictory to its essence. A man can have many other things besides whiteness, or blackness, and humanity."

This rather lengthy quotation shows wider horizons, seen with the eyes of an experienced historian of philosophy who investigated the history of some philosophical conceptions and expressed it in his masterful work, *L'être et l'essence*[18]. The consequence of affirming only abstractly-seen essences of things which are sensibly cognizable not only led philosophy into error—the whole of essentialism is a true child of the acceptance of such a position— but it also fragmented and scattered all sciences. In the history of philosophical thought, there took place a curious objectivizing of "how" we know and a confusion with *"what"* we know. Besides the objectivizing of human cognition already occurred once, in a somewhat different area, with Plato, when the generality of concepts was understood as an objective trait, which generality in the thing itself is only a way of human conceptual cognition. In effect, this position had equally far-reaching consequences, both in the theoretical as well as in the practical area.[19]

Undoubtedly, the manner of human, intellectual, conceptual cognition is general and hence, this knowledge is generally essential because of the fact that the essence, which is grasped and understood in a definition is an abstraction of the objects of sensible cognition. The abstraction from sensible data and the essential generality ultimately do not contradict the fact of conceptual cognition.

In spite of these reservations, we must recognize that our conceptual cognition—even if it does not exhaust the entirety of intellectual life, since it is in the framework of judgments and through judgments that complete human cognition is attained—does not reach the fundamental structure of being. It likewise reaches being but it grasps this being from the side of content and incompletely. For we can distinguish within being its two sides, its two fundamental elements: essence and existence, but a real essence can exist only when it is this essence of an existing being. Hence a real grasping of the essence is an actual grasping of being from one side, from the side of its content. It is for this reason that even our conceptual cognition—even if we grasp the essential traits of a thing in the widest understanding of essence—puts us in touch of a thing because it is in contact with essence which belongs to existence; and which finally becomes understood through the existence of this being whose essence it is.[20]

As it is commonly known, however, alongside conceptual cognition man also makes use of an even more noble "judgmental" cognition. For concepts express within us only ontic contents which are, in some way, permanent and necessary and grasped in a universal manner. We do not take any personal intellectual responsibility for conceptual cognition, which is detached from knowledge attained through judgment.[21] For a purely conceptual cognition does not, as yet, express our personal "engaged" relationship to a known reality: it does not exist in a detachment from a knowledge achieved through judgment. The history of philosophy knows the tragic misunderstanding in its effects, caused by the above-mentioned "spirit of abstraction," in whose thought even judgmental knowledge leads to the production of a new concept. For effort was made to reduce the entire cognitive process and its results to the acquiring of a new "concept" about reality, so that the results of the process of abstraction would be primary concepts, which can be enriched by establishing them in judgments. A judgment which arises from a composition of concepts will give, as a result, a new, higher and better reflected-upon concept, and a group of judgments would lead to the construct of an even more excellent concept, a kind of super-concept.[22]

In later times, perhaps a Platonic theologism was at fault: for man's intellectual life was understood on the model of divine ideas. God's intellect was supposed to have been a "pleroma," a noble collection of ideas and his intellectual life would lead to a vision of himself and the world in the ideas. In God, there would be only one idea: His own essence or in the order of the supernatural: LOGOS, who is the most noble and first idea, in which God knows and acts: "The Word was with God . . . through Him everything was made . . . what was made in Him was life."[23]

It was observed that intellectual cognition adequately expresses itself in the idea. For this reason, various cognitive activities in man were reduced to the production of a new idea. The ways of producing this new idea were various: either through abstraction, or through judgment or through reasoning. However, all of man's cognitive operations were to terminate in the production of a new idea or in the improvement of an idea which he already had. The wiser a man is, the less he has need for particular ideas, since he sees more in "higher" ideas than less intelligent people are able to perceive in a whole series of particular ideas.

But the matter is quite different than the suggested indications of Plato and the solution of Aristotle, as well as that of Latin Aristotelianism. For our judgments—to which we have already directed cursory attention—both existential and predicative, are something structurally and qualitatively different from concepts, and they contain within themselves such elements which are not reducible to concepts. Due to these new, structural and qualitative moments symbolized by the expression "is," our judgments designate being. The affirmation of being which is effected through judgment is different in existential and predicative judgments. In existential judgments: "John exists," "Rome is," we fundamentally affirm the fact of the actual existence of some concrete thing. This existence is given us either directly when, for example, I see my friend near me and I can affirm his existence, or else in indirect existential judgments of the type as "God exists," where an entire series of intellectual steps is necessary in order to articulate this judgment in a meaningful manner.

The direct affirmation in an existential judgment of the existence of some concrete thing is, at the same time, an affirmation of being, given us in the most primary knowledge—what used to be called in philosophical tradition reaching back to mediaeval times— *"ens ut primum cognitum"* —being as the primary cognizable object. In an existential judgment, the very fact, or otherwise, the "act" of being is that which strikes us as the most important in being itself. For "before" I know what is the content of being, "before" I realize the character of the being which I know, I first know that it exists.[24] The fact of the being's existence is the foundation of the "be-ing" of a given being. Without the real fact of existence, there are no other real contents, no other real entity. For this reason, too, the affirmation of the fact of existence is our most primary act of cognition, an act of pre-reflective cognition. Only on this act of cognition—which is so obvious that it gives way to an oversight as involving no problem—can other cognitive acts be constructed.[25] On the basis of an affirmation of a being's existence, we can accomplish the next act: of abstraction and of creating abstractive concepts. However, it is impossible to abstract from that which, in general, is not given us as existing. Then, and only then, can I create for myself a concept about a thing, since the thing itself was first given me as really existing.

Here also arose a misunderstanding in the history of philosophy. For, from the times of Aristotle, it was observed that the foundation of intellectual abstractive operations is the sensible perception of the object. The object must be given me in a sensible perception, so that I might accomplish an abstraction from concrete sensible data. The process of abstraction was discussed in detail, against the background of omitting individual-sensible traits. All of this is true. But we must still add that this type of activity of abstracting from sensible data pre-supposed the very fact of the existence of a concrete object of our sensible perception. No sensible perception of an individual object would take place, if this object did not exist in itself and its existence were not affirmed by us either formally in an existential judgment or equivalently, at least virtually, against the background of real experiences in cognitive sensible perception. And hence, something more primary in our act of human cognition, even more primary than the consciously sensible perception, is the human cognitive perception of the fact of a known being's existence.

In addition, it is a truth that man's cognitive function is accomplished in totality and that we do not have in us only sensible perceptions, to the exclusion of intellectual cognition. For there is only one cognitive function with sensible, as well as with intellectual accents. Finally, the reason for sensible as well as every kind of intellectual cognition of a thing is the primary affirmation of the fact of existence, accomplished in existential judgments which are a completely pre-reflective act.[26] Various other cognitive acts already point—in, at least some embryonic way—to the subject and object of cognition, while in existential judgments, there is not, as yet, a generally designated, cognizing subject. Here, we are completely "objectivized;" the existence of being completely absorbs us and it is the reason for achieving a real cognition, of whatever kind, of real traits of a known object.[27]

It is precisely existential judgments which bring us in contact with the very be-ing of being. This is done very imperfectly; nevertheless, the first cognitive step of contacting non-subjective reality becomes really achieved here. Without a primary affirmation of being, it would not have been possible to accomplish any other cognitive act, which is the construction of concepts and next, the issuing of judgments and reasoning. Because of existential judgments which put us in contact with reality from the side of that which is the "root" of the reality of things, from the side of actual existence, further stages of our abstracting and selective knowledge are, however, connected with reality. Every kind of cognitive operation has its foundation in being, in reality. And even if, in the process of abtractive cognition or in one or another aspective and selective knowing, there took place a somewhat strong shift of emphasis and, as a result, there came into being an incorrectness of knowledge and mistakes—nevertheless, there is always the possibility of returning to the primary sources, to the very roots of cognition and verification at the foundation—whether actually and in what measure, the conditions of things which have been affirmed in selective and abstracting cognition, are real or, at least, they have a foundation in reality. Without a pre-reflective contact with being which exclusively is the "nourishment" of our thought and our knowledge, we must stand on the grounds of cognitive idealism and this idealism could not have been removed in any way. Besides, the history of philosophy points to abstraction, only to a knowledge of contents as the primary basis for human cognition. At the same time, it shows the necessary consequences of a cognitive idealism which inevitably accompanies certain primary cognitive foundations.

Besides the existential judgment in which we ascertain the existence of a concrete being, we also have other judgments that are completely different and which are not deducible from them, about which logic speaks widely— predicative judgments. These are normal judgments in which there are a subject and predicate, joined together in a sentence by the copula "is" (*resp.* "is not"). Judgments of this type are—at least in the area of philosophy and pre-scientific knowledge[28]—bearers of truth because they bring us in contact with being, with reality. We should constantly recall here a theory of Thomas which is not as yet appreciated: "If there are both essence and existence in the same thing, truth depends more on a thing's existence than on its essence, just as the very name of being (*entis ab esse*) comes from be-ing (existing). And intellectual action itself which grasps a thing as it is (exists), owing to its particular similarity to the thing, produces this agreement which constitutes the essence of truth."[29]

Normally, it is customary to emphasize that the sentence-copula "is" constitutes the very "soul" of a predicative judgment. As we have previously observed, the predicative sentence, e.g., "Man is white" means the very real being itself, since such a sentence can be understood as an abbreviation for "Every being which possesses trait 'x,' possesses trait 'y.'" And hence subject and predicate of a predicative judgment which appear as universal are two general traits of the very being which is composed and whose component elements can be understood through general traits (universals), which are evident in the judgment as "subject" and "predicate." Hence "every real cognition" has simultaneously an essential and an existential character. The fact that cognition begins with being does not mean at all that that which is later is not being. Being is first but it is always. Being accompanies all our representations. And even this is said too weakly, since basically, all cognition is "cognition of being." Cognition does not go beyond being, since beyond it is nothing. The classical example so frequently quoted by scholastics contains, in spite of its banality, a profound truth. That which I first see only from a distance is initially, for me, only something: being; if the object comes closer, I see that it is an animal but it remains a "being." If it were to come even closer, I would see that it is some kind of man, and, in the end, that it is Peter; but all the successive designations of the known object are always only steps of a more precise cognition of being. ". . . Being, therefore, is the first object of intellectual cognition, not only in the sense that it would already be contained in the first known object but, likewise, in this sense that it is contained in every known object and that every cognition, without regard for its object, is likewise, and even before all, a cognition of being."[30]

III. THE SUBJECTIVE NON-CONTRADICTABILITY OF THE ACT OF KNOWING

There is a rich set of issues falling under this title which, by itself, can constitute a separate treatise. For we are dealing with the ultimate explanation (in the sense that we are not appealing to any other cognitive discipline), of the possibility of man's intellectual knowledge. There is an extensive literature on this question, which is connected with different philosophical trends which propose, in different ways, the solution of the problem of the possibility of man's intellectual knowledge. These propositions can be divided, in a most general way, into three groups:

a) A system of innate ideas or a priori categories making valid knowledge possible;

b) A system of empiricism and, connected with it, a concept of concrete abstraction;

c) A system of empirical rationalism with the notion of universal abstraction and its non-contradictory elements.

Each of these possible solutions has a series of separate formulations and attempts toward its resolution, which we shall mention, as need arises. The first two proposed solutions, which are diametrically opposed to each other, will then be shown to be wrong because of the absurd consequences that are linked with them. The third position, in principle, avoids the absurd consequences but its explanations will have a negative, rather than a positive character. And in this sense it will recall the general solutions indicated through metaphysics.

A. A PRIORI SYSTEMS OF INNATE IDEAS

The problem of a valuable and rational knowledge appeared almost simultaneously with the origin of Greek philosophy. Should one trust sense knowledge or should one rise above (beyond?) it and reach another world, a pure thought which is not blemished with mutable, unstable, and constantly changing sense perceptions? This conflict became especially acute in the case of Parmenides, who became aware of the fact (he presented his reflections on this problem in the form of a religious revelation), that there is a fundamental opposition between the intellectual and sensible trend of knowledge. These are, as it were, two roads on which man must go. And once gone, he cannot leave them, since they are roads that lead in different directions: to truth: the way of intellectual knowledge; to error: the way of sensible knowledge. The way of intellectual knowledge leads to truth because it is the way of being. Being manifests itself to the human intellect as an immediately given object of knowledge; and to such a degree that to think and to be are one and the same: NOEIN TE KAI NOEMA TAUTON.[31] This connection between being and intellect has appeared in the history of philosophy in various a priori ways of knowing. We can mention here names and, linked with them, theories of intellectual (particularly conceptual) knowledge: Plato, St. Augustine, Descartes, Leibniz, Malebranche, Gioberti. According to these thinkers, our intellectual concepts do not arise by way of an intellectual activity on empirical data but rather they are somehow given along with human nature. Hence they are innate or they also appear at suitable occasions. Obviously, every one of the above-mentioned authors presents his own individual solution. The only factor common to all of them is that intellectual conceptions are connected with the human intellect because man is fundamentally a spiritual entity who lives his own intellectual life.

To avoid the charge that our assertions are without foundation, let us glance briefly at the solutions proposed by the above-mentioned eminent proponents. Plato's theory of innate ideas presented in the *Phaedo* and *Meno* is well known. Man, as soul, knew ideas directly before he was joined to the body. He knew them in previous incarnations. "The soul, then, as being immortal," Plato writes, . . ."and having been born again many times, and having seen all things that exist, whether in this world or in the world below, has knowledge of them all . . . for as all nature is akin, and the soul has learned all things, there is no difficulty in her eliciting or as men say learning, out of a single recollection all the rest, if a man is strenuous and does not faint; for all enquiry and all learning is but recollection."[32] ". . . knowledge is simply recollection, if true, also necessarily implies a previous time in which we have learned that which we now recollect. But this would be impossible unless our soul had been in some place before existing in the form of man."[33]

St. Augustine, who accepted the notion of a soul using the body, but, on the other hand, as needing illumination for knowledge of necessary, changeless, and eternal truths was searching for the source of this truth: "Now where could our mind discover these characters of truth? Not in things, for all of them are contingent, and since they all begin and end in time, none of them is either immutable or eternal. Nor can our mind discover these characters in itself, since, like all created things, it is contingent, mutable and enduring in time. The only way to account for these characters of truth in the human mind is to admit that every time it forms a true judgment our mind is so to speak, in contact with something that is immutable and eternal. But to say 'immutable' and 'eternal' is tantamount to saying God. The existence of immutable truths in mutable minds is the proof of the existence of God . . . God is the inner master who teaches the same truth to all the minds that seek after it. He is, so to say, the Intelligible Sun which enlightens the minds of all men."[34]

According to Descartes' opinion, there exist in us certain innate ideas, as for example, the idea of "things," "thoughts," "truths," "God," along with acquired ideas, such as hearing thunder, feeling fire, seeing the sun, and ideas formulated by a knowing intellect, e.g., idea of a siren, griffin, centaur.[35] "Among these ideas, some seem to be born with me, others to come from without, and the rest to be made by myself. For I have the ability to conceive what is generally called a thing, or a truth, or a thought; and it seems to me that I do not conceive this from anything but my own nature."[36]

According to Descartes, ideas are inborn in the same sense that certain talents are inborn with nature or sicknesses in certain families. Just as children at birth do not show actually inherited psychical traits but only an inclination in a given direction; so too, in the human intellect, there is a power which, without the cooperation of material things, brings out the innate ideas which are the objective representations of things. These ideas do not belong to experience, even though their use takes place jointly with sensible knowledge.

Leibniz, beginning with the premise that it is impossible for one thing to have causal influence on another—"the monads are self-enclosed and have no windows"—is of the opinion that the soul, as chief monad, attains a knowledge of the world not under the influence of material things, but completely automatically, on the occasion of sense perceptions. An innate emanation of knowledge is only equated with a previous act of knowledge which can be recognized as the sufficient reason for the following act of knowledge. Acts of knowledge, however, correspond to reality, as a result of the activity of "Pre-established Harmony," in virtue of which, God has so ordered the world, that the activity of one thing corresponds to the actions of another thing. This theory gives rise to a false causal interpretation of the world.[37]

Yet another modification of a priorism can be called a system of ontologism, according to which the idea is not only a psychic human product but its own reality, distinct from it. Intellectual, conceptional knowledge would take place not through psychical intellectual forms but through an immediate union of the knowing soul with its object, who is God himself—known, however, not in his essence but only in his attributes, like "infinity,"[38] "idea,"[39] "being."[40]

The foundations for this kind of position flow from the conviction that our knowledge cannot refer to subjective ideas, since the latter are only modifications of our own psyche. For this reason, only something objective and eternal can be this object. As it is evident in human knowledge that the known "essences of things" are necessary, eternal and changeless, and hence have divine attributes, it is not surprising that what is first in the ontological order is also first in the cognitive-psychical order, if there exists a connection between knowledge and being.

Obviously, such reasons flow from far-reaching misconceptions and a failure to distinguish between the mode of cognition and the mode of existing; or between the different modifications of signs, which are found in the fact of knowing, etc. But above all the absurdity of the consequences which flow from such an accepted position falsifies the accepted assumptions. It is useless to speak here any further about such consequences. Suffice it to recall that they lead to postulating either a pantheism or an angelism or, finally, a denial of knowledge itself.

B. EMPIRICISM

Empiricism, as it is found in the thought of Locke, Hume, Stuart Mill and others, represents an opposite direction in the development of the problem of knowledge. Clearly this is not the place to describe their points of view in detail. It is sufficient to bring into relief only some fundamental aspects of their position, so that against this background we can perceive the subjective conditions of man's cognitive functions.

From a certain point of view, English empiricism can be treated as a continuation of Descartes' ideas. For both Locke and Hume based their entire philosophical systems on an analysis of the epistemological point of departure, previously proposed by Descartes. The difference between them and Descartes reduces itself (in the point of departure) to a greater and more fundamental emphasis on the empirical character of our ideas. For Descartes held that the basic ideas are inborn in us, while the English empiricists, who accepted the validity of the starting point in philosophy for an analysis of the ideas themselves, accepted that these ideas are empirical in character.

It was precisely Locke who substituted general images for universal concepts and, further, in keeping with the remainder of the Cartesian tradition, called them "idea." This idea is to be a hazy, typical image whose individuating notes have been obliterated. These general images, in spite of their imperfection, are needed by man for communication with others and for expansion in knowledge. Locke understands abstraction in a strictly concrete manner as a kind of separation of certain notes of an image from other, coexisting and co-appearing ones in a concretely saturated image. The result of such an abstraction is an abstract image. It becomes general (in a certain sense) because it can represent and replace all the particular images of this attribute.[41]

If Locke asserted that general images are something fictional, created only by our mind and existing only in it, it was Berkeley who held that, in general, ideas of this kind do not exist when our consciousness is not aware of them. Particular representations can be called "general," insofar as they replace a series of similar representations; in other words, that they perform the function of general representations, even though they are not such in reality. Likewise, there is no abstraction in the sense of "detaching" and separating certain representative notes from others. Abstraction is merely a function of attention, since "to abstract" means to direct attention to certain notes. Therefore abstraction in a positive sense is only the concentration of our attention on certain notes of the representation; negatively, it is a failure to direct this attention.[42]

But Berkeley left unanswered the unexplained questions of uniting the name with the particular representation which performs the function of a universal representation. D. Hume[43] clarifies this lacuna. He distinguishes between concrete impressions, sensations and ideas. An idea arises from an impression, which is more lively and more permeated with concreteness. Ideas which are the result of impressions are simple or complex, as a result of the intellect's activity which unites elements, according to their contiguity, similarity etc. All ideas, however, are concrete representations of singulars. Particular representations become as if universal, because of their connection with a word which is the common name for a whole series of representations. And owing to habit, it is not only a particular representation but of others similar to it. For concrete representations which are endowed with a common, general name, perform the function of conception by the fact that it receives a general meaning, resolving itself into the psychic function of habit and association.

Empiricist views find their strong continuation in the person of Stuart Mill,[44] according to whom general terms evoke certain representations. Perceiving the meaning of general terms depends not on some kind of general representation of conception, but on a series of particular images, which unite according to certain notes that our attention isolates and brings out in relief. The mind, (which is the collective name of the different states of an attentive and conscious being), concentrates its attention on only certain aspects of representations. It leaves others in the area of an increasingly diminishing consciousness and, for this reason, it can designate the course of this or that association of representations. As a result, there are present in our consciousness, connected (associated) representations—complex ideas—which arise on the basis of attention and association. It is Stuart Mill's position that our consciousness does not register universal concepts and universal representations.

H. Taine[45] brings to a close the associationist concept of representations. His position is that we have no universal concepts; neither do we grasp any universal notes. We merely have a tendency to call things by a common term. When we are thinking about something abstract, we have in our consciousness only words, which are accompanied by hazy and indistinct representations (images) like traces or echoes of previous experiences. On the other hand, what corresponds to an abstract concept is not this hazy and indefinite representation but the word, which evokes more or less clear representations that belong to a class connected with the name. The fact, however, that names have a certain meaning, or that we understand them, is explained by a property of a two-fold asssociation: between the name and representation of a certain class and among representations, because of which, there is a tendency to give a general name to a whole group of similar representation. A substitute function of words and mutual association of words and representations suffice to explain "universal concepts."

The author who called attention to the fact that, with the help of purely nominalistic assumptions, one cannot explain the fact of knowledge, was the French psychologist Ribot,[46] who submitted to introspective investigation words that have a meaning and those that are meaningless. He asserted that the recognition of one group takes place differently from the other. He accepted as a hypothesis that the unconscious plays an active role and it contains something that gives the word meaning and the ability to stand for the designated thing. And because meaningless words obviously evoke "nothing" in consciousness and meaningful words do evoke something, the hidden element allows itself to be more or less defined, if we investigate the way in which we come to grasp (understand) universal names. Ribot expresses the conviction that so-called "universal concepts" are habits or individual dispositions that are formed in the area of representations. Similarly, as in the development of a habit, so in the development of universal concepts there comes an end to the strain and effort and a facility and speed develop in their use. For thinking is nurtured and supported by hidden and unconscious activity, which glimmers in the direction of the consciousness. The hidden knowledge is composed of an ensemble of notes drawn from the representations; in proportion as the number of notes decreases, the universality of the concept increases. A universal concept is, therefore, composed of a series of elements: habit, memory of prolonged characteristics extended from representations, and an activity omitting changing characteristics.

If a priori rationalistic theories accepted the intellect as a specific power or a quality of soul contacting directly a spiritual or ideal object, the second group of theories stands on the position of denying the existence of the intellect as distinct from a sensible apparatus, especially of representations, of a cognitive power.

Both groups of theories do not address the basic facts which are realized through the ego's acts of cognition of equally material and immaterial contents. Neither do they seem to deal with the fact that our abstractive, intellectual cognition is very intimately connected with a sensibly representational cognition.

Therefore we must search for an interpretation of the observed cognitional facts on a middle course, where there will be affirmed a connection between intellectual knowledge and sensible sources—emphasizing, at the same time, the different structural character of the acts of intellectual cognition, which points to direct structure of the subject of knowing acts, i.e., the intellect.

C. STRUCTURE OF THE INTELLECT

If in agreement with our constructed analyses, we hold the position that, on the one hand, the nature of our universal expressions and judgments is fundamentally different from singular, changing and sensible expression which are subject to time—and, on the other hand, we observe the simultaneous co-appearance of the same sensible expressions as the necessary foundation and unique source of the cognitive contents, then we cannot agree with either of the extreme empiricist positions, nor, likewise, with the position of a priori nativism of various kinds. In a word, we must affirm the sensible realm as the single source of the contents of knowledge about the world, even though the character of the knowledge which has been gained or fashioned is qualitatively different from the sensations themselves. In such a case, the solutions proposed either by extreme rationalism or by extreme empiricism cannot be accepted.

From among the philosophical theories pertaining to the fact of human knowledge, the most coherent concept, and one which is most in agreement with facts and which does not fall into absurd consequences of extreme views, seems to be the concept of knowledge proposed by Aristotle and completed by St. Thomas Aquinas. It has been continually defined more precisely, throughout the centuries, by all kinds of authors who have accepted the mode of thinking of classical philosophers.

This concept can be expressed in three fundamental theses:

(a) the foundation for our human knowledge in regard to its contents are sensible perceptions; a denial of this fact would make our contact with the world unthinkable;

(b) the contents of human knowing testify that they come from a special, immaterial power, called the intellect, which differs from senses;

(c) since we wish to preserve the receptive character of knowing, we must accept an a priori (in the ontic sense) power, which makes possible (non-contradictory) the very fact of knowing universal contents.

The artificially constructed theses, however, express essentially-connected points of the theory of human cognition in classical philosophy. This does not mean, however, that there is some uniformity in their area, in regard to the particular formations, or some general agreement, which excludes discussions and (at the same time), the possibility of more precise explicitness. It is proper, however, to examine the contents of the particular theses.

(a) The unique foundation for the contents of our human knowledge are sense perceptions.The question here is about the cognitive content with which we operate during our entire conscious life. From the time of Locke, the ancient Aristotelian formula became prevalent, namely *nihil est in intellectu quod non fuerit in sensu*. But the content of this statement differs in Aristotle and in Locke. The latter gave a superficial meaning to Aristotle's ancient thought, by reducing all kinds of cognitive contents, practically to sensible ones, while the Stagirite observed correctly that senses are also the primary and irreplaceable foundation for the contents of our intellectual knowledge. And when this knowledge is achieved by the intellect, it is essentially different from the structure of sensibly cognitive acts. Nevertheless, sensible knowledge is the unique and irreplaceable source of various contents with which we nourish ourselves in our cognitive life.

A substantial portion of the Aristotelian Tractate *Peri Psyches* contains analyses of sensible knowledge as the most perceptible structures of human cognition. Similarly, our everyday experiences, as well as experimental psychology, confirm the conviction about the complete dependence of our intellectually cognitive contents on given data of sensible knowledge, so much so that the lack of some sense organ makes it impossible to fashion for oneself a conception based on the function of the given sense. This is also the reason why people who are blind from birth do not have an adequate understanding of colors, etc.

The necessity of sensible knowledge as a basis for intellectual content can also be inferred from the consequence of rejecting apriorism and ontologism. These positions held that knowledge comes directly from the sphere of the spirit alone; whether our, or some other, namely God. This kind of position basically cuts us off from the material world in which we are born, through which we live and which we constantly transform through culture. A cutting off of the contents of our cognitive knowledge from the senses would be equivalent to a cutting off of our knowledge from the actually existing world. Various theories of a monad, unfolding according to a pre-established harmony, or likewise various changes of occasionalism are only an inefficient and artificially constructed attempt to explain our real contact with a material world by simultaneous contradiction—that this very world of matter constitutes the source of the contents of our intellect. The meaning of human life in a world of individual and changing matter, without a direct knowing of that matter as changing, in the course of sensible perception would be, in short, inexplicable and bizarre.

Furthermore, man's very structure as a psycho-physical being indicates that, within the reality of the human functions of our psyche—and human cognition is indisputably such a function—there stands out a very essential connection between the spiritual side of our cognition and our material side. To express it briefly, man's union of body and soul, his structure as this kind of natural entity, as in fact he is, would be completely unintelligible if man did not draw his cognitive contents from sensible perceptions. For if, indeed, the union of the body and soul is not a union counter to nature but, on the contrary, it precisely constitutes this nature, the soul likewise draws its benefits from this union.[47] This can be achieved only in its proper sphere of acting; hence, in intellectually cognitive functions, in which the material-sensible aspect is involved. Since, on the other hand, the body and matter do not enter into the structure of intellectual ideas, they could only be present, for this reason, at the genesis and articulation of the intellectual structure of the ideas themselvs. The senses thus furnish cognitive contents which the intellect accepts in its own way. They also constitute their exemplification through a so-called activity of "returning to images," which we shall discuss below.

Sensible knowledge, which is the basis for strictly intellectual concepts, performs (according to St.Thomas' view), yet another function: namely its own instrumental causality.[48] For our images do not conduct themselves completely passively in intellectually knowing functions, but they impress their stamp in an active sense. The instrumental function of our representations in the process of forming concepts, as well as the entire cognitive process, deserves more careful attention.

(b) The intellectually-cognitional contents, as we have already pointed out above in our discussions of the meaning of general expressions and of universals, do not contain anything material in them. For if, indeed, we use universal concepts which are immaterial in their very structure; and if they constantly arise within us; then they also contain their own source, their own power, as a potentiality which produces these very concepts. This power is precisely the mind, which is the direct and efficient cause of concepts. The necessity for the mind's existence as the direct source of cognitional knowledge is something indisputable, if we wish to account for the fact that we, human beings know universally, really, and necessarily with the help of judgments and reasoning. The mind which is directly responsible for our intellectual cognition and thinking (and hence, not only for the objective understanding of the content of the things themselves, but also for various cog-

nitive operations in conceptions, as well as affirmations in judgments and finally, constructional reasoning)—stands at the basis of the entire human
culture. And hence, just as there is a great difference between animals and
men, between animal and human knowing so, too, there is a great qualitative difference between intellectual cognition and sensible, representational
knowledge.

And even though sensible knowledge never appears in man in a pure
form, as it does in the case of animals—insofar as we can judge about this
on the basis of animal reactions resulting from their knowing—nevertheless,
the sensible aspect of human knowledge is essentially different from the intellectually-cognitive aspect. For we atttain sensible knowledge along with
images under the influence of physical and physiological stimuli. Our
sénses, in conjunction with the images are open to the activity of the material surroundings but, at the same time, they do not go beyond the limits
of matter. However, by basing ourselves on this very sensible and representational knowledge, we come to a self-awareness and a recognition of a
spiritual content, or even of negation, of defects or of relation. And for this
reason, we must affirm that such a different kind of knowledge postulates
a separate knowing power which we call reason.

Availing ourselves of an analysis of various cognitive acts and of various
aspects of knowing, we find it is possible to multiply arguments, almost to
infinity, for the existence of reason as a special spiritual source of our ideas
and of the affirmation of existence, especially in judgments. However, an
especially convincing proof for the existence of reason is our self-cognition
which is an instance of full reflection that grasps "oneself," one's own "I,"
insofar as it is the performer of cognitive acts and the objects and contents
actualized through the cognitive "I." Self-cognition testifies to the cognitive
experience of the cognitive realm which is delineated by the two extremes:
"I" as the permanent performer of cognitive acts and other acts of mine
(hope, love, hatred, fear, etc.), as well as "objective" contents which intrude
themselves on me, but which are never "I," and which are usually gathered
from the surrounding world.

Self cognition testifies to a spiritual source of knowledge, comprehending
cognitive acts, insofar as they are accomplished through my own "I" and
they affect "non-I." Likewise, the comprehension of the relation between the
performing self and the object as performed in the act of cognition, raises
man above everything,—which can only be cognitive by experience—and
which does not outlive itself as the source of its own acts performed by itself.

Reason, as the adequate source of intellectual cognition manifests itself as
a "power" different from the senses and imagination; namely, as an automatic source of cognition; this obviously does not mean that the factual

functioning of reason in man was not connected with sense operations and imagination. To slacken the operation of reason and the imagination (keeping in mind the specifically essential and human structure) would be tantamount to striking at man's "beingness."

A denial of the intellect as a source of our universal necessary knowledge, of our judgmental knowledge in which we not only unite and compare concepts among ourselves—something which already demands a knowledge of the relation of universal content grasped in the concepts—but something which is essential for judgments: to execute an affirmation of the identity of things (*resp.* to negate the ontic identity), would be equivalent to a denial of a phenomenon in nature, which is MAN himself. For, on the one hand we would notice the uniqueness of the phenomenon of the "human fact" in nature. On the other hand, we would not accept any commensurable essential reason, i.e., any cause which would allow us to understand the non-contradictable motives (real, efficient reasons) of this very uniqueness. All these indications of uniqueness can be easily reduced to this, namely that in his act of cognition, man is fundamentally somewhat different from animals, that is to say, that man possesses a different power of knowing than animals and this power is precisely the reason, intellect or mind. These are but different names allocated according to its dependence on a concrete function and on its concrete designation, as well as its dependence on a concrete object. They are different names of the same source of knowledge which is characterized, above all, by the fact that it is a power capable of grasping intellectually, being as it is in itself, and not only such contents (meanings) which are helpful (necessary) in adequate relations for a being which achieves knowledge.

(c) If this is clearly the case, then we must accept in man the existence of an apperceptive power, a power which is essentially connected with intellectual cognition and which makes knowledge possible and which acts in a stable and natural manner. This power has been called from the times of the classical Greek philosophers the "agent intellect."[49]

Only Aristotle's and principally, Thomas' theory of the agent intellect and possible intellect (properly, knowing intellect) enables us to avoid the stance of sensualism on the one hand and of idealism (in its various forms) on the other. For, indeed, if we draw our cognitive content from sense impressions, then, there must come into being the necessity of abstraction, which changes these very concrete contents into universal ones, which elucidate the necessary connections. For abstraction to become a reality, there absolutely must exist some kind of intellectual power which will make possible perceiving the intellectual, universal, and necessary contents in given sensible representations.

The philosophical theory (hypothesis) of the agent intellect presupposes a vision of a cognitive context. Man, who lives in a material world constitutes one portion of it because of the fact that he possesses a body. Hence, man's body and the surrounding material world constitute immediate conditioning—a kind of environment of human cognition, and a gradually awakening human thought. For a thought, even though it is immersed in a material world is not, however, completely absorbed by matter. It does not reduce itself to the rest; but, on the contrary, it can penetrate matter. It governs it, dominates, and orders it for its own purposes. Against the background of the relation of thought to matter, there came into existence the problem of the possibility of knowing this matter. For, on the one hand, thought is immaterial in its ontic structure; on the other hand, its object is fundamentally material. It is only due to a knowing of the material world that man can develop intellectually. Furthermore, "to know" means to grasp and make one's own, in an objective manner, those contents that present themselves to us as an object. To know does not mean "to create" objects but to grasp them in agreement with their "ontic" structure. And so, to understand is, in a way, "to grow" (in a particular way because it is objective), of the known thing (content)[50] and, in this aspect, to pass from potency to act. How can we reconcile all these elements of knowledge?

First of all, we must reject the hypothesis of the immediate influence of matter on the intellect as on a knowing power, with respect to fundamental considerations: namely, the impossibility of operations of a non-entity on a being. For matter, in relation to an immaterial intellect has an aspect of non-being to being.[51] A thought can neither be evoked nor annihilated by means of a bayonet or cannon. If matter and material conditions were to act directly on the intellect and on thought, then we would be forced to accept the materiality of both intellect and thought. But this hypothesis has been rejected.

But there is another possibility, namely that thought should act on matter and make it conform to its needs. Such a possibility could be accepted, but not at the moment of the origin of the cognitive act. For thought must spring up: it must be, since prior to the actualization of the cognitive act, thought does not, as yet, exist. If thought were to exist prior to the actualization of the cognitive act, we would be forced to accept some kind of idealism, namely that thought exists before knowing, or that knowing does not consist of a union of object and the "pro-creation" or articulation of thought. If, in the cognitive act, thought itself or the intellect would already be acting on matter, we could not hold the position that to know, in the first phase, means "to receive" content from reality, to become informed of its status. Knowledge would be only a production unrelated to matter. Such a concept would not be in agreement with the established fact of "passiveness" (a "complete dependence" of our intellect on the content of the object of knowledge.

After having rejected two diametrically opposed propositions, we must finally accept the third. By observing the conditions of a material activity, we assert that the body can act within the domain of material spatio-temporal, changing and contingent conditions. And for this reason, too, matter (understood as a spatio-temporal continuum), cannot influence the spirit which, since it is something immaterial, does not also contain extended and contiguous limits. It is not something spatial or changing with time. For this reason, matter cannot influence the intellect as some immaterial source of knowledge. It cannot determine the intellect to know "itself" directly. Of itself, matter cannot be an object influencing the spiritual power. If objects were to determine their individual contents directly through themselves, then the intellect would know them individually, concretely, materially and mutably, just as senses know them in their sensibly cognitive act. For, if intellectual knowledge does not evidence itself to be material in its acts (conceptually-cognitive), then this proves that it is not matter which determines the intellect directly through itself. Rather, the intellect itself, in a certain sense, is active in relation to existing, material objects; it itself uncovers immaterial structures in matter and thereby it itself liberates and somehow "structures" the immaterial in a given material object, so that it can now directly influence the intellect as a knowing power. In other words, the intellect as agent constitutes intellectually cognitive forms: it constitutes them in sensibly-cognitional data. Obviously, there is no kind of "substantial" change of a thing here. For a material thing, concrete and individual, remains the same thing and it is unchanged in itself. Only the sense impression, created by man who is knowing sensibly becomes subjected, as it were, to a "shining" by a naturally active (and hence, agent) intellect which reveals notes that are structural, necessary, and separated from matter (because of this it universalizes). If, in the sensible impression, necessary and essential notes which are invisible to the senses "shine" it is through this same kind of impression as being "de-materialized" that it becomes proportionate to it, so that it could already have an effect on the intellectually-knowing power (called the knowing, possible intellect) and it could determine it to the knowing of this very "shining" sensible impression (image).[52]

Therefore, just as soon as the sensibly-knowing impression has been formulated in and by man—owing to the fact that it was formulated in a human knowing subject—it is immediately "dematerialized," in virtue of the natural activity of the human, spiritual-psychic powers. And hence, individual, changing and temporal elements are freed from the relation which they have with the structurally and formally essential elements, with which they constitute a unity. This same impression (image) is also simultaneously "read" by the senses and, at the same time, dematerialized and prepared for reading by the intellect. This natural dematerialization of impressions; and especially of images—with respect to the fact that they are also naturally subordinated to a further "reading" by the mind (possible intellect)—is performed by a psychical power which is connected with intellectual cognition. This psychical power which dematerializes images we call the "agent intellect."[53] This power, however, does not bring about the act of knowing but makes knowing possible by constituting an object proportionate to intellectual cognition. For the object (as a dematerialized image), is able—as proportioned in its ontic structure—to affect the intellect and to determine it to know "itself." The moment that the possible intellect (actually knowing) unites with the dematerialized image, as already with an intellectually-cognitive form, the act of universal, necessary and essential knowledge takes place.

If the knowing intellect can properly be only passive in relation to its object of knowledge (this means that it cannot generate it for itself but it can only submit itself to it as to something which has already been made and which exists), the result of the receptivity of our understanding and its realism is the necessity of accepting the existence of such a psychical power. This power is directly connected with the intellectual act of conceptual knowledge, which actually constitutes the object of intellectual knowledge. For in themselves, objects of intellectual knowledge as material things or only as representations or sensible images are only potential objects of intellectual knowledge.

Cajetan, a commentator on Aristotle and Thomas Aquinas, in his *Commentary* on the *Summa Theologiae* of St. Thomas (In I, q. 79, a.3, n. 111), argues in the following manner for accepting the theory of an agent intellect: "Everything which is in potency becomes actualized by a being-in-act. In relation to the objects of its knowledge, our intellect finds itself in potentiality because only the object of intellectual knowledge is capable of actualizing it. Hence, since the object of intellectual knowledge in act, does not exist of itself but only material objects exist—which are only potentially objects of intellectual knowledge—therefore, an actual object of intellectual knowledge must be constructed and produced. For this reason, there exists in man, a natural power, constituting actually objects of intellectual knowledge and this power, connected by nature with the knowing process, we call "agent intellect."

The essential function of the agent intellect is the production of intellectually-knowing forms, which can become the proportional object of our intellectual knowledge. Intellectual forms which are so constituted have the power, through themselves, of determining the intellectually-knowing power of the so-called "possible intellect," to know precisely this object which is presented by an intellectually-knowing form that has been freed from material and singular conditions. We call our psychical powers which are con-

I-MAN: AN OUTLINE OF PHILOSOPHICAL ANTHROPOLOGY

IS NOT A STUDENT TEXT BOOK. IT IS A "SOURCE"

BOOK WHICH PHILOSOPHY PROFESSORS USE IN PREPARING

CLASS LECTURES.

FOR STUDENT TEXT, CF. OP. CIT., P. XI.

nected with the process of intellectual knowledge, "agent intellect" and "possible intellect" (as if passive), not as a result of their mutual relation, but from the point of view of their relation to the object itself. For the agent intellect fashions from the sense data (image), an actual and dematerialized object of intellectual knowledge—*facit objectum esse in actu*—and this is precisely why it is called an agent intellect. The possible intellect becomes moved and roused from its knowing passivity by the dematerialized form which, through the very fact of its dematerialization, becomes an actual object of intellectual knowledge. Therefore, the possible, knowing intellect, in relation to its object of knowledge is "passive"; it is in potency to knowledge. The knowing process arises at the moment when the intellectually cognitive form determines the cognitive power of knowing exactly oneself.

The theory of the agent intellect can, on the one hand, make possible the realism of knowledge but, on the other hand, it can preserve man's specificity as a being in his own spiritual and immaterial structure. While this has not been accepted as a postulate, it does present itself as a "human fact," fundamentally different and not reducible to nature.

The theory of the agent and possible intellect arrived on the scene of the history of human thought, namely the history of philosophy,[54] against the background of ambiguous statements by Aristotle on this subject. The Stagirite himself did not know how to develop properly the matter of universal and conceptual knowledge. The arguments which were presented in the *Phaedo* were so convincing that there was no way to rise above them to an everyday order. With Plato, the whole theory of knowledge was a very simple matter. For Plato observed that there exist in the intellectual world, just as in the material world, actual objects of knowledge. These are the Ideas which constitute the object of conceptual, necessary knowledge. Aristotle rejected the possibility of the existence of Ideas "beyond things." This would lead to the absurdity of realizing an infinite series. Consequently, he was forced to formulate a theory of intellectual knowledge. Aristotle accepted two intellects: agent and possible (passive) because there could never be a process of abstraction without an agent intellect. However, he did not accept some kind of "agent sense," since the material objects of sensible knowledge are proportional to the produced, cognitive sensations and even cognitive images. Because he rejected an "agent sense," he was forced to accept the hypothesis of the existence of an agent intellect, whose function would be the furnishing of immediate and adequate conditions of knowing to the possible intellect, as its own intellectually knowing power.

However, his explanations on this point in the *Peri Psyches* were so equivocal and obscure that they became the occasion for the formulation of various theories. For the Stagirite's statements that "the agent intellect is separate or separable, capable of being separated and unmixed," were interpreted in the sense that there existed either some kind of superhuman divinity, called "agent intellect" (while the possible intellect would be, like man, mortal—a materialistic interpretation of Alexander of Aphrodisias), or some kind of divinity which was a common light for all men—the theory of Themistius.

The views of Alexander and Themistius endured in Latin and Arabic philosophical conceptions. With Themistius, there already appeared a combination of Neoplatonic and Aristotelian elements. With the Latin philosophers, there was joined to the Neoplatonic and Peripatetic elements, Augustinian illumination which takes on most varied expressions in the Middle Ages. And, in such a form, (William of Auvergne, Roger Marston and others), there appeared a theory according to which only God is an "agent intellect" and there are no personal agent intellects in individual people. The moderate theories (Roger Bacon, Henry of Ghent) expressed the position that in reality there exist agent and passive intellects in individual people but they suffice for knowledge of a lower type. The higher knowledge takes place only through God's intervention as *"intellectus agens"* in the full sense of the word. In the mildest form (Gundissalinus of Spain), there was recognized the existence of an uncreated agent intellect, like God, which exists under the name, *"illuminator communis"* or *"lux divina radians."* Furthermore, both intellects, agent and possible, were supposed to be powers of individual people.

Thomas Aquinas knew all these various theories when he was forced to take a position in the face of Aristotelianism pressing on one side and Augustinianism on the other. Both extreme positions agreed on the ontic unity of the human person and they recognized man's inability to know the truth by means of his own natural powers. Thomas, however, who accepted Themistius' statement that "both intellects are something with the soul," held the position that they are powers of the human soul itself. The statement that the agent intellect is "unmixed," he accepted to mean that there existed a spiritual faculty which possessed no bodily organ. Obviously, this did not exclude God's causality as the first agent, first truth and first intellectual light. In this way, he showed a realistic and, at the same time, a moderate explanation.

IV. THE PROCESS OF INTELLECTUAL, CONCEPTUAL KNOWLEDGE

In accordance with the theory of St. Thomas, who is a classical example of one who analyzes in detail the non-contradictable agents of the whole process, the process itself goes through the following three stages:[55]

1. Sensible knowledge is the foundation of every content of man's knowledge, which is testified to by the character of our knowledge, as well as of our thought.[56] This is completely in agreement with man's structure as a psycho-somatic being, as well as with the investigations of experimental psychology. These testify to the complete dependence of our concepts on appropriate sources of sense knowledge (the possession of proper concepts is conditioned by the possession of an adequate sense which furnishes the basic content of knowledge). Finally, this position affirms negatively the possible absurd consequences following from a denial of the role of senses, as the singular foundation of our conceptual knowledge.

2. Sensible knowledge, especially images, is subject to the activity of the agent intellect. Since it is to become proportioned to intellectual knowledge. therefore, the agent intellect actualizes the object of intellectual knowledge in the given images.[57] "To actualize" means the same as "to immaterialize an image" and dematerialization (according to an ancient Greek concept of matter as an element of being), means the same as "dissolution" of the relation of individual notes of a given image from its ontic content, which expresses itself (from the side of the content, essence) in an ensemble of constitutive notes.[58]

3. The image which has been dematerialized by the agent intellect becomes the actual object of knowledge for the possible intellect. Hence, it acts on the knowing intellect by impressing on it, its form or the dematerialized, cognitive picture of the material thing. For the image is a representation of the thing which is to be known intellectually and through the dematerialized content, it determines the intellect to know that which, in its image, is expressed as a representation of the thing. Prior to the "activity" of the agent intellect, the image is singular and material; for this reason it cannot determine the intellect to a knowing of the content (meaning) represented by itself. It can "affect" at once, when it has been "shined" and hence, proportioned to intellectual knowledge, since it has been dematerialized and dissolved from its materially-individualizing relation.

We can still distinguish in this "dematerialized" image, a two-fold aspect of immateriality: (a) its own ontic side of dematerialization as the result of the agent intellect's activity, and (b) the intentional immateriality for the reason that the image itself is already an intentional representation and the "form"of the thing.[59] "State A" by reason of its ontological status permits the dematerialized image to act on the possible intellect, whereas "State B" remains transmitted to the intellect, due to which, the latter is aroused from cognitive indifference. The transmission of "State B" to the intellect ("State A" does not need to be transmitted to the intellect, since it is immaterial), that is to say, of a knowable form, does not take place in some sort of mechanical way, as if "that very form itself," which was in the image, "wandered on" to the intellect. Rather, it merely evokes in the intellect, a process of intellectual knowledge or, at least, the state which becomes the birth of this intellectual knowledge.[60]

4. Hence, this is an evoking of an intellectually-knowing form, in the intellect. For if the intellect is in potency in relation to its object and it cannot, by itself, pass from potential knowledge to actual knowledge, there exists a proportional agent which determines it to knowledge and which releases in it, the process of this knowledge. For the intellect possesses within itself, this agent that is traditionally called "form"[61] and which is the inbred reason—precisely a knowing one—of the intellect's activity.[62] For knowing is an inbred act, an act of the knower and not of some kind of known thing.[63] In view of this, the known thing does not itself act but rather the intellectually-knowing subject who must determine himself to the knowledge of the non-subjective content, though precisely, of the known thing. Hence, the known object is in the subject but only intentionally as contents, but the reality of the intentionality is constituted by the subject itself.[64]

Hence the content of the object which exists in thought, exists according to the way the subject and man exist. It is, however, an objective content, i.e., of the known object. It is called an intellectually-knowing form which determines the intellect to the process of knowing this content, which is expressed in the form. Obviously, this form as the inborn reason of an inbred knowing process—if the knowing process has arisen, it has its own inbred "beginning," which is called a knowing form and it has an inbred terminus, called "conception"—this form neither is nor can be something conscious.[65] For the form is a determining and directing agent of intellectual knowledge; it is that power *a tergo,* which—since it is a non-contradictable agent of an inbred process—cannot become something conscious. Only the end of the process becomes conscious—the known contents and not the non-contradictable agent of the origin of these contents. Physiological agents within us, which actualize knowledge are similarly unconscious but they likewise do not contradict the fact of sensible perception. The concept is (becomes) immediately conscious and we can make it the object of our reflective knowledge.

5. The causative conditioning of an intellectually-knowing form. The question here is: What can be recognized as the causative reason of this very form which conditions the origin of our thought? At the basis of the schematic considerations which we have presented here and, before all, referring to the theory of St. Thomas, who undeniably of all the philosophers, devoted the greatest amount of space to this very discussion, we can accept the position that it is precisely our image, insofar as it is dematerialized, while act-

ing—just as the object of cognition is proportioned to its own power—is, indeed, the causative agent which releases a knowing form in the intellect. Before its dematerialization, the image is not the actual object of intellectual knowledge because it is not, as yet, proportioned to it.[66]

In such a situation, St. Thomas advances the hypothesis that the image which is being dematerialized can be known in itself, as an instrumental agent (strictly causally-instrumental): "Images act as an instrumental and secondary agent but the agent intellect is as a fundamental and primary agent . . . images are like an instrumental agent."[67] In the process of instrumental activity, the result resembles the prinicipal agent rather than the instrument.[68] If the dematerialized image is the causative agent of the existence of the process of knowledge (since it is a synthesis of the activity of the agent intellect and the imaginable content), this very image—insofar as it is not "shined" by the activity of the agent intellect—can be recognized as a potential agent of our knowledge. But the "light" of the agent intellect (is) the principal,[69] actualizing agent, obviously, only insofar as we can generally speak of a principal agent and an instrument, since man is the chief agent and all his powers of activity are more or less connected instruments.

We are using here a simplified and schematic language, only to call attention to the fact that there are, among powers, as instruments of human psychic activity, agents which lead, determine and form. These powers are, as if, more active than the others which perform a rather passive, material and determinate role.[70] At the basis of things, however, it is man and his human nature which act in a complicated ensemble, not immediately accessible to our knowledge. The speculations which Thomas made here have, as their purpose, to explain and to make more imaginatively understandable those agents whose activity is solely the non-contradictable moment of our intellectual knowing. It does not seem, however, that speculations which pertain to knowledge and its phases were completely useless and nonsensical because they indicate certain limiting and rather negative points that direct our knowledge. Keeping in mind such a hypothetical and only negatively-explanatory role of Thomistic speculations on the subject of the process of conceptually-intellectual knowledge, we can make a further analysis of Thomas' thought.

And so, according to his conception of the intellectually-cognitive form, we can look upon it as the "thing" itself, grasped in its concrete entity and also as a picture or representation of a thing.[71] In the first case, it is a concrete and accidental manner of the existence of our "I." In the second case, as an *imago*—a picture and representation of a thing—it does not differ from the thing itself. And for this reason, we grasp the thing and its picture in a simple knowing-act, that is to say, in the picture, we see the represented thing itself.[72] The intelligible form is singular in existence and universal in representation. Being singular, it is also something immaterial, as already the property of an immaterial intellect (for it originated in an immaterial intellect).[73] But at the same time, it is universal in its representation and precisely because it represents a thing, it is the reason for the cognizability of a thing.

By representing the known thing in a universal way, the form, in its own way of existence, as a property of the intellect, is something more perfect than the thing itself. From the point of view of the representation, however, the form is not something more perfect than the thing, since it presents only certain, selectively-grasped notes of the thing. Therefore every universal cognition (representation!) is, of its own nature, something imperfect because it does not grasp things in their wealth of notes but only in a very selective manner of making things present. We must emphasize, once again, that the traditionally called "immateriality" of intellectual, cognitive forms comes from the subject of their non-independent existence, i.e., from the intellect and not from the manner of their representations. The manner of presentation may be called "immaterial" only in the Aristotelian meaning of "immateriality," namely in regard to the content in its non-potentiality. In such an instance, however, we are dealing with a fundamentally equivocal expression of immateriality, since in one case it pertains to the manner of being in an existential sense, and in the other in a formal (Aristotelian) sense.[74]

6. The intellect which has been fecundated with an intellectually-knowing form achieves, in proper sense, a knowledge of things which culminated in the production of a concept. We usually say that the intellect knows the essence of the thing: *intellectus apprehendit quidditatem rei*. What does this mean exactly? In agreement with tradition, this expression should be understood in the sense that we grasp a thing's attributes cognitively, usually in a very sketchy way. Hence, these are selective, sketchy cognitions about incompletely specified contents and, as a result, we have a rather negative knowledge, i.e., one which basically differentiates being from non-being or a content from negation.

On the strength of its own natural inclination, our intellect is constantly abstracting from the object which is presented in sense knowledge: that which can become the object of thought, that which can be apprehended. Everything that exists can be apprehended—everything, insofar as its constituent agents do not mutually exclude themselves and do not verify a contradiction. For everything that exists, or can really exist, can be grasped intellectually, thanks to an internal structure which excludes contradiction. This internal structure that excludes contradiction and determines the possibility of the existence of a subject and the possibility of thinking by means of our intellect can be called, in a most general way, "essence." Obviously, a real possibility demands not only a structure which excludes contradiction but also a real existence, in which this "non-contradiction" could be noted in the subject. As a result, we know in a most general way, from the point of view of non-contradiction and, by the same token, of being, if we agree that non-contradiction is a manifestation of being itself.

The human intellect, which is directed to the knowing of the essence of a thing that is represented in an image, recognizes this essence under the aspect of being (the process of spontaneous abstraction) as *quid intelligibile*. This kind of very incomplete knowledge—usually ordered to the practical goals of human life—can be analyzed more deeply in further processes. However, all the disclosed elements or moments will be a fuller expression of this very essence which was first expressed as *quid intelligibile*.[75] This process of intellectual knowledge which we have just outlined and which is based on Thomas Aquinas' considerations and proposals accepts completely man's sense knowledge. At the same time, it distinguishes, in an indubitable manner, intellectual knowledge which is genetically connected with sensible knowledge. Finally, it not only shows the factuality of conceptual knowledge but it ultimately translates it by constructing a hypothesis of the process of the act of intellectual knowledge itself. Obviously, this matter concerns conceptual knowledge which terminates in the production of a concept.[76] For further acts of judgmental knowledge—in predicative judgments—are the object of conscious work and reflection, which brings to the surface everything that takes place "in consciousness," in a way that is occasionally mechanical and sometimes concealed.

V. FUNDAMENTAL AREAS OF INTELLECTUAL LIFE

Everything which bears a human stamp is, in some way, derived from intellectual cognition. There are many derivative areas: science, technology, art, morality, social services and the like; in sum, culture and civilization, understood in the widest sense, are essentially bound with the life of the human intellect.

There is need for some kind of even preliminary arrangement of all spheres of intellectual activity. As in many other matters, so here too, there came from Aristotle some very interesting—and recognized today as classical—propositions of arrangement and connection of these various fields of human activity. For the Stagirite distinguished three activities of human life: THEORIA, PRAXIS, POESIS, usually translated as respectively contemplation, behavior and productive activity.[77]

Although there is doubt while reading carefully the Stagirite's text—whether the classification he proposed was conducted according to the same basis of division, whether it was complete and separate, which means: whether every human act should be one of contemplation, of behavior or productive activity, (Aristotle himself testified to the verifiability of one area to another)—nevertheless, Aristotle's suggestion has endured throughout the course of the history of philosophy. And it has acquired, on the part of its commentators (for instance St. Thomas Aquinas) many new and valuable insights. Today also, it does not seem useless to emphasize its analogical character, so that we can bring into relief moments which were fittingly perceived by Aristotle and Thomas.[78] We must focus our attention here only on the specificity of the three designated areas of knowledge. For surely it is clearly known that in the normal course of events, it never—or very rarely—occurs in a "clear" or "distilled" state. In the accompanying analysis, we shall direct our attention, for the sake of clarity, to these areas in their "ideal" state, because it will enable us to understand better those forms of human activity in which various types of man's activity are intermingled and established.

With Aristotle and Thomas, we meet the basis for the proposed demarcation, with respect to the goal of knowledge. For if human knowledge was ordered exclusively to truth, it was called theoretical knowledge (contemplation); if it was related to activity, practical knowledge; if to an external production in matter, productive science. But along with the basis for demarcation with respect to goal or purpose, we likewise have—especially in the case of St. Thomas— a basis with respect to the kind of object of a particular area. Obviously, the formal character of the object was connected with the purpose, but the very structure of the object was emphasized, which was called *speculabile, agibile* and *factibile.*

The first, *speculabile,* is the object of a purely theoretical knowledge of man who, by means of the cognitive act, strives to inform himself about the factual state of a thing. It is for this reason that such a kind of knowledge is beginning to be called today "informational knowledge," with truth as the principal criterion of this knowledge.[79] For truth is both the purpose of this knowledge and also its ultimate criterion of value. The second kind of knowledge,[80] *agibile* concerns itself with the entire moral conduct of man; this knowledge actualizes itself in acts of conscience which direct moral decision. The third group, however, *factibile* directs creative, aesthetic and productive knowledge. This is a specific knowledge, as we shall see later, which is connected with the entire area of man's culture (creativity understood in the widest sense).

We must now look more closely at these separate areas of human intellectual life, so that we may be able to understand the basic disposition of man. As we have already observed, these areas appear rarely if ever in their "pure" or "distilled" state. For, in every type of knowledge, we are dealing with moments borrowed from another area. But we must emphasize the characteristic elements to enable us more easily to make clear-cut distinctions.

The first type of knowledge—informational, theoretical—stands at the basis of other areas of knowledge. When informational knowledge, however, appears in the guise of theoretically-scientific knowledge, it pre-supposes its pre-scientific state, which likewise belongs, fundamentally, to the area of informational knowledge. The prescientific type of knowledge which is called everyday or common sense knowledge is the foundation and starting point for everyday science. For these can be developed only through a precision and a direction toward a determinate goal and a grounding of everyday knowledge. And this is why it is customary to consider a spontaneity, lack of proper foundation and organization as characteristic traits of everyday knowledge. Scientific knowledge would be characterized by its own methodology, organization, and proportional justification which is intersubjectively verifiable.

In prescientific knowledge, man is rather passive, and reality which surrounds him in the form of nature and men, acts upon him in an active way, thereby causing a development of knowledge itself. On this level, the intellect develops automatically, without any direction pre-established beforehand, without any method of organization and of overcoming any obstacles to knowledge. Prescientific knowledge is very rich and varied and perhaps there is no area of human life—for fundamentally, human life itself is based on prescientific data of human knowledge—which would not find its expression in prescientific knowledge. And even if it is not an organized and proportionally gounded knowledge, nevertheless it is not an unrestricted and completely uncritical knowledge. And precisely because it is a fundamentally passive knowledge, it is ontically grounded in this sense, that some kind of reality corresponds to the particular existence of these cognitive contents. It is not a knowledge proportionally based on proclaimed convictions or assertions because, above all, on this level of knowledge, there are, as yet, no organized positions. There is no methodically intentional directivity. There is also a lack of logical tools, with whose help experienced convictions can be justified. Nonetheless, it is prescientific, everyday (commonsense) knowledge that the organization of human life bases itself, as well as everything that can be said about a commonsense type of knowledge, about its role and its extent—everything which pertains to prescientific knowledge.[81] Obviously, the extent of prescientific knowledge broadens over the centuries, since many achievements of purely scientific knowledge through-out a practical life in a community, penetrate to a prescientific knowledge. Hence, we can observe today in the treasury of prescientific knowledge and of common usage, certain contents which only yesterday were available ex-clusively to people of high specialization, e.g., of a practical competence in using radio, television and refrigeration.

For theoretically-scientific knowledge (since it is likewise informational knowledge), as well as a prescientific knowledge, possesses these charac-teristic elements which are lacking in prescientific knowledge. Hence it is a methodical, reflected and directed knowledge and, by the same token, a knowledge which is organized according to some model and proportionally grounded according to accepted theses. But this does not mean that all these traits should appear to a highest degree in every kind of scientific knowl-edge. Just as every area of human culture is constantly improving, so, too, is knowledge. And sciences are likewise developing, not only through the creation of new branches of knowledge, but also through a homogeneous and intense development of knowledge and a continuing elaboration of more efficient investigatory methods, as well as increasingly improved systemati-zation and precise refinement of foundations.[82]

Scientific knowledge passes through two phases. The first consists in gathering information within the extension of a given science, above all, in school or under the directorship of a master. This is already scientific knowl-edge because it is organized, methodical, grounded, and oriented toward a determinate end. But one who acquires this information does not as yet make any new intellectual discoveries. He is only somewhat "led" intellec-tually, and he only becomes better acquainted with the contemporary state of knowledge. This first stage of knowledge embraces a wide range of "learning"—from elementary school to further advanced, higher, and spec-ialized studies. The moment, however, when man makes personal dis-coveries in his studies, he arrives at a phase of scientific knowledge, explanatory scientific knowledge in a most strict sense. It enriches man-kind's universal understanding of the world. It furnishes new and hitherto unknown information about the investigation of the world.[83]

In the tradition of classical philosophy, however, what are the characteris-tic notes of scientific, theoretical knowledge? Generally, this type of knowl-edge is defined as *recta ratio speculabilium* or the correct use of reason in the sphere of *speculabile*. Hence it is the work of reason (of a discursively knowing power), insofar as it is properly directed by the very constitution of things, the constitution of ontic elements which are the basis for estab-lishing "the law of learning"—in a word, *speculabile*. However, what are the notes of this *speculabile,* the object of theoretical knowledge? This first and most characteristic note (trait)—even more, the constitutive moment of *speculabile* from the times of Plato, was considered to be *necessity,* with the result that theoretical human knowledge presented itself as necessary knowledge. Obviously, "necessitariness" of knowledge was variously understood: from the maximalistic concept of necessity in Platonic-Aristotelian science to the necessity of a probabilistic type, which is connected with contemporary concepts of science and Hume's induction, along with a logic of probability, which is linked to it.

If we were to ask about the objective foundation for this necessity, it would be proper to refer to two fundamental solutions known in the history of philosophy: Platonic-Aristotelian and Kantian. According to Plato and Aristotle, as well as all those who stand on the ground of cognitive realism, the source of the necessity and that which explains the cognitive necessity, is the ontic arrangement of things. Plato indeed pointed to the Ideas as being "behind" a thing as necessity itself. Aristotle, however, made the well known correction by "incarnating" the idea in a material thing, which through the incarnated "idea-form" is what it is. The form which organizes matter and constitutes the ontical contents of a thing is the ultimate element that establishes existence and knowability, which are not optional but, rather, necessary and articulated, in real, essential definitions. Such formulated definitions then become premises in a syllogism.[84]

Kant has a different explanation for the necessary character of knowledge. He observes that necessity flows not from things but from the structure of the knowing mind, which is then an a priori category of the mind. Hence various scientific knowledge is a knowledge which possesses, in itself, a degree of necessity. For the a priori (logical) category of necessity is a projection of our ego. "All necessity, without exception, is grounded in a transcendental condition. There must, therefore, be a transcendental ground of the unity of consciousness in the synthesis of the manifold of all our intentions, and consequently also of the concepts of objects in general, and so of all objects of experience, a ground without which it would be impossible to think any object for our intuitions; for this object is no more than that something, the concept of which expresses such a necessity of synthesis."[85]

As we have already mentioned, together with the basis for probable necessity in empirical sciences, are inventive notions connected with the name of Hume. In general, the basis for probable necessity is a widely understood measure of a thing, and not its internal structure. However, there always exists some type of necessity in theoretical scientific knowledge.

A necessary knowledge, however, can take place within the limits of general concepts: whether universal or analogico-transcendental. If the knowledge of things, the detection of their laws and the establishment of structures takes place through univocally-universal (general) concepts then indeed we are dealing with particular sciences. For these sciences (or all non-philosophical sciences) strive to become informed explicitly and precisely about some segment of reality by applying their own methodology of knowledge. And particular sciences are specified according to their dependence on the way concepts are formed, and from the separated object of knowledge. Their number is constantly growing, and it will surely continue to do so, since it is possible to investigate the same segment of reality with the help of variously formulated and defined concepts. But we can also find—and we are constantly finding—new areas of reality for investigation.

If, on the other hand, knowledge of reality, the establishment of its fundamental and ontic "laws,," is achieved with the help of transcendental concepts, then the ensemble of acquired positions already belongs to the area of philosophy.[86] For only analogically-transcendental concepts disclose, in the application of a suitable method of philosophizing, the non-contradictable, ontic agents of the fact of existence of analogically universal being, as well as of particular forms of being, which are of interest to philosophy.

Along with the attribute of necessity, it has been traditionally customary to distinguish also the attribute of the immutability of knowledge, as well as its universality. Immutability of scientific knowledge is very closely connected with the characteristic of necessity. It is a certain emphasis of necessity in relation to the fact of perpetual motion in nature. Immutability, which has its foundation in things but which is formally attained through schematization and the cognitive grasping of the necessary structures, places an emphasis on permanence and likewise, through it, on the value of science itself. However, the universality of scientific knowledge, that is to say, its value for more than one exemplar, was linked, in the history of philosophy, with the characteristic idealism of Plato and all those who were of the opinion that the fundamental condition of a thing is its universal idea or some kind of "third nature." Such a position, however, is faulty and it cannot be substantiated in a verifiable way. It seems that the basis for the universality of affirmations (concepts) is, fundamentally, not the thing itself but the human intellect which—inasmuch as it is immaterial—accomplishes the schematization and, through abstraction from material, singular notes presents to us the universal science when it is "anchored" in things.[87]

In theoretically-informational knowledge, Aristotle had already distinguished three fundamental phases of development:

1. NOUS, or the introductory phase, relies on the perception of the first principles in being. Simply stated, in order to reason and to accomplish various knowing operations, there must be their beginning, which consists in reading (*intus-legere,* hence, "intellect") of the fundamental, intelligible

contents. The first intelligible results flowing from a contact with reality, and which are the foundation for a further intellective process, are precisely the so-called "intellection (understanding) of the first principles." The question is whether someone is intelligent in a theoretically-cognitive sense and whether he "sees" matters which do not need proof, as e.g., that what is—is and that being is not non-being. In every area of knowledge, there in an initial state of intellection.

2. The second phase of theoretically-informational knowledge is called in Aristotle EPISTEME, or "science." However, in fact, it is "reasoning" in the widest sense of the word. For in different branches of scientific knowledge, there exist methodically-cognitive, organized and well-founded steps, which are precisely a kind of reasoning. This type of reasoning is somewhat adjusted to every science, but it is always found in every type of theoretical knowledge. A general and specialized methodology of sciences discusses the subject of the kinds of reasoning, its value, its extent, etc.[88]

3. Finally, the concluding phase which crowns man's intellectual-theoretical knowledge is, according to Aristotle, SOPHIA, wisdom, which can be recognized today as philosophy. This phase is the final judgment, equally of the fact of knowledge as well as of the most universal, analogical object of human knowledge, which is being. (Obviously, I am omitting here the question of its type.)[89]

The three phases of informational human knowledge present a certain totality. If we should understand theoretical knowledge as a certain psychical process, then it possesses its own starting point (intellection of first principles), its various phases and determinations—in other words, reasoning. Finally, it can lead to its own judgment of the entire intellective process, to its own wisdom which, as knowledge, is likewise subject to a methodological rigor. But from the side of its extent and limits, it is a knowledge of an ultimate kind, which does not appeal to any further, ultimate sciences.

The specific and thorough character of the particular phases of human informational knowledge investigates the theory of scientific knowledge and the methodology of various areas of science, understood in the widest sense—including also a philosophic knowledge of an elucidating kind, such as was formed in the history of classical philosophy.[90]

The second broad area of human knowledge, which stands at the basis of human conduct and hence, also, the morality of man, is so-called practical or prudential knowledge. In the history of philosophy, it was Heraclitus of Ephesus who called attention to this type of knowledge, when he observed that radically changing reality can be understood only by a concentrated awareness of that which, in the changing data, is one and common—logos.[91] Practical, prudential knowledge does not appertain to reality as it presents itself in permanent, necessary structural aspects, rather, it appertains to me—myself—as one performing actions. For if I am to accomplish something as a person—and hence, consciously and freely—I must first knowingly determine myself to action: to emanate, within me, an action and to constitute a causative reason for the act which I have begotten. For human action is not determined, ultimately, through nature but through knowledge, precisely through intellectual knowledge that appears in the form of a practical judgment: "Do this now, in such and such a way." The issuing of such a judgment presupposes a concrete knowledge of a changing situation, a knowledge and acceptance of some kind of rules of conduct and of locating oneself as having to act concretely under all these concrete conditions.[92] Hence, we are dealing here with a specific area of intellectual life, a directly related and ordered conduct.

Just as in the area of theoretically-informational knowledge, we can differentiate here three most general stages of this area of knowledge. The first and fundamental phase is knowledge (awareness) of the principal rules of conduct. These rules derive from an expressed recognition in us, of a natural, rational law of acting, that can be expressed in the form of a judgment, "Good should be done."[93] This is an affirmation, in practical language, in language of the area of prudence. This foremost law of conduct of man's rational nature (a natural law) sets forth the whole order of morality, leaving to the concrete recognition of human reason, what is good and under what conditions something is good, and how this good is to be attained or realized.[94]

A second differentiating aspect of practical knowledge is the act of conscience (of practical reason), improved through prudence and forming a decision about acting, or not acting. The mechanism of making a decision is complicated. However, in every act of decision there occurs a concretely-knowing moment that appears in the form of a practical judgment (practically-practical), with the aid of which we determine ourselves (autodetermination) to this or that action. Whether the practical judgment which determines us to proper action is the last factually-determining judgment, we ourselves decide by freely choosing the judgment which need not be the best nor the most rational. The union of the moment of choice of the practical judgment (the moment of the will's freedom) and the contents of a judgment, which decides (determines) the character and factuality of our action, constitutes the essential aspects of a decision. This decision is always a moral one because it is not possible to disengage it from a relation to a norm of human conduct. This norm is the good which is recognized by man.[95] It is for this reason that moral order fundamentally occurs in personal (*resp.* interpersonal) circles and hence, of a good that is essentially connected with the person. This personal good which is seen and recognized by a man undertaking a decision, takes on the form of duty which should be performed in the right way, that is, the execution or non-execution of an act which realizes a knowingly (prudentially) affirmed good. Obviously, the realization of a seen good, as well as its "seeing," demands an improvement in this order: the ancient and mediaeval thinkers called it prudence. It is for this reason that prudential activity exerts a particular impress on man's conduct and, from the prudential character of undertaking a decision, the entire practical order of conduct was called "the domain of prudence."

Finally, the third stage which is the zenith of the area of practical knowledge would be the practical wisdom of experienced people. A longer period of time is presupposed here, which would enable man to attain this experiential wisdom, so characteristic of older people and which is so highly prized by mankind. A worldly wisdom, originated from experience has fulfilled and can further fulfill the role of moral philosophy, of the philosophy of human conduct. In this type of wisdom, there arise theoretical judgments which, however, did not arise as a result of argumentation and cognitive analysis, directed by methodological rules, but rather as a testimony flowing from a varied realization of a good in rich, personal contexts.[96]

The third area of the human spirit designates a so-called poietic knowledge which is sometimes also called a creative or productive or constructive knowledge. In each instance, the area of knowledge is different from the two previously mentioned types of knowledge: informational and practical. Fundamentally, the difference resolves itself into differences of structure and purpose of intellectually-knowing operations. For if the purpose of informational knowledge is the disclosure of the structure of reality and agreement with the thing and thus, the goals connected with the truthful functioning of our intellect, the purpose of practically-prudential knowledge is the realization of the good which man has acknowledged. Hence, in agreement with almost all philosophical directions, the goal of creative knowledge is neither information about reality nor a realization of the good in the strict sense. In the same manner, both the Greek as well as the contemporary tradition of philosophy has accepted, as the goal and basic criterion of such a knowledge, beauty itself in its widest meaning, understood in a transcendental sense.[97]

When, however, the question concerns the character of creatively productive knowledge, it expresses itself above all in the construction of new, intentional objects from the elements given us in informational knowledge. For, if we are given to know, in informational knowledge, what man is, what a lion is and what a bird is, then, we can, as it were, "break apart" the achieved unities of informational knowledge into different elements to construct a new object, for example, a sphinx or some other production which was fashioned as a result of creative knowledge.

Creative knowledge stands at the basis of all kinds of cultural creativeness and it constructs—by the application of its own criterion which unites a given construct—all kinds of objects that belong to the area of man's culture. The intellect here remains active, by accomplishing the same construct whose individual elements were previously given us in a normal, informational knowledge, whether prescientific or scientific. Our constructive knowledge is a real knowledge only because of the informational knowledge that causes us to adjust with reality, since all the elements of the construct are real. However, the construct itself and its uniting criterion (most generally called beauty, in which ugliness is also included) derive from a subject which accomplishes this kind of knowledge.[98]

Just as we encountered a characteristic threefold phase in the preceding areas of informational and practical knowledge, we can also perceive, without difficulty, the same threefold phase in the area of creative construction. Usually productive knowledge is distinguished into (1) its purely creative and artistic phase (2) its productive phase (when we transmit creative ideas to a production in external, non-psychical matter), and (3) its phase of aesthetic perception.

The first stage, which recalls the first phases of the previous two types of knowledge, resolves itself into a so-called "artistic vision." Classical philosophers had little to say on the subject of this vision. The psychologists were more concerned with the process of cognitive creativity. In ancient Greece, artistic knowledge was scarcely emphasized in the expression *architechne*. It was assumed that this type of knowledge exists, but there was no further analysis of it. It was considered, in general, that artistic ability is a special gift from the gods, as Plato testifies in *Ion* and *Phaedrus*. "For all good poets who compose good poems do so not through art but by power divine. God enters into them and being inspired, they speak these beautiful poems and the music writers do likewise . . . And one can do nothing until God enters into him, until he has lost his senses and his reason. . . . These beautiful poems are not human, or the work of man, but divine and the work of God; and that the poets are only the interpreters of the gods by whom they are severally possessed."[99] . . . "He who having no touch of the Muses' madness in soul, comes to the door and thinks that he will get into the temple by the help of art—he, I say and his poetry are not admitted."[100]

Hence, it was considered that artistic creativity is a special gift which cannot be learned, and that the artist, in his creative madness, sees differently from other people. Not everyone is gifted with an artistic vision; there are special chosen ones of the gods.

If, however, the artistic vision was something exceptional, then TECHNE or the performance of some kind of artistic picture is something that demands study and training. In this respect, it was proper for the mind to be trained and educated and for this reason, it was mandatory that art, understood as execution, should be *recta ratio factibilium*: reason directed by the content (of law or structure) of that which should be made. *"Factibile,"* however, is not only something material and hence clay, stone, wood, paper or cloth but it is —additionally and above all—an idea, thought, plan or cognitive construct that exists in the mind and which should be incorporated into particular matter. This idea may be "incarnated" in matter either correctly or incorrectly. Hence, one must learn art, the technique of realizing in non-psychical matter, one's own or another's artistic idea that originated in the mind. The technique of "incarnating" thought in matter fascinated both Antiquity and the Middle Ages, and for this reason, the entire cycle of the area of artistic (aesthetic) knowledge was named from its creative, productive, technical knowledge; *ars.*[101]

As a result of R. Ingarden's outstanding studies in this area, we can also emphasize a third phase of knowledge which is connected with the perception of works of art—with aesthetic knowledge and the fashioning of an aesthetic picture within oneself, i.e., of the recipient. Hence we must obviously distinguish at once between two types of knowledge of works of ART: one, a theoretically-critical knowledge that belongs to the normal area of informational knowledge and the other, which has for its aim, the pleasure that follows from the knowledge of artistic works—and this is precisely aesthetic knowledge. There were already certain references to this theme in Greek Antiquity which suggested the "individuality" of this type of knowledge. Plato writes in the *Philebus* (51A): "Protarchus: Then what pleasure, Socrates, should we be right in conceiving to be true?" Socrates: "True pleasures are those which are given by beauty of color and form, and most of those which arise from smells; those of sound, again, and in general those of which the want is painless and unconscious, and of which the fruition is palpable to sense and pleasant and unalloyed with pain." And the familiar text from Plato's *Symposium* (210E–211D) about the perception of beauty in itself and which aroused raptures—" . . . only on this level is life worth something—if it is worth anything in general—when man beholds beauty in itself."—was always the inspiration for thinkers who wondered about the problem of knowing beauty.

In the aesthetic perception of beauty and in the construction of an aesthetic picture, we can distinguish, most generally, three phases (in closer analysis, it shows itself to be more complex). R. Ingarden both analyzed and called attention to this fact: (a) initial emotion, which directs our knowledge to a given object in such a way that it "excludes," for the time being, the knowledge of other objects (b) a collection of cognitive acts that concern the artistic object in which we must grasp a certain foundation and an ensemble of coordinated elements (c) finally the phase—which the previous ones make possible—of a personal pleasure that flows from a contemplative type of knowledge of an object which is given us for an aesthetic "look." The coordination of emotion and of acts of contemplative knowledge decides about the proper character of aesthetic knowledge and performs, in man's life, a function that purifies and integrates the human spirit.

CHAPTER VI

INTENTIONALITY OF KNOWLEDGE
AND CULTURE

In considering those things which relate to knowledge, its central role in human life and its connection with fundamental areas of human activity, we must give at least cursory attention to everything that is called "culture," since its connection with the act of knowledge and of cognitive creations is beyond dispute. At the same time, it is proper to outline more closely the relation between culture and the cognitive contents.[1]

In spite of numerous publications on the theme of culture, its essential character—its connection with nature and man—an open problematic always exists in the very matter of understanding culture, as well as its essential expression. This is, after all, understandable because in the dependence on philosophical currents, in the dependence on a different aspect of analyses, even within one particular system, there appears a somewhat different aspect of the same issue.

In our proposed considerations, we shall emphasize those moments of the general understanding of the problem which emphasize the connection of culture with man. Specifically, these will be: the general meaning of the expression "culture;" an understanding of intentionality and the intentional aspect of cultural works. Obviously, the question is very extensive. Hence we must deliberately consider the essential moments, so that we will not become entangled in discussions and disputes on themes which are not considered here because this would demand monographic studies and not a working sketch.

I. GENERAL MEANING OF THE TERM "CULTURE"

Overlooking a purely verbal explanation (*cultura* from [the Latin] *colere* "to cultivate;" precisely, "till the soil"), we use this term to denote everything which comes from man as human activity or production.[2] And if human activity or production, along with the product, is always achieved in existing material—in natural creation (nature, in the widest sense of the word)—then we can understand by culture, the kind of transformation of nature which is capable of expressing, in it, beauty. This beauty is characteristically human; and, hence, it is a trait of rationality: for reason makes man to be what he is.

We could agree that culture is the rationalization (intellectualization) of nature[3] if by "rationalization" or "intellectualization" we will understand the engrafting in natural material, not only of the human concept-idea in the narrow sense but also various activities of the intellect. We shall also understand their various possible applications to materials—NATURE—indifferently, whether this transformed material will be man himself—in all his various dimensions which are subject to a rational improvement—or whether nature which surrounds him is subject to human activity.

For various creations of nature:—both nature in its most varied forms, as well as man himself, since he is also (not exclusively!) a creature of nature and all his natural activities—to the extent that they are subject to human rational activity in the widest sense—are a kind of manifestation of culture.

When understood in such a wide sense, culture would include everything which exists in nature as natural and which is or was subject for transformation under the direction of the intellect. Hence, manifestations of the human spirit, insofar as they are guided by the intellect, human work and activity caused by the human intellect and creations of material nature which have been changed by the human intellect, constitute, in the widest sense, the domain of culture. Understood in such a way—as precisely the rationalization or intellectualization of nature in its range of possibility—culture embraces in its scope everything that is called culture in its narrow sense, and civilization in its historical sense.

If we keep in mind such a broad but, at the same time, appropriate understanding of the expression "culture," nothing prevents our recognizing a narrower meaning which underscores its important moments or also commonly appropriate ways of using this culture.

And in reality, we are witnesses to the fact that the general understanding of culture has been very fragmented, especially with regard to the different moments that are located in its general analogical understanding. However, it seems that today, the more the various meanings of the expression "culture" that are restricted, singled out and differentiated, the more we must keep in mind its principal analogically common (single) understanding. We must do this, since it allows for a comprehensive view of culture, of an analysis of its essential character and, because of it, a more fundamental evaluation of the role of culture in particular areas of life, as well as its role in what is called "the meaning of human life in general."

By indicating only superficially certain areas and manifestations of culture, we shall easily observe that within the limits of the proposed understanding of culture, there are also located so-called objective, functional and subjective culture, by taking into consideration that which we submit to the productive or adaptive power of the human mind: (a) objects of nature which have been modified by human thought, (b) the human subject itself, to the extent that it is capable of being subject to the human intellect in a permanent or only a transitory way (c) human activities themselves, at whose forefront stand the acts of the intellect, which can be further intelligently improved in the most varied, objective directions.

Within the range of culture understood in a wide sense, there will also enter its natural and supernatural character in its dependence on the following: What additional elements will be acting on the mind—whether only those which the mind itself discovers and verifies or whether also those which it accepts under the influence of the will and of grace.

By referring to proper bases of division or differentiation, we can distinguish culture from civilization: culture in the biological sense (furnishing man with some niche which nature does not provide) and culture in the eschatological meaning which reaches beyond to the TRANSCENDENT.

We can also restrict the meaning of the expression "culture" with respect to a more immediate need of analyzing or using it. There are or can be an unusually great number of these particularizations, dependent on which activities of culture we shall concern ourselves and which manifestations and aspects or moments we shall concern ourselves and which manifestations and aspects or moments we shall subject to an analysis. Hence we are permitted to use—for a suitable reason—the expression "culture" with its most varied adjectives as: individual, social, of the masses, of various social groups: of different areas of human life—national, state, philosophical, scientific, religious, literary and artistic, of painters and musicians, agrarian, industrial, etc.

All the particularized understandings of the expression "culture," however, presuppose its primary meaning which, to a certain degree, (proportion) will be realized in a selective or a particularized understanding of the expression "'nature." And this foremost sense is the rationalization (*resp.* intellectualization) of nature. The intellectualization itself, however, from the times of Plato and Aristotle was connected with the function of exemplar causality insofar, namely, as man objectifies his ideas and gives them the function of a MODEL, which is realized in inner and transitive activities. This proposed conception of culture, however, is wider in its range than the model. This is so because it concerns not only acts that are the result of reflection but also spontaneous ones of our higher psychical powers, insofar as they are the expressions of the rational side of man.

II. UNDERSTANDING OF INTENTIONALITY

After a schematic and general observation about culture, understood in a wide sense, we must next examine the question of intentionality, which has received some very penetrating study in the last one hundred years—especially in the understanding of F. Brentano, of phenomenologists, and in other contexts of contemporary Thomists. Divergent understandings of this problem created a situation which can even be called a "dispute" on the subject of intentionality. A resolution of this dispute demands a more detailed study, and hence we must examine here only some, and, in my opinion, essential moments of this dispute, whose one or other resolution has a bearing on the question that is being analyzed here.

The primary understanding of intentionality is connected with the philosophical and theological conception of St. Thomas.[4] The picture of reality which is shown through theology and philosophy is a pluralistic one in the sense that there exists only one self-intelligible being, a being who possesses completely within himself the reason for his existence. It is the Absolute: God. All other beings in their vast multitude only participate in divine existence, since they do not possess in themselves and from themselves the reason for their existence. Their participated existence, even of the more excellent beings besides God, is a derivative existence, constantly dependent, since their existence is imparted to them. It is, as if an "influx" from an Absolute to a particular being. Thomas called it *"esse fluens:"* partial, flowing, not firm, as if "hurrying" from God to creatures who share in it. He also recognized a manner of existence, understood in such as way as *"esse intentionale"* —an intentional existence. Intentionality of this type is equivalent to a participation of existence. Used in this sense, the expression does not explain anything special, and it therefore did not take root in any further history of Thomistic thought. It is so general a term that it was replaced by other technical expressions. Perhaps one moment in the conception of intentionality did remain unappraised, namely, the derivation of all beings, of all reality from the Absolute by way of the intellect. By using lan-

guage extracted from the description of the psyche, we can say that all beings were radiated through Absolute Consciousness and they are as if a realization of this Consciousness.

But along with the conception of the intentionality of existence, there was
likewise known to St. Thomas the intentionality of activity, especially in the
case of the activity of efficient-instrumental causes (activity of a pen in relation to writing), where the power of the instrument's activity actualizes itself under the influence which flows through instruments of the activity of
efficient causality. The intentionality of causal activity which St. Thomas
observed was a very suitable way of elucidating the lack of self-intelligibility
of various beings about the character of consequential existing. For, in such
a case, self-intelligibility belongs to cause but the self-intelligibility of being
belongs only to the Absolute who is "pure existence."

Aquinas likewise knew and used extensively the conception of intentionality in explaining the cognitional way of existence of objects in senses and
in a knowing intellect. For everything which we came to know exists in the
soul of the knower in a manner proper to "conscious psychism" and hence
as a "material" intentionality in the case of sense knowledge and as "non-
material" intentionality in the case of intellectual knowledge. The intentional
manner of existence of cognitive objects (in the act of knowing) becomes a
reason for establishing further analyses, whose aim is to establish a manner
of existence of the knowing psyche itself. However, St. Thomas himself did
not investigate the manner of existence of objects known by the psyche;
neither did he directly concern himself with the subject of the intentional
manner of existence of objects which result from the human cognitive
psyche and hence, for example, artifacts.

As we have already recalled, F. Brentano, in the nineteenth century referred to the idea of intentionality. He called cognitive objects, and hence,
those which are in consciousness insofar as the latter is "directed toward"
those objects, intentional objects; and he reduced them to a psychical form
of existence. E. Husserl protested against this by emphasizing that the meaning or essence of an intentional being is, in no degree, reducible to psychical
acts themselves.

And what, in this context, is intentional being for Husserl? It is that meaning which discloses itself in acts which represent the object. For we must
emphasize more pointedly the difference between acts of consciousness and
the object which is presented. Only the meaning which is presented in the
acts is an intentional meaning and an intentional object. And in an intentional object, understood in such a way, we must distinguish: (a) that which
is perceived: *Gegenstand welcher intendiert ist;* (b) the manner in which it
is grasped; *wie er intendiert ist;* for example, in representation of judgment;

(c) the aspect under which we see it, for example as a whole, as a part, etc. Naturally, the intentional object is different from the transcendental object itself in relation to consciousness. An intentional object can likewise be called intentional matter which is found in a qualitatively different form, e.g., conceptual or judgmental, cognitively presented in relative aspects. When, for example, I speak of an equilateral or an equi-angular (isogonic) triangle, I change the aspect of the understanding but the intentional object remains the same. In each case, matter and quality are moments constituting an intentional *"Erlebnis."* One moment cannot be reduced to another.

R. Ingarden likewise referred to Husserl's conception and he developed his theory extensively in a series of works in the area of aesthetics, as well as in his chief work, *A Dispute on the Existence of the World.* Ingarden begins the analysis of intentional being with an analysis of notion which is realized in sense perception and in which he distinguishes three moments that constitute, in general, one entirety:

(a) The moment of intention as opposed to intentional. "I introduce this distinction," he writes[5], "in order to preserve the term 'intentional' solely to signify products, *resp.* the objects of acts containing in themselves the moment of intention. On the other hand, 'intentional' is to signify solely that which, in the act containing the intention is the essence of this intention . . . referring to something. . . . Corellatively, this moment causes an object to be subordinated to a subject. Because of this (moment), the object of the subjective act, i.e., the object as the correlate of the act is separate from the act. The object is in the act, conceived as something that: (1) lies beyond the limits of the act itself (from outside the act) (2) in a certain distance from the subject . . . The moment of intention is a moment completely non-autonomous. It is led by . . . the content of the act."[6]

(b) The content of a non-evident conception: "The content of the act is in it (a directive moment), that which determines it and in what direction the act directs itself and what object it concerns."[7]

(c) The moment of grasping reality. The directive moment gives a non-evident content of the the the act's reference to the object, whereas the content of the act gives to the directive moment, a single or, eventually, a multi-meaning direction which is somehow made precise. In this direction the subject, who is performing the act, reflects and, through this act, effects a material limitation of the object. Taken together, the one and the other create what we usually call an "intention:" a conception included in the act. Only in the case of sickness, according to Ingarden, the intention constitutes an already closed "wholeness" of act, in which there is a lack of a moment of assertion of the existence of an objective act. To these three moments which have been enumerated, especially the third, there can be, and usually are, added other moments that "formulate" the wholeness of the act. To these, we can add moments of love, hatred, positive and negative evaluation, desire, repugnance. These moments surround pure conceptions. According to Ingarden, Husserl was inclined to maintain that these possess their own intending moments. These moments color the object emotionally.

If it is a question about the very structure of the intentional object then, according to Ingarden, we are dealing with a different construction than in an individual and independent object. What is especially striking is the "double-aspect" of its formal structure. Ingarden writes:[8] "It has two sides as if two cheeks which, in spite of their diversity, belong to each other precisely because of the intentional causation producing it by the act. . . . One side is precisely what we call the 'contents' of a purely intentional object; the other, however, is what can be called its 'intentional structure' of the intentional object itself. . . . Its intentional structure reveals itself to us when conjecturing about it, we direct attention to its 'structure' or also when we reflect on what makes it an act, we pass from itself to its intentional equivalent. . . . In its contents, the intentional object 'is' exactly such as is conjectured. 'It exists' in the way marked out for it in the act which designates it through a moment interwoven within itself, which seizes or, in a given moment, bestows existence. And precisely because all this is only thought about, 'conjectured,' 'attributed,' this constitutes a being of a purely intentional existence which, as we know, is a special instance of an essential (ontic) heteronomy."

In other words, we are dealing here with what was already known to St. Augustine in his theory of signs. For the intentional object can be conceived as such and such and as something which represents and designates. Ingarden writes a little further on: "There appears, therefore, in a purely intentional object—if we can express it so—a 'double subjectivity' of its own kind, in the fundamental opposition to an independent individual object where something similar is fundamentally excluded. . . . In the contents of a new intentional object, there can come forth anew an intentional object with a new content, with its 'two-sidedness' of structure etc., *in infinitum.*"

The content of the object can have a *lacuna,* an indefinite place and, for this reason, the law of the Excluded Middle does not apply to it, even though this principle is fulfilled in the intentional structure itself.

According to Ingarden, intentional being is the weakest manner of existence in relation to real, ideal and absolute being. Non-independent moments characterize intentional existence: of non-subsistence, derivation and non-actuality.

In an intentional being, e.g., in some kind of artifact, we must distinguish the following moments:

(a) The author's creative experience or the reproduction of the recipient. This is accomplished through acts of consciousness which are characterized by intention or directed to some sort of object. The intention can focus on independent and eventually real objects, but it can also focus on the kind of object which is not really given but exists because it was "constituted" through an intention as an object.

(b) A physical foundation of works which constitutes an inter-subjective foundation of the identity of a given artifact, e.g., printer's ink on paper and so forth.

(c) The work itself or the intentional object and hence, that which remained constituted as an object through the directive act of consciousness. And even if such an object has nothing of itself that could constitute it — since it exists only because of the directing acts of consciousness — nevertheless, it is not nothing because it can be the object of true judgments that are intersubjectively accessible.

(d) The concretization of artifacts or the result of the acceptance of this work by the recipient. Because the intentional being is indefinite, since it is only schematically outlined and has a suitable physical foundation for its identity, this being can be constructed by another person in the same way.

Concretization can be of two kinds: either cognitive or aesthetic. In the latter case, we are dealing with an aesthetic object. The first and second stages (a and b) are types of really existing being; however further on, they are already an intentional being and they show more clearly the presented traits of intentional being.

The conception of an intentional being presented by the phenomenologists is the result of a penetrating analysis and description of the data of consciousness; and to this extent, as a description, it undoubtedly constitutes a valuable *novum* in the history of human thought. Its weakness lies elsewhere: in its characteristic approach to reality. For, as G. Kalinowski[9] correctly observes (he quotes N. Moreau), Husserl's phenomenology does not leave the area of gnoseology and finds its most important issues in a theory of objectivity which, however, does not arrive at a contact with ontology (metaphysics). Husserl's gnoseology is not a theory of knowing real being. It is raher a *noezology* or a theory of thinking: *cogitatio*. This is why it brackets by definition and a priori, the real existence of the thinking subject as well as the real world. And, at the very beginning of such a thinking, we are not dealing with a REAL AND ACTUAL EXISTENCE. And hence, in further areas of an analysis of the act of thinking and through it, an analysis of the kind of intentional being that appears in directing acts of consciousness, it is impossible to reach factual and real existence which had been initially bracketed. And if we later speak of even an INTENTIONAL EXIST-

ENCE, this "existence" will be understood in different way than was the primary and everyday understanding of the existence that constitutes the factuality of the world and hence, of an existence which realizes the ontic meaning. Intentional existence which makes its appearance in phenomenological analysis can be recognized at best as a kind of "price" of a thought object. A careful reading of the texts of phenomenologists on the subject of the character of intentional existence convinces us that we are not just dealing with real existence, but rather with some kind of suitable selection of qualitites that is sometimes called either absolute, ideal, real, or intentional existence.

The consequences of this statement are far-reaching in the area of metaphysics, where we are analysing the undeniable elements of the existence of being and not only some kind of "price" of a thought object, whose existence is bracketed a priori.

We must agree, however, that initially intentional existence does appear in acts of our knowledge, insofar as it is a realistic understanding of an existing being. Only on the boundary of knowing with the support of cognitional acts is its projection possible in metapsychical activities. In brief, informational knowledge is the basis for the creative, productive knowledge; hence, intentional existence, which is given us in a cognitive experience, is requisite for understanding the intentionality of the creations of culture.

If intentional being is primarily realized in the act of human knowledge, then we must, above all, differentiate between the cognitive meaning and the cognitive act itself. The meaning is usually given me from the outside: it is something which is "cast" at me. It is always "not-I," it is precisely objective, as the Middle Ages expressed it: *"est in statu obiectali.* This "not-I" of the cognitive meaning is something immediately given in every cognitive act. And there never follows such a moment in which the meaning of knowledge would be reduced to a cognitive act that would "bear" or also construct this meaning. And even if I were to become an object of knowledge for myself, there is always that characteristic reduplication: "not-I" of the cognitive meaning, and the "I" as manifesting myself in the cognitive act. The known meaning "objectively" refers to the known thing, to a transubjective object. The known meaning which finds itself within me, which is known and which endures as a constant "not-I"—as an essence of the thing in its purely essential contents—does not differ from the real meaning of the thing itself. Obviously, the meaning which is constructed in my cognitive acts and which refers to the thing itself, which really exists outside me, is not an exhaustive understanding of everything that constitutes the meaning of the real thing itself. But in the selectively understood traits, it is nevertheless identical with the thing's meaning. This means that nothing that constitutes the meaning of the cognitive act was taken "from nowhere;" but it is recognized as coming from the thing. The selectively grasped traits which present the thing's meaning in an indeterminate way (as Ingarden says), in that what they present, they identify (from the point of view of the meaning!) with the meaning of the thing itself.

But besides the contents of the cognitive act, there exist acts that construct or "accept" some kind of meaning. These acts are likewise constantly recognized as my acts. In some manner, I make myself present in these acts. Every cognitive act is performed by me. These acts are bearers of a known meaning which really exists only "in" my acts. The known meaning did not arise independently of acts of my knowledge; nor does it possess an existence that is independent of the knowing acts. For real existence is the existence of something which is a this or that existing subject. A non-subjective non-existence and only an objective one is a contradiction because it is a "non-existing being," if by "being" we understand an existing subject.

Hence we cannot agree with Ingarden that existence should belong to a set of cognized relations and something expressed in a thought object. The objection about existential monism is worthless, since a real and hence only subjective existence is different in every ontic case; it is not reducible to a second existence. The differentiation, however, of the four manners of existence (and, fundamentally, of some kind of objective existence because it is the result of mental combinations) is, in relation to real existence—which the phenomenologists bracket in the beginning—something entirely equivocal.

For this reason, intentional being possesses, in the cognitive act, its existence only as subjectivated in the human psyche. This is not a return to a previous Brentanoism and psychologism, because in intentional being there is specifically the fact that its meaning is objective, self-imposed from the object, and existence is in relation to this heteronomic meaning. In the case of man, it exists through the existence of the subject.

Even though intentional meaning would have as its own endowment, a weakest existence, it cannot be inferred from an analysis of such an understood intentional being about an existing subject, and hence, about man, his soul etc. This is so because an intentional being which is so thought, even existing in the weakest manner, would not make possible an immanence (presence) of the ego (it would be something external in relation to an existing being) in all cognitive acts.

For our cognitive acts are an existing bearer and subject of cognitive meaning which—because they do not have their own objective existence— exist solely through the existence of the subject, in this case, of man. The objection of psychologism would perhaps be justified, even though the entire intentional being would be solely the product of the human psyche. In the meantime, the intentional meaning is foreign, self-imposed, objective; and its existence is only the existence of the subject. The intentional meaning which is unreal through and in itself becomes real through the subject (more strictly: the existing cognitive acts construct in themselves the meaning in the presence of the influence of the existing meaning of a thing.) This content which performs the cognitive act, selectively chooses, as it were, and expresses this meaning in itself as in a subject, giving it a different kind of existence than it had in the thing itself. The intentional meaning in the act of cognition acquires an immaterial character because it exists through the existence of the knowing subject.

Consequently, the structure of an intentional being appears differently in its existential character than Ingarden had described it. The consequences of this position in the area of philosophy are fundamentally different.

III. THE INTENTIONAL ASPECT OF CULTURAL WORKS

Contents which originally exist only in the mind through thought can be expressed externally because they can be "subjectivated" in another, i.e., in transpsychical material. We are dealing here with a linked system of signs. Primarily and in a spontaneous way, the linkage of a system of signs occurs in speech and in everyday language, where we are dealing with MEAN-INGS, which are experienced in a cognitive and aspective way as identical with the content of things; at the same time, with conventional signs which constitute words and sounds of our speech. For in the same speech we already meet: (a) conventional signs, e.g., *"pies," "canis," "Hund," "dog";* (b) one meaning which is the natural and transparent sign, aspectively identical with the content; and (c) a really existing concrete dog.

The linkage of formal, transparent and conventional signs which constitute human speech belongs to the essential manner of man's being in the world. For man not only enriches himself internally through the knowledge and expression within himself of the content of things, but also, by expressing externally to another person the acquired cognitive content. The ability to externalize and manifest externally experienced and hence conscious contents, in the form of a suitable choice of signs and symbols, is an expression of the psycho-physical, essential structure of man, who is neither a pure spirit nor only organized matter.

Just as speech and articulated sounds are the external expression, symbol or sign of internally living and conscious contents of the spirit so too other actions, deeds and their more or less permanent effects can be the same kind of externalized expression and symbol. It is customary to point to human mimicry, to man's gestures, to his behavior, his labor and various works which arose under the influence of human activity. Some works are only a rational modification of the actions themselves and, at the same time, transient as, for example, song or dance. Others, however, have a more permanent manner of its symbolic, abstract, ontic existence, with respect to a basic permanent foundation in which they were expressed. It is sufficient to point to works of art, painting, sculpture, architecture and the like. Such a type of external expressions of human cognitive experiences should be added to a system of conventional signs, to a system of symbols in relation to an internally marked and more or less conscious intentional content.

But it is precisely here that a certain doubt and difficulty arise. Are all human activities and works, and hence works of art, of human technology, like roads, bridges, cities, factories, truly only a symbol of internal cognitive experiences? Are they in some sense only an external sign of that which takes place within the human cognitive psyche?

Let us proceed very carefully in our analysis and let us establish elements which are established beyond any doubt. And undoubtedly the "drama" of human creativity takes place within man in his cognitive sphere. Obviously this does not mean that there are no other psychical powers beyond the cognitive ones, which are involved in the cognitive experience. For in cognition, we must deal with suitable "meanings," ideas which are primarily an aspective comprehension of the content of the things themselves. Through the fact of aspective identity of the comprehended meaning and content of the thing, we can speak about cognitively experienced meaning as about a formal and clear sign of the thing itself. This means that whenever we experience some content in the cognitive act, we are referring it to the thing itself.

Along with the experienced inner "meaning," however, we are witnesses to an external manifestation of this experience. Here, the matter becomes more complicated. For we meet a spontaneous manifestation of internally experienced contents, e.g., in shouts, speech, gestures and with a reflected-upon manifestation; e.g., in a controlled and scientific speech, in literature, and in works of art and technology. In the second instance when we direct ourselves by reflection, we choose a suitable, external expression-symbol for an adequate expression of our internal experiences. Every creative worker knows how much effort a suitable selection of an external expression demands, since it is a kind of symbol-sign for revealing internally nourished cognitive experiences.

The matter is further complicated by the fact that the external expression as a sign or symbol can more or less adequately express that which the knowing subject proposes to say. And this depends on the formal construction of the sign, symbol itself (and hence on the aggregate of well chosen qualities which should indicate internally the intentional content), and on the basic-material, which has its rights in regard to the constitution of the material itself. For one works differently on paper, with paint, differently with stone, cement, iron, etc. And of course every material can be used by man for an outer human, proper manifestation of his experience. And it is precisely here that the third element, the purpose of the manifestation, appears. For we express our intentional experiences for purely cognitive purposes in a different way than we do for practical-moral purposes, than for aesthetic purposes; and still differently, for practical purposes. Obviously, we do not have a mutual exclusiveness among the above-mentioned purposes, but this exclusiveness varies appropriately in relation to different surroundings and a hierarchy of purposes.

We should also call attention to an important psychological moment in the formation of the intentional contents of human experience. By distinguishing connected signs in an analysis, we do not change in any way, the direction of creativity. If man is a psycho-physical creation, it can and often does happen that the internal formation of intentional being is accomplished in close connection with an external use of symbols. And sometimes the external use of symbols and work on symbols helps or simply decides about the formation, within the psyche, of the intentional being that expresses itself externally by means of a suitable symbol. By establishing here a system of signs, we merely call attention to the formal structure and not to their genetic conditionings. These latter ones belong rather to the area of the psychology of creativity and not to a philosophical analysis of the structure of intentional being.

And so, after having differentiated between intentional contents which are experienced within the human psyche, the external conventional signs and symbols of internally experienced ideas, as well as the purpose of their use—in relation to the essential character of this same material in which we express our symbols—we must still point out that the very formal structure of the internal signs, i.e., of symbols, can also be more or less lucid in relation to the designated contents. For clarity in designation, is quite a long distance from a naturalistic drawing to alphabetical or clay-tablet writing.

However, all human works are formally dependent in relation to the intentional content, since we can understand them as a result of exemplar causality.

Clearly there are certain levels of dependence and connection of a nature, transformed by the intellect with internally-psychical intentional contents. Man expresses himself more forcibly or more weakly in his external works.

Sometimes in magical manipulations, we are dealing with only an external appropriation of a thing's name, which is not derived from man. It was only known that the thing itself is in human possession, that it is at man's service—from whence the tendency to know the thing's name or, in some religious dealing with magic, to know the name of the appropriate god or demon. Today, however, with the use of modern technical means, we witness the production of new substances in the shape of permanent chemical compounds which do not exist in nature. Everywhere, however, we are dealing with a bond between a human product and spiritual experience which stands at the foundation of a work's origin.

If we are going to take under consideration this very aspect, namely the influence of inner psychical, intentional contents on external work, we have a basis for recognizing the intentionality of various works which come from man. *For everything which remained in this existing transpsychical material built by the human spirit (its intentional content), is subsequently intentional,* since it is some kind of sign-symbol of a cognitive sense experienced by human thought. The secondary intentionality of a work is read and basically used only in relation to the human spirit. Truly, this may appear strange; for example, in the case of using roads, dwellings, clothing, and gastronomic creations but on closer consideration this strangeness and apparent paradox disappear. The intellect is always the reason for using and availing oneself of or also enjoying secondarily intentional works. Even more, it is precisely in relation to the specific structure of man, in whom the human intellect plays the dominant role (in general, the spirit) that the actualization of human potentialities is slowly accomplished as well as man's gradual up-bringing with respect to his initial non-adjustment to the natural environment. There appears the necessity of constructing a cultural niche from the self-realization of the purposes of human life.

Therefore creations of the human spirit are derived from the experience of inner psychical, intentional contents; and at the same time they are ordered to the human spirit as to a recipient. Since external cultural creations are cultural and since they are signs-symbols of the cognitive sense—in separation from the human cognitive psyche—they lose their meaning because they are not "open" as signs for the spirit. In some hypothetical case of the disappearance of all humanity from the earthly planet, all cultural works would not be works of culture but they would be only an accumulation of matter.[11] Their value—if we can speak generally in such an instance about some kind of value (for value appears in relation to the spirit)—would be only the value of the material. For if cultural works as secondarily-intentional are a sign-symbol, the entire meaning of the sign lies, as it were, mid-way between the intellect which "marks" and another intellect (or the same one as another), which receives and reads a designated meaning in the sign. In such a supposition, it is difficult to recognize as valid, Hegel's claims about a purely objective Spirit, which is realized in the works of a so-called subjective spirit. Eventually recognized, (in other systematic suppositions, however), the objective spirit would be exclusively secondarily, an intentional way of existing and precisely with respect to that intentionality, it could be called an objective spirit.

With such an outlined understanding of cultural works, we can end by way of conclusion, about the destiny of everything that constitutes the area of culture. It is an inner ordering of the human spirit and speaking more precisely, of the development of human personality. Therefore this area arose as the result of the activity of the human spirit (intellect) and it is used by reason of the human spirit.

Such an assertion is joined to another one: it is possible to speak about a hierarchy of value of cultural works, since works alone which are united more directly with the development of human personality, fulfill more fundamentally their essential destiny. In concrete cases, the hierarchy of these values is based not in an abstract and schematic way, but precisely through the human spirit which makes a decision about that, which in life's changing conditions, is more or less necessary for him. Man is constantly "compelled" to make a decision in selecting such cultural values which are more or less connected with an internal development of his personality.

If, however, we should wish to establish some kind of analogically general hierarchy of cultural values, then we could only accept the assertion that cultural acts, within the compass of the human spirit, are of greater value to the person than are non-spiritual ones. On the other hand, among acts and trans-spiritual works, those that are connected directly with man and his body, to the degree that it is an instrument of the spirit represent a higher value for the human person than non-human cultural works, i.e., those realized in a non-human material and hence, creations of nature which have been changed by the human intellect. However, in this instance, such an assertion is only partially substantiated.

Finally, since cultural creations do not exist in and for themselves but derive from and for the spirit, we can accept the assertion about a permanent and non-permanent manner of culture's existence. By this we can indicate its somewhat eschatological character. Cultural works which are objectivized in matter—from the viewpoint of the material character of their real "subjectivated" existence—are subject to the laws of matter: motion, change and cessation. And they have no likelihood of a permanent, atemporal existence. If they *can* survive, it is only in and through the human spirit (obviously insofar as it is immaterial and immortal). By constructing a culture, the human spirit in which, for the first time, the intentional content of the works expresses itself and exists through the existence of this same spirit, is above time in its extra-temporal duration. Similarly, in a constructed work which is known theoretically, practically, as useful or also aesthetically, a second person "reads" the content that has been symbolized in the material subject and primarily made intentional. And it gives a new a way of spiritual existence that is above time, as a cognitively-grasped content remains embodied as a subject in the human spirit.[12]

In sum, various works which have come from the spirit and are assigned to the development of the soul have a chance of survival through the human spirit.

CHAPTER VII

MAN AND HIS FREE ACTIVITY

Questions pertaining to man, his neuralgic moments of activity, his structure and destiny, are always timely.[1] Each human generation, increasingly enriched every now and again by new achievement of knowledge and technology, necessarily returns to these questions in order to become more and more fully aware of the meaning of its existence.[2]

In the life of every human being there are many threads of activity, but only one moment of human action "severs" man from the whole of nature and sets him in opposition to it (even though this nature were the human organism), the essentially human moment, decisive of the human, personal, unrepeatable, unique aspect formed "from within." This is the moment of decision. For each of us decides from within what to do or not to do in relation to the various "objects" of our activity in the broadest sense.

For some, the necessity of decision is so "dreadful" that they simply decide not to decide personally, restricting the exception to compliance with or submission to some kind of system and, concretely, to another person or group of persons who are supposed to take "in their hands" the burden of the decision and of the possible responsibility (*resp.* irresponsibility). Escape, however, is futile, since from decision—even from indecision—there is no possibility of evasion. And when we decide to put our very decision into another's hands, we thereby make a real decision about the "right and wrong" of the decisions of those who are supposed to decide for us. In addition, we form for ourselves the impersonal face of that system in whose name someone decides for us.[3]

Moments of decision are therefore inseparable from man; they are in fact nontransferable; they are that element which constitutes the human character of individuals called *homo sapiens*.

185

I. FREEDOM AS A FACT OF CONSCIOUSNESS

The very fact of human decision and of its every experience reveals to each of us our inner freedom of activity and choice. Consciousness of this freedom accompanies us irresistably in the process of making a decision: it is also an inner fact which, when reflected upon, can amaze us—and amazes us continually—yet it is a fact given to us immediately in inner experience.

Of course, the fact itself of the consciousness of the freedom of our decision is still not its justification or explanation: it is still not an answer to the question: whether we are actually free in our decisions, and how is it possible for us to be truly free in these decisions? And therefore the arguments of various philosophers and thinkers (Descartes, Bossuet, Bergson, Maine de Biran, Mercier, Boyer, and others) which appeal to the fact of the consciousness of the freedom of decision for its justification—evidence fundamentally a confusion of the fact with its philosophical interpretation. For it is necessary, first of all, to ascertain the facts (although even here one must realize that the ascertained facts are already in that moment involved in some kind of, at least, embryonic theory); and then one can give interpretations and a theory, more or less, of the ascertained fact.

The question of the knowledge itself of the fact of making a decision is, however, rather complicated, both on account of the character of our knowledge, as well as on account of its relation to the volitional moment in "making a decision." Most often the recurring misunderstanding in this matter is a kind of tendency to treat knowledge univocally.[4] For we already possess worked-out models or patterns of knowledge and, in the normal course of things, we try to transfer them to our internal life, to impose them, as it were, on the moment of making a decision. Models of knowledge can be diverse, as for example those of which H. Bergson wrote. In his view, our knowledge was fashioned together with the needs of human beings as tool makers. The human intellect specialized in the cognitive sphere of inanimate matter, and this to the extent necessary for the production of tools for itself. Trained and improved in this aspect, the intellect henceforth feels comfortable in the sphere of inanimate matter, and is inclined to transfer one way of knowing which was proper in the service of inanimate matter for the use of tools, to all other objects of knowledge, and especially to the sphere of life, which is a constantly flowing, new becoming. Naturally, the model transferred to this sphere of becoming, formed in the service of inanimate matter, does not suit the context at all; it distorts the object, petrifies life, and eventually leads to pseudo-knowledge. This could also be a rather different model, suggested by Aristotle's theory of scientific knowledge and, namely, a type of general, necessary, and unchanging knowledge. Such a type of knowledge was necessary for the formation of science as valid knowledge and was valuable for many people and for a protracted period of time.

The search for such models (*resp.* types of knowledge) in inner experience during the moment of "making a decision," of "choosing something," would be a futile exertion or endeavor. Human moral experience, principally expressing itself vividly and distinctly in the moment of "decision," does not even have the kind of context in which the above-mentioned models of knowledge could somehow be applied. For individual, changing, concrete experience is constantly emerging in ever varying conditions, always unique; this is, in the full significance of that word, the moment of the "coming-into-being" of a human act, expressed from the point of view of the very foundations of this coming-into-being. Therefore, all types of knowledge "immobilizing" the object of knowledge cannot have any place here, because there yet is no object, but it is only to come into being in the outcome of "making a decision," since it is to come about precisely as a result of an inclination of the will. Even Aristotle himself already realized this when he postulated a new type of knowledge, useful precisely for guidance in the sphere of the coming-into-being of human action, for the sphere in which a person "decides" about some act; in a word, for the sphere not of the theoretical but precisely of the practical. He borrowed this very model of knowledge from Heraclitus (he—from the poets), who thought that for knowledge of the changeable world, of the world which is like a dialectical entity of mutually opposing forces and tensions, knowledge of the detached, noetic type could not suffice, and he postulated a type of more intuitive knowledge called PHRONEIN. This knowledge, in the conception of Heraclitus, was like a deeper, inner insight into changeable reality, for the sake of uncovering and getting a glimpse of the fundamental law governing the changeable world of mutually opposing forces and tensions.

The sphere of practical life distinguished by Aristotle, in which a person knows not in order to become informed about the necessary, stable, and universally valid state of reality, but in which he knows in order to act, in order to release from himself a human, unique, unrepeatable action, since it can never appear again in literally repeated circumstances, is guided by precisely that kind of phronetic knowledge, and hence by that type of knowledge which "here and now" must in a practical way indubitably direct me to decide on precisely this act and not another. The general theoretical type of knowlege here would be of no avail, since the purpose of practical knowledge is also different. Through it I am to make an act of decision; as efficient cause, I am to constitute a new, concrete being formed from my will,

a being which is not at all necessary, even relatively (in its ontological structure). Therefore, knowledge must find expression here corresponding to the
context of the variable, individual decisions which we ourselves to some extent determine. And therefore, knowledge standing at the basis of decision
unites together with our inclination. For when I say to myself, "Do this and
that," "Act thus and so," I am constantly vigilant (I have awareness of this)
cognitively over my inclination, and I want to know individually that toward
which I decide and how I decide. In a word, in the course of deciding, I am
aware (that is, I have knowledge) of my freedom of deciding.

The specific consciousness (also resembling a type of phronetic knowledge) of freedom in our acts of decision was emphasized by M. Scheler, although no doubt he overemphasized some things: "That which is freedom,
we understand only within the compass of our volitive life and never through
theoretical reflection (?—M.K.). Of all the contrasts between an affirmation
of freedom and determinism, the deepest and also least obvious from every
possible cognition . . . lies in the dissimilarity of the fundamental attitude
which we are here considering:

1. whether we take the attitude of wanting, of acting, which precisely
stands before some kind of serious decision included in the living drama of
our acts—as if there, where the degrees of intention, of plan, of resolve, escape from the chaos of the inner agitation of mind and of the initial dance
of thoughts and tend only toward increasing definiteness and resolution.—

2. or whether we treat the whole process from the outside as an 'object,'
as a stream of something that is happening, and then we divide it into parts,
not looking into that inner living frame of acts and not experiencing those
acts anew, as it were. If we look at the formation of the will in the second
of the above-mentioned ways, then we already place the whole into the objective order of time and we bind to one another the separate stages of the
process, its phases and contents. Some part—which becomes clear only in
its experience, in the doubts, the risk, the effort, etc., and is transformed in
certain 'experience,' which can be considered cognitively, which possesses
definite characteristics, attributes, traits—is here, in addition, related with
its antecedent and eventual consequent. . . . Determinism knows nothing of
the making of decisions, of the swelling of life from which they flow in an
evident way, but establishes them as already completed and takes note.
Then, in addition, it joins them together in their subsequent and causally
conditioning processes, but it does not at all perceive with this the occurrence of each of these processes from the side of life's inner activity. Consequently, this second kind of treatment of things never leads to the sort of
experience of them which could somehow be covered by the meaning of the
word 'free,' and likewise does not lead to its opposite—'constraint.' If we

were creatures who viewed the world only as theoretical observers, then we would never arrive at the consciousness of either the idea of freedom or the idea of constraint."[5]

Scheler's observations concerning the difference of the immediate (involving, probably, cognitive moment of the type *phronein*) experience of freedom in the course of "making a decision" and of the theoretical consideration on the subject of the knowledge of freedom, of the consideration which is unable to lead to the seeing and making us aware of the fact of freedom, can be better understood and recognized only in the context of the conception of knowlege which he employs in his phenomenological considerations, and not in any kind of knowledge whatsoever. For the consciousness of freedom "within the compass of our volitive life" is, after all, "consciousness," and therefore is intellectual knowledge, admittedly of a different type, but always knowledge nonetheless. It is "accompanying" knowledge, knowledge "on the spot," occurring at the time when my acts are being accomplished, are taking place within me, when they have not yet ended and have not taken on a final, i.e., determinate form. From the moment they end and at last take on a final character, they already appear as "determinate," and then from external observation, it is difficult to say whether they are free or constrained.

Just as from one side this is a proper differentiation of the knowledge of the fact of the "freedom" of a decision from the knowledge, seemingly "external," of the fact of a decision already made and from the theory of that decision; so also from the other side it is not a proper claim about the impossibility of "external" knowledge of the free character of our decision. Above all, it is not proper because a differentiation is not the same as a separation. We make, after all, (or can make and construct a theory) deliberations on the subject of a cognized fact, on the subject of a process experienced by us. Then our knowledge, which accompanied us in the course of making a decision, is still that same intellectual knowledge (admittedly of a different type) which works out a theory of this fact or process. Ultimately this theory is brought about through knowledge carried on in the realm of our intellectual judgments which penetrate both the whole of our act of decision and its particular elements and phases. If our knowledge were merely an external inspection, like the visual inspection of some color or shape, then Scheler's assertion concerning the impossibility of a knowledge of freedom after the process of decision is completed would be justified. If, however, our knowledge penetrates the whole of our act of decision and its individual phases, and if it is this same intellectual knowledge which accompanies the whole "constructing" of the decision, then there seems to be no reason (apart from possible preconceptions splitting up consciousness) for which a given experience would not be able to be placed in a network of theory regarding that very experience.

Describing further the fact of making a decision, Scheler distinguishes the freedom of the act of deciding from the idea of undeterminateness, which entails unpredictability: "How little the opposition of undeterminateness and determinateness has in common with the opposition of freedom and constraint is best shown by the following: If someone in the positive experience of a free act of his own doing made up his mind always in a free manner to observe the order, to do the same thing in these conditions: if further— that resolution were extended in every circumstance to inner consent, and if this someone possessed also the strength to accomplish it, then the external picture of his behavior, of his actions, would not contain anything 'unpredictable.' He would be entirely predictable, and in spite of this act would be no less free. Theoretical determinism would hold and not indeterminism, and yet freedom would exist in the strictest sense of the term. . . . That which allows us 'to build' on the character of a person, e.g., to trust that a wife when absent will be true to her husband, that she will not yield to any sort of temptation that might change her feelings and behavior, that which allows us to believe in a promise and does not allow us to accept that in the course of time the influence of the act of a promise will be overcome by certain situations and desires related to them, etc.; this is precisely a faith in the freedom of a given person, a faith in this, that in the face of changing impulses and inclinations, he can oppose something which removes their determining influence on his behavior. In this sense, the person is the more predictable the more free he is. On the other hand, e.g., a 'capricious' person (the language speaks clearly: 'unpredictable') is relatively unfree or such that all situations and the impulses freed by them have decisive and at the same time defining consequences for his behavior (with someone insane, and therefore entirely 'unpredictable,' freedom is precisely excluded the most; his behavior and experience is closest to the determinateness defined by the laws of nature). . . . Indeed, such an essential relationship takes place that the more freedom with which an act is performed, i.e., the more the person 'alone' defines it, and not his relationships with situations and specific experiences, the longer that act endures and penetrates all mechanisms and systems of the spiritual life of the person."[6]

Reflecting, on the other hand, on the "point of departure, or the so-called "moral experience," the "generative moral situation," metaethicists write: "Both the content of the act as well as the act itself stand before me as absolute tasks to be performed, and not on the other hand as something optional for a conditional acceptance. In the moral situation immediately given to me I discover myself as placed in a situation of an absolute call to act. . . . Furthermore, an act establishing the alternative of departure from duty does not remove duty at all, but only departs from it. . . . But that very act is proof of one thing . . . namely, that I am capable of opposing absolute duty, I am capable of breaking the "absolute moral law.' The absoluteness of duty does not determine me completely to . . . the good. If through the act I declare myself 'for,' that is my choice, my free decision, that is my act. If through the act I declare myself 'against,' that is also my choice, that is also my act. The 'alternative of good,' just as the 'alternative of bad,' is an 'alternative of freedom.' The coerced act not only could not be either good or bad, it could not be . . . an act."[7]

Therefore, freedom appears in us—and of this we are conscious—as the ability of self-determination both for action as well as inaction, both for action toward this as well as toward another object. We know the circumstances of our self-knowledge, that we do not feel coerced from without in order to act rather than not to act, in order to choose this rather than that. And if someone tries to force us from without, we know too from our inner experience how much our freedom "rebels" against such a behavior, and sometimes the very fact of coercion to something is already enough in order to set in motion in us—in defense of the freedom of our decisions— mechanisms aiming at the removal from us of the external constraint.

At the moment when I make a choice, and through it the self-determination to "this here" act, I am conscious of it, and I preserve this consciousness for a long time, sometimes in the form of the "remorse of conscience" that I myself determined to do just what I did; that I could not have done this but precisely I myself wanted to and therefore I did it; that the decision comes from me; that it is I who am the originative cause of this act which I myself form "within me," applying my will to want (rather than not to want) and to want in precisely this way and not in another. And so, bringing forth from myself this very act, "I become," "I am built," the same as is the act brought forth from me: lying: I myself "become"a liar; standing in defense of the weaker: I myself "become" a defender, etc. And so in practical behavior in a way I "create myself as a human being: I form for myself, through my deeds which I would not even reveal externally, a personal face. The realm of free decisions is that only realm in which a human being "constructs" himself and by this transcends nature, which gives all other beings a determinate nature and a way of acting determined by nature. The person must "constitute" for himself his personal nature through acts of his free decision and be determined to that very way of behavior.

"If we look without bias at experience," writes M. Scheler, "then human life appears as an edifice composed of actions and endeavors running in phases. They are accompanied by the sense of determination, of passive compliance, of coercion or behavior out of sheer habit. However, these phases run in free acts of various degrees, ranging from the relatively free act of will in the choice of direction of a street—in contrast to an automatic walk, to go just anywhere—to decisions concerning acts in which 'we radically change' our whole life and its innermost purpose. . . ..

"It is charged of this immediate consciousness of freedom, however, that it is basically some illusion and that it could deceive in all those circumstances when the determining motives of our actions are hidden from us, and when either we accept in their place other motives or do not accept any. . . . But his accusation misses its mark because it contradicts a certain phenomenon. I or someone else can arbitrarily make mistakes regarding every concrete circumstance of my freedom or his, but that there exists freedom, this is given even in illusion."[8] And if in the content of illusion the idea of freedom is clearly given to me, I ascertain it all the more at the time when I experience my human decisions.

The consciousness of the freedom of our decision, given to us immediately, is the fundamental fact in our moral, personal-human life. This fact, as fundamental for our private life and society, demands many-sided explanations, particularly philosophical, which alone can reveal to us the noncontradicting elements of the awareness of the fact of the freedom of human decisions.

II. INTERPRETATION OF THE FACT OF FREEDOM

The philosophical interpretation of the world acquires livelier colors when we focus it on the microcosm of the human being. Although it is true that the human being in large measure is an "unknown being" and, as Goethe remarks, "he is as strange today as in the first days of creation," still let us try at least in the most general contours to detect and explain the coexisting "nerve of humanity" standing at the basis of all culture, namely, the attribute of human freedom. Usually we speak about the freedom of the human will, but in fact what is in question is the freedom of the person, since the will is only a dependent element of the human structure. The concrete person is the one who acts rationally or non-rationally, freely or unfreely. That person is the being of whom the powers and attributes are: reason, will, and ways of acting.

Therefore, in order to be able less inaccurately to clarify the problem of the freedom of the human being and to sketch the most general contours of the solution to this question, it is necessary first a) to take into account and call to mind, important in this problematic: the ontic aspects of human existence; b) to articulate the idea of freedom; c) to make an analysis of the mechanism of free human action, and through this to realize d) in what way the fact of human freedom, continually developing, is connected with the dignity (and also with the tragedy) of the human person.

In these inquiries we will employ the method suitable to classical philosophy, because we have to state precisely the facts given to us in pre-scientific knowledge, as well as to explain them giving such reasons of which the negation would be a possible negation of the facts or also of the fundamental propositions of the system. For the fact of the freedom of the human being cannot be interpreted apart from the system and its more primary propositions, since these facts are not the first and basic object of philosophy. They presuppose (in the explanation) a philosophical interpretation of being in general and of the being of humans in particular.

The analyses made here are found within the framework of a particular system which, however, does not hinder, but helps to specify the basic conceptions and makes the argumentation more to the point. For if the philosophical "system" by means of which we interpret the world takes advantage of the the achievements of the theory and methodology of the sciences, if it is not an *a priori* system encumbered with nonrational influences of an imprecise, reflectively unenlightened, and superficial method of knowledge, then it gives the guarantee of a more competent and efficient cognitive "tool."[9]

Approaching analyses within the framework of a particular philosophical conception, one must also have this in mind, that a system of philosophical thought is not something external to the person, as e.g., the tools which the physicist uses, but that it is constructed within the person-philosopher proportionate to his increasing depth in precise and methodical thought.

A. THE HUMAN BEING: A SPIRITUAL MATERIAL CONTINGENT BEING

In wanting to know the nature of the human being better, we surely never stress too strongly his ontological contingency. The contingency of our being manifests itself not only in its very structure, i.e., in its complexity, divisibility, transitoriness, but above all in the mode of its activity. For all human activity, as an expression and manifestation "on the outside" and "to the inside" of human nature, bears upon itself a stamp of contingency. Just as the very fact of the contingency of being, revealing itself in coming-into-being, alterations, and death, testifies that Heidegger is to a large extent correct in calling human duration a "being toward death," so too, the activity of the human being bears the mark of transitoriness and the tendency toward death, i.e., of contingency, which in intellectual knowlege appears in the possibility both of true as well as of erroneous knowledge, and in volitive aims assumes the form of effective and ineffective, of good and evil desires, of spontaneous and free desires as well as of unfree tendencies marked by necessity. If contingency comprises the fundamental attribute and is even the constituting moment of the being of the human individual,[10] then that very character of contingency will manifest itself also in all human acts, and especially in the specifically human act which we call free choice, decision. Thus, the very structure of our contingent being already provides the foundation and proper perspective of the judgment of our free acts and of their character.

One should not, therefore, expect *a priori* that free choice would be ontically more perfect than the structure of the human being himself. As human contingency in the order of knowledge is manifested not only in knowledge that is aspectual, successive, but even sometimes erroneous, so too in the order of choosing the diversified limitation of choice will be manifested.

This limitation of freedom is accentuated all the more because the contingency of a human being concerns not only his ontological-existential side, but also his ontological-essential side, in the order of so-called human nature. For if the human being is not a spirit "imprisoned" in matter, as Plato taught, but on the contrary—a spirit (speaking less precisely) being "liberated" through matter, a spirit which self-existing requires matter in order to be able to act, in order above all to become aware of its very self, that is, to achieve self-knowledge through matter being organized to the dignity of the human body, then the mark of the determinism of matter will be expressed everywhere. But the particular place in which the laws of matter find their expression are the acts of human nature through which the human being is expressed as a human being. The act of decision is that place in which in a most explicit manner the spirit is united with matter, the personal moments and the moments of nature (i.e., of something that is determined). Attention should especially be drawn to the fact of the organization of the body itself by the human soul. For the human body is a unique creation in nature. It cannot be placed on the same plane as the organisms of animals which sometimes, from a biological point of view, and especially because of adaptation to the environment, are "more perfect," more specicalized than the human organism. And yet only the human organism is a "body," i.e., it is organized for the expression of the spirit and the possibility of contacting the spirit with all that makes up the content of the world. The body is a phenomenon fundamentally ordered to the spirit and its affairs. Therefore illnesses of the body, especially those that incapacitate or impede the "expression" of the spirit in the body and through the body (particularly the so-called psychic illnesses) are considered to be something profoundly abnormal.

The body, therefore, as matter organized by the human soul, brings in to the sphere of the spirit a large dose of natural, denumerable determinisms, since matter itself, being determinate, "transfers" its manner of being onto the manner of activity of the being of the human, of which it is an essential component.

Indeed, such a general view calls to mind many factors of the Aristotelian conception of the human being, but yet essential differences occur here since for the Stagirite the human being was essentially an animal, admittedly rational, but always an animal.

The Aristotelian conception seems to have been close to the biblical conception of the human spirit, according to which every person is more "body" than spirit and the existence of the human being in eternity can occur only at that time when the body arises from the dead.[11] The idea of a resurrection was, in relation to human "fate," a principal idea. Today in Christian circles, accepting the creation of every soul by God, we perceive an oscillation of thought between two conceptions of the human being: either as an embodied spirit or as spiritualized matter. Always, however, the human being appears as a composite being, a being who is one in the multitudes of elements co-constituting him. Nevertheless, the unity of the human being (this was perceived and substantiated by Thomas Aquinas) is not the effect of the organization of matter: it is not the result of the "arrangement" of the constituent acts of human nature, but it is essentially an ontological unity, i.e., a unity grounded on the single act of existence-life. For the act of existence of a human being is not constructed as a result of the organizing of the body, but on the contrary, the very organizing and constructing of the somatic side of the human being is then harmonious when it occurs "under" a present single existence. Therefore, the life of a human being is his unique existence, bound with the human soul through which, as through form, the whole human being exists. For there are possible only two ultimate solutions to the problem of the relation of human existence to its "I-soul." Either this existence is the consequence of the organizing of the human body, and then life is an emanation and result of the organization; but in such case the "disorganization" causes the disintegration of that existence, which would then be something accidental, relational—it would cause the "manner of being" of an organism, that is to say, of cells and tissues reciprocally arranged. Or else the organization is the result of the existence of an ego-soul. And only then can one speak of the self-existence and non-relatedness of the human ego and, consequently, of the essential connection of the activity of a human being with his ego-soul.

Understood in this way, the ontological structure is able to manifest itself and indeed does manifest itself in the specific activity of a human being. What should be emphasized here above all is the unity of action. The human being is a single entity and all of his acts are characterized by unity. For they proceed from one "center," "from me," and have as their aim the unity of the being: "me." Just as human knowledge bears upon itself the mark of functional unity, so too human aspirations are an expression and as if an "extension" of a single human being. The functional unity of activity does not obstruct his structural complexity and multiplicity. This is clearly disclosed in knowledge. For we know that everything which we call human knowledge arises from me, composes one great "sequence" of my specific, conscious knowledge. However, in this conscious contact with the world, various cognitive structures take part, such as sight, hearing, memory, imaginations, intellect. And just as the stream of light penetrating into a gothic cathedral through a many-colored stained glass window gives, thanks precisely to the structural composition, one picture, so too do we absorb cognitively, in a single, functional, cognitive continuum, the external world through the various sources of knowledge. Sometimes we accentuate the sensory-material side of knowledge, while at other times its spiritual-intellectual side. Always, however, there are in the acts of human knowledge— roughly speaking—two great cognitive structures: sensory and spiritual.

A similar thing occurs with the desires of a human being. For there are no purely spiritual acts-aspirations (spiritual feelings) without simultaneous sensory and material inclinations (sensory feelings). In connection with such a state of affairs, it is usual to distinguish in human volitive aspirations:

a) A system of neuromuscular movements, encompassing reflexive, instinctive, habitual movements. Alone in themselves they form a closed motor mechanism, the manner of performance upon which the will does not have direct influence. The will intentionally makes use of this mechanism, incorporating its energy toward purposeful aims or incorporating it in subordination to cognitive representations as well.[12]

b) The cognitive representations, such as perception, images, ideas, and judgments, constituting also the element of volitive activity.[13]

c) The group of sensory feelings-desires toward ("to" or "from") the desired object.[14] The consequences of this precisely affective (involving various feelings) intensity are observable motor movements in the organism.

d) Finally, the essential, volitive element—"wanting" itself, being an intellectual delight in the object, under the influence of the judgment of practical reason, of a particular aspect of the object.[15]

The structural multiplicity should not, however, obscure the functional appetitive-volitive unity, just as the view of a human hand in a dissecting room, where there are separated groups of tissues, should not obscure the actual function of the hand in the organism. Therefore, whenever in further considerations there will be reference to the free activity of the human being, called "free choice" or "free will,," it will always be necessary to keep in mind the unity of the function and the various composition of this activity in consideration of the structure and the source. Because of these diverse structures, appetitive human activity is diversely conditioned: it has its free and determinate sides; it is also in different aspects both free and unfree, since this is the activity of a single being with a composite structure, and at the same time of a contingent being, of which the being finds its concrete expression in acts of decision.

B. FEELINGS AS FACTORS INTENSIFYING DESIRE

The question of feelings (and their role in the psychic life of the human being) is so extensive that it could become the object of numerous monographic works. Having in mind, however, the mechanism of human activity and free choice, we ought at least in the most general way draw attention to the affective factor which so overwhelmingly intensifies activity, and sometimes even decisively influences the choice of what is desired, detested, feared, or causes irritation.

Just what is feeling in the human being? How does it manifest itself? What are its basic forms? What is its relation to activity? These are questions which should somehow be taken into account in an attempt to outline the role of feelings in our life.[16]

Feeling, sometimes called (for some definite group, especially in consideration of intensity) emotion, is a specific appetitive-qualitative, psychic experience, being characterized initially by the acquisition or loss of the state of psychic indifference toward the "stirring" object. There arises a characteristic, more or less intensely felt, appetitive movement "to" or "from" the concrete thing.

If, however, the realm of desire is two-fold, intellectual and sensory, then feeling is connected with the sensory sphere of knowledge, although in the Polish language it is common to speak also of spiritual feelings, of love, hate, sadness, anger, etc. Spiritual feelings, however, related to the side of intellectual knowledge, are in fact acts of the will, something yet to be discussed below. Feelings in the strict sense are acts of sensory desire and, as such, must be internally connected with physiological changes of the organism. As sensory desire, they comprise a specific synthesis of the psychic and physiological element. In addition, they are a manifestation of originative desire, or, more precisely, they are connected with the knowledge of the subject, and in this they differ from so-called natural desire which is an inclination of a being (as a result of its ontological structure) to its own proper good. Natural desire, also called "natural love" in the sphere of classical philosophy, is in fact the disposition of a being to an activity, and through it to some object, a good.

To express the matter differently: natural desire is an inner manifestation of the purposefulness of the being, revealing itself in its ordered potentialities which are actualized in our life through acts not necessarily presupposing knowledge, whereas feelings as acts of sensory desire necessarily are connected with sensory knowledge. At first glance it is difficult to distinguish feelings as acts of sensory knowledge from feelings of a higher order—acts of will. Ultimately, however, the main difference resolves itself into the independence of acts of will from physiological changes, while in acts of sensory feelings this bond is indissoluble, since it belongs to the very essence of the feelings.

Ordinarily, three integrating elements of sensory feelings are distinguished: a) appetitive-psychic, b) physiological, and c) cognitive-sensory.

The first element is characterized by a particular appetitive "movement." For just as a material-local motion brings the subject of motion toward or away from some object, so also the appetitive movement psychically inclines "to" or "from" a concrete thing.[17]

The characteristic trait of "movement" is typical, after all, not only of sensory feelings, but also of all appetitive states, as well as of the higher, volitive states in which there also appear adaptation and motion "to" a beloved, or aversion from a detested object.

The second element of affective experience is physiological change to a degree easily perceived,[18] such that there are ordinarily distinguished: a) more intense nervous and biochemical phenomena, e.g., in breathing, circulation of blood, endocrinous secretion (alteration of the rhythm of breathing, increase or decrease of the capacity of the heart and blood vessels, change in the gastric juices, in the secretion of the liver, kidneys; change of the composition of the blood, etc.); b) the facial expression accompanying different affective states, greater or lesser muscular tension, gesticulation—the result of which the expression of the face and of the whole configuration of the bearing of the human being is different; c) also the accompanying voluntary facial expression finding its manifestation in symbolic gestures. (Congratulations, greetings, condolences, are occasions of the manifestation of this facial expresion generated by social life.)

The third integrating element is the sensory movement which often precedes or at times follows the two initial elements. Feelings are united with impressions or images and accompany them. Not only the quality of feelings depends on the content of impressions, but also at times their power. Focusing attention on the object awakening the feeling increases the strength of the feeling itself, and cognitive occupation with a different object weakens the former feeling.

The influence of knowledge on feeling, and vice versa, contributed to the emergence of a theory of affective-thought and "affective-logic," which was said to play a more significant role in human life than the logic of reason (e.g., A. Comte, A. J. Mill, T. Ribot). The differences between these logics would be revealed in this, that purely rational thought spins out conclusions from premises regardless of the resulting life consequences, whereas affective-thinking does not tend toward a true conclusion, but toward a kind which responds to the dominant feelings.

If a specific appetitive movement and physiological change make up the essence and the very heart of feeling, then sensory knowledge is not a necessary element, but merely an accompanying one.[19]

One can regard feelings from a different aspect, and according to this, work out a classification. By attending to both their functional as well as genetic manner of manifestation, one finds it necessary to distinguish in a most general way pleasant and unpleasant feelings (function!) as well as bodily and sensory feelings (genesis!). An entirely different domain is the issue of the different formal objects of sensory desire, and the classification in consideration of the isolated object of affective life.

The pleasantness or unpleasantness of the sensations penetrates all feelings to the degree it happens that the same feeling can be both pleasant and unpleasant from different aspects: when at the same time the states of pleasure and pain follow immediately upon one another, they are significantly intensified. There are various theories explaining the phenomenon of the pleasantness and unpleasantness of feelings. The theory of Aristotle, it seems, has in no way become obsolete.[20] For it observed that all acts of a sensory nature either are or are not agreeable. If sensual acts occur without impediment, they carry along the quality of pleasantness; if, instead, an obstacle arises in their fulfillment, then a painful and unpleasant moment follows.[21] For sensual acts are ordered to the good of sensory nature, which is the preservation of the individual and the species. For this reason acts following this line are good for nature. The pleasure felt in sensory functions is that which regulates activities (especially in animals); pain, that which disrupts activities.

If it is a question of the genesis of feelings, it happens that sometimes we experience bodily feelings which have their origin in organic changes, passing afterward into their conscious feelings: satisfaction or pain; sometimes, on the other hand, into sensory feelings which are derived from cognitive impressions or sensory images, passing through the realm of likes and dislikes and finding their outlet in physiological reactions within the organism. Finally, there may arise the situation (not infrequently encountered) that bodily feeling is transformed into sensory, when the process which originated in the organic changes is received through the sensory-cognitive apparatus and intensified.[22] The distinction of feelings into sensory and bodily has its application in the field of morality, where bodily affective experiences have a different character (pre-moral) than sensory affective experiences.[23]

When we take under consideration the question of the formal objects of affective experiences, then we notice that we behave differently toward a concrete pleasurable good which is attainable without difficulty; and still differently toward a good which is difficult to attain, one which must be won.[245]

Good easily attained is appealing, moves and guides desire directly to itself. Attraction springs up, purely sensory love.[25] Such concrete love is the first reaction which some concrete good proper to sensual nature stands before us. But when, instead of a pleasurable good, an unpleasant thing, a concrete evil, stands before this same nature, there arises an act, contrary to love, of affective aversion or of specific dislike or even hatred.

Love and aversion (hatred), the initiating motion of affective life, can be converted into a further phase. For when a concretely appraised good is not yet possessed by us, then the original love is converted into desire (and sometimes longing, when that desire is constant and prolonged); and when we attain it—then satisfaction, a pleasurable state. A threatening evil, on the other hand brings about affective flight, repugnance. But when this evil becomes real and unavoidable—it causes sorrow. Ordinarily the feelings of these two series do not co-exist. This means that love, desire, and joy can exist without the second series, repugnance, aversion, and sorrow, but not conversely, since ultimately every feeling presupposes the original attraction—love.

The question of the affective life is complicated to some extent by the emergence of additional obstacles in conjunction with an attractive good or when it is difficult to overcome a threatening evil. There follows a kind of appetitive restraint, and there springs up the concrete task of the conquering of the constant inhibiting difficulties. If the possibility of the overcoming of the difficulties connected with the good is assessed positively—the person takes stout heart (in the spiritual order: hope); if the possibilities are assessed negatively—discouragement arises. Of course, this state develops further and leads either to joy or to sorrow, according to the degree the difficulty has been overcome. Unfulfilled expectation and discouragement turn into sorrow. It is known, however, that states exist in which it is hard to avoid an evil awakening aversion. At such a time there stands before us the alternative: either this evil appears as possible to overcome and then a feeling of courage arises; or else it appears as concretely impossible to overcome and then fear arises. Courage and fear are particularly dramatic feelings because of the threatening evil which can sometimes become present. As we know, a present evil produces sorrow. But it happens that present evil still does not destroy, still appears as possible to remove, one needs only to attack and overcome it. Then anger grows as a feeling destroying the former affective situation. When we are overwhelmed with evil, then in some moment a first attack arises—anger, which retaliates on the present evil. Anger expresses a higher degree of tension—like an explosion, and therefore it cannot last long since it ends either in vengeance on the evil and through this in an attained good causing joy, or in an unsuccessful act and sorrow.

The eleven distinct fundamental acts[26] of the affective life do not exhaust the entire objective structure of affectivity, but present its most simple manifestations.[27] From their different combination are formed more complex affective states, such as melancholy yearning, being desire colored by sadness, or shame, being the integration of a number of affective acts, e.g., aversion and fear, jealousy, regret, which already are made up of more acts of our affectivity. Of course, the source of all affective states is the primary attraction called love. Every subject has his own way or manner of affective response particular to him. Still, however, there are certain general patterns of the manner of affective reactions, which are called the temperament of the subject.[28]

As was already mentioned, acts of feelings are coupled with acts of will, such that sometimes they bear those same names. For there is not in our emotional life some sort of isolated states, although in the analysis one must distinguish and contrast them. The affective life, then, is coupled with emotions of a higher order, i.e., acts of will, if these are formed also under the influence of reason. This does not mean that reason would destroy our affective life, would expel it or replace it with higher acts. Reason and the volitive life (the so-called higher feelings, spiritual) can activate our affective life and with its help, as with a good tool, they can obtain a stronger means for the realization of personal goals.

Of course, feelings which precede the activity of reason (such as anger or spontaneous fear) demand calming, since they determine us too strongly to rash action. Accompanying and intentionally awakened feelings, however, assist spiritual strengths, give them greater power, and can also be conducive to the development of lasting, good dispositions of action. Such a role of feelings in the personal life of the human being is their essential sublimation.[29] The process, however, of sublimation and of the purposeful arrangement of feelings in our activity is long and arduous, but contributes to the harmonizing development of the individual. Feelings not trained and left to themselves, to their spontaneity, can result in a great deal of destruction and incapacitate or at least radically weaken our freedom.

C. THE WILL AND ITS FREEDOM

The question of the will can be looked at from a twofold point of view: a) the more general, and then by "will" one can understand a particular way of acting, a certain manifestation of one's own "personality" and an expression of the character of our ego; b) the strictly philosophical, when we analyze the ontic character of human rational tendencies, ultimately decisive of the formation of the human being.

When we turn our attention upon the will as upon an expression of human activity, it is not possible to resolve it into some simple and primordial psychic element. In such a state of affairs, the will is manifested as a synthesis of many different psychic states: imaginations, ideas, inclinations, desires, biological-unconscious dispositions, i.e., of all those factors which make up in some moment the characteristic of the behavior of the person. Being a synthesis of these many different elements and psychic states, the will so broadly understood becomes the expression of the personality of the human being. For the psychic states of the person together with the elements constituting them are not loosely arranged side by side, but display a unity, and thereby point to such an element or moment that organizes and gives to the person its own psychic mark, generally called the personality of the individual. In this sense, too, the "will" is sometimes in a state of psychic peace, when the person does not experience inner conflicts, or in a state of inner strife. In the first case, the personality can be regarded as an harmonious arrangement of various psychic (as well as pre-psychic) factors, related to some aim conceived as a personal good.[30] In the second case, when inner conflicts appear, we would denote by our will an overall reaction to particular, decentralizing psychic aims. These conflicts, in the opinion of some thinkers from the sociological circle of Durkheim, occurring in the realm of our consciousness, would reveal the character of the will as the personality of the human being. For as a result of inner conflict, the person leans in the direction of the winning idea and makes a decision in accord with it. But why does a particular idea conquer? This is the result of some kind of collective imperative; for society determines the person, forms in him these and not other attitudes, which overcome our personal desires. Social regulations place curbs upon personal aims and bring about their restraint. This very restraint would be called the will.

Of course, the will so broadly understood does not exclude, but on the contrary, demands the existence of its own psychic-spiritual strength, decisive ultimately of "self-mastery," of making a personal, nontransferable decision. For we experience in ourselves a kind of desire that is directed toward the good known intellectually, insofar as some object, both material and immaterial, is the good. Further, sometimes we entertain in ourselves such aims that demand self-mastery, as e.g., the serving of a sentence out of justice; the apology of one person to another, although this act demands humbling oneself, etc. Hence, psychic tendencies toward the good, both material and immaterial, pleasant or unpleasant, personal or social, have their psychic source called precisely the will in the strict sense. The sources of these psychic tendencies cannot be reduced to other known, purely cognitive, psychic powers or to a group of suitable feelings, since the entitative character of the cognitive processes and affective-sensory tendencies is completely different from that of the spiritual-psychic tendencies toward the good cognized intellectually. Precisely this spiritual-psychic tendency toward the good, organizing and not excluding various sensory-appetitive tendencies that sometimes in struggle must be overcome in the name of the good seen intellectually, is in the strict sense the will united directly with intellectual knowledge, together with which it constructs the spiritual, personal image of the individual. More precisely: the person, through knowledge and through the will organizing itself ultimately in decisions, constitutes himself as a psychic personality. Therefore, one can speak of the existence in us of a power revealing itself in acts of the tendency toward intellectually cognized good.

In the tradition of classical philosophy there are distinguished, following Thomas Aquinas, two kinds of acts of will ordered to an intellectually perceived good: natural, emanated acts and dictated acts (Translator's note: cf. Glossary, #2, 3.). The first, natural, emanated acts, have the will itself for their directed cause, and therefore they are called "voluntary" acts, for they have in view a perceived aim as good, toward which they tend straight from their source; the will. The fundamental act brought into being by the will is love, which can assume various forms, depending upon the good toward which it tends, e.g., the form of desire, joy, hatred, sadness, hope, despair, fear, anger, courage.[31] Of course, these acts normally appear together with the "lining" of analogous sensory feelings.

Natural acts brought into being directly by the will have the good for their formal object, which in concrete circumstances is always "this here" good, although "this here" good from the ontic side presupposes the good as good, i.e., the good in its analogous generality, which "qualifies" the will as its formal object, just as being "qualifies" the human intellect. This good in analogous generality, being the object of the natural acts of the will directly brought into being by it, stands at the basis of the experience called "happiness in general." Clearly, it presupposes the intellectual vision of being as being, of which the consequence is the natural, rational inclination (will) toward good, being personal happiness.

Apart from natural acts directly brought into being by the will, there also exist acts dictated by the will as originative cause and performed by other powers of the human being, e.g., reason, the motor powers, the hands, etc. Having in view natural acts, voluntary and dictated by the will, and executed by other psychic or motor powers, one can notice that these last are subject to coercion, whereas voluntary acts solely in relation to the good in general are subject to necessity, but not to coercion. On the other hand, in relation to any other good, not being the good in general, they are free acts.

In order better to comprehend the nature of the formulated position, it is necessary to analyze briefly the concepts of necessity and coercion as conditioning a deeper understanding and justification of freedom itself. If the free is that which is not necessary and performed under coercion, then in that case what is necessity itself and coercion? On this point, however, there appears a considerable difficulty. For a strict and unsystematic definition of the concept of necessity is not easy and even impossible. It could be defined in prescientific knowledge, but such a defintion would be obscure, imprecise, and one could even say "contains in the definition that which is being defined." Or we might attempt to define that concept even more precisely, but then we would have to enter the terrain of a particular system. Taking both routes, however, we notice that the systematic endeavor is only a clarification of a prescientific understanding of necessity, which most generally can be called all that which cannot be. And although we realize that such a definition is very far from precision and clarity, since the very expression "can" or "cannot" is still more obscure than the expression "necessity," we use it sensibly, assuming that we are dealing here with some kind of primary conception, intuitively understood, and that one cannot define all concepts strictly. Aristotle and Thomas also used this definition, since it was verified in the qualifications of ontic necessity, i.e., of the necessity connected with the very nature of a thing, expressing itself in the activity of the so-called "four causes." And precisely having in mind the Aristotelian theory of the four causes, one can specify the prescientific understanding of necessity and conceive it as that of which the negation is the negation of being (in the given aspect in which the very act of negation takes place).

The real justification of necessity is connected with the function either of the "internal" causes, i.e., material and formal, or the so-called "external causes," which are efficient and final causes. And thus, in the Aristotelian system, matter necessarily is potentiality, since this constitutes the concept of matter. The human being necessarily is rational, since rationality is an element constituting the essence of his being. On the other hand, the external cause of necessity can be twofold, the first of which is connected with the activity of the final cause and forms the so-called hypothetical necessity. For if someone wants to attain an intended end, (the hypothesis), then he must use means leading to the realization of that end. Therefore, the means are hypothetically necessary for achieving an intended end. If, on the other hand, the justification of necessity is an external efficient cause, physical and moral alike, in that case we have coercion. When, however, the subject of coercion is any kind of being having natural inclinations opposed in relation to the act of coercion, then this last takes on the form of violence. Consequently, if a person acts not because he determined for himself the object (end) of his activity, but because someone from without imposes this end upon him and compels the act itself through some physical force, then he will not be in a real sense the source from which the process of activity emerges, and at least he will not be its fundamental source, since it is outside himself in that being which compels the coming-into-being of the fact of the activity and chooses for itself its particular end. The acting human being, however, becomes only an enslaved tool of the activity of a stronger agent, which uses the mechanical powers of the person for the realization of its ends. The person, however, can in his interiority, in his will, not consent to what he performs externally and under coercion. Clearly, it is not this type of action that is being considered when we analyze the conditions and mechanisms of the free choice of a human being. Free choice can occur solely at the time when the person constitutes himself from within as the agent of the activity; i.e., when he chooses for himself an object, aim, i.e., an end of action, and when from within his very self he commands the emergence of the appropriate act.

It follows from this that our will (we ourselves, when we act from within) in relation to the analogously general good, which is our happiness in general experience and not determined, is subject to necessity, and not to free choice. This means that our will (we ourselves) cannot want good, if good is the formal object of the will. For in relation to its formal object the psychic power cannot be indifferent. Therefore, if we ascertain the will as an intellectually appetitive psychic power, then it has its own necessitating formal object, which can be the analogously apprehended good. In relation to the good as good we do not have any inner freedom, since all acts of will tend toward their object from the point of view of good, even at the time when we perform an objective evil.

On the other hand, the will in its freely formed acts cannot be subject to coercion, since these acts flow from an inner source, from the will itself, and they remain in the will itself. Hence, if the will thus precisely forms them, then it can do this in accordance solely with its formal object, with its structure. Therefore, no one externally can command free inner acts of will. It is evident that acts of will comanding the performance of something external arise differently. Such acts can be and often are coerced as a result of violence and force.

Our freedom of action, called freedom of will, refers therefore solely to inner decisions directly formed within ourselves, in relation to the wanting of all goods that are the necessary good., i.e., the analogously general good. For no concrete goods (even God, who appears to us solely indirectly in the light of conducted reflective discourse) coerce the will to the necessary wanting of themselves. Hence, this freedom can be defined as *the rule of the will over its acts in relation to all goods that are not the infinite good.*

Thus conceived, freedom appears in the form of the so-called "freedom of choice" *(libertas specificationis)* and "freedom of action" *(libertas exercitii).* On the strength of the first, the will is not necessarily determined to the wanting of precisely this object rather than another. For every concrete object can appear to me cognitively as a limited object, as an object "with shortcomings," in consequence of which I do not have to choose it. On the other hand, on the strength of the freedom of action, we can actually perform (or not perform) the very acts of the wanting of something. And so, thanks to the one and the other freedom, I can choose between objects "A" and "B," and even in relation to this same object "A," I can want it at one time and at another time cease wanting it.

D. THE MECHANISM OF FREE CHOICE

Before we come to a consideration of the mechanism of free human action, we will inquire yet briefly about the possible main determinants of a human being, capable of ruling out his free and independent choice.

In the history of philosophy and rational psychology, attention was turned to a variety of factors determining a human being to basically necessary action, and only seemingly free as a result of the unconsciousness of necessity of the determining factors. Depending on the nature of these possible factors, determinism was proclaimed: theological (God in some way would determine beforehand the human will); psychological (the human being would be necessarily determined to some kind of greater or more attractive good): materialistic or physical (manifesting itself in some type of natural determination) mainly as a result of the activity of the laws of inanimate or animate matter. All these and other types of determinisms limited or simply annihilated the possibility of the free choice of a human being. He would not always be fully aware of their existence, so that the consciousness of the freedom of a free action of the person would be rather the unconsciousness of the existence of determining factors. Does not a reflection of this kind contain certain pertinent intuitions, or is it entirely mistaken, or does the consciousness of freedom, and even its reality, exclude the existence of various determining factors? These are the questions for which one must, in considering the mechanism of the free choice of the human being, give yet further answers.

First, however, we will briefly analyze the mechanism of free choice. In classical philosophy one must always realize the complicated nature of this issue and, therefore, in explanatory analyses, attempt to take into consideration a minimum number of factors, in order not to get completely lost in the interpretation of the process of "free choice." It is clear that the human being performs this choice, but not with all of his powers. Above all, there participate here those psychic sources of action that are proper to a human being as a human being, and special emphasis should be placed upon their function as well as upon the mechanism of their activity. This does not mean that other powers do not play any role here. On the contrary, as already previously noted, these powers actively participate, since the person does not act with some sort of isolated powers, but through powers united in one great function. More exact knowledge of their activity would allow us better to understand many difficulties existing in this matter. Despite this, however, for a better and also easier perception of the essential moments of freedom, we are purposely limiting ourselves to the analysis of only those elements of free choice that ultimately determine the freedom of human decision. These are the acts of intellect and will, which presuppose the whole rich material of pre-psychic (unconscious and subconscious) life, in which appear the profoundly conscious acts of free decision. This, of course, does not mean that the consciousness of freedom experienced in decisions would be the consciousness of absolute freedom; but on the contrary, it is the consciousness of a very limited freedom, of a freedom that oftentimes is won with difficulty, and therefore it sinks into our consciousness so deeply.

A human act has above all two characteristic features: it is conscious, and it is performed with a sense of lesser or greater freedom. It is therefore an act uniting intellect and will as the ultimate factors decisive of the human aspect of our decision, which does not at all mean that only these two psychic powers would be present in the act of decision. But if we take under consideration only these two ultimate determining factors, then there also appears a difficulty. For how can one speak of the freedom and "nondetermination" of human action, since reason necessarily "determines," because it presents for realization some definite contents or definite plans? It is not satisfied with this merely general indication of the direction of activity, and then thereafter blind, but it examines the circumstances and analyzes the good that it is to obtain in the performance of a given act. And if this is precisely how the matter stands, then does not the intellect determine our will in detail?

Indeed, the intellect enters minutely into the concrete determination of having to perform a choice of the will. The relationship of the intellect to the will illustrates to us in the broadest sense the common example of the cooperation of a strong, but blind person with a paralytic, but keen sighted one. There can arise such a situation that both, mutually needing one another, resolve to coexist. The powerful blind person places the frail paralytic with sharp vision on his shoulders, and together off they go. The sharp sighted one fully informs the blind one of all he sees. Further, he fully examines the things and situations that become objects of interest for the blind person, but he is at the mercy of the blind one who carries him wherever his own fancies point. And it could happen that the blind person learns from the one with sharp sight (who is unable to lie and reliably tells of all he sees) about the existence of a pool of very filthy warm water, gets into the pool in spite of the warnings of the paralytic, and takes a muddy bath that gratifies his fancies. Or it could happen that he learns of tasty fruit in someone else's orchard, goes to get it, not allowing the one who can see further warnings, but demanding only particular information about how to get into the other's orchard unobserved and snatch the favorite fruit.

This comparison limps, as do all. In it, however, there is an interesting thought that can help illustrate for us the relationship of intellectual determination (which here represents the frail, but keen sighted paralytic) to the choice of free will (which in the example represents the strong, blind individual). Acts of intellect and will mutually intertwine and remain in a dialectical clasp with one another, forming one whole in decision. Therefore, every intellectual indication of particular contents responds to some type of assent, choice of the will. The intellectual indication of content is especially important in concrete decisions that concern the selection of means to some generally planned, or for some reason previously chosen, end. The choice of means is carried out in great detail. For we are dealing here with the sphere of practical life, in which a person knows not in order to become informed of the necessary, unchanging, and generally significant state of reality, but exercises concrete intellectual knowledge in order to act, in order to release from himself a human, unique, unrepeatable act, which never again will appear in exactly repeated circumstances. Such a type of knowledge, called "phronetic" in the peripatetic tradition, is supposed to direct and determine me in a practically indubitable way to bring forth a decision concerning the performance of precisely this and not another act. The general theoretical type of knowledge would be of no use here, since it woud not be capable of the determination of an individual concrete action. Therefore, there must here come to the fore a knowledge commensurate with the cognitive context, i,e., with changeable, individual decisions situated in a context of individual-changeable circumstances.

The type of "phronetic" knowledge is the so-called "voice of conscience," or the act of practical reason ordered to the sphere of concrete knowledge of that which does not exist and which is to be done in order to exist. This act of knowledge, which continually suggests to the person: "Do this," "Don't do that," "Do it this way or that way," is an act of the intellect in the practical sphere, analogous to an act of the intellect in the theoretical order when it brings forth "existential judgments." Just as existential judgments establish the first real data in the sphere of theoretical knowledge, since they are judgments ascertaining the existence of concrete beings, so the "voice of conscience," i.e., the act of phronetic knowledge through which we are determined to act, performs an analogous role, since it is a concrete judgment(practically-practical) concerning the existence of a being that we are to make, that we ourselves are "to produce" as its efficient cause. For a human being making a moral decision thereby makes a decision to become the efficient cause of a new being that previously did not exist.[32]

Hence, the essential drama of the moral experience of a human being—of free choice—occurs not in the theoretical phase of the merely general intended act, or in the phase of its physical performance, but precisely in the moment of the making of a decision, i.e., in the moment when the person resolves to perform, or not to perform, some act, whether it be internal or external, but which affects society.

This is the moment of the "free choice" of some concrete means ordered to the realization of the general aim of human life. In the eyes of the great thinkers, generally the personal aim of life, which is happiness, flowing from the union with the final and objective good, appeared as the final reason of every action of a human being. The fact that a person chooses this action rather than another demanded special justification and explanation. The choice of precisely this act and not another was considered as consent to the best *hic et nunc* means leading to the final end of human life. Hence, the whole "drama" of decision is played out precisely in the field of the choice of appropriate means to the objective, final end.

In the moment of this choice, i.e., in deciding upon a deed, the above mentioned cognitive act is at work, which takes on the form of a practically-practical judgment commanding what should be done and in what manner.

Ultimately then (in the sense: finally and most fully-concrete), the determination flows always from the intellect. Hence, the will and our choice (the act of the will) always follow a practical judgment of our intellect, determining us personally to the performance of this here act. And the will designates the final judgment of the practical intellect. Is the will still free in these circumstances? Yes! It is free since it precisely decides which judgment of the practical intellect is to be this final judgment: finally determining us. The will can interrupt the process of intellectual inquiry and command: I will have it so. It selects for itself the final judgment and determines itself by the cognitive content of the final practical judgment. And so, in the case of a person who is going to act, there occurs self-determination. It must occur, if some act is to be brought forth in the person. The person, however, determines himself with the help of his rational powers of reason and will. But this, that he determined himself precisely this way and not otherwise, is regarded as the moment of the freedom of the person.[33] Here is a schema that somewhat clarifies the relationship of the intellect and will in the sphere of action.

Intellect	**Will**

I. THE ORDER OF INTENTION AS THE BASIS OF ACTION

1. A general-analogous grasp of the apprehended good	2. Love of the good as the general desire of personal happiness
3. The intellectual vision of a concrete good	4. The wanting of this good

II. THE ORDER OF CONCRETE ACTION— CHOICE OF MEANS TO THE END

5. Pondering over the means toward realizing the good	6. The approval or disapproval of the will

7. Practical judgment about a concrete action
  a) theoretically-practical judgment
  b) practically-practical judgment
	8. Free choice of the will decisive of self-determination as the source of human action

III. THE ORDER OF EXECUTION OF THE FREE DECISION OF THE PERSON

9. The command of reason regarding the performance
   a) by concrete direction concerning how to do it
   b) by signalling the will to move the motor powers

10. The movement by the will of the motor powers of the person

11. Intellectual bliss from the attained end—*fruitio*

12. Gratification of desire—*quietatio appetitus—delectatio.*

In this schema is shown the moment of the free decision of a human being who finally acts through his two psychic powers: intellect and will, mutually conditioning one another. Also illustrated in the schema is the preservation of the law of causation, in the form of the self-determination of the will through the practical judgment of reason. Hence, each of our acts has its real efficient cause in our will, which finally through the selection of an appropriate judgment determines itself as the author of an act with such content as is presented by the practical judgment of our intellect.

What, however, is the ultimate justification of this moment of freedom? Why is the will able to decide "freely" that precisely *this* practical judgment will be the final judgment through which the person will be determined to a free action?

Most generally, note that the justification of the moment of free self-determination is the nature of our intellect and will. For if the intellect has as an object of knowledge being existing in any manner whatsoever, then because of this factor a person is not limited in his knowledge. Hence, he can know everything, provided that what is cognized presents itself to him in the form of a material being, and thereby in some way being possible to visualize. Having an unlimited range of knowledge, at the same time and through this, the person is necessarily ordered to unlimited, analogously general good. Every concrete being, however, can appear to human reason as a being with some shortcoming, a being in some limited form, thereby— if we stand on the ground of metaphysics ascertaining the real identity of being and the good—as a limited good, a good "not attracting" necessarily, i.e., such, to which a person can cognitively and emotionally remain at a distance. In order that such a concrete good actually (really) attracted the person and inclined him to the choice "of itself," it is first necessary that the person alone through intellect and will would determine himself to the choice of precisely this and not another good. For if some good does not attract necessarily, then one cannot release an action with a view to the necessary pursuit of this good. Hence, in order that an action might come to be, there must first come to be the necessary and sufficient conditions, which are: the determining source of the appropriate direction of action (the choice of this particular good) and the factual release of the process of action rather than inaction (freedom of action). All this the person himself must do, determining himself through a practical judgment to such an act and not another, and to action rather than inaction. Therefore, freedom of action and choice enters into the very structure of human action—and the cancellation of this freedom is also the cancellation of the necessary and sufficient conditions of human action.

From the nature of the intellect itself—being able to know in an unlimited way, and from the will, tending to analogously general and thereby to infinite good—an act of free activity emerges, if concrete beings and goods do not have coercing and captivating power, attracting to necessary action. For every concrete object appearing as a good, beyond infinite good, (but seen only intuitively, directly[34]), has its shortcomings that can cause the human will to "turn away" from it, and thereby to relinquish the action or to choose another object, admittedly also with "deficiencies," but for some other reasons more attractive to the person's taste. Therefore, too, the will has the ability of control over its acts in relation to all goods that are not adequate to the infinite good. Hence, the freedom of a human being toward all goods, apart from the final good appearing to us analogously general, is also an argument for the existence of a concrete, infinite good—the Absolute, which, however, can attract the person necessarily only when it appears as a good seen in itself and intuitively.

The justification presented here of the consciousness of the freedom of human decisions also confirms the spontaneous human conviction in the inner freedom of will, confirms the human practice of responsibility, even judicial, for the free behavior of the person, confirms the sense of all morality. For cancelling human freedom of decision, we would also cancel the bases of human morality.

Hence, according to the presented argumentation, one cannot agree with the theses of radical determinism, in whatever form (theological, psychological, materialistic or naturalistic), that the freedom of will of is only the unconsciousness of necessity. Above all, because we experience this freedom consciously, and the act of consciousness is not unconsciousness of self; in addition, the fact of consciousness not only has a complete explanation, but what is more—has an explanation of the necessitating order, of which the consistent denial entails the affirmation simply of the absurd. Beyond this, it is not sufficient to negate freedom of the will and later explain this negation with unascertainable hypotheses, but one must, for the denial of the fact of freedom, negate on the basis of positive argument the very fact of the consciousness of freedom and eventually explain the feeling of freedom as a disease or as a derivative mechanism formed on automatisms. . . .This kind of explanation, however, immediately appears absurd and incomprehensible.

E. THE DEVELOPMENT OF FREEDOM IN THE HUMAN BEING

The theoretical conception of freedom of the will sketched here and its justifiction are basically simple enough that one ought to be able to make them concrete and fortify them with ascertainments of more detailed conditions, also flowing from the perception of human nature. For the human being, as repeatedly emphasized, is not only a spirit acting with the help only of intellect and will. The mechanism of action limiting itself merely to spiritual, psychic powers is proper for beings which theology calls angels or pure spirits. Undoubtedly, in many textbook analyses and explanations, and also definitions of human freedom, there appears some mark of angelism and, strictly speaking, of scholastic schematism, which has worth as its own cognitive endeavor but not, however, as a true picture of reality. For the human being, as has already been observed, is a contingent and material being; matter penetrates the human be-ing which is one, in spite of the composition from spiritual and material elements. If the human being acted entirely immaterially, he would cease to be a human being, he would become a pure spirit. This does not mean, however, that the previously conducted analysis was faulty. No. It was conducted only by taking under consideration the essential moments of human decision, which are the acts of intellect and will. These acts ultimately crown the whole complex of prepsychic and psychic processes, which must also be taken under consideration in analyzing the issue of the freedom of the will.

After the ascertainment of the moment of freedom in human choice, more careful attention should be directed to the material determinants accompanying human choice. From agelong human practice, we know how much it is possible to influence a person and limit the possibility of his free choice. There are many and very different kinds of material determinants, as a result of which the real possibilities of choice, although they do not disappear entirely, remain nonetheless restricted, and often practically almost demolished. For it is possible to create for a person such conditions of action in which the normal function of the psyche undergoes such far-reaching determinations that nothing remains for the subject but to agree to the existing determinants, since the possible lack of accord can destroy human life in general. Hence, for the preservation of higher values, the person resigns from lower values. This does not mean, however, that human life would always be a higher value than the value of protest against existing material determinations; but in such circumstances there already are needed truly superhuman and heroic powers in order to choose freely the loss of one's life rather than submit to material determinants which one cannot control.

Hence, the very practice of many ages of the life of humanity indicates the fact of the narrowness of the boundaries of free human choice. If we would imagine a scale of determination and self-determination, then on a given hundred degrees—self-determination can occur in normal circumstances between, for example, the fortieth and sixtieth degrees. All the degrees above and below make self-determination practically impossible. In some rare conditions this border can move, but always at the price of heroic efforts.

Futhermore, in the existing and factually possible degrees of self-determination, i.e., there where we freely form our acts of will as free, there also appears—as secondary (like a "lining" of free human action), more closely unknown and unknowable to us—a quantity of material determinations, if the human being acts as a human being, i.e., as a psychophysical or physicopsychic being. For everywhere that empowered potentialized material factors enter into play, there also exist their laws of matter and, amid them in some way also, determinism. Therefore, each of our actions, originated in consequence of self-determination, i.e., each of our free acts, always has an unfree aspect and side because it also occurs in a material, and not purely spiritual, environment. The activity of our reason occurs in connection with matter. For the human being without sensory knowledge, including both external sensory knowledge, as well as internal,e.g., imaginative, could not arrive at the formation of concepts and judgments, which in their structure admittedly appear as immaterial, but in their functioning are very essentially connected with matter. For our intellectual, cognitive life is like a rational melody emanating from musical instruments. The meaning of the melody is rational, but its function is not possible for a human being in separation from the activity of the senses and their material subsidiaries. A similar thing exists in our wanting, which is also entangled in the web of human emotions, that sometimes must be expanded and agitated in order to add a more powerful drive to our acts of will, manifesting themselves in the form of wanting.

The function of our intellectual knowledge as well as the function of our aims-desires, is closely connected in us with our sensory-material substratum. And this substratum, as is known, is found—being matter—in constant motion. Indeed, our spirit, penetrating matter, penetrates and unites the various phases of movement into one, but it nevertheless cannot rule out the essential function of matter which is continuous motion, unceasing change. Precisely as a result of this, we are not able somehow to stop the course of matter and arrange it as we please, but we must make our decisions somehow "in the course," constantly running into the unknown, of the vehicle of our life. In virtue of this, too, our decisions, our discernments, are not at all perfect acts of knowledge and wanting; they are connected precisely "with the course" of matter unceasingly flowing through us, the course over which we do not have full control, and deciding "in the course," we decide in many cases provisionally, constantly postponing for later more thoughtful, more, as we hope, reflective and improved decisions. Of course, this is an illusion, since those same circumstances in which we made the less free and more faulty decisions are never repeated in the future. There is in this, nevertheless, a great amount of truth, since just as a driver of an automobile learns and improves his movement in the course of driving, so too a human being both can and ought to become educated to ever more perfect and more free decisions.

Therefore, in our activity we are free according to the measure of a human being. If we educate ourselves in the aspect of the intellect, of physical proficiency, so too can we educate ourselves "to freedom," i.e., to the making of decisions with greater and increasing independence from material determinants. For each and every human being, on the strength of his entitative structure, has given powers with the help of which he can develop himself in the direction of freedom and independence from various forms of necessity. The development, however, presupposes action, the actual performance of liberated acts, through the actualization and development of our knowledge, reflection, through acts of self-mastery. Especially these last—not known in the world of matter (as was observed by E. Schrödinger[35]), as fulfilling the command: "I ought," and thereby realizing values that still are not, and that one ought to call into being—are in us the moments of the development and construction of human freedom. Hence, through the conscious performance of free acts of decision, we can more fully control the mechanism of self-determination and thereby, in an ever fuller sense, create in ourselves a human, personal face open to the Absolute. Admittedly, as a result of the human situation resembling the situation of a vehicle in progress, we will never come to the abstractly and systematically fixed conditions of fully free decision—and precisely therefore we await the moment of death conceived actively,[36] in which we ultimately fulfill our knowledge and possess the clear will of choice—yet nevertheless, through acts of our freedom, ever more fully attained, we will direct ourselves toward the aim of life, toward the final good. In this sense, too, the saints can be regarded as those who reached greater proficiency in free decisions, because they liberated themselves more fully from the material determinants of their wanting.

In the "construction of freedom," it is necessary still to turn attention to the possibility of the reverse direction of development. Having given psychic powers "towards freedom," we can, submitting passively to the pressures of various kinds of determinants, gradually and imperceptibly decide to follow the stronger and more pressuring psychic impulse, and thereby resign from genuine choice, not taking under consideration the more difficult alternatives. An especially threatening case of the deterioration of the freedom of a human being is public pressure organized by a power, such as that which took place in fascist Germany, where the conditions for making free decisions were taken away. As a result, not only the citizens of that country were deprived of freedom, but also the citizens of the neighboring countries of the enslaved nation. A human being, however, deprived of the possibility of free decision, or also depriving himself (through passive submission to the surge of material determinants) of the freedom of choice, ceases slowly to be in a psychic sense a person, and becomes an "object," an element of the material world.[37] And M. Scheler rightly observes: "There occurs even such an essential connection, that the greater the freedom with which some act is performed, i.e., the more the person 'himself' qualifies it, and not his connections with the situation and individual experiences, the more this act endures and penetrates the whole of the spiritual life of the person. Of course, one cannot judge by the external expression of behavior whether someone always behaves in the same way due to habit or due to freedom. And after all, habit is some kind of coerced activity, and consequently the opposite of freedom. The fact that the more a person is part of a collectivity, the more he succumbs to pressure and becomes unpredictable, is explained by this, that freedom indicates precisely the predictability of an individual, and coercion—unpredictability. A collectivity is unpredictable, capricious, hysterical. It is worthy of notice that the more the activity of a certain person can be conceived and explained in a given situation by means of the ordinary operation of human impulses, the less we need take into consideration his personality in order to understand his life; the more we are able to 'explain' him 'according to the law of nature,' the more unpredictable he becomes for us, the less we are able to 'understand' him, i.e., reduce to a unity the given actions, looking at them inwardly from the side of his intention and his 'I' . . . . It may appear that faith in the phenomenon of freedom, in the factual existence of alternatives in the life of a human being, his proper call to a determination concerning the reality and unreality of various contents—is synonymous with a kind of annihilation of every certitude, of the possibility of trust, and leads to chaos. This picture, sketched by determinism—painted in the most vivid colors from the time of Hobbes—is actually the product of 'dread in the face of freedom.' We all know this dread, above all in insignificant and empirical matters, which for philosophers-determinists grows into some vague dread in the face of absolute license and chaos."[38]

It is understandable, that in a chapter having as an aim to turn attention upon human freedom of decision, its construction, maturation, it is difficult to enter into discussion with various deterministic positions which, in the name of the preservation of order and neatness, throw overboard considerations of the possibility of the freedom of human decisions. The indicated formulation of Max Scheler suggests that the matter can be presented the other way around: that only freedom makes something ultimately comprehensible. But the concern here is not a comprehensive response, but an indication of the direction of the solution. And precisely here there appears still one theoretical difficulty, connected with the maturation of a human being "toward freedom" and with the action of the Absolute on the world and on the human being. For already M. Hartmann, accepting the freedom of a human being as a fact and foundation of morality, indicated the impossibility of the existence of God in connection with the acceptance of such a state of affairs. For the existence and action of God on the world would cancel out the freedom of the human will.

Opinions on this subject flow most often from the inadequacy of our language not only in relation to supernatural reality, but also ordinarily to naturally transcendental reality, especially in relation to the Absolute. For we use an objective language, formed on the basis of knowledge of a material world. The categories of freedom, necessity, coercion, are derived from precisely this world. This is why it is so hard for us, for example to make use of the category of freedom, since in the empirical sciences we have become accustomed to express contacts which take place between things in necessitating categories. Further, precisely such a manner of expression assumed the rank of scientific knowledge. But meanwhile, God and the manner of his activity are transcendental for human understanding. God in his activity is not connected with the categories of "freedom" and "necessity" derived from this world. As Absolute, he is not at all limited to definite ways of acting—and such precisely are the freedom and necessity of contingent beings. The manner of activity of God is, after all, according to the measure of God, i.e., higher and embracing at the same time necessity and freedom. In addition, whatever the Absolute does in nature, as Creator of all nature, is natural, because nature does not come from itself but from the one who created that nature. Therefore, the whole problematic of the determination of God in free human activity, the problematic that once kindled to red-hot the passions of the Jesuit and Dominican schools, is basically only a linguistic misunderstanding based, after all, on the anthropomorphic tendencies of the theology of that time.

*   *   *

Hence, our personal freedom of decision is a primary selfconscious fact that is explicable and intelligible in philosophical interpretation. For freedom is a necessary aspect of the will as a psychic power that, through its free acts of love, enables us to live "for-another-person." The functioning of freedom, although it is difficult, can increase in our life when we rise above material determinants through self-mastery; but it can also decrease—when we decide to conform to psychic, social, or material determinants that are for some reason stronger. Nevertheless, by making a decision, free in its core, we always bear responsibility toward ourselves and other persons, and even toward the person of the Absolute.[39]

CHAPTER VIII

MAN IN THE PRESENCE OF MORAL GOOD AND EVIL

The realm of morality constitutes an essentially human field of activity in which man is necessarily situated, and from which he cannot escape because of his own personal ontic structure. Hence morality with its aspects of good and evil becomes the next object of investigations, since these will enable us to understand more fully the meaning of human life which—as is evident from internal experiences and the history of all humanity—takes place on the axis of good and evil.

As, from one side, the theory of moral good and evil occurs in the context of a particular system and whose understanding and acceptance are presupposed in the construction of this same theory—so from the other side, it appeals to certain everyday intuitions, not only as common sense criteria but also as elements which are to be included in a realized philosophical conception. This theory is to be an expression of understanding what, ultimately, is moral good and evil, which we constantly experience and of which we are not always aware, as elements which constitute both morality itself and good and evil acts. Moral good and evil are a particular instance of good and evil existing in the world and which affect us directly.[1] If, however, considerations about good and evil in an analogical generality have an impersonal character which is somewhat "detached," investigtions which concern morality from the aspect of good and evil are, from the nature of things, closer to us, since they are "fused" with the subject.

219

I. FOUNDATIONS OF MORAL BEING

For a fuller understanding of the problem of moral good and evil it is proper to examine it in a three-fold area: (a) man as a subject of morality; (b) the constitution of things cognitively grasped in our intellect; (c) as well as the first constitution of ideas or of the so-called "eternal law" as the ultimate norm of moral conduct.

The general considerations of these three areas will allow us to orient ourselves in the nature of morality itself and of its good and evil directions.

A. MAN AS THE SUBJECT OF MORALITY

The first and fundamental area of moral good and evil is linked with man, his structure, his capabilities of both cognitive and volitional acts directing a rational conduct.

From the aspect of his ontic structure, man is a single and entire, undivided and subsistent being. This ontic oneness we discover and establish by way of analyzing various personal acts which point to the existence of a single subject. For all these acts and, especially, intellectual-volitional acts, carry with them a stamp of a definite individuality. They are acts of "this here" man who determines his own activity in a definite manner. The activity of a human subject is not a duplication of typical functions of some kind of particular "human species." Rather, it is an individual, unrepeatable reproduction of an individual exemplar of personality, of an individual way of existing and of actualizing a potentiality which, only analogically and not univocally, constitutes every composed human individual be-ing. In addition, in his consciousness, man "recognizes" himself as the author of his actions. He feels himself as a single "I," a single distinct subject responsible for his own actions.[2]

Taking into consideration the composed structure of the human person— really existing through a unique unrepeatable act of existence which serves the entire "entity" by reason of the human spirit that exists independently and is, at the same time the form of its body[3]—we can now turn our attention to the functional side of this person. The ontic oneness and subjectivity of man manifest themselves best in those acts in which are engaged the individual powers of acting, i.e., those which equally distinguish the human individual in his relation to nature and to other persons. These powers of activity are the intellect and will. For the human person expresses himself most completely in those acts in which the activity of these powers is joined together in one harmonious whole, and enables man to perform his own self-conscious and proper activity. Acts of this kind are called decisions.

A decision is that which constitutes an essential expression of a human person's autonomy. Through acts of decision (through a series of them, in relation to various objects of human activity), man becomes the author, the creator equally of his own personality as also (in a certain sense) of the object of his activity. Consciousness and freedom and hence autonomy of the human person are not "given" in a ready and changeless form. Rather, they are "pre-given" it, and through it they carry the stamp of potentiality in the same measure as the entirety of human existence. They form and concretize themselves in activity and, thereby, activities take on improvements and a permanence—to the measure of permanence of the subject of action himself.

In turn, man does not acquire these habits independently of other persons. In this sense, man's autonomy is genetically and functionally conditioned by heteronomy in relation to the external world but, above all, to other persons.

The development of personality in the direction of autonomy is the development of the capability of intellectual knowledge in its various forms and manifestations and of free choice of one's own good, above all, of the kind which can become the object of personal love. It is also a development connected with those capabilities of making a reliable decision, i.e., of a personal ordering for oneself of a known and loved good as the proper aspiration. In an act of free decision which is composed in this way, man recognizes, against the background of a concrete object, natural law[4], which appears in the form of a practical judgment: "Good is to be done." At the same time, he accepts this law through an affirmation of this particular object as a good which directs him to a personal and, at the same time, a common good. Hence, natural law is "inscribed" in the rational nature of the human person, and it always actualizes and fulfills itself at the moment of a personal decision in the presence of "this here" good. At this same moment of choice, man applies natural law (the performance of good) to his own personal nature and individual situation. And in this sense, he accomplishes a personal intellectual reflection—self-cognition and concrete choice—and he applies a law to himself, which is also proportionally (analogically) a law for other people. The guarantee of the objectivity of this law is the intellect which "reads" the necessary aspects of the object as a concrete good. Only in the light of the essentials of the property of human nature (an objectively knowing intellect and a will which chooses freely), as well as of common good, can a norm-law bind every man internally in conscience. It becomes a regulative-law for persons only to the degree that it is accepted in an act of free decision, as an element which binds human autonomy with heteronomy, human individuality and independence with interdependence of nature and other persons. The acceptance of natural law in every act of decision is a basic and indispensable element for the develop-ment or actualization of the human person who acts "with nature" (a rational one!) in the direction of common good.[5]

To make a decision in which the focus is on moral good and evil, natural law, responsibility, actualization of the person—if obviously the decision is to be morally good—is irrevocable as its own "most primary foundation," a so-called "right desire" called in Latin terminology *rectitudo voluntatis*.[6] Without the latter, we do not even have, in a strict sense, a truly moral human act. The fact of right desire follows upon intellectual knowledge and precisely a knowledge which specializes in the practical area and hence, in the area which directs human conscious and free activity. Fundamentally, this is a question of a type of knowledge in which we improve our vision of the natural law: "Good is to be done" by confronting it with fundamental areas of human life, where the right of acting and realizing good is espe-cially important. The improvement of the practical intellect in these very fundamental areas of procedure bears, in philosophical tradition, the name *synderesis,* human conscience.[7]

Man is born neither good nor bad morally, at least basically, even though he is replete with hereditary inclinations, of which some are helpful in build-ing moral good, and others are not. In addition, we can detect in man a kind of natural flaw which reveals itself in an internal disharmony, which Cath-olic theology explains as original sin. In spite of this, man is, by nature, or-dered to the knowing of truth, as well as loving the good (which as yet is not "moral good!"). This natural disposition of man (of his will and his de-sire) to actual objective good is precisely what can be called in a fundamen-tal meaning "right desire of the human will." The will which is linked with an actual and objective good (it presupposes exactly acts of an intellectual, normal knowledge) does not direct itself into the area of the conduct of the practical intellect in such a way that it would satisfy all kinds of distorted desires (in such a case as already somehow a wrong will) and hence, would choose only such concrete judgments that would answer to wrong will. On the contrary, because man in his knowledge sees a real good, he binds him-self with it; he relates himself to the attainment of good and in his phronetic knowledge, he gives such judgments which will be the element of auto-de-termination of free will, choosing a real good, objective in the act of the will and responsible in decision.[8] Only the rectitude of the will, which is con-tinually and endlessly forming itself by ordering itself to real and objective goods, gives a guarantee to undertaking morally good decisions or the a-voidance of moral evil. However, it is not possible, practically, to seek first the rectitude of the will itself rather than other concrete goods. This is so be-cause the rectitude of the will constructs itself in us, along with the rightness of our decisions. Hence it is something dynamic in us; it can increase and diminish along with the increase and diminution of a morally good life and, hence, a permanent and continuous choice of concrete, real and genuine goods.

The question here, however, is about establishing a priority (in both a formal as well as a dispositional aspect), concerning the examination of the relation of synderesis and "rectitude of the will." If synderesis is, in the order of practical knowledge, equivalent to that which, in the theoretical area, constitutes an intellectual intuition of first principles (being a varied cognitive explanation of the content of being, thing, oneness, truth and good),[9] together with their fundamental, wise synthesis, then, in the order of action (conduct), synderesis also constitutes the first foundations of moral life, which rests on the natural law of "realizing good." Since good is the object of desire in the practical order, it is the same being which is the object of knowledge in the theoretical order. And, as in the theoretical order, being and the transcendentals (thing, one, truth, good, beauty) can be expressed in the form of first principles so, too, in the practical order, good appears cognitively in the form of a judgment. This judgment is the essential expression of the natural law: good is desirable and it should be desired (be done); evil (which is, as yet, only spontaneously and non-reflectively only) arouses repugnance and should be avoided. The particularization of this fundamental law-judgment are the first moral precepts that regulate the realization of good in fundamental, human, natural inclinations. Since we possess these very first principles in our psychical disposition as an application of the natural law to fundamental human inclinations, we possess, by the same token, an aggregate of first moral principles, traditionally called *synderesis*.

The functions of the practical intellect, which occur in the form of a judgment expressing natural law, as well as of first moral principles called synderesis, are formally prior, as auto-determining elements from that which is determined—hence, from will and its rectitude. The acts of the intellect are the absolute, indispensable and primary element of moral life, which reveals itself in human decisions. Their distortion or incorrect functioning is the basis for what can be called the principal and perhaps incurable moral sickness—a kind of inability of a correct viewing of the good, as a kind of *moral insanity*. A lack of synderesis testifies to the inability of leading a moral life and it is usually connected with some kind of psychical sickness. This sickness, clearly, is "graduated," but its most sensitive "barometer" is precisely the capability of a correct moral evaluation, particularly in fundamental laws for human conduct.

With respect to the primacy of intellectual functions in relation to the rectitude of the will, we must observe that rectitude of the will itself facilitates normal, correct functions of the practical intellect which reveal themselves principally in synderesis. For rectitude of the will is the fundamental attitude of a person in his aspiration toward an actual good revealed by the intellect, toward a good which is fundamentally suitable. For only a suitable good can be recognized as an end in itself for human conduct, since such a good is ordered neither to "usefulness" nor also exclusively to pleasure.[10] Hence, a stable attitude of the will toward an actual good enables the intellect to perceive practical truth, and makes it easier for it. For the will does not obscure the intellect's field of view but it draws it nearer, since it is connected with good. Rectitude of the will, therefore, precedes the disposing acts of an intellectual intuition of the primary moral principles.

Keeping in mind the human subject who expresses himself in acts of decision, in the presence of choosing a concrete good—what presupposes on the one hand, the presence of the practical intellect which reveals itself in the form of a judgment about doing good and of first moral judgments; (synderesis) and on the other hand, the fundamental rectitude of the will—one can and should realize in this area the meaning of morality itself.

In the tradition of realistic ethics, morality was called the relation itself of agreement (in the case of moral good) or of disagreement (in the case of moral evil) of the human act; more precisely: of a human decision with a rule of practical conduct. This relation is known as a so-called "transcendental relation" and hence, necessary and inseparable from a human act, a human decision. This means that as often as a decision or a human act takes place—and hence a conscious and freely-willed act (it is already achieved internally in man under the form of a practically-practical judgment, along with a choice of the will)—this identically same act, even if it were not revealed externally and realized physically is nevertheless the same moral act, in a positive or negative sense, since it is bound to a necessary and inseparable relation with the rule of conduct.

The rule of morality, however, or the rule of conscious and free conduct is the human conscience—practical reason, insofar as it gives judgments, beginning with the primordial judgment, "Good must be done," through the most varied particularizations of this judgment with respect to the concrete character of a good which can be chosen and is the occasion of choosing this good. It dictates in a categorical way *hic et nunc* that one should proceed in this concrete instance precisely in this way and not otherwise. The rules of conduct or practical judgments are obviously based on a vision of the structure of the concrete object as a good, about which we shall speak further on. The final rule of man's conduct is the Absolute (Eternal Law) which, having created man's nature and the world of things, is the ultimate guarantee of the rightfulness of natural rational inclinations to actual goods

Obviously, between God (His Eternal Law) as the ultimate rule of moral conduct and concrete human prudential knowledge, which appears externally, in the form of a dictate of practical reason or so-called conscience, there still exists a series of intermediate instances. We can mention, for example, society or various groups of people who are bound through mutual cooperation, who can indicate to each other mutually general norms of conduct in concrete, lived instances. And through this, they can educate themselves mutually in the moral order through common decision: what values and what eventual norms should be taken under consideration in a decision defined by actual conditions—with respect to the fact that the object of that decision is in agreement either with human nature (social) or with the will of God, Who intervenes through revelation in human history.

External intervention of the human community in the establishment of the rules of moral conduct is not, however, the most essential for moral activity. For the sphere of morality concerns basically only the interiority of man and it is precisely that necessary relation of agreement or disagreement of human decision with the rules of conduct. This relation is contained in every action, in every human decision which cannot not be a decision taken under the influence of the intellect and it cannot be indifferent in relation to a good which is realized by the will. Hence human decision—insofar as it is directed by the practical intellect in the perspective of a concrete good—is the nature of morality. For every "conduct" or "behavior" is something external and heteronomous with relation to the autonomy of human will, which must determine itself through a practically-practical judgment about the choice of precisely this good and no other, and precisely in this manner and no other.

Keeping in mind the fact that every human act, insofar as it is human is directed by the intellect with respect to the good, or that no conscious or freely-willed human act can be indifferent in relation to good, we observe that no human deed-decision is indifferent to natural law as a command to do good. For each is a realization of a good: either actual or ideal. For if natural law appears in the form of a judgment: "Good must be done," then every act is a realized good. From this title, natural law is internally bound with morality. We must emphasize that if the realized good is only an ideal good and if we admit that we evaluate it precisely as ideal, we oppose natural law and, in truth, we equally find ourselves in the moral order. The moral sense in this case, however, is negative and the decision is morally wrong, since we are not choosing such a good that can unite us with common good, but that which separates us from that good.

The area of the subject which we have analyzed here and in which the entire "drama" of moral decision takes place, still demands a completion by means of objective elements which are connected with it. Admittedly, natural law which appears in man in the form of a practical judgment about doing good, as well as acts of the intellect which direct the decision, are already objective elements. However, it is still proper to emphasize their objective character by an exegesis of a so-called "objective constitution of a thing" in whose context human life and moral survival are effected.

B. CONSTITUTION OF THINGS

The second area which has a decided influence on moral good and evil is precisely the objective constitution of things. For man is born, and he develops in a naturally-communal environment. And without this environment, human life, in any order—and hence likewise in the moral order—would in general not be possible. The objective constitution of things which is likewise nature as society and as everything which was made by man in the cultural-creative process, is the necessary context of moral decisions, and it demands a special emphasis with respect to the dangers of moral subjectivism.[11]

The objective constitution of things can be examined in the light of spontaneous and "prescientific" cognitive data. Hence they are the kind of data which are proper to every man as one who normally uses his reason in everyday problems; and once given, they suffice for the constitution of a morally acting subject. But we can and should reach by means of a philosophical elucidation of the problem of moral good and evil toward a better organized metaphysical knowledge, so that we can establish the objective foundations of the moral order itself.

If we realize that in "prescientific" and spontaneous knowledge, nature and society are not an accidental creation of elements assembled in a disorderly way, but that they have their objective laws and structures, which manifest themselves in a more or less permanent and necessary activity, this conviction both grows and acquires fresh confirmation in a metaphysical analysis. One of the first and most basic philosophical laws established in the area of metaphysics is the thesis about the intelligibility of things. The point here is that equally the existence of particular beings taken analogically, as well as the commensurable content of the existence of these same beings, is somehow capable of being read by our intellect and in certain limits, understood (the limits in their dependence on the intellect and the state of investigations of both general and particular sciences can proceed almost to infinity). Being is known by us when it expresses itself in the form of first principles: Identity, Non-Contradiction, Sufficient Reason, Finality. If indeed these primary principles are only an epistemological expression of the same thing and if these principles constitute the ultimate basis for intelligible knowledge; and if because of them knowledge in general is possible (for whatever we know is being), then being in itself is rational and intelligible and the laws of being are the laws of our thinking. The totality of intellectual knowledge concerns being, and there is nothing in thought that somehow did not come from being. In other words, the intellect can carry out its cognitive operations only when it is specifically joined to being. Everything which reveals itself in the intellect, constitutes its real content or it somehow comes from it. Hence, if the accumulation of cognitive activities is called rational life, this rationality, above all, serves being as the object of intellectual knowledge.

The objective constitution of a thing, understood analogically as being, therefore, furnishes our thinking, laws and cognitive contents. Nothing which we cognitively experience in a subject is independent of the objective constitution of a thing. For our intellect neither creates nor constructs the contents in an act of knowledge; rather, it "receives" them from the thing. In essence, our knowledge is the "receptacle" of the contents of the objective constitution of a thing. Thus there is no danger of subjectivism in our really experienced moral life, since we live by objective contents and laws of being. Subjectivism can appear along with philosophical explanation and interpretation of moral experience. But philosophical explanation and justification is not an experienced moral fact. It is only its interpretation that is dependent on the entirety of the system.

In the arrangement of the things themselves, we should emphasize on the one hand, the analogy of concrete beings, their uniqueness, specificity, their non-schematization—in a word, their individuality. And, on the other hand, keeping in mind the impossibility of our profound, individual, conceptual knowledge of concrete particulars, and at the same time the impossibility of uncovering individual ontic structures, and as a result—how very important—of individual inclinations and purposes (especially with people), we must use universal, univocal concepts in the formation of "laws" as judgments about being.

Since the analogical state of existence reveals itself in the fact that being cannot be understood monistically but only pluralistically—which is synonymous with the statement of the existence of independent and undivided beings—every essentially-concrete being is different from another being. It is an essentially-concrete distinct being. Even within the extent of one so-called ontic class or "kind," there is no ontic univocity but there exists a substantial, essentially-concrete separateness. But separately essentially-concrete ontical objects create through categorical, necessary and transcendental relations, a relative and analogical oneness and they point, at the same time, to their ultimate common source of origin, to its ultimate ideal or model. For at the moment when we realize that multiple, changing, analogous being is rational and this rationality identifies itself with existence itself, we observe the basis for the fundamental presentation of the questions: whether such an analogical being is a being which ultimately explains itself and its rationality; whether it is also rather a being which comes from such a being which is a pure intellect? When we observe that essences of things are not the reason for their existence and that their existence itself is generated and can be lost, we must admit that it comes from another being, who is Absolute Existence. And for the same reason, since the intellect is derived from it, being is intelligible. The Absolute-Being, as the source of all contingent and analogical beings, is most intelligible in itself. Hence it is the kind of being in which ultimately the composition of a cognitive power and knowing of the object disappears. Hence the Absolute is the Intellect itself, which is the object of his knowledge; and he knows himself in himself and everything which is derived from him as accidental, multiple, composite, and analogical.

Appearing before us in metaphysical knowledge, the composition of analogical beings as intelligible beings, orders us further to call attention to the essential, analogical structure of individually-separately existing persons and things. If particular beings are essentially-analogical, it means that they are composed of the most various elements, which create in each being one unity which is like a network of real and necessary relations. A concrete composition of relation means an inclination to this and no other activity. The ordering of being to activity and through it, to a commensurate realization for a given nature of good can be recognized as a foundation of a natural law of particular beings. In every being, this law is specific, distinct and analogical, just as the composition of real relations that constitute being itself is specific, distinct and analogical. However, in spite of the different, distinct existence of natural law so understood (more precisely: its foundation), we notice a proportional common or analogical inclination of various beings (in particular of persons), as existence itself is analogically common.

By grasping the natural inclinations to activity, and realizing through them suitable goods of a given nature, in common understandings and judgments, we can form in our knowledge, a judgment-law about the nature of beings belonging to various classes. And in our conduct, and hence in a conscious and free decision, we must reckon with the nature of a given being or classes of beings, from their inclinations and purpose. Such a being-object can be everything in our conduct and acts of decisions: from material objects all the way to the world of people, even ourselves and our spontaneous, as well as reflective, cognitive acts, to our own acts of love. For we can take everything as the object of our practical knowledge and our acts of decision. By undertaking these very decisions, we must reckon with the nature of object-beings, in whose presence we are acting.

C. CONSTITUTION OF IDEA—ETERNAL LAW

The third area in which we arrive at a philosophical understanding of morality and of deficiencies which occur in it or of moral evil, is the existence of the Absolute as the ruler of the world or the existence of so-called Divine Law from time immemorial which is the prototype of things themselves. So understood, Divine Law—according to St. Augustine—is the ordering of divine wisdom, insofar as it is the ultimate ruler of all acts and movements and hence, it so created things that, as the result of their substantial construction, they hasten towards commensurate goals which have been assigned them. Hence from time immemorial, Divine Law is the ultimate ontic reason of suitable essential structures, their inclinations, their link with their own purposes. Philosophical knowledge, both metaphysical as well as ethical, cannot ignore Divine Law as the ultimate ontic reason of the structure, inclinations and purposes of really existing things.

St. Thomas, who kept in mind the universal order of the derivation of things from God, when he was writing the *Summa Theologiae* (where he availed himself of the general Neoplatonic theme: the derivation of things from the First Principle), first pointed to the eternal Divine Law. Next, he gave a short, almost outlined explanation of Natural Law and he affirmed that it is only a "participation" in Eternal Law but he did not explain any further on what this participation depends. In philosophical knowledge, however, (contrary to theological knowledge as presented by St. Thomas), we direct our attention, above all, to existing things themselves and we point to God as a final, non-contradictory reason for existence and being. A rejection of God's existence leads to contradiction in the ultimate explanation of the world. Hence, God is the ultimate cause of the intelligibility of things and of their inclinations and purposes.

In considering the Eternal Divine Law as the ultimate basis for the intelligibility of things and, thereby, also the highest law of moral conduct, we can assert that a failure to reckon in our decisions with objective nature and inclinations of beings—which we take as the object of our activity—is, ultimately and basically, a failure to reckon with the Eternal Divine Law as the ultimate reason of the existence of things (but it may not, if someone does not realize the connection which exists between them). And, on the other hand, to reckon in the undertaking of moral decisions with nature, the inclinations and purposes of things—especially when these beings are human persons—is, at the same time, an affirmation of the Eternal Divine

Law. It is, at the same time, an affirmation of God as the ultimate cause of contingent beings. For an affirmation or a transgression of the Eternal Divine Law does not take place in an abstraction and directly in relation to God Himself. Rather, it takes place through the composition of things (in the wide sense of the word, including in it—above all—persons)[12] with which we either do or do not reckon in our conduct. God appears as the ultimate law of our conduct insofar as He is the Creator and Ruler of things.

Obviously, the question here is about the purely natural motives of our moral conduct. For there can, and do come into being, supernatural motives for our moral decisions.[13] God himself can intervene in human life. According to Catholic theology, such an event took place when God became man in the Person of Jesus Christ. In such a context, the question of God as a law of moral conduct acquires completely different dimensions. The contact between God and man becomes, in such a case, a personal and direct contact, insofar as he himself "dwells within us" and directs human conscience from within: "God, Who created the world and everything in it, he who is Lord of heaven and earth, does not dwell in temples built by human hands and he does not accept service from human hands, as if it were something he needed because he himself gives life and breath to all and all . . . He is not far from each one of us because in him we live and move and exist" (Acts, XVII, 24). We are dealing here with supernatural motives and rules of human decisions.

The theory of such conduct is moral theology which takes into account supernatural contexts of human activity.

We, however, are basically interested in the purely natural motives of human decisions, as well as in the natural elements of moral acts, since supernatural elements cannot annihilate everything that is natural.[14] This obviously does not mean that the supernatural cannot ennoble all that which is natural.

After having distinguished a threefold area of moral life and, hence, the subject of moral decisions, their objectification in the form of the composition of things, as well as their ultimate reason of intelligibility, who is the Absolute, understood as the Eternal Divine Law, we can in conclusion examine now more closely the structure of the moral act.

II. MORAL BEING

Just as we distinguish in the theoretical order a fundamental understanding of being in existential judgments: first, the clarification of the content of being in the form of primary principle-judgments, such as Identity, Non-Contradiction, and Sufficient Reason, next, the particularization of such a type of knowledge in the form of a very differentiated particular knowledge, so, likewise, in the order of practical knowledge we can discern a specific, analogical unity of various cognitive acts which are connected with activity. If we should wish perhaps to bring into relief, somewhat artificially, a parallel between both kinds of knowledge (theoretical and practical knowledge), we would notice that the role of understanding being and first foundations here—in the practical order—is filled by judgment. This judgment is the expression and enlightenment of one by natural law, "Good should be done," as well as *synderesis* as the complex of first foundations of moral conduct. Natural law and *synderesis* can be developed in the form of general ethics as a more or less reflected upon and established theory of moral conduct. For man can possess his own prescientific ethics, understood as a living, practical wisdom of moral conduct. Ethics, understood in a very general way can be the foundation for stating concrete judgments concerning proper conduct with relation to this or that object-thing.

Having outlined the parallel of theoretical and practical knowledge, as well as the moral syllogism which has been presented below, we must take into account that we are dealing with a certain schema which helps only to understand the mechanics of a decision and of explaining the structure of a moral act. However, we cannot apply this schema directly to a living moral activity which is incomparably richer and more complicated. Above all, in the case of human cognition, it is not as if we are dealing separately with intellectual knowledge and acts of the will. For we use and, sometimes, to a preponderant degree, elements of sensible knowledge, of our feelings and passions. In great measure, we are "animals" and the mechanics of knowing and acting, which are proper to animals, are likewise our lot. Obviously, they are sublimated by the very fact that this type of knowledge is joined with intellectual and volitional activity, but their sublimation[15] is, as yet, not their negation.

In various types of manuals which are devoted to discussions of ethics or moral theology, moral choice is presented as a kind of object of a deductive method. The described schema proceeds in the following manner:
(a) natural law and first principles of moral law called *synderesis* (b) ethics or moral theology or also living wisdom and moral experience (c) knowledge of the nature of the object of moral decision, (d) concrete act of practically-practical act of the intellect: "Do" or "Do not do," in relation to a concretely viewed object which appears as a moral good or its denial.

From among the four would-be mentioned premises, the first two (natural law, along with *synderesis* and ethics), would constitute the major premise of a moral syllogism. The knowledge of the nature of the object in concrete conditions would constitute the minor premise. The conclusion of the moral syllogism would be a practically-practical judgment: "Do" or "Do not do."

The syllogism of a moral decision which has been presented here is in a-greement with the schema which explains, for example, an outlined conception of knowledge which comes from Aristotle's *Second Analytics:* unity and, at the same time, a structure of a practical knowledge. But, at the same time, this schema can be very deceptive if we should wish to conceive our moral life on the model of scientific living and of a specified concept of science. For, as it is known, even in the area of science (beyond the formal disciplines), there is no purely deductive knowledge. All the more, there neither is, nor can there be, a purely deductive knowledge in the control of moral conduct. For especially in the area of human moral behavior, there occurs a complication and appearance of the most varied structures, motives and cognitive and desiring acts. Even if man's knowledge is only functional as an indication of the ontic unity of a particular person, nevertheless, in a single cognitive function—as in one current of a great river—there stand out very differentiated structures and currents which are dependent not only on the object of its character but also, on the knowing subject itself, on its structure, inclination, behavior etc. The question here, of course, is about practical knowledge and, hence, knowledge that is essentially linked with man's activity as an autonomous being. For this reason, when we order the functional knowledge of man to activity, of its nature, it finds itself under a stronger influence of sensible perception than what takes place in scientific theoretical knowledge.

Cognitive sensible perception is further strengthened in a person who is weighing a decision, especially an important experienced one, by the flow of the activity of instincts. At that time instances can and often do happen so that the knowledge which is to warrant a proposed decision is obscured and sometimes nullified. And hence—if we use the outline which we had previously presented, in so-called premises of acts of conscience (or a higher motivating knowledge), there sometimes occurs a so-called knowledge of the nature of the thing, its internal relations, its purposeful relations, its relations to Eternal Law. But there can and usually does follow an immediate decision-act which, by the fact of a diminished reflective consciousness becomes a morally diminished deed, to the extent to which there was a lack of knowledge of variously directed relations, which *de facto* enter into the object-good of moral acitvity.

A diminution of a moral deed also takes place sometimes in relation to the greatest pressure of our emotions and passions, which do not allow the intellect a more calm examination in a situation but which incline, through the will, to the giving of the kind of practical judgment which follows the line of emotions or internal passion. These diminished moral deeds appear very frequently in our moral life and they are the rule rather than the exception in human activity. For a right moral decision, we must train ourselves in self-control and reflection, since the pressure of biological forces and a lack of spiritual control are by nature very great. This is why we cannot underestimate the role of the irrational elements in the analysis and explanation of a moral decision. This means that in a concrete situation, it is exceedingly difficult to outline to what extent an undertaken decision was truly free and to what extent the choice followed the overpowering of irrational aspects.

In spite of this, in an analysis of moral good and evil, we should take into consideration somewhat ideal states, which have been "distilled" from "preconscious" and sub-conscious pressures, because in a contrary case, we could never realize the essence of a moral choice and the nature of good and evil.

Hence, in an ideal moral act and, therefore, where we have a full intellectual consciousness flowing from a knowledge of the nature of good, which "stands before me" for choice and a complete freedom (concretely, this is an extremely difficult thing to verify and to what extent we have freed ourselves of constraining elements and, for this reason, we can only speak here of a moral certainty), we can observe the following agreements or disagreements with the essential elements of our conduct:

1. Agreement of our free choice of the will with the act of the intellect, a so-called practically-practical judgment. This agreement exists always. Only cases of mental sickness can break the bond of the act of choice and a practical judgment because a practical judgment and an act of free choice constitute one being of a moral decision. There is no moral decision without the mutual existence of a judgment of the practical reason as an element constituting an act of decision. This judgment determines the content of the act and of the act of the will which decides whether a given judgment of the practical intellect is actually the final judgment that truly determines to this and no other kind of conduct. It is also for this reason that the fundamental thing is precisely the rectitude of the will of its right freedom which can increase or diminish along with a formation in good or also an abandonment of this training.

2. The agreement of our practical judgment with the theoretical judgment about the thing-good or with a knowledge of the nature of the thing, its inclination or its purposes. Hence, a knowledge of the object-good in the presence of which we undertake a decision is something very important for moral good and evil. For I cannot "use" an object-good inconsistently with its nature, purpose, inclinations especially—and above all in the area of morality—when this object is a human person: I myself or my neighbor.

3. If my practical judgment which impels me to make a decision which

is bound with a theoretical knowledge that indicates, more or less exactly, the nature of thing-good, its inclination and purpose, is ultimately in agreement with the inclinations of the thing itself and its purpose, then, it is likewise in agreement with Eternal Divine Law or the disposition of divine ideas about a given thing. Then, too, my deed is morally good because there is evident a relation of agreement (a) of a free choice with practical judgment, (b) of a practical judgment with a theoretical judgment about the nature of thing-good, its inclinations and its purposes, (c) of the nature of the thing itself with the disposition of divine ideas or the Eternal Divine Law. Undertaking such a decision, I realize natural law: "Good should be done" in a concrete case which discloses itself to me as a good. I actualize my personal potentiality by enriching myself with real good. I affirm good objectively as the ultimate reason for the intelligibility of things.

On the other hand, concrete moral evil emerges in the lack of agreement between elements of a moral composition. These absences present themselves:

(a) In the inadequate knowledge of a thing's nature, its inclination and its purposes. Even though in itself, it is a fundamentally intellectual evil not a moral one, nevertheless, this lack of a cognitive—even a theoretical agreement with the nature of things (precisely of a human person as the chief object of moral behavior), can bear the character of moral evil, while theoretical knowledge already becomes for me, a kind of premise or motive for making a practical judgment. And when we recognize the nature of a thing in the perspective of conduct, the effort of the cognitive agreement must be proportional to the weight of the undertaken decisions.

(b) If, in the resulting theoretical failure to recognize the nature of a thing-good, there is also lacking a correct practical judgment about our conduct in the presence of an observed good, then there is also no moral evil but only an intellectual error—insofar, clearly, as the theoretical knowledge was not true in an uncommitted way and insofar as the union of a practical judgment with theoretical knowledge was essential and necessary.

(c) If there is a proper cognition of the nature of the good-object, its inclinations and purposes, and the practical judgment which results from the influence of some kind of causes of a depraved will is not in agreement with the nature of the good-object, then, there is a lack of agreement of our practical conduct with the object-good. At the same time, there is a lack of agreement of practical cognition with the theoretical. *This lack of agreement is a depravity from within man* who makes a decision in the presence of an object-good which presents itself to him. This inner distortion of personality constitutes the essence of moral evil. It is an expression of disagreement between man's conduct and the nature of the thing itself and its eternal and ulitmate guarantee: the Absolute.

Is moral evil, therefore, which is commonly called sin, an "offense" against this Absolute-God? Likewise, in the light of the considerations we have made here, as well as taking into consideration the very expression "offense"—we can form the conviction, without any further difficulty, that in this supposition, we are using metanomic language, which is proper, after all, in the area of various theologies. Of course, metanomy—or if we consider the question in an ever more general sense—metaphorical analogy has its own rules of usage in a specified area of knowledge. But rules of usage of metaphorical analogy in the field of theology are clearly delineated and they amount to this: namely that no metaphor used in biblical and theological language is an independent, cognitive intervention but it enters into the context of transcendental analogy and the analogy of faith. However, in spite of these provisos, metaphorical expressions do not give any clear-cut cognitive pictures; neither is theoretical knowledge their exclusive purpose. Principally, the role of metaphorical analogy leads to evoking in man certain determinate positions in the presence of the Transcedent Being (God), which involve not only man's intellect but also his emotional aspect.,

Hence in the expression "offense against God," the question is about the development in man of such attitudes which would make difficult the realization of evil in relation to very important consequences linked with the presence of evil in a human subject. For a subject which is afflicted with moral evil becomes incapable of bringing forth from itself personal acts which are necessary, according to the date of faith, for human development or also "spiritual life."

Strictly speaking, however, moral evil as evil does not fulfill a function of transcendence, and it strikes a blow only at the subject and not at God. Since it is a lack, it does not perform the function of any causative or proper reason or goal, and hence of those reasons that bind one being with another. If, however, it is possible to speak about an "offense against God," it is only indirectly said, insofar, namely, as the human person burdened with evil becomes incapable of performing specific good acts, in this way, deforms itself and, at the same time, makes itself incompatible with the "eternal idea" which the Absolute has of it. Such an incompatibility of an accidental being—caused by it freely—with the Absolute, constitutes, in the spiritual order, a deep confusion.

Moral evil, as every evil, does not exist through its own existence but through the existence of the subject in which it resides. For this reason, it cannot be, of itself, an object either of any cognitive endeavors or also of others that are connected with activity. The subject himself as the bearer of evil is the object of equally cognitive and, in a certain sense, implementing endeavors. For this reason, we cannot directly fight evil without simultaneously fighting, in some measure, the subject itself of this evil. For if evil is not a being, then only the subject-bearer of evil exists as being. Accordingly, a positive battle with evil is, above all, a battle with an already weakened subject which carries deficiencies within himself—namely evil. A total eradication of evil is possible only through the annihilation of the subject. As long as the subject exists composed in its structure, there can always appear deficiencies in him. Hence a direct and immediate battle with evil is an unsuccessful trial of the hypostasizing of evil, and it really strikes, above all, at the subject as the bearer of evil. Meanwhile, the subject of evil is a being and thus, good. A direct battle with evil (always concrete) would cause more harm than good because it would actually strike at being and good. Hence from a philosophical point of view, it is proper not so much to remove evil (for only that which exists can be removed and not that which does not exist), as to strive for good as well as the entirety and perfection of the thing-subject.[16] Evil can be "fought" through a healing of the subject and by providing it with goods which it does not possess. And perhaps against this background we can understand properly the theory and precept of the Gospel of non-resistance to evil.

CHAPTER IX

MAN AND SOCIETY

The theme suggested in the title includes a series of questions which concern the personal structure of man, insofar as it guarantees a basis for the organization of community, and the various mutual relations between society and the individual, whose comprehensive treatment would demand an extensive monograph. Hence we must necessarily make certain limitations with the result, that the basic problem can be expressed in the form of a question: Whether and under what conditions does a community guarantee personal development? Above all, the question here is a consideration of the ontic conditions of the mutual relation between the individual and society, by way of an analysis of (a) the ego—of a being that is open to a "Thou" and "we," (b) the essential character of community, as well as (c) the basis for a social common bond, which is called "common good." The general answer to the problem formulated in this way is contained in the familiar concept of personalism. It seems, however, that we should emphasize more strongly than it has been done to date, the organic connection between the theory of society and the concept of ego, which is open to a "Thou" and "we," as well as that of common good.

I. ONTIC CONDITIONS FOR THE RELATION BETWEEN INDIVIDUAL AND SOCIETY

In contemporary philosophy, we can observe a special growth of interest in the problematic of man, particularly in his social conditionings. The problems were investigated by J. Maritain and E. Mounier, as well as by contemporary existentialists (M. Heidegger, K. Jaspers, G. Marcel, J.P. Sartre,

237

L. Lavelle, R. LeSenne). However, Kierkegaard had already directed attention to the existence of man in reaction to the absolute idealism of Hegel. Kierkegaard declared himself against the functionalization and objectification of man—he emphasized man's individuality which manifested itself particularly in religious experiences.

Just as Kierkegaard—although independently of him—G. Marcel came out against the functionalization of human existence. He discredited the view of the human individual who, "in his own eyes and in those of others, presents himself exclusively as an agglomeration or accumulation of functions."[1] This position is also common to other existentialists, e.g., Sartre and Camus. For the human person does not lend himself to be reduced exclusively to a social function, i.e., the fact of being a clerk, a priest, a doctor, a laborer, a professor etc. The existentialists also emphasize the distinctness of the human person in relation to nature. For man is someone "for-himself," even though "from nature," man "exists" (*sistit ex,*) even more—man constantly exceeds his limits; he performs acts of transcendence with relation to nature and himself.

Personalistic theories, especially those of Maritain and Mounier distinguish between an individual and a person. They call attention to the fact that man's individuality alone, which is a function of matter, does not separate him with respect to a social group, but it subordinates this group in imitation of a biological cell to the entire organism. On the other hand, man as a person surpasses the community which should be subordinated to him.

The problematic of man which is outlined in personalistic theories demands, however, a renewed consideration, since the problem of the relation of an individual to society is always current and vital and it possesses a significant, practical meaning. A renewed and better organized linkage of this problematic with the tradition of classical philosophical thought also appears necessary.

A. AN OPEN EGO

The theory of a personal being possesses its own rich history and it extends to the earliest philosophical concepts on the subject of man. In particular, Plato's considerations, Aristotle's analyses and the investigations of St. Augustine and the Church Fathers—which attempted to integrate Christian faith with Neoplatonic speculations and, this, against the background of Christological disputes—have an important meaning for the establishment of personal being. Contemporary concepts of philosophers, especially of the phenomenologists, have cast light on the understanding of man as a subject, who performs his actions both in relation to the world and to another person who is a partner in human experiences; and also finally, in relation to the kind of community about which we can say "we."[2] These considerations complete the kind of picture of the human person which the tradition of classical philosophy has outlined.

Hence, keeping in mind the structure of personal and, especially, of human reality, as well as the basic consequences of the accepted fundamental structure, (which is the object of a separate study), we must also emphasize in the personal "I," those moments that stand at the basis of interpersonal, as well as of general-communal relations, in the broadest sense of the word. For these moments are closely connected with their manifestation of our psychic-personal living. By pointing to these very characteristic manifestations, we can detect in the very structure of personal existence—or at least we can postulate—such states which do not contradict these characteristic ways of existing on the level of "I-world," "I-Thou" and "I-we." By anticipating somewhat the results of our considerations and by basing ourselves on our previously developed analyses of the structure of the human being and its characteristic manifestation in the order of knowledge and desire, we must now state that they resolve themselves into a personal "openness" of man. This is an openness with respect to the possibility of "communicating" in the order of being, with which we have come into contact in our knowing and loving. These ultimately find their expression in our acts of decision. This assertion recurs constantly as a leitmotif of all the considerations which have been deveolped here. Obviously, however, it does not dispense us from the obligation of reflecting on these matters, on the canvas of the analysis of man from the perspective of society.

As we have already said more than once, man is born into the world; he is brought up, matures and dies. He is thrown into the world without his consent. He is immersed in the world to the degree that he draws from the world, all his various vital powers, not only for his biological life but also for his psycho-spiritual life.

Without the world, man would not come to a self-knowledge; he would not be able to become aware of himself.[3] The material world is necessary, not only for an "awakening" of his spirit, but it is constantly necessary to him for his development. And even though man is immersed in the world— as M. Heidegger has observed—he uses the world of things as a means for himself and for self-expression. Nevertheless, in his attitude of "using"[4] things, he conducts himself differently than animals. Only man keeps a distance from the world of things. He communicates with things "adequately":[5] he has regard for the structure of things and for their existence, that is to say, he communicates with the world under the aspect of his being.

For the animal, the world is its surroundings, since it is a kind of extension of its organism, which the animal knows concretely and is unerringly able to utilize for its "own" individual or specific nature. On the other hand, in order to be able to use the world for his own or specific nature, man must first know a thing, that it exists and that it has some sort of ontic structure, whose use may be correct or wrong or erroneous, striking at the very reality of the individual. Man communicates with the world not as with closed and comprehensively adapted surroundings, whose use he knows unerringly, but as with a "world" which is a stranger to him, a collection of things, of entities which he can utilize only after he has come to know them; at least after a most general understanding of their ontic structure. Hence, man is not limited to a segment of reality; he is open to all reality. This openness places the world of things as an "object", as something which is distinct from the "I." And even though the awareness of one's "I" as something radically distant from the world of things takes place through the world, through grasping the contact of things which they have with me, this contact is fundamentally a contact with being. The fact that a thing exists and has a well-defined structure is, for me, the basis for entering into a closer contact with it. It permits me to be better aware of my own individuality. It allows me to recognize the "I," not only as the *centrum* but also as the subject of my activity, through which I communicate with the world which is different from the "I."

Undoubtedly, "I," in such a measure, amounts to self-cognition, in which I communicate with the world from the aspect of its entity and of a reality of its most varied particularization—manifesting itself in the different forms of culture, which constantly grows in the history of mankind. If man could—*dato non concesso*—divest himself of his presence in the world, by that very fact, he would divest himself (in a specified way), of the feeling of his own self, which testifies to his own reliance on those contents which constitute what we call "the world." But in like manner, the "immersing" of oneself in the world with the arrangement of the world's contents for my own "I" as for a subject, causes an impoverishment of my own "I" and a failure to attain the world of things as a being. A lack of reference of the world to the "I," an absence of an ontic connection testifies—if we can express it so—to a "diminution of both the 'I' as well as the world in which we are immersed."[6] The kind of tension that exists between the world and the "I" is thus a fundamentally human area, while the communication between "I" as the center and subject and the world is a *communication of being and hence of that through which something exists and it is something defined in itself, which must be known so that it could be used.*

And yet, man does not consider the world in which he lives and the whole of nature as partner of his dialogue. Even though it can happen in mythology or poetry, that the world of things (the world of nature) is personified and there is established a human dialogue with such a personified world on the basis of a partnership, nevertheless all this takes place in the name of an agreed upon fiction. Dialogue or a mutual communication of intellectually-knowable contents (*dia-logos*) is achieved between "I" and "Thou," with the result that "Thou" is apprehended as another "I" or as a being in itself and for itself—as another person. For the personal "Thou" possesses all these features which we distinguish in an analysis of the self as a personal being.[7] And just as in an analysis of my own personal being, I distinguish "I" as the subject and performer of my acts by the fact that these acts are precisely a coordinated "I," since I "begot" them from myself—and hence, I treat myself as a subjective being in the full sense of the word—in the same way, I observe all these moments in another "Thou." I treat another person as an autonomous subject of all the acts of which "Thou" is the source and final end. Hence he is the same kind of personal being, a being in itself and for itself as an "I." "Thou" is another "I" with whom contact and communication are accomplished precisely on the basis of recognizing "Thou" as another "I." And hence everything which I experience in the world, so, too, the "Thou" experiences, and just as "I" am open so, likewise, is "Thou" open. This is why all the acquired experience and wealth can be communicated and transmitted in a specifically personal way through acts of knowledge and love to another "Thou." And because he is a being in and for himself, he is, at the same time, his own end in his personal activity for the "I." In a word, another "Thou" is an equal partner for "I," not as a world of things which is, for us, an impersonal world, a "something," as M. Buber said—an "It" a being in itself but not for itself.

Our partnership with another "Thou," understood strictly personally and not as that of an object is accomplished on the basis of an openness, particularly in a three-fold area: knowledge, love and freedom. Even the word "dialogue" points to the possibility of one's communicating an intellectual content. And just as the world which is before me is not closed in its knowable order but it is open to my cognitive faculties and I can "read" this world through my acts of knowing and I can make my own these contents which constitute the ontic structure of the world and I can state these contents or inform myself of them, in the same way, I can present these contents and express them, by means of signs, to another person, another "Thou." The communication of known contents is human speech which constitutes the essential means of interpersonal communication. As an inter-human communicational "vehicle," speech presupposes, before all, (a) an act of knowledge (b) a readiness to transmit these contents to another person and (c) an act of factual transmitting through the use of a system of conventional signs.

In the act of knowledge, as we know, there takes place an aspective union of a knowing subject with the object, by grasping a desirable (examined) substance of a thing. Thinking is precisely the vivifying in the soul of the meanings of known things. These meanings which are the natural signs of things (which have been grasped in an appropriate way), we express externally, through suitable conventional signs of a given language. By communicating through conventional signs we can, by means of them, arouse in another's intellect, the same meanings which we are entertaining. We must only wish to disclose in our own knowing apparatus (the intellect), the meanings and to transmit them, through conventional signs, to another person. In the process of communication, "I" and "Thou" are open, both in relation to each other's partner, as well as in relation to the transmitted contents (cognitively grasped meanings). At the basis of communication (as also in the relation of being in the world), there is a being but one which is not fully apprehended. For not only are the communicated cognitive contents a kind of existing contents (as we have shown in the Chapter, "Man and Knowledge"), but two independent subjects communicate these contents to each other, since they are beings in themselves and for themselves.

Besides a cognitive communication of knowledge between "I" and "Thou," there also exists the possibility of communicating mutual love.[8] This love is understood not only as an attraction in a previously known object, not only as a dynamic disposition of another to do good and to communicate with him under the aspect of goodness (love understood in this sense as the communicating of a good to another is, at the same time, the communicating of being, if being and good are interchangeable, transcendental values), but it is also the offering of an "I" to a "Thou." The moment of offering oneself to another person is the most sublime moment of the act of love, since it is an expression of the highest degree of existential communication.[9] For the subject who is a person (a most perfect being because he is a being in itself and for itself) offers himself to another person and encounters, in the perfect act of love, a similar offering of another "Thou" to the "I." Hence, there arises a characteristic manner of existence between "I" and "Thou," a manner of being "for another," through which "I" offers himself to another and, in meeting with a similar act from the side of the "Thou" he not only does not lose any of his inner riches but, contrarily, he enriches himself in everything which the other person has acquired and what he personally presents.[10] In the act of love the "personally-existential openness reaches its zenith, since there occurs here another person's communication, not only of his objective, existential, intentional and cognitive contents that have arisen as the result of an individual person's work, but something more, the offering of the very person's subject (of the very being) who, while presenting himself to another person, *adopts the manner of being-living-for-another-person.*"

In like manner, the possibility of communicating cognitively, and even further, the possibility of begetting an act of love as an inner liking, acting and offering of oneself presupposes a person's spiritual freedom. It manifests itself in that communication in its cognitive aspect and even more so, as an act of love is, in one way or another, a freely willed "wanting" by a personal subject. No one can force me to cognitive communication and even less so, to communicate in love. For this is a matter of my freedom which I exercise in one way or another, with respect to another person—obviously, presupposing in like manner, the freedom of another person, who may not wish to communicate in one way or another. This freedom which is the basis and manner of communicating with another person demands a mutual trust, a respect for the freedom of the other person and a real "encounter." Undoubtedly, we are using here a metonymical language but it lends itself exactly to the expression of those interpersonal states that arise in line with the "I-Thou" relationship.

To elucidate the manner of being for another person, we accept hypothetically the states which are extremely opposed to those which we have described above. Having accepted the possibility of the existence of a "closed" person (obviously, this is impossible from the side of the ontic structure, even though from the side of psychological activity, there can happen to be a far-reaching restriction of openness and even an inhibition of interpersonal communication), one can speak of meeting men, for whom there is no other "Thou" and there is no dialogue. There is only a constant and permanent "monologue" (and again, the monologue is already a dialogue with a fictitious "Thou"). Such a conceivable personal being would see the unique goal of activity only in himself and all others would be treated only as a thing, as an "it," as a means to an end. In such a case, there would not be another as an authentic partner.[11] The result would be that the "I" of such a person would become increasingly enclosed; it would become impoverished and would approach a psychical degeneration because there would be a lack of communication on the personal level—which uniquely actuates and arouses development of the dynamism of man's personal being.

On the other hand, if we were to accept an inordinately open personal being, which would have no regard for itself but would completely "hang" on the "Thou," a different consequence would follow. A total forgetting of oneself with a complete subservience to the other person would be, as a matter of fact, a state in which "I" has nothing more to express to the other person. For one who constantly searches for another, while forgetting about himself, cannot find the other, since he has nothing to offer to the other, for he does not possess a developed, personal *centrum*. He does not possess an "I" as a distinct personal countenance, constantly living for another person. Having lost his own "I," he cannot gain another real "Thou" whom one encounters in a partnership—a meeting which presupposes a developed personal *centrum;* it presupposes an "I."

We have presented obviously extreme examples which have, for their objective, the bringing into relief, the personal role of "I" and "Thou" and their mutual subordination, which does not negate the personal sphere. On the contrary, by establishing a way of being "for another," it adds to a stronger formation of a personal center and a personal subject as a being in itself and for itself. Eventually, both extremes destroy this person-subject centrum. For an encounter with another person, through acts of knowing and love in freedom, presupposes precisely a personal "I" who actualizes himself through interpersonal communication in the order of being.

"I-Thou" relations lead to a completely new form of interpersonal life, which can be called "we" and which is equivalent to a social form of living, that constitutes some kind of new, distinct, real and truly human way of life.[12] For it can happen that the "I-Thou" relations are a perfected form of egoism, called a "dual egoism," if they exclude the characteristic form "we," which depends on significant and broadened values of that which gave a basis for the form of living as "we-two." For it seems that there exist such values which cannot be realized in a pair; these values are common to a larger number of people and, for that reason, they have been called COMMON GOOD[13], whose constitution needs the entire collective body which constitutes "we." In addition, different persons can participate in such a created or commonly viewed "being-good" and, by participating, they bring about their own internally-personal development. Precisely because they have, as their aim, the development of their personal potentialities, we observe that it is impossible to develop them, either in isolation or as a pair (even though the interpersonal relations "I-Thou" do permit, to a greater degree, a development of fundamental, natural and personal inclinations than is possible in isolation). There arises the necessity of constituting a basic, social group and with its help, the establishment of a community which will enable not only the creation of objective values that surpass the potentiality of particular individuals (or groups: "I-Thou"), but also is a guarantee of an internal, personal development of particular individuals. In a word, the basis for the establishment of some kind of community is COMMON GOOD, which can be variously understood. Nevertheless, one understanding of common good (about which we will speak below) is necessary—specifically, the kind which becomes the goal of aspirations in inner-personal development of particular human individuals.

Values which surpass the possibility of particular human individuals are, undoubtedly, cognitive values, values in the sphere of human volitional-emotional acts, as well as values in the area of productive-creative activity.

The first ones stand at the basis of a science, understood in a sociological sense and, hence, of various social arrangements which are ordered to a scientific knowledge and an objective development of scientific thought, not merely for the use of only one person, but for the use of a great number of people, even for generations of people. For the basis for human welfare and progress are, fundamentally, cognitive achievements, especially scientific. Scientific progress which takes place, before all, in its specializations surpasses the capability not only of an individual man, but even of smaller social groups. Scientific progress, in its transmission to the next generations demands collective effort in the attainment and consolidation of theoretical achievements. For this reason, too, value and genuine good which flow from scientific knowledge are something universal communal, something that exceeds the possibility, production, and attainment by one individual. Hence, a communally existing form like "we" is necessary—a form which has for its object a realization of scientifically-knowing value.

In like manner, the good will of an individual man is not enough for the realization of a good—even if a purely moral good—as, for example, of a communal justice, living in peace, the liquidation of threats from the side of biology, as well as any kind of external agents. Only a society can effectively guarantee the realization of an interhuman moral good.

Finally, the entire area of creativity, which is linked with industry and technology, clearly exceeds the possibility of an individual and his/her particular good. Everything that is the product of human work (both intellectual and physical) is a common good that could not have arisen without the form of living in which people perceive themselves as "we" who have, as their goal, a common good that transcends particular and individual goods.

Above all, a man's birth, his upbringing, his development and attainment of human perfection, within the limits available to man are possible only in the branches of the various forms of communal existence. In this connection, community becomes the form of personal existence, linked with the development and perfection of the person, in a purely and clearly personal order. Obviously, this does not prevent the same society from guaranteeing man's life, even as a biological individual, which can be more clearly observed in highly organized communities.

However, the development of the personal "I" takes place through the relations, "I-Thou," which presuppose a personal "openness" of a person and which enrich man and establish more securely an existential communication than the relations "I-world." This is so because these relations guarantee a communication of two beings in themselves and with themselves because the relation "I-we" makes possible a communication in common good, which is the only good (at least in the highest understanding of common good), not antagonistic to community. If "I-Thou" relations have regard for another person as person, then "I-we" relations allow a participation in common good, for insofar as a set of created values, it is the necessary means for authentic human life. Insofar as it is a form which perfects personal being, through an enrichment in the order of intellect, will and creative powers, and finally, insofar as it is a common good, which has been objectivated and understood as a goal of all spiritual aspiration, it makes possible the ultimate fulfillment of the human person.

These various aspects of realizing a common good must be assured by society, which is understood as perfect (possibly) expression of what is called "we." It is here that individual persons participate in a common good, not by virtue of some external "allocation," but by a subjective participation in a common responsibility for a realized good. A purely material participation in the production of a material or materially-spiritual good is not enough. This participation in virtue of some kind of distributive justice is essential, but it does not as yet create the kind of community or society which is the real expression of the category of the existence of a human "we." A participation in a good which is only material (on the strength of a real benefitting from common services), does not go beyond the relation of some part to the whole. An authentic human, personal participation, which is the realization and expression of "we," demands that the participating persons be really responsible for the integrity of the common good and that they have an influence on its realization. It further demands that by participating in common good, they could really make possible, two further aspects: (a) a common good as a form which would actually perfect an individual person (the point here is that man could, by participating in society, actually attain scientific, moral and creative qualifications), and (b) that there be no excluding of the possibility of realizing a common good—understood as the ultimate objective end of human aspirations.

Society as precisely an expression of the human category of the realization of "we" constitutes, ultimately, a "human environment," where a personal development is guaranteed. Here, too, individual persons participate as subjects by realizing that which constitutes the highest personal values and which ultimately opens it to the highest degree, by opening itself to an absolute, objective good, namely the Absolute Being.

The most fundamental form of social life which fulfills, in its order, the most perfect human category "we," is, from one point of view, the family; and from the other, the state.[14] Between these two communities, there exists a possibility of a whole series of social groups, which are organized from the point of view of some limited or more particular aspect of common good. Families, kinship, tribes, peoples, societies and trade unions' classes, are social formations located in the field created by two extremes, family-state. This is why so much attention is devoted to these two fundamental forms of social life.

In the normal course of events, the family is the basic social entity which begets and brings up man as a participant in wider forms of social life. The family is this basic "we" in which "I-Thou" relations take place and in which there already comes into existence the question of common good, which transcends the "I-Thou" relationship. The "I-Thou" relationship between husband and wife and next, between child and parents, is the first chance and, at the same time, the first and perhaps most important form of "personal opening" of oneself to the world, to another person and to common good. For it is only through the family (in the normal course of events), that man who arrives in this world has the possibility of surviving biologically, of forming within himself all the necessary biological factors of the psychical life and of the first contact with the being of things and being of human persons. Furthermore, it is only in the family that a man learns to perceive common good, transcending individual dimensions and through the family, that man becomes a participant in a community; he creates the first "we." For this reason, the role of the family in the formation of a personal attitude can never be overestimated, which does not mean that that there are no theories which irrationally are resolving the relation of the family to wider communities.

A perfect (obviously in the natural or innate course of things[15]) human community is the state, which constitutes the ultimate inborn human expression of "we." The theory of the state, its fundamental constituent elements, its foundation and end are too vast a problem that could be, somehow, determined here definitively and essentially, or even explained in a more detailed way. We are only interested in emphasizing the point that the state, as a perfect community has all the means to take care of the actual common good of the participants of a national community. In our times, this community is increasingly expanding and it has a tendency to outgrow national states and to envelop slowly all of mankind into some kind of future, universal model of a chief political system. This system differs greatly from the character of communities which will enter into the composition of the universal national community. Concerning these matters, we can only speak of a tendency that appears in the form of various kinds of supranational outgrowths which are the embryo of a future nationalistic human community.

B. THE DYNAMIZATION OF THE HUMAN PERSON

In an outlined general conception of an open person, insofar as it is the basis for a collective living, those moments interest us, above all, which determine its social character and can become a foundation for establishing the relation of "person-community." Usually when we say that man is a social being, we mean above all that since the human person is a contingent being and therefore a being endowed with potentialities, he is not in a position to actualize his "nature" differently than through his own activity and through the cooperation and help of other people—in other words, this full development of personal life can be attained only in a community.

Every independent, concrete, contingent being, who is the object of our empirico-intellectual knowledge, is a complex being, even though he is authentically and actually undivided. Understood in this way and with mental reference to his existential aspect, man is bound to his necessary and transcendental relations, which constitute him as one entity.[16] We detect in him a whole series of "component parts:" as for example, integral parts which constitute man's body; essential parts as matter and form (soul); substantial parts: substance and accidents, essence *(natura)* and concrete individual existence etc. It is especially important to call attention to two types of composition: one, of so-called "integrating parts," and the other, of substance and accidents. As a result of a composition of "substantial parts," the human organism finds itself in constant motion and flux of matter. Within the human organism arises a whole series of new cells and genes. The organism develops from an embryonic stage to full maturity, However, the development proceeds slowly. Likewise, since man is a composite being from this point of view, he is at the same time a particular individual substance, which acts through its properties or so-called "powers of acting." These are cognitive powers (intellect, as well as internal and external senses), volitional powers, concupiscible and irascible powers, which constitute the emotional-concupiscible side of man; the motor powers, along with the vegetative ones, which make biological living possible; the intake and assimilation of food, as well as reproduction.

The living-material conditionings are one of the aspects of the person's potentiality; at the same time, they explain the person's relationship to other persons. The human person is a concrete, individual *compositum,* in whom material-sensible, as well as rational-volitional elements constitute a specific unity—a dynamic unity that underlies the entire development and improvement. A slow, multi-sided and multi-staged and conditioned development of all the powers of human nature, a human existential "lack of self-reliance" which spans almost a quarter of man's life, make him subject to other persons. They also constitute one of the foundations of the fact of organizing human individuals into social groups of all kinds.

Endowed with potentialities, the whole of man's life embraces all kinds of aspects, as well as the character of interpersonal bonds which join man with all kinds of social groups; it is also correspondingly varied. That which is essential in every one of these bonds is the fact of interhuman interdependence in a successive arrival at the fulness of personal being of every human individual. For its entire complex structure constitutes a basis for the existence of the relation: "person-community." Although the human person constitutes a certain whole and complete "world-in-itself," nevertheless, he cannot develop himself (about which we have already spoken); he cannot realize his potentialities nor his powers which constitute the fulness of a "personal" world without cooperating with other persons.

It appears that an independent, human individual "creates himself" in the process of this many-sided interaction between persons. He is a "being-in-himself"—independent and complete—insofar as he is, at the same time, a "being-for-another," as well as a social being. The potentiality of human nature explains the essence of a common bond from the point of view of so-called internal causes, which constitute this particular being a concrete individual. But not only is the development of individual "portions" and of individual nature conditioned by the existence and participation of man in some kind of community, a personal development, a development of that which came to be called "I," needs this participation. By nature, man inherits only a disposition and natural inclinations which he must develop and transform by his work into a personal individuality. Intellectual, volitional, creative, religious and aesthetic potentialities are much more profound than natural potentialities. It is precisely when we have to deal with "nature" that we must deal at the same time with a stable source and, basically, with a well-ordered activity. For nature is a determining factor.

On the other hand, a person is freedom, as we can express it with certain emphasis. Freedom constitutes one of the essential manifestations of a personal being. For this reason a personal being must determine himself; he must actualize himself from within. But this cannot be achieved without participation in common good and the help of other people. Hence, for the actualization of personal life, for the development of knowledge, love, creativity, of finding and creating oneself through spiritual acts of a personal individuality, there is need for help which leads to a real participation in common good that is the basis for social life.

A fuller explanation of the nature of society as the "being-relation" among persons therefore additionally demands a consideration of the purpose, that is to say, of a common good as the ultimate reason for the existence of society.

Society is for man a kind of ecological (cultural) niche, which makes his biological, as well as psychical-personal, development possible. Community, so understood, includes, among others, the totality of all physical phenomena which give a gathering of people a determinate character of an organization that flows from the psychical feeling of order. Obviously, such a psychological phenomenon in the theoretically-knowing area, presupposes some kind of object towards whose experiences these are directed; in sum, some kind of social being is presupposed. Therefore, the psychological aspect cannot be accepted as primary in the analysis of social being. This is so because psychical experiences already presuppose a corresponding subject and object—they presuppose being.

From a philosophical (metaphysical or ontological) point of view, community is undoubtedly a certain actuality, a certain being. However, it is not an independent being as, for example, man or some other physical, living being is an independent entity. Society can be understood only as a *group of people bound together with relations*. The relations which bind people (from the philosophical point of view) are not relations which constitute being in the substantial order. Rather, they are relations which constitute a "social reality," a relational one, into whose "composition" enter particular subjects as independent rational beings.

What is this "social being" which is not a substantial being regarding an essential immanent unity of acting? There was no theory proclaiming the substantial unity of a social entity. Besides, such a theory would necessarily negate the substantial unity of individual human persons—which would be frankly absurd. For, if a social entity is a gathering of people—of persons— then it can be understood only as a unity of relation among persons. However, in such a "unity of relation," or even more closely, in an undefined "relational being" (unity and being are transcendental, equivalent values), we can distinguish three moments: (a) the foundation for the existence of relational unity (b) the fact of its existence, and (c) the character of existing relational unity.

Ad (a): The foundation for a relational unity or social reality are the transcendental relations of the human person to a common good as an ultimate end.[17] For a human person who is in the process of dynamization cannot develop himself and reach the good, without other persons who create a "we."

Ad (b): The actualization of real, transcendental and necessary, ontic, relations takes place by the fact of the existence of categorical relations. This existential moment or the very coming-into-being of a categorical relation of persons, one to another, is equivalent to the fact of the origin of society. The coming-into-being of categorical relations is something necessary since otherwise, transcendental relations could never be realized.

Ad (c): The manner of existence of categorical relations, which are necessarily liberating, differs according to the different social creations, e.g., family, tribe, class, state, Church.[18] From the metaphysical point of view, relations which constitute a social entity are not absolutely but only relatively necessary, and the unity of relation that constitutes a certain social entity is only an analogical unity with a large margin for variations.

From the philosophical point of view, the only matter of importance is that the social entity is a creature of necessity in its foundations (transcendental relations). At the same time, the appearance of categorical relations of persons to each other is also necessary. On the other hand, the character of these relations which create the concrete content of a social being is relatively necessary. Besides, the character of societies is constantly changing. However, relatively necessary relations which constitute society can become the object of necessary knowledge and, therefore, the object of social philosophy.

Community therefore is a gathering, a "bond" of categorical relations, binding human persons so that they can develop, in the most possible, comprehensive manner, the dynamism of their personality (not every individual in all respects but different individuals in various respects), *for the purpose of fulfilling the common good of every human person.*

Obviously, it would be a gross misunderstanding to consider society as an intentional being, if by an intentional being we mean cultural creations that come from the human intellect and are realized in matter which is both human and non-human. Every intentional being is fundamentally an optional construct (of one's own choice) which comes from human thought and not from human nature as such. Community, on the other hand, is a natural creation which is necessary for the realization of common good.[19] A broad understanding of intentional being by St. Thomas identifies the concept of intentional being with the concept of a being which comes from the Absolute and, for this reason, it is not useful in a philosophical analysis of social being, since it does not differentiate it from other creatures of nature. The concept of social being applies not only to the smallest social groups but also to various groups, along with national states which, in these times, show themselves as a transitory creation—of a "historical category." Such a designation of community also applies to the relationship of the whole of humanity (universal state), whose most varied relations are discerned in the form of work. Its productions in various societies are mutually linked with peoples of various origins, states, nations and so on. We are—as we have already mentioned—witnesses to the present creation of supranational communities as e.g., the United Nations Organization. Their goal is cooperation in assuring conditions for the personal development of every individual. In like manner, its goal is a vigilance for the protection of the existence of all humanity, in the face of the danger of total war; as well as bringing relief to starving peoples, to those culturally neglected etc.[20]

C. COMMON GOOD

In the concept of man and community which we have presented and which was also known to the Greek thinkers, Plato and Aristotle—and which ·can be called finalistic[21]—there appears the problem of common good as the basis for the rise of community and the binding force of its laws. In the framework of this concept, a philosophical explanation is necessary of the very structure of common good—for as a good, it is the goal of the aspirations in the activities of human persons.

But what is "common good?" An answer to a question presented in such a way is made possible by analyzing the meaning of the two expressions that stand out in the question: "good" and "common." In the course of analyzing these two meanings, we must keep in mind the concepts of human nature and human personality, with which common good is linked and specifically: to which it is ordered, since it is the object and goal of its activity.

In the beginning of the *Nicomachean Ethics*, Aristotle wrote: "Every art and every inquiry, and similarly, every kind of activity, as well as decision, seems to be hastening toward some kind of good and, for that reason, to an accurately defined good as the end of every aspiration." The concept of good which Aristotle accepted was a concept of finality and, hence, one which explained good as a reasoned goal, and not only as an aspiration. In this place, the Stagirite placed in opposition another concept of the good—an ecstatic one—which was known to Plato and was later accepted by Plotinus, in which that was called "good" which, being perfect in itself, "diffuses itself" in other beings and thereby imparts existence to them.[22]

As the purpose of every aspiration, the good will disclose itself more clearly, when we turn our attention to the dynamic character of being. For we know the nature of every being in the context proper to the activity of this being. And this activity becomes understood, in turn, in the light of a proportional object: the end. Activity—the act of being—is the inclination, proper to each being, to realize a manner of existence determined by nature. For the nature of being discloses and improves itself through activity in which being, so to say, "manifests" its be-ing. The good-end of activity is but the object of the appropriate inclination of a given being: it is also called "desire." The end does not differ from the good objectively but only formally: it involves a relation to an actual desire when we say about the good that it is "desirable." For the good is being, insofar as this being becomes the reason of the desire (the end of desire). But so that there might be activity rather than non-activity, there must be a commensurate reason for the existence of this activity, thanks to which, some kind of being—which previously did not exist—is now existing rather than not existing. This reason can ultimately be only "being-good" which, by the fact that it becomes a reason of desire (it is desirable), can constitute the end of the being's activity. Briefly: Being arouses desires because it is good and since it is good it becomes the goal of desire.

The "good-desirability" of being becomes "intelligible" particularly in the case of an analysis of the activity of an intelligent nature, i.e., of man. Only the good can constitute the basis for an existential explanation of the fact of human activity—both from its objective as well as its subjective aspect.[23] The fact that man acts for a specified end can be explained only by the fact that the object of desire appeared to man as worthy of desire—as a good. And only because of that good, man desires it—"wants it." Keeping in mind the social aspect of human life (human nature), we shall call that object of human activity "good," which can become the particular end of every personal desire and, in this sense, it can be analogically common to all persons living in society.

Thomas observed: " . . . actions are indeed concerned with particular matters, but those particular matters are referable to common good, not as to a common genus or species, but as to a common final cause, according as the common good is said to be the common end."[24] Thomas' text correctly points to the only rational possibility of understanding common good as the basis for explaining human activity in general, as well as law in particular. Strictly speaking, it refers to human activity insofar as it is directed by law. This matter is obviously subject to a further explanation which is already linked with an analysis of the fact of law. The fact of law, however, presupposes the same liberation of human activity or the fact of existential human activity. For human activity (as an existential fact), explains itself only as a good and this, equally, with respect to purely objective, as well as subjective considerations.

Keeping in mind the objective considerations, the good which is really identified with being, can be constituted in its objective, (i.e., ontic) content by the same "element" or "moment" that constitutes being. For as we know—in agreement with a notion of philosophy which has been established elsewhere—the element which constitutes be-ing is the act of being, commensurable with a concrete individual nature. For existence is understood as the most perfect moment of being, since this existence is the ultimate act of everything that is called real being. For no perfection would be a real perfection if indeed it did not exist. Nothing more perfect can be added to the act of existence.

The existence of a being is understood here as that which ultimately actualizes all the potentialities of being that belong to a given nature of being. In the case of man, we have in mind not only the "naked" existence and, because of it, a fictitious existence of human nature, but also such an existence or such a real "being-a-man," which calls forth all the conditions of a real, concrete and human person—insofar as he becomes a perfect being, i.e., one that develops both biologically and rationally. If we understand existence as concrete, "formed" and really existing, it is precisely this kind of being that we identify with the good.

In philosophical systems, according to which it is not the act of existence but a variously-understood "form" (e.g., Aristotelianism, Platonism, Augustinianism, Scotism), that determines being, a distinction is usually made between be-ing given us without its perfecting additions—and hence, a be-ing constituted by an undetermined "pure" form—and a form which has been perfected and enriched by additional forms of being—for example, in the case of man, "being-wise" and "being-perfect." Then a distinction was made, namely that the simplest and as yet undetermined existence is not a good in its proper meaning, ("*ens simpliciter est bonum per accidens*"). It is only a be-ing which is perfected, developed, and enriched that is a proper good ("*ens secundum quid est bonum simpliciter*").

Good has always been understood as a "developed" entity, an analogically perfect one which—as it is especially apparent in the human act of the will—causes (it is the reason) a desire of itself, and through it, it is the reason for desiring. It becomes the basis for explaining this very fact, especially the activity of the human being. In order to attain the good—"ontological perfection"—man has established science and various other occupations that supply him with new "good-beings" which can fulfill and perfect him. Through analogy—and not a metaphorical but a proper one which is based on the metaphysical structure of the acting being—it was understood, in the Peripatetic system, that the concept of the good stands at the basis of the justification of every activity, especially human activity.

For man, the good is the constantly fuller actualization of the potentiality of his nature; in every other instance, there is another actualization—analogically understood. Man hastens "to multiply" his manner of existence, to enrich himself. Man's natural inclinations which exist within his intelligent being, prompt him to act in the direction of a personal good or the realization of his essential status. By reason of his intelligence, man can—he has a right to—recognize and accept them personally and, at the same time, to make a free selection of the means for their realization. The existence of these inclinations in every individual of a rational nature, along with the existence of a subject-person, find their ultimate foundation in the Absolute Good, to whom every being, and in a particular way, a conscious and free being, is oriented.

And this fuller realization (in proportion to the natural potentialities of the individual) of his ontic aspirations in the area of knowing, loving, free auto-determination, is this "attracting force," this good which is the reason for the existence of every human person's activity. And in this sense, i.e., of an analogically identical end, it constitutes common good.

Likewise from the view point of a person-subject, good appears as a foundation for human activity. Since human reality is contingent, it is, by the same fact, limited and inasmuch as it is dynamized, it does not actually possess, in itself, those perfections which it needs for a complete internal and external development. And since vision and also a constant survival of its contingency are an expression of realization, they are, at the same time, a concretely-experiencing of its own incompleteness of being. An incompleteness and limitation of being testify to the "hunger" for a desired good, which is longed for and is not possessed. And at the same time it is viewed as a good which, in some way, belongs to man. Hence the persistence of a lack of good testifies to an activity which has, for its own goal, the fulfillment of that lack. This it does by supplying a suitable good through which—in a given aspect—the fulfillment of human be-ing takes place.

And only the good can become the common property of all people. The character of this good designates human personality. For when we speak about common good, by that very fact, we also speak about the kind of good which concerns people as bearers of a right—of dynamized beings—who are in potentiality and who have a right to a personal development (for personal beings who are not in the process of dynamization are not guided by this right).[25] In such a state of affairs, common good is attainable with the help of human acts as personal acts, and these resolve themselves above all into acts of the intellect and free will. Hence, in line with the actualization of the intellect and free will, there lies, fundamentally, the good which can become the common good of all people. It is a personal good in a particular sense. It expresses itself through the most varied actualizations, according to an inclination and disposition of our nature and, at the same time, the need of other persons, of actual conditions, etc., of agents that determine concretely every human activity.

The intellect and free will—more exactly man through the activity of the intellect and will—can actualize himself by way of systematic acts and training, through which he can attain higher standards in various areas and through which the human personality enriches itself with various improvements. In this respect, we also find science, with its vast range of specializations, those which already exist, and those that will come into existence, as well as art; and, finally, moral and religious enrichment. And only in this order of a purely personal good, which is attained by the intellect and will, can there be no contradiction between the good of the whole community and of particular persons as its members. Further, it is only in such a conception of common good, which is the goal of the personal activity of every man, that we can posit the principle that the growth of an individual person is at the same time the growth of common good of the whole society. For the enrichment of personal development cannot be achieved at anyone's cost, but it serves everyone. For this reason, the goal of the community is making possible the fullest realization of common good; i.e., the creation of the conditions for personal actualization to an unlimited degree.

It is clear that the very actualization of personal good, which is, at the same time common good, demands in the normal course of events such material means as: nourishment for the continuation of biological life, which also conditions psychic life; inhabitancy and technical improvements necessary for them. These are needed so that human life—which is measured equally by material energy as well as by its use—could be easier and, at the same time, could create conditions for the development of specifically personal goods. On this point, there can occur conflicts between the individual and the whole society concerning division of material means which serve the realization of common good. Thomas already had called attention to the fact that *nemo potest superabundari nisi alter deficiat.* For it can happen and, in practise, it does very frequently happen that there is an unequal division of material goods and, therefore, the task and the purpose of social powers is not only to divide proportionally, i.e., justly, the goods of all the people. But at the same time, it is also its task to organize work in such a way that, in effect, it could increase the material means for making possible the simultaneous realization of essential personal good and common good. But all material goods, whether considered separately or jointly, cannot be recognized as common good in the proper sense; and, by the same token, they cannot be understood as a reason for the existence of law and social order.

Material goods will remain important, sometimes indispensable, but always only a means to a proper end. For if a particular material good does not possess within itself the reason for an ultimate good; that is to say such a goodness that draws of itself, a proper and, all the more a final cessation of human desire and activity; then the sum of material goods does not acquire this reason through a quantitative addition. For being does not arise from non-being, and non-being of itself does not pass to being.

We can observe a certain hierarchy in the order of material goods; there are goods of a higher and lower rank, more and less valuable. Undoubtedly, vegetative human life is more valuable than vegetative animal life or plant life for the reason that it is "immersed" in the personal life of man, subordinated to personal good; and that there is no good beyond the individuality of the human person. Goods suitable for the sustenance of personal life have a greater value for man than goods suitable for the most comfortable living etc. For if we notice in the process of analyzing human activity and its goal that many goods are desirable, not because of themselves but because of a higher good—in the first place the good of the person himself who is desiring—we can also state that just as in the order of nature, there exists a hierarchy of beings—there are "stronger and weaker" beings and, at the same time, the entity of the Absolute is the foundation of everything—so, too, there exists a hierarchy of goods, since good and being are really the same.

Hence the highest objective good is also at the same time the highest Absolute-Being, whom religion calls God. This good can be "attained" only through acts of being of the highest order, as are personal acts—acts of the intellect and free will. Likewise, only the highest Good can be the objective Good which is common to every person and to the entire society; and the making possible the attainment of this very Good is the reason for the existence of society and of the same law which binds in society. No community can exist against its own proper way of being and issue such laws which, in any way whatever, should seek to make impossible or hinder the attainment of common good, or to condition the attainment of this good with the help of rules-commands that, of their very nature, were not necessarily bound with common good. All such norms or decrees can be recognized as being only pseudo-laws, which cannot in any way, bind in conscience, a human being who is ordained to the attainment of common good. Obviously, this does not mean that it is always easy to detect and indicate whether and how much, concrete laws, which are issued by some community, make impossible the attainment of common good—or, that they limit its attainment and condition the compliance with other laws not necessarily connected with common good.

Human acts which border on common good, or personal acts of knowledge or love can grow in a person endlessly; and their growth not only does not harm anyone but, on the contrary, it enriches society by adding to a fuller bond of community with common good. On the other hand, other human acts which do not tend to a goal directly but have material goods as their object—and hence, corporeal, external goods in the area of animate and inanimate matter—must be subject to social control. They must also be regulated by statutes and ordinances to make it possible for every human person to fulfill that fundamental right, which is a real possibility of a favorable subordination to a common good, through a development of his personal potentialities.

St. Thomas' text and its interpretation, which we have quoted above, shows the inadequacy and, in this sense, the error of other ways of understanding common good. These ways have been formed in different theoretical contexts, even though there were attempts to transplant them into St. Thomas' system. We are speaking here, for example, about the theory of setting in order people to common good in the manner of individuals according to kind or type, or of components to a group. According to such theories, common good is not a personal good of a human individual, and by itself it cannot attain common good. Common good can be realized only with the common effort of all individuals together, as for example, a tree, by itself, does not constitute a forest, and one individual does not constitute a complete mankind. Theories of this kind which seek within common good both a suprahuman and suprapersonal good that an individual man cannot attain, are not acceptable because they deny the essential trait of personality; namely, its "wholeness" or "completeness." According to the assumptions of these theories, the form of an aggregate entity of a collective or some suprahuman formation would be a higher form of existence than that of an individual person, whereas there are no independent "fuller" forms of existence than the human person. Community is only a relational creation (in spite of its necessity) and it cannot usurp the place of a human being. For if some kind of higher whole should be placed above man-person, to which man would be totally ordered and this higher whole would represent a sterling value of being, it would constitute a "whole" that would be "completely" capable of making man happy. It would fulfill every human aspiration because it would possess a "knowledge" of that which man lacks. Such a personification of a social creation (creature) would be totalism, which rules out the nature of human personality in its fundamental qualifications.

Understood in a finalistic way, common good presents itself to man as his own personal good, grasped by the intellect, and hence every person can and should understand it; and understanding it, each should cling to it. The binding of a human person by this good is an internal binding and not an external one, which is an irrational command that is not accepted by man-person in a conscious and free manner. A command which is imposed externally by a community but which is neither understood nor cherished internally by man, is a moral violence which by its nature is something immoral. To understand common good, we must therefore see its essential character and the role of community in such an education of man for a rational freedom, so that he can see internally and cherish freely both common good and himself as its participant. A different way of binding man with community by means of law leads to a cancelling out of human nature, understood as a free personality which can undergo the process of actualization.

II. FORMS OF SOCIETY AND MAN'S DEVELOPMENT

The sequence of considerations, which we have outlined here and which establishes the essential elements of the development of human personality permits us to delineate possible general answers to the question: What kind of social organism is not contrary to the basic moments of man's development? And just as in many other areas, we can similarly point here to a threefold line of development in which is stressed either (a) the side of the social organism in its relation to the individual or (b) the right of the individual with respect to the social creation, or finally (c) where various mutual arrangements (and subordinations) between the human individual and community are shown.

A. Considering the matter from a historical point of view, one does not find it difficult to observe that social organisms appeared as "more powerful" creations than the human individual. In ancient times, man was completely subordinated to the power and will of the whole, so that his entire private life—as B. Constant had already observed at the beginning of the 19th century—was subject to strict control. There was no freedom in the choice of a particular occupation, profession of religion etc. The human individual was lost in the state.

A monument and, at the same time, a frightful "model" of an ideal concept of the state is Plato's *Republic*.[26] Coming from the highest Athenian aristocracy, in spite of the fact that he was formulating an apparently very noble philosophy, Plato nevertheless was passionately enamored of politics and, as Jaeger asserts, Plato's entire creativity was closely bound up with politics and education for citizenship.[27] His conception of the state and political systems influenced world events, for there was never any lack of those who were anxious to realize the ideal of the Platonic form of government. In this form of government, the spiritual or worldly "wise men" were prone to thrust upon the people certain exemplars of authoritative happiness, without regard to their free-will acceptance.

Let us turn our attention to Popper, author of the famous work, entitled *Open Communities and Their Enemies*,[28] as well as to Jaeger on Plato's concept of the structure of community. The essential goal of this structure was to be the education of man: "For ultimately, the Platonic State concerns itself with man's soul. What we read about the state itself and its structure; namely, the organic concept of the state . . . serves only for a greater reflection on the human soul and its inner structure. But fundamentally, Plato comes to the problem of the soul, not from a theoretical, but from a practical point of view, namely as an educator of souls. The education of the soul is that lever with whose help the Platonic Socrates sets the entire state into motion."[29] Plato did not think very highly of people who were subject to the state since, in the eyes of the sage, the relation of citizens to authorities is equivalent to that of a shepherd and swine: "When they praise some tyrant or king, one has the impression that he hears praises of a shepherd, e.g., of swine or cows who admire him because he milks them well." But to tell the truth, this sage does not have any better opinion about the tyrant either . . . "He considers him a worse beast than the other animals and more crafty than people who graze and milk cattle."[30]

People must be trained by the inculcating of virtue in them. The structure of community must correspond to the structure of man, who shows himself to be composed of variously-ordered "souls," among which must exist harmony and justice. Jaeger writes: "Since justice can be found equally in the soul of an individual and in the entire state, these characteristic traits can be better perceived and understood if we will observe them from a distance and on a state-wide scale, rather than if we observe them in a single soul. . . . In Plato's judgment, both the state and an organized soul equally possess an identical inner structure and this, equally, in its healthy as well as in its degenerate state."[31] And just as a rational, spiritual and vegetative soul exists in man, so too there necessarily exist in the state, hierarchically arranged classes: the wise men who rule; the guardians who should protect the organization and security of the citizens; and the workers, farmers, craftsmen who must support the entire state. The harmonious co-existence of these three classes is an excellent realization of justice and, at the same time, a fulfillment of educational assignments of the community in relation to man. Here is how Jaeger sees the fulfillment of this justice: "Plato sees justice in the state in this, that every member of society fulfilled his specified functions in the best possible manner. The rulers, guardians and workers have their own clearly defined assignments and if everyone in these three classes will take care to perform his function to the best of his ability, the state which arises from their cooperation will be the best that we can imagine. Each of these classes possesses its own characteristic virtue: the rulers should be wise; and the warriors, brave. The third virtue, which is a prudent self-control (SOPHROSYNE), is not connected exclusively, it is true, in a similar way with the third class; nevertheless, it does have a special meaning for it. The mutual understanding of the classes is based on this virtue, with the result that those who are inferior by nature, freely subordinate themselves to those who are superior. It should be equally characteristic of the rulers as well as of the ruled, but it does make the greatest demands on the class of whom obedience is expected."[32]

Plato's concept of society—as K. R. Popper constantly points out in the course of his work—is a consequence of his extreme rationalism which transforms itself, in social manners, into a doctrinairism which does not recognize any plasticity, tolerability and historicity of human activity, especially of social activity. Guided by this rationalism, and at the same time recognizing—in opposition to the Pre-Socratic philosophers—a significantly advanced sphere of man's freedom, this Platonic concept of society seeks to locate this freedom in the branches of explicitly formulated law and an inexorably established social order, wherein there is no longer any completely private life—everything is a social function.

As A. Kasia[33] correctly observes: "The ideal Platonic state was, in essence, a police state of unheard-of severely, executed moral-religious laws. . . . In his state, absolutely nothing could escape notice of the "Guardians of Order". . . . Plato thereby introduces very exacting regulations of life, which bind equally every citizen of his state. . . . The rulers should take every citizen of his state under their scrupulous control and protection, without exception from birth until death. . . . The law-giver should watch diligently over their sorrows and joys, over the longings and fervor of various desires in mutual association—says Plato;—he should impart rebukes by means of laws or bestow fitting praise on those who deserve it."[34]

The crowning achievement of man's relation to the community is to be a total and complete submission of man to the state, even to the choice of marriage and begetting of children, so that, against this background, justice can be realized as a religious and saving goal. No wonder that only in the mind of an aprioristic doctrinaire could the following advice originate. It is contained in *The Laws,* and although it is true that it is directed to the soldiers, it nevertheless is obvious from the context that it is universally obligatory. Popper reproduces it on the jacket of his work: "It is of paramount importance that no one should ever remain without direction, whether man or woman, so that he could not become accustomed to deal on his own and in his/her own way—whether in matters of importance or recreation. Both in war and in peace, everyone should have his eyes constantly directed toward his superior. He should submit to the latter's direction, even in the slightest matters. Hence he should stand when ordered, march, train himself, wash himself, eat food, arise at night and stand guard. . . . In a word, all must become accustomed and trained so that, not even thinking that something can be done individually and separately from others, and not knowing how to proceed in general, they should always unite their efforts and act in unison with all. One must learn to rule with others and to listen to others, for all lawlessness must be extirpated from the life of people and animals that serve man."[35] Hence even animals must bear a citizen's lot in the Platonic state.

The Platonic concept of community—as Willamowitz-Mollendorf maliciously asserted and his pupil, Jaeger, affirmed[36]—reminds us of ecclesiastical organization. In fact, it is equally based on the totality of an a priori system, especially in its concept of man as a fallen god who, to the mind of its wise founders, must be "redeemed." Therefore Plato did not seek, nor did he investigate more fully, man's nature; but he had a vision of a total, authoritatively given happiness of man. He was the first to give a theory of human happiness—admittedly, in spite of itself but in agreement with the views of the sages who exercised power.

The concept of a state which totally brings up a citizen—even though it never disappeared from the scene of history—nevertheless did have, in different periods, its own particular profound recurrences, especially in view of an insufficiency of individualistic-liberalistic political systems. These, in theory, fell into another extreme but in practice they similarly led to an undermining, or even a denial, of the foundations of life of large groups of people. Contemporary theoreticians of the state and of law who experienced fascism point to the characteristic traits of the system of government, connecting it with the servile forms of the ancient and Platonic ideal of the state. J. Messner[37] even establishes characteristic traits—which are an application of Plato's conception—of such a system of government. In summarizing, he states that a system of government that is based on Platonic models can be designated as the kind of government in which the human person is not the end but only the means of realizing the ends of government, and his value is only that of a means.

Like Plato, who recognized only the totality as genuine reality, Hegel, many years later, accepted that only the "whole" is true and real. By "reality," he understood absolute being as such. Parts however—therefore in a community, people—are only "dialectical moments" of the whole, and nothing more. Hence the community, and not individual people, represents a real value. For in itself reality is not constituted by substantiality but by relation. For it lacks substantiality, and that which can be called substantiality is only an aggregate and a bond of relations. The individual man—a person—is thus completely, in all aspects, subordinated to the community. In a word, he is a function of this community.

Society exerts, (or attempts to exert) total control over man's thoughts, his technical and artistic creativity. The social authority establishes man's goals and the means of attaining these goals so that, as a result, he is deprived of the possibility of realizing his personal goals and, thereby, the means which could assure him some kind of independence in relation to society. Man and his creative initiative find recognition only insofar as they realize the goals of the community. A man, who attempts to protect his own non-conformist goals becomes known as an enemy of society and is destroyed by it. As a result, such communities bring back slavery.[38]

B. *Liberal individualism* constitutes a second, equally extreme alternative of realizing the relation: man-society. This theory is based on epistemologically nominalistic conceptualizations. For when we look around us in society, we see only and exclusively people. "Humanity" in such a context, represents, in a realistic way, nothing other than only separate and exclusive human individuals. This family, for example is nothing else than its individual members: father, mother, children, aunts, etc. Consequently, society as some kind of reality is a fiction; only people exist, of whom some have power and others do not. Individual people, in relation to each other, act in a definite and more or less free manner. What we call "society" is, simply speaking, a shortened way of expressing ourselves about people. Obviously, in such a conception, there are no social obligations, no laws and, for this reason, such an extremely individualistically understood theory had no important representatives, with the exception of M. Stirner,[39] who seriously denied social rights and obligations. J. J. Rousseau has the reputation of being the inspirer of individualistic-liberal conceptions, along with his theory of "social contract,"[40] which starts with the undeniable enunciation that "every man is born free"—which, in his understanding, means that every man enjoys an inalienable state of freedom which he possesses from birth. This is not a question here of the freedom of human decisions, freedom of choice, but rather the manner of man's existence. This existence is independent of others and this independence is innate in man. On the strength of this independence, man cannot be subject to anyone. He can be obedient only to himself and his own commands.

But because people desire to live more comfortably, they organize themselves into a society. And here, at once, arises a problem: In what way can we reconcile, in social life, the basic demands of natural law with a social association? How "can we find a form of association which would guard and protect, with all its common power, both the person and the goods of every member of the association—thanks to which, each person by uniting with all, would obey only himself and would remain just as free as formerly?" Rousseau sees the solution of this problem in the social contract which guarantees at the same time equality and freedom: ". . . each one of us gives up his own person and all his power for the order of all, under the guiding direction of the general will; each individual, however, becomes a member of the whole as an indivisible part of the whole." In this way, equality was realized.

The reconciliation of freedom with community results from a different understanding of freedom: "Freedom depends less on a manifestation of one's own will than on not being subservient to the will of another. That will is truly free, against which, no one has the right to present opposition. Through general freedom, no one has the right to that which is denied him by the freedom of another." In order that freedom be guaranteed in its fulness, and that no man should be subject to another, legislative authority must not only be exercized by all, but it must also apply to all. Statutes must be an expression of general will and, at the same time, they must contain a general object that applies to all. The will must be manifested personally and hence, according to Rousseau, only the referendum is uniquely the legal form of the functioning of authority.

In the conception of a freely united society, where every member is sovereign, it must of necessity lead to a denial of authority which, is a formal element of society. In such a case, authority is not an act of reason, nor is it of an intellectual nature for whose development social unions are necessary, so that through them, it could develop more fully in personal aspects, at the cost of introducing social and distributive justice. If individualistic liberalism were to stand at the basis of a social union of men, by the nature of things there would be no place for the realization of any common good,—and hence, a good which is, at the same time, the good of the individual and of the entire society, a good in whose realization there is no contradiction between the human person and the whole society. Meanwhile, there would exist only the good of the individual as the ultimate goal in itself alone, without common good. Such a state of affairs could end in anarchy or the ultimate annihilation of social existence and of all laws. By the same token, interpersonal relationships would be reminiscent of a state of struggle for existence, which Darwin describes—where only the biologically strongest individuals would rise, without any moral scruples, above the surface of life. Social anarchy would be the consequent result of liberalism understood in this way.

There is still another possible consequence of a doctrine understood in this way, i.e., of a totalism which, *de facto,* was the ultimate stage of the evolutionary process of individualistic liberalism. Proudhon foresaw and indicated this evolutionary process.[41] In such a hypothesis, the human masses both are and are not the subject of sovereign authority, since they perform their governance through delegates who act in the name of the masses. Such delegates battle among themselves, and they weaken the government. In the face of a debility of warring parties and delegates, there arises a need for strong, dictatorial rule by an individual or a group who would direct wholly and totally the community it rules. And in such a sense, individualistic-liberal democracy would actually degenerate—as history testifies—into a government of either one party that totally solves all difficulties, or of one race, or of one nation, or of one "providential" leader.

C. *If human personality* is a real being with potentialities of self-realization and which needs society for its personal development and if (a) society is equally a real being, not truly substantial but only relational and which exerts a basic and necessary influence on man's development—for whom it creates a cultural and ecological niche (just as nature which furnishes a suitable habitat, creates a biological niche for animals), and if (b) community constitutes itself as a relative unity through the formal element of power— which is the work of a rational nature—then, the relation between a human person and the community cannot be composed according to the extreme models that were previously presented. For extreme solutions lead, in the end, to a denial of a human rational nature and they thereby create circumstances which threaten a distortion of the development of human personality.

We should, therefore, take real factors under advisement and hence: (a) an autonomous substantial and self-contained personality which needs community for its existence, (b) community, understood as a relational being (c) common good which possesses its objective and subjective side and hence such a good that unites all to a common goal which is, at the same time, the goal of every individual. Realization of common good is the only foundation for the coming into being of a community and for authority that coordinates the genuine rights of individual persons. A society thus understood is a society of persons, and hence of rational free persons, who realize common good through acts of love, of persons who are subjects of laws, of beings "for themselves" and, through real acts of knowledge, love, and creativity are also beings "for another." Hence a community of persons is above all an organization directing itself rationally and, in the last analysis, appealing to reason, which is the basis for freedom. Laws, constitutions and regulatory ordinances that obligate with their binding force draw out, with understanding, an acceptance of these very laws in consideration of common good. Community, thus understood, is therefore an accepted form of government above all "from within," through the consciences of free persons.

Community, therefore, is not a kind of autonomous substantial totality, as it appears in Hegel's conception, which really exists solely through a dialectical unfolding, of which people are only moments. A community is not above persons but, on the contrary, human persons as independent beings surpass community. It seems proper and fitting here to recall the Aristotelian theory of categories. The fundamental category which decides existence is substance. The Stagirite did not even hesitate to make the assertion that being—that which truly exists—is substance, or such a way of being that has autonomous existence. Properties of being, however, and among them relation, are only modifications of the way a substance exists.

Keeping both man the human individual and society in mind, we must emphasize that despite Hegel's view, the real and autonomous beings are people, i.e., human persons, and that society, which is a relational association of these persons, is only a real way of existing and of man's life and development. For man does not acquire his be-ing from society, but the latter receives its be-ing from real individual people, just as various relations, which are non-independent modes of existence "among" already independently existing beings, are ultimately explained by and resolved into substantial being.

Community is therefore really and fundamentally ordered to man as a being, as a person, since a personal being is the same as a free and conscious human being. A social structure which subordinates man and completely leads him to a social function is fundamentally wrong, evil and without a goal. Such a community is a servile community, which deforms the personhood of its members, since it is not in agreement with the fundamental ontic structure of man and of existence. Something abnormal would then enter in, since existence, autonomy and substantiality would be at the service of that which, of itself, is not a being—something which is constituted by a set of relations, which presupposes an autonomous being and which is its property and is ordered to it.

Factually, in servile societies which subscribe in practice to Hegelian idealism, where society is some kind of autonomous whole, and for which people are a reflection and dialectical moment, only power as the formal element of society would have the status of a full personhood. It would in truth be a being in itself and for itself, while all other persons would merely be the means which enable the power to live and to be used. It is for this reason that in the conception of society there are fundamentally two opposing theories of society: (1) one according to which the totality the whole, is truly being (Platonism and Hegelianism) and (2) the other, in which true being is the individual man. In the first conception, man is for the sake of the whole. In the second, the "whole" which constitutes only a relative unity, built on autonomous beings and ordered to the good of individual and self-contained beings, i.e., people; is really and basically for the sake of these people who are knowing, free and capable of love, and who have their personal life and not one which is ordered by the "whole." A social whole exists for the sake of a person. It exists so that it could make possible the development of the realization of personhood. For this reason, a social organization is better, insofar as it serves individual people. A personal life resolves itself into a development of the full man from the point of view of knowledge, love, freedom, and all that is linked with the development and improvement of the so-called "human spirit."

Liberal individualism is therefore a distortion and an error in the social structure. It is more dangerous with respect to its consequences (anarchy and the possibility of an unscrupulous domination of some individuals, a denial of authority as the coordinating agent and a negation of common human good), than in its basic human foundations. An understanding of community as a "whole"—a being in itself and for itself—is, on the other hand, an a priori doctrinairism, based on a disregard for human nature. For according to this hypothesis, man is not what he is by nature, but he is and must be fashioned into the kind of man that the a priori system wants him to be. And it is all the worse for facts if they do not agree with the system.

Making use, however, of the "order of nature" is likewise deceptive, as it is evident in the case of Aristotle who committed such a grave error that he recognized slavery as a "natural state." Worse yet, he justified this state of affairs. Despite this, there is no other ultimate reference system than precisely the inner structure of a thing which manifests itself in activity, and which we call "nature." For when we take human activity under consideration, undoubtedly we should take into account a hierarchy of human acts. The fundamental criterion in establishing human activity is above all the goal which is the common good of the activity of the individual man and of the entire community. Hence, with respect to the goal and the connection between human activity and common good, we must qualify human acts (activity) as more or less worthwhile.

In such a state of affairs, specifically personal activity, e.g., cognitive-volitional activity (within it is included the entire range of expressions of personal life) is, for man, the most valuable, noble and most lasting, especially when we take into account man's personal immortality. From the viewpoint of these activities—which, on the one hand, permanently ennoble man, and, on the other, bind this person more directly with common good— we can accept it as a fact that man is that "entirety" which is superior to society. This is so because it improves autonomous personal being as the highest "whole;" it endures beyond time and transcends material conditions, including death. On the other hand, human activity which is internally involved in materiality in its changes, and which depletes itself in material changes, cannot be recognized as specifically man's personal activities. Everything that is "common" to man and to animals, as well as to plants—although it arises from a personal subject—nevertheless does not possess a specifically personal goal. In this respect, it is subject to community and to the exercise of its authority.

Does this mean that there exist in man separate ontic structures of being which constitute a personal order and separate structures which constitute the singularity of a human being? Aristotle and after him, St. Thomas and their followers held, the position of existing separate ontic structures. For Aristotle, matter constituted the principle of individuation. Thomas likewise believed that quantified matter (of definite or indefinite quantity—undetermined more precisely it is not known) individualizes material beings as well as man. But the perspective of Aristotle's and Thomas' questions about individuation is completely different. For the Stagirite, who was under Plato's influence, the essential cause of being was form, which is universal and understood by itself and which, through its individuation and intermingling with matter, becomes at all times individual. On the other hand, for Thomas—for whom being is real not because it has a form, but since it is organized through form, it possesses the act of existence—the question about individuation resolves itself into indicating non-contradictory elements of individuation—not as a being but as a strictly potential and receptive element which restricts the manner of an existing being. Such an element is precisely quantified matter which, for the same reason, is the cause of everything that can be called "individual." This matter is understood as a limited and limiting manner of existing, since it is bound with alteration (organizing and dissolving of matter) of a material being.

In this sense, we can agree with St. Thomas' position that there exist ontic reasons of an individual who is understood not as a separate being (man's be-ing is the same as his personal moment!), but as the reason for human activity, which does not transcend formally the alteration of matter. For there are present in man activities of a vegetative and animal type which are so intermingled with matter that they are finally exhausted in it, since they have as their goal the attainment of some material change. And there are activities in man which are linked with the essential goal of the human being as a person, and these transcend the mode of being matter.

Consequently, we should speak not so much about the individual structure of man as subordinate to the community and about personal structure as subordinating this community to itself (theory of J. Maritain), but rather about the ontic foundations of activity of an individual and personal type. In such a state of affairs, the theory of personalism would be more intimately bound up with the character of human activity (qualifying the relation, "man-society" from the point of view of the character of activity!) than with the manner of existing. For it is not possible to divide in a personal human being, layers of an individual; or of a relatively autonomous layer, or of a personal layer which would already be independent of matter. The proper evaluation of human, personal and "individual" (material) activity would have a place with respect to its connection with the goal as common good.

A practical determination of "man-society" relations is extremely difficult. Man's personal development as an actualized and materialized being likewise takes place through material means, which cannot be separated from the actualization of man's spiritual potentialities. The same man must submit himself to society with respect to the distribution of material means, which have the realization of common good as their goal—which good is always the personal good of the human individual. Material means are always limited and, for this reason, society and its authority should be aware of, and concerned about, serving the foremost goal of society to the highest degree, which is the total development of the real person. Society should also provide for the proportional development of all members of this society.

Man is ordered and subordinated to society and conversely society is ordered and subordinated to man, but from different points of view. Since the dignity of the human person is the highest good, man is free and independent in his personality and his purely human actions, and he can and should develop himself in his personal life without any commands. Commands bind only insofar as man acknowledges himself to be bound by them in conscience, with respect to the necessary disposition of being which must be perceived by him personally. For wherever material goods come into play—even at the time when, in an exceptional case, the material good is a human life—as a way of existing in matter or another corporeal good, all the more external, material good for whose use and possession, a second man equally has or may have a right,—in all cases, the individual is ordered and subordinated to the community. From the view point of these goods, society has the authority and it rises, somewhat above man who, in certain concrete cases can lose the right to an uncontrolled use of material goods.

The fact is that it is extremely difficult in practice to establish, without conflict, a relation of man-society. Such relations in their negative form remain established in a foremost statute, a so-called Constitution. Presently, additional help in the area of legislation is given to states or social organizations by international organizations, as for example, the United Nations Organization, Papal Encyclicals, etc.

Since personalism—if we were to keep the traditional term—is only a philosophical theory which points to the basic and general foundations of affirming personal and social truths, it cannot become a social theory which would determine, in a concrete manner, the organization of a given society. This is so because establishments which concern the relation between person and community are accomplished in the branches of a particular cultural situation. To a great degree, they are marked by conditions in which the entire society is developing. In brief, they constitute a historical category.

This does not mean that one could not try to establish, at least in a negative sense, man's rights which are inalienable from the point of view of the character of the human personal being, as well as of the goal of human activity. Such attempts are actually being made today, especially by the United Nations Organization, as well as the Apostolic See in its universal teaching. However, the attempt to establish the rights and duties of man is only the first and introductory step, not so much as a guaranteeing to a concrete man a realization in regard to these determinations, as an appeal to a wider social consciousness. Only after this thought has come into being and has taken root in the universal consciousness of people, can we approach an institutional guarantee of these rights of each individual, so that man could attain these rights—in a truly effective way—in his relations with various social institutions.

In any case, in line with the general demarcation introduced by a philosophical theory of personalism, human nature cannot be changed in an a priori way; neither can man's aspirations which flow from his nature be accepted as fundamentally erroneous. But it is uniquely proper that, by analyzing the natural inclinations of the human rational nature—in agreement with these same people as various interested and free persons—we should establish concretely the way in which the structure of society should be formed, so that common good could be actually realized.[42] It can be seen from mankind's experience until the present, that generally social reforms which are accomplished in the name of philosophical or theological a priori doctrines are not in agreement with life and, in practice, they do not serve man in his personal development. On the contrary, they deprave and pervert man and, on the other hand, these reforms succumb to a modification under the pressure of life which in its dynamism is more powerful than the various constructs of thought which have no anchorage in life.

CHAPTER X

MAN AND RELIGION
By Zofia J. Zdybicka

I. INTRODUCTORY PERSPECTIVES

In his existential unity, man comprises two ontic areas: matter and spirit. Corporeity and spirituality indicate a type of man's immersion in the cosmos, as well as a type of transcendence of the human person in relation to the whole world of matter. Therefore, since man is "an existence-in-himself" and "for-himself," he is equally a being in the world of things and the world of persons. Man is a "dynamic" being,i.e., one who develops and actualizes himself by entering into various relations with these two realities. By his actions, the human person as if "creates" himself, or at least transforms himself. The activity of the human person—of a material-spiritual being—is multi-dimensional. Possessing various types of dispositions, man develops himself through varied activities. We can therefore speak about various levels or spheres of human existence designated by appropriate dispositions and capable of establishing values in:

1. a material-biological sphere and, therefore, the area of life-giving and economical-technical values, which generally satisfy the biological needs of man. Man produces this type of values by mastering his natural environment, so that it can be better adapted to his needs and so that the world can become at the same time a better place in which to live. Almost all modern science and techniques are based on this type of values and therefore on the fullest development of such dispositions which enable man to transform his environment.

2. The cultural sphere which satisfies man's psychic needs. Here we must include all cognitive, aesthetic, and social values, for example, ethical and the like.

A special type here are moral values, which define the manner of man's existence as a person, and hence as a subject who comes into contact primarily with other person-subjects. These indicate a person-to-person-relationship, as well as religious values which bind man with something that transcends the world of nature and culture.

All nonreligious values revolve around their relationship of "being-in-the-world." Their purpose is to develop the human dynamism which tends to shape the world in accordance with human measures; that is, to establish an individual life-style in a community increasingly worthy of man. For that which determines specific religious values is the fact that they bind the human person not only with a reality equally distinct from the world of things, but also with persons, with a transcendent reality. These values point to the vertical dimension of human existence, from which point of view other dimensions draw new meaning, intensity, and depth. From a religious perspective,—at least in those defined by higher forms of religion proper to our culture—human life becomes not only coexistent with other human persons, but coexistent with another personal "THOU"—with the person of the Absolute.

Here however appears a basic problem: To what degree is man genuinely open to the sphere of religious values? At the same time is this openness indispensable for the "fulfillment" of the person? There is no doubt as to the openness of man to the world of things and persons. Of course, the characteristic which distinguishes man among living beings is not so much the power to transform nature and to become independent of it, as it is the ability to form new values: of truth, goodness and beauty. However, there is a wide range of difficulties, once we recognize that man is directed to the transcendental sphere, that he is a being "toward God" and a realization of such a direction is necessary for the fulness of human existence.

Although religion always existed as a general criteron of human life, it never created a problem which, in our present worldwide community, has acquired its own importance: What is man's religious perspective and what does it mean? Where does it come from? Is it rooted in the human being? Is it an essential trait of man which belongs to his nature or is it an accidental trait which presents itself in regard to some occasional biological, psychological or social circumstance of nature—and hence, with respect to education, tradition, a feeling of solitude, a condition in nature and dangers connected with it? From the time of Feuerbach, a second important problem made its appearance: Does there really exist—independently of human consciousness—an equivalent of a transcendent reference and an object of man's religious activity? What is its nature?

This matter as the history of human thought shows, is neither simple nor easy with respect to a final solution—both in regard to the solution of the contents as well as to the formal aspect of the given problem.

The difficulty lies in the character of the religious phenomenon and consequently in the character of man's traits. Speaking most generally the religious phenomenon is a relation between man and a reality distinct from him, namely, a higher and transcendent one. The religious dimension of man is not therefore an absolute property; that is, it is not expressed or realized in man himself, independently of his relations to other beings. Rather, it determines a relative trait, in the sense that it supposes reference to a reality which transcends man ontically, and which is inaccessible in direct knowledge.

And so *homo religiosus* as an anthropological category always poses a problem while, for example, *homo sapiens, homo esteticus, homo socialis, homo oeconomicus* or *homo faber* are considered indisputable definitions of human existence. This is understandable, if we consider the fact that they express either unconditionally the absolute properties of man realized in himself, without any necessary reference to other beings, or the relative characteristics whose existence and nature do not cause any restrictions because they are given empirically. For example, in the case of the definition *homo socialis*—the social character of man constitutes indeed a relative characteristic, which presupposes the existence of other persons. These beings, however, are of the same category; they are accessible in direct experience, and for this reason there is no greater difficulty in confirming the character and fundamental interhuman relationships: the openness of the human person to other personal beings.

The recognition of the religious dimension of human experience or its denial, especially a knowledge of the character of religion and its value, establish not only a knowledge of man himself, not only a knowledge about facts and religious experiences but, above all, the solving of the problem of real existence of the transcendent object of religious actions. On this, of course, depends the outlook on the nature of religion and its functions in individual and social human life.

Hence the question about man's religiousness belongs to the core problems of theoretical knowledge about man, as well as to the most important practical questions. For we are concerned with a determination of the final perspectives and dimensions of human life. Little wonder, then, that the manner of solving this problem is a matter which divides philosophical systems and currents; sometimes it denotes epochs. On this point we can agree with Feuerbach that the great eras in human history differ, above all, in their relation to religion. We can cite, as an example, the religiously oriented Middle Ages, which left an indelible mark on present-day forms of human activity; and our present times when culture is, above all, linked with values which are bound with the material-biological sphere. As much as religion was for the Middle Ages the principal value, and that which was either worldly or religious penetrated individual and social life, so in modern times, a very sharp division is drawn between these two realities. In itself, this phenomenon is good because the progress of civilization requires a greater division of functions and value. A danger lies in the fact that a one-directional growth of modern civilization can disturb the norms, balance and harmony of the development of human personality. There is a fear that man may be engrossed to such a degree in the values of material culture and civilization, that there will be no room for any other cultural values, especially for religious ones!

The problem of the place of religion in the life of a human person and in social life defines itself today more sharply than ever, as the results of certain currents of thought which have questioned the necessity of religion for man and, what is more, have pointed to its negative meaning in the development of the human person. Under the influence of identifying religious consciousness with "ill-fated consciousness" by Hegel and the views of Feuerbach, who perceived in man himself the birth of religious contents and acknowledged the subject of religion as hypostasized traits of a human type, Marx stressed the postulate of the destruction of religion as an activity which limits the autonomy of man and hampers the dynamism of his development. The phenomenon of "Promethean atheism," according to which man judges that he can subordinate the earth for himself through knowledge and technology if he dispenses with God, is undoubtedly complicated. Its origin was due not only to philosophical interpretations of religion; but also to improper resolutions of many individual and social problems of life, effected by persons or religious societies. At present, we are witnessing a conflict in thought and life of two fundamentally different types of humanism: (a) immanent humanism, according to which man is a completely autonomous being, the most valuable of all reality and whose development takes place through the actualization of horizontal relations. This type of humanism is struggling for the supreme position of man, for his development, his worth and his complete happiness; (b) in like manner, a humanism which recognizes the human person as being of the highest value in the realm of created entities, and which points to timeless perspectives of human life. It immeasurably broadens human existence, since it is the ontic consequence of a psychological and moral union of a human person with a personal transcendent Being. Both atheistic and theistic humanisms and personalisms concentrate within themselves all the most general and most important problems relating to the question: Is religion necessary for acknowledging the proper dignity of man and appreciating his full development?[2]

As we have already noted, this is a difficult question. Nonetheless we hereby present it with a comprehensive knowledge of man, along with the religious phenomenon. From the critical point of view, precise methods of knowledge have been developed and attention has been given to both human existence as well as to religious events. In the last several decades, we notice a development in the philosophy of man and religious knowledge. The preceding century (second half of the nineteenth and first half of the twentieth century) is exceedingly rich in its research, which both denies and affirms the necessity of man's bond (union) with religion.[3]

In the mid-nineteenth century, there arises a dynamic progress of "positive" knowledge about religion which assembles facts in a scientific manner and which bases its investigations on it. (Of special interest were archaic and Oriental forms of comparative religious knowledge.) Next arise other branches of religious knowledge: psychology, sociology, along with its own philosophies of religion, which constitute not so much one of the philosophical disciplines, as rather theories of religion, dictated by the general foundations and tendencies of the system, within whose framework they came into existence.[4]

Marx, Nietzsche, Freud and later, Sartre, are the chief modern critics of religion, who consider it to be an event deprived of permanent, necessary and real foundations in man's nature. Religion is not a primary phenomenon, essentially connected with the structure of human existence. It is something secondary, which comes into being as a result of various social-economico-historical conditions. Most often, it is the result of unfavorable, frustrating situations and conditions of man's existence in the world of nature or the world of social bonds, and it can be liquidated once these are improved. Hence we have the postulate of destroying any religion, precisely for the dignity of man, for his emancipation from illusory bonds which inhibit the development of the natural and uniquely real forms of human life.[5]

Alongside the reductionist theories in the last century—in a certain measure as a reaction to the improper interpretation of religion—there arose theories portraying the originality and the irreducibility of a religious phenomenon to other spheres of man's existence. The anthropologically oriented philosophy at the beginning of the twentieth century, resulting from subjective-consciousness analyses, proved to be a perfect climate for the growth of phenomenology and the philosophy of religion. There was no concern here (as in the history of religion or comparative religions), only for the collection of religious facts or for the search for and description of the beginnings of religion, but for the discovery and establishment of the essence of religious actions, the essence of divinity, of holiness and the like. Undoubtedly the philosophy of religion owes its greatest achievements to the adaptation of the phenomenological method, even though there remains the influence of the interest and method of presenting philosophy by the existentialists. Rudolf Otto[6], Emil Brunner[7], Martin Buber[8], Mircea Eliade[9], Romano Guardini[10], Henri Duméry[11], Gerard van der Leeuw,[12] and, above all, Max Scheler,[13]—are pioneers and promoters of this discipline in our century.

The phenomenologico-existential method, which strives to grasp acts of consciousness, their structure, as well as the methods of constituting objective counterparts and meanings, is successful in examining man's experiences, taken in their unrepeatable concreteness and in relation to that which is exterior with respect to consciousness. Therefore this method proved to be very fruitful in the area of examining religious experiences. The achievements of the phenomenology of religion are immense. Phenomenological descriptions and analyses of religious experiences constitute a permanent contribution to knowledge about this area of human activity. In the opinion of the most eminent philosopher of religion, Max Scheler, religious actions grasp their object directly and intuitively. Therefore they have an objective character; that is, they do not create their objects but cognize them. Divinity and holiness then are not, as Feuerbach and his followers affirmed, the product of man, but something that exists beyond him and something that he discovers, when he feels and thinks. By means of phenomenological analysis, we ascertain not only the essence of religious actions but also the characteristic relation between man and religion, pointing to the transcendent object of such actions in relation to man's subjectivity.

The phenomenologico-existential method then examines the contents, the subject matter of the religious phenomenon with regard to what constitutes it. In this process, we receive much valuable and highly probable information about the religious man, who stands out very vividly in their descriptions as "one calling" for transcendence. In this way, we reach a knowledge which is truly significant and indispensable but only descriptive and, thereby, incomplete; because ultimately, it does not explain the religious fact. Therefore, there is a valid need to explain the philosophy of religion; that is, of one which, originating in an empirically given religious fact (a religious phenomenon) would interpret it in philosophical categories and endeavor to reach its ultimate explanation. Since the religious event is connected with man's essence, the explanation of such an event requires consideration and a universal investigation of every aspect of reality in which man lives and acts, as well as those which are attained.[14] Thus there is a need of a more objective treatment of the phenomenon of religion and of discovering its final, ontically non-contradictable reasons. The following sketch will be an attempt to define such an understood explanation of the religious fact. This sets the course for further inquiries. First, we shall give a description of the phenomenon of religion from the point of view of its object, as well as its subject, and we shall determine its relation to other spheres of human activities, such as cognition, morality and the arts. Then we shall consider the event of religion as a philosophical category and finally, we shall show the ultimately non-contradictable relations of religion which are both objective (they are linked to the personal structure of the human being), and subjective (they are linked to the existence of a Personal Absolute and his relation to the world—the transcendental participation of being).

II. THE RELIGIOUS FACT (PHENOMENON OF RELIGION)

The history of human culture and especially, the history of religion, supply us with much empirical material so that we can say with great probability that religion is inseparable from human life. Wherever man appears, he develops a religious activity. As E. Fromm rightly observes, there was no such culture and, as it seems, there cannot be any in the future, which would not contain religion.[15] The universality of the appearance of religious acts is hence beyond discussion. But a highly controversial issue with which students of religion are wrestling is an exhaustive answer to the question: What is religion and what are its ultimate sources?

The difficulties in giving an exhaustive and universally valid answer are caused by the great number of historical and contemporary religions. (They differ both in the character of the religious object and in religious experience.) Other difficulties are caused by the wealth of forms of religious life and especially in the specificity of experiences and religious acts, which are acts of the person, not of the nature, and as such are unrepeatable and united with what is, as if irrational, in its individuality and spontaneity. All this makes the area of man's religious behavior a very difficult object of analysis and interpretation, especially a philosophical one. Many philosophical concepts and trends add to the compositeness of the religious phenomenon.

In our consideration, we shall first deal with the most general characteristic of the religious fact, that is, we shall search for those elements which would be common to all religions. But first, we must establish certain distinctions in terminology. How should we understand "a religious fact," the "phenomenon of religion?" In religious literature these terms are used to define various realities, for example: prayer, sacrifice, faith, revelation, concretely, existing religions (historical and contemporary) such as Judaism, Christianity, Islam and to denote man's self-reference to a reality other than himself and to society in which he lives; that is, to some transcendent object, defined by modern students of religion as *sacrum,* insofar as this reference expresses itself in a specific activity.

What is the mutual bond in the above-mentioned phenomena? The religious fact in the original, basic meaning is man's very reference and direction to a transcendent reality. This is given in religious experience, but it discloses itself basically and originally in man's special behavior expressed in religious acts. Prayer, sacrifice and cult are therefore religious acts or the realizaton of such a reference. On the other hand, individual religion as a compilation of truths and directives concerning religious behavior, along with institutions, constitute an integrated cultural fact, which includes man's behavior together with a determination and organization of man's religious activities, which is the result of such reference to a transcendent reality.

A closer description of a religious fact, which is a specific reference of man to a transcendent reality and which reveals itself in man's attitude and in certain types of acts, can be accomplished by: (1) an indication of what constitutes such a reference and, hence, what is the transcendent object: (2) how is such a reference given to man (is what kind of human acts): and (3) in what relation does the religious fact remain toward other human facts (cognitive, moral, aesthetic).

In religious and phenomenological literature, there are many particular analyses of concrete acts, religious behavior or determinations of the character of the objects of religious reference, which enable us to recognize the quality of the religious phenomenon. In the following sketch, we cannot follow this "inductive" way. Instead, we shall limit ourselves to a citation of typical analyses in the literature of the religious fact, so that we might discover in them elements that are essential to it.

The Ancient and Middle Ages frequently used etymological definitions. Thus Cicero derives the term "religion" from *relegere,* defining it as a "diligent observation of that which is connected with divine worship." Lactantius, on the other hand, derives this term from *religare,* understanding religion as a "binding and union with God." St. Augustine and St. Thomas also refer to this definition. The former defines religion as a union (bond) with God, but Thomas defines religion as a virtue, which subordinates man's relation to God and, as such, constitutes an act of the virtue of justice. Nevertheless the understanding of religion as a union of man with God (as a personal reference to a personal God) is interspersed throughout his entire work. It even finds expression in the structure of the *Summa Theologiae,* whose composition portrays man as God's work, and as one who came from

God and is hastening toward him by a moral life with the help of Christ's sacraments in the Church.[16]

In modern and contemporary definitions of religion, the subjective element is usually stressed: the cognitive, volitional or emotional. Hence, Hegel defines religion as "an absolute consciousness in the consciousness of self or absolute consciousness of the subjective spirit;" Kant, as "a recognition of a divine command in all obligations;" Schleiermacher, as "a feeling of coexistence with the Infinite." James considers religion "as feelings, actions and experiences of the individual man, insofar as they refer to a bond with anything conceived as divine;" Söderblom, as "a relation between man and a supra-terrestrial power in which man believes and to which he feels a belonging, a relation which expresses itself in trust, fear, faith, prayer, sacrifices and ethical behavior;" Schlund, as "an attitude, a complex of active and effective relations between man and a superhuman power, with the purpose of attaining salvation;" Brunner, as "man's efforts to find a support in supra-mundane powers and thus reach salvation;" Hessen, as "life's relation to the holy;" Smith, as "a relation of the kind that occurs in a living experience between an individual and the object of worship, which evokes in us respect and love;" Fromm—as "every system of thought and actions, shared by a certain group, which provides the individual with a structure of orientation and an object of worship," Otto, as "an experience of mystery which is realized when man opens himself to impressions of eternal realities which reveal themselves on the path of temporality;" Wach, as "an experience of the *sacrum*." According to Jung, religion is a "solicitous and scrupulous observance of what Rudolph Otto accurately called *numinosum*; that is, the observance of the dynamic existence or effect not caused by an arbitrary act of the will. On the contrary, this effect embraces and overcomes man who is always its victim and not its creator." Gruehn calls religion "the kind of spiritual attitude which refers to God or, more simply speaking: if a soul has some kind of union with God—which surpasses all creatures, if God directs it." According to Van der Leeuv, "religion is not only a broadening and deepening of human life to the limits of potentiality, and even beyond these limits, in order to attain 'something different;' but above all, it is an intrusion into our life of that which does not belong to it."[17]

The above-mentioned definitions, so varied and already containing a certain interpretation of the religious phenomenon, indicate several basic elements essential to it. (1) a peculiar character of the limit of man's reference, which is always some sort of reality, higher than man, which is defined by a general term of: "deity," *sacrum, numinosum,* "God" or an "object of worship;" (2) an attitude of man toward this reality (faith, respect, fear, honor, love, certain responsibilities); and (3) a moment of active (redeeming) intervention of a transcendent reality in man's life.

Religion is therefore a specific, conscious reference of man to something different from and superior to him: it is a bilateral contact with someone (or something) that appears in a definite form and in a special human activity. The religious attitude is formed according to that which is the object of this type of contact and it specifies the character of the religious phenomenon.

A. ANALYSIS OF THE OBJECT OF THE RELIGIOUS FACT FROM THE ASPECT OF REALITY—A RELIGIOUS RELATION

In the above-mentioned deifinitions, we notice a tendency toward the widest possible understanding of the religious object. It is designated by the term "mystery," *sacrum,* "something higher," *numinosum,* "deity" or "God." The history of religion and the presently-existing religions furnish us with a wealth of material on whose basis we can answer what actually is the end of man's religious reference. These differ both in regard to their content as well as their form. Hence it is very difficult to find a designation of religion as a common human phenomenon, in such a way as to avoid associating it with a specific type of religion. The object of religion can clearly be either a personal, or impersonal, or spiritual, or material being. It may have a moral character or it may be some type of technical power. This gives a basis for differentiation of certain types of religion, for example: totemism, fetishism, animism, polytheism, pantheism and monotheism.[18] Considering the great variety of religious objects, it would be difficult to find an informative and common definition of the religious phenomenon. For this reason, we must distinguish religion in a broader and narrower sense.

In a broader sense, religion would be a reference to a suprahuman reality, understood in a most general sense. This may be some undefined, impersonal magical power (*mana*), concentrating itself in certain objects (fetishism); a vital power (like the sun), a life-giving element (totemism); a superior basis of all that is (*logos*); an impersonal dynamic reality; an active basis of the whole world (pantheism) and the like.

A narrower understanding of religion is connected with a recognition of the personal character of the object, in which man searches for the genesis and meaning of life. The question here is to have a definite conviction that the partner of a religious union can be a person, but not necessarily a most perfect person. All types of religion which accept faith in spiritual beings, especially in the spirits of ancestors (animism), as well as all types of polytheism must be considered here. Polytheism implies the conviction that for every living being, god is a living entity, who excels man; and all human events can be explained by a living person who does not die and who makes decisions concerning human fate. Thanks to the gods, man possesses everything that decides about his life as a person and, above all, he does not feel helpless in the world of surrounding things and powers of nature.

In such an understanding, religion definitely means man's reference to some one and not to some thing: to some one who possesses, at least in some respect, attributes of a personal being (life, freedom, love, immortality), as well as the quality of holiness which is understood, above all, as a separation from that which is "every-day," ordinary and starkly visible (mystery, and transcendence). A decidedly personal and monotheistic character of the object of religious reference is found in Islam, Judaism and Christianity. Scheler limits the religious phenomenon to this type of reference only: "Only where the Transcendent "Thou" surpasses the world as a totality—do we have a right to speak about a religious act."[19]

The newest definitions and interpretations of the religious phenomenon stress the personal character of the object of religion, as well as the personal character of man's reference. By observing carefully the history of religion, by gaining a deeper insight into the character of different deities as acknowledged by various religions and man's relationship with them, it seems that we could have found sufficient material illustrating and verifying the thesis; that man as a person has always searched—even in religions considered to be cosmic, dynamic or pantheistic—for some one and not some thing, who could answer his question about the meaning of life, and who could help him in life's difficulties. From the beginning of history, man was aware that only nature or impersonal powers cannot be a justification for his personal life but rather, a powerful and loving person, even though he sometimes portrayed this person in a very naive manner. If he gave divine honor to the sun, it did not always mean that he adored material phenomena. Most often he treated them as "hero-phanies," that is, manifestations of a mysterious power and it was this power that he adored.[20] The worship of cosmic objects was therefore always connected with the conviction that they are the revelation of divinity. For example, heaven occupies an important place in many religions in China, India and Greece; it seems, however, to be a manifestation of the greatest deity and it expresses a moment of his transcendence, namely that he is inaccessible and superior to man.[21] Another characteristic is the process of the personification of deities who are a physical reality. When Zeus commands Themis to summon the deities to a meeting, "there come, besides Ocean, many gods of the rivers, the Nymphs who inherit the forests, the clear founts and groves and flowery meadows."[22] In the Persian religion, even though the object of religious worship are chiefly the four elements of nature (light, water, earth and air), that is, forces on which life depends; nevertheless, there also appear personified powers: *Mithra, Varuna, Indra.*[23] An interesting expression of satisfying the need of a personal deity is the unity, under a certain aspect, within deity of the most perfect human and animal elements (*Re-Harachte*) in the Egyptian religion.[24] According to Babylonian myths, the gods are good, just and formidable masters. Man should serve them with trust, humility and fear.

The personal character of the object of religion is usually linked with Western-European tradition, where the personal being was always treated as the highest manifestation of reality and where the awareness of the person's distinction from the other beings was explicit. But we can give many examples of Eastern religions which, in addition to the recognition of an impersonal power or impersonal law, understood pantheistically, accept personal beings with whom man comes into religious contact. This applies, for example, to the religion of India: "Along with the depiction of an eternal, impersonal law governing the world already in Veda . . . other depictions appear: about a personal being, who governs according to a self-established law."[25] In Jinnism, many deities render various blessings to people, even though they themselves are subject to the operations of the karma. The Pantheon of Japanese deities, whose leader was the goddess of the sun, *Amaterasu,* are also personal beings who enter into kinship in hierarchical dependence and the like.[26]

Even though the moment of personification or personal understanding of the object or a religious bond did not appear in all religions, at least from the point of view of the subject (man), religion was always treated as a search for the foundation of man's personal life. If, in the primitive systems of religion, man searched for an answer to the question of the meaning of his personal actions and personal life in natural objects, it was always a question of his personal life. Every object of religious reference influenced man's life, thanks to which man confirmed, developed and preserved his life as a person. We have excellent testimony of this in various types of myths. Even though there is a question in mythical understandings between some sort of previously existing world—whose beginning and nature cannot be doubted—and the human world, nevertheless, myths do not refer only to the primitive procedure of things: all most fundamental and practical affairs of human life; such occupations like farming or hunting; the first moments of a new-born infant, the coming to maturity, matrimony, birthdays, death; in brief, the whole human life in its permanent elements does not belong to the world of mundane affairs. In mythical times, it possesses holy archetypes in which it participates. In the mythical world, gods and heroes performed eternal feats of work, love, war, and death; human life is only their reflection.[27]

Christianity brought about an exceptionally interesting moment in the understanding of the object of religion. It is the personal Absolute who is simultaneously a community of persons. There is as if an actual fulfillment of the ideal of a person, whose constituting element is the possibility of interpersonal communication. So understood, a Triune God is for man an ideal model of religious union, which contains in itself a relationship with a "transcendent Thou" and, at the same time, with other persons in a horizontal perspective (one commandment of love of God and neighbor).

B. ANALYSIS OF THE RELIGIOUS FACT FROM THE POINT OF VIEW OF THE SUBJECT—RELIGIOUS EXPERIENCE

Since we defined religion as a union of man with transcendent reality which justifies human life as a personal existence, and after indicating the character of the other member of the religious reference, a question arises: In what manner is this reference given to man? How is it expressed and what is its function?

Phenomenology of religion and especially psychology of religion has devoted much attention to this question by analyzing and describing *religious experience* as a path one takes to enter into a personal, conscious contact with divinity and as a manner of experiencing—especially from man's side—a relation with it.

Despite many valuable works in this area—especially those of Otto and Scheler and other modern psychologists of religion—a determination of the character of religious experience still remains a difficult matter, especially if one would want to indicate the elements common to all religions.[28] This is related to a variety of religious attitudes dictated by a different understanding of the religious object, as well as by the character of proper religious activity, which is suitable to a given cultural milieu, to the multiplicity of religions and, above all, by the individual and very personal character of religious experiences. Spontaneity, unrepeatability and "non-measurability" are greater here than in any other area of human life. As a personal experience, it involves all the elements of the human psyche (and even the body): cognitive, volitive, emotional, and just as a person is unrepeatable in his individuality, so are his most fully personal experiences unrepeatable and unmeasurable.

Keeping in mind such a type of conditions of a subjectively understood religious fact, we shall nevertheless try to indicate the fundamental moments and elements of a religious experience, always being aware of the fact that we are achieving an approximative typology of events, which elude every systematization.

In this greatly complex and rich human experience which is the religious experience, we can distinguish three basic phases which consecutively constitute the composite processes.

(1) *Contact* with a religious reality (*sacrum*) which is a religious perception and which supplies certain information about the religious object. It is a phase which is analogous to cognitive and aesthetic perception in a cognitive, moral and aesthetic experience. The subject here is as if passive; it is the receiver. Activity is on the side of the object which reveals itself, shows its presence and "strikes" the subject and arouses it from its previous state. While the subject is passive in this phase of the experience, it is nevertheless capable of receiving this "blow" from the side of the religious object. Two types of potentialities come into play here: natural potentialities (cognitive and volitive-emotional powers), as well as so-called obedient potentialities which are spoken of in Christian theology. This is a help (grace) which flows from the side of God and which strengthens the perceptive abilities of man in this area. The result is that the ability to receive the "blow" from the side of the religious object in a human subject is commensurable neither with the relation to the acting object nor with the natural powers of man. The religious "stimulus" can act in various ways, and it can also find a very different response in the receiving subject.

The main problem linked with the first phase of religious experience is the manner in which the religious object manifests itself and reveals its presence. In other words, whence come the cognitive contents which man affirms and which constitute the source of religious acts?

All scholars of religion are quite in agreement that the religious object (*sacrum, numinosum*) is not directly accessible, in all its grandeur, to the subject. To express the cognitive transcendence of the religious object the term "revelation" is used. All religious experiences, and hence all religions, imply a revelation, either natural or supernatural, or an acknowledgement that the religious object in some way "speaks" about itself, but it does not reveal itself directly (cognition is by means of signs). These may be linguistic word-objects or oral word-signs which God himself "pronounces" about his existence and life, and also his aims in relation to man (supernatural revelation). Moreover these two ways of revelation are complementary rather than exclusive.

Otto and Scheler devoted much attention to religious experience and its accompanying problem of cognitive perception, indicating the individuality of religious experience. In his analysis, Otto attempted to include all religious experiences, whereas Scheler limited himself to an analysis of religious experience proper to religions which recognize a personal God.

According to Otto, the religious object, *numinosum,* is inaccessible to man in a conceptual type of cognition. Instead, it is a power which affects man, and which incites in him natural responses rather than emotional ones. It fills him with terror, fear and, at the same time, it fascinates and attracts him. A cognitive attainment of the *numinosum* is impossible; but what is possible is the existence or feeling of divinity, thanks to a special ability of the human spirit, which Otto describes as *sensus numinis*. Thanks to it, man experiences *sacrum*. The feeling of *sacrum* is a specific original affection which results in man's search for communication with *numinosum*.

Numinosum, according to Otto, is possible to man in a particular emotional response which it invokes in an experiencing ego: "It is in this way that it moves the human ego with such and such a determinate feeling." Otto reduces these feelings to several typical ones: a feeling of mystery full of fear *(mysterium tremendum)*, expressing absolute inaccessibility; "otherness" of this *numinosum*, a feeling of absolute omnipotence *(tremenda majestatis)*; admiration *(mirum)*. The feeling of the mysterious religiousness is something strange and odd; something which eludes generally the range of common, understood and known things and hence, its own; in view of this it is hidden and contrary to what is common and, therefore, it fills man with a thrilling feeling of the unexpected. Qualitative content *numinosum* given in a religious feeling is from one aspect, a repulsive element *tremendum* together with *majestatis* and, from another, something very attractive, glamorous and fascinating; something that together with the repulsive element *tremendum* enters into a personal contrast-harmony. Thus from the "revelation" in the human feeling *numinosum*, there arises an appropriate means of experiences and achievements (religious actions).[29]

For Scheler, the religious phenomenon begins only when a personal God comes into play. What unites both thinkers is the emphasis of a specific religious experience and the stressing of the intentional character of the religious act. Their perception in the area of religious perception can be defined as "intentional feeling." It is stressed in such a way that religious experience can be understood only from the point of view of the object which determines it and, at the same time, that it has a quality of engaged cognition, in which volitive-emotional moments participate.[30] These pertinent accents, however, do not adequately characterize cognitive perception in a religious experience. To describe it, it is absolutely necessary to consider that reality which is linked with "revelation" and "faith." Cognitive perception in this type of human experience is not so much a seeing and "inspiration" as "hearing" God, as One who reveals his presence and his plans, who speaks to man, who is capable of accepting the word directed to him and who responds to it with faith. Faith refers to precisely such a reality which is not directly accessible to cognitive perception. Therefore the assertion of a cognitive content in religious experience is not super-imposed by the state of affairs or objective evidence or reasoning, but it is an action produced under the pressure of the will, as a result of understanding the personal value of the religious object, with respect to motives of credibility (confidence). Therefore faith has a character of personal involvement, since in this manner it involves the will whose activity has the character of pursuing a good (love) which has been seen.

The moment of a volitional acceptance for the sake of "personal" motives is the essential element of faith. In differing from a purely cognitive perception, where cognitive experience has a character of an objective "vision," religious experience deals even in its first phase, with a personal cognition which is engaged and conditioned through love.

To the extent that the word and response to these are the proper manner of interpersonal communication, we are dealing here with religious perception. Its nature is the realization by a knowing subject of the presence of a living God. God speaks, and man responds in the form of faith, hope and love. Therefore religious perception is a recognition (with the whole psyche) of the presence of the Absolute. If the trait of every cognitive experience is the disclosure, the revealing of an object, as a result of which man gains information about it, and he himself does not create the cognitive contents, then this becomes true to a greater extent in relation to religious perception. In this perception a personal God reveals himself by means of words. God is present in man, who does not see him, but whose "voice" he is capable of hearing and responding to it.

It is essential for religious perception that the initiative should come from the side of the object, from the side of the revealing God, who announces Himself, and not from the side of man. This proves that God wishes to enter into contact with man, that is, religious experience has the character of an interpersonal dialogue. Therefore religious perception is in essence dialogic (communication by means of word), just as every religious act possesses the character of dialogue. Scheler writes: "The religious act requires, in distinction from all other acts of cognition, even in the area of metaphysics, a response of some contrary or especially reciprocated act from the side of the object, to which it hastens in agreement with its intentional being. This in itself already proves that we can speak about religion only when its object has the form of a Divine Person."[31]

2. In the second phase of religious experience, there follows the "taking-over" of the activity by the subject which has been "struck" by the religious object. Since man has perceived the religious object as the highest personal good in religious perception, he is involved personally. The reaction of the subject to the revelation of the religious object, and its recognition as the

highest good worthy of love, is the desire to enter with it into personal contact. This is expressed in a series of interior and inner-exterior acts which can be most generally defined as *"pietas,"* an attitude of worship and respect, which again takes on the most varied forms in particular cultures and in particular persons. Without doubt, contact with the religious object can evoke all the emotional types described by Otto and other scholars of religion, but it expresses itself most deeply when it is brought into contact with a personal deity, in faith, hope and love. However, the final aim of a personal contact with deity is not the attitude of worship or respect, but aiming toward union with it. Religious perception contains an appeal to action, whose aim is not only to worship, to present petitions, or to adore, but also to prepare the subject for a union with a deity who is acknowledged as the highest good worthy of love. Man desires and pursues this union with it, and to be absorbed by it.

The activity of the subject in this phase of religious experience—just as analogically, his perceiving ability in the preceding phase—has both a natural and supernatural character. Man's activity concentrates on preparing himself for dialogue, since he is aware of his own distinctiveness and unworthiness in relation to deity. All religions clearly contain the acknowledgement of the need of purification to enable us to come into contact with deity. They prepare special techniques of "interior life" (Buddhism, Hindu yoga, Neoplatonic asceticism, Christian asceticism and mysticism), which should help to attain—variously understood—a union with it. In Christian mysticism, natural activity is supported by a special grace which acts in man and prepares him for union with God. This implies, however, methods of interior purification described by the great Christian mystics: for example, John of the Cross or Catherine of Siena, called the purification of the senses (night of the senses) and purification of the spirit (night of the spirit), which, by purifying man first in his bodily-emotional part, and then in the spiritual, should lead to a union with God. The subject's own activity is pervaded by the action of grace so that the mystical experience in Christianity is not commensurable with an applied technique. It is the fruit of the Holy Spirit's activity in a suitably prepared soul.[32]

3. In the third phase, there follows an actualization of the conscious bond with God through action (religious act) oriented toward the religious object. Only then does the religious action have a crowning religious qualification or it fulfills the religious function of sanctifying.

Just as human persons are different and unrepeatable, so with a varied involvement of intellectual, volitional and even motor powers, there take place religious acts which have for their aim, a fuller actualization of a union with God. The final completion of a religious activity takes place when the entire action of Transcendence (God) meets with a full attunement of man, when Transcendence finds a complete resonance in him. In Christian theology, such religious activity is realized by the working of the Holy Spirit (theory of the gifts of the Holy Spirit). Under his influence, the subject reaches as if a certain connaturality with God, with the result that man becomes ready to engage in a dialogue; open to all aspirations for good, he reaches the so-called state of passive (infused) contemplation.

Thus to a certain degree, in all religions but especially in Christianity, the religious experience develops from a passive acceptance of God's action (first phase), through various types of activities, which have as their purpose an increasing freeing of man from limitations—an ever greater "spiritualization" and direction toward God (second phase)—up to the state of mastering and actualizing the bond, the union which is an introduction to, and preparation for, a full life with God and in God, which is to be man's portion after death.

Christian mysticism differs from all natural mysticisms in the fact that the final union with God is not a result proportional to the activity of the subject, but it is a gift; it is caused by the Holy Spirit dwelling in man. There is also a difference in purpose. For example, as much as "sanctification" for Eastern mystics depends on a fuller awareness of an immaterial element which is in man, so much in Christian mysticism, "sanctification"—even though it is rooted in the immaterial ego of man—is ultimately the work of the Holy Spirit.

C. BASIC FORMS OF RELIGIOUS ACTIVITY— RELIGIOUS ACTS (RELIGIOUS DEED)

There exists a great variety of religious acts by which man expresses his relationship to deity and actualizes in religious perception the conscious perspective of "being-toward-Transcendence." While we are aware of their richness and very individualized character (they are acts of persons), we can place them in several basic categories. They are: prayer, sacrifice, cult, asceticism and moral perfection. The union of religion with practical conduct is so intimate, that when Thomas Aquinas speaks about religious acts, he distinguishes two types: (1) proper, by which man refers directly to God himself (prayer and sacrifice), and (2) secondary, which condition the contact with God or they are the result of that contact. They refer either to other persons, or to the very subject of religious experiences or even to other things (moral behavior).[33]

a) PRAYER—constitutes the most basic and common religious act, which appears in all religions and attests to man's personal attitude toward a deity, however it may be perceived. The partner in a personal dialogue may be either some invisible power, or some other object, but it is always considered as someone who listens and in some way responds. We can speak about prayer in the strict sense only when there appears a real awareness of a spiritual bond with a personal God. Then it is a dialogue between a human "I" and divine "Thou;" it is man's response to God's word directed to a man (a response to a call). Therefore prayer establishes faith in the existence of a personal God. It establishes a dialogue with God whose direct presence man experiences.[34]

Prayer may assume various forms (adoration, thanksgiving, petition); its basic task, common to all forms, is the interior integration of man and a fuller actualization of the spiritual bond with God, and not the informing of God about our needs or our situation, which he already knows. St. Augustine expresses this task of prayer when he says that we pray not to inform God, but to "create ourselves" (*ut homo construetur*) as persons directed to God.

As a spiritual act, prayer also releases spiritual energies; it is the source of spiritual activity which has a concrete result, either in the relationship to the praying person, or to the one for whom man prays, or in some wider context. The posture of concentrated meditation—prayer—is the greatest of human activities: it constitutes the activity of the human spirit which brings about concrete results. The existence of persons who choose prayer and contemplation for their chief form of personal and social activities is thereby justified. (Here we mean congregations of contemplatives in the Christian culture, and individual religious vows or religious communities in other religions and cultures.)[35]

b) SACRIFICE—at the basis of every religious relation—at least in its personal forms—is love, which flows from the feeling of one's distinctness and inferiority, as well as from a desire to overcome them through a union with God. All religious activity is the striving for this union. The active quality of love depends on the fact that love is fundamentally a *giving*, and not a receiving. The ability to love consists in giving oneself to another. This is also realized in the relationship of man to God. Therefore "sacrifice" as a giving of oneself appears in all religions, and its fullest expression is found in the Christian religion. The moment of the gift constitutes here the symbol and the expression "being-for-God," "being-toward-God." It includes either some material goods (something that is mine) or spiritual goods (concern, love, solicitude), and finally, it should lead to the *giving* of oneself, which constitutes the deepest bond with God—it is the union with him in love.

D. RELIGIOUS FACT AND SCIENTIFIC COGNITION, MORALITY, ART

The specificity of the religious fact—given in a widely understood religious experience and revealing itself in the particular activity of man—will be seen more clearly by comparing it with other specifically human facts, especially in the area of cognitive, moral and aesthetic experiences and conduct.

1. Cognitive experience. The essential moment for cognitive experience is contact with the object, which reveals and discloses itself to the cognizing subject. The fundamental purpose of cognition is to obtain information about reality (theoretical purpose), but the realized value in cognitive acts is the value of truth, which is the agreement of the knower's thought with the known object. The cognizing subject is somewhat passive here (in the case of cognitive contents, he reads them but he does not create them). He assimilates the contents given him from without. The assertion (the moment of realizing the truth) is imposed upon the subject by the objective state of things: objective evidence or some type of demonstration; emotional moments should not come into play here. Relations which constitute the cognitive act are defined as personal-factual relations, not as interpersonal ones. In a cognitive experience, even if the object should be human beings, it is treated as a "thing," or as a set of qualifications, which are to be known, but not as a "person" with whom one establishes a personal contact. In a religious experience—as seen in the considerations presented above—the motives of assertion are of a different, i.e., a personal, type, for example: confidence in a person whom we believe; a conviction that believing is worthwhile.

Thus volitional-emotional moments (love) enter into the very structure of religious perception. All religious cognition then has a quality of involved personal cognition which induces one to action.[36]

2. Moral experience. It is important to become aware of the proper character of the moral fact and to ascertain the relationship to religious facts, because morality often identifies itself with religion (for example, Kant), or relationships are improperly established between these two activities of man. Moral experience—similar to religious experience—has many phases and it is practically oriented, i.e., to the act. In the first phase, it takes on the form of an experience of duty, as a result of recognizing such a situation which appeals to the cognizing subject that he should perform a particular act. It implies an experience which refers to moral values (moral good or evil). The experience of duty and moral values passes in the next phase into an experience creating a moral behavior actualized in a moral act (moment of decision). By means of an act which is in harmony with duty, man creates a good being (goodness) which, above all, enriches the subject or the author of the act. It makes him "better;" it makes him more human, for by his moral acts and moral works, man creates and transforms himself—"builds" himself as a person.[37]

There exists a strong analogy between moral experience and religious experience. Moral experience, similar to religious experience, is focused on action. It expresses itself in the action which develops and "creates" the subject himself, insofar as he is directed to another person. Both religious perception and perception implicated in a moral experience contain an appeal to action. Mere thought about duty, or mere knowledge about values, has no moral value, just as thinking about God, or knowledge about sanctity, has no religious value. But the object of a moral act is different: human beings are its object (and the very subject of the moral experience as a person), while in a religious experience, the subject is directed straight to the Transcendent Person. Religious value, which is the result of a religious act, appears to be a very complex composite value, built upon another type of values and, hence, it implies a value of good, although it is not exhausted by it.

3. The aesthetic experience—similar to religious and moral experiences—is complex. In the first phase, contact with the object produces in the perceiving subject, a certain emotional and appetitive state, with the result that the subject concentrates his attention on the object. Hence aesthetic perception takes place as the result of a certain emotional state and it contains a set of cognitive acts, which grasp the qualities of the artistic object (its harmony of elements and the like). It evokes, in turn, certain volitional-emotional states; this oscillation from a cognitive attitude to a volitional-emotional reaction is characteristic in an aesthetic experience. These states are expressed in the approval or disapproval which results from satiety or from discouragement in relation to the preceding phases (pleasure, delight, or disappointment in regard to the original emotion). Articulation of this emotion assumes the character for an aesthetic judgment (it is pleasing or not). The realized value is the value of beauty and the function of the aesthetic experience—that which Ossowski describes as "life of the moment." Hence it is an escape from business, work and objects of everyday life and a transfer to a new dimension, "disinterested" from the practical point of view.[38]

It is precisely through such a disinterestedness and a kind of "getting away" from the everyday affairs of life—which brings no measurable material profit, since it really enriches man emotionally, and extends his existence to new dimensions—that we sometimes identify it with religious experience. Beauty may doubtless be something religiously-creative, precisely because of the capacity for disinterested behavior. Likewise, it always plays an important accompanying role in religious experience and in religious acts (religion and art). Nonetheless, there exists a great difference in the object and aim of one and the other type of experience. In a religious experience, the object can ultimately be only a Transcendence; that is, a really existing and loving Person, and the purpose of religious activity is the pursuit of a union with It. In view of this, a religious experience is focused on action, leading to the attainment of a real union (love) with God, while the object of an aesthetic experience may be every being—natural or derived from man—which furnishes the experiencing subject specific experiences, but it does not fulfill a personal existential role. As much as aesthetic experience diverts attention from practical reality and causes, as it were, "life of the moment," so religious experience fulfills a directly opposite function: it takes root in something changeless (in eternity). If, in a certain sense, it draws one away for a while from everyday practical matters, it does this only to become aware of the full perspective of life and even to include in it, daily activity. Besides this purpose of religious life, there is a certain reinterpretation of the entire human life which, in the perspective of "being-toward-Transcendence," acquires a new, deeper sense.

III. RELIGION AS AN AREA OF CULTURE

A religious fact—being a specific reference of the human subject to a transcendent object, given in a religious experience and realized through religious acts whose center is the object of religion, usually understood in our culture as a Personal Absolute—constitutes a special field of cultural-creative activity of man. This field differs from other areas of culture because it is a conscious cooperation with God in constituting a spiritual bond between human persons and a transcendent "Thou."

The human person, which is a dynamized being and open to another personal "Thou" in a horizontal perspective, realizes his openness to Transcendence, in a certain measure, in union with other persons. Although religion is a most personal and individual matter, it does not cease being a social affair, for the relationship to other persons mutually constitutes the very personality of man. In addition, the openness of the human person to Transcendence determines, as everything else in human life, a certain potentiality for realization. This realization requires not only the personal effort of the human spirit, but also the cooperation of other persons, more than in any other area because the spiritual reality which it reveals and to which it leads, is more difficult to attain than any other. Mutual help of human persons is absolutely necessary.

We must now indicate the structure of religion as precisely a cultural happening (religion in the objective sense), which embraces a certain area of human knowledge and activity, directed to some kind of Transcendence. The value of activity in this area is holiness.[39]

Therefore a religious fact determines: (1) a set of truths, (2) a program of religious activity and a set of directives for religious conduct, and (3) institutions whose purpose it is to help man in realizing his religious activity.

A. A set of truths. Every religion contains a theory of a religious object, of the world and man, of his situations and perspectives, truths which inform us about the mystery of man's destination. In the religious doctrines of all modern and historical religions, we can observe certain common elements. For each one embodies: (a) a determination of an ontic and moral ideal, (b) an acknowledgement of the ontic and living insufficiency of man or some kind of weighing down with guilt (element of a loss), and (c) an indication of a way of delivering man from an unfavorable situation (*mysterium salutis*).[40]

(a) Every religion presents a certain reality respectively or absolutely perfect, superior to man with respect to ontic moral perfection, or with respect to power. This can be a personal Absolute or properly, a Perfect Personal Community as in Christianity—a certain archetypal event or somehow understood as *sacrum,* which performs a two-fold role in relation to man: it is the source of his personal life, as well as his ultimate end. Contact with this ideal gives the proper sense to human life and indicates man's permanent and unlimited perspective.

(b) The essential element of every religion is man's conviction that his existence is far from the presented ideal from both the ontic and moral points of view. The desire to be united with it is joined with the awareness of one's insufficiency and therefore, a feeling of deficiency, frequently connected with a feeling of guilt and the realization of the need for help from the side of the transcendent reality.

(c) "Savior," "deliverance" constitute an absolutely indispensable element in every religion which takes on a very varied form in particular religions. The expression "deliverance" of man can be understood in different ways, depending on the degree of awareness of such a lack. Sometimes it appears in the form of help in everyday affairs (protection from sickness, catastrophies, injustice). In higher forms of religion, especially in Christian religion, it is a question of supernatural salvation, which frees man from sin and enables him to unite with God. The Person of Christ, God-Man, most fully expresses the idea of salvation adequate for a human person. Since Christ is God and Man, he unites in his person what is divine and human; he is the one who "reconciles" God with man and establishes the sign (sacrament), through which salvation is achieved. He is also a personal model of that to which religious activity should lead: to a union of human "I" with the transcendent "Thou."

Religions which exist concretely in the realm of doctrinal content and hence, in view of the nature of a religious object, the condition of man and the manner of deliverance, differ greatly. This constitutes the area in which the history of religion or the study of comparative religions is interested. The object of research in the philosophy of religion is frequently the epistemological character of the proper cognition for religion. We have already examined this question somewhat when we discussed the nature of cognitive experience in religious experience. Here we shall focus our attention on the specificity of religious doctrine and religious cognition in relation to other types of human cognition, especially of specialized sciences and philosophy. Relations between these areas of knowledge are not always interpreted correctly.

Cognition contained in religious doctrine differs from scientific and philosophical cognition in extent, formal object, source and type of assertion.[41] It differs in extent, since it deals with such areas of reality which are not proper to scientific cognition, nor even to philosophy (for example: spiritual life of God). The difference also concerns the formal object. Inasmuch as scientific cognition is concerned with the acquisition of information about a certain area, or about a certain aspect of reality (the question here is about theoretical cognition), so, from the beginning, religious cognition concerns itself with involved, living and practical truth. There is no strictly theoretical cognition in any phase of religious cognition. Likewise the source of religious and scientific truth is different. In fact, religious doctrine can contain certain truths which may be attained by one's own reason (for example: truth about God's existence and the existence of the soul), but they are not characteristic sources of religious truths. Here, the ultimate source is always some type of revelation. Religious doctrine (theology) consists in the reading and interpretation of supernatural revelation. In the Catholic religion, interpretation of revelation is achieved according to definite rules (analogy of faith, personal involvement of the theologian, acceptance of the Teaching Authority of the Church).[42]

The most essential trait of religious cognition, which distinguishes it from all other types of cognition, is the manner of assertion of religious truths. This is achieved not as a result of the object's evidence or of some kind of reasoning, but on the strength of trust in the person who presents the information. Hence the motives for assertion in scientific and philosophical cognition differ from those in religious cognition. The cognitive foundation and the cognitive side of religion is faith, which depends on a reasonable explanation in theology. Faith is the kind of cognition which takes place in interpersonal relationships; it is a special act of the will, that is, of a power whose fundamental activity is love. In this sense, we can say that at the basis of religious cognition is love, which further affirms the personal character of man's reference to Transcendence.

This does not mean that religious experience does not have an important cognitive role in religion. God cannot have any meaning for a person if he does not present himself in a personal experience. But this is only a specific experience, resulting not so much from a particular inspection of the person who is ontically and cognitively transcendent, but it is the result of an awareness of its presence by means of a "sign." In revealed religion (that is, in supernatural revelation), this sign assumes the form of a "word," whence we say that religious cognition, faith, is "from hearing." If we can speak here about experience, then it is an experience of a specific type, which is the awareness of God's presence in the soul, resulting from the power of grace. (Its special form is, for example, mystical experience.)[43]

When we speak about the character of religious cognition, there is a definite need of distinguishing it from a philosophical cognition of God that is often considered in competition with it—which is a result of improper interpretation of one or another type of cognition.[44] In characterizing religious cognition, we describe it as a cognition which is directly conditioned ethically, and which possesses a personalistic character. Often there is no clear consideration that this kind of cognition considers, in its point of departure, personal relations, and that it is a confirmation of presence on the strength of faith. Perceiving God's presence in the cosmos (confirmation of the symbolic character of the world) or in one's own soul is something secondary to the recognition of God's existence on the basis of faith. Obviously, cognitive acts in religion lead to an increasingly deeper cognition of God; religious experiences allow for a closer approach to his mystery, but only when one accepts, at the beginning, the fact of the existence of God with whom the religious dialogue takes place.

A natural and entirely neutral cognition of God's existence, of the kind that takes place in metaphysics, is achieved, on the other hand, on the basis of knowing the structure of reality and its explanation. It is always a direct and theoretical cognition (whose result is only in a determined activity). It is a natural cognition which implies a moment of reflection (it is not direct; it does not constitute an intuition). Even though religious and metaphysical cognitions of God concern the same final designation, they fundamentally differ nevertheless in character. It is another matter that theology profits from metaphysical cognition, since it seeks to indicate the natural foundations of religious beliefs and thus the conviction about God's existence which flows from faith.

B. A program of religious activities and a set of directives for religious behaviors. Contact with Transcendence calls for and releases in man a special type of activity, whose aim is the achieving of a union with It. It is a personal activity and hence very spontaneous and difficult to express in some kind of rule. Nevertheless, since man is a person, he is a social being and a being who has potentiality. Even in this most personal area, he can develop his activity with the help of other persons. It is also possible to formulate certain most general rules for these activities (schools, methods of interior life), whose knowledge can help man in this most difficult area of his activities. Since man is a person who has potentiality, he "learns" "to-be-to-ward-Transcendence," just as he learns "to-be-toward-another" man. Therefore human society develops methods and patterns for religious behaviors; it organizes common prayer, sacrifice, forms of cult; it controls the principles of morality, implicated by the religious foundations. Particular religious communities (churches) usually conduct a planned activity which manifests itself in proposing and organizing special actions, whose aim is the development of some type of religious activity. Hence one can speak about a certain type of "politics" of religion, just as one speaks, for example, about "politics" of science.

C. Religious institutions are designated for social help for a human person in the realization of his/her activity. Religious society depends on the recognition of a common faith by various individuals. This faith is upheld by common experience (tradition) and a suitable organization. Membership in the specific religious organization (the Church) indicates the autonomy, as well as the social character of the human person. The realization of the human person, even in his direction toward God, is achieved through and together with others. Just as the Person of the Absolute has a social character (in Christian religion), so the religious dimension of the human person is inseparably joined with its social dimension.

When the potential and social character of the human person are taken into consideration, there appears the problem of religious upbringing, guided both by the family and religious community (church) from earliest childhood. Its need seems to be the same as the need for teaching the child knowledge, development of family feelings, moral and aesthetic attitudes and the like, and especially of that which may be called teaching of "being-for-others." Just as children are taught from childhood to know and to love those near to them, even when they do not understand what cognition is, nor who the other person is and what value he has in their life, in the same manner a man who is a being in potency and, therefore, one who develops his dispositions, should learn "being-toward-God" even when he is not yet in a position to understand the character of his reference or who is his goal. The moment of rational verification of convictions acquired in childhood, and of religious foundations, must take place at a later period, along with a general intellectually-personal development, but its proper result depends to a large degree on the level of religious education.

IV. PHILOSOPHICAL FORMULATION AND EXPLANATION OF A RELIGIOUS FACT

A religious fact, given in an interior experience and expresssing itself in empirically-ascertained manifestation, requires interpretation and a detailed explanation. This cannot be accomplished automatically. We must make use of a certain philosophical system, and hence of many reflections and theories explaining religion. And because it is a human fact, it needs, in a philosophical explanation above all, a consideration of the theory of the human being and a theory of being itself. For it is within the framework of anthropology and metaphysics, that we can interpret and ultimately explain any type of human fact. Consequently, in further investigations, we shall refer to a knowledge analyzed within the framework of such philosophical disciplines. We are limiting ourselves in this respect to philosophy of the classical type, that is, to one which searches for ontical factors, which ultimately condition and explain (so-called non-contradictable factors), a fact which interests us.

A. RELIGION—AN INTERSUBJECTIVE RELATION ("I-THOU")

In modern philosophy, Scheler achieved perhaps the fullest characteriza- tion of religious acts. According to his statement, these belong to human consciousness, as well as acts of thought, will, memory and the like. They are primordial elemental and elementary manifestations; they have no empir- ical genesis in this sense: i.e., that they do not arise in conjunction with other psychical acts. Scheler thought the most important attributes of religi- ous acts to be the transcendence of their purpose, the satisfaction of their as- piration only by God, and the awaiting for an answer from God and mutual love.[45]

According to Scheler, just as all spiritual acts, so too the religious act is directed toward an objective sphere, that is, it does not construct its object, nor does it ascribe anything to it. Its completion depends upon the actuali- zation of intentional contents through its passive intuition. Therefore a religi- ous act distinguishes itself by immediacy of the experience *sacrum* which, according to Scheler, constitutes an *a priori* axiological idea (idea of divinity) which is given to man intuitively. Therefore *sacrum* constitutes the primordial phenomenon (*Urphänomen*). The idea of holiness is not reducible to any historical category. As a primordial value, *sacrum* is not subject to definition. It can be described, drawn nearer, but it cannot be defined exhaustively. Scheler does this by borrowing many elements of description from Otto; yet the overtone and intention of his statement are different. The basic constitutive ele.nent of *sacrum* is, according to his statement, infinite love.[46]

Even though Scheler interpreted the religious phenomenon as an interpersonal relationship and he identified the concept of *sacrum* directly with a personal God, he nevertheless did not indicate the ultimate ontic sources of a religious relation. Rather, under the influence of Scheler and Otto, there grew a widespread opinion that the object of religion is *sacrum* as the greatest distinct axiological category. Corresponding to it, is man's psyche "absolute sphere," from which flow religious acts (Scheler) or *sensus numinis* as an a priori ability of experiencing *sacrum* (Otto). An experience of that which is holy creates the empirical contents of *sacrum*, which manifests itself in human experience.

In connection with such an understanding of the religious act and its sources, a number of problems arise which must be solved in order to determine the character of religious relations. The question here is whether there really exists in man an absolutely personal sphere or a special *sensus*, thanks to which he experiences a transcendent reality. Is *sacrum* a special primordial category? On what does the function of religious acts depend?

Now, if a religious act would result from a "distinct" sphere or from a definite disposition of the human subject, then religion would be one of the manifestations of human existence which do not reach the foundations of human existence. The need for transcendence toward God seems to be conditioned much more deeply. It is called for by the very personal structure of the human being and, by its roots, it reaches a conscious ontic situation of man in a surrounding world of things and persons; and its function depends on the actualization of the human person in his fullest and deepest dimension.

To a great degree, inquiries in the contemporary philosophy of the "subject"—especially certain types in existentialism—have contributed to an emphasis on the character of religious relations. They have revealed the "openness" of human existence, a multilateral openness which is also an openness toward something transcendent.[47] The course of argumentation in favor of such a position proceeds as follows: The human person is not a pure spirit; he is not an "I" independently of the body. Therefore he does not constitute a "closed interiority," which would only pass through incarnation, as for example, Plato regarded man (as an incarnated god). He is a spirit which "completes itself" in corporeity; he is "I-in-the-world." Since the human person is a "being-in-itself" and a "being-in-the-world," he is also a "being-for-another"—he is open to other personal beings. The world of things and the world of persons constitute a natural environment for the man who enters into the most varied relationships with them, and thus creates himself, his "subjectivity." An awareness of self is therefore an awareness of the cognition of the "I-in-the-world" and "I-with-others." Man realizes himself in a humanized world, which is called such because it bears traces of human presence. Presence in the world necessarily entails relationships with other personal beings. Man becomes himself (a person) in confrontation and communication with them. The subjectivity of the human person is therefore formed in interhuman relationship and in the use of the material components (*der Stoff*) of this world. Cut off from others, man could not have realized his personal life. If man becomes a person through contacts with others, or authentic human life implies the presence of another person—and this is a twofold presence: real (physical) and presence by the word in which one believes and trusts—then from a purely athropological point of view the realization of human existence requires revelation and devotion through faith, which constitutes the basic categories of human experience. Hence, in the personal structure of man, there is engraved an openness to personal existence which manifests itself through its word.[48]

How does man recognize his direction toward the transcendent "Thou?" As Marcel writes, man is a direction to the Transcendent Being, a trust in God. He is an "invocation." The entire human being is a "call."

Man becomes aware of his being "rooted" in the world and, at the same time, of his distinctness from the world. By realizing his concrete relationships with the world, he knows that he does not enter the world of nature as its part or as a function of it, but as a personal being, who is able to choose the object of his cognition and love, and it is through this type of freedom that he transcends the whole world of nature. As such, he is the only being for whom his own existence (life) is a problem and at that, a most basic one. It is precisely in the question about the meaning of life that the transcendence of the human person appears most in relation to all other beings. Only man is interested in the entire existing universum of being, and the position he occupies in it. Hence, he asks the question about the meaning of his own existence, and he needs an answer to it. As Heidegger observes, man is a being who in his existence is preoccupied with his being, and the question about "being-in-general" is a manner of "being-a-man."[49]

The religious dimension of human life is linked with the ability to ask about the "direction" of existence. Man asks a question not only from the aspect of the "whence" but also of the "whither" of his being. In searching for the foundation of his existence, man searches not only for his origin but also for his purpose. There are many human purposes which correspond to many possible modes of a human "being-in-the-world." But no concrete purpose constitutes man's end which would adequately satisfy his "natural desire."

As a "self-grounded project," who is actualized in his transcendence, man fails completely when he is considered as a "project-in-the-world." A "natural desire" of human existence must be understood as man's orientation toward the Transcendent Being, which is essential for the human personality. Man does not desire to be God, but he desires to see God.[50] As Marcel writes, man is pointing toward the Transcendent Being, a thrust toward God. He is the "invocation." The entire human being is a "call" (having a "thrust") toward God.[51]

An "openness" of the human being to Infinity which is widely described by existentialists and experienced by the individual, points to certain dispositions which already concern the ontic structure and ontic situation of man in the world, and can constitute, from the side of human experience, a convincing basis for a philosophical explanation.

An all-embracing ontic perspective which man is able to encompass constitutes the explanation of the possibility of the appearance of the religious fact. Briefly we can say: man is a religious being because he is a thinking person and a metaphysical being (as understood by the existentialists). The religious posture is found in the personal nature of man and his roots in the ability to think. God reveals his existence to us through our existence. Religion, as F. C. Copleston rightly observes, depends on the experience of the contingency of the human person.[52] The experience of our own being shows us that we are a "being-in-ourself" and a "being-for-ourself"; and simultaneously that we realize "ourselves" to the extent that we are open to other beings. By experiencing ourselves, we experience our own incompleteness, dependence, finiteness, and contingency. In a word, we experience our own contingency which takes on a specific intensity in view of our becoming aware of the limits of human experience—in the presence of death. The human being who is not self-sufficient is aware of his/her contingency and the contingency of the external world. This primordial awareness postulates the existence of a full, absolute being who would be a justification and completion of man's personal life.

The awareness of our own ontic status, of relations with the world of things and, above all, postulated interpersonal relationships, lead to the recognition of a desire for intersubjectivity with the transcendent "Thou."

What we have discussed thus far has the character of a phenomenological description rather than an ontological explanation. Such a description of the experiences of a personal being, however, helps to achieve a philosophical grasp of the phenomenon of religion. We shall try to reformulate ontologically the characteristic which has been presented above.

1. The foundation for directing man to God is the non-necessary (contingent) ontic status of human existence. Man as a being (something which exists) is not a primordial necessary being: existence does not belong to his essence. Therefore he shares the ontic status with all remaining elements of the world (he is a caused being). Knowledge about the ontic situation of man, which is acquired in metaphysics, is given to man, in a certian way, in the personal experience and awareness of his transitoriness, frailty and lack of necessity.[53] Because the experience of this contingency is a transcendental, since it is the lot of all people, the religious act which arises from this very awareness of man's own existential situation in the world is a common phenomenon. This "reaction" of man to something transcendent, as a result of the whole experience of contingency, cannot be reduced exclusively to restricted, specialized capabilities, or only to certain spheres of human life. Consequently, because a religious perspective is linked with the nature of human existence, it pervades as it were the whole man in what is most essential to him: the human ability of cognition and love.

2. The goal of religious destiny can be only an absolute person. For if man is a person, a conscious being who is loving and free in determining the object of love, then the respective partner of his life can be only a world of persons. Because the capacity of his cognition and love goes beyond contingent persons, he can be united only with a personal fulfilled existence, freedom and love. By taking into consideration the personal ontic status of man, we must agree with Scheler's reason, that the end of a religious relation cannot be some kind of material being, some kind of personal dependent being. Only a personal Absolute constitutes an adequate "Thou" for human existence.[54]

3. In connection with the above observation, it would be difficult to agree with Scheler or Otto that "the value of holiness" constitutes the primordial or an a priori category. It seems that it occurs in man as a result of experiencing his own contingency. Obviously this transition from an experience of contingency to "perceiving" something which this contingency implies, can be so spontaneous that it is almost unnoticed; nonetheless, it is essential for understanding the character of religious experience and of the religious fact in general. Such a solution seems to stress even more fully the personal character of a religious relationship.

Considering everything that has been said thus far, we understand philosophically a religious phenomenon as a relationship of a person to person, or for a person, that is, as a relationship between the human "I" and the absolute "Thou." This is a particular type of relationship:

(a) Existential—it is a real union, whose posture is written into the structure of persons and which requires for its realization a suitable practical activity.

(b) Intersubjective ("I"–"Thou"), that is, it occurs between personal beings who are "beings-in-themselves" who determine themselves especially in the sphere of cognitive and free activity. It has a dialogic-responsive character; that is, one of mutual meeting, and mutual giving of oneself. Both subjects existing "in-themselves" simultaneously exist "for-one-another."

(c) Dynamic—it establishes in man a potentiality for "being-toward-God" which can be realized only through proper human—that is conscious and free activity. The mere potential direction toward God and the whole transcendent sphere does not as yet constitute religion. For religion as a conscious and voluntary actualization of a potential reference through religious acts (passing from potency to act). The religious bond created by religious activity is not however the work of man alone. From his side in such a type, God also has an active part. Dynamism then refers to both members of the relation. In Catholic theology, God's action in constituting a religious bond is described as Providence, sanctifying and actual grace, and also a special help of the Holy Spirit, which has for its aim the perfection and spiritualization of man as a preparation for a full union with God (gifts of the Holy Spirit).

(d) Necessary for the full realization of the person as a material-spiritual being, who becomes more and more a person through spiritual activity tending to self-spiritualization (in the ontic and moral sense). Religious union with God is necessary, so that man would truly become a man. In a certain sense, necessity also affects the other member of the religious relation. Since God created man out of love and since he is Love, the Fullness of Goodness and Truth, he cannot not love us, that is he cannot not *desire* the fullest development of the human person. And since the human person attains the fullest development through union with God, then God cannot not desire this union because he himself is the "Author" of man's nature.

(e) "Reversible"—it is that kind of relation which can be described as a relation of a human person with the Person of the Absolute for a person; of the kind that perfects the human person most fully. It may be said that all cultural activity, that is, cognitive, moral, and aesthetic, develops the spiritual aspect of man and perfects it. But the activity which leads to the realization of the relation with God (religious acts) perfects, more than all others, the very person in the highest degree. This is true because, for exam-

ple, the moral act perfects the acting subject, but it is simultaneously adapted to the good of others. In like manner, cognitive activity usually has as its goal a reference to a practical result and cognition, while truth serves as a means of transforming or creating something. Similarly, artistic activity perfects some material and results in an artifact; hence it is a transitive relation. A religious act perfects only the subject (man perfects himself). The aim of the relation is therefore the fullness of all perfections, an act which is complete in every respect. In view of this, religious activity precludes any gains; therefore it is completely directed to man, completely disposed to his fullest actualization (perfection).

Human existence is therefore an existence in the perspective of the transcendent "Thou." This perspective gives to all of man's activities, not only to religious ones, a significance and worth without changing their interior contents.

A religious act, as an experience and real expression of the personal bond of man with the transcendent "Thou," involves the whole person and penetrates all areas of his existence and actions. It unites with itself the cognitive, volitional and emotional elements into one whole in the deepest personal core of man. Hence, the whole human ego is involved in a religious act. Religious experience is a most engaging, most complete, and consequently most integrating act in which the human subject does not lose his individuality but, as Kierkegaard rightly observes, by being in contact with the divine subject, he discovers and grounds this individuality most fully. If exterior and interior acts shape the personal "I" of man, then religious acts do this in the highest degree; man becomes here in the highest degree a person and a "spirit."[55]

In view of this, how can we describe the function and value achieved by religious acts? It is generally accepted that the value is one of holiness. Now arises the problem: What is its essence, and what is its relation to other values, of goodness, truth, beauty?

When the character of religious acts which we have described above is kept in mind, it seems that the value realized through them (holiness) is not a separate category of value alongside of truth, goodness and beauty, as a basis for the spiritual creativity of man. These values have their counterparts in the characteristics of being (transcendental characteristics). There does not exist, on the other hand, a distinct transcendental characteristic of holiness, which, analogically to other values, man could (recognizing beings, transforming them) create (acquire). Holiness seems to be a value which is "built" on all the remaining ones; it consolidates them, and it is essentialy united with man, not only as a material but, above all, a spiritual being, who is developing in the perspective of the Pure Spirit, and striving to become united with him. Because the existence of a human person is the existence of his spirit which organizes matter and frees itself through an activity which has, as its assignment, the creation of truth, goodness and beauty, man is a being in the perspective of the transcendent "Thou," who is a Pure Spirit.

In religious activity the action is aimed directly at the Spirit, and its direct aim is the "spiritualizing" of man. The matter here is, as it were, something spiritual, i.e., a function of spiritualizing man. This function is understood in an ontic sense, as a fuller subordination of the body to the spirit, as well as in a moral sense, as a greater and more spiritual love, a fuller freedom and the like.

Understanding in this way, the value of holiness as a value of "spirituality," and understanding the function of religious acts as a "spiritualizing" function (spiritualization), seems to be more in agreement with the nature of the human person and the nature of the Divine Person because they encompass the whole human person and his spiritual activity.[56]

In religious experience and in religious acts, there is a completion of the proper manner of the existence of a human person, who lives in time and who is actualized and has an unlimited dimension because of his spirituality. Hence interior and exterior religious acts form the personal "I" of man in the perspective of his life which, to a certain degree, is his lot here and which will be a mode of existence after death. If the human subject as if creates himself or at least transforms himself, by means of his acts—especially spiritual acts—then, this applies to the fullest extent to religious acts, through which man actualizes himself as a spiritual being and, as it were, divinizes himself. Thomas Aquinas does not hesitate to call man "god through participation."[57] The entire religious activity of man is directed to such a divinization. "Being-in-oneself," "being-for-oneself" is simultaneously "being-for-another" and, above all, "being-for-God" and since it is "for God," it is more "in-oneself," "for-oneself" and "for-others."

Since man is a material-spiritual being, in whom spirituality expresses itself through matter and in some way "emanates" from it, he can constitute this relation to the transcendent "Thou" only through gradual interior and exterior activities. A realizaton of this bond is the fullest development of man, both as a person and as a spirit. The entire process of the realization of man—creation of a human person—can be described as a process of spiritualization: gaining an ever fuller freedom in relation to determining factors of matter (even though we know from Revelation, there will always remain a certain reference to matter),[58] gaining an ever greater truth (authenticity—being truly yourself), goodness, love, interior freedom and the like. It is precisely because of his spiritual element that man has a relation to God and his union with God demands a certain connaturality and, hence, a "spiritualization" and a certain moral perfection. Such exactly appears to be the function of religious acts—the realizaton of man in his spiritual aspect. Christian theology provides information about the special adoption of man by God (adoption in Christ). Nonetheless, grace founds nature. Moreover, in the very process of spiritualization (sanctification), man is aided by special strength (grace). The religious act, as we have observed above, is achieved not only by the personal activity of the subject, but it presupposes a special help from God's side. Encounter, dialogue, faith, hope and love in relation to the transcendent "Thou" are conditioned not only by man's strength but also by the special power imparted by God (sanctifying grace). Nevertheless, even in such an interpretation, sanctification has, as its object, a participation in the life of God who, being a spirit, can develop dialogue with a spiritual being.

B. MAN, A DYNAMIZED PERSON, AS THE SUBJECTIVE BASIS FOR THE RELIGIOUS FACT

Man is a material-spiritual being who experiences his existential unity (of his "I") and his subjectivity; namely, the fact that he is the doer of specifically human acts which, above all, are intellectual cognition and volitional desire (love). As a substantial being who experiences his own identity, man is a dynamized being, i.e., one who has certain dispositions and who realizes (actualizes) them in contact with the world and other personal beings, through respective activity in relation to their potentialities. Man realizes himself as a person through adequate acts in relation to his potentialities; he develops himself and achieves a fullness in the needs and limits of is nature. Dynamization (and thereby actualization) of the human person has a two-fold direction: a) internal and b) external.

(a) Man actualizes himself internally through cognition, love and freedom. How is this accomplished? From the metaphysical point of view, act is a perfection; potentiality, on the other hand, is a state of imperfection. Hence it follows that activity, which is the act of the doer, is his actualization or his perfection. Man develops himself (as a doer) through his activity, especially specific human acitvity, which is intellectual cognition and deliberative desire (*intelligere, velle*).

Man's highest potentiality is his intellect as a cognitive power, as well as his will, an an appetitive power. Potentiality perfects itself; that is, it actualizes itself, in agreement with its object. The object of the intellect is truth, and of the will—goodness, because the human intellect is disposed to the cognition of truth and the will to the attainment of goodess. Man can know intellectually everything that exists and he can love everything. His potentiality in this area is unlimited because, ultimately, it is oriented to the Absolute. Precisely, the proper object of the intellect is the essence of material things and it actualizes itself insofar as it cognizes the essence of these things. But since the end of intellectual cognition is all (truth in general—universal truth) by cognizing the essence of material things, man cognizes their ontic character as of beings that are caused, effected, and derivative and he remains in the state of inquiry and potentiality, as long as he does not cognize their cause—of an Absolute Being who is the Absolute Truth. Therefore, none of the fragmentary truths actualizes fully the potentiality of the intellect. Not even the affirmation of God's existence does this because at present, it is always an incomplete cognition. A full actualization of the intellect's potentiality can be assured by a direct contact with the Absolute Truth who—as the limit of the actualization of the human intellect's potentiality—shows itself as the ultimate goal of human cognitive activity.

A similar situation takes place in another manifestation of human potentiality, which is the will. Just as the human intellect is oriented to the cognition of all truth, so the will is oriented to all goodness (good in general), universal goodness.

By cognizing the most various goods (being and good are interchangeable), man makes them the object of a special desire; he directs himself toward them in order to unite himself with them. The essence of volitional desire (love) is an entrée to a cognized good, a union with it. Man, who cognizes everything—can love everything; he can unite himself with everything in an act of love. For a personal being, the adequate object of love is a cognitive and loving being—therefore a human person who is uniquely capable of returning love for an act of love and with whom an "encounter" and union can take place. Love of any relative good, even if it should be a most loving and loved person, does not fully actualize the human potentiality in this area. The ultimate object which it will realize can be only the Complete Goodness. The ultimate goal—the aim of human love presents itself as the Absolute Goodness.

An analysis of human activity, especially of cognitive and volitional acts in which man's nature manifests itself as that of a dynamized person, leads to a discovery of that which constitutes his natural end—his maximum. This is, as we have shown above, a contact with the Complete Goodness which cannot be lost. Such an unforfeitable Goodness which would completely satisfy natural human aspirations and would constitute the goal of cognition and love, cannot be any contingent being, any material being, not even any human person, but only a fully perfect Person: God.

Such is "the capacity" of human cognition and human love. Only a personal bond with the personal Absolute assures man of a total satisfaction which is in proportion to his potentiality (to nature). It assures him of a full realization, as Thomas Aquinas describes it, of a complete happiness. We are not concerned here with some kind of emotional state or some kind of psychical satisfaction or feeling of complete happiness. Thomas understands happiness in a dynamic way: as a complete actualization of the human person's potentiality, which is achieved only through the union of man's intellect and will with the Person of the Absolute.[59]

"Being-toward-God" also manifests itself from a negative aspect in human freedom. The human person is determined neither in the choice of the object of cognition nor especially in the choice of the object of love. A person decides and is aware of his/her freedom in this sphere of choosing goods, with which one unites through love. This affirms the truth that man's powers are not determined with relation to any contigent being, and that man himself directs his own conduct, and that, in this act, he transcends the entire world of nature whose activity is always determined in the direction of a definite goodness. In a conscious and free manner, man decides even on the choice of the Full Goodness, which is not apparent to him in its full distinctness as long as he lives on this earth.[60]

As an analysis of human activity indicates, the final end of man—union with the Highest Good and the Highest Truth—objectively speaking, is not chosen by man; it is given to us objectively (the Highest Good must be as if desired by man out of necessity). Man cannot not want union with the Full Truth and the Full Good, just as he cannot not aspire to the full development of his natural potentialities. Freedom concerns the way and the manner of aspiring to attain the ultimate end. Therefore it concerns goods which are the means to its attainment. But a paradoxical situation takes place here—a lack of "freedom" in relation to the Highest Good is, at the same time, the greatest freedom.

A further justification of the transcendent dimension of the human person is his subordination "toward death" which again affirms, from the negative side, the potentiality of the human person who—as long as he/she is living in temporal dimensions—is only in the phase of actualizing himself and not in the state of actuality. Contemporary philosophy has called attention to the dynamic character of death as the end of self-actualization and as the way to full actualization. We speak of death as the moment of an ultimate decision in relation to the Fullest Good. Hence death is considered as "man's most important act through which he ultimately fulfills his existence."[61]

If the absolute goal of human existence were to take place with death, then man would not have the potentiality of achieving the goal of his life—full actualization. If this were really so, then the human being would be something irrational, internally "false," unnatural because, by his nature, he would be directed to something which is fundamentally inaccessible to him.

(b) A potential human person actualizes himself externally through interpersonal bonds. Hence the natural context of a person's life is a community of persons (family, nation and the like). Man comes to life in a community; he lives in it and develops. However, the goal of a human person's potentiality is not the human community. Although it is a necessary condition of life and development, it is not that which constitutes the person, nor ultimately justifies him nor is it his goal. Man transcends not only the world of things but also the world of persons. Since man is the highest being in the ontic hierarchy, (a person is a substantial being and a community is a relational being), a person is ontically the purpose of the community and not vice versa. Ontically considered, community perfects person. Therefore a human person preserves his autonomy and his freedom in relation to all social relationships. This is possible only when a person accepts the existence of the Absolute, toward whom he is directed and who is his ultimate end. Transcendence of the human person in relation to society also manifests itself in the fact that the person is not only an object but also the subject of laws. This means that man can choose goods which he recognizes as proper means leading to the realization of the ultimate end which he has chosen. And because he is not the only personal being, there must be a mutual agreement in the use of goods, so that other persons will not be deprived of the goods that they need to realize their ultimate purpose.

The transcendence of the human spirit manifests itself in the context of bonds with nature and in the context of social bonds. Man as a reflecting "I" who is aware of his distinctness and freedom, is not a function of the world of persons or of things, even though he is immersed in them. Since he is immanent in relation to the world, he transcends it and he is capable of directing himself dynamically toward God. As a conscious subject, man is oriented to the absolute subjectivity, the source from which his own existence flows and toward which he tends as a being, especially in his spiritual aspect. Ultimately, he draws his subjective completeness and dignity from the "being-toward-God" and "for-God."

Religion therefore constitutes a relation between the human person—a potential being—and the Person of God—a Pure Act. By religious acts, we should understand every kind of conscious and free actualization which brings the person of man, as a potential being, closer to the Pure Act. Therefore religious activity includes the perfecting of man in truth, goodness and beauty, if all this is done in the perspective of the transcendent "Thou" and for the sake of him. The essential characteristic of religious activity is that it is immediately and directly guided to the final goal and purpose of human existence and not to the means which lead to its realization, as is the case in all other areas of human activity. But the means can also be justified (with the remaining activity) that they may be given religious value, in virtue of the intention which directs them to the final goal.[62]

The non-contradictability of the religious fact, that is the relation (bond) between a human person and the Person of the Absolute, is therefore the ontic status of human existence, which is personal and simultaneously contingent (dynamized). The goals and limits of human activity, especially of the intellectually-cognitive and deliberatively-volitional type, constitute the objectively conditioned possibility of the coming into being of a union with the Transcendent Person, of the kind of contact that is realized precisely in man's religious activity.

Even though the human person is directed immediately to the transcendent "Thou," in the case of religious acts, and thereby, the proper dimension of human existence is realized, nevertheless, we also find here the potentiality of the human being. This is always only a phase of actualization—never in temporal dimension—a state of actualization. In addition, such a direction, as everything else in human life, has a character of disposition which may or may not be actualized to a lesser or greater degree. Actually, such an activity of man presupposes an involvement of another element of a religious relation—God who, even in this instance, honors human freedom. This explains why it is possible for people to live in a faulty manner (incorrectly), whether they are religious or whether the area of religious activity does not constitute an object of special concern for them.

C. OBJECTIVE JUSTIFICATION—RELATIONSHIP OF THE WORLD TO GOD (ONTIC TRANSCENDENTAL PARTICIPATION)

In addition to the openness of the human subject to absolute subjectivity, whose acceptance appears necessary as a result of the analysis of a dynamized personal being's structure—which constitutes the foundation for a religious relationship from man's side—we can point, in another direction, to broader and more widely existing foundations of an ontic union of man with God which, from an objective point of view, does not contradict the religious fact. The issue here is to confirm the existence of God as a personal being, who is the ultimate efficient, exemplar and final cause of everything that exists. This is accomplished in metaphysics which has a universally-ontological (transcendental) perspective. It is difficult to review, in a short sketch, a more detailed way by which we can arrive, in metaphysics, at the affirmation of a personal Absolute. We shall necessarily limit ourselves only to an indication of that direction.

The fact of the existence of many changing beings (ontic pluralism) which are evolving and are linked with other beings through various relations but retaining their own distinctness—beings which are cognizable even though they are not necessary—indicate that their origin is from the Absolute Being, Who is a personal Being. This Being creates through cognition and therefore according to a certain "plan," "thought" and "idea" (the world is rational), and in a free manner (since beings which compose the world do not have the character of necessity and cannot come from the Absolute by way of a necessary emanation). Our factual human existence, as well as the existence of the whole world, which is a collection of non-necessary and yet intelligible (rational) beings, would be incomprehensible and inexplicable without the existence of God, the Absolute of Existence—of a free and loving Person. Only he, as a self-knowing and free being, forms the basis for the justification, explanation and understanding that everything which is changeable, passing or transient, actually exists. He is the source of the world's existence (the efficient cause); he planned the world (exemplary cause); and he who, above all, desired the world (loved it: final cause). Hence the world was created out of love and exists by the power of participation in God's existence.[63]

The metaphysical (ontic and ultimate) explanation of a really existing world indicates that we ourselves and everything around us, the whole world in its most profound structure, is united with God by means of necessary ontic relationships. Therefore there exists a real, actual and most internal union—since it enters into our very ontic structure—between the world and God who is the source of every life-existence. Whatever exists, exists in virtue of its participation in the Absolute, that is, whatever exists, comes from him; it is the realization of his thoughts and his desires. We can therefore say that we ourselves and the entire context of our existence are, in a certain sense, religious, precisely because we are really united through existence with God. In explaining the relationship between the world and God, the philosophy of being meets with revealed truth, which St. Paul expresses: "Because in reality he is not distinct from each one of us, since we live, move and exist in him."[64]

Because we ourselves and everything that exists, exist in virtue of our participation in God, for this reason, everything comes from him and is directed to him (returns to him). Hence everything can be for man—a rational being—a sign, a symbol of God: in a word, everything through which God speaks (also our own existence).[65]

Because they reach so deeply into the very "roots" of being, these bonds of man—who is a personal being and therefore cognitive and free—should be recognized and expressed personally. By recognizing his ontic bond with

God, man must, as it were, bind himself with God through cognition and love, because man recognizes that God is the source of his life. He created him out of love and destined man to dialogue with Him (*religare: religio*).

Because they reach down so deeply into the very "roots" of being, man's bond and those of the whole world with God—which belong to the order of nature—constitute an ontic foundation for a supernatural order. Revelation refers to it as the order of grace, which gives a new dimension to man's union with God (adoption through grace in Christ) and which does not destroy the deepest structures of nature.

The fact of transcendental participation (everything that exists, exists in virtue of its participation in the existence of the personal Absolute) constitutes the non-contradictability of the religious fact from the side of the object. It also indicates from this point of view that only a religious fact understood as an interpersonal union, which occurs between a human person and the person of the Absolute, constitutes for man, the only suitable and adequate type of religion. All other "dispositions of orientation and objects of worship," regardless of how they are understood, would be not only insufficient for man but also incompatible with the dignity of the human person, with his potentialities, nature and ontic structure. Only the personal Absolute and the Fullness of Existence, Unity, Truth, Goodness and Beauty, constitute that *sacrum* or *numinosum*, in which man can believe, trust, love and aspire to unite with him.

The ontic union of everything with God (transcendental participation) also points to the way of the human person in his realization of "being-toward-God." It does not take place directly, by neglecting the world but rather through a relation with the world and with human persons who as participants in the Absolute, aspire through the world and together with it, to a union with God. Obviously, this does not exclude the special intervention of God in the history of the world, which occurred in Judaic and Christian Revelation and especially in the fact of Incarnation. The fact of Incarnation, in reality—more clearly than anything else—points to the way of spiritualization and, in a certain sense, to the divinization of man.

As a result of the completed investigations, we can respond affirmatively to the question presented at the beginning: Is man a "religious being," just as he is a rational, social and moral being? Man as a person is directed to the transcendent "Thou." This means that he is ontically united with God. In virtue of his personal structure, man has, of necessity, the need to enter into a psychological and moral union with God and he actualizes these potentialities in a free manner. Hence the "religiousness" of man (religious dimension of the human person as a manner of "being-toward-God") is not a variable, accidental and historically conditioned trait, but it constitutes a property rooted in the very nature of the personal being, viewed both in itself and in relation to God.

Because the cognitive approach to the second member of a religious relationship is difficult (we are speaking here of a strictly natural cognition), the discovery of the necessary, ontic and objective foundation of man's religiousness requires a greater effort than the solution of any other problem related to man. In a similar way, the actualization of the ability, disposition "being-a religious-man," the actualization of an openness to the transcendent "Thou," a complete actualization of the disposition of "being-toward-God" encounter greater difficulties than the actualization of other potentialities of the human person. This also explains the possibility of errors or "deformations" in the area of this type of human activity or the far-reaching weakening of the actualization of man's openness "to the Absolute."

CHAPTER XI

THE PERSON—AN EGO OF A RATIONAL NATURE

The problem of the "person" has its own abundant literature both in the past as well as in the present.[1] Nevertheless one feels that there is a lack of a synthesis which would not limit itself to a summary of investigations made up to the present time, but which—by taking into account the results of analyses—would show especially the fundamental characteristics of a human person, because a human person is a foundation and model for an analogical understanding of a personal being.[2] However, one statement on the theme of the person is perhaps the common good of various philosophical directions and demonstrated attempts of solutions: the person is understood as the highest and most noble formation of being.

It is precisely from this point of view that in philosophy the concept of person is inseparably joined with the concept of being. And the understanding of person as the supreme formation of being is, or should be, the model for understanding analogical being. For a person is more a being than structures which are below him. And even if, under the influence of the nineteenth-century economy of thought, it was customary to think that less composite and more simple structures achieve a more perfect model of thinking (*resp.* of cognition), nevertheless in the realm of philosophy, the simplest formations of being are not and cannot be a model of the intelligibility of reality. On the contrary, personal being can be such a model which is accessible to our cognition and which fulfills most adequately the fundamental traits of existence; a subjectivity and subsistence or that which G. Hegel emphasized in another context: *an-und-für-sich-sein*. For subjectivity and subsistence emphasize simultaneously the be-ing of being, its autonomy, indivisibility, internal uniqueness, truth (intelligibility), goodness—and

313

hence, those traits of analogical reality that bear the name of transcendentals.

It is difficult to distinguish at once what elements or entitative moments determine what beings are persons and which are not; there are various solutions. However, against the background of the history of the problematic of the person, we can clearly distinguish two different approaches; (a) the historical approach which leads to the attempt of discovering the person through an analysis of nature and (b) the phenomenological approach which, by means of a description of conscious human experiences, strives to reach the ultimate personal substratum of the human being.[3]

Let us try to sketch both ways, so that against this background we can recall the characteristic personal traits which Thomas Aquinas already mentioned on different occasions and which we must now analyze more fully.

I. THE CONCEPT OF NATURE

Admittedly, one of the greatest discoveries in the area of rational cognition was the concept of nature (*physis*).[4] For once the concept of nature, understood as a permanent structure, as the source of regular activity was established, it was possible to explain various phenomena by pointing out definite, permanent, necessary and even universal structures whose "emanations" should be observed and stated in order to elucidate facts or activities. To strengthen the matter of scientific explanations, the ancient Greeks emphasized the necessity and permanence of the structure-natures which stand at the basis of various activities.[5] Furthermore, Plato and Aristotle stressed the primacy of universal natures over the individuals so that they might precisely make the accidental activities of beings a necessity. And although from the time of Aristotle, philosophy had as its ultimate goal, the explanation of the world given us in the sensible domain, nevertheless this explanation was achieved by basing itself on universal concepts (which were shown in the form of an Aristotelian type of definition) which expressed universal natures—and which of necessity did not reach directly to truly ontic and actual singulars.

To understand the world which is given us in daily experience, man reached out to the universal nature-essences. These were grasped and understood in themselves and could as such be clearly expressed in a definition. Through it, our cognitions were more strongly linked with the activity of the mind; but when "put upon" the concrete being, especially a living being, they were unable to grasp concrete and individual life. The concept of nature-essences could be truly multiplied, widening or restricting their extensions (some indeed accented the extensional side of conceptual knowledge). Nevertheless, the cognition of abstract nature-essences—precisely because it was ABSTRACT cognition (it abstracted from life, motion and change of individuals)—was of necessity inadequate for a concrete living being, especially for the spiritual life of a person. Despite this, however, it was necessary to use concepts which grasped various aspects of a substantial being (about which Aristotle told us the most), and uniting once and for all, conceptual cognition with substantial being. But after the analyses conducted by the Stagirite, it was realized that so-called "first substance" (the real living Socrates) is something different from "second substance" (the universal concept which we have about Socrates). And within the limits of a so-called "first substance," men searched for and perceived some kind of universal nature understood as TO TI EN EINAI. This nature and not the individual concrete being was to be the object of scientific cognition.[6]

And hence on this basis, a question could arise: What elements must be "added" to second substance, namely conceptualized nature, and what elements to substance as general nature, the bearer of *to ti en einai,* so that one or the other could become the real particular Socrates? Basically, however, such a question did not enter the mind of the ancients. The meaning of the question was noticed only after the Christological controversies in Christian times. If, indeed, as faith taught, Christ is true God and, at the same time, true man then, since he is one personal being—as the Council of Chalcedon taught—he could have two natures as the source of his divine-human activity.

The Council solutions indicated such a unique being who, although he is a man nevertheless he is not at all a human person, but exclusively a Divine Person. In the light of the Council determinations, it was demonstrated that human nature is not automatically a human personal being because it was "taken over" and fully realized by the person of the *Logos* in the historical Christ.

And because they wanted to link the doctrine of the faith with philosophical culture, and especially with the thought of the Greek philosophers, Christian writers used philosophical terminology determined principally by the Neoplatonists. They posed the question about the essential constitutive element (or also moment) of the person. They noticed that one can speak about a person only within the area of so-called "rational natures." Thus beings who are bearers of non-rational natures are *a limine* excluded from the whole problematic of the personal being. For in the area of rational natures, the most varied kinds of known elements of analyses of substance in Aristotelian philosophy were distinguished and emphasized: essence (*to ti en einai*), universal, matter, form and those characteristics called accidents.

Nowhere however is it possible to penetrate into the essential and constitutive element of a person, since neither characteristics (among which there are also individuating elements connected with matter) nor matter, nor form, could determine about a person (being a formally constitutive element) as the most perfect formation of being. As a result, men resorted to certain ideas connected with Platonism and Neoplatonism and they searched in some kind of *forma totalis* or a substantial modification of an individual being, for that which determines a person.[7]

Most frequently, however, the person was taken as a model of an individual, as an exemplar of a determined species—in this case, a species of a rational nature. In truth, species as a universal is understood in itself; nevertheless, species "distributes itself" to individuals, since it exists through singulars. The moment of "distributing to another being as to an autonomous subject ranked as a sign of an ontic incompleteness. Hence personal being began to be comprehended quite universally as a "fulfilled" being which cannot "communicate itself" with another being as with a subject. Ontic autonomy and subjective fulness in the sphere of a group (species) of a rational nature became the characteristic trait of a personal being: and Boethius' definition of a person expressed this: *rationalis naturae individua substantia.*

But such a solution was only an apparent one because it was precisely a question of indicating the moment "thanks to which" subjective fulness follows. It was only with the solution given by St. Thomas that the matter became better clarified. For he observed that only that element of a rational being constitutes a person which fundamentally constitutes being—and hence an individual existence of this rational nature. For if Jesus Christ is only a divine Person and not a human one—this is due solely to the fact that he possesses only one existence—i.e., divine. Divine existence actualizes human nature, making it a real source of real human activities which nevertheless were the "property" of the Divine Person.[8]

Although St. Thomas' solution was taken into account in later times (especially by Capreolus[9]), nevertheless in the so-called Thomistic school under the influence of Cajetan, another, a Neoplatonic and ancient version of the personal being, was accepted, a version which exercized no small influence on the conception of man, his soul and immortality.[10]

With the appearance of Cartesian thought and method, the problematic of the personal being was linked with consciousness, since only consciousness understood as *cogitatio* (because basically it was an operation on idea-concepts) would constitute the essence of a spiritual substantial being; and hence only the human soul could be such a being. Henceforth, in the current of the philosophy of the subject which looked for its starting point of philosophical analyses in the data of consciousness, finally the question of the person began to be linked with various phenomena and forms of conscious life.[11]

Attempts to show the specifics of a personal being came from an analysis of nature understood in one way or another, with the result that from the time of Descartes, a change of perspective is noticed. Clearly it is connected with a change of manner of philosophizing and of turning away from the problematics of being—generally understood analogically—in the direction of the thinking subject. The philosophy of the subject and its characteristic understandings by various authors constitute the second current of the explanation of the person, especially the person against the background of the description of what man experiences in his consciousness, elucidating not so much the states of being, but rather as fundamental moments of the human mode of existing.

II. AREAS OF HUMAN CONSCIOUSNESS

Consciousness and the so-called "areas of consciousness" became the privileged object of philosophical analyses.[12] It is only in the area of consciousness that truly human experiences take place and, therefore, consciousness appears as its own "ontic horizon," encompassing everything that can be explained philosophically. Obviously the problem of the "ontic horizon" is also linked with another problem: namely, the aprioristic conditions for the cultivation of knowledge—more strictly speaking (and more in agreement with this direction) with the act of thinking because not every thinking is already a cognition.[13]

When we turn our attention to the characteristic data of conscious human experiences, we can observe their twofold aspective trait or also their twofold aspect, which fundamentally differentiates man from all other creatures of nature. And from that, we can also observe that which, since the time of the Greeks, can be called "nature," understood as a determined source of activity. This nature is either a "reasonable" manner of activity which characterizes itself most generally by its own "going out of itself" for the purpose of entering the thing in itself,[14] or it is a completely conscious activity[15] in the manner of comprehending that which manifests itself in cognition.

What is the question here? In contrast to animals who are completely suited in their natural activity to their environment and "set" in it, man is constantly transcending his milieu, because he transcends himself as a subject of activity. For specifically human activities and hence those that flow from man's rational cognition or which are connected in any way whatsoever with rational cognition do not have a goal or purpose—as animals do—of only an individual or so-called "species-nature." In his cognition, in his acts of decision, in his love, man "conspires" with the thing in himself, or he acts in such a way that he reckons with the thing's inner structure, understood in a wide sense. Things or beings possess their own particular structure and their characteristic manner of activity, and man has fundamentally these moments in view when he carries out his activities, through which he "goes out of himself" for the purpose of arriving at the very thing itself. Hence what we can briefly call "reasonableness" is one of the primordially grasped traits of human activity.[16] This "reasonableness" manifests itself in all acts of rational cognition in which we attain the so-called essential structures of things. We attain being in itself even if our intellectual cognition in its foundation was not to reach being but only a cognitive grasping of phenomena, since we then understand these phenomena as something definite, something in itself, as something that exists—and this is precisely what we call being. "Reasonableness" in intellectual cognition is connected with the intentional character of our cognition because we are disposed, above all, to apprehend the content of the thing itself.[17]

The "reasonableness" of human activity finds its specific expression in acts of decision and free choice,[18] since we are sometimes "forced," as it were, to choose something, "conspiring with a thing," which is foreign and hostile to us (as to a biological subject and a source of activity). The acts of decision, especially the difficult ones, manifest to us very explicitly this transcendence toward being which is characteristic for such a reasonable manner of conducting oneself. But the highest form of proper human activity is an act of real love in which the transcendence of the subject is the greatest. This is so because love not only places us in harmony with the object of our loving, as Aristotle taught; it not only "leads us out of ourselves," as St. Thomas emphasized; but it demands a "giving-of-oneself" to another person, to another "Thou" and establishing a way of "being-for-another."[19] The "reasonableness" of human activity also manifests itself in social life, since the very conception of reasonableness is a mode of being for man.[20]

The "non-reasonableness" of human behavior manifests itself in those places in which the described mode of being is entirely absent. Nevertheless, the absence of this reasonableness can occur at certain moments or "parts" and at such a time, we are not dealing so much with something unreasonable as with a less reasonable mode of being, as for example, a utilitarian mode of being in which we place ourselves as an end and everything else as a means to the end.[21]

Besides "reasonableness," we notice in ourselves, especially in the area of cognition, a total mode of apprehension. It shows that whatever we understand is always as it were something cut out of a greater totality. Each content is, as if a determination or part of such a totality which covers itself with the entire horizon of our consciousness. There is no comprehension of a thing—"creation"—which would exhaust our potentiality of cognition and which would cover itself with the area of consciousness constituted by grasping analogical being.

We can say that just as "reasonableness" is comprehending a being from the side of its content, so "totality," which characterizes our understanding of things is likewise a grasping of being, but, as it were, from the side of its extensions. But "reasonableness" as well as "totality" characterizes such a mode of human activity which indicates being an analogical reality and not merely those objects that satisfy man's natural, biological or psychical needs.

The foundation which explains the fact of "reasonableness" and "totality" of our psychical acts is the spirit[22] which manifests itself in these acts. The spirit is understood by Max Scheler as a person. However, it is only one aspect of man's personal being. We can speak of the spirit only insofar as it manifests itself in spiritual acts which are varied and differentiated in their content, and among which we find a unification and subordination. Spiritual acts are simple and not able to be resolved into some more fundamental components. In contrast to other human activity, they are not subject to the laws of motion and change (likewise of aging and dying). They constitute a separate sphere of the spirit which is not subject, for example, to sickness and physiological changes. (The contents of comprehensions and of judgments, acts of spiritual love, are the same when one is healthy as when one is sick.) Spiritual acts complete and perfect the subject which produces them.[23]

Such acts seen in their mutual subordination in effect give a kind of profile of a man, his characteristic and permanent attitude in activity which directs him in choosing a criterion proper to himself alone. Such a stable mode of activity which is the result of organization and a hierarchy of spiritual acts can be called "self" (*osobowość, Selbst*). Its fundamental characteristic would be oneness in the manner of acting. Obviously, man's "self" can change as the result of some kind of internal transformation (e.g., conversions) or a new "self" can organize itself as the result of accepting a new value criterion of human activity.

Along with the self, his own self-organization (through subordination) of acts of the spirit, one can distinguish in man and in the whole of his activity, his own "I," which is called the "phenomenological I."[24] Since man "has been cast into the world involuntarily,"[25] he must establish in himself, in relation to external objects, a kind of dispositional center, by means of which he will be able to master more or less effectively the things surrounding him. Man who lives in the world, treats things as suitable means-values for his life. As Heidegger correctly observed in *Sein und Zeit,* external objects are useful *"um-zu-Sein"*; and in the sphere of this usefulness, man builds for himself a "pyramid of value." In this manner, we fashion from childhood a dispositional center called the "phenomenological I" because by separating ourselves from things we treat ourselves as a distinct center which disposes external objects. This phenomenological "I" grows with the passage of time and declines with the weakening of human strength, as we increasingly diminish the sphere of our activity, and as the world of things escapes the sphere of our decisions. This phenomenological "I" which increases and diminishes is not yet the "I" which we shall examine in future analyses. It is not the "I" of a human being or the ontological "I" which reveals the be-ing and subjectivity[26] of a person, which encompasses the totality of human experiences, both spiritual and psychical (joined with the physiology of the nervous system), as well as with biological and subconscious experiences.[27]

It is precisely this "I" as subject and being that manifests itself in the course of philosophical analyses—insofar as we regard given cognitions both immediate and mediate which reveal the contents of human acts by indicating the subject's ontic character.[28]

III. THE PRIMORDIAL FACT OF MAN'S CONSCIOUS EXPERIENCE

When we use a strictly philosophical method[29]—namely of the non-contradictability of facts or contents given us either in direct or indirect cognition—we notice, above all, as a primordial fact a kind of twofold division of our experiences; for the cognitive experience "I" is completely different from the cognitive experience "mine." For the "I" is constantly present in all acts which are called "mine." "I" am always present, conscious and aware in all my acts. At the same time it manifests itself as a *centrum,* the performer and subject of these same acts.

As we have already indicated, there is absolutely no need to prove this subjectivity of "I." Every one of us knows that he is the subject of his own actions. To be a subject is something more than to be a *centrum* from which these acts emanate and, as it were, gush forth. If the awareness of being the *centrum* of all my psychical experiences can be recognized as a psychological category—and hence as a manifestation of a normally functioning healthy psyche which perceives that all acts flowing from it affect it, then subjectivity is already most strictly a metaphysical category. To be a subject means the same as to be a being, because there is no being which does not exist as a subject. For subjectivity or be-ing "I" is inescapably given us in cognitive experiences.

The experience of subjectivity is something immediate, something which needs no proof. On the contrary, all proof—as a psychic process—presupposes the awareness of a subjective "I." For the recognized condition of man's initial accountability is his consciousness, which is nothing else than the experience of being the subject "I" in relation to MY acts. For the immediate data of our cognitions do not demand any proof; but, conversely, all proofs depend on and presuppose these immediate data as a fundamental starting point.[30] For this reason too, the experiences of being-a-subject "I" in relation to "my" acts is indubitable.

Obviously—and this is extremely important—the subjectivity (be-ing) of an ego is given us only from an existential aspect. This means that we know that we exist, that we are aware of our existence as a *a subject who performs "my" acts*. This performing—or effecting—manifests itself especially strikingly in some regions of psychic activity; notably moral acitivity. But no less in relation to "my" acts do we feel ourselves the authors of "my" acts and their ultimate ontic origin. Yet a direct experience of subjectivity from the existential aspect is not, at the same time, a direct cognition of one's nature. Hume committed a very grave error in this respect when he denied the subjectivity of the "I," because he was unable—and correctly so—to "discern" anywhere the authentic content of this "I" neither in the analysis of the idea nor in the relation between ideas. Hence he was forced to recognize the human "ego" as yet another psychic habit.[31] Meanwhile the ego is constantly present and conscious, but only as an existing subject[32] for "my" acts. I can learn about the content of "I," or about my own "nature," only through an analysis of "my" acts. This is, however, a roundabout way, which presupposes far-reaching philosophical analyses.[33]

Along with D. Hume's error, we can also perceive another significant error of Max Scheler who perceived the human spirit and its highest value, but who denied at the same time the subjectivity of every spirit, which, according to his statement can be only a function. The subjectivity and, because of it, the be-ing of the spirit would be an illusion flowing from the tendency of objectifying, by means of human cognition, everything which is only a function. Functions and activities possess no subjective existence, but only we people who, in achieving cognition of whatever function make it, at the same time, an object (*Gegenstand*) and by means of it—in M. Scheler's understanding—a being. However, to be a being or an existing subject is not the same as to be an object, especially in a philosophical tradition which finds itself under Kantian influence, as is the case with M.

Scheler. For in Kantian philosophical tradition, objectivity is constructed—a direct experience of the ego as a self-subsisting subject is reducible neither to an experience of the content nor to an experience of a cognitive objectivity.[34]

Hence we avoid both errors and widespread opinions in relation to a direct experience of the subjective "I,"—which manifests itself only from the aspect of the fact of experience, i.e., from the existentialist aspect. The disclosure and cognition of the content of that "I" which exists and is conscious in all "my" acts, depends on the recording of this relation—of "mine" to "I"—as well as on an analysis of the ontic character, i.e., the ontic structure of "my" acts. Now a matter of first consideration here is the constant testimony of our consciousness that, in identically the same measure, I am the source and author of "my" spiritual acts, of a type such as intellectual, conceptual, judgmental and reasoning cognition, as well as acts such as breathing, feeling and muscular activity. Sometimes I experience acts of pain which are "mine" much more than are acts of intellectual speculation. I feel myself as the subject who performs equally spiritual and physiological actions. "I" am equally conscious in material acts as well as in immaterial ones.[35] The "I" transcends all the contents of "my" acts and, as it were, threads" them on itself. It is immanent in all these acts but, at the same time, it does not exhaust itself in any one of them, so that we cannot say that in immanent cognitive acts, the "I" would be bound more closely with the spirit than with matter. The conscious "I" which exists as a subject transcends all "my" acts, and it gathers them by integrating them into one being, by acting in a purposeful way from within.[36]

As we have already recalled, the area of moral activity, the area of human decision, is the particularly privileged place in which the "I" is as if most conscious, most subjective, and performing and creating "my" acts.[37] For in the act of decision through free choice of such a practically-practical judgment in which I determine myself to action, I grasp with fervor and ardor my own causation. I perceive how I am precisely causing a new (but truly contingent and, however, non-autonomous!) being, which did not exist previously, and for whose existence I an "responsible."[38] It is previously "I" who decides on some kind of activity or non-activity, who decides on the constitution of a new being or not. The bond of the "I" with that which is "mine" and that which "gushes" from the "I" freely, is best grasped in an act of decision and which has always been the object of great descriptions in world literature. There is also the conviction which constantly accompanies us about the responsibility for everything which "I" perform.

Keeping in mind the relation of a subsistent subjective "I" to the performance of "my" acts, we perceive as it were *in fieri*—in the act of creation, a relation between man and nature which is described in the classical philosophy of being. This subsistent "I" who is conscious of both "my" spiritual and corporeal acts is nothing other than that sought-after person, about whom St. Thomas said that he is HIS OWN EXISTENCE AND PROPORTIONAL TO A GIVEN INDIVIDUAL NATURE,[39] and who can be defined in agreement with the current classical philosophy as the I OF A RATIONAL NATURE. We perceive that "I," who is at the same time transcendent and immanent in all "my" acts, is an epression of the transcendence of person above nature. As a subjective subsistent "I" (given to us in cognition from an existentialist aspect), the person organizes or—as Aristotle and after him, St Thomas expressed it—forms for himself a concrete individual nature: a concrete individual source of rational activity. Obviously this organization of man's individual nature is accomplished fundamentally through spiritual acts because we are concerned here with a "nature," understood as the source of man's activity from a purely human aspect. It is not a question that "I" should organize according to my pleasure my corporeal nature which is given me in great part through my genetic formation. For the organization of one's body and material nature is also dependent on biologico-material laws and on all those determinants that compose a natural order. As a causing and subjective "I," the person is involved with laws of nature when he is forming and organizing his body. Although he has a primacy over the organized body, at the same time, he heeds this body in order to express himself, to be aware of himself, in order to be a man. In all of this which manifests itself through and in the body, man is "related" to other creatures of nature and he is subject to the laws which are discovered in nature.

Despite this, man transcends nature and he manifests his own personal traits of activity, which are the consequence of a created personal "nature" (understood as the source of activity) which can be roughly identified with the personality profile of a man who is constituted as the result of the hierarchization of spiritual acts. And in this sense, "I," as a subject who exists (to a higher degree than the organized body), transcend the contents of spiritual acts and their stable manner of activity. Man chooses his acts, and through them he expresses himself and intervenes in the world as he finds it.

Hence in acts of decision, I select (accept and reject) such acts of determined content that suit "me." A selection of actions suitable for oneself (always with a definite content which has its influence on the character "I"), is precisely the creation of one's personal nature. It is the "construction" of a personal individuality; it is—if we can borrow and at the same time change the sense of J.P. Sartre's saying—"the creation" of oneself. On this level—as the author of definite spiritual acts with a determined characteristic personal trait—I experience my personal existence in a different way than I experience the existence of other beings. For this reason, too, K. Jaspers observed accurately that I experience the judgment "I am—exist," differently that I experience the judgment, "You exist," or "It exists." I affirm my own personal existence in a completely original manner because I experience the existence of a person-subject from within. I affirm a personal-subjective existence in the purview of fulfilling myself and of organizing my nature. I affirm my existence by transcending the nature which I am organizing. On the other hand, I affirm the existence of another being (even a personal one) as "thematized," as objectivized, as a thing in which I truly affirm an act of being through an existential judgment. But it is completely determined by its content. Conversely, I "heatedly" affirm to myself my own personal existence which, as it were, "threads" on its own act of existence the organized and transcendent contents; it brings into relief this "I" from an existential aspect, from the side of facticity of life, from the side that it exists.

And hence the direction of Christian thinkers, who were under the influence of Greek thought and who sought persons through an analysis of nature as the supreme moment of nature's activity, was wrong. The priority of nature, so brilliantly observed in the activity of the whole cosmos is deceiving—in the case of applying it to man's acitvity—since man is not merely some kind of determined nature, some kind of "human nature" that is particularized in relation to a general "idea of man." Rather, man is, above all, a subsisting, personal being who is conscious and who experiences as an "I"—as a subject who organizes his own individual nature by producing acts which are equally spiritual and physiological—which are acts about the contents that are given by the "I." And although I do not feel that spiritual acts are more "mine" than physiological ones, nevertheless it is through spiritual acts that I fundamentally form my individual "nature" as a stable source of activity with definite personal traits. For actions which are bound with matter must take into consideration the laws of matter and, thereby, determine as it were the transcending person in the form of a subsistent subjective "I." Nevertheless we are witnesses in our "personal" life that it is exactly I who is organizing, through performed or freely emanated acts, a personal individuality and my own nature. And hence "human nature" is not so much given to me; rather, the transcending person "I" creates this nature from the accumulated elements of nature—from the aspect of matter which is subject to the laws of nature.[40]

The state of affairs which we have described is nothing else than the familiar theory of St. Thomas Aquinas who underscored the subsistence of the human soul in relation to the body whose form it is.[41] For man exists differently than the entire universe; not as the result of the organization of matter, nor as the result of nature's acitvity but he subsists as a soul; he creates for himself and organizes, i.e., he "forms" his body which, since it is material must be subject to the laws of matter and thereby hands man over to the "bondage" of material laws.[42] Man himself is not the result of the organization of matter, but the organization of human matter is an essential, formal function of a subsistent soul which expresses itself in spiritual and corporeal acts as a subjective, subsistent "I," who animates all the material elements and calls them to human existence. The human being is not the consequence of the organization of matter. Some acts of the subsistent "I" testify about this character—for example, acts of intellectual cognition, love, creativity and decision which manifest themselves as immaterial, unquantifiable, immeasurable and not subject to time and space. Rather it transcends matter from many aspects even if it is essentially bound with it. Since the transcendence of a personal being in relation to nature is always a determined source of activity (a person is a free and self-determining being with respect to activity and hence he constitutes his own individual "nature"), it is an unusually important perception because a personal being is a being in its fundamental meaning. As we have already mentioned, to be a being in the proper sense means to exist as an independent subject (various "objective" types of existence are an equivocation since, in large measure, they are the consequence of particular systematic cognitional positions). An independent subject, however, i,e., a being existing in himself is a perfect subject since he not only exists im himself but also for himself; he is *pleno sensu* a PERSON. This takes place only in the case of a personal being who, as subject, is at the same time the author (performer) of his acts, through which he not only "expresses" himself but also "constitutes" himself in the sense which we have given above.

In addition, it is proper to recall here once again what we had already pointed out previously; that the personal being becomes, in the area of philosophy, the model of a fundamentally self-intelligible being who is as if a kind of principal analogue in analogically metaphysical cognition.

Under the influence of the nineteenth century, the model of a self-intelligible being for science was acknowledged to be the simplest material being or at least one composed of matter. And such a model of intelligibility began to be transposed to all cases of being. Consequently the most intelligible beings were the simplest cases of material beings; and they became the ideal of intelligibility. On the other hand, beings which existed truly subjectively, personal beings, became, in science and rational knowledge, something completely unintelligible. The epitome of unintelligibility would be the Absolute Being—God and not because of his transcendence, but precisely because of his unintelligibility. By accepting the model of intelligibility as a personal being, there appears a different character of rational cognition.[43]

IV. THE THEORY OF PERSONAL BEING

In examining the traditional theory of personal being, in classical philosophy—it was customary to emphasize the two-fold transcendence of the person: (a) in relation to nature, through spiritual acts of intellectual cognition, love and freedom; and (b) in relation to community—through acts bound with the moments: subjectivity of right, completeness, dignity.[44] Doubtless the seeds of the theory of personal being are perceived very accurately and it would be proper to develop an analysis and considerations of the meaning of this topic by also taking into account phenomenological expositions and reflections. And in great measure, such reflections exist in philosophical literature, although they are not linked with the conception of a personal being.[45] The tradition of classical philosophy which emphasizes these mentioned moments and characteristic traits of the personal human being is in this measure more compact. But it seems necessary here to make certain qualifications. Hence it is not proper to separate from each other the moments of cognition, love and freedom. Even though they are different structures of being, nevertheless in inner personal life, they are very closely linked and they mutually condition each other, like angles of a triangle which are different from each other but by mutually joining with each other create a single geometric figure.

For man can be considered as a *res naturae,* and hence as a particular biological exemplar, who lives and responds to the stimuli of the environment and the world. And in this measure, the differentiation of ontic cognitive structures of love and of freedom is seemingly most justified when, in relation to definite objects of activity, these manifest themselves as definite structuralized functions. We should examine as much as we can the structure of these functions so that we can understand man as an agent cause in the world or in a kind of natural-cultural environment.[46] An analysis of the acts of cognition, love, decision and freedom is indispensable since it alone can show the ontic structure of these acts, and in turn it projects on the ontic structure of the subject, "I" who "emanates" these acts. For we have only a roundabout and indirect way—only through an analysis of our spiritual acts—of cognizing our own human ontic structure. Consequently the character of our cognition, love, freedom, their process and subjectivity, enable us to catch a glimpse of our ontic character. In an analysis of acts of cognition of love or freedom we are hastening, above all, toward the establishment of the character of their particular object, which by specifying the act itself, points to its ontic character. For our process of cognitive analysis is directed by the determined nature of the object defining the character of the act. This is the way designated by the ancient Greeks (chiefly by Aristotle in the books *On the Soul*, a way from the analysis of a proper object to an analysis of the act; for this way points to its source as a real potentiality of acting. In this cognitive process the concept of a determined nature is put to good use.

But we must also look at man as a being who is forming from within his spiritual image internally—and hence as a person. And viewed in this way, man appears as one who acts cognitively through love with consciously experienced freedom. Three acts : knowledge, love, and freedom mutually condition personal life. Even our cognition is not a merely natural function. This is so because we not only modify our cognition correspondingly with love and free decision, but we also make selections as if a priori. There exists within us a natural cognitive selection in relation to the world. For we are so constituted that we possess our cognitive as well as sensible and spiritual apparatus which is selectively disposed: we retrieve from the environment stimuli which are particular and adjusted to our cognitive retrieving apparatus, leaving behind many other stimuli just as a radio receiver is adapted to the reception of wave lengths of only a certain range without profiting from other frequencies. But besides this natural selectivity, for example through acts of abstractive knowledge (we grasp in them that which we commonly call the "essence" of a thing and that which is possibly the result of a lengthy process of accommodating ourselves to the environment), we still possess a cognitive selectivity of personal nature. By becoming involved inwardly (and hence some form of love), man freely disposes himself so that he is either receptive or nonreceptive to a suitable informational-cognitive content. Under the influence of love which he has chosen freely, man can intensify his cognition to a significant degree; he arrives in some cases at a commonly known "cognitive passion" in some area of science or life. Cognitive sensitivity which has arisen as the result of a free choice or also a decision strengthened by love decides, to a marked degree, man's personal activity.

In this connection, St. Augustine had frequently called attention to the role of love in cognition, which sometimes approaches extreme formulations of cognition through love. And even if we cannot agree on an extreme formulation which leads to a confusion of concepts, nevertheless it is proper to emphasize the role of love and its involvement in cognition. For love of an object under investigation, or motives of love in an examination sometimes intensify a difficult process of examination; in addition, they establish the area of selected investigations. And even if acts of cognition are and should be "cool" and not permeated with emotion, their release, their endurance and their intensification are indivisibly bound with love and involvement.

To a greater degree, in personal life and its transcendence above nature, there is linked a human, personal love as above all a liking and spiritual giving of oneself to another person, because obviously love fulfills itself fundamentally and in its proper meaning in relation to another person, less so and only in a secondary sense in relation to a non-personal object.[47] There have been many analyses written in the current of classical philosophy about the connection between love and cognition, as well as about the character of love itself. Perhaps it is worthwhile merely to call attention to thinkers like Aristotle, St. Thomas Aquinas and in contemporary times, Blondel and Marcel, who made great contributions to the understanding of the problem of love as a personal action. If the Stagirite undertook a discussion of love in the categories of motion and "transformation" so-called by an acceptance in a loving subject of the "form" of the loved object—which is to become the source of the act of love—St. Thomas observed that the act of love has a different character than an act of cognition and there is something more here than merely a moment of "transformation," a disposition of a loving subject so that he permits in himself a permanent and continuing dynamism of activity (*actio immanens non habens se per modum res operatae sed per modum operationis*).[48] This is similar to what Augustine recalled, *ponderibus aguntur omnia; pondus meum amor meus; eo feror quocumque feror.*[49] Continuing this same thought Marcel added that properly love is ultimately the spiritual act of giving of oneself to another person. And as a result of this giving of oneself—equivalent to death and ultimately a fulfillment of oneself at this moment—it constitutes in man a way of "being-for-another-person." The highest possible act of love is the giving of oneself to the Absolute Person at the moment of death understood in the active sense.[50]

When it is a question of strictly free acts, of free decision, it is through love and commitment that it best directs the entire personal life. Only J. P. Sartre affirms excessively that man is freedom. In our personal life through acts of decision which are really continuous, we constitute ourselves as the source of activity. Through acts of decision, we affirm ourselves as an acting subject and we form our personal individuality. For acts of decision affect not only the external world and external objects; but they rather, affect fundamentally the subject himself as an acting being. The external world is only in an intermediate way the object of our decision through our own acts which we bring into existence from within ourselves. For man's freedom and his acts of decision affect our practical judgments through which we determine ourselves to activity. And so I myself through a free act of free choice (through a free act of love) choose for myself this particular practical judgment (sometimes neither the best nor rational), which determines me to activity. Through freedom, I constitute myself the source of activity. And in this sense, we can agree with Sartre that man is complete freedom—he is freedom as a person in relation to acts of performance, especially practical activity.

At the same time man, who lives in the world and who is related to nature through his body, possesses within himself deterministic moments; hence he is not only freedom but also to a great extent, nature which must be gradually transformed into "freedom."

As Max Scheler correctly observed, man is the kind of being who, in relation to his natural drives can say "no"—*"Der Mensch als nein sager"*; and in this way man can "protest against" his natural acts. We can also see in this situation one of the very characteristic human traits which differentiate man and beast, which even in death confirms its instincts. For if man can "objectify" himself in relation to his natural acts—he can subject them to the spirit—he can make of them an object of his free choice and he thereby transforms "nature" (the course of activity determined by natural structure) in freedom (the kind of activity which flows from auto-determination).

These three acts: cognition, love and freedom mutually complement each other like angles of a triangle: they give a characteristic feature of the transcendence of a person above nature and above the nature of the world, which man possesses in himself through his body, which is composed of the elements of nature.

Three further moments which are underscored in a personal-human being are likewise a sign of a person's transcendence even in the subordination of creations of social life. Above all, the subjectivity of law binds man as a person with common good which, in an objective sense, is ultimately identified with the Absolute.[51] Only man is a subject of a legal relation, for he has the right that another person should do something (or should cease doing) for this reason, that each person is subordinated to an internal development of perfection in the order of his powers and personally spiritual dispositions, which obviously is equal to a realization of common good as the only good that is not antagonistic to society. For common good which is the internal intellectual-moral development of the human person is realized the more that individual persons perfect their own personal potentialities: intellect and will. For the ultimate object who actualizes these human potentialities to the fullest is the Absolute. Now to be the subject of laws is nothing else than to have a relation with respect to another person, whose activity or non-activity is due us because of a proportionate common good. The foundation of law thus understood is our objective subordination to the ultimate good. For each one of us, who is perfecting himself from within, can demand from another person (people) a certain activity of cessation of activity, insofar as it is due us because of a necessity of realizing a common good.

And if society is a gathering of people for the sake of common good—otherwise man would not be able to develop his personal potentialities—then the particular personal being who is realizing common good can demand that another man either act or cease acting in such a way that the realization of common good understood subjectively can be made either possible or impossible. For the subjectivity of law is the primary and fundamental moment of transcending a human collectivity by a human person. This transcending is possible only when man's personal being transcends the various forms of nature and determination; when it is not only exclusively a creature of nature but, on the contrary, it is from certain aspects, an organizer of this nature.

Common good is also the ultimate foundation for joining together dynamized human persons into free personal societies. For community is not only the work of an instinctive nature (as in the case of ants, bees or termites), but it is a necessity dictated by the dynamization of the human person, whose full development is impossible without life in a community, because the perfecting of human cognition, human love and human freedom would be impossible. This perfecting is very tedious and lengthy, but its result is the constituting of a person as a "being-for-another-person."[52] This process assumes many forms: from the elementary biological form, in which one can see through a difference of sexes, a mutual ordering of individuals of the opposite sex, to the highest regions of the spirit, such as contemplative cognition and love, whose development and object are conditioned by a personal context. For both acts of intellectual cognition and acts of love, as well as moral conduct and artistic creativity in the wide sense, arise, develop, and perfect themselves in a real or virtual dialogue with a "Thou" of another person. For even in cognition, which is most eminently a common activity, because we want to know most definitively, we "express ourselves" so that another, could also understand. Spiritual acts which are constantly performed in the perspective of the "Thou" of another person, constitute such a characteristic mode of being that it can be called "being-toward-another-person." In summary, this means that a person's life, his spiritual development, and his achievement of perfection as a rational being, is impossible without establishing his entire interior life on the level of a dialogue with the "Thou" of another person, whether contingent (person of another man), or unconditionally transcendent (person of the Absolute).

As an essential form of human life, community neither enslaves nor exhausts personal life. As a person, man transcends this community because as a personal being, he is the highest form of a totality which social life does not complete in the subsistent-existential order, but only makes this total completeness possible. Because man is a person he does not cease being a corporeal nature and part of nature. Because he is a synthesis of person and nature, he strives as a person to subordinate community to himself. But as a relational creature who has a corporeal nature and is part of nature, he strives to be subordinate to the same community.

The two real sides of the human being: personal and naturalistically-natural possess their own necessary structural conditions. The fact that they constitute the same human being complicates the matter even more, since it is impossible to rank man univocally in a definite ontic context. Simplifications which appeared in the history of human thought constitute serious warnings with respect to the logical consequences that accompanied oversimplified solutions. For if man as a person were only a reflection of some greater "totality" (Hegel), then it would be necessary to accept the priority of the totality over that of the person, who would really have to be subordinated to the "totality" and its developmental laws, because the derivation of such a type would cancel *a limine* the transcendence of personal life—as it is observed from another point of view. If we were to grant that man is only a monad which unfolds itself from within, a subject which constitutes being (ontic contents), then, as a result, community would be only a meaningless margin, or it would mean only as much as an individual monad would want. Obviously these are extreme, aprioristic solutions which do not take into account the human fact.

By respecting fundamental facts, we must recognize man as a personal being whose development is accomplished in and for the subject. For even the manner of "being-for-another-person" which is observed in spiritual acts, enriches, fulfills and actualizes the personal subject himself. As a person, man has his own personal end which is not realized through community as such.

A concrete delineation of limits which subordinate man as a being of nature to community, or the subordination of community to the personal human being, is exceedingly difficult and usually utterly impossible. By means of his conscience the individual man must continually build these limits, and he must mature spiritually toward an increasingly higher personal life.[53] At different stages of internal development, man perceives and affirms differently his relation to community.

Finally, the third moment which is the dignity of the personal being, is linked with the fact of religion. As a person, man lives fundamentally not so much in the context of a naturalistic nature but rather in the context of a person. This means that the real justification of personal human life is not primarily nature—not pure relations with objects—which does not mean that man could live somewhere else than in the world. The fundamental human "existential" is precisely "being-in-the-world," so much so that beyond the world we cannot imagine any real human fact which we explain in anthropology. Yet man who lives in the world, and who gathers all his biological strengths from the world, nevertheless transcends this world in a specifically human order, in a spiritual order. He perceives that he is some-one who is a subjective being, distinct from the world and "thrown" into this world. He is not merely the sum of fortuitously chosen accidents, a synthesis of the laws of matter. At the same time, man knows, experiences and some-times succeeds in explaining that his spiritual acts and inner spiritual life are not the accidental activity of the powers of nature, and that the most select and complicated assembled powers of nature do not ultimately explain what is specifically human: the life of the spirit.

This life of the spirit, which is inseparably joined with the "Thou" of another person, becomes better understood and explained by means of inter-personal relations, than through a content-thing relation that flows from the presence in the world of a non-personal nature (of nature understood as *"natura"*). As soon as relations based purely on things (which constitute the order of nature) are cognized by man, they become the domain of science. Mindful of such a state of affairs, I do not live—in my personal aspects—in the context of scientific principles (in the illustrated manner), but rather in the context of personal principles. For if I love, hate, perform acts of deci-sion, if I live what is called a personal life, then the fundamental and essen-tial explanation of such a kind of life is not a relation based on things and, consequently, a science (as a cognitional understanding of relations based on things),[54] but that which gives a foundation and makes my human life mean-ingful can be only another person—another "Thou." Hence, again, personal life structures itself as a form of being "for-another-Thou," and in an ulti-mate perspective—for the THOU OF THE ABSOLUTE PERSON. This is precisely the fundamental moment of religion. We can therefore say that man as a person is fundamentally a religious being because he is the kind of being whose *raison d'être* of being and development is another person and ultimately the ABSOLUTE PERSON. This "ultimateness" is engraved in every interpersonal experience.

And perhaps young people in love are not that much in error when they mutually "adore" each other; when the lover tells his beloved "You are ador-able." She is "divinity" or the reason and meaning of the lover's life in a real and proper sense, even if incomplete, and she really fills this role in-sofar as she participates in the person of the Absolute. And so, interpersonal unions which give a foundation and meaning to a personal life as being most worthy make the same person SOMEONE WORTHY in himself and usher in the moment of religion in the most essential sense.

Ultimately, the context of a person's life is the TRANSCENDENT PERSON in whom persons of human existence participate and constitute the vertical horizon of man's personal life. As a person, man creates a nature for himself and he elevates it to a participation in a person's being as a manner of "being-for-another." Since he is a man and consequently the unique existence of the subjective "I" in ITS PSYCHO-ORGANIC UNITY (which is essentially present through the immanent function of continuous forming of the body as a co-worker and at the same time its first expression), man creates himself through his personal acts unto the fulness of personal life. In this current, he joins other persons and in the ultimate context the PERSON of THE ABSOLUTE as the highest FULNESS.

CHAPTER XII

THE HUMAN BEING IN THE PERSPECTIVE OF DEATH

I. THE FACT OF DEATH

The focus of all anthropological questions, in the sphere of philosophy, is undeniably death, toward which every human being inevitably tends, which is inscribed in all the acts of our life, which intrudes itself not only as a basic theme of human existence, its meaning or meaninglessness, but which also constitutes the constant "lining" of all our human experiences. If—as M. Heidegger accurately expressed it—a human being is a "being-towards-death," then too an ultimate understanding of the human being becomes more complete when, in the general considerations, we also take into account the moment of death as a fundamental and necessary perspective of human life, before which all other questions pale, since they are not always a necessary fact, they do not always affect all human beings, they are not always truly enduring questions.[1]

Death and the group of questions associated with it have always been an object of the reflections and considerations of the greatest geniuses of thought. Cicero attempts to identify even philosophy itself with a *commentatio mortis*.[2] Even though we were to regard this type of view as exaggerated, having in mind the classical conception of philosophy that ultimately explains the being originally given to us in sensory experience, yet the being thus given is transformable from within, is a disintegrating being, and in the case of a human being that disintegration is simply the realization of the process of death viewed from without. An investigation of the process of the transformation of a being reveals to us and discloses the inner structure of the being itself, its place in the context of other beings, and also the essential meaning of its existence.

In order to be able more closely to examine the question of the death of a human being, one must first view this fact from without, look at it as far as possible as an objective observer, and then one must also take into account the inner moment of inspection, namely, the way we ourselves personally see our own death, so that against this background the process of death might be related still more to the inner structure of a human being. Such introductory analyses will allow us in the second part of the chapter to make a thorough analysis of the problematic of death understood as a personal experience, i.e., death understood actively, insofar as it is the fulfillment of the personal process of the actualization of a human being. Hence, if the first part of the chapter will be devoted to the problem of death insofar as it comes to us from without and is "inflicted" upon us, then the second part will consider the question of death as the fulfillment of the personal life of a human being.

The method of the reflections conducted here follows the convention employed in classical philosophy (and not transcendental philosophy[3]), i.e., an indication of the fact as well as its description, and then a consideration of those factors that do not contradict the fact given to us for explanation. A rejection of the noncontradictable factors is necessarily tied to a rejection of the very fact given to us for ultimate (or the kind that does not presuppose still further) explanation.

A. THE FACT SEEN FROM WITHOUT

Death is an obvious and natural fact for a human being, insofar as the understanding of human death in general is concerned. We know, after all, that every human being who was born goes through a period of maturation, aging, and finally death, as the natural completion of the course of life, which, regardless of whether it turned out to be nothing but successes or nothing but failures — seen from a natural perspective from the biological side — is an inevitable journey toward death. From the biological point of view the life of a human being could be represented in the great metaphor of a *tauromachus*. This was magnificently done by P. L. Landsberg,[4] and it is worth citing his grand vision here:

"The bull that enters the arena knows nothing of what awaits him. He rushes joyfully from the obscurity of his prison and rejoices in the vitality of his youthful powers. Dazzled by the sudden light he feels himself master of the closed circle which becomes his world and which still seems to him a boundless plain. He tosses up the sand of the arena and rushes in every direction, with no other sensation than that of joy in his power.—Thus the infant leaves the body of his mother and soon begins to play in a luminous world which still conceals his destiny and its attendant dangers.

"The first adversaries enter the ring. It is still a game. Combat is natural to the bull. The struggle intensifies his awareness of life and of his own strength. These little vexations at the beginning merely build up his anger. It is the rage of the strong which reaches full measure in this provocation. The struggle calls forth the attacking animal which lies hidden beneath his every-day existence. There is nothing disagreeable beyond the limits of the game. But slowly a painful element is introduced. The game is rigged. The adversary is too cunning, he provokes and then retreats. Although the weaker of the two, the adversary becomes the stronger, because he is bad. The redness of the cloth becomes exasperating; it is no longer the happy pretext for a fight.

"Thus the adolescent at school and elsewhere has his first encounters with a guileful world against which the sincerity of his struggle is unavailing. But the fatigue of youth is not important.

"The fight only becomes serious for the bull with the entry of his enemies on horseback. From high above him the picadors strike at him with their lances and wound him from a distance. The bull attacks: he surpasses himself in his fury. His rage is now magnificent, blind and suffering; its frenzy secretly inspired by a despair of life, but constantly reinforced by a perpetual victory over this despair. It is the innocent old horse which suffers worst from his stubborn attack. The wily picador disappears when his bloody task is completed.—So does man enter on the real struggle of his life. He can never overcome evil. If he destroys any one of is adversaries, he will only have destroyed an innocent. Here all are innocent; our adversaries are only masks for the Evil which we shall never destroy.

"At this moment the bull is still strong. But from now on his reserves are failing. He looks stronger than he really is. His grip on life is shaken. The wounds from the lances were deep and his blood is flowing. And now the action is held up by an intermezzo. He is to be decorated, and also wounded again. There is both respect and mockery in festooning this gallant fighter with bandilleros. And the heroic beast provides an almost comic pretext for the elegant dance of the bandillero, the man who garlands him with these lethal darts, and succeeds in planting his weapon, in spite of his own fears, thanks to the very grandeur and slowness of the driven bull. —Thus man in his maturity attains honour and success at the very moment when he is weakened by the wounds of life. And even worldly glory is only a more secret wound, a traditional and almost ridiculous decoration, a travesty of victory. For he has conquered nothing. No one is victor in this world. We pretend that he has been victorious, as if true glory lay at the disposal of man. This is indeed an insult. The bull, at least, does not believe in his new honours. Perhaps he has even the foreboding that the world only glorifies those whom it is about to sacrifice.

"Then with the matador, the high priest of the mystery, death enters the arena. Behold it! It is the sword, beautiful, supple and inevitable, hidden under the terrible red of the cloth, but hidden only from the one destined to receive it. The others behold this death, and the weakened bull enters his agony, and in transcending this agony reaches a deeper, though not yet ultimate gravity after the tragi-comedy of the interlude. The tragedy begins, or rather the tragic significance of the whole spectacle is finally disclosed. A good bull remains dignified, a fighter to the end. I do not think that he still believes in victory. But though almost without intelligence, he is not without an obscure awareness of the approaching moment, an awareness which has been brusquely sharpened by the adventures of the past twenty minutes, which comprise a lifetime. There have been struggles and attacks, withdrawal and return, on both sides. There has been success and defeat. The combat has not rested on a purely physical plane. The matador, summoning up his will, tries to lead and dominate the bull, maneuvering him into the only position which will allow of a mortal blow. He waves the red flag of death, so that it masters the bull, compelling him to follow it, like a lover dying beneath the spell of a sovereign mistress. And suddenly the bull is killed. His massive body wears the sword like a last proud cry of despair. For a few seconds he seems to resist. But death comes, the death that has so long been present, identified with the sword, identical with its source, the matador who wields it. The dead animal is carried away, like a thing.— Thus we all come to death in this world. Every battle with death is lost before it begins. The splendour of the battle cannot lie in its outcome, but only in the dignity of the act. The definitive is the inevitable."

The general reflection on human destiny assumes a more painful and personal expression when death takes someone close to us, in relation to whom we had shaped our life on the basis of a partner in dialogue. The absence of the person occasioned by death changes not only the external situation— as a result of which the very same house, the very same dwelling-place or surroundings, sometimes become "unbearable" for us because they testify to the constantly present absence of the person "filling" the environment and context of experiences—but to a great extent our "interiority" also changes through the change of a perspective of viewing, through the absence of more than just intellectual and emotional experiences of the partner. We notice that people, after the death of dear ones, become "different" in their outlook, in their love, in their opinions. Death has sown a desolation that is constantly present, although a person may even become accustomed to this absence—as time goes by.

St. Augustine expressed this experience of the death of a dear one in his *Confessions*:[5] "My heart was made dark by sorrow, and whatever I looked upon was death. My native place was a torment to me, and my father's house was a strange unhappiness. Whatsoever I had done together with him was, apart from him, turned into cruel torture. My eyes sought for him on every side, and he was not given to them. I hated all things, because they no longer held him. Nor could they now say to me, 'Here he comes,' as they did in his absence from them when he lived. To myself I became a great riddle, and I questioned my soul as to why it was sad and why it afflicted me so grievously, and it could answer me nothing. If I said to it, 'Hope in God,' it did right not to obey me, for the man, that most dear one whom she had lost, was more real and more good to her than the fantasy in which she was bade to hope. Only weeping was sweet to me, and it succeeded to be my friend in my soul's delight."

The death of a dear one affects us very directly in our personal experience. For if the "Thou" of another person is like an objectified, "I," all that happens to the "Thou" of the partner, on the strength of intrapolation [*intrapolacja*], affects me as well. Consequently, the experience of the death of another person is in large measure the intrapolated [*intrapolowane*] experience of my own death, which awaits me in the world. But despite this I can, with the passage of time become accustomed to the absence occasioned by the death of a close partner, since along with the passage of time there also occurs a process of the rationalization and seeming justification of the fact of death. For we ultimately understand the objective necessity of the death of a human being as a natural biological process.

Death seen from without—even the death of persons closest to us, accepted with rebellion, protest—is ultimately a normal, explicable, phenomenon for us. It is a work of nature, which has its determinants, its necessities—this allowed some to define living creatures as things that are able to die.[6] To the Stoics nature explained everything, including death: "But the time and the period is fixed by Nature; sometimes by your own nature or constitution, as when you die in old age; but always by the nature of the whole, whose parts being continually changing, the whole universe is preserved in perpetual bloom and vigor. Now that is always good and seasonable, which is conducive to the advantage of the whole. The termination of life, therefore, cannot be an evil to any one, as there is no moral turpitude in it; for it is neither subject to our choice, nor adverse to society. Nay, it must be good, as it is seasonable and advantageous, and conformable to the order of the universe."[7]

B. THE FACT SEEN FROM WITHIN

An understanding and even a general acceptance of the fact of death—especially when it concerns strangers—nevertheless takes on the form of a protest when it concerns personal death. The views of theological thinkers quoted by Pieper[8] also point to this: " 'Human death is frightening and mysterious, no matter how plausible it may be scientifically. For death is the downfall of what is bent on life'—thus Hermann Volk. And Romano Guardini in his essay on *The Last Things:* 'Bread is meaningful in itself, as are light, truth, love—human death is not' . . . The Protestant theologian Oscar Cullmann flatly calls death 'unnatural' and even 'abnormal;' from the point of view of the New Testament, he says, he would 'not venture to join Karl Barth . . . in speaking of 'death as natural.' ' "

Is it not a puzzling matter that in fact the real thinking of one's own death is not possible? I can imagine that I am on the death bed, that I have died, that I am lying in a coffin, that they are carrying me to the cemetery, etc. But in each such thought experience (basically imagined!) I make use of certain cognitive contents, which either radiate from me, from the ego, or somehow are established on the ego. That "I," however, is present everywhere, immanent and at the same time transcending the experienced contents, even if these were the contents of one's own death. I cannot really think of the nonexistence of the subject of thinking, since every act of thinking presupposes the immanence in this act of the very subject of thinking. An act of thinking is not possible without establishing it in subjective existence. And if death were the negation of the very subject, its annihilation, then the actual thinking of the nonexistence of oneself would strike at the existential foundation of thought itself, at the immanence of the subject in relation to thought contents. Hence, any thinking of mine about my own death is nothing but a constructional, artificial thinking, transferred from the view of other subjects and an imposition of that view on the "I;" with this qualification, however, that in thinking of our own death, we thereby affirm this "I" as thinking, i.e., surviving, because it exists (thinking is after all an important form of existence) in the experienced cognitive contents having to do with our own death.

The very thinking of one's own death is a concealed affirmation of the transcendence of existence in relation to its various forms, if I cannot think of the real nonexistence of myself. Even the speaking about the "nonexistence of oneself" after death is talk of a different form of existence, since every utterance concerning content is always established in existence—if not of a subject that is spoken about, then at least of a subject that expresses itself.[9] A real utterance concerning content, without the establishment of it in the existence of a speaking subject, would be a nonentity, a nonbeing. The affirmation of one's own subjectivity, of the existence of one's own "I" (of one's own act of personal existence), is this unique event of ontical affirmation in all of our cognitive acts, which cannot be denied and from which one cannot "escape" due to the very character of the act of cognition. For there will be no real act of cognition if there is no consciousness, the presence of the real immanence of the existing "I" in everything that is "mine," i.e., in my cognitive contents. I can make up the most arbitrary and fantastic cognitive contents, but all of them are established in the "I" that "nourishes" them. Therefore, I can think of anything, but I cannot really think of the nonexistence of the "I," since then I would be thinking not only of non-thinking, but I would be thinking of that which is the ultimate negation of the very ground of thinking.

Every cognitive act occurs on the cognitive "axis:" subject-object. And I cannot think reflectively, in a controlled manner (when I control my thinking), so that the cognitive axis would disappear, cancelling one end of this "axis"—my "I" as the subject of thinking; I cannot really think of the "nonexistence of myself," since all thinking is precisely established upon the affirmation of my existence. Hence, in trying to think of our own death, we must objectify ourselves, make a "thing" of ourselves, and somehow separate ourselves from the thus reified subject in order to be able to represent "ourselves" no longer with the "attributes" of life; to imagine ourselves as nonliving. This kind of cognitive objectification of one's death is not an authentic cognitive experience of it, if the experience presupposes an affirmation of the existence of oneself as subject. Experiencing our death represented cognitively, we really experience it precisely as the death of "someone else." Even this impossibility of an authentic cognitive experience of our own death is extremely significant and stands as the basis both of questions concerning the existence of the soul after the death of a human being, as well as of the characteristic experiences analyzed below.

Although we are not able cognitively to experience our own death in some isolated cognitive act, yet we constantly experience it in an "accompanying" way (just as a shadow accompanies our moving about in the sunlight) in our various cognitive-appetitive psychic experiences. And these are just the processes that must be considered, since their analysis provides informative material for the understanding of the human being as a "being-towards-death."

The actual thinking itself about one's own death is basically a thinking about one's own existence whose form fundamentally changes, which ceases to be in relation to the world but which, changing forms and content, continues to ENDURE in other changed dimensions and contents unknown to us. And perhaps this is just where one ought to look for the grounds of the solution to this age-old experiential dilemma between the conviction concerning, on the one hand the naturalness of the death of a human being, and on the other hand, the rebellion and inner nonacceptance of personal nonexistence.[10] Death as a work of nature, i.e., determined to a proper activity of nature, of biology, is something ultimately understandable, since it is the natural dissolution of that which is ordered toward this dissolution—and which, after all, is constantly occurring in us through catabolic processes. Given such a state of affairs, death would be a kind of radical falling apart and disintegration of the organism, i.e., of the body unceasingly organized by the living "I." Biological death is a necessary work of nature, which occurs on the strength of the inner factors of determination that go into its make up. It may even be painful, especially when it affects me in some sense, but it is understandable.

Death is not, however, and cannot be understood as referring to my personal life, as referring to the person. After all, it is not possible to think of personal nonexistence both on account of the very structure of the act of cognition in which there is the presence of the "I" transcending "my" contents, as well as ultimately on account of the structure of personal being itself, which, subsisting, does not have in itself an inner ground of nonexistence,[11] if the body exists through the existence of the soul. The human being as nature and the human being as person—here is the reason, on the one hand, of the naturalness of death and, on the other, of the rebellion against death and the fact that it is deemed the worst evil that can befall a human being.

Of course, such an explanation does not rule our still other forms of an explanation of the rebellion against death—namely, the conception of death as a punishment.[12] For if the personal acts of a human being are basically human acts, and in just these acts human death is something incomprehensible (death as referring to the person who is given to us in cognitive experience from within, solely in personal inner experience)—then the factuality of human death can still in addition be explained through an appeal to guilt and punishment. This, however, is an additional and complementary explanation by reason of freely accepted acts of faith.

C. THE ONTICAL FOUNDATIONS OF THE FACT OF DEATH

The perspective of personal death, the inevitable fact of it, in spite of inner rebellion and the impossibility of even actually thinking about personal death as nonexistence, has always induced people to search for some ontical foundations, the perception of which would be able to explain to what extent the process of death and the very fact of death annihilates the human being.

In large measure the fact of human death stimulated reflection upon the ontical structure of the human being, which was to become the basis of the explanation of the ultimate factuality or else some mere appearance of death.[13]

Practically every philosophical theory about the human being initiated, adopted, or simulated a kind of conception of human nature that "did not fear" death any longer, since it would be something merely apparent for the human being. In this regard the attitude of Epicurus is typical: "Death is nothing to us; for the body, when it has been resolved into its elements, has no feeling, and that which has no feeling is nothing to us."[14] "The dread of death," writes Krokiewicz,[15] "resolves itself into the concrete fear either of the pain of dying, or of suffering after death, or of nothingness. Fear of the pain of dying can intensify the terror of suffering after death as well as the terror of nothingness, because while a human being is dying, he or she is still alive, and so that pain belongs to the pains discussed in the fourth part. . . . There remain two mutually exclusive causes of dread, namely, fear of suffering after death and fear of annihilation. On the whole, the ancients related very suspiciously to belief in the individual immortality of the human being. It tended more to frighten them with the presage of judgment and punishment for offenses committed in life, than to gladden them with the promise of a doubtful happiness and reward for rather uncertain merits." Epicurus vehemently teaches that one should not fear any suffering because with death the human being utterly ceases, since the person's atoms are dispersed and the human organism perishes irrevocably. Epicurus stresses the nothingness of death: "We were born once; one cannot be born twice. Life passes away and will never again return. Not being certain of tomorrow, you put off joy for later, and meanwhile life is frittered away and each of us dies in the treadmill." And so there is only this short temporal life and it ought to be affirmed, since death ends everything.

The position of Aristotle and the Stoics was similar in its metaphysical expression, since their conception of a human being affirmed nature alone as acting in the measurable, concrete, material conditions. Accordingly, given the acceptance of such a position, the ultimate expression of wisdom is the opinion of Seneca: "No evil is great which is the last evil of all. Death arrives; it would be a thing to dread, if it could remain with you. But death must either not come at all, or else must come and pass away."[16]

A radically different solution of the problem of death against the background of a specific structure of human nature is given by Plato, whose considerations on this topic, reaching their high point in the *Phaedo,* fully deserve to be quoted verbatim: "It looks as though this were a bypath leading to the right track. So long as we keep to the body and our soul is contaminated with this imperfection, there is no chance of our ever attaining satisfactorily to our object, which we assert to be truth. In the first place, the body provides us with innumerable distractions in the pursuit of our necessary sustenance, and any diseases which attack us hinder our quest for reality. Besides, the body fills us with loves and desires and fears and all sorts of fancies and a great deal of nonsense, with the result that we literally never get an opportunity to think at all about anything. Wars and revolutions and battles are due simply and solely to the body and its desires. All wars are undertaken for the acquisition of wealth, and the reason that we have to acquire wealth is the body, because we are slaves in its service. That is why, on all these accounts, we have so little time for philosophy. Worst of all, if we do obtain any leisure from the body's claims and turn to some line of inquiry, the body intrudes once more into our investigations, interrupting, disturbing, distracting, and preventing us from getting a glimpse of the truth. We are in fact convinced that if we are ever to have pure knowledge of anything, we must get rid of the body and contemplate things by themselves with the soul by itself. It seems, to judge from the argument, that the wisdom which we desire and upon which we profess to have set our hearts, will be attainable only when we are dead, and not in our life time. If no pure knowledge is possible in the company of the body, then either it is totally impossible to acquire knowledge, or it is only possible after death, because it is only then that the soul will be separate and independent of the body. It seems that as long as we are alive, we shall continue closest to knowledge if we avoid as much as we can all contact and association with the body, except when they are absolutely necessary, and instead of allowing ourselves to become infected with its nature, purify ourselves from it until God himself gives us deliverance. In this way, by keeping ourselves uncontaminated by the follies of the body, we shall probably reach the company of others like ourselves and gain direct knowledge of all that is pure and uncontaminated—that is, presumably, of truth. For one who is not pure himself to attain to the realm of purity would no doubt be a breach of universal justice. . . .

"Very well, then, said Socrates, if this is true, there is good reason for anyone who reaches the end of this journey which lies before me to hope that there, if anywhere, he will attain the object to which all our efforts have been directed during my past life. So this journey which is now ordained for me carries a happy prospect for any other man also who believes that his mind has been prepared by purification. . . .

"And purification, as we saw some time ago in our discussion, consists in separating the soul as much as possible from the body, and accustoming it to withdraw from all contact with the body and concentrate itself by itself, and to have its dwelling, so far as it can, both now and in the future, alone by itself, freed from the shackles of the body. Does not that follow? . . . Is not what we call death a freeing and separation of soul from body?"[17]

That ultimate victory of soul over body, which is the essential content of the *Phaedo* and of many of the other Platonic dialogues, constitutes the expression of the very act of philosophizing and of the profound hope a human being possesses on the strength of his or her own nature, on the strength of the structure of his or her psychic acts, which are constantly being incompletely fulfilled in life. And although the conception of the soul's connection with the body and its imprisonment in the body is the reception of an orphic revelation in Plato, yet he greatly enriched this concept (which in spite of everything is not in accord with nature and inner experience, since neither he himself nor any of us was eager to escape from the body—and we regard our body as a great good, not an an evil), and in it he perceived real factors, based on an analysis (or perhaps an intuition?) of the fulfillment in us of our spiritual acts.

Although the general concept of the structure of the human being presented by Plato is erroneous, yet it was undoubtedly he who most brought into relief those moments of personal life that clearly transcend matter and that are the foundation of the basic formulation of assertions concerning the continuation after death of what Plato called soul; not just because Plato said it, but because an analysis of personal acts constitutes sufficient reason for assertions of this type.

Therefore, having in mind the structure of the human being, manifesting itself through the structure of personal acts such as intellectual cognition—both conceptual and judgmental—as well as our reasoning and reflection, and also the structure of our acts of love, of decision, one can perceive that they are immaterial and as such testify to the immateriality of the ontical subject, which forms such acts from itself, causes them and gives them a characteristic structure, defined in the analysis precisely as immaterial. The immaterial, ontical structure of the acts testifies to the immaterial structure of the subject itself, which—existing—causes and sustains these acts in existence. In accordance with the tradition of classical philosophy, we can call that subject the human soul, which admittedly does not appear to us immediately in our cognitive experiences, but which is the ontical ground of our perceptible spiritual and immaterial acts, given to us immediately in inner experience—the "I" and that which is "mine." Indeed, one cannot identify the soul with the "I" as the personal subject subjectivizing "my" acts, but one can and ought, in that immediately given "I," performing both material as well as immaterial acts, to distinguish (through noncontradictable philosophical thinking) the immaterial soul as the reason of being of psychic acts that are immaterial in their structure, as was already mentioned earlier.[18]

Consequently, if there are spiritual, i.e., immaterial (not having matter in their inner structure) acts existing in us, then too their subject as the reason of being likewise cannot be something (someone) material, and speaking generally—matter, since then one would have to agree to the absurd in this sense, that "nonbeing" (body) is the reason of being (spirit), i.e., that nonbeing (body) is the same as being (spirit).

The soul, being in itself a subsistent entity and imparting existence to the body—as the proper and essential core of the immediately experienced "I"—and being an immaterial entity, but together with the body co-constituting the human being, is at the same time the "form" of the body.[19]

In order to remove the difficulties appearing in connection with the problem of the understanding of the term "form," I would like to stress that the point here, in short, is that a human being is not some sort of contingent conglomerate of spirit and matter, but is a single being of two components necessarily ordered to one another: soul and body. The relation of these components to one another is expressed in the widespread Aristotelian terminology as the relation of matter to form or potency to act. What this means is that analogically the very same function that, according to Aristotle's system, form fulfills in some living body, is likewise fulfilled by the soul in the human organism, making it the body, i.e., the kind of organism that is essentially connected and ordered to spirit, to its activity, and to not only its inner "expression" but also to its inner enrichment, i.e., the actualization of the potentialized person.

The concept of the composition of matter and form or more generally of potency and act is not only a suitable concept, but also the only admissible concept for the expression of an ontical state in which numerous factors or component elements are able to be discovered (as in the case of the human being), on the condition that at the same time the essential unity of being is also preserved. Despite the multiple composition of ontical components, in the human being there is really one being, one ontical existence. And wherever a multiplicity of ontical components can be distinguished with the simultaneous preservation of the unity of being, the composition of potency and act is realized. There can be many potencies in a different sense, but they are realized as being through one ontical act, i.e., one existence.

Consequently, if the soul is—using Aristotelian language—the form of the body or, speaking more clearly, is the human being's one act of being, then this means that it is not only the ground of the existence—of the life— of the human being, but also that it unceasingly organizes matter to be human matter—a human body. This does not mean, however, that the soul is altogether submerged and immersed completely in matter (i.e., is a function of matter alone), since it also performs specifically immaterial functions, which are the acts of intellectual cognition and acts of will. Acts of intellectual cognition and will, neither having any attributes of the temporal-spatial continuum nor being changeable-potential in their structure, require that the immediate sources of these acts—the powers performing the acts of cognition and will—would not be some material bodily organ. Granted that sometimes the brain is spoken of popularly as the instrument of cognition, yet the brain itself is not an intellectual-cognitive organ, in spite of the fact that it is a necessary instrument of cognition, just as for an artist an instrument for playing is necessary, e.g., a piano. This does not mean, however, that a piano concert is the work of the piano itself. For in the performance of psychic acts with an immaterial ontical structure, the whole human being participates, i.e., even matter, and in particular the human being's central nervous system. For in the human being we perceive a functional unity, which nevertheless does not rule out the structural-ontical difference of the components of the human being and ultimately the distinct character of the human soul as the subsisting subject for spiritual acts.

Having in mind, then, the fact of the ontical subsistence of the human soul and its noncorporeity, one can perceive the real ontical foundations of its immortality. For if the soul—being the essential factor of the ego—possesses its own existence, is a subsistent being (which expresses itself unceasingly in our self-cognition and manifests itself in judgments of "I am") organizing for itself the body, which exists by the existence of the soul, since for the body to be means to be organized by the soul, then in the moment of the decomposition of the body and its total disorganization the subsisting and immaterial soul, as the ultimate subject of acts that are immaterial in their ontical structure, cannot cease to exist. It would perish only if its existence were the result of the bodily organization. But then the absurd would follow: being arises from nonbeing; the body, which is not spirit, organizes itself in the form of non-body, i.e., "creates" the spirit that manifests itself in all human cognition and wanting. Hence, the essential ground of the immortality of the human soul is its subsistence, i.e.,—expressing it in the language of the philosophical tradition—the fact that existence (ascertained in the judgment, "I am") belongs immediately to the soul, which is also the form of the body.

If existence belongs immediately to the soul, and to the body only and exclusively through the soul, then the annihilation of the body does not entail the annihilation of the subsistent substance which is the human soul-ego. Thomas briefly observes: "That which has existence through itself cannot either come into being or undergo destruction, except through itself. For this reason, too, the soul cannot come into being by way of generation, i.e., material alterations, since it has an immaterial existence; and likewise it cannot cease to exist by way of natural destruction."[20] There would have to occur a special intervention of the Absolute, who would annihilate the soul, since the soul of itself, being in its essence an uncomposed spirit, cannot forfeit existence. Only the Absolute, therefore, is the reason of the generation of the soul, and only the Absolute could—obviously acting contrary to the natural order—annihilate it.[21] The annihilation, however, of an immortal being is contrary to its ontical structure and natural inclination. Furthermore, it would not have any reason of being (nonbeing has no reason!), and finally—as St. Thomas properly observes—it would be contrary to divine justice.[22] Therefore, not having sufficient reason either in the structure of the being or in divine activity—annihilation would be an unnecessary and irrational "miracle."

We daily encounter the problem of immortality and thereby its germinal solution in the unceasingly posed question: "Will we continue to exist after death, and is our ego immortal?" These questions are posed not only directly in precisely the form of questioning sentences, but also equivalently in one way or another, a question such as this is the whole of human activity, i.e., rational activity. The very character of our cognition, the use of necessary, general concepts; the character of our judgments in one way or another affirming be-ing; the simplest acts and declarations of love manifested externally with the help of the great quantifiers: "forever," "never;" the whole of creative and cultural work, attempting in the course of changeable and transitory matter to leave behind a lasting trace of our thought; everything that is somehow a rational expression of the human being—is an expression of a transcendence beyond changeable matter; is at least the really posed question: "Will we continue to exist when the changeable state of matter entering into our ontical structure carries out the still further, still more radical alterations, called death?"

Since we do in fact pose precisely these existential questions through the whole of rational activity, and we pose them in the course of unceasing material changes—because the matter, after all, which we now animate constantly continues to pulsate its changeability—as a unique, precisely human group of beings in the world, then there does exist a real and sufficient ontical foundation of the appearance of these questions. And our immaterial ego, ordered to endure beyond time, is precisely such a sufficient ontical foundation. For if there are real questions (whether expressed in words or in deeds), then there is a real foundation of the possibility of these questions arising. And this is already in principle a solution in the positive sense of this typically human question that every human being poses directly or equivalently.[23]

II. DEATH AS A PERSONAL EXPERIENCE

If philosophical reflection begins in wonder, then the fact most conducive to wonder is our personal death. This matter is so unusual that one cannot even cognitively experience this particular fact authentically, despite the constant awareness that there awaits us an end of life in the body.

Having in mind the necessity of death, constantly accompanying us—like a shadow—one finds it necessary first to reflect upon the concept of death itself, and then to indicate those real forms of spiritual life which, with regard to their ultimate fulfillment, occur in the moment of death conceived as a personal act.

Insofar as the so-called definition of death is concerned, it is possible to set forth various propositions on this topic: a) one can speak of the clinical death of a human being, i.e., of the cessation of the functioning of the central nervous system, the heart, or some other important organs; b) one can and should distinguish clinical death from biological death, i.e., real death from the biological point of view, the irreversible cessation of the vital functions of the human organism; c) one can also conceive some philosophical and perhaps even religious definition of the death of a human being as e.g., "the separation of the soul from the body," assuming that the human being either "has" a soul, or "is composed" of soul and body, or "is" a soul using a body. All of the possibilities, however, presuppose that both the soul and the body are individual substances-things that are separable from one another.

Of course, the philosophical or philosophical-religious definition of death as a complete separation of the soul from the body is at first glance very simple, since one can easily form an imaginary model of the "separation" of one thing from another, but the same definition understood in actual fact is immearurably difficult and complicated, because in separation from a systemic backing it says little or nothing, because it says a great deal and badly.[24] Hence, one can understand such a definition of the soul only in the context of a system; for one must first determine the real relation of the soul to the body and properly conceive the soul and the body individually, as well as the personal whole.[25]

One can speak yet of another concept of death, namely, as the completion of life in time, and thereby of such a state or the attainment of such a state of the human spirit, in which the human being ultimately is constituted a truly personal being, capable of making ultimate human decisions.[26] What is at issue here?

Let us assume for the present the hypothesis, which we will justify in subsequent philosophical analyses of this chapter with the use of an appropriate method of philosophizing, that the moment of a man's death is that particular moment in which change, and thereby time (as the measure of material change), precisely is ended and there no longer follows a "transition" to a further temporal moment, as that which occurs in all changes where a temporal moment is the link of the phase of movement ending, but not completed, and at the same time turning into the next phase, which is beginning, but also will not be completed because it will "turn into" a still further phase. In the moment of the death of a man we are, therefore, dealing with the real, temporal (because changeable) end of "duration-becoming," if it is also to be (although in a different aspect, because already nontemporal and unchangeable) the beginning of a possible unchangeable duration. This particular moment in which the "fulfillment" of the time of human being occurs is the moment in which all personal acts (i.e., acts of cognition and love) arrive at fulness, because they arrive at completion, at fulfillment. This moment, which will become the beginning of a new unchangeable state, a state of nontemporal duration, must precisely be completed, fulfilled, in order for fulness to occur, if it is to occur at all. Hence, too, the moment of the end of time is the moment in which converge, as though in a keystone, the personal human acts continually begun but never ultimately completed (because performed in essentially changeable conditions) in the course of human life. And if we were to call that completion-finale of human life death, then we would avoid the systemic definitions of the death of a man as the "separation" of soul from body and—consequently—we would avoid at the very outset an analysis of the problem of death in the context of a system. This does not mean, however, that in further considerations it will be possible to move away from this particular context, since philosophical thinking, if it is orderly, is a "system" of thinking.

Accepting the concept of the death of man as a completion and not an interruption of personal life, we also propose a hypothesis connected with this other concept, and which it will be necessary to justify; namely, that only the moment of death as the moment of the fulfillment of all personal (cognitive and appetitive, acts of man is precisely that moment in which man becomes truly in actual fact fully capable of making a decision in relation to his life, in relation to an ultimate choice of value, in a word: an ultimate decision concerning the meaning of his existence, that is to say, first and foremost, the acceptance of God, since only this moment of a human being's life is a moment in which his personality, understood in a dynamic, psychological sense, is fulfilled. This does not mean that a human being prior to the moment of the completion of his life would not be a person. He is one, but he is one in a potentialized sense, because he can continually become more complete; he is one in an incomplete sense, because he can always become more perfect; he is one in an ontical sense, which means that he has the circumstances of his existence. The moment of death is the ultimate completion of the changeable process of psychic life, such that further development actualizing the potentiality of the human being is not possible. Death, being the completion of the actualization of the personality, presents thereby the culmination point in which all changeable acts begun in the course of human life find their fulfillment, in consequence of which the human being in the moment of death becomes ultimately perfectly enabled psychically to make his decisions concerning the meaning of human life, the affirmation of God, and his ultimate end.

Of course, when we speak of this moment of death, this does not mean that it could be experienced experimentally by someone. The experimental experience of death and a return to the temporal, changeable conditions of duration are a contradiction. For that which is "terminated" is not something not completed. That personal experience of death also does not seem possible in conjunction with the participation of material organs, the brain, since such an experience is precisely connected with change, motion, while—in this hypothesis—death is supposed to be an experience of the human being in which time ends and change ceases. Consequently, such an experience of death occurs "after" the biological death of man, "after" the cessation of the material changes taking place in the human body.

Still another demarcation is important here, allowing the question under consideration to be brought into relief. What is at issue is the differentiation of death accepted passively and actively.

Death in the passive sense is the decomposition of the human organism. This decomposition, after all, is constantly occurring in the course of organic human life. The ultimate decomposition is the biological death of the human being who, being subject to nature in the aspect of the organization of matter and, moreover, being in a certain sense a creature of nature—is subject whether he wants to or not to the laws of nature. The ultimate result of subjection to the laws of nature is precisely biological death, is the decomposition of the human body. The human being in this sense is condemned to die and must "undergo" this death, i.e., experience it. This is the so-called "passive" experience, independent of the human person and his psyche. The "passive experience" of death occurs beyond consciousness, and the famous aphorism of Epicurus can here be applied: "Death is nothing to us, since so long as we exist, death is not with us; but when death [in this sense] comes, then we do not exist."

But if a human being is a thinking being, and if spiritual life (cognition and love) is connected with the human ego understood as a soul that is to survive the decomposition of the body—then besides death understood passively one must distinguish death understood actively, that is, death as a real experience of the human spirit. This experience cannot occur in conjunction with the co-activity of the brain, because all material activity has already ceased. It can occur autonomously in the sphere of spirit if the spirit brings to an end the changeable states and changeable activity of its powers. This kind of experience of death—transtemporal—still belongs to the human being, whose spirit completes the acts of cognition and love initiated and performed incompletely in the changeable, potential conditions of his life. That bringing to an end of changeable life is a bringing to the ultimate moment in which the spirit is able to express itself.[27] Precisely this ultimate spiritual "expression of oneself," performed against the background of the completion of the changeable states of the psyche, is the moment of the making of ultimate decisions, is death understood in the active sense. Without death understood actively, a human being would be a "thing," and not a person consciously experiencing the most important moments and sides of his life. There arises, however, a question concerning what sort of spiritual acts can tell us something about death thus understood.

a) When we take, as the object of philosophical analysis, our human cognition expressing itself in everyday speech, i.e., in subjective-predicative language, then we notice—something to which, after all, various thinkers and philosophers have drawn attention down through the ages—that the expression "is," being a sentence copula in predicative sentences, fills an essential although very mysterious function in our human intellectual cognition.

The problem of the expression "is" and its role in judgments, i.e., in responsible human cognition, has a substantial literature containing many penetrating analyses. There has also appeared a theory according to which, using subjective-predicative language containing the sentence copula "is," we already thereby affirm God's existence *implicite*. And although this theory of Maréchal[28] does not seem acceptable in its original form (because then the problematic of God's existence would be reduced to an awareness of the acknowledgement of God's existence contained in speech itself, which either would be a pseudo-problem if we were to understand it in Kant's sense, or would not be the problem of God's existence if it were conceived in the psychological sense), yet the character of our natural language, insofar as it expresses human cognition, bears witness to the fact that cognitively we apprehend existing reality—really existing being—and in apprehending being we also apprehend, obscuring and imperfectly, the ultimate reason of being, which is the Absolute. For this reason, too, along with many reservations flowing from the necessity of appealing to the explanatory thinking that philosophy affords us, we can say that to every human being is given a spontaneous, imperfect, and obscure cognition of God's existence in the form of some "judgment " taking the shape of a question, a doubt, a conviction, or else a conjecture concerning the existence of God.

A mature human being in some way "justifies" this imperfect and spontaneous judgment, ultimately affirming the existence of God or denying it, depending upon which type of explanatory cognition he will use: philosophical or scientific cognition, or else he will resign from a justification, contenting himself with fideism as the blind affirmation of the original and natural conviction.

In connection with the philosophical interpretation of the spontaneous and original judgment concerning God's existence related to the function of the expression "is" in our ordinary language, it is necessary above all to note the objectivism and realism of human cognition. Our cognition is a specific psychic grasp of the objective states of things, and not an arbitrary construction. This means that our cognition expressed in judgments has the attribute of truth, i.e., it is in accord with the factual state of things. But the factual state of things first and foremost actually exists. And we ascertain this in very simple and original existential judgments of the type: "John exists;" "this here table upon which I am writing exists;" "my thinking exists." Such a type of cognition, expressed in existential judgments, is the cognitive grasp of being "on the spot," spontaneously, and most originally. Even before I know what the thing is, I perceive that a concrete thing "is," i.e., "exists." This original human cognition is so natural; and spontaneous that we usually pay no attention to it, but concentrate on the cognitive grasp of the very content of the thing. On the other hand, a fuller cognitive grasp of the content of the thing occurs in a judgment in which the expression "is" again appears as its core, when, for example, I ascertain that "a human being is a mammal." We meet the expression "is," therefore, both in existential judgments in which we assert the real existence of some concrete, individual being, as well as in predicative judgments in which we ascertain the belonging of some attribute (predicate) to a subject. The "is" of the one and of the other judgment is different and fulfills a different function: the ascertainment of real existence in existental judgments and the ascertainment of the belonging of an attribute to a predicative judgments.

There have indeed been attempts to identify the two meanings of the expression "is" (that of existential judgments and that of predicative judgments), but these attempts are surely doomed to failure, concerning which, after all, there is already sufficiently abundant literature. Regardless of such interpretations or others, however, the very expression "is" is conditioned by the cognitive grasp of really existing being, without which human cognition would not be possible at all. Still, the intellectual cognition of really existing being is the cognition of being that is merely contingent, changeable, i.e., not self-intelligible, and so it is the cognition of the kind of being that has the reason of its existence beyond itself in the Absolute. In other words the Absolute ultimately accounts for the fact that contingent being exists rather than does not exist, although of itself it is "indifferent" both in relation to existence and nonexistence alike.   .

Consequently, if all cognition making use of subjective-predicative speech is evidence of an intellectual cognition by us of being that is not self-intelligible, and if all philosophical interpretations, even though accurately executed, appear very seldom and are executed by only a few and with an admixture of errors (*a paucis, raro et cum admixtione erroris*)—then there arises in every human being a natural need for an ultimate cognition of the real foundations of realism, no longer with an admixture and risk of errors. There arises a need for a concrete and indubitable cognition of the ultimate reason of being, noncontradictable with regard to the existence of the world and ourselves, namely the Absolute, in religious language called God. Without a real, indubitable (since in some sense intuited) cognition of God as the reason of the existence of the world, of ourselves, and of all that we cognized "as though in a riddle," our intellectual life would be unfinished in a fundamental and most important point, and the human being as a person would no longer be a "someone" but an unfinished "something," not finding a concrete answer for the spirit to that question which was involved in every act of human intellectual cognition. The human being would turn out to be his own existence and the existence of the whole world would constantly be preying on his mind and, in the vast majority of cases, either he would obtain no answers at all, or he would obtain answers requiring an elite higher education.

If, then, in the moment of the completion of the changeable way of existence, i.e., in the moment of death, he would not bring to an end, i.e., to a concrete solution, the existential questions involved in the whole of human cognition, then it would be necessary to accept the assertion that a human being is an unnatural being. The whole course of human nature as human, i.e., in cognitive moments, being the pursuit of the discovery of the meaning of existence—a pursuit, after all, included objectively in every act of intellectual cognition—would be a pursuit never fulfilled, and the human being would not have practically a real possibility of an accurate and indubitable solution of his existential questions. But since these conditions do not prevail in the course of changeable duration, because changeable duration merely gives rise to the whole of this problematic but does not solve it, consequently only in the moment of the completion of this duration, i.e., in the moment of death, can this pursuit be fulfilled, when God as the ultimate reason of being stands concretely and intuitively before the human intellect in its final, full, cognitive act to which the whole of psychic life was ordered, just as beings that are contingent, changeable, and not self-intelligible are ordered to the Absolute as the only noncontradictable reason of their existence. Cognition is merely a reading of that particular relationship.

b) We come now to a description and analyses of other (volitive) typically human psychic experiences to which, after all, other philosophers drew attention, but not always making the description and analyses in the perspective of death. We are concerned here with the general experience of happiness against the background of concrete human decision as well as with the experience of love.

A convenient point of departure is the description of the structure of human wanting, of human will. Thomas Aquinas,[29] and recently M. Blondel,[30] carefully attended to a charactertistic division in this sphere. The latter perceived that the human will is always disposed toward something more than it concretely wants. No concrete wanting equals the continually living capacity of the will, which is disposed toward infinity. In Thomas Aquinas that division of the will was called *"appetitus naturalis"*—the natural desire of the will, and *"appetitus elicitus"*—the desire concretely elicited in relation to a concrete good. In conjunction with this, he observed that no concrete good constituting the object of acts of the will fulfills, satisfies, human desire, which, on the strength of natural desire (on the strength of its structure), is directed toward universal good. That direction toward universal good is the natural desire for happiness, never extinguished by concrete goods. That universal desire for happiness, being the dynamic source of all concrete desires and at the same time accompanying every elicited act of desire, is the natural never-extinguished desire for the Absolute-God. A human being is not always concretely aware of this; and even though, being aware of his unsatisfied desire and being an atheist, some human being wanted to resign from that "desire for more," from the desire for infinity, this would not be possible. On the contrary, if a human being is ever richer in knowledge, richer in material means, richer in love of others, then the conviction constantly accompanies him that he has not possessed happiness, that something that can satisfy him is constantly beyond him.

That division of the will into the desire for ultimate happiness and the desire for concrete goods, although it can be explained in philosophy by turning attention to the derivation of infinite desire from the intellectual, cognitive apprehension of analogously general being (in which we obscurely apprehend God as the reason of being)—yet, as the natural desire for "something more," bears witness to the fact that the subject itself (the human being, the soul) is, in its nature disposed toward infinite good, since it manifests this unceasingly in every expression of wanting-desiring. If this is a desire of nature, it has a chance of being fulfilled precisely as a work of nature (nature is nothing other than the constant order of some thing being fulfilled), and that division of desire into the desire for the infinity of an ultimate unnamed happiness and the desire for a concrete something (for this here object) will be fulfilled when infinity and abstract happiness stand before the human soul no longer as an abstraction but as something concrete, and thereby as a real good drawing the human *psyche* to itself. That "meeting" of the roads of abstract, infinite, and concrete, real desire, of desire that occurs in a nature still human, is possible only in the moment of the completion of life, its finale, when God, although still not in a supernatural vision but as a concrete and intellectual-volitive experiential good, will stand before the human spirit in order to show it that concrete and real good that, encoded and in the veil of the world, appeared to the human being's spirit during its journey through life. On the other hand, with the human being everything of value has pointed precisely to this good, which in itself is, exists, and which has influenced us through the changeable world of goods that do not satisfy the infinite desire of a human being. Therefore, human desire is divided until the moment of death; and then, in the highest moment of human life, God will stand before the human spirit as a concrete good (just as all goods that the human being actually wanted and toward which he tended were concrete) and at the same time as the infinite good, which, as analogously general good, as happiness in general, constantly disturbed the human will. God, realizing concreteness and infinity, can actually appear before the human spirit only in the moment of the nonreversible finale of changeable human life, i.e., in the moment of so-called death. Without the appearance of God—this should be stressed—human nature would not have a rational ontical structure, since the pursuit of nature would be objectless. And an objectless pursuit is not a pursuit of nature. If, therefore, we want to treat human nature rationally, then we cannot ignore the natural inclinations. And if this is how the matter lies with human desire, then one ought to accept the fact that in the fulfillment of the human being's time, which is called death, God will stand before us in order to draw us to himself like a magnet, no longer through the world of things, of changeable beings, but through his very self. The world of things and people prepares, enables, and suits us for this more intense adherence to him when he appears. Hence, death would be the fulfillment of the natural desire of the human will. Only in this moment—if it happens at all—can there occur a total confrontation of human desires and decisions with concrete and infinite good, because in no other moment of human life is such a confrontation even possible due to the factual, changeable, human will.

c)   In other works of the most outstanding writers there is related a co-occurrence of two states in certain peak moments of a human being's experiences: love and death, as the perceived aspects of the same reality. The myth of Orpheus and Eurydice, writes Marcel in *Présence et Immortalité,*[31] stands at the very heart of my existence, since only the deep experience of love allows for the possibility of the greatest accumulation of the spiritual strengths of our ego, strengths that are normally scattered and diffused. That accumulation of personal strengths in love permits the most expressive manifestation of "me"—of "my ego." For I only then become conscious as an "I" when I set myself in opposition in the aspect of the "I" not to objects-things, but when beside the "I," I perceive a "Thou" as a correlate. And, therefore, for a human being to be a human being, i.e., to be a conscious and loving ego, means basically to be a correlate of a "Thou." Hence, for a human being "to exist," "to be" precisely as a human being i.e., as a person, means "to-be-with," "to co-exist." The human being was born as a product of love and exists in love and for love. In the very heart of the personality, in the very core of the "I" is an enchanted inclination to a "Thou," thanks to which inclination and its realization through acts of love we accent and develop our "I" ever more strongly. Without love our ego is weak, is without support; moreover, it is not formed as a human ego. The "I" of every human being has been formed in actual interpersonal contacts (which are always some modification of love.) Hence, real bonds of love stand at the basis of an understanding of the human ego, of its existence, since this existence as precisely human existence is expressed in love, i.e., in the union of an "I" and a "Thou."

An essential manifestation of love is the "giving of oneself." Nearly all thinkers, ancient, medieval, contemporary, and especially G. Marcel, took note of the fact that in the act of love we coordinate ourselves with the "Thou" as the object of our love, we give ourselves to the beloved "Thou," and through this act of the "giving of oneself," of the spiritual "surrender of oneself," we do not become impoverished but, on the contrary, we become fulfilled, we become a fuller "I," we experience (for some short time!) the fulfillment of human existence.

If the human being is "built up" and constituted in his human existence through love for another "Thou" and through it reaches the fulfillment of his existence in assuming the features of "co-existence," then the basic factor organizing that existential "giving of oneself," the limiting, determining, individuating element, in a word—the element that not only subsists (exists in a human, conscious way), but rather "is possessed," is our body. For if we were to agree with the previously presented thesis (in Part I) that our ego subsists, and the body exists only through the ego-soul, then in that case our body's manner of existence would be precisely not so much the kind of existence as the ego-soul lives, but would be the first manner of a "possession." In the terminology of G. Marcel, we are dealing with the famous distinction of "*être*"—to indicate the manner of existence of our ego-soul, being constituted in the dialogue of love, and "*avoir*"—the "possession" of that which is originally "mine" and which is precisely our bodily organism, organized by our ego, and it exists by the existence of ego-soul.[32]

This body of ours, as the thus conceived element limiting and determining ontical activity both to the manner of bodily surrender as well as to the individuation of matter, would be that factor which, on the one hand, makes possible the development of the spirit, our ego, and, on the other, unceasingly combines it with individual, individualizing, atomizing forms of activity.

In the moment, therefore, when after biological death this form of limiting activity will cease, our ego will attain the condition of full self-expression in love for the transcendent "Thou"; it will attain the condition of full "giving of oneself," and thereby of full constitutedness in a perfect psychic personality, which is a cognitive existence for the love of and union with the absolute "Thou." Hence, if all the acts of love that we experience in life are acts of our ego's "giving of itself" to another "Thou," then only death experienced actively (i.e., not the passive, biological death, conceived as the cessation of the functions of animated matter) creates the conditions for the outburst of personal love that ultimately constitutes the personal "I" in relation to the transcendent "Thou" as a concrete and absolute good. Death, thus understood, then, and love are the two sides constituting the human personality. Without the coming-into-being in human life in the moment of death, i.e., in the moment of the cessation of bodily changes, of the full conditions of love—all the impulses of great genuine love would be something pathologic and unnatural rather than the work of a spiritual human nature. This liberating nature of love, freeing us from atomizing forms of existence, was intuited by the great poets, and they gave expression to this in prophecy and poetry in which great love was combined with death, since often biological-changeable duration without love is not a life worthy of a human being. Love, therefore, as a form of human existence conquers biological death, and moreover, only at the moment of the cessation of biological changes attains the conditions of full self-expression, full freedom, and full constitutedness of the human personality, which is joined in the act of love with the cognitive, ultimately fulfilling, transcendent "Thou," toward which every real human love of the "Thou" of another person had led to fulfilling in a limited way. Without the perspective of the fulfillment of personal-human acts (cognition, the desire of love), i.e., without the real as well as concrete possibility for every human being of the eternal endurance of that which already now has appeared in biological forms of duration as transcending matter, the very acts of cognition and love, if they were ultimately to succumb to change and time, would be yet another monster of nature, would be simply meaningless. Death, then, experienced actively, becomes the factor ultimately making human life meaningful.   .

One could thus analyze the various aspects of the psychic life of a human being and perceive death being realized everywhere in human existence, death understood from one side biologically as the cessation and passing away of determinate, atomized forms of activity, and from another—death as a liberation toward fulness, as precisely the fulfillment and necessary fulfillment of that which transcends in human activity, of that which cannot be reduced to any purely material category. One could point here to such human psychic acts as precisely the poetry and creativity addressed to a transcendent recipient who understands anxiety, sadness, tragedy, or the need of happiness and love; one could thoroughly analyze acts of human decision, which always turn out to be somehow partial, incomplete, not expressing the capacity of our ego and leaving behind themselves a feeling of non-completeness and ulitmate non-self-expression, which is always "lined" with a certain "melancholy of existence." One could point to the conditions of human freedom, which is always freedom from a certain aspect, freedom determined also by material factors, as a result of which freedom is more a postulate and point of destination—precisely in the moment of the fulfillment of the personality—than a point of departure in making ultimate human decisions. One could finally point to that which St. Paul already once observed, that there exist opposite directions of development: biological and psychical. The biological direction goes from an original vigor toward a gradual diminution and disappearance as the years go by, whereas the developmental psychical tendencies, the so-called "inner man," develop and mature with the passage of time. This notion is not refuted by the general ascertainment that an old human being is psychically less competent and sometimes becomes childish. For these sides of a human being are connected precisely with the decline of biological competence. Nevertheless, the developmental tendencies of the biological and psychic lines are in different directions. With the crumbling of the "bodily home"—as Paul says—the moment of death reveals an inner, psychic, personal edifice.

The various aspects of psychic life—here only some, perhaps the most essential, were considered—can be subjected to an explanatory analysis in the perspective of death being realized. Further analyses of this kind would reveal just what was illustrated above based on examples of psychic-personal experiences, namely: death is the moment of the full constitution of the personal ego, i.e., of such human existence that has the complete conditions for the concrete cognition of values, for the cognition of a transcendent, absolute person, and for entering into an ecstatic act of love; that act of love as a fully cognized, fully free, loving bond or our "I" with the transcendent "Thou" embraces, fulfills, and perfects all the personal and transpersonal values that we attained in the changeable forms of life, that we intuited or partially cognized.

The considerations conducted here situate the human being somewhat differently in the perspective of death, for which it is also necessary to employ a different model than was in use up to this time: some sort of "division of soul and body." For the separation of the soul from the body is only one of the aspects of death, and that of death understood passively as the occurring dissolution in a man of his material elements; that dissolution over which we have no control or power. It "happens," but it is not caused by personal human acts and therefore such death cannot be experienced actively and in a free manner. In the passive experience of death we are not so much a person as a decomposing material object. And surely that is not what is at issue in the personal experience of death. What concerns us is an active, free experience. And here death as the completion of the changeable manner of existence appears thereby as the fulfillment of all that which, through the personal acts of the human being, was continually begun and, to be sure, never fully completed, since the changeable biology of life did not produce the full conditions or the real possibility of the kind of development of the human ego that is designated by its spiritual, i.e., infinite, capacity. In conjunction with an active conception of death, a different model of death will be very useful, namely, a model of maturation and birth.

Just as the human being in the embryonic state in the mother's womb forms all of his organs for life beyond the womb, for life in the open world, life more subsistent and independent—so likewise our life already subsistent in the open world reveals such psychic activity, activity most valuable, personal, which does not fit in the nature of that world, which unceasingly transcends the world of nature to the degree that the human being is forced to create for himself a special "ecological niche"—a cultural one, in order to be able to exist and develop psychically. And if we were to assume a certain fiction, namely, that the child in the mother's womb leads a psychic, conscious life, then the moment of its birth would be regarded—by this hypothetically consciously living child—as the moment of its death. For it loses everything at once in the moment of birth: nourishment, air, all the real conditions of existence. The cutting of the umbilical cord would be regarded as the ultimate act of death. And, meanwhile, in just that moment it passes into another manner of existence, independent existence. We can apply the same model of birth to death in which the human being is able for the first time to make use of the continually initiated, imperfect acts of his personal structure in relation to the infinitely extended cosmos and, above all, in relation to the transcendent "Thou." Just as the formation of the organs of the embryo points to their full employment in a life outside the womb, so the acts of the human psyche, acts of cognition, love, our decisions, creativity, and rational work transcending the changeable world, organizing that same world, point to the full realization of all that which is now only begun, which is as though in an embryonic state.

The psychic acts now brought forth fit and prepare the psyche for the first cry of an independent existence, full of love and freedom. And that precisely is the experience of death by the human person, the personal experience, and not the so-called passive, biological one, which is only the experience of undergoing decomposition.

In such a perspective it is difficult to call death the "separation of the soul from the body," because—as K. Rahner[33] properly observed—not only do we not know whether it is possible to designate death in this way, but, moreover, since the days of Augustine and Thomas Aquinas[34] there exists a tradition according to which the soul, as spirit transcendentally, i.e., necessarily, ordered to matter, cannot dispose of this relation without the simultaneus cancellation of its be-ing. If it were possible to speak of a separation of soul from body, then at the very most we might be able to speak of a separation from the "here and now" quantified body; and a separation in this sense, after all, goes on continually during our biological duration as the cells previously constituting "us" are sloughed off.

Consequently, if in the moment of biological death more individualized matter in the form of body departs all at once, then our soul still does not thereby lose the relation to matter, because it cannot lose this relation. Rahner, following Thomas, says that in the moment of death there would occur a much deeper bond of the soul with the cosmos than existed through the assimilation of nourishment, namely, there would occur a bond with the cosmos in its fundamental, crucial connections, which are the foundation of the rational organization of matter, of that organization which appears to human thought in the form of laws. Of course, this is a hypothesis, but an interesting and fruitful one, revealing the ever wider entrance of spirit into the world of matter to which it first submits, which it cognizes, which it directs, and which it finally—as Christian revelation says—is to subject to its laws. This hypothesis would well explain the special status of the human's psychosomatic being. For the spirit, forming the body for itself in the mother's womb with the participation of the parents, attains objective knowledge in human life of matter in an embryonic state, and the same spirit, ultimately attaining to the fullness of self-consciousness in the moment of death, unites with the very heart of matter, which is rationally taking shape, in order to bestow upon it ultimately—time is not at issue here—its own personal, spiritual visage.

APPENDIX
By
Stanisław Kamiński

NOTES ON THE METAPHILOSOPHY OF MAN

In modern times, one readily observes an increasing interest in human matters. This causes the development and origin of various disciplines concerning man. In addition to the sciences which study man from a limited point of view—anatomy, physiology, psychology, ethnology, naturalistic and humanistic anthropology, for example—there exist numerous attempts to create a universal science of man and to answer thoroughly the questions: "What is man?" "What is his essence?" These are questions of an indubitably philosophical character. But along with the great diversity of types of philosophy arises a diversity of formulations of philosophical anthropology. And the matter does not end here. The contemporary explosion of anthropocentrism was caused not so much by a desire on the part of thinkers as by, above all, the needs of practical disciplines. The most complete picture possible of man proves to be indispensable particularly for theology, ethics, pedagogy, politics, and medicine (especially in treating psychological and protracted illnesses). This seems to demand that the philosophy of man not limit itself to speculative investigations (an applied metaphysics of some sort), but realize the fullest possible integrating vision of human nature and, in the course of doing so, take advantage of all the findings of the particular sciences. In such a situation, the essentially accurate and methodologically correct conception of the philosophy of man becomes an enormously important problem, and, at the same time, an exceedingly difficult one to solve. It cannot be avoided, however, if we are striving for a reflective participation in the anthropocentric direction of our thought. In our quest for a philosophy of man, we have to know what we want, and why.[1]

The following remarks will attempt to demonstrate, against the background of various summarized views of philosophical anthropology, that its

363

conception is most comprehensively validated within the framework of the classical philosophy of being; that it can most adequately comply with postulates of a world-view and be of service to practical disciplines when propounded under the auspices of the classical philosophy of being; and that it thereby does not have to disregard universally required criteria for rational knowledge. First, let us look briefly at the history of the formation of philosophical anthropology.

The history of philosophy only gradually became interested in man. In antiquity, the primary object of philosophical interest was the cosmos. Man was only barely treated as one of its elements.[2] Protagoras' thesis about man's being the measure of all things was not developed philosophically. Even if there were investigations about human affairs, these investigations almost always focused exclusively on the cognitive or moral aspects of such affairs.[3] Similarly, the establishment of man's ontic place was not undertaken universally in straightforward fashion, but within the framework of the philosophy of nature. Hence, the problem of the soul as a form differentiating humans from other changing beings became, in fact, a part of cosmology. It is another matter that the attempts of Plato and Aristotle to determine the nature of the soul and its relation to the body can be theoretically and methodologically incorporated into ontology.

Among Christian thinkers, a rather theological conception of man was formulated according to which man became the element of order of divine affairs (the *imago Dei* in Saint Augustine, for example). Man's salvation, not his being, occupied the attention of those engaging in philosophy in the early Middle Ages. Likewise the celebrated theocentrism of Thomas Aquinas was not conducive to a separating out of the anthropological problematic in philosophy. By this time, however, certain principles in the theory of being and action, along with an account of the dignity of the individual, were already formulated in anticipation of a philosophical anthropology.[4]

Only during the fourteenth century did philosophers noticeably begin to focus on man as a knowing subject, and on everything else cognitively given to him. Nicholas of Cusa raised the dignity of man even more, by emphasizing his individuality and creative abilities.[5] Renaissance humanism became more of a slogan than a thematic and methodologically defined philosophical proposal. Admittedly, there was passionate searching for an answer to the question, "What is man?" but this search was not carried out on the ontological plane. There was penetrating deliberation about the art of human life (Montaigne), and a great deal of moralizing (La Rouchefoucald, La Bruyère). Man's greatness and nothingness, his mystery, and the other inconsistencies within him intensely interested Pascal. There were even attempts to present human individuality in terms of surpassing what it produces so as to form new works better corresponding to reality (Bacon).[6] For the most part, however, in the early period an introspective approach was taken. Later, an historical approach was explored which meant that these investigations only began to approach philosophy in insignificant ways. Then, because of the arrival of psychology, pure anthropological notions finally appeared.[7]

Epistemological anthropocentrism found expression in the seventeenth century. There ensued, however, a return to man not in his entire, concrete structure, but to man as a pure subject. With Locke and Descartes, human consciousness as the exclusive subject and object of philosophical analyses became the source of human knowledge, as well as the criterion of its worth. The philosophy of knowledge was not an introduction to, or fragment of, philosophy; now, if the philosophy of knowledge did not replace philosophy, it basically absorbed it. A clear indication of the emphasis on a partial treatment of man is Descartes' definition of him as, above all, *res cogitans* as opposed to *res extensa*. This became stronger in the eighteenth century.[8] In his theory of the autonomous and active reason, Kant treated the latter more as an internal object of philosophy. Apart from that, when natural anthropology was established, (J.F. Blumenbach), the great critic from Königsberg extracted from philosophical anthropology a so-called "pragmatic anthropology." It was intended to consider the person as free and creative, and especially as self-improving ("man aims at culture and civility").[9] This separate discipline, however, did not have a philosophical character; it was simply a cultural-historical theory of man. But in seeking the principles of human nature, the eighteenth century (particularly Hume) anticipated a philosophy of man.

The nineteenth century presents a great diversity of approaches to the enigma of the human being. On the whole, the German idealists treated man as absolute reason. Emphasis on the activity of the human mind led in Hegel to objective idealism. The object of thought was everything: and everything existed dialectically and evolutionally. With this Hegel made the theory of culture, as evolutionary, the most important branch of philosophy. Thanks to him, there began to arise a reaction against rationalism and idealism which paved the way for ontological anthropocentrism, i.e., for approaching the theory of reality from the side of man, and, thereby, grasping him concretely.[10] Feuerbach gave man the most prominent place in philosophy (philosophy = anthropology), but conceived him as the most perfect creation of nature (naturalism) and cultural reality as his projection. Continuing in that direction, Marx formulated the premises of the materialistic philosophy of man: the theory of alienation and of socialistic humanism.[11]

The so-called development, during the nineteenth century, of exact sciences, and of humanistic sciences in particular, did not favor the formation of an autonomous philosophy of man. The human person neither found himself at the center of the universe, not could he be an object of precise investigation. Scientists excluded human questions from the realm of scientific consideration. Humanists frequently proclaimed a relativism of cultural and, consequently, of human values. Philosophy concerned itself mainly with a self-likeness of man but it did not do this skillfully. It described separate aspects of man, such as: *homo religiosus, homo faber, homo creator, homo ludens,* etc.

Another outgrowth of the philosophy of the subject is Kierkegaard's existential anthropology. According to him, it is the philosophical analysis of consciousness that directly and best leads to authentic being. For Kierkegaard this means concrete human existence whose uniqueness consists in self-reflection, in the relation of the self to its own self, along with the tragic choosing between contrary alternatives (Christ or nothingness, infinity or finiteness, freedom or necessity, eternity or temporality). The task of human existence, however, is self-perfection. Confusing idealism with a naturalism and an evolutionism (and even with a glorification of the brutality of the instincts) lies at the basis of the anthropology suggestively expounded by Nietzsche.[12] Here the fundamental anthropological category is human life. It was in such an intellectual climate that, around the year 1900, there originated an attempt to treat all of philosophy as a theory of man, and identify man's life with philosophy. Bergson, Dilthey, and later Klager are interesting examples of this. Each in his investigations tried in his own way to give prominence to human life, emphasizing, in general, the irrational and creative moments in it.[13]

Against this setting emerged M. Scheler, the creator of philosophical anthropology as autonomous (in relation to the particular sciences) and as the discipline most characteristically grasped by the modern mind. According to Scheler, the philosophy of man neither synthesizes findings of the particular sciences, nor philosophically interprets them, but studies human nature ontically. Thanks to the use of the phenomenological method, the philosophy of man becomes *die Selbstproblematik des Menschen* in all of its spheres: knowledge, existence, activity, experiences, etc. It is almost a philosophical self-consciousness of man,[14] who is not an element of the organized world, not the highest product of biological development, but a spiritual personality who turns his attention toward himself and who transcends the world. Hence even metaphysics becomes a *Metaanthropologie.*

A full-blown philosophical anthropocentrism was established by existentialism, a current of thought also grafted onto the tree of philosophical subjectivity (generally, objectivizing the "I" is not allowed). Initially, the philosophy of man was treated as an introduction to metaphysics (a *regionale Ontologie*). Later, however, philosophical anthropology replaced the philosophy of being (Heidegger), and sometimes had little in common with it. The very mode of human existence ("the relationship with existence") was acknowledged already as philosophizing (Jaspers and Marcel). Philosophical anthropology is a theory of man's authentic existence. Human existence is not only the primary fact and central object, but is, likewise, the completely proper theme of philosophy.[15] Regardless of how existential philosophical anthropology, is based on self-experiencing or self-understanding, it takes as its starting point various moments of the human phenomenon, and accents various types of problems connected with that phenomenon. At times, these problems can be closely linked with ethics (Sartre. for example) or with theology (Buber, Bultmann, Brunner, Bonhoeffer, Tillich, Rahner). Depending on the choice of one, and not another, aspect of human existence, the entire philosophy of man becomes interpersonal (in Buber, for example), or personal, more or less hermeneutical, and, finally, more strongly or weakly linked to the tradition of ontology.[16]

Frequently, one comes upon types of philosophical anthropology, which retain an existential starting point and phenomenological method, and try to construct an objectivistic metaphysics of man. Although the autonomy of such a metaphysics is not denied, these anthropologies probably rarely view it as a segment or thematic aspect of classical ontology, cosmology,theodicy, and ethics. Nonetheless, the conception of an autonomous philosophical anthropology appeared and took on a certain determined form constructed entirely within the framework of the classical philosophy of being. Then, philosophical anthropology was treated, for the most part, as one of the disciplines of a so-called "particular metaphysics" seeking the ultimate ontic grounds of human behavior.[17]

Sometimes, propositions of philosophical anthropology as a type of synthesized culmination of particular sciences about man are put forward with great ingenuity. Most frequently, this is done on the basis of one leading discipline. It does not always have to be only a generalization extrapolating an ordinary positivistic synthesis. Sometimes it constitutes those theoretical complements of particular sciences that are closely linked with metaphysics or ethics. H. Plessner's model is just such an example of an intermediate philosophy of man (between the theory of being and natural science).[18] A Gehlen also attempts widely and amply to take advantage of material provided by particular sciences in carrying out a philosophical "disclosing" of man's essence.[19] A. Portmann practises anthropology primarily against the background of biology and comparative studies of human behavior.[20] Based on a far-reaching extrapolation of the results of cosmo-and bio-genesis, P.

Teilhard de Chardin sketches an alluring vision (though tinged with mysticism) of man and his place in the universe.[21] Even medicine has provided some with a basis for the construction of a philosophy of man.[22]

Finally, in the course of the development of psychology, there frequently are philosophical attempts at forging a comprehensive picture of man. For this, it is believed that it suffices to take into account all human experiences as a point of departure.[23] But philosophcial anthropology seems to have the fullest support in the humanities. From that vantage point, one can distinguish at least three kinds of philosophy of man, embedded more or less clearly in the neo-Kantian, Marxist,and structuralist tradition.[24] A separate type of philosophical anthropology arises in connection with futurology (D. Gabor, N. Rotenstreich, Bromberger, Pendell, Kostler).

The sketched panorama of today's typical models of philosophical anthropology still must be augmented by an interim, syncretic, and fragmentary conception. This has to do not with the completeness of this presentation, but with the attempt to answer the question: Which of the best known conceptions of the philosophy of man can adequately satisfy philosophical concerns about life, perform the role of fundamental knowledge for the humanities and practical sciences pertaining to human activity; and, simultaneously, meet basic epistemological and methodological requirements?

In general, it is unanimously admitted that philosophical anthropology cannot replace either another science or group of sciences about man. However, the divergence of views already begins in the evaluation of the sufficiency of the above-mentioned tasks of such a philosophy, which is a meta-science in relation to disciplines concerned with human affairs. It is not difficult to agree that the logical or semiotic analysis of languages or the theories regarding the methods of particular sciences about man, or the critique of knowledge occurring in those sciences by no means lead to solidly based solutions to the questions that revolve round the mystery of man taken as a whole. For man's nature, existence, and position in the cosmos call for objective investigations of topics pertaining to the human structure in its most profound sense. Besides, restricting philosophy to cultivating a meta-science generally has proven to be not only ineffective in dealing with the fundamental problems formed by century-old tradition, but also consistently unrealizable.[25]

The quality of philosophical anthropology viewed as a synthetically generalized superstructure, built on the base of comparative knowledge about man, creates even more controversy. This superstructure takes on various forms. First of all it can be some encyclopedico-synthetic elaboration of the results of natural, cultural, and also psychological and sociolgical anthropology (which would provide a mosaic-like vision of man). Or it can be a general extrapolation of the most theoretical claims of the above-mentioned sciences (a so-called inductive philosophy of man). Finally it can be a concluding synthesis of scientific achievements, which occurs in the area of one leading discipline, either in superdisciplinary fashion according to the particular use of a discovered controlling idea, or even a preconception of man (which unusually creative minds achieve after appropriate scientific and practical preparation). Or it can be an analytic-critical reflection on facts from the realm of human affairs generally entertained in the sciences. This approach aims at the construction of a reasonable answer to the fundamental questions about the nature of man, his place in the world, and the meaning of his existence.

The encyclopedico-synthetic formulation of philosophical anthropology does not provide necessary conclusions in the construction of a world view. For, in reality, it does not go beyond the results of the particular sciences about man. While providing a mass of regional information about man, it does not succeed in viewing him from a new, comprehensive perspective, which would include his primal unity and integrity, and only mechanically sums up partial aspects of him.[26] Likewise, it is not in a position to be the base that the humanistic and practical sciences about man wish to have because it is, in reality, only a concise juxtaposition of the result of those sciences. Effectively to assemble significant, particular trends of thought, one first has to understand what it means generally to be a man. For the elucidation of particular, partial aspects of man and his works, one must have recourse to ideal or model types of human behavior, as well as a theoretical model of human activity. Such types or models cannot be generalizations of observation, but must be the result of a separate intellectual conception of the nature of man; i.e., of his ontic identity. Here we have a paradoxical situation. The more the philosophy of man is linked with particular sciences, the less able is it to perform its function as their basis and its role as a theoretical foundation for a world view. A similar situation occurs with the philosophy of man as an extrapolation of the most general theses of thematically appropriate disciplines. Here, it cannot really arrive at new points, and the epistemic-methodological values of such an inductive philosophical anthropology, to the extent that it is withdrawn from strictly scientific knowledge, quickly diminishes. Results reached in this fashion neither can be verified scientifically, nor can they contribute to the solution of those problems that most disturb us concerning the ultimate reasons of existence and meaning of human life.

Nor are the models of the philosophy of man that either analytically-critically or synthetically, cap the achievements of appropriate sections of the humanities and natural sciences, free from the above difficulties. For a poliscientific theory of man does not have at its disposal either a method or common language for the various sciences about man that, at the same time, complies with axioms of the logic of knowledge.[27] The thought given to human matters by these sciences either does not exceed the limits of a particular discipline, or does not fit into a particular discipline and become an autonomous science. In the case of the latter, it must grasp data for the explanation of facts by means of its conceptual apparatus, and use its own method of validating proposed hypotheses. Suggesting as a compromise that philosophical anthropology derives initial facts from particular sciences and, at the same time, interprets them in a profound manner, showing the ontic grounds implied by them, does not really solve the difficulty of choosing the proper path of scientific-philosophic collaboration. For scientific facts are not written in a language independent of a particular theory of explanation.[28] Hence, there are not, strictly speaking, common scientific facts for truly differentiating a natural, humanistic and philosophical theory. Each of these has for itself its own proper facts to explain. Each investigates reality in a specific way, and each constructs for itself different cognitive objectives.

The above comments are not at variance with arguments about the usefulness of knowledge, apart from particular sciences about man and an autonomous philosophical anthropology, that is built on the former. Such knowledge certainly contributes to ordering diverse information about man. It allows one to eliminate more easily the gaps and unintentional discordances within this information, and perceive knowledge-forming analogies and correlations between the particular areas of knowledge themselves. Similarly, such knowledge does not deny the need for philosophy to know the main findings of the particular sciences. Independently of performing an all-embracing cultural function, such findings indirectly provoke and prepare questions for the philosophy of man, and, on the negative side, help isolate its starting points. Finally, in opposing a "scientistic" conception of philosophical anthropology,such knowledge does not justify any type of irrationalism. There exist important historical reasons in favor of the possiblility of an autonomous philosophy of man which does not appeal to suprarational sources of knowledge, and which conclusively provides an empirically-validated solution to problems that disturb people and are not found in a place to be investigated in the realms of various types of extraphilosophical knowledge.

Nevertheless, it does not seem, advisable to have to proclaim an anthropocentric (as is the case with many phenomenologists) or ontological (characteristic of the existentialists) theory of knowledge to appreciate the full weight of man's mystery and role. Man, admittedly, appears as a being who is unusual and privileged in his activities and position in the world. He even seems to be the unique keystone of ontic diversity in the cosmos. This is because human consciousness allows for grasping one's own person as one's own "I," and grasping everything else as data of the subject or his activity. Nevertheless, a philosopher should not speak about man exclusively in the first person. People do not exhaust the entire range of philosophical interest, and, even more importantly, cannot become the most profound reason which explains all possible reality. Man is also an element of the cosmos. That is why there is need for a theory concerning other than human types of being, as well as an overall theory of being, to explain completely and definitively all that does not necessarily exist. Self-experiencing, self-understanding, self-perfection, although important factors in the process of self-definition, do not exhaust human knowledge, and, even less, human activity. Knowledge attained extraspectively and extrasubjectively is indispensable.

Philosophical anthropology, therefore, is not a philosophical reading of propositions about nature, society, and knowledge from the point of view of man, but a distinct part of philosophy. Acceptance of such a view is joined with yet another consequence of previous considerations. A philosophical interpretation of human facts is not safeguarded by a subjectivism and its implications, unless knowledge of the basic structures of objective reality is also included within the point of departure, alongside self-experiencing and self-understanding. This should not be taken to mean that the philosophy of man is only a development of ontology, or that reflection on the nature of philosophy leads by itself to such a view. Philosophical anthropology cannot be an instantiation of general metaphysics and still remain metaphysics. Philosophical anthropology has separate data to explain.[29] The phenomena grasped in the starting point are situated on the horizon of being, but being of the human type: they are essential and fundamental for man and his existential position. But since these phenomena are not only situations of my "I" exclusively, but of a relation of a first person to a second, to another thing, to the future, and to the entire universe, they do not explain themselves conclusively in terms of their own nature. Their thorough interpretation must occur within the domain of a metaphysical type of knowledge. Hence, in explanations that are the most theoretical, one must have recourse to the method of the philosophy of being and its cognitive apparatus. This method, of course, becomes enriched in conformity with a modified point of departure within philosophical anthropology. But it is language that transforms general metaphyscial terms into expressions with new meanings (based on analogy). Analogy creates new conceptions, and also characterizes them in relation to general metaphyscial ideas. Consequently, one can maintain that human existence is explained conclusively and fully by means of man's intra-existential structure which is common, to a large degree, to all being and, which, even more importantly, co-participates in absolute being.[30]

The conception of philosophical anthropology outlined here requires, therefore, that its system methodologically presuppose a so-called general metaphysics as well as a philosophy of nature, and surpass metaphysical psychology, ethics, aesthetics, and the entire philosophy of culture. Philosophical anthropology explains human phenomena by their ontic structure and what follows from that, namely, by their existential position among beings. This requires metaphysical propositions about the composition of being, the properties of being, and the hierarchy of its types.[31] Once again, other disciplines already mentioned such as particular metaphysics, make use of propositions from the philosophy of man in interpreting the events with which they begin.[32] But in the course of carrying out a complete metaphysics, one cannot sharply mark off stages that pre-arrange a separate sphere of metaphysics. The most significant characteristic for the latter is the procedure of cyclically returning to contacts with reality, repeatedly seeking analogies between various types of existence, and constantly expounding these already reached from that point of view. A metaphysical reflection having interpretative value, and the experiential grasping of the phenomenon together with its primary understanding interpenetrate each other.

To one not well versed in classical philosophy, the proposed model of philosophical anthropology may seem too abstract, taking too little account of the findings of the sciences concerned with man, and, above, all difficult to control with respect to the empirical validation of propositions. Many of these apprehensions can be dispelled. For despite the relatively metaphysical character of the evaluation of the above theory of man, the theory is neither obsolete, nor far removed from life. It was precisely the contemporary mentality's needs that gave birth to it. Particular sciences today do not provide answers to questions about who man is, taken as a whole, and what kind of relations he has with other entities (species, society, culture, nature, timeless value, the Absolute). The sciences do not tell us whether man is simple or complex in his ontic structure, nor what type of existential ties belong to human nature, nor, finally, what is the meaning of man in his ontic perspective. It is not known how to resolve definitively the following dichotomies: person—world, freedom—necessity, immanence—transcendence, dualism—unity of the soul and the body. Philosophical theories, also, are not sufficient for solving such problems of partial perspectives of the human person, even in expressing the various functions of man as variations of the same theme. Consequently, philosophical anthropologies such as the theory of perception and aesthetic creation of M. Dufrenne and M. Souriau, the theory of knowledge of E. Husserl, the theory of morality or natural law of

Fichte and Sartre, the theory of religion of Schelling, J. Bachofen, and Ricoeur, the theory of existence itself propounded by Heidegger, or the theory of the creation of a sign developed by E. Cassirer, do not solve the above-mentioned problems. For man in all manifestations and activities appears as ontically identical, though of various diametrically opposed aspects. A perspective in the philosophy of man that achieves complementary formulations should be found. The antagonism among conceptions of philosophical anthropologies up to the present does not favor such a pursuit. Meanwhile, the responsibility of humans for the reality in which they live and by which they create, is increasing. The problems in adopting the best posture in our present civilization are not at all diminishing (despite the tremendous advance of science and technology). There is no escaping conflicting situations. One must constantly judge, and lasting criteria are lacking.[33] It is clear that a theory which studies man from the point of view of his existence, and which conclusively indicates explanations for him within his ontic structure, can provide satisfactory and rationally well-founded principles for the unraveling of that intricate, unfathomable, and rich human reality. The riddle of death, or of sin and suffering, is not solved unless man is situated in the ontic perspective of the Absolute (man is called to eternal happiness). The philosophy of man has to reveal his transcendence (openness, relatedness) not only to a human, but also to a divine "Thou." For the Absolute, defining itself as "Thou" for man (Rahner), is man's explanation and good. In these general statements is concealed a ground adequate for the validation of a basic theoretical world-view and concrete principles of action. There, particular sciences about man find the expression and justification of their implications. All this simultaneously constitutes empirical verification of the propositions of the philosophy of man. The latter also checks its own authenticity in the very concrete phenomena provided in the point of departure. In any case, however, this method of carrying out philosophical anthropology is not any less epistemologically and methodologically correct than the method which assigns a place for anthropological investigation among religion, art, and science, or in the private sphere of contemplation.

CHAPTER I

Notes and References

[1] In general, "We must state that Biblical anthropological interests are minimal. They limit themselves to questions connected with the practical, especially to an explanation of ethical conduct. There exists a peculiar dialectic between anthropology and moral studies in the Bible. The Biblical author takes into account anthropological assumptions and he does not deal with them. He understands them only as a function of moral life . . . For example, the struggle between soul and body (*sarks*) does not exactly correspond to the traditional Biblical distinction between soul (*psyche*) and body (*soma*). It constitutes a synthetical Biblical understanding of man, who matures in the midst of ethical demands towards a complete perfection and resurrection. And so it is a kind of over-simplification to speak of a Biblical anthropology. Because if, for example, the New Testament understands the notion of soul as a basis for a new faith in God's existence and the body is a manifestation of a life that removes itself from God's sphere—these are theological rather than anthropological designations. L. Stachowiak, "Biblijna koncepcja człowieka" w *W nurcie zagadnień posoborowych* (The Biblical concept of Man in *In the Wake of Post-conciliar Questions*) Vol.II, Warszawa, 1968. p. 226.

[2] "The first concept, which is not altogether accurately called "monistic" is proper to almost all of the Old Testament books. It considers man as an undivided whole, with psychic activities that are inseparable from the individual organism. Special organs, like body, the life-giving element, soul, heart, nerves—these are not parts of man in the strict meaning of the word but rather, functional manifestations in a specified range of activity." *Ibid.*, p. 210.

[3] *Ibid.*, p. 224.

[4] M. Adriani, *L'Anima nell'Antico e nel Nuovo Testamento* in *L'Anima*, (Brescia, 1954), pp. 9-27.

[5] The Orphic movement develops in the Sixth Century of our era and is a reflection of the universal longing for a liberation from moral and political chaos, that reigned precisely during this period. In Orphic sources, there stood out, above all else, a great moral survival: a feeling of evil and a desire to be liberated from it. A symbol of the inner struggle is the history of Dionysius-Zagreus. Zeus' younger son, Dionysius, according to a myth, received from his father, the government of the world, but the Titans, as the personification of evil and the bodily element, were lying in wait for his life. Finally, they succeeded in imprisoning him, even though Dionysius concealed himself by taking on the appearance of a bull. The Titans tore to pieces the body of the bull-Dionysius (*homofagia*) and they ate it, but Athena was able to save his heart which she offered to Zeus. Zeus swallowed the heart and a new Dionysius was born, who was a revival of the former one. He struck the Titans with bolts of lightning for their godlessness. From the dust of the Titans were born men, who are composed of two elements: the Titanic element, which is the bodily; and the Dionysian, which is divine. It is for this reason that there rages within man, a constant battle between the elements of good and evil and there resides a cause of an inner tearing apart of man and hence, a desire for liberation." Cf. W. Jaeger, *Die Theologie der frühen griechischen Denker* (Stuttgart, 1953) pp. 89-98.

[6] Cf. P. G. Faggin, *L'Anima nel pensiero classico antico* in *L'Anima*, pp. 29-69.

[7] Cf. Jaeger, *op. cit.*, also *Religions of the World* (Warsaw, 1957) pp. 245 ff.

375

[8]Cf. Faggin, *op. cit.*, p. 31 note.

[9]*Ibid.*, p. 34.

[10]Cf. Jaeger, *op. cit.*,p. 104.

[11]Aristotle, *Metaphysics,* Lamdba, 8 passim.

[12]Cf. Faggin, *op. cit.*, pp. 38-49.

[13]Cf. Plato, *Timaeus;* W. Jaeger, *Paideia,* pp. 247-253.

[14]Cf. Jaeger, *Paideia,* p. 247.

[15]Plato, *Phaedo,* 66B-67A.

[16]Cf. Faggin, *op. cit.*, pp. 43-45.

[17]*Ibid.*

[18]*De Anima,* II, 1 (412a 29).

[19]*Ibid.*, II, III, passim.

[20]*Ibid.* III, 5 (430a 13).

[21]This perhaps results from Aristotle's text and this is how Alexander of Aphrodisias explained it but the question is open to discussion.

[22]*De Anima,* III, (430a 13.)

[23]Cf. Faggin, *op. cit.*, p. 52.

[24]This was under the influence of the Pythagoreans. In *Tusc. disp.*, I, II, 24, Cicero writes on this subject" . . . quid de Dicearcho dicam, qui nihil omnino animum dicat esse."

[25]Cf. Faggin, *op. cit.*, p. 52 n.

[26]*Ibid.*, p. 53.

[27]*Ibid.*, p. 55. The Stoic Seneca, however, professes some kind of faith in a nearer undefined eternity for the soul. "Dies iste, quem tamquam extremum reformidas, aeterni natalis est" (That day which you dread as the end is the birth of eternity." *Ep.* 120, 14.

[28] Cf. C Fabro, *L'anima nell'eta patristica a medievale* in *L'Anima,* pp. 71-102.

[29]*Ep. ad Diognetum,* VI, 1-4; *Die apostolische Väter,* (Tübingen, 1924), pp. 144, 23-28.

[30]Cf. Fabro, *op. cit.*, p. 80.

[31]"Ad nihilum reductae (animae) interitionis perpetua frustratione evanescunt . . .mors vera, cum animae per longissimi temporis cruciatum consumetur igni fero." Arnobius *Adv. Nat.,* 14-15.

[32] . . .materia animae in colore . . quodsi anima ignis est, sicut ostendimus." Lact. *Div. Inst.,* II, q. 22; Fabro, *op. cit.*, p. 78. The author cites texts which testify to the orthodoxy of Lactantius.

[33]Cf. Fabro, *op. cit.*, p. 84. Soranos of Ephesus was the author of *Peri Psyches.*

[34]*De Anima,* ed. Warzink, p. 31.

[35]Cf. Fabro. *op. cit.*, p.82. The author points out that Tertullian is a witness to the crisis of thought of early Christianity, when there was literal acceptance of some of the Gospel texts and, on the other hand, a borrowing of formulations from various philosophical systems.

[36]Origenes, *De princip.*, VI, 2:. "Hi vero (spiritus) qui de statu primae beatitudinis moti quidem noti sunt, non tamen irremediabiliter moti, illis, quod supra descripsimus, sanctis, beatisque ordinibus dispensandi subjecti sunt ac regendi; quorum adjutorio usi, et institutionibus ac disciplinis salutaribus reformati, redire ac restitui ad statum suae beatitudinis possint. Ex quibus existimo, prout ego sentire possum, hunc ordinem humani generis institutum, qui utique in futuro saeculo, vel supervenientibus saeculis, cum caelum novum et terra nova erit, restituetur in illam unitatem."

[37]" . . . Unusquisque ergo descendentium in terram pro meritis, vel loco suo quem ibi habuerit, dispensantur in hoc mundo in diversis vel loci, vel gentibus, vel conversationibus vel infirmitatibus nasci, vel religionis vel a munus piis parentibus generari."—*Ibid.*, IV, 23.

[38]Cf. Fabro, *op. cit.*, p. 86.

[39]*Ibid.*, p. 87.

[40]"Hinc apparet quoniam non est naturaliter omnia incorruptibilis, sed gratia Dei per fidem et justitiam et intellectum perficitur incorruptibilis."—*Super Petrum*, I, 9.

[41]"Super animae statu memini vestrae quaestiunculae immo maxime ecclesiasticae quaestionis: 1. utrum lapsa de coelo sit, ut Pythagoras philosophus omnesque Platonici et Origenes putant; 2. an APORROIA Dei substantiae et Stoici, Manichaeus et hispana Priscilliani haeresis suspicantur; 3. an in thesauro habeantur Dei olim conditae, ut quidam ecclesiastici stulta persuasione conficiunt; 4. an cotidie a Deo fiant et mutantur in corpora secundum illud quod in evangelio scriptum est; pater meus usque modo operatur et ego operor; 5. an certe ex traduce, ut Tertullianus Appolinaris et maxima pars occidentalium autumat, ut, quomodo corpus ex corpore, sic anima nascatur ex anima et simili, cum brutis animalibus conditione subsistat."— Hier. *Ep.*, 126, 1, 2; PL 22, 1085.

[42]*De Trinitate*, VII, 4,7, 829.

[43]*De quantitate animae*, XII, 22, PL 32, 1048.

[44]Cf. E. Gilson, *History of Christian Philosophy in the Middle Ages*, (New York: Random House, 1955).

[45]Ph. Böhner, E. Gilson, *Christliche Philosophie: von Ihren Anfängen Bis Nikolaus von Cues*, Padenborn, 1954.

[46]*Civit. Dei*, XXI, 10.

[47]Cf. Böhner, Gilson, *op. cit.*, p. 203.

[48]*Ibid.*

[49]*Ibid.*, pp. 118–128.

[50]Cf. on this subject, M. Kurdaiałek, "Koncepcja człowieka jako mikrokosmosu" w *O bogu i o człowieku*, (The concept of Man as a Microcosm in *On God and Man*), Vol. II, Warzawa, 1969, pp. 109–125.

[51]"Ita fit, ut qui probitate deserta, homo esse desierit cum in divinam conditionem transire non potest vertatur in beluam."—*De Cons. Phil.*, IV, 3.

[52]Cf. Böhner, Gilson, *op. cit.*, pp.262–276.

[53]Cf. G. Verbeke, *Le "De Anima" d'Avicenne, une conception spiritualiste de l'homme*, in *Avicenna Latinus*, (Louvain-Leiden, 1968), pp. 71–73.

[54]In principle, I am limiting myself to a presentation of the above-mentioned work, since it includes all hitherto scientific research on this subject.

[55]The reference here is to Aristotle's *Politics* (cf. *Pol.*, I, 2 [1253a 3]), pointing out, simultaneously, that to live in a community is an expression of (man's) nobility. "Hoc autem est propter nobilitatem ejus et ignobilitatem aliorum animalium." *De Anima*, V, 1, p. 70, 14. In Avicenna, we already have a declaration of communal togetherness: "esse homini est co-esse."

[56]"Homini autem necessarium est quaedam addere naturae . . . primum eget homo agriculturae sicut et reliquis artibus." *De Anima*, V, 1, p. 70, 16–23.

[57]*Ibid.*, p. 72.

[58]*Ibid.*, p. 74 n.

[59]*Ibid.*, p. 76, 99.

[60]"Nihil autem horum est anima humana, sed anima est id quod habet has virtutes et est . . . substantia solitaria, id est per se." *Ibid.*,pp. 80, 58.

[61]Which does not mean—about which we shall speak later—that he held the position of a separated instrumentalism of senses in the area of intellectual knowledge.

[62]Cf. Verbeke, *op. cit.*, pp. 20–35.

[63]Avicenna holds the position of an instrumental creation of the world.

[64]Cf. Verbeke's analysis on this subject, *op. cit.*, pp.. 59–73.

[65]"Cum autem anima liberabitur a corpore et ab accidentibus corporis, tunc poterit conjungi in-

teligentiae agenti, et tunc inveniet in ea pulchritudinem intelligibilem et delectationem perennum." *De Anima,* V, 6, p. 150, 71.

[66]Thomas Aquinas' investigations on the subject of man, knowledge, love, decision, moral good and evil transcend—in my opinion—the treatments of many other, as well as, contemporary thinkers. For this reason, I shall strive to present, against the background of contemporary issues, St. Thomas' development of thought, on the premise that it is manifestly precise, creative and, above all, reasonable.

[67]Since Descartes lived at the College of La Flèche for 12 years, he knew well the theory of man's possession by the devil (analyzed in scholastic philosophy), and he knew that the demon has no access to the intellect and will but only to the senses.

[68]R. Descartes, *Meditations on First Philosophy,* Med. VI.

[69]*Ibid.,* Med. VI.

[70]*Ibid.,* Med. VI.

[71]On the subject of Descartes, cf. E. Bréhier, *Histoire de la philosophie* (Paris, 1960).

[72]Descartes, *op. cit.,* Med. VI.

[73]*Ibid.,* II.

[74]*Ibid.*

CHAPTER II

Notes and References

[1]A life which is based on common-sense knowledge does not concern itself with effects, which frequently flow from *a priori* philosophical systems. On the question of the relation of common-sense knowledge to philosophy, cf. my work, *Realizm ludzkiego poznania (Realism of Human Cognition)* Poznań, 1959, pp. 97–115.

[2]A critique of the concept HOMO-ANIMAL RATIONALE, presented, among others by J. Möller, *Man in the World* (Paris, 1969), pp. 9–26, 95), resolves itself into an explanation: *obscurum per obscurius*. Additionally, history (strictly as events or occurrences), does not seem to be excluded from the designation, *"animal rationale."* To the contrary, it is clearly implied, since to be an animal is to occur but rationality indicates not only an occurrence but rather directing. Besides, the universal characterization as *"animal rationale"* does not pretend to a role as defining everyone who demonstrates *what is man*—but it points to a human reality as a creature of nature and simultaneously as transcending nature. Other designations do not exclude the traditional one; but they are only particularizations of it.

[3]The well known concept of Gehlen (*Der Mensch, seine Natur und seine Stellung in der Welt* Bonn, 1955), is based on biological anthropology. The author, however, attempts to transcend biological aspects and he even indicates that culture, and above all morality, is a biological necessity of human reaity. "Sittlichkeit ist eine biologische Notwendigkeit." (p. 410). Although we mention Gehlen's concept, we do not intend to evaluate it or the discussions of anthropologists and philosophers on this subject. Gehlen's concept has opened up many interesting insights about which we shall speak later on.

[4]In the same place, the author in question writes, " . . . die Kultur gehört zu den physischen Existenzbedingungen des Menschen." In criticizing Gehlen's concept, M. Landmann (*Philosophische Anthropologie,* Berlin, 1955), warns that so-called "defects" about which Gehlen writes are not defects but rather positive conditions for the development of the spirit. Gehlen's position is similarly criticized by F. Büchner (*Vom geistigen Standord der modernen Medizin* in *Mensch und Welt,* Freiburg, 1957, pp. 71 ff) and by the famous biologist, A. Portmann, (*Biologische Fragmente zu einer Lehre vom Menschem,* Basel, 1951). The latter arrives at an interesting notion about man, namely that he is a spirit building himself a body.

[5]Obviously, this refers preeminently to the famous dialogue, *Phaedo,* although the concept is found scattered throughout many of Plato's works.

[6]A characteristic Aristotelian trait in the theory of knowledge was the reduction of intellectual knowing to concepts. Even judgment was to express itself in the formation of a new and more excellent concept. Concepts, however, were subject to a certain hierarchy patterned on the hierarchy of a natural class. Such a stand became entangled in insuperable difficulties, e.g., in the case of the classical definition of truth. N.B. These difficulties become apparent when we focus on the specificity of judgmental knowledge in relation to conceptual knowledge and on the mutual non-reduction of both types of intellectual knowledge.

[7]Strictly speaking, Descartes was the first to identify images and concepts with ideas.

[8]Cf. P. Chojnacki, *Pojęcia i wyobrażenia w świetle psychologii i epistemologii (Concepts and Representations in the Light of Psychology and Epistemology),* Kielce, 1928.

379

[9]These points are clearly presented in J. Bocheński, *Philosophy: An Introduction* (Dordrecht, 1962), pp. 73–82.

[10]Plato's *Phaedo* provides an excellent testimony to this fact.

[11]Cassirer attempts to present this thesis in his work, *An Essay on Man* where, beginning with Neo-Kantian assumptions, he sees the meaning of human life in cultural creativity. E. Rothaker, *Probleme der Kulturanthropologie* (Bonn, 1948), likewise perceives the problem of cultural creativity as a factor of human nature. Problems of contemporary anthropology in German literature are examined by H. J. Schoeps, *Was ist der Mensch?* (Gottingen, 1960).

CHAPTER III

Notes and References

[1]Cf. E. Mascall, *The Importance of Being Human,* New York: Columbia University Press, 1958.

[2]*The Uniqueness of Man,* pp. 9 ff.

[3]*Ibid.*

[4]*Ibid.,* p. 15.

[5]*Ibid.,* p. 32.

[6]*Op. cit.,* p. 13.

[7]For the presentation of P. Teilhard de Chardin's doctrine, the translator is using the following English editions: "My Universe," *Science and Christ,* New York and Evanston: Harper and Row, 1958; "The Phenomenon of Spirituality," *Human Energy,* London: Collins, 1969; "A Mental Threshold Across Our Pacific: From Cosmos to Cosmogenesis," *Activation of Energy,* New York: Harcourt, Brace, Jovanovich, 1971.

[8]"My Universe," *op. cit.,* p. 44.

[9]*Ibid.,* pp. 78 ff.

[10]"The Phenomenon of Spirituality," *op. cit.,* pp. 95 ff.

[11]*Le phenomène humain,* p. 187, quoted in Mascall, *op. cit.,* p. 7.

[12]"The Phenomenon of Spirituality," *op. cit.,* p. 95.

[13]*Ibid.,* pp. 96 ff.

[14]Cf. *ibid.,* p. 98.

[15]*Ibid.,* p. 100.

[16]*Ibid.,* pp. 103 ff.

[17]*Ibid.,* pp. 108 ff.

[18]*Ibid.,* p. 108.

[19]*Ibid.,* pp. 108, 110.

[20]"From Cosmos to Cosmogenesis," *op. cit.,* pp. 262–63.

[21]*Ibid.,* p. 263–64.

[22]"My Universe," *op. cit.,* 63–64.

[23]*Ibid.,* pp. 65–66.

[24]On this topic, cf. my article, "Religion and Science," in *Znak,* 7–8, (1967), 861–887.

[25]An interesting examination of P. Teilhard de Chardin's doctrine is found in O. A. Rabat, *Dialogue avec Teilhard de Chardin,* Paris, 1958. For another presentation, cf. C. Cuénot, *Science and Faith in Teilhard de Chardin,* London, 1967.

[26]On the Marxist conception of man, cf. Schoeps, *Was ist der Mensch,* (Göttingen: Musterschmidt, 1960). pp. 33–57.

[27]Cf. A. Schaff, *Marxism and the Human Individual* (New York: McGraw-Hill, 1970), pp. 168 ff.

[28]*Karl Marx/Friedrich Engels Collected Works* (MECW), (New York: International Publishers, 1975 —): "Contribution to the Critique of Hegel's Philosophy of Law," MECW, III, p. 182.

[29]A concise and very informative presentation of the problematics of philosophy of man can be found in T. Slipko, "A Conception of Man in the Light of Contemporary Marxist Anthropology

in Poland," in *Zeszyty Naukowe KUL*, 2 (1967), 3–16. Perhaps the most complete presentation of the Marxist theory of man can be found in Lucien Sève, *Marxisme et théorie de la Persona-lité*, Paris, 1972.

[30]This thesis resembles the position of Teilhard de Chardin, of course after removing everything which comes from Revelation.

[31]Schaff, *op. cit.*, p. 70.

[31a]MECW, V, p. 7, footnote added by translator.

[32]A different presentation of this question can be found in Slipko, *op. cit.* Cf. also R. Garaudy, *Perspectives de l'homme*, Paris, 1959.

[33]Cf. J. Prokopiuk, "Posłowie" (Epiloque) in Z. Freud, *Człowiek- religia -kultura*, Warszawa, 1967, p. 315.

[34]B. Suchodolski, "Wstęp" (Introduction), *ibid.*, pp. 13 ff.

[35]Prokopiuk's proposition, *ibid.*, p. 321.

[36]C. Thompson, *Psychoanalysis: Evolution and Development*, (New York, Thomas Nelson & Sons, 1950) pp. 19–20.

[37]*The Standard Edition of the Complete Psychological Works of Sigmund Freud* (SECPWSF) (London: Hogarth Press, 1955); ——, "Three Essays on Sexuality," *SECPWSF*, VII, p. 165.

[38]*Ibid.*

[39]"Group Psychology and the Analysis of the Ego," *SECPWSF*, XVIII, p. 91.

[40]Prokopiuk, *loc, cit.*, p. 323.

[41]Thompson, *op. cit.*, pp. 30 ff.

[42]*Ibid.*, pp. 50 ff.

[43]Prokopiuk, *loc. cit.*, pp. 326 ff.

[44]Cf. *ibid.*, p. 327.

[45]Thompson, *op. cit.*, pp. 34 ff.

[46]*The Neurotic Constitution*, New York: Moffat, Yard and Co., 1917.

[47]*The Collected Works of C. G. Jung* (CWJ) London: Routledge & Kegan Paul, 1953: "The Psychology of the Unconscious," CWJ, VII: *Two Essays on Analytical Psychology*, pp. 40–43.

[48]*Ibid.*, pp. 64 ff.

[49]*New Ways in Psychoanalysis*, New York: W. W. Norton & Co., 1939.

[50]Thompson, *op. cit.*, pp. 206 ff.

[51]*Ibid.*, p. 211.

[52]Cf. P. Watté, "L'idéologie structuraliste," in *Bilan de la théologie du XXe siècle*, (Paris: Castermann, 1970), pp. 339–45.

[53]We have quoted chiefly from Lévi-Strauss who, as the founder of structuralism, is outlining here the basic tenets of a structuralist view of man. For the epistemological consequences of a structuralist method, cf. P. Watté *op. cit.* A similar presentation can be found in P. Blanquart, "Ateismo e strutturalismo" in *Ateismo contemporaneo*, vol. II, pp. 493–520.

[54]This section of the chapter is meant to be, insofar as it is possible, a compendium of C. Lévi-Strauss' pronouncements. My concern is that the well known themes on the subject of structuralism, which have appeared in numerous publications, should be not only examples illustrating the pronouncements but, on the contrary, that from these same pronouncements of the chief spokesman of structuralism, a picture of man would be outlined, which would be the result of an accepted method and cognitive position. At the same time, the ultimate cognitive foundations of structuralism would be revealed. The picture of man which appears here (*resp.* lack of picture), is basically in agreement with accounts which have appeared in philosophical literature on this subject.

[55]Cf. Blanquart, *loc. cit.*, pp. 497–99.

[56]C. Lévi-Strauss, *The Savage Mind* (Chicago: University of Chicago Press, 1968), p. 252.

⁵⁷*Ibid.*, p.. 267.

⁵⁸As B. Suchodolski points out in the *Introduction* to C. Lévi-Strauss' *Structural Anthropology*, Pol. trans. K. Pomian, Warsaw, 1970: "His conception of structure differs fundamentally from the opinions which were in force during the beginning of the twentieth century, when structure denoted an independent building of an individual totality. According to Lévi-Strauss, 'structure does not refer to an empirical reality but rather to models constructed on its foundation.' This very important designation permits us to separate the methodological conceptions of the French anthropologist from all those theories which accept empirical reality as the object of investigation." (p. 25) Further on he says correctly: "In this way the methodological principle is realized, according to which science is not concerned with objects of reality but with 'objects of investigation' which it constructs. In this way, linguistic investigation is the model example, since language in understanding, to which it is suited, is precisely such an object of investigation and not of human reality, of concrete speech. 'Almost all linguistic behavior,' affirms Lévi-Strauss with enthusiasm, 'is situated on the level of unconscious thought.' In the process of speaking, people do not give an account of these linguistic matters which they obey and which science reveals. The disclosure of such matters can be accomplished without harming abstract thought . . . But the meaning of linguistics is greater. For this discipline pertains to facts which, according to Lévi-Strauss, are basic for understanding culture and man. Language is not an instrument which expresses human contents. It is an agent which creates them." (p. 27).

⁵⁹Lévi-Strauss, *The Savage Mind*, p. 262.

⁶⁰*Ibid.*, p. 263.

⁶¹Lévi-Strauss, *Structural Anthropology* (New York: Basic Books Inc., 1963), vol. I, p. 21. In *The Savage Mind*, there are longer passages on history (pp. 248–63). On page 263, Lévi-Strauss confesses: "We need only recognize that history is a method with no distinct object corresponding to it to reject the equivalence between the notion of history and the notion of humanity which some have tried to foist on us with the unavowed aim of making historicity the last refuge of a transcendental humanism: as if men could regain the illusion of liberty on the plane of the 'we' merely by giving up the 'I's' that are too obviously wanting in consistency."

⁶²Lévi-Strauss, *The Savage Mind*, p. 262.

⁶³*Ibid.*, pp. 249 ff.

⁶⁴*Ibid.*, p. 248.

⁶⁵*Ibid.*, p. 249.

⁶⁶*Ibid.*

⁶⁷Cf. Blanquart, *loc. cit.*, pp. 510 ff.

⁶⁸Lévi-Strauss, *The Savage Mind*, p. 248.

⁶⁹*Ibid.*, p. 252.

⁷⁰*Ibid.*, pp. 252 ff.

⁷¹*Ibid.*, pp. 255 ff.

⁷²*Ibid.*, p. 252.

⁷³*Ibid.*, p. 247.

⁷⁴*Ibid.*

⁷⁵*Ibid.*, pp. 255 ff. I repeat this quotation because of its signifance.

⁷⁶In his "Renewal of the Doctrine of Man," in *Theology of Renewal*, vol. II Montreal, 1968, pp. 420-63, Ch. Moeller develops a critque of structuralism viewed from a Christian conception of man. According to Moeller, who agrees with other critics, especially J. Lacroix, we are dealing in the area of structuralism with the most radical atheism of all time. A denial of man's subjectivity is a denial of the foundations of transcendence because it leads to a denial of the presence of a subjective spirit in the world.

⁷⁷Paul Ricoeur *(Esprit,* 11 [1963] 652, note) made this objection some years ago in his remarks

to C. Lévi-Strauss. He called attention to the fact that the ideas of the author of structuralism constitute ultimately a combination of agnosticism (in the final analysis of a philosophical system). For ultimately a dependence on the law of chance is an admission of a radical agnosticism, as well the supraintelligibility of the syntactical structures of language. On this point we can observe again a continuity with some notions of neopositivism.

[78]David Hume's principal philosophical work has the significant title, *A Treatise on Human Nature*. I have already presented briefly (in Chap. I), Descartes's anthropological theory and hence I am omitting any reference to it here.

[79]*A Treatise,* ed. by L. A. Selby-Bigge, Oxford: Clarendon Press, 1978, I, Pt. IV. par. VI.

[80]CF. also Chap. VI, "A Person's Identity" *passim.*

[81]*Ibid.*

[82]A. Wawrzyniak, "Metaphysics and Man" in *On God and Man,* vol. 1, Warsaw, 1968, p. 625.

[83]Ultimately we are dealing with a voluntaristic interpretation of fundamental metaphysical notions.

[84]Cf. F. Ueberweg, *Grundriss der Geschichte der Philosophie der Neuzeit,* bearb. M. Heinze, Bd. II, Berlin, 1897, par. 2,3,5: cf A. Landman, "Przedmowa" (Foreward) to the Polish translation of G. W. F. Hegel, *Phenomenology of the Spirit,* Pol. trans., A. Landman, Warsaw, 1965.

[85]*Ibid.* "With the development of postkantian philosophy," writes Wawrzyniak (*op. cit.,* p. 265), "the conception of a transcendental subject was changed, which after Fichte's elimination of the thing-in-itself, became the single source (foundation) of the entire reality. In connection with such an ontological outlook on the constitution of the world, there is expressed an increasingly fundamental role of subjective cognition in philosophy. And even if this transcendental subject is raised beyond the individual subjects in Schelling's and Hegel's systems, and it ceases to be an aspect or element of human consciousness, its method of cognizing . . . forms itself further, as if in opposition to subjective cognizing."

[86]Hegel presents his theory of philosophical anthropology in *Philosophie des Geistes* (*Sämtliche Werke,* ed. H. Glockner, vol. X, Stuttgart, 1958).

[87]*Ibid.,* para. 400, pp. 122ff.

[88]Hegel, *Phenomenology of the Spirit,* pp. 114 ff.

[89]*Ibid.,* p. 132.

[90]*Ibid.,* p. 159.

[91]Wawrzyniak, *op. cit.,* p. 266.

[92]On this subject, cf. Schoeps, *op.cit.,* pp. 58–83.

[93]He presents his theory in his seminal work, *Sein und Zeit,* Tübingen, 1960

[94]Cf. Schoeps, *op. cit.,* pp. 149–60; 164–79.

[95]Heidegger was born in 1889. He received his Habilitation in Marburg, where after World War I, he succeeded to Cohen's chair but in 1928, on the recommendation of Husserl who was retiring, he was transferred to Freiburg. His *Sein und Zeit* which deals with an analysis of man first appeared in 1927 as Part I. Part II has never appeared. Heidegger changed some of his conceptions of philosophy.

[96]*Sein und Zeit,* p. 7.

[97]*Ibid.,* pp. 59–63.

[98]*Ibid.,* p. 386.

[99]Cf. Schoeps, *op.cit.,* pp. 186–93.

[100]"Ich, als Sein bin in der Wurzel verschieden von allem Sein der Dinge, weil ich sagen kann: 'ich bin'" *Psychologie der Weltanschauungen,* Berlin, 1966, p.2: Schoeps, *op. cit.,* p. 186.

[101]Cf. K. Jaspers, *Das Umgreifende des Erkennens* in *Von der Wahrheit,* München, 1958.

[102]In discussing M. Schelers's views in a greatly abbreviated form, we are directed to Schoeps' previously cited work, *Was ist der Mensch?* pp. 202–12.

[103]*Philosophische Weltanschauung,* München, 1955, p.62.

[104]Darmstadt 1930, München, 1947.

[105]*Ibid.,* p. 110.

[106]*Ibid.,* pp. 45 ff.

[107]Cf. Schoeps, *op. cit.,* pp. 205 ff.

[108]*Ibid.,* p. 206.

[109]*Die Stellung* . . . p. 77.

[110]Cf. Schoeps, *op. cit.,* pp. 207 ff.

[111]Scheler himself suports such a position in *Philosophische Weltanschauung:* " . . . wer zugleich als geistige Person am höchsten hinaufreicht in seinem Sebstwesstsein in die Lichtwelt der Ideen, der nähert sich der Idee des Allmenschen und in ihr der Idee der Substanz des Weltgrundes selbst—in der steten werdenden Durchdringung von Geist und Drang." p. 104.

CHAPTER IV

Notes and References

[1]Cf. M. Kurdziałek, "Koncepcja człowieka jako mikrokosmosu" (The Conception of Man as a Microcosm) in *O Bogu* . . . Vol. II, pp. 109–25. Kurdziałek, among others, writes: "In patristic anthropology—as Nemesius testifies—there came fully into prominence tendencies that had already appeared more clearly in Philo of Alexandria and were also familiar to the authors of the 'hermetic works' as well as to the then extremely numerous adherents of Pythagoreanism, Orphism, and Platonism. They all aimed at uniting the knowledge of man and the world in a coherent interpretation of doctrines handed down in so-called 'revealed books'" (p. 120). "Medieval, ascetic-theological microcosmism derives from the same assumption as does psychological-theological. If, however, the former seems to 'succumb' under the pressure of Platonic-Augustininian-Dionysian spiritualism and psychologism, then the latter seems in turn to succumb to the 'magnetism' of Cynical-Stoical moralism. According to this hypothesis, man is a microcosm because in his moral life there occur the same law and order that we observe in the macrocosm. . . . Man ceased to be a microcosm in the physical sense of that word; the ancient cosmological meaning of this term was extended to the structure of the soul or else to the 'qualities' constituting it; eventually, owing to self-observation, there were brought into relief such characteristics of human nature as the attainment of knowledge (*scire*), the execution of choice (*velle*), the realization of one's potentialities (*posse*). This microcosmic thread . . . found an eminent continuator in the person of Nicholas of Cusa, and through him influenced the contemporary philosophy of man" (pp. 124 ff.).

[2]Admittedly, St. Thomas was fundamentally a theologian and exhibits a theological (ordered to eternal salvation) view of man, yet he learned from St. Albert the Great to distinguish orders (about which, unfortunately, certain publicized postconciliar theologians have forgotten—and have thereby pushed theological thought back into the pre-Medieval period, and all this in the name of "realism," "historicity," with a disregard for a fundamental condition of cognition: point of view or formal aspect [*aspectowości*])—and therefore even in the *Summa Theologiae* he presented a picture of man that is disclosed in and through philosophical interpretation.

[3]Man, however, in the formulation of Thomas Aquinas, (but not of his commentators, who succumbed to the influences of fifteenth-century Aristotelianism and Scotism) did not appear as a "synthesis" of spirit and matter, but as a person, i.e. an ego of a rational nature (which will be discussed below).

[4]The schematizing approaches to man gave an *a priori*, "rational" solution in the sphere of the moral and political sciences, but unfortunately not taking into account the structure of the human being, i.e. a spirit, which in matter and through matter organized by it, progresses toward the fullness of life.

[5]The immediate data of consciousness here are the legitimate point of departure, since they refer precisely to that which in consciousness and through consciousness manifests itself and attains human expression. This does not mean, however, that a strictly phenomenological description and point of departure would be accepted here, or that consciousness would be something primordial in the philosophical analysis (cf. my article "O realizm metafizyki" [On the Realism of Metaphysics], *Zeszyty Naukowe KUL*, 1969, no. 4.). It means merely that the self-cognition

that each of us has of himself is, in the sphere of philosophical anthropology, something that is primordially given.

[6]J. Alfaro properly formulates this matter in somewhat different terminology (*Teoria ludzkiego postępu [Theory of Human Development]*, translated [into Polish] by S. Głowa, Warsaw, 1971, p.53): "The reflection of man upon himself discloses his fundamental and vital experience in the existing tension (which belongs to the essence of man) between *subjectivity,* as the clear presence of himself in the indestructible consciousness of his own 'Self,' and *objectivity,* as the considered content of something that exists beyond consciousness. Man cannot catch himself at the empirical experience of himself, but only through the reflective act in which he presents to himself something opposed to his self-presence. One cannot think (subjectivity) if one does not think about something other than one's reflective act (objectivity), just as one canot think about anything whatsoever without the thought of oneself. Consciousness, being the presence of an object to oneself, characterizes man as a *spiritual* subject and constitutes the primordial and fundamental data of his being." The author, however, using still other terminology, makes a series of inaccuracies here, confusing the subjectivity and objectivity of the act of cognition with the subjectivity of the immanent ego in "my" acts, which also have their subjective and objective side.

[7]An analysis of the "ego" reveals its existential side (the fact that I am) and its so to speak content side (the fact that I exist as a subject actually subjectivizing my acts of a different type).

[8]The concern here is with the emphasis of the fact of the basically simple conceptualization of the "Self" conceived as the correlate of "my" possessions, broadly understood. If we conceptualize, and objectivize the "Self"—then it basically refers precisely to the thus broadly understood phenomenological "Self."

[9]The person as a subject of law can become evident in light of the analyses of both the very fact of law as well as the theory of personal being, which, however, will be treated below.

[10]The expression "Self" is often understood differently, depending on the character of the science (particular or general), the cognition (prescientific or scientific), the philosophical system. In such circumstances, it is difficult—without a treatment of the various types and spheres of cognition—to make some sort of classification of the meanings of "Self," but this is not necessary for the course of the present considerations. When, however, I speak of the "Self" broadly understood, then I have in mind that which later in the analysis will be called personal being, and which is connected with all "my" acts, both purely spiritual as well as physiological acts, since the ego is the author and aim, i.e. the performer of all these acts, and thereby encompasses the whole of man's being. In addition to this broadly and comprehensively understood "Self," it is still possible to speak at times of some narrow understanding of the "Self," which, however, is not given to me immediately, but rather is co-given in acts of a spiritual type (cognition, love), and which it is necessary to clarify, explicate, and that in systemic cognition bears the name "soul." The cognition of this restricted "Self" is basically the work not of primary, immediate cognition, but of philosophical cognition (by means of a system). But that narrowly (not most strictly!) understood "Self" (as soul) is co-given in the higher psychic acts. Concerning the subject of the different types of "Self," there will yet be mention in the analysis of the question of person.

[11]Concerning such expressions as "center," "subject," "cause," "performer," "aim,"—I understand them as follows: in our immediate cognitive experience, the "Self" initially appears as the "focal point" and "center" of "my" functions. To be a "focal point" and "center"—is the initial understanding of "subject;" for it appears that this "center" radiates, emanates, acts from itself; furthermore, it produces them, since we are conscious of the causation of our acts by us. That production is also ordered to the "Self" as causing those acts; hence, the "Self" as the cause and aim of my acts is their performer. But to be the performer of acts means the same as to

subjectivize those acts. Hence, we register the "Self"—observing the fundamental human situation—as the subject in the act of subjectivizing.

[12]This means that "my" individual acts are separated from the "Self," but the function of the subjectivizing of these acts—the fact that the "Self" always appears as performing certain acts—is not separated and is inseparable, although it is differentiated.

[13]This materiality may quite well be through conformity or organization, but not necessarily through identity.

[14]We do not encounter the differentiation of "Self" and "non-Self" (which will be discussed below) anywhere apart from man. For only consciousness of one's subjectivity as subsisting allows the differentiation of everything that is "non-Self" from the co-ascertained "Self." For this is the experience of personal being, apart from which there is no "ego" and no feeling of being oneself.

[15]Cf. the analyses conducted below of the sphere of the structure and process of cognition.

[16]A more detailed explanation of the problem: how is it possible that the "Self" could be understood both as material and immaterial?—is carried out below, when the "Self" becomes "connected" with the soul organizing the body, of which it is the essential form, for itself.

[17]ST I, 76, 1.

[18]This is clearly in itself superfluous—given the "consciousness of the immediate data" of one's inner experience. The concern here is merely with the systemic confirmation of what the data do not directly accentuate. The primordial data, however, are the ultimate end of the process of reasoning, both from the side of the point of departure, as well as the point of arrival. The systemic confirmation defines and reveals the justifications, the rejection of which is either absurd or leads to the absurd; that—in this case—being is non-being, when it does not possess autonomous existence and when it is not subjectivized in that which autonomously subsists, i.e. in a substance. And although at first sight the expressions "substance," "accident," are not accurate in relation to man, who is fulfilled in his functions, they should be taken analogously..

[19]Continuing Jaspers' thought, it can be said that when I affirm: "I exist"—I affirm a factuality, the act of the existence of the subject as subjectivizing; of the subject in the act of subjectivization. I perceive myself differently than all other beings, even other persons closest to me. They are affirmed from the objective, and not the subjective, side. I perceive only myself in an aćt not only of immanence, but also transcendence; I perceive that not only am I present in "my" acts performed by me, but that these acts transcend, that it is I who cause them, that they are not an adequate expression of the ego, that the ego actually predominates over them. Therefore, seeing them from within as the one emanating, causing, calling into existence"my" acts, I see my own be-ing as the being of a subject existing and radiating the existing acts from itself.

On the other hand, I see other persons and things from an objective side, through a description of their properties and attributes, which are not able to be a being not being subjectivized. I do not perceive, the subjectivity of another being directly, through attributes—the properties and reduced reflection non-contradicting the be-ing of these same properties. Hence, there is a great difference between objective cognition and the intuition of one's own existence of the ego as a subject in the acts of subjectivization. This state of affairs has fundamental meaning for the affirmation of one's personal being, which will be discussed below in the treatment of the concept of personal being. On this topic, cf. K. Wojtyła, *Osoba i czyn (The Acting Person)*, Chapter II.

[20]*A Treatise of Human Nature,* ed. L. A. Selby-Bigge (Oxford: Oxford University Press, 1968), Book I, pp. 251–2.

[21]Between the substantiality of man and other creatures of nature there also occurs this difference, that (expressing the matter briefly) they are a specimen of a definite "class," while man through his personal acts of cognition and love forms his own personal "nature." For each of

us differently, "personally" arranges for himself the same fundamental constitutive properties of analogously general human nature.

[22]Potentiality and act, as two non-dependable "elements" of the same being, are necessarily commensurate with one another, if they are components of the same individual. Cf. my work, *Struktura bytu (The Structure of Being)*, Lublin, 1963, pp. 120–64.

[23]Of course, in Aristotle the question of the human soul is a separate question. Here we are concerned with the observation that the ontical structure of man is one of the many instances of the so-called "hylomorphic" composition of being from matter, as the potential, variable (and being the ground of variability) element, and from form (*eidos*), as the element actualizing, organizing matter. In such a case, man was an almost typical example of a being composed of form-soul and matter-body. The soul as the form of the body exists—in the Stagirite's opinion—by the existence of the whole: of man. Neither the soul nor the body is capable of existing alone, for they are not capable of acting alone, but human activity is the activity of a con-crete, and therefore of something that is a "fusing" of soul and body. Furthermore, nowhere in the variable universe was there possible the coming-into-being and the activity of such a being which, being changeable, would not be changeable "from within"—and hence be composed of matter and form. Both of these elements, as components of one being, are something real in one real being and through that real being composed "of them." Therefore, the existence both of matter and form is possible solely in the logical consequence (and hence: due to the composition). The act of existence of man—in Aristotle's eyes—was the consequence of the realization of the composition of soul and body. In short, the existence of man was the result of the organization of matter under the influence of a set of forms of nature, and ultimately of the human soul, which received existence through the composed whole. This problem, however, was wrongly posed and wrongly resolved, because it was, in the issue of human existence, merely the particularization of a general system, and not an interpretation of the immediate data of human experience. The "hylomorphic" conception of man, basically naturalistic, was attacked and also improved in the course of the long history of philosophic thought. Such names as Aristotle, Theophrastus, Nemesius of Emesa, Themistius, Avicenna, Albert, and Thomas, can serve as the stages of the development of this conception.

[24]Cf. my work, *Metafizyka (Metaphysics)*, Poznań, 1966, pp. 345–414.

[25]Iin Aristotle's system only one form was subsistent, without matter—the Aristotelian god as self-thinking thought. Even the forms of heavenly bodies were united with "matter," which constituted the so-called "fifth essence"—*quinta essentia*—ether. Ether, as the "body" of forms of perfect pure intelligences, was not subject to "corruption" and changes from within.

[26]It is difficult to establish indubitably the meaning of the very obscure Aristotelian conception in this regard, as is evidenced even in the later history and commentaries on this same conception. Cf. G. Verbeke, *Themistius, Corpus Latinum Commentarium in Aristotele Graecorum,* Vol. I, Louvain, 1957, pp. XXXIX–LXXII.

[27]Cf. Böhner, Gilson, *op. cit.,* pp. 121–24.

[28]This position synthesized Platonism with Aristotelianism. This appeared especially clear in Avicenna. Cf. G.Verbeke, "Introduction" in: *Avicenna Latinus . . . , pp. 9–30.*

[29]Admittedly, in the whole Platonic and Neoplatonic trend, the soul was conceived as a subsisting being; indeed, even Avicenna wrote: "*anima est . . . substantia solitaria*" (*Ibid.,* pp. 80, 65)—yet in this trend the soul was not acknowledged as the form of the human body in the proper sense. But whenever, on the basis of Aristotelianism, the soul was acknowledged as the form of the body in the proper sense, then its materiality was also acknowledged, as Verbeke shows (*Ibid.,* p. 21) in the example of Pomponazzi. Thomas Aquinas was the one who synthesized the Neoplatonic and Aristotelian conceptions and acknowledged the substantial subsistence of the human soul, and at the same time its function of the "formation," i.e. of the or-

ganization and animation, of the body. Such a theory, well-founded, was something exceptional and unusual, and at the same time not understood even in the "Thomistic school." Cf. E. Gilson, *Elements of Christian Philosophy* (Garden City, New York, Doubleday & Company, Inc., 1960), pp. 203–219.

[30]For the human body to exist—means to be organized and formed by the soul. The body, therefore, does not possess an individual, separate, ontical existence of some sort; it exists due to the fact that it is matter organized by the human soul. The process of the organization and disorganization of the body is continually in motion. The disorganized matter of the body is no longer the human body. The phenomenon of the human body calls for special studies in this light, which would be able to show, on the one hand, its link with nature, and on the other, its distinctiveness, specificity, and precisely human nature.

[31]Cf. *Q. Disp. De Anima*. Here are some of Thomas's statements: *"Quia unumquodque agit secundum quod est actu, oportet quod anima intellectiva per se habeat esse per se absolutum non dependens a corpore. . . . Intellectus animae humanae habent naturam acquirendi cognitionem immaterialem ex cognitione materialium, quae est per sensum. Sic igitur ex operatione animae humanae, modus esse ipsius cognosci potest. Inquantum enim habet operationem materialia transcendentem, esse suum est supra corpus elevatum, non dependens ex ipso; inquantum vero immterialem cognitionem ex materiali est nata acquirere, manifestum est quod completmentum suae speciei esse non potest absque corporis unione . . . "* and *ad* 1: *"Licet anima habeat esse complementum non tamen sequitur quod corpus ei accidentaliter uniatur; tum quia illud idem esse quod est animae communicat corpori . . . "* ST,75, 2 (*passim*) and 76, 1. The analyses conducted in these articles are characteristic. Cf. Also on this topic the commentaries of S. Swieżawski to Thomas's *Traktatu o człowieku (Treatise on Man)*, Poznań, 1965; "Introductions" to questions 75 and 76). A correct emphasis by Swieżawski on p. 15 on Thomas's principle: *'Cognoscitivum aliquorum nihil eorum habet in sua natura.'*

[32]René Le Troquer, *What is Man?*, trans. Eric Earnshaw Smith (New York: Hawthorn Books, 1961), pp.32–3.

[33]Ontical subsistence is something different than fullness in the aspect of the so-called "species." For soul-ego is not man, but through it man exists as a being of a definite "species." Cf. Thomas, *Q. Disp. De Anima*, a. 1.

[34]Cf. my article, "Człowiek w perspektywie śmierci" (Man in Perspective of Death), in *O Bogu . .* , Vol. I, pp. 143–45.

[35]*Op. cit.*, pp. 39 ff.

[36]The functions of our cognition particularly witness to this. Le Troquer rightly observes: "It is not an intellect that thinks, it is the whole man, that is an intellet served by a sensibility and a sensibility penetrated by intelligence. Through the union of these two functions in his cognitive act, [strictly speaking, we are dealing here with a single cognitive function of two different structures; the author's expression is somewhat imprecise, but what is at issue is the general idea—M.K.] man is able to experience concrete reality in an experience which is neither purely intellectual not purely sensitive, but human, that is, both. This experience, in fact, can be neither purely sensitive, since if we confined ourselves to sight we should never know what we are seeing, nor purely intellectual, since to intelligence there corresponds an idea which, being abstract has no existence outside ourselves, It follows that the intellect lives, in its own mode, the reality of which it understands. . . . The body is present not only in the act of understanding but also in the act of the will, which is love . . . It is through the gestures of the body in all their manifold forms that we are able to express our love to the beloved, and these gestures, indispensable to every human lover, become the real signs of our affection." *Ibid.*, pp. 40–41.

[37]There are different types and forms of "composition"—from the purely quantitative, integrating subject, through the accidental-substantial, essential composition, to the ontical composition of essence and existence—all are adequately expressed in the concept of the composition of potency and act. Cf. my work, *Metafizyka (Metaphysics)*, Part II.

[38]Cf. the analyses in *Contra Gent*. 1168, 69,70,71,72.

[39]Cf. G, Manser, *Das Wesen des Thomismus*, Freiburg, 1948, Ch. 11, par. 4.

[40]Cf. ST, 76, 2, 3. *E. Gilson, *Elements of Christian Philosophy*, p. 209. [footnote added by translator]

[41]Cf. a series of papers in *The Concept of Matter*, ed. Ernan McMullin (Notre Dame: University of Notre Dame Press, 1963).

[42]Cf. my article, "Z filozoficznej problematyki badań nad koncepcją materii jako składnika realnego bytu" (On Philosophical Problematic Investigations on the Concept of Matter as a Constituent of Real Being), *Studia Phil. Christ.*, 1967, no. 2, pp. 17–48.

[43]Cf. I. Dąmbska, "Z teorii instrumentalnego poznania," (On the Theory of Instrumental Cognition) in *O narzędziach i przedmiotach poznania (On the Instruments and Objects of Cognition)*, Warsaw, 1969.

[44]This is shown rather clearly in Baeumaker (*Das Problem der Materie in der griechischen Philosophie*, Münster, 1890).

[45]In the whole of scholastic philosophy, this position was in force: *"immaterialitas est radix cognitionis."*

[46]Cf. *The Concept of Matter*.

[47]*A fortiori* one cannot, on the basis of empirical cognition, assert the impossibility of the existence of a being not subject to such cognition.

[48]The analysis of the very fact and course of cognition reveals that the cognitive union of object with subject is something entirely unique and occurs differently than what takes place in any possible union of matter. Cf. my work, *Realizm lukzkiego poznania (The Realism of Human Cognition)*, Poznań, 1959, Ch. XIII.

[49]SCG. II, 66.

[50]Cf. A. Stępień, "Zagadnienie genezy duszy ludzkiej z materii" (The Question of the Genesis of the Human Soul from Matter), *Zeszyty Naukowe KUL, 1960, no. 1, pp. 109–17*.

[51]Cf. Chojnacki, *op. cit*. The author presents the conclusions of the works of the Würzburg school, showing the distinctions of concepts and images.

[52]Cf. Stępień, *op. cit.*, pp. 110 and 114 ff.

[53]Le Troquer, *op. cit.*, pp. 27–30. If we were to go a step further and ask on what that "becoming-present" of the world in me depends, we ought to consider the process of the very act of cognition as an example at least of conceptual cognition (exercised through concepts), which also is the part (as though material) of cognition exercised through judgments. For cognition occurs in part through the formation and becoming-present of the cognitive "object" in the cognizing subject. For through the act of cognition we do not change the object itself, but we ourselves change. Under the influence of the object acting on me, I myself begin to act, cognizing the object that I as yet did not know a moment ago, and I form in myself and make present for myself an image of that object (in imaginative and conceptual cognition). Owing to the image or representation formed and made-present for myself, the object is no longer in me in the mode of the existence of the object itself, but precisely in my mode of existence. For whatever exists by the existence of a subject takes on the mode of the existence of the subject, as already was observed long ago: *"quidquid recipitur ad modum recipientis recipitur."* If, therefore, the representations-concepts, judgments, existing in me are immaterial in their structure, then they obtain immateriality not from the side of the cognitive object, which precisely is ma-

terial (often material), but from the side *of the subject forming the concept and conferring its own subjective mode of existence. Therefore, the existence in me of cognition is a confirmation of my immaterial mode of existence.*

[54]Cf. St, I–II, 8; 13, etc. In various places in his writings Thomas devotes a great deal of attention to this problem.

[55]The problem of death and immortality will be discussed in Chapter XII.

[56]St, I, 75, 6. Cf. *Contra Gent.* II, 79.

[57]*Elements of Christian Philosophy,* p. 219.

[58]Extremely instructive in this problem is the somewhat lengthier exposition of Gilson who, concerning himself with this problem in *Elements of Christian Philosophy,* writes: "In the writings of Thomas Aquinas himself, there is really no distinct problem of the immortality of the human soul. Assuredly, there always comes a moment when the question has to be expressly asked, but when it comes, the problem has already received its answer. This is visible in the *Summa Contra Gentiles,* Book II. After first demonstrating that, among the intellectual substances, there is something in act and something in potency (chapter 53), and then that to be composed of act and potency is not necessarily the same as to be composed of matter and form (chapter 54), Thomas proceeds straightway to prove that 'intellectual substances' are incorruptible, (Chapter 55). For if 'intellectual substances' are incorruptible since the human soul is an intellectual substance, it is incorruptible. . . . In the case of a being composed of soul and body, such as man is, the disintegration of the body entails that of the being. Man dies when his body dies, but the death of man is not that of his soul. As an intellectual substance, the human soul is the proper receiver of an act of being. Having its own being, it itself is a being properly so called (*habens esse*). This act of being belongs immediately to the soul; that is, not through any intermediary, but *primo et per se.* Now that which belongs to something by itself, and as the proper perfection of its nature, belongs to it necessarily, always and as a property inseparable from it. . . .

"The reason the proofs of the immortality of the soul seem difficult to understand is that all are tied up with the mysterious element hidden in the notion of *esse.* . . . By far the worst obstacle to an understanding of the doctrine, however, remains the impossibility of imagining the act of being. And, because it is not imaginable, many infer that it is not intelligible. One does not need to go out of the school of Saint Thomas himself to find philosophers and theologians who are convinced that the doctrine of the Master becomes vastly improved if we eliminate from it this cumbersome and somewhat queer notion. . . .

"The decisive part played in this problem by the notion of *esse,* or act of being, is not a historical construction; it is a fact. In the *Summa Theologiae,* I, q. 75, a. 6, Thomas proves that, since the soul has an act of being of its own, it cannot be corrupted in consequence of the corruption of another substance, be it even man: 'That which has *esse* through itself cannot be either generated or corrupted except through itself.' For the same reason, such a soul cannot come to be by way of generation (because no creature can cause actual existence), it can only be *created* by God. Conversely, such a soul cannot cease to be by way of natural corruption. In order to lose its act of being, it must be annihilated by God, for only He Who gave the soul existence can take existence away from it. . . .

"Since he [Duns Scotus] could not admit that the soul had an act of being of its own, the immortality of the soul remained for him an object, not of knowledge, but of faith: *sed haec propositio credita est et non per rationem naturalem nota.*

"A re-examination of this conclusion is provided by the extraordinary case of Thomas de Vio, Cardinal Cajetan, Minister General of the Dominican Order, a quasi-official interpreter of the theology of Saint Thomas Aquinas, who, in the evening of a long life spent in the study of the Angelic Doctor, finally subscribed to the conclusion of Duns Scotus, and did so for the very same reason. . . .

"Cajetan himself had offered demonstrations of the immortality of the soul, but he had done so in a curious way. In his own *De Anima*, as well as in his Commentary on the *Summa*, Cajetan seems to have undertaken to prove the immortality of the soul on the strength of two truly Aristotelian propositions: the soul exercises acts in which the body has no part; and, the soul has at least one power (its intellect) whose existence is independent of the body. Now, these propositions permit the conclusion that there are, in man, operations immaterial in nature, but they do not justify the further conclusion that the cause of these operations is an intellectual substance endowed with an act of being of its own and, therefore, able to survive the death of its body. Obviously, on the strength of the principles of Aristotle alone, Cajetan could not prove what Aristotle himself had not been able to demonstrate. It is small wonder that Cajetan failed to convince, be it only himself, that he had found a real demonstration of the soul's immortality.

"The facts are known. Years later, in his *Commentary on the Epistles of Saint Paul*, speaking of the mystery of predestination, Cajetan was to write that he could not see how it could be reconciled with free choice. 'I do not *know* this,' Cajetan says, 'just as I do not know the mystery of the Trinity, as I do not know that the soul is immortal, as I do not know that the Word was made flesh, and the like, all things which, nevertheless, I believe.' So, at the end of his life, the immortality of the soul, which he had hoped to demonstrate by the principles of Aristotle alone, and without resorting to those of Saint Thomas Aquinas, had become for Cajetan a pure object of faith, exactly like the mystery of the Trinity" (pp. 210–18).

For this reason, at the Fifth Lateran Council, on December 19, 1513, Cajetan did not agree with the papal constitution prescribing the possibility of the demonstration of the soul's immortality on the basis of rational inquiry alone. Cajetan's position was consistent in relation to the assumptions of pure Aristotelianism accepted by him. In Aristotle's system there was no place for the act of existence as an act of being—just as there was no place in the system of Duns Scotus. And in this manner Cajetan—a Thomist—was closer to Duns Scotus than to Thomas.

CHAPTER V

Notes and References

[1] E. Gilson, *Elements of Christian Philosophy,* p. 220.

[2] *Ibid.*

[3] Originally in Plato and later in Avicenna through a distinction of "third natures" which henceforth became the province of philosophers' speculations and as a set of pure possibilities, things in' themselves, the province on ontology etc.

[4] Toward the end of the last century, Galton began systematic investigations in this area. He became known for his theory of "composed, typical representations," which give to a certain degree the effects of intellectual concepts. For just as a single blurred print of some type of man appears on a photographic plate (if we had photographed a whole series of people of such a type) so, too, the representations are superimposed on each other as the result of the similarity of traits. They create an apparent general concept which is, in point of fact, only a "composite representation," a "typical picture" of blurred individual traits.

[5] *Op. cit.,* p. 37.

[6] A. Forest, *La structure métaphysique du concret selon saint Thomas d'Aquin* (Paris, 1930), p. 80 writes correctly: "C'est qu'il-y-a de commun entre plusieurs réalités de notre expérience, ce n'est pas une chose, une partie, mais c'est une loi, c'est-a-dire l'identité de raports qui se retrouvent toujours les memes dans les sujets ou ils réalisent."

[7] Cf. I. Bocheński. "Powszechniki jako treśći cech w filozofii św. Tomasza" "Universals As Content-Traits in the Philosophy of St. Thomas," in *Philosophical Review,* 1938.

[8] Usually many arguments are presented as classical proofs for the existence of reason as a different cognitive power from the senses (including the imagination). Some of the most frequently used arguments are: (a) The existence of general concepts in man which are different from representations. The fact of the real existence of such concepts testifies to their real source which is called intellect (reason). (b) The fact of cognizing immaterial objects testifies to a proportionate faculty likewise immaterial, which is capable of achieving such a cognition. (c) The fact of affirming existence in judgmental acts testifies to the existence of a power which affirms be-ing. (d) The manner of intellectual cognition is radically different from that of sensible cognition. We are able to cognize everything, all forms, and articulations of matter. Hence this power is immaterial because a material cognitive power can achieve a cognition of only a certain portion of matter and in a concrete way. (Thomas called attention to the fact that "cognoscitivum aliquorum nihil habet eorum in sui natura.") (e) The fact of objectivization of the area of consciousness, of self-knowledge.

Sometimes there is talk about the "thinking" of computers. Obviously we cannot identify human thinking—even if it is understood in a most primitive way as an "operation on ideas" (Cartesian conception)—with the "thinking" of electronic machines even if there is a certain similarity directed to one of the areas of activity. For if we distinguish in human cognition three "strata" of signs: (a) conventional signs: speech and writing (b) natural signs: the meaning of general expressions and (c) individual signed things, then, we meet in the activity of computers only an operation dealing with conventional signs but not with meanings and even less with designations. In addition, an operation dealing with conventional signs is accomplished basically from a syntactical aspect. This means that the electronic machine is fully capable of translating the language-symbol, insofar as it fulfills the syntactical function. But a man is needed who could decipher, by means of a living intellect, the meaning of the coded verbal signs that were fully converted with respect to their assigned direction of translations. Hence computers operate on only one level of language; they deal solely with conventional signs from a syntactical aspect which is only an external "instrumental" side of thinking. What is foreign to the machine is that which, in its minimal understanding, is thinking: an activity dealing with meanings which only human reason can accomplish, i.e., understanding the meaning of conventional signs.

[9]"Not-I" is "dependent" on "I."

[10]Such a generally delineated picture of things finds its many reflections in numerous writings of Thomas Aquinas when he discusses man's intellectual cognition, e.g., St. I. 84–89

[11]A work devoted to an analysis of this problem is S. Adamczyk, *De objecto formali intellectus nostri secundum doctrinam S. Thomae Aquinatis,* Rome, 1933.

[12]Gilson, *Elements,* p. 228.

[13]*Ibid.* P.p. 228–29.

[14]On this subject cf. my works, *Teoria analogii bytu (Theory of the Analogy of Being),* Lublin, 1959, *Struktura bytu (The Structure of Being),* Lublin, 1963: *Metafizyka,* Poznań, 1966.

[15]Mediaeval philosophers are familiar with the theory of *conversio ad phantasmata* or a return to representations following the process of abstraction. This return has as its aim not only to illustrate but also to aid in understanding the abstracted content.

[16] Cf. analysis in preceding chapter as well as ST. I. 76. 1.

[17]*Op. cit.,* p. 155.

[18]*L'existence et i 'être.* Paris, 1942 *(Byt i istota.* Warszawa, 1963).

[19]On the theoretical level, idealism is the principal consequence. On the practical level, however, there are tendencies to form totalitarian social regimes in which the human (living) individual would be a realization of the abstract which would do only this or that as the presupposed totality decided.

[20]Obviously this contact with "essence" (understood however in an abstract and selective [exemplary way] way) becomes real cognition (an element of cognition) only when the comprehended "essence" of being is the comprehended essence of a real being and hence of an existing one. For the process of separation in abstracting from a real existing context is, at the same time, a separation from real data. And it can happen (as the history of philosophy gives us examples especially in the case of idealistic currents), that man will be managing very well with abstracted contents which will exist only through logical connections and conclusions and which will no longer designate concrete reality. This does not mean that such thinking would be worthless; it only means that it has ceased to be a philosophical interpretation of existing things.

[21]A personal intellectual responsibility is the assertion of truth: when I assert that something is "thus," and in verifiable reality it is so.

[22]This is connected with the Aristotelian epistemological current for which "to know" means to create a concept. For this reason, too, in the renaissance of Thomism under the influence of 15th century Aristotelianism, "judgment" as well as an act of cognition was considered to find its highest expression in the production of a new concept.

[23]Prologue to the Gospel of St. John.

[24]The term "before" concerns chiefly the indication of a reason: the reason for knowing a content, an essence, is its existence affirmed in an existential judgment.

[25]This does not mean that I first enuntiate an existential judgment which asserts a contentless existence. (By means of an existential judgment), I affirm an existence in being. I affirm this existence as affecting the content which I know better with each additional act of intellectual

cognition. But the reason for all further operations is the primordial affirmation of the existence of being.

[26]In the process of forming and becoming aware of our existential judgments, there is a series of increasingly intensified expressions of the "meaning" of this judgment which originally appears in the very "striking" of the "fact of the world" in our cognitive apparatus. It ends with a reflexive cognition of the character of this judgment which is the reason of grasping the real cognitive concepts of various types.

[27]The cognitive axis of subject-object which would seem to be the fundamental location of all cognition (in the case of German idealists, especially Schelling it is an absolute starting point), is fundamentally the "conscious" starting point in the pursuit of philosophy. It so happens that all philosophical systems, from the Ionians to Sartre, constitute one succession of philosophical thought located in a conscious area by the subject-object poles. In philosophical anthropology, such a situation is really primordial and it expresses itself in the correlative "I-mine," but this is not a primordial situation of human cognition in general. Neither is it the foundation for philosophy because there are more primordial situations where this cognitive axis does not appear. Such a situation is present in the primordial affirmation of existence where no "hiatus" of subject-object as yet exists and where we still have a pure objectivization, where the fact of the "world's" existence strikes me and immerses me in the order of real being. It is at this point that a metaphysical analysis should begin.

[28]Cf. S. Kamiński, A. Krąpiec, *Z teorii i metodologii metafizyki* (*On the Theory and Methodology of Metaphysics*). Lublin, 1962, pp. 133 ff.

[29]St. Thomas, *Sent,* I, d. 19, q 15, a 1.

[30]Gilson, *L'existence et l'être*, p. 253.

[31]On the subject of Parmenides, cf. K. Reinhardt, *Parmenides und die Geschichte der griechischen Philosophie*. Bonn, 1916; W. Jaeger, *Die Theologie der frühen. . . .* pp. 107-36.

[32]Plato, *Meno,* 81, C, D.

[33]_____, *Phadeo,* 72E.

[34]Gilson, *History . . . .* pp. 76-77.

[35]Descartes, *Meditations,* III.

[36]*Ibid.*

[37]Cf. E, Bréhier, *Histoire de la philosophie, La Philosophie moderne,* vol. II, Paris, 1960, pp. 234-73.

[38]Cf. N. Malebranche, *De la recherche de la vérité,* 1, III, p. II, c. 6

[39]Cf. V. Gioberti, *Introduzione all studio della filosofia,* vol. II, c. 3.

[40]Cf. Rosmini, *Teosofia,* sect. 1, c. 5,6.

[41]Cf. Bréhier, *op, cit.,* pp. 276-99. A different kind of apriorism can be explained as an attempt to resolve the problem of the origin of universal concepts. Different forms of apriorism would be hypothetical, non-contradictable origins of ideas and in this sense would perform the analogical function of NOUS POIOUN.

[42]*Ibid,* 336-58.

[43]*Investigations Concerning the Human Reason,* ch. XII; cf. Bréhier, *op cit.,* pp. 402-22.

[44]Cf. J. S. Mill, *System of Logic,* Pol. trans, Cz. Szaniawski, vol. I, pp. 38 ff.

[45]Cf. Bréhier, *op. cit.,* p. 938.

[46]Cf. Chojnacki, *op. cit.,* pp. 16 ff.

[47]The theory of the human person emphasizes the personal character of a human being who actualizes himself in and through matter. The body becomes not only a "place" but also a co-element constituting man. Cf. ST, I, 56.

[48]Cf. below for a description of the process of the origin of concepts. The theory of instrumental activity performs a very important function in the system of Thomistic thought. It explains

for example such problems as the function of senses in the process of intellectual cognition; the theory of the operation of the sacraments, Biblical inspiration etc.

[49]There is a whole series of monographs on the subject of the Aristotelian theory and the history of the agent intellect. Cf. Verbeke, *Themistius* . . .

[50]Aristotle's saying: "The knowing soul becomes all things" (anima cognoscendo fit quodammodo omnia) received a more profound understanding in the creative philosophy of St. Thomas through the elaboration of the theory of the *species* as intellectually cognitive forms which represent in the mind the contents of what is cognized.

[51]Cf. my work *Metaphysics*, pp. 271 ff.

[52]Cf. This is connected with the problem *sensibile per se est intelligibile per accidens*. What is directly known through sensible cognition is known indirectly through intellectual cognition. We are dealing here with the fact that the same material object is known both materially and intellectually in its different aspects and reasons. In sensibly grasped contents there are also structures which are "unreadable" to the senses but which must be grasped by the senses so that they could be "readable" to the intellect. Hence there is an uninterrupted cognitive sequence passing from "readable" sensible structures to necessary structures disclosed only to the intellect.

[53]Cf. ST, I,79, s; SCG, II, c. 77; *De Spirit. Creat.*, a 9; *Comp. Theol.* c 83; *De Anima*, a 4; *III De Anima*, lect. 10.

[54]Verbeke, *op cit.*, pp. 59-73; cf. De Wulf, *Histoire de la philosophie médiévale*, vol. II, Paris, 1936, pp. 390 ff. I am afraid that the interesting considerations of M. Gogacz in his work, *Istnieć i poznawać*, Warszawa, 1969, esp. pp. 220 ff., make the role of the intellect a bit too independent while it is only an affective power and as such it does not seem to fulfill the individuating functions of be-ing.

[55]I am basically presenting here the theory of Thomas Aquinas because, to my mind, it is the only theory which takes into account different undeniable facts and which gives a concrete definitive explanation.

[56]Cognition is information about reality whereas thinking is an activity on concepts acquired in cognition.

[57]Thomas writes in *Contra Gentiles* II, c. 77: Determinatas rerum sensibilium naturas praesentant nobis phantasmata, quae tamen nondum pervenerunt ad esse intelligibile . . . est igitur in anima intellectiva virtus activa in phantasmata, faciens ea intelligibilia actu; et haec potentia vocatur intellectus agens.

[58]"Phantasmata sunt quidem actu similitudines rerum quarumdarum; sed sunt potentia immaterialia. Unde nihil prohibet unam et eandem animam, inquantum est immaterialis in actu, habere aliquem virtutem per quam faciat immaterialia actu, abstrahendo a conditionibus individualibus materiae." ST. I, 79, 4 ad 4. Cf. *Q De Anima*, a.2; *De anima*, III, lect. 10; *De Verit.*, q. 10, a. 6 ad 1. Thomas emphasizes that the dematerialization of an impression depends on changing it from a potential state of being an object of intellectual cognition to an actual state, in which appear the constitutive ontic traits (at least non-contradictability) of a thing. Cf. ST. I, 79, 3 ad 2; 84, 5; SCG, II, c. 59; c. 73; *In III Sent.*, d. 14, q.1 ad 1; *De Anima III*, lect. 10; *Q De Anima*, a. 3 ad 18; a. 5 ad 17; a 16 ad 11; *Quodl.* 7 a. 3; *De Unitate Intellectus*, passim.

[59]Cf. SCG, II, c 77; *De Spirit. Creat.*, a. 10 ad 17; *De Pot.*, q. 5 a 1 ad 5; SCG II, c 84; *Quodl.*, 8 a. 3.

[60]"Anima humana similitudines rerum quibus cognoscit accipit a rebus illo modo accipiendi, quo patiens accipit ab agente; quod non est intelligendum quasi agens influat patiens eandem numero speciem quam habet in seipso, sed generat sui similitudinem educendo de potentia in actum." *Quodl.* 8, 3; cf. ST I, 85, 1 ad 3; *I Sent.*, d. 17, q. 2 a.1.

[61]" . . . illud, quo intellectus agit comparatur ad intellectum intelligentem ut forma ejus, quia forma est quo agens agit." ST, I, 55, 1.

[62]"Per speciem intelligibilem fit intellectus intelligens actu: sicut per speciem sensibilem sensus actu sentiens. Comparatur igitur species intelligibilis ad intellectum sicut actus ad potentiam." SCG. I, c. 46.

[63]"Operations animae, sensibilis dico et intellectivae, non sunt tales ut in exteriorem materiam transeuntes, sed in operante persistunt, sicut intelligere et velle. Velle enim et intelligere non sunt actus voliti et intellecti, sed intelligentis et volentis . . . . Harum igitur potentiarum operatio non terminatur ad res exteriores, neque sicut ad principium agens, neque sicut ad subjectum potiens, sed ad eas terminatur sola relatio potentiae operantis; quae quidem relatio consequitur formam operantis per quam operatur; sicut imaginatio per formam relictam a sensu, habet operationcm propriam in imaginatione consistentiam; ad rem vero exteriorem, quam imaginatur, habet relationem per formam qua informatur, et ex hac relatione contingit quod. imaginando congnoscit rem imaginatam. Et similiter intellectus, per forman intelligibilem qua intelligit, refertur, quadam similitudinis relatione ad rem extra, quam intelligendo cognoscit." *Ibid*, c. 52.

[64]The specific modification of a cognizing intellect takes place here.

[65]The reason of that which is conscious cannot itself be conscious. The logical reasons of a concretely conscious content can be conscious, but not the ontic reason of consciousness in general because then there would be an infinite regress which is a contradiction.

[66]"Phantasmata per lumen intellectus agentis fiunt actu intelligibilia, ut possint movere intellectum possibililem." SCG, c. 59. "Phantasma movet intellectum prout est factum intelligibile actu, virtute intellectus agentis." *Q.D. De Anima*, a. 3 ad 18; cf. a.. 4; SCG, II c. 59. 90.

[67]*De Verit.*, q 10 a. 6 ad 7; "Intellectus agens quod facit rerum similitudines in intellectu possibili. Phantasmata autem, quae a rebus exteriores accipiuntur sunt quasi agentia instrumentalia." *Quodlib*. VII. a. 3.

[68]Cf. Krąpiec, *Metafizyka*, pp. 497 ff.

[69]Cf. *De Verit.*, q 10 a. 6 ad 7; *III Sent.*, d 14, q 1, a. 1; q 2.

[70]Cf. *III Sent.*, d 14 q 1 a 1, q 2 where Thomas states explicitly: "Nulla potentia passiva in actum exire, nisi completa per formam activi, per quam fit in actu. Impressiones autem activorum possunt esse in passivis dupliciter: uno modo per modum passionis, dum scilicet potentia passivi est in transmutari; alio modo per modum qualitatis et formae, quando impressio activi jam facta est connaturalis ipsi passivo. . . . Nec sensus nec intellectus possibilis operari possunt, nisi per sua activa perficiantur vel moveantur. Sed quia sensus non sentit nisi ad praesentiam sensibilis, ideo ad ejus operationem perfectam sufficit impressio sui activi per modum passionis tantum. In intellectu autem requiritur ad ejus perfectionem quod impressio sui activi sit in eo non solum per modum passionis, sed etiam per modum qualitatis ei formae connaturalis perfectae, et hanc formam habitum dicimus."

[71]Cf. *De Verit.*, q. 8, a. 3 ad 18.

[72]It is completely "transparent" in the thing with which, from the side of the representation, it identifies itself from the point of view of the comprehended traits. This is a unilateral identification, i.e., of the form with the thing and not of the thing with a form, because the thing in itself has a richer content.

[73]The side of the immateriality of accidents testifies to the immateriality of its foundation. We learn about the immateriality of the ontic form by means of an analysis of the structure of its content, or from the side of its intentional contents. But we are dealing here with a two-fold meaning of immateriality.

[74]The concept which arises as the result of cognition through an immaterial form in relation to designated things is potential and not actual. It is actual from the aspect of a comprehended meaning and not of a designation.

[75]If we should want to present schematically, in a simplified way, the process of cognition, we must emphasize the following phases: (1) The representation of the object of potentially intellectual cognition. (2) The activity of the agent intellect on the potentially intellective representation. Next comes the dematerialization. The dematerialized representation can act as a stimulus on the possible intellect. "Efficiuntur quodammodo homogeneae intellectui possibili." *De Anima,* III, lect. 10, 3. (3) As a result of the "striking" of the dematerialized representation in the intellect, an intellectually cognitive form arises and takes shape in the intellect. (4) As a *species impressa,* the form begins the process of intellectual cognition which terminates in an internal "utterance" a *dictio* which assumes the form of the concept as a *species expressa.* (5) The produced concept becomes the intermediary between the "transparent" cognition and the contemplation of the thing itself and a further process of cognition.

[76]We could also ask about the structure of the concept as a representation of the thing. These questions however are linked with the metaphysics of cognition and have been presented in another work. *Realizm ludzkiego poznania (The Realism of Human Knowledge),* chap. 17. We have resorted to some repetition here because it was necessary for an integrated interpretation of the fact of human cognition.

[77]Cf. J. Kalinowski, *Teoria poznania praktycznego (The Theory of Practical Knowledge,* Lublin, 1960, p. 11.

[78]*Ibid.*

[79]The objective treatment of the matter which is considered as the goal can be better known, to my mind, as a criterion. Kalinowski comes to a similar conclusion (*Ibid.,* pp. 14 ff.).

[80]"Aristotle's teaching on knowledge," writes J. Kalinowski, "is closely connected with his outlook on vital activity. . . . The first vital activity, contemplation, is a cognitive activity if by a certain understanding of it, we can say there are still other functions composing it, but only in the way of auxiliary ones. On the other hand, behavior and production are not cognitive activities. However, they cannot be developed without performing certain cognitive activities." (*Ibid.,* p. 14).

[81]On the subject of common sense knowledge and its role, especially in the area of philosophy,of. *Realizm ludzkiego poznania (Realism of Human Knowledge),* ch. 1.

[82]On the subject of the nature of science and its components, cf. S. Kamiński, *Pojęcie nauki i klasyfikacja nauk (The Notion and Classification of Sciences),* Lublin, 1970, pp. 144-91.

[83]Obviously this does not mean that the aspect of learning and the aspect of scientific creativity are in practice separate.

[84]On the subject of the Aristotelian concept of science, cf. Kamiński, *op. cit.,* pp. 58-66.

[85]I. Kant, *Critique of Pure Reason,* p. 211.

[86]It seems that the difference between universalizing and transcendentalizing cognition is essential for the distinction between the individual sciences and philosophy, especially of its classical source. On the subject of transcendentalizing knowledge, cf. Kamiński, Krąpiec, *op. cit.,* Part I.

[87]Cf. above considerations.

[88]Cf. Kamiński, *op. cit.,* pp. 51-143 where the problem is presented in a historical way.

[89]Not only are there different philosophical directions but also different conceptions of philosophy. It is customary to speak of a philosophy which explains (chiefly classical philosophy); of a philosophy which elucidates (chiefly phenomenology); and of a philosophy which expresses (principally existentialism).

[90]In Polish literature, cf. Kamiński, *op. cit.*

[91]Cf. Jaeger, *Die Theologie der frühen* . . . pp. 127-46.

[92]Cf. below, Man and His Free Activity.

[93]Cf. my article "O tomistyczna koncepcje prawa naturalnego. *"W nurcie* . . . (On the Thomistic Conception of Natural Law) in *In the wake.* . . . vol. II, pp. 11-39.

[94]Cf. Below, "Man in the Presence of Moral Good and Evil."

[95]It is only after good has been seen that a vision and obligation follow. Duty does not present itself to us a priori. Rather, it is merged, as a relation, with a concrete decision which is coupled with different elements.

[96]This wisdom can be identified with natural ethics.

[97]Such a transcendental beauty also includes usefulness. In this union every creativity would ultimately have as a goal a transcendentally understood beauty, even if this is not always directly discernible.

[98]Cf. my article, "Intentional Character of Culture," in *Logos i Ethos* Kraków. 1971, pp. 203 ff.; cf. below, "Intentionality of Cognition and Culture."

[99]*Ion*, 533-534C.

[100]*Phaedrus*, 245A.

[101]The problematic of *ars* in the creativity of St. Thomas has a special meaning because it becomes the notion of orderly activity not only for man but also for God.

[102]*Studia z estetyki (Studies in Aesthetics)*, vols. I-III.

[103]Quoted in W. Tatarkiewicz, *Historia estetyki*, vol. I Wrocław, 1960, p. 157.

[104]On the subjectivity of aesthetic cognition, cf. R. Ingarden, *Studia z estetyki*, vol. III. Warszawa, 1970.

CHAPTER VI

Notes and References

[1]The close connection between culture and all areas of human life is beyond question. The basis for these connections is, however, the act of cognition.

[2]Here, I wish to call attention to the most general basic meaning of the expression "culture." Insights of colloquial language point to the existence of some kind of general understanding which is found at the basis of a more particularized understanding.

[3]When we speak of culture as an intellectualization of nature, we must emphasize here the agent of intellectualization as the intellectualization of nature. Obviously such an intellectualization can be joined with other values—either good or bad. This, however, is a further matter whose understanding presupposes a more basic and more primordial understanding. Unfortunately, even concentration camps were works of culture but of a degraded culture with respect to an evil use of the intellect.

[4]A listing of literature on the subject of Thomism and of the Thomistic conception of intentionality is contained in the work, A. M. Heimler, *Die Bedeutung der Intentionalität im Bereich des Seins nach Thomas v. Aquin (Forschungen zur neueren Philosophie und ihrer Geschichte,* Bd. XIV, Würzburg, 1962

[5]*Spór o istnienie świata (Dispute on the Existence of the World),* Vol. II. Kraków, 1948, p. 230.

[6]*Ibid.,* pp. 230-32. (Transl. note: We are indebted to Prof. Władysław Stróżewski, of the Jagellonian University for assistance in translating these passages into English

[7]*Ibid.,* p. 232.

[8]*Ibid.,* p. 250 and note.

[9]*Querrelle de la science normative,* Paris, 1969, p. 113.

[10]When I assert that cultural works bear the character of a sign or symbol, (a) I do not wish to move to a Neokantian position, especially that of E. Cassirer who holds that human cognition is of its very nature a symbolic cognition. In order to locate myself, I assert something diametrically opposite by affirming realism. (b) I am concerned with a very fundamental understanding of a sign, the kind that St. Augustine already knew when he said". . . signum est res, quae praeter speciem quam ingerit sensibus aliquid aliud facit de se in cogitationem venire." I am not concerned here with emphasizing some most particular function of a sign, i.e., as referring to something, representing something, expressing itself, a signal etc. because these are further particularizations of the problem.

[11]Obviously this does not mean that the intentional content of the sign magically disappears when some person is not looking at it and, likewise, that it miraculously reappears when it is viewed by someone else. Because it exists through the existence of matter in which it has its foundation, it can even exist "eternally" (i.e., very long as for example on the moon). But when the intentional content of the sign is separated from the human intellect, it is neither a symbol-sign nor is it "read" as an intellectually expressed content which is subordinated to another human being. Hence in an absolute separation from the human spirit, it is generally not a cultural work. The hypothesis of an absolute separation of a cultural work from the human spirit is clearly an unattainable hypothesis. It is only a question of a theoretical expression of the

problem and at the same time of emphasizing the connection between culture and the human spirit; more specifically, of man as a person who, from a certain aspect, is a "being-for-another-person" and who expresses himself externally and manifests himself to another person through "a spirit incarnated in matter" and who is in his formal composition a psychical, intentional sign-symbol of personal experiences.

[12]It is clear that the eschatological character of culture demands further and more differentiated analyses. At the same time it seems to me that by making this general affirmation, I am in agreement with investigations made thus far. For if the only real manner of existence is the existence of some being as a subject—(obviously this object may sometime be a being in itself or a so-called "substance," or also if one presupposes a substantial existence, it can be a substantial accidental existence and even, and this is very important, an inter-subjective relational existence)—then cultural works that lack a purely "substantial" existence can exist only as "substantiated." And if only the spirit resists the destructive forces of time and change, i.e., if we accept the immortality of the human spirit, then we can affirm the persistence of cultural works in man and by man insofar as man himself is a spirit which organizes its matter and which expresses itself in matter.

CHAPTER VII

Notes and References

[1]Sometimes the anniversaries of tragic human decisions, such as the anniversaries of a declaration of war, the anniversaries of decisions of aggression, make us more profoundly aware of the sense of human freedom and of the responsibility towards other persons connected with it. The responsibility for tragic though free decisions can never be extinguished, if the structure of these decisions is timeless. For this reason they may always serve as timely examples of theoretical analyses.

[2]By "the sense of human existence" we understand here both the structure of the being of humans as well as the causally-purposeful conditions of human activity broadly understood, necessarily connected with such a structure.

[3]For all other intellectual-cognitive and creative actions are directed by objective "laws" and conform to those already determined laws. But in acts of decision, presupposing freedom, we ourselves determine and become the originators of the act as an "extension" of our way of being.

[4]In the cognition of "the fact of making a decision," it is necessary to differentiate a) the reflective knowledge of what occurs within me in the moment of the making of a decision—this will be discussed in part II of the chapter; b) the very act of cognizance, entering into the composition of the decision, of the act of phronetic knowledge, i.e., of the detailed practical judgment, being an element of the decision, and this is just what is under discussion here; c) general consciousness, awareness, being the virtual reflection performed in the course of all cognitive acts. Precisely this general consciousness, manifesting the unity of the psychic life, is conditioned by the derivation of all intellectual-cognitive acts from a single source of knowledge, the intellect, which has the various functions of which Thomas writes in *Summa Theologiae* I, 79.

[5]"Zur Phänomenologie und Metaphysik der Freiheit" (Translated into Polish by A. W., *Znak*, 1963, no. 11, p. 1275).

[6]*Ibid.*, pp. 1226 ff.

[7]S. Kamiński. T. Styczeń, "Doswiadczalny punkt wyjścia etyki" The Experimental Point of Departure of Ethics), *Studia Philosophiae Christianae*, 1968, no. 2, pp. 48 ff. In the examination of this article doubt may arise, however, whether the described point of departure is the moral decision itself, or the moral act, or—as the article seems to suggest—consciousness, called even the "sense" of moral obligation, or also the sense of the duty of making a decision *(de futuro)*. It seems that consciousness and the sense of the duty of making a decision still are not a moral act, but a uniquely necessary condition of this act, which besides appears in the analysis of the moral "act" as one of the elements, very important—but precisely "of the elements," not, on the other hand, the act itself. Have not these matters been confused, failing to distinguish the act of decision itself from consciousness and the sense of duty to perform this act? In a word, have they not proceeded backward one step too many—perhaps under the influence of Maritain and Kant—in the analysis of the immediate data of "my" consciousness concerning the moral act? The consequences of such a step are far-reaching, because in such a supposition they would not start from the "existential fact" in the analysis of the moral act,

but solely from the consciousness of the obligation to accomplish such a fact. Consequently, they would remain only in the sphere of consciousness and of the conscious manifestation of that which occurs "within me." In this condition, they would remain in the field of phenomenology, and not of explanatory philosophy. We would have, in such circumstance of analysis, descriptions of a very unusual moral situation, in which duties were disclosed to us in an absolute way. Normally, however, a man does not always "know" how he should proceed, he has doubts, he seeks counsel, he longs to reach "moral certitude," i.e., the kind which minimally suffices for moral acts. A man, however, always knows what decision he has made. Hence, the analysis of the already existing and accomplished decision, and not the consciousness of its obligation, can become the foundation and also the "object" of philosophical, classical, explanatory treatment leading, on this background of the philosophical analysis of moral act, to the construction of ethics as the theory of that act. I have already considered these issues in the article "Przeżycie moralne a etyka" ("Moral Experience and Ethics"), *Znak*, 1965, no. 9, pp. 1129-46; these issues will also be touched upon below in ch. VIII.

[8]*Loc, cit.,* p. 1280.

[9]A work by S. Kamiński and myself, *Z teorii i metodologie metafizyki (On the Theory and Methodology of Metaphysics),* (Lublin, 1962) is precisely such an attempt (as yet perhaps the only one in this field in world literature) in the area of the metatheory of metaphysics.

[10]The be-ing of men as well as of every entity, constructs in a real sense the existence proper to the subject. This existence is not identical with essence, and therefore is contingent.

[11]On the topic of the findings of biblical anthropology, compare the interesting and careful formulations of L. Stachowiak (article cited, pp. 209-26).

[12]Of course, the neuromuscular system is relatively autonomous and its dependence on the cognitive apparatus is limited.

[13]In the previous chapter there was carried out a consideration on the theme of intellectual knowledge. There was not mention, however; of sensory knowledge. Therefore, in a most abbreviated way we must here call to mind matters generally known from psychology. Traditionally, a distinction is made between the so-called "external" senses, of which the object of knowledge is the external world, and the so-called "internal" senses, namely those which, for the object of knowledge, have the impressions of the external senses. Although there are many external and internal senses, their cognitive function is one, running through the various senses as through various "structures," extracting from the world a cognitive object specific to themselves. From the time of Aristotle, there are distinguished among the external senses: the sense of sight, having for an object the vision of colors; the sense of hearing, recognizing sounds and noises; the sense of smell, detecting various odors; the sense of taste, recognizing flavorful qualities; the sense of touch, being a general sense, perceiving extension from the side of its resistance. Contemporary psychology, within the general sense of touch, distinguishes a series of other senses, such as: temperature, weight, the sense of balance, kinesthetic, etc. Each of the distinctive senses possesses its particular organ which, receiving in itself the effect of a physical stimulus, produces a physiological stimulus, together with which in the living and experiencing organism the sensory impression is effused, as a cognitive form of the thing grasped in the aspect of the appropriate knowledge of the sense.

This impression of the individual external senses comprises the object of knowledge for the internal senses, of which four are traditionally distinguished: a) the common sense, uniting in one objective whole the impressions of the individual external senses, e.g. the color black, the sound of barking, the scent and appropriate tactile impressions in this same object, which reason calls (symbolized by the name) "dog"; b) the estimative sense—instinct, through which "is read" the concrete usefulness (and its form) in the perceptible object for the knowing subject; c) imagination, which preserves the united images, perceived under the absence of the sensorially known object; d) memory, which in knowledge "adds" the temporal factor, knowing the object as already previously known (re-knows).

The internal senses, receiving impressions from the external senses, fundamentally transform them into images, at the same time enriching them in the concrete form of usefulness: what is entire, temporal, or useful for the cognizing individual. In the person, sensory knowledge, grasping the concrete content of the material thing, is closely related functionally with intellectual knowledge, together with which it forms one cogntive process of the human being.

[14]Concerning feelings as elements of inclination (of desire) see below.

[15]This inclination is precisely the act of spiritual love.

[16]The short exposition about feelings I will present is based on the classical analysis of Thomas Aquinas (ST, I–II, q. 17, 7–9; q. 23; q. 25; q. 56, and *De ver.* q. 25; q. 26; q. 20 a. 2). The author conducts his inquiries against the background of an analysis of objective conditions, which is unique in world literature, and in addition to presenting an objective (due to the object!) analysis, also takes into consideration the subjective states. Cf. on this topic the very interesting volume 10 of *Suma teologiczna (Uczucia [Feelings],* translated into Polish by J. Bardan, commentaries provided by F. W. Bednarski, London 1967.)

[17]Thomas writes, characteristically: "Ex consideratione naturalium motuum veritas accipi potest. Si enim accipiamus in motibus naturalibus accessum et recessum, accessus per se respicit id quod est conveniens naturae, recessus autem per se respicit id quod est contrarium." ("The truth of the matter is to be found by considering natural movements. For if, in natural movements, we observe those of approach and withdrawal, approach is of itself directed to something suitable to nature, while withdrawal is of itself directed to something contrary to nature.") ST, I–II, 36, 1.

[18]Describing the experience of the feeling of fear, St. Thomas observes: "Exteriora membra frigida remanent"—"consequitur sitis, interdum solutio ventris"—"tremit etiam labium interius et tota interior mandibula"—"crepitus dentium." ("The outer parts become cold"—thirst ensues; sometimes indeed the result is a loosening of the bowels"—"the lower lip, too, and the lower jaw tremble"—"chattering of the teeth.") Cf. ST, I–II 44, 3 ad 1, ad 2; q. 47 a 4; *De ver.* 26, 8, etc.

[19]Against this background also there would appear descriptively the integrating qualifications of feeling as of the specific appetitive movement related to the organic change and to the accompanying sensory knowledge.

[20]Cf. P. Siwek, *La psychophysique humaine d'après Aristote,* Paris, 1930 pp. 121-50.

[21]For this reason Thomas wrote: "Quando constituitur in propria operatione connaturali et non impedita, sequitur delectatio." ("When a thing is established in its proper conatural and unhindered operation, delight follows.") ST, I-II, q 31, 1 ad 1.

[22]Cf. St. Thomas, *De ver.* q. 26 a. 2 and 3; J. Woroniecki (*Katolicka etyka wychowawcza [Catholic Educational Ethics],* vol. 1, pp. 153–56), devises this sort of consideration on the theme of the appearance and reciprocal influence of bodily and sensory feelings upon one another. "Bodily feeling originates from some kind of physiological process in our organism which, when it reaches the process of intensification, makes us aware of it as something which causes us satisfaction or discomfort. Here there will be, therefore, both the normal vital functions in our organism, such as hunger, cold or warmth, the impulses of the sexual organs, as well as abnormal occurrences, indispositions of some organ which, when we begin to feel them, cause us unpleasantness or pain. This general state of our bodily affectivity is that which we call frame of mind. Not much is needed to disturb it; sometimes it is unfavorable, although we do not know its source; we feel a kind of dread, although nothing threatens us, or we are in an angry or sad mood, although there is nothing to account for it. These moods are apparently occasioned by something which is located in our organism, which is reflected sub-

sequently in the nerve centers of appropriate feelings, reaches our awareness and causes in us certain lesser or greater discontent. On the other hand, the normal functioning of our organism gives our consciousness a sense of tranquility and occasions a favorable mood, a kind of sensory satisfaction of life, which we call a sense of well-being. The successive order of the elements of bodily feelings appears as follows: 1. some alteration in the organism; 2. awareness of it, feeling of it; 3. satisfaction or unpleasantness.

Sensory feelings develop in an entirely different way. They begin from the knowledge of some object, from the sight of something, the sound, or the apprehension by smell or even merely from the thought of something and its representation to us in imagination. If the object thus perceived is indifferent to us, i.e. says nothing to us, as we commonly say, it does not awaken in us any feeling. If, on the other hand, it is not indifferent to us, then either there arises in us a liking for it or a dislike, and from these two fundamental attitudes toward the object emerge all other feelings. . . . This movement of our soul towards or away from a perceived object resounds, as it were, in our organism, calling forth in it numerous rather varied reactions, according to the kinds of feelings the given object elicits. The successive order of the elements of sensory feelings appears, therefore, as follows: 1. the perception of some object; 2. liking or aversion; 3. a physiological reaction in the organism.

If we now compare these two types of appearance of affectivity, then we are first struck by the reversed direction of the process in them: in the first, from body to soul; in the second, from soul to body. Next, and most importantly, we are also struck by the superiority of sensory over bodily feelings, due to their richness of content. Bodily feelings are cognitively very poor, since they resolve themselves into only the one sense of touch, or sensibility, which, diffused in a way throughout the entire body, allows us to feel and become aware of changes in our organism when they reach a certain degree of intensity (this is done by the systemic sense!—M. K.). And the appetitive reaction is here, accordingly, a great deal poorer, since it resolves itself into satisfaction or dissatisfaction being able to reach as far as pain. How much richer in content are the sensory feelings, taking their stimuli through the external senses from the world existing beyond us and transforming them then in the laboratory of the internal senses! In the human psyche their wealth increases the constant connection and mutual interaction of both levels on one another—sensory and mental. Thanks to this, our sensory feelings become in a way spiritualized and can be brought under the control of moral dispositions i.e., of virtues. . . .

Besides these two aspects, there is yet a third, relying on this, that new bodily feelings are being transformed into sensory feelings. The way this happens is that the desire of the first initiates the second by evoking in the imagination a representation of the appropriate object, and this strengthens or maintains the physiological movement. In this way the felt hunger or thirst (bodily feeling) awakens in the imagination a representaion of tasty food or drink and its desire holds within the sphere of consciousness the physiological process of hunger and converts it into the appetite for food or drink. This can be observed much more clearly in the sexual realm where in the first phase of bodily feeling there is no image of another person; the other appears only when in the excited imagination there is sketched some picture which becomes an object of desire, and through it sustains or even strengthens the physiological movement. The process of the passage of bodily feeling into sensory we can thus depict in the order of its elements: 1. some change in the organism; 2. awareness of it, feeling of it; 3. satisfaction or discomfort; 4. emergence of an image of an appropriate object in imagination; 5. liking it and desire of it or dislike and aversion; 6. maintaining the physiological process or else a strengthening of it."

[23]The process described here has, of course, influence on the moral experience of the individual and acquires different evaluations. For if the feelings are beneath the threshold of moral appraisal, then sensory feelings—due to the possibility of their coordination with choice, with reason—cross the threshold of moral evaluation and become morally good or bad.

[24]For this reason also classical philosophers in the Middle Ages thought that there exist in us two distinct emotional powers (like two hands): appetitive, which have for an object the concrete good known by the senses, easily attained, and irascible (aggressive), having as an aim the attainment of difficult good, with the inclusion of a whole mechanism of combat, or the removal of evil.

[25]As already mentioned, the terminology for the expression of states and acts of feeling is shaky because feelings do not appear in us in a distilled state or in a state isolated from the higher emotional, spiritual experiences. It so happens that the acts of our feelings frequently occur coupled with acts of will in one appetitive sequence. Then to this emotional state we give a common name: love, hate, sadness, hope (taking heart), etc. For this reason also common terms for the designation of affective and volitive states still do not attest to a nondifferentiation of affective acts from acts of will, since it oftens happens that acts of will in relation to acts of our affectivity are able to say "no" and conflict or also discharge the affective states which become recognized as e.g. morally evil.

[26]Only very general references were given here. St. Thomas conducted an analysis on this topic in his treatise on the feelings in ST, I–II, 22–48, where he discusses the problem of feeling in general, and then in detail analyzes the character of particular acts of our affectivity. The matter merits a special monograph, although F. W. Bednarski inserted very many interesting observations in a commentary to the texts of Thomas in a book cited above.

[27]When we compare feelings within the compass of just one series, then among appetitive feelings the following genetic order is usually set down: love, desire, joy; whereas in the order of intention and purpose it is reversed: joy, desire, love. Feelings in relation to evil are always later, after the appropriate opposite feeling. In the series of irascible feelings we notice first hope, then courage, finally anger. Whereas in relation to evil—discouragement is opposed to hope, fear to courage. Fear follows after discouragement. Whereas anger follows after courage. Hence, the eleven basic feelings in order of emergence are arranged as follows: 1. love, 2. hatred (aversion) toward its opposing evil, 3. desire and 4. flight in the face of evil, 5. hope and 6. discouragement, 7. fear, 8. courage, 9. anger, 10. joy from attained good or 11. sorrow from present evil.

[28]If permanent ways of affective reaction in the person form his temperament, then the feelings occurring with great force of intensity can be called emotions, whereas to emotions are contrasted sentiment, as a quieter state, not shaking the psychic and somatic side of the individual so strongly.

[29]The question of the sublimation of feelings is extensive and has its various theories, e.g. of Freud, M. Scheler, E. Kretschmer, Bovet, S. Baley. These theories are of course related to certain models of man, useful in some special cognitive or educational sphere. A theory of the sublimation of feelings against the background of the structure of human existence was also given by St. Thomas. The basic text of the study of Thomas on this theme is found in ST, I–II, 56, 4; q. 17, a. 7–9; *De ver.* q. 20, a. 2. The sublimation of feelings in the understanding of Thomas is the constant conformability of the affective life with the exigencies of reason.

[30]Of course, in the personality so broadly understood, a fundamental factor is the hierarchical arrangement of spiritual acts, which will be discussed below.

[31]As was already said, we use these names in the primary sense for the designation of the various acts of our affectivity.

[32]Basically, however, in an act of decision we choose not a good or external objects, but we choose (and this lies entirely in our power) our practical judgment, through which we determine ourselves (self-determination) to some action (or inaction), and through our action to the real causation of something which still does not exist.

[33]Therefore, the freedom of a human being is an experience, a personal way of action; it is

played out in the interiority of the person; it relates to external things only indirectly, i.e. through the released action. Action is inconsistent, however, if it is not determined at the very source. The determining moment is my practical judgment (reason), which I choose for myself. This choice lies in my power, since it occurs in my personal inwardness in which, by an act of will, I choose for myself from my various possibilities such an intellectual determinant that suits me.

[34]Of course, such a good can only be the Absolute God revealing Himself directly in his divinity, if this is participated in intellectual-volitive life. The theological theory of the "beatific vision" deals with this issue.

[35]*Geist und Materie,* Braunshweig, 1956, pp. 7 ff.

[36]Cf. my article: "Człowiek w perspektywie śmierci" (*The Human Being in the Perspective of Death*), in *O Bogu.* . . .Vol. I, pp. 123–48.

[37]The existentialists, especially J. P. Sartre, focus attention on the possibility of the "objectification" of a human being, already even in the unreflective knowledge of oneself. Cf. *L'être et le néant,* Paris, 1957, pp. 310 ff.

[38]*Op. cit.,* p. 278.

[39]Responsibility does not necessarily appear in the context: "toward" someone—but always: "for" such an arrangement of things or relations that "I" brought about and that no longer will be possible to separate from the causing "I."

CHAPTER VIII

Notes and References

[1]On the subject of evil, cf. my monograph, *Pourquoi le Mal? Réflexions philosophiques*. Paris, 1967.

[2]More extensive considerations of this subject are contained in the work of Cardinal K. Wojtyła, "Osoba i czyn na tle dynamizmu człowieka" w *O Bogu* . . . (Person and Act Against the Background of Man's Dynamism, *On God*) vol. I, pp. 204–19; likewise *Osoba i czyn*, Kraków, 1969 (*The Acting Person*, Boston, 1979). The latter work constitutes a very valuable contribution to the formation of the theory of the person against the background of an analysis of man's actions (especially moral ones). A reading of this work drew my attention to the subjectivity of "I'" as the chief form of a personal being.

[3]This is Thomas Aquinas' conception of man (ST 90, 2 and 75, 2; 76, 1), along with a seminal theory of a personal human being.

[4]On the subject of the conception of natural law, cf. my article, "O tomistyczną koncepcję prawa naturalnego" w *W nurcie* . . . (On the Thomistic Conception of Natural Law in *In the Wake*) vol. II, pp. 11–37.

[5]If we understand natural law as presenting itself as a necessary judgment, "Good must be done," then everything which appears in the intellecutal (phronetic) cognition of an acting subject as a good, obligates its realization precisely as a realization of natural law.

[6]Cf. ST, I–II, 19, 9; 94, 4 ad 3; II–II, 104, 4 ad 2.

[7]*Ibid.*, I–II, 94, 1 ad 2; I, 79, 9; II–II, 47, 6 ad 3. In the last text cited, Thomas says significantly, "Synderesis movet prudentiam, sicut intellectus primorum principiorum scientiam."

[8]Cf. preceding chapter.

[9]On the subject of first principles, cf. my work, *Metaphysics*, pp. 104–78.

[10]The bases for distinguishing between a proper, a pleasant, and a useful good in human desire constitute various manners of desire-love. If one desires some good or loves it only for itself, then it is a just good. Such a good can be only a person. If we desire some good because the function itself of desiring some good is desirable, we are dealing with a pleasant good. If, however, we desire some good with respect to some other good, we realize a useful good which is fundamentally a means to an end. This does not exclude the possibility that some good, for example some loved person, could perform the functions of all three goods.

[11]In life, we deal not so much with moral as with ethical subjectivism and therefore with a subjective interpretation of moral facts. The guarantee of moral objectivity is always intellectual cognition of the object. In its spontaneous cognitive process (phronetic cognition in moral decisions is of this kind), the human intellect is "objectivated" and matters of the intellect are matters of the thing itself.

[12]The area of morality locates itself on the human level (likewise interpersonal). For our moral decisions always affect people, at least ourselves as those who are making decisions. For if our decisions directly affect things (and not persons), then this thing is treated as the object of the eventual authority of another person. We speak about the so-called "objective order of things" only in order to emphasize moral objectivity. The same "objective order of things," however, is fundamentally and in a primary sense a "personal order."

[13]These motives are understood in the theological virtues of faith, hope, and love. Through faith, new and supernatural (broadened) horizons of behavior are shown to man. Man is being located in new contexts; he is shown as one who has been redeemed and adopted through the grace of the Son of God, called to an eternal Trinitarian life of God. Through hope and love, man gains new impulses always to make difficult decisions (especially heroic love of neighbor, love of enemies) as the Gospel demands. In connection with the fact that the area of morality affects human activity, the question presents itself: Does Christianity demand from a believing follower acts of moral decision which are essentially new in their content with respect to new and hitherto unknown rules of moral behavior? Or, in relation to rules of moral behavior which bind all people, does it merely furnish new motives and incentives and show new perspectives of human moral life? If the answer to the second question would be in the affirmative, then the difference between moral theology and ethics as systems which interpret human activity would be fundamentally reduced to delineating other positions for a believer and the presentation of new motives for heroic moral activity. Church regulations of human moral behavior in some area of life would be a somewhat different matter. There would come to the fore such discussions as the Church's precept of participating in religious worship on designated days, the observance of fasting etc.

According to St. Thomas, the obligation of this type of precepts flows from the need to observe essential laws and hence of a Christian position. The essence of a Christian position is precisely sanctifying grace, freely given by God and which shows itself in action through the three theological virtues; faith, hope, and love. Article I of the 108th question in the I-IIae of the *Summa Theologiae* is unusually interesting on this subject: "Utrum nova lex aliquos exteriores actus debeat praecipere vel prohibere?" Thomas' characteristic thoughts follow: ". . . convenit ut per aliqua exteriora sensibilia gratia a Verbo incarnato profluens in nos deducatur: et ex hac interiori gratia, per quam caro spiritui subditur, exteriora quaedam opera sensibilia producantur. . . . Et talia sunt opera sacramentorum quae in lege nova sunt instituta, sicut baptisma, eucharistia et alia hujusmodi. . . . Alia sunt opera exteriora quae ex instinctu gratiae producuntur . . . quae in fide per dilectionem operante consistit. . . . Alia vero sunt opera quae non habent necessariam contrarietatem vel convenientiam ad fidem per dilectionem operantem. Et talia opera non sunt in nova lege praecepta vel prohibita ex ipsa prima legis institutione, sed relicta sunt a legislatore, scilicet Christo, unicuique secundum quod aliqua curam gerere debet. Et sic unicuique liberum est circa talia determinare quod sibi expediat facere vel vitare" etc. I have purposely given this text without any translation because it is too revolutionary for our common-place way of thinking. Certainly none of the moralists has gone that far in interpreting the obligation of positive law.

[14]It is proper to apply here the theory of the twofold (natural and supernatural) specification and objectification of this same act-decision.

[15]St. Thomas' conception of sublimation appears in *Summa Theologiae,* I–II, 56, 4 and 5; 74, 3 and 4.

[16]Likewise community can be "separated" from the subject of evil if this is necessary.

CHAPTER IX

Notes and References

[1]Quoted in F. Copleston, "The Human Person in Contemporary Philosophy," in *Contemporary Philosophy*, London, 1956, p. 106.

[2]Questions on the subject of the structure of personal being (cf. Chap. XI) are fundamental for the accomplishment of these investigations. For such relations which can be observed in "groups": "I-world," "I-Thou," "I-we" presuppose a suitable ontic structure and hence a personal independence, intellect, will and characteristic manners of activity on the part of these principal powers.

[3]Cf. St. Thomas, ST, I, 76, 5, "anima autem intellectiva . . . secundum naturae ordinem, infimum gradum in substantiis intellectivis tenet; intentum quod non habet naturaliter sibi inditam notitiam veritatis . . . sed oportet quod eam colligat ex rebus divisibilibus per viam sensus."

[4]We are reminded of the Biblical saying, "Go and subdue the earth." *Gen.* I, 28.

[5]Cf. Chap. XI.

[6]Cf. note 3 in this chapter.

[7]Cf. J. B. Lotz, *Ich-Du-Wir*, Frankfurt a M., 1968. A reading of this work caused me to take notice of the described relations, I-world, I-Thou, I-we. My treatment of this subject, however, differs from that of the author.

[8]The problem of love is the object of very interesting analyses by St. Thomas (ST, I–II, 26–28) in which he considers the question of the nature of love, its causes and effects.

[9]A further discussion of this subject will be found in the next chapters.

[10]Obviously, just as in the case of cognition so, too, in love the reason of generating it (at least very frequently) is that which can be called in general "human body." It enables these acts to come into being but it is not the goal of their actualization. In the case of love, we are dealing with an extremely delicate matter where, especially in marital love, the body is the reason of giving oneself and although it is simultaneously the reason of giving oneself and also the gift, it is not that which leads man to the highest point of love and which constitutes him in love.

[11]Obviously this would lead to pathological conditions and a kind of psychic degeneration.

[12]This real, new and separate manner of existing leads to a complex of categorial relationships which are based on a transcendental relation to common good about which we shall speak below.

[13]Even though we shall analyze the notion of common good below, we cannot omit a discussion of it here in connection with a consideration of the notion, "I-we."

[14]The question of the state and family is an entire subject in itself and I mention it only to complete the picture of community. Besides, Aristotle had already expressed this thought: (*Pol.* c. I), "Every state is a community of some kind and every community is established with a view to some good; for mankind always acts in order to obtain that which they think good. But, if all communities aim at some good, the state or political community, which is the highest of all and which embraces all the rest, aims at good in a greater degree than any other, and at the highest good. . . . The family is the association established by nature for the supply of men's everyday needs. . . . The state is by nature clearly prior to the family and to the individual, since the whole is of necessity prior to the part." In the second chapter he says, "Seeing then

411

that the state is made up of households, before speaking of the state, we must speak of the management of the household. The parts of household management correspond to the persons who compose the household." Aristotle's last affirmation survives today in the conception of states as a family of families but it seems that such a concept is too dangerous for the individual concrete man and it can lead to a disguised form of fascism. For the human person is not merely a function of some kind of society but he is also a being "in-itself-and-for-itself."

[15]There exist societies whose purposes are supernatural as, for example, the Church.

[16]If every composite being which is essentially one is by the same fact the bond of necessary relations, then this composition of elements which are realized in every being (essence and existence) is an expression of transcendental relationships.

[17]This is a question of common good understood in a primary and objective sense.

[18]As we have already pointed out, all social groups find themselves on the "communal field" created by two poles: family and state.

[19]This does not mean that intentional creations should appear even in the first places in communities. For if intentional structures are the foundation for all kinds of cultural forms, then it is only in the social context that so-called intentional "beings" appear. In a strict sense, however, community itself is not an intentional creation as a product of cognition. Rather it is a natural relational being which is subordinated to the good of human persons who constitute a "we."

[20]In his *De Civitate Dei,* St. Augustine saw such an ideal social organization which realizes itself, however, in people. This organization is bound with the realization of the individual good of personal beings.

[21]A community which is subordinated to the realization of the good of individual persons and of the totality.

[22]Such a conception of the good contradicts the accidentality of being; it affirms the necessitarianism of pantheistic gradualism. This does not mean, however, that the "diffusion" of good is not true but one cannot seek in it an element which constitutes good as good.

[23]In order that there might exist any kind of free activity which previously did not exist, there must be a reason for the existence of the fact of acting. Such a first reason is a motive because of which one acts rather than not.

[24]ST, I–II, 90, 2 ad 2.

[25]In the general conception of law, a distinction must be made between the existential fact of law and its essential aspect which involves content. By law interpreted as a fact, I understand a "relation between acting persons whose activity (or non-activity) is mutually due them with respect to a proportional common subordination of these persons to a common good as a goal." When law is understood in this way, it possesses its content aspect which may be defined in agreement with tradition as "a rational regulation with respect to common good which has been given and promulgated by one who is in charge of a community." Cf. my article, "O tomistyczną koncepcję prawa naturalnego" w *W Nurcie* . . . ("The Thomistic Conception of Natural Law" in *In the Wake* . . .) vol. II, pp. 11–37.

[26]To put the matter in a rather exaggerated way, I "blame" Plato to a certain degree, even though I cannot fail to admire him. Plato's political conceptions were also justified in large measure by his painful experience and decadent conditions of the Athenian state in which the wisest and best people like Socrates were condemned to death. Plato wanted to give a theory of an ideal state. It became a grim twist of history that such ideals became realized.

[27]Cf. Jaeger, *Paideia,* vol. II, p. 246 ff.

[28]I am using the German edition, *Die offene Gesellschaft und ihre Feinde,* Bern, 1957.

[29]Jaeger, *Paideia,* vol. II, p. 255.

[30]Cf. *Theaetetus,* 24 D.

[31]*Paideia*, vol. II, p. 255.

[32]*Ibid.*, p. 288.

[33]A. Kasia, *Antynomie wolności. Z dziejów filozofii wolności (Antinomies of Freedom. From the Chronicles of a Philosophy of Freedom)*, Warszawa, 1966, p. 28.

[34]*Laws*, 631 E; 632 A.

[35]*Ibid.*, 942.

[36]*Paideia*, vol. II, p. 262.

[37]J. Messner, *Das Naturrecht*, Tyrolia Verlag, Wien, 1969, pp. 279 ff. (1) The authority of the social power is absolute and the aims of the authority are, at the same time, the goal of all organizations subordinated to the supreme government, so that there can be no mention of a contradiction or independence of the groups' aims and that of the government. (2) There are no associated groups which do not fulfill the will of the supreme government. (3) There is no law against the supreme government because the individual cannot assume the role of a judge against the supreme government. (4) The supreme government possesses the only official public opinion. (5) The source of power goes "from the top to the bottom" and this is the same direction which orders and decisions follow. (6) There is either no representation of the citizens or it is a decorative organ of power which performs only a propaganda role. (7) The social government is fundamentally a government of force, where the individual can be completely trampled upon by external pressure. (8) In such a government, there are no organs for the control of power. (9) In such governments there is no freedom of thought and speech. (10) Neither is there any possibility of organizing legal opposition. (11) Man's rights are not generally respected in such governments. (12) Basically, the government is the only true possessor of goods.

[38]I am purposely presenting this matter in an exaggerated way because I am interested in a theoretical emphasis of the foundation and direction rather than in their factual realization. We can accuse even St. Thomas of an over-emphasis of power. Gilson's text is characteristic in this respect, *Elements*, pp. 257 ff (in Polish translation).

[39]Cf. his famous work, *Der Einzige und Sein Eigentum*.

[40]I am using here the following work: Peretiatkowicz, *Filozofia prawa Jana Jakuba Rousseau'a (Jean-Jacques Rousseau's Philosophy of Law)* Kraków, 1913.

[41]Cf. the insightful observations on this subject in J. Maritain, *Principes d'une politique humaniste*, Paris, 1945, pp. 37 ff.

CHAPTER X

Notes and References

[1]Cf. for example A. Dondeyne, *La foi ećoute le monde*. Paris, 1964.

[2]There is an extensive literature on this subject. I am citing several sample positions: J. Arntz, "L'Athéisme au nom de l'homme? L'Athéisme de J. P. Sartre et de M. Merleau-Ponty" in *Concilium*, 16 (1966) 59–64; I. Herman, "L'Humanisme total, signal utopique coexistence et pluralisme," *ibid.*, 139–56; J. Moltmann, "L'Esperance sans foi. Réflexion sur l'humanisme eschatologique sans Dieu," *ibid.*, 45–48; R. J. Nogar, "L'Humanisme évolutionnaire de la foi," *ibid.*, 65–72; S. M. Ogden, "Proclamation chrétienne de Dieu aux hommes de soi-disant 'Age athée'," *ibid.*, 97–104; H. de Lubac, *Athéisme et sens de l'homme*, Paris, 1968.

[3]Cf. for example M. Nédoncelle, "Philosophie de la religion" in *La Philosophie du milieu au vingtième siècle*, vol. II; cf. also Jaworski, "Kronika współczesnej filozofii religii" (A Chronicle of Contemporary Philosophy of Religion) *Znak*, 9 (1966) 1132–50.

[4]Philosophy of religion constitutes an area of knowledge about religion which is marked by a great vitality but, at the same time, it gives rise to many questions and reservations about its formal character. Its methodological status is especially undetermined. The variety of conceptions of the philosophy of religion is explained to a certain degree by the plurality of conceptions of philosophy or of concrete philosophical directions. For philosophy of religion is the application of a general philosophical theory to the religious fact. There are problems which concern still other matters, for example: What is the object of the philosophy of religion: religion in general, natural religion, or concrete revealed religion? There is also a discussion concerning the subject of a suitable method of investigating the religious phenomenon. On this subject, cf. M. Jaworski, "Problem filozofii religii" (The Problem of the Philosophy of Religion) *Studia Philosophiae Christianae*, 2 (1967) 169–92. Different conceptions and directions in the philosophy of religion are found in H. Fries, *Die katolische Religionsphilosophie der Gegenwart*, Heidelberg, 1949; P. Ortegat, *Philosophie de la religion*, 2 vols., Paris-Louvain, 1948: J. Hessen, *Religionsphilosophie*, Bd. I–II, München, 1955; J. Collins, *The Emergence of Philosophy of Religion*, New Haven, 1967; L'Ourre, "Themes in Contemporary Philosophy of Religion," *New Scholasticism*, 4 (1969) 577–601; K. Schmitz, "Philosophy of Religion and the Redefinition of Philosophy" *Man World*, 3 (1970) 54–82; G. van Riet, *Philosophie et religion*, Louvain-Paris 1970; J. K. Roth, *Problem of the Philosophy of Religion*, Scranton, 1971.

[5]Although every one of the above-mentioned thinkers interprets the phenomena of religion differently, they all come to the unanimous conclusion that religion impedes the full development of human potentiality. Marx explains the religious fact as an historical event which arose under the influence of man's inability to dominate the forces of nature or improper social structures. Religion is a certain form of social consciousness which should be transcended because it is truly a form of protest by man against material and social misery. Nevertheless it is a helpless protest because it transposes man into an "illusory" reality and it restrains his practical activity. At the same time, it restrains the process of social development. Nietzsche looks for the genesis of religion in weakness and even in a sickness of the will. Religious faith arises as the result of dread before a decision. It is also an escape from responsibility, an escape from man's psychic immaturity, from feelings of threat, and other such pathological psychic states. Freud held

414

that religion has its source in man's helplessness in the presence of the forces of nature and of inner instinctive powers. Instead of using his intellect in order to dominate them, man stifles or directs them with the help of other affective powers. Sartre, on the other hand, holds that belief in God alienates human freedom which is both incarnated and located within us. Z. Czarnecki, *Filozoficzny rodowód marksistowskiej teorii religii (The Philosophical Genealogy of Marxist Theory of Religion)* Warszawa, 1971; S. Freud, *Totem and Tabu,* New York, 1960; W. Gromczyński, *Człowiek świat rzeczy, Bóg w filozofii Sartre'a (Man, the World of Things and God in Sartre's Philosophy)* Warszawa, 1969.

[6]Rudolf Otto, *The Idea of the Holy: an Inquiry into the Non-rational Factor in the Idea of the Divine and Its Relation to the Rational,* London, 1950.

[7]Emil Brunner, *Religionsphilosophie evangelischer Theologie,* München, 1927.

[8]Martin Buber, *Ich und Du,* Leipzig, 1922; _____, *Eclipse of God,* New York, 1952; _____, *Good and Evil: Two Interpretations,* New York, 1963.

[9]Mircea Eliade, *Traité d'histoire des religions.* Paris, 1964.

[10]A bibliography of Romano Guardini's works is contained in M. Jaworski, *Religijne poznanie Boga według Romano Guardinego (Religious Cognition of God According to Romano Guardini)* Warszawa, 1967.

[11]Henri Duméry, *Le problème de Dieu en philosophie de la religion,* Paris, 1950.

[12]Gerard van der Leeuw, *Phänomenologie der Religion.* Tübingen, 1933, 1956.

[13]Max Scheler, *Vom Ewigen in Menschen.* Berlin, 1933. We must distinguish clearly between two kinds of phenomenology of religion: (1) Phenomenology of religion as a humanistic science: Religious phenomena and those connected with religion are described as they are given in all kinds of empirically accessible areas: historical, psychological, and sociological. In this interpretation, certain general structures are distinguished, and various phenomena are classified in order to arrive at an understanding of religious concepts. The pursuit of this science is in agreement with a humanistic philosophy formed by existentialism, structuralism and hermeneutics. The resulting conception of religion is almost philosophical (G. van der Leeuw, M. Eliade). (2) Phenomenology of religion as an eidetic science and hence somewhat philosophical, since it observes phenomena in consciousness and through a so-called essential inspection (*Wesenschau*); it apprehends and describes the essence of religion in a most general way. The exponent of a phenomenology of religion understood in this way is M. Scheler. His phenomenology of religion was applied to a phenomenological method, shaped to philosophy to an understanding and clarification of religious phenomena. For Scheler, the initial material of the first order was an experience of a Christian type.

[14]On the limitation of a philosophy of religion which is severed from metaphysics (Phenomenology of Religion) among others cf. W. Stróżewski, "Erich Fromm: Perspectives and Reductions" *Znak,* 5 (1967) 593–636. Phenomenology of religion investigates only sensibility and not reality which corresponds to acts of a religious object. In this connection, even the factual genesis of sense does not come within the area of its concern.

[15]*Psychoanalysis and Religion,* New York, 1972.

[16]Cf. ST, I–II, 81, 1–8.

[17]There is an enormous number of definitions of religion. R. Pauli, *Das Wesen der Religion,* München, 1947, cites approximately 150 definitions. Cf. L. Kaczmarek, *Istota i pochodzenie religii (The Essence and Orgin of Religion),* Poznań, 1958; E. Kopec, "Co to jest religia" (What is Religion?), *Zeszyty Naukowe KUL,* 2 (1958)73–85; J. Keller, "Religia: pojęcie, geneza, klasyfikacja, struktura" w *Zarys dziejów religii* (Religion: Its Notion, Genesis, Classification and Structure" in *Outline of the History of Religion)* Warszawa, 1968, 9–14; A. Stanowski, "Fenomen religijny" (The Phenomenon of Religion) *Więz,* 7–8 (1971) 60–72. The definition of religion constitutes one of the chief and likewise most controversial problems of

almost all religious disciplines. There are many positions concerning this problem. Cf., for example, W. Cohn, "Ist Religion Universal? Problem der Definition von Religion," in *Internationales Jahrbuch für Religionssoziologie*, Bd. II, Köln-Opladen, 1960, 201–13; M. E. Spiro, "Religion: Problems of Definition and Explanation," in *Anthropological Approaches to the Study of Religion*, ed. M. Banton, London, 1966, 85–128; F. J. Streng, "Studying Religion, Possibilities and Limitations of Different Definitions," in *Journal of the American Academy of Religion*, 40 (1972) 219–37. The problem of religion was likewise widely debated and discussed by Polish scholars of religion, especially in the fifties. Cf. articles in *Euhemera* for the years 1957 and 1958.

An attempt to delineate the definition of religion is contained in an article, S. Kamiński, Z. J. Zdybicka, "Definicja religii a typy nauk o religii," (Definition of Religion and Types of Studies of Religion) in *Roczniki Filozoficzne*, 22, (1974) z. 1.

[18]Concerning the object, distinction is made for example between dynamic and personalistic religions (Stanowski, *op. cit.*); between cosmic and revealed religions (cf. J. Daniélou, *Dieu et nous*, Paris , 1956; between authoritative and humanistic religions (Fromm, *op. cit.*); monotheistic and polytheistic and pantheistic deistic religions. Among scholars of religion toward the end of the nineteenth and the beginning of the twentieth century, there were strong monistic tendencies which aimed at reducing cosmic and revealed religions to a common denominator. The present attitude is that this position is quite impossible.

[19]M. Scheler, *op. cit.*, p. 530.

[20]Cf. Eliade, *op. cit.*, p. 145 (Polish translation).

[21]Cf. Daniélou, *op. cit.*, p. 16 (Polish translation).

[22]Homer, *Iliad*, XX, 7–9. Concerning a personalistic understanding of the object of religion in the mind of the Greeks, cf. E. Gilson, *God and Philosophy*, New Haven, 1941.

[23]Cf. F. Machalski, "Religie Persji" w *Zarys dziejów religii* (Religions of Persia" in *Outline of the History of Religions)* p. 305.

[24]C. Kunderewicz, "Religie Egiptu" (Religions of Egypt) *ibid.*, p. 344.

[25]E. Słuszkiewicz, "Religie Indii" (Religions of India) *ibid.*, p. 51.

[26]W. Kotański, "Religie Japonii" (Religions of Japan) *ibid.*, p. 151.

[27]Cf. Daniélou, *op. cit.*, p. 20. Such an interpretation of religion as a repetition or a reference to an archetypal event comes chiefly from M. Eliade, *Traité d'histoire des religions*.

[28]An analysis of religious experience from a psychological aspect is made, for example, by W. Gruehn, *Die Frömmigheit des Gegenwart*, Münster, 1956; L. Kaczmarek, "Człowiek—istota religijna" w *W nurcie . . .* ("Man a Religious Being" in *In the Wake . . .* vol. II, pp. 171–208.

[29]Cf. Otto, *Holiness*, *passim*.

[30]Cf. B. Häring, *Das Heilige und das Gute*, München, 1950.

[31]Scheler, *op. cit.*, p. 535.

[32]On this subject, cf. Daniélou, *op. cit.*, as well as Garrigou-Lagrange, *The Three Ages of the Interior Life*, St. Louis, 1947–48.

[33]Cf. St. Thomas, ST, I–II, 81, 1.

[34]Cf. Häring, *op. cit.*, pp. 18–31; F. Heiler, *Das Gebet*, p. 489; St. Thomas, ST, I–II, 83, 1–17.

[35]It is worth noting that *religio* in Latin also means "religious order." This term which is used to indicate persons or fellow-religious points to the essential meaning and aim of this type of life, whose constitutive element is a conscious and freely willed "being-toward-God." Its fundamental activity is that which aims at an increasingly fuller realization of one's own union with others and with God.

[36]Cf. S. Kamiński, "Od spostrzeżeń do poglądu na świat" w *O Bogu . . .* ("From Observations to Opinions on the World" in *On God . . .*) vol. II, pp. 127–45.

[37]Cf. M. A. Krąpiec, "Człowiek wobec dobra i zła moralnego" (Man in the Presence of Moral Good and Evil) in the above-mentioned book; cf. also T. Styczeń, "Doświadczenie moralnosći" in *Logos i Ethos*, Kraków, 1971, 327–55.

[38]Cf. S. Ossowski, *U podstaw estetyki (At the Basis of Aesthetics)* Warszawa, 1958, pp. 271–79; also R. Ingarden, "Przeżycie estetyczne" w *Studia z estetyki* ("Aesthetical Experience" in *Studies in Aesthetics)* vol. III, Warszawa, 1970, pp. 97–102.

[39]Cf. Kamiński, *Pojęcie nauki . . . (Conception of Science . . .)* p. 202.

[40]Cf. E. Smith, *Experience and God*, New York, 1968, pp. 169 ff.

[41]Cf. Kamiński, *op. cit.*, p. 202.

[42]For a more detailed discussion of the question cf. M. A. Krąpiec, "Religia a nauka" (Religion and Science) in *Znak*, 8–9 (1967) 861–87; cf. P. Chauchard, *Science et religion*, Paris, 1962; *La science, la technique et l'homme de demain*, Paris, 1967.

[43]The question of religious experience, especially since the time of W. James, constitutes one of the important problems in the theory of religion. Interesting considerations on the subject of the character of religious experience are outlined in the book *Experience and God, op. cit.*, pp. 21–67. This problem requires a special investigation.

[44]I have in mind religious cognition as it is presently presented, for example, by Hessen and Guardini. In Polish literature, cf. M. Jaworski, "Religijne poznanie Boga" (Religious Cognition of God), *Zeszyty Naukowe*, 3 (1961) 39–58; _____, *Religijne poznanie Boga według Romana Guardiniego (Religious Cognition of God According to Romano Guardini)* Warszawa, 1967; A. Nossol, "Idea religijnego poznania Boga" (The Idea of Religious Cognition of God) *Zeszyty Naukowe*, 3 (1963) 15–24; _____, "Religijne poznanie Boga w świetle nauki Kościoła" (Religious Cognition of God in the Light of the Teaching of the Church) *Collectanea Theologica*, fasc. I (1971) 53–69.

[45]*Vom Ewigen in Menschen*, p. 535. "A religious act cannot, by itself or with the help of thought, construct that which presents itself as the object of an idea, of contemplation, of man's thought which realizes it. In some way, he must accept the truth toward which he aspires, which saves him and brings him happiness. This he 'seeks' precisely through the mediation of that being which he seeks."

[46]The impossibility of meeting in general with holiness when one wishes to draw it from any other objective area, from any other class of value has its basis in the very fact that, in an a priori way, so called from the top, Scheler establishes it as the highest class of value. "The ontic synthetic axiom for religious consciousness extols that which is completely only through itself of full value and is of a kind of value of holiness. This type of value cannot pass away or be lost in any other group of values, whether they are logical values, cognitive values, axiological, moral, or aesthetic etc. *Ibid.*, p. 390; cf. also Häring, *op. cit.*, pp. 120 ff.

[47]We should mention here, above all, M. Buber who introduced the theory of man creating himself in relation to the world, to human persons, and to God. The fundamental aspect of human existence is a dialogical relation of partnership which constitutes a personal "I," carrying on a dialogue with another "Thou" who is received in a free manner. The divine "Thou" constitutes the basis and the a priori of this relation. Cf. M. Buber, *Werke*, Bd. I–III, München, 1962–64.

[48]Cf. E. Schillebeeckx, *Dieu et l'homme*, Paris, 1965, pp. 144 ff. It is worth noting the title of K. Rahner's work, *Hörer des Wortes* (Hearer of the Word) München, 1963, where he presents the conception of a philosophy of religion which, according to his statement, is a fundamental theological anthropology which indicates that the understanding which man has of himself, assumes the possibility of receiving a factually existing theology.

[49]Cf. W. A. Luijpen, *Existential Phenomenology*, Pittsburgh, 1962, pp. 344 ff.

[50]*Ibid.* "So long as being-man is understood as absorption in "being-in-the world," so long as

his destiny is sought solely in the possession of the world, there is no hope for man. Hope finds its source not in being-in-the-world but in the being-in-the-world-but-transcending-it (*in-der-Welt-über-die-Welt-hinaus-sein*) which is real in love." *Ibid.*, p. 354.

[51]Cf. G. Marcel, *Du refus à l' invocation*, Paris, 1940. "If we can believe in an Absolute Thou, a Being in whom unfaithfulness and betrayal are impossible, if I could believe in this Being's Love for me and if I were permitted to love this Being, then I would be able definitively to consent to myself. This awareness of orientation is called 'hope'; it is the belief in Love." Luijpen, *op. cit.*, p. 355.

[52]Cf. Copleston's declaration found in P. Ortegat, *Philosophie de la religion*, vol. II, Louvain-Paris, 1948, p. 810.

[53]This concerns an indication of the direction of inquiries. As much as man reflects on himself as an existing object, so much does he perceive the problem of a relation to an existing subject, who is God. In this kind of process, there is always present a moment of reflection; it is not merely a clear-cut direct experience of God.

[54]In this respect, it is difficult to agree with Fromm that a personal God does not have to be for man "an object of reference and adoration," provided that he performed a positive role in human life. Such a position in the matter of the object of religion does not seem to take into account the ontic nature of man for whom the object of a religious reference cannot be an ontically inferior being. Cf. M. Jaworski, "Człowiek i Bóg. Zagadnienie relacji znaczeniowej pomiędzy osobą ludzką i Bogiem a problem ateizmu" (Man and God. The Question of a Meaningful Relation Between a Human Person and God and the Problem of Atheism) *Logos i Ethos*, 115–28.

[55]Cf. A. Usowicz, *Psychologia religii w zarysie (Psychology of Religion in Outline)*, Kraków, 1951; Gruehn, *op. cit.;* Kaczmarek, *Człowiek—istota religijna (Man: A Religious Being)*.

[56]This is not be understood as an indentification of the value of religious acts with individual values: truth, goodness, beauty and consequently as an obliteration of the difference between the area of religion and secular areas. The essence of a religious act is a direction toward transcendent reality. The perspective which religion designates, however, is one that involves everything which, above all, constitutes man and which develops him in a spiritual sense. And in this meaning, it can be said that the value of holiness is built on the value of truth, goodness etc. E. Smith proposes some interesting solutions on the subject of the relation of that which is holy (religious) and that which is worldly. He says that what is holy indicates the ultimate purpose which makes prominent and gives clearness to all individuals of worldly existence. That which is worldly, however, is the model and means by whose help that which is holy comes into full reality. Without the profane, the holy would become a sphere of a "pure spirit," which is impossible when we take into consideration the ontic state of man. Cf. *Experience and God*, p. 61; A. Levi, *Religion in Practice*, New York, 1966.

[57]ST, I–II, 3, 1.

[58]The Christian truth about the resurrection of the bodies and about the "new land" emphasizes the necessity of some kind of material element in the life of a human person, even after death.

[59]St, I–II, 3, 5.

[60]Objectively considered, the ultimate end is "given" to man; subjectively, it only appears to man that he selects this end. Beyond this, until God does not reveal himself fully as the Absolute Good and Truth, he can actually recognize him or not recognize him as the conscious end of life.

[61]K. Rahner, *Zur Theologie des Todes*, Freiburg i. Br., 1958, p. 85. At the moment of death, man's period of actualization, his "being-on-the-way" comes to an end. For this reason, the moment of death is the moment of the fullest actualization. Christian theology calls attention to the religious character of death. . . . Man's final move which he brings to a close and, at the

same time, terminates his earthly existence as a wanderer, is an act of rendering love. In this act, man accepts his appointment with death. He gives himself to God and commits himself to him, along with his fast vanishing life." J. Pieper, *Tod und Umterblichkeit*, München, 1968.

[62]This does not have to change the content of extrareligious activity. The relation between religious activity and extrareligious areas of human life is not always understood correctly, whence arise certain misrepresentations and conflicts. Cf. for example A. Zuberbier, "Religia a doczesność" w *W nurcie . . .* "Religion and the Mundane" in *In the Wake*) vol. I, pp. 207–35.

[63]The problem of the ontic relation between God and the world is examined in greater detail in my work, *Partycypacja bytu. Próba wyjaśnienia relacji między światem i Bogiem (Participation of Being. An Attempt to Explain the Relation Between the World and God)*, Lublin, 1972.

[64]Ap., 17, 28.

[65]I have in mind here ontic signs and symbols which man can read, in an intermediate way, i.e., by reflection, as signs of God's existence. The problem of symbolic cognition in religion constitutes a separate question which I shall not discuss here.

[66]Theories which explain the connection of religion with some social situation (Marx), or a psychological one (Fromm), or a biological one (Kołakowski) do not consider sufficiently the universal ontic status of the human person. A discussion of this type of considerations, however, goes beyond the established limits of this outline.

CHAPTER XI

Notes and References

[1]Cf. for example, M. Landmann, *Der Mensch im Spiegel seines Gedankens* (München: Karl Alber Verlag, 1962). The author lists at the end of his work some 1,458 bibliographical titles.

[2]In the history of philosophy, "person" has been treated as an analogical-transcendental value which is realized even in the Absolute, who is a person.

[3]This does not mean that the second way and not the first, reveals personal being but, rather, that it proceeds in a different way from the first, by considering important human moments which must also be emphasized.

[4]On the subject of the discovery of the concept *phisis (natura)* cf. for example Jaeger, *Paideia*, vol. I chap. IX, esp. pp. 181 ff. L. Strauss presents an extensive exposition on the subject of *phisis, Natural Right and History*, Chicago, 1953, pp. 79–113.

[5]Almost all the first philosophical works of the ancient Greeks were entitled *Peri Physeos*. These indicated some element or structure which was to make the world intelligible.

[6]Cf. my work, *Arystotelesowska koncepcja substancji (Aristotle's Conception of Substance)*, Lublin, 1966.

[7]I am pointing to only the most acute moments of the problem. In the history of the problematic of the person, there was a search for a constitutive element in some (ontic) traits of being. It referred to a neoplatonic source, according to which, the emanated hypostases represented determined ontic traits. Usually these traits had a positive character: some form of unity. But there also arose theories (John Duns Scotus) which pointed to negations (*negatio dependentiae actualis et aptitudinalis*) as moments which decide the character of personal being. This union of person with a determined ontic trait is, of course, understood against the background of essentializing sources of classical philosophy.

[8]The theory of the personal being of Christ is connected in St. Thomas with an explanation of the dogma of the Incarnation. It signifies above all the duality of Christ's nature and the singleness of person who is the Divine Word. The person of the Logos "assumes" (*assumit*) in itself and gives be-ing to the human nature of Christ. "Humana natura ergo in Christo . . . non hypostasis dici potest quia assumitur a principaliori, scilicet a Dei Verbo." (*De rationibus fidei ad cant. Antiochen.*) c. VII, *Opuscula*, ed. Mandonnet, p. 264. Another text of Thomas emphasizes even more strongly the moment of assuming: "Quia humana natura in Christo non per se separatim subsistit sed existit in alio id est in hypostasi Verbi Dei, non quidem sicut accidens in subjecto, neque proprie sicut pars in toto, sed per ineffabilem assumptionem, ideo humanna natura in Christo potest quidem dici individuum aliquod . . .non autem potest dici vel hypostasis vel suppositum vel persona." (*De Unione Verbi Incarnati*, a. 2)

If human nature were in some manner separated from the Person of the Word, then it would possess its own act of existence and, by this fact, it would become a human person itself. For this reason, the act of existence as the highest ontic perfection (*De Pot.* q. 7 a. 2 ad 9), as the element which ultimately bestows unity (*Quodl.* IX a. 3 ad 2), as an ontically integrating element (*ibid.*, XII q. 5 a. 5), as an innermost element which penetrates everything (*De pot.* q. 3 a. 7)—this act of existence decides about the being-person: ". . . esse pertinet ad ipsam constitutionem personae." (ST III, 19, 1). St. Thomas discusses this question at length in *Quodl.*

II a. 4 ad 1. He excludes the possibility that the element constituting a person might be some trait lying on the plane of essence because, in such a case, the nature which has been "assumed" by the Person of the Word would possess deficiencies: "Naturae assumptae non deest proprio personaliter propter defectum alicujus quod ad perfectionem humane naturae pertinet. (ST III, 4, 2 ad 2). Consequently, the existence of the person of the Word of God in Christ is one and it actualizes this human nature. Hence Christ is one person, a divine person. He is, however, man because the person of the Incarnate Word possesses and actualizes in the ontic order, Christ's human nature. With respect to the relation of the human nature of the existing person of the Incarnate Word to the same act of existing, we can (with respect to this relation) call it an existence of a kind of "second order." A second order existence, however, is nothing else than the real relation of Christ's human nature to the existence of the Divine Person. This existence really actualizes the human nature. It constitutes only one entity, only one person. "In Christo autem suppositum subsistens est persona Filii Dei, quae simpliciter substantificatur per naturam divinam, non autem simpliciter substantificatur per naturam humanam. . . . Et ideo sicut Christus est unum simpliciter propter unitatem suppositi, et duo secundum quod propter duas naturas; ita habet unum esse simpliciter propter unum esse aeternum aeterni suppositi." (*De Unione Verbi Incarnati,* a. 4)

[9]Capreolus' texts are found basically in J. Capreolus, *Defensiones Theologiae Divi Thomae Aquinatis,* ed. Paban-Pegues, Turonibus, 1904, vol. V, pp. 105–18; vol. I, pp. 234–38.

[10]The principal texts of Cajetan are found in the Commentary on the *Summa Theologiae,* p. 111 (Ed. Leonina, vol. XI. Cajetan's conceptions are the result of his theory of being. The consequences of such a theory found their expression in connection with the preparations by Leo X for the Fifth Lateran Council, when Cardinal Cajetan answered that he does not see the possibility of a rational (outside of faith) demonstration of the immortality of the human soul. Such a position was clearly in contradiction to the views of St. Thomas.

[11]Sometimes there was an emphasis on the cognitive moment (R. Descartes), sometimes on the volitive (Maine de Biran), and sometimes even on moments of social consciousness (Del Valla).

[12]By making the *cogito* a point of departure for philosophy, R. Descartes linked philosophy with consciousness as the place where activity concerning ideas takes place. For the English empiricists, impressions and ideas were the object of philosophical analysis in the point of departure as well as in the ultimate argumentations. For Kant, the operational conditions of a conscious subject contituted the ontological situation.

[13]To cognize means ultimately to inform oneself about the state of a cognized being. To think means either to construct concepts or to operate on concepts. The result is thinking rather than cognizing.

[14]An analysis of a reasonable manner of existence and of man's activity is described by H. E. Hengstenberg in the first part of his work, *Philosophische Anthropologie,* Stuttgart, 1966.

[15]A totally conscious manner of apprehending as *totalité* is emphasized by the French philosophical movement, e.g., J. Y. Jolif, *Comprendre l'homme,* Paris, 1967, which is not without the influence of Cartesian thought.

[16]And moreover not only in activity but even in the manner of existing because the human body is "reasonable" and it is linked with "reasonableness" in all kinds of subordinations.

[17]The trait of a reasonable manner of cognizing appears in various cognitive structures: in direct simple apprehension, in acts of judgment, and in reasoning. We observe everywhere a fundamental "reckoning with" things, their structure, their manners of existence.

[18]Acts of decision through which man expresses himself as a man and hence as an autonomous, self-determining and conscious source of causation, constitute a special place for the manifestation of "reasonable" activity, since a decision is for the sake of the production of a new being, whose author is the person.

[19]The theory of the act of love which we shall discuss later, presupposes a mastery of the investigations of Aristotle, St. Thomas and G. Marcel. (I am referring to the principal thinkers.) The initial understanding of the act of love was linked with the schema: *movens — motum; transformans — transformatum*. The loving subject was "routed" out of his passivity by a loved good which simultaneously "transformed" the subject. This internal "transformation" (*transformatio*) would explain the act of love. St. Thomas called attention to the fact that even if such a conception explains much, nevertheless this "inner change" cannot be treated in the manner of cognitional changes (conceptions), because the act of love is dynamic and the transformation in question has a strictly dynamic character: an impulse which compels activity in the direction of a real uniting of the subject and object of love, of constituting a union between them, and even of a real unification. In this process of uniting through love, there enters a process of giving oneself to the beloved. Frequently, our body makes possible this process of "giving oneself" but in the ultimate giving of oneself, although the body is the initial reason, it makes impossible a giving of oneself which is complete and timeless. Hence acts of love even postulate death (myth of Orpheus and Eurydice), in order to achieve a giving that is complete and irrevocable.

[20]Along with *community* as a reasonable form of existence, there appears a *bond* as a fundamental and useful form of social being; on the other hand, *masses* appears as an unreasonable form of social being.

[21]The highest point of "unreasonableness" is disinterested hatred in the evil of another person.

[22]The spirit which manifests itself is a function rather than a subject. The considerations which we have treated below in another context are a repetition (but a necessary one) of that which had been pointed out above.

[23]H. E. Hengstenberg presents a detailed analysis of spiritual actions in his work, *Philosophische Anthropologie* (Stuttgart, Kolhammer Verlag, 1957) pp. 137–219.

[24]This is a more profound level of human psychism.

[25]M. Heidegger in *Sein und Zeit* denies the suitability of Aristotelian categories of being in their reference to man. In their place, he accepts socalled "existentialia" as forms which better characterize the human being. Among these fundamental existentials is *Geworfenheit*, an involuntary casting of things and people into the world.

[26]To be autonomously a subject is fundamentally to be a being.

[27]There exists a double polarity in man: one, in which the poles are the spirit and the biological structure and the other, on the confines of the biological structure where again, the poles are psychism and a physiological structure.

[28]On this subject, cf. Hengstenberg, *op. cit.,* p. 131.

[29]On the subject of the philosophical method of argumentation, cf. Kamiński, Krąpiec, *op. cit.,* pp. 223–54. The most general and most non-contradictable fact given us in philosophical explanation depends on showing the kind of reason whose contradiction would be either absurd, or would lead to absurdity or, finally, to a denial of the very fact which was given us to be explained.

[30]Cf. Aristotle, *Post. Analyt.,* I, c. 1, where he indicates conditions for argumentation.

[31]Hume writes " . . . nor have we any idea of *self,* after the manner it is here explained. . . . It must be some one impression that gives rise to every real idea. . . . But there is no impression constant and invariable. . . . It cannot, therefore, be from any of these impressions or from any other, that the idea of self is derived; and consequently there is no such idea." *A Treatise,* vol. I, IV, VI, ed. L. A. Selby-Bigge, (Oxford: Clarendon Press, 1978), pp. 251–52.

[32]We must strongly emphasize the fact that to be a subject is fundamentally to be a being, to exist as a being. The conception of a subject rather than an object is more strongly bound with the conception of being. For the object can be a cognitive construction (as, for example, in Kant) but not a subject which can exist independently, since all real existing is always the ex-

istence of some subject. Moreover, the level of subjectivation is at the same time the level of existing. This means that the more some being is subjectivated, i.e., it is in itself and for itself, it is thereby a more powerful being.

[33]For in indirect cognition when I am analyzing the content and ontic structure of "my" acts, I use such conceptions as materiality and immateriality, corporeity and spirituality, nature and activity, etc. And an understanding of every such pair of conceptions is always interconnected with an interpretational system.

[34]The existential "I" as given directly in a cognitive experience, escapes every philosophical critique to date.

[35]I am not analyzing here the conception of matter which is closely bound with the conception of science and being. I have called attention to these matters, to a certain degree, in an article, "Z filozoficznej problematyki badań nad koncepcją materii jako składnika realnego bytu" (On Philosophical Problematic Investigations Concerning the Conception of Matter as a Constituent of Real Being) in *Studia Philosophiae Christianae,* 2 (1967) 17–48. In footnote 58, I called attention to the fact that in the thought of Thomas' system, against the background of act and potency, existence is the immaterial aspect of being: " . . .if existence is the existence of a non-composite substance, we may then speak about an ontic immateriality of being. Absolute immateriality can exist only where Pure Existence is present, as Pure Act." A careful reading of this quotation should not cause any misunderstanding, which happened in the case of Fr. Kłosak.

[36]To this extent, St. Thomas' analysis in *Summa Theologiae,* I, 76, 1 is very significant, especially his central opinion: " . . . ipse idem homo est, qui percipit se intelligere et sentire; sentire autem non est sine corpore." This is an expression of a fundamental human experience as an immediate given fact.

[37]Cardinal Karol Wojtyła correctly called attention to this fact and he expressed it in the entire structure of his work, *Osoba i czyn (The Acting Person).*

[38]When I use the expression "responsible," I understand it in the sense of responsible for something and not responsible to someone or in the presence of someone. To be responsible for something means to establish a new relation in the ontic order, which relations are either made possible or impossible (they either facilitate or make difficult) the realization of personal good among people. This responsibility does not exclude a responsibility in regard to someone who watches over the fulfillment of common good. The one and other meaning of understanding responsibility results in the genesis of a third meaning, of a responsible man, of the kind who is prudent in his behavior with regard to a vision of the consequences of his behavior.

[39]Cf. ST, III, 19, 1 ad 4; *Quodl.* II, a. 4 ad 1; on this subject, cf. J. Szuba, *Tomistyczna teoria metafizycznej struktury osoby (Thomistic Theory of the Metaphysical Structure of the Person),* Lublin, 1953.

[40]A transcending person actualizes and fulfills himself in his acts. Ultimately, fulfillment of a person can be achieved only through an act of death, experienced from within as an ultimate affirmation of the Absolute, toward whom a person was hastening while this person was affirming and fulfilling analogical and partial truth, goodness and beauty. Cf. Chap. XII, "Man in the Perspective of Death."

[41]Thomas' basic statement on this subject is the following: "Anima illud esse in quo ipsa subsistit, communicat materiae corporali ex qua et anima intellectiva fit unum; ita quod illud esse quod est totius compositi, est etiam ipsius animae. Quod non accidit in aliis formis, quae non sunt subsistentes. Et propter hoc anima humana remanet in suo esse, abstracto corpore, non autem aliae formae." ST, I, 76, 1 ad 5. This affirmation of St. Thomas preceded the analysis of the pivotal article which was an explanation of a fundamental, existential and directly obvious affirmation: "ipse idem homo est qui percipit se intelligere et sentire." (*body of article*)

Obviously Thomas' texts speak about the soul and this is important. They say nothing about the person. Another perspective appears in them which only makes easier an understanding of the analyses which have been made here. Thomas did not present the question in the area which interests us.

[42]The affirmation that man exists previously as a spirit is not equivalent. The problem of man's coming into being is always linked with the fact of the process of birth. But it is precisely in this process of being born that man's spirit is, as if, a composite, ontic reason, which later makes itself aware through the body as a subjective "I." This means that existence serves man through the spirit which expresses itself only in the body and through the body. As an ontic act, existence does not serve man in the result of the organization of embryonic life. In such a case, man would be a being as a result of the organization of matter and there could never appear in human life an act of transcending matter—which is not true.

[43]A self understanding being would ultimately be, in the area of metaphysics, a subsisting, uncaused being or one whose essence is existence.

[44]The establishment of the relation of person to nature and to the community is not only useful with respect to the fact that the human personal being grasps what are man's most appropriate dimensions, and what has always been emphasized by thinkers, namely, relation to the world (*Geworfenheit*) and to men (*Besorge*), but it shows, at the same time, the essential manifestations and basic structural traits of the person's existence. For the primordial conscious experience "I" expresses and manifests itself through actions which are its fundamental emanation. They manifest themselves against the background of the most characteristic conditions of personal life (in the context of other persons).

[45]These works are not so much the result of analyses of a personal being but rather the sphere of a philosophical anthropology as, for example, Hengstenberg's quotation.

[46]And this is what was also done in scholasticism: a bright picture of a thing was gained but, as a result, it was a picture representing *membra disjecta* of acts in relation to one personal being, who "expresses himself" through his acts.

[47]When we direct our attention to an analysis of love conducted in the Middle Ages and especially by St. Thomas (ST, I–II, 26–28), it is evident that all the conditions necessary to achieve an act of love can be fulfilled only by a person in relation to another person, who alone is capable of a proportionate response to the act of love. And only a person as a subsisting being can be recognized fully as *bonum honestum* or the kind of good which is the goal.

[48]Cf. *QQ Disp. De Verit.*, q. 4, a. 2 ad 7.

[49]*Confessions*, XIII, c. 9, PL 32, 849.

[50]Cf. my article, "Człowiek w perspektywie śmierci" w *O Bogu* . . . ("Man in the Perspective of Death" in *On God* . . .) vol. I, pp. 123–43.

[51]There exists a subjective and objective order of common good, understood from the point of view of finality, as the goal of human rational aspirations. The subjective (personal) order expresses itself in such human activities which add to the actualization of man's personal potentialities, i.e., they bring about the perfection of man as a person. Of the first order are: cognitive acts, acts of the will, of love, of free decision, which realize spiritual values. Acts of this type which perfect man realize, at the same time, the good of not only a particular individual but also of all people. For if the individual becomes better, the entire society is enriched because of this realized good. Hence acts that realize the good of the individual are acts which realize common, universal, human good which is the only good that does not antagonize people.

To the order of a common subjective good corresponds the objective order: realized goods, all of which as being, are a participation in the self-subsistent Good, the Absolute. Finally, man is called to a recognition of the correlation of a common subjective and objective good, namely, to a recognition that man's personal perfection takes place when a personal development leads to an ultimate and irrevocable affirmation of the Absolute.

[52]Expressions formulated in this way have their tradition from the time of Hegel, who perceived very important moments in the evolution of "Idea-Totality" and he introduced the expressions: *An-sich-sein, Anders-sein, An-und-für-sein,* emphasizing the characteristic moments of human existence. And precisely such a moment of human living, as Heidegger correctly observed, is "being-for-another-person" as a special "existential": *Fürsorge.*

[53]Personalistic philosophical theories only indicate a direction: they do not give concrete solutions. Moreover, a univocal solution is impossible because the realization of common good in the case of every person is unrepeatable.

[54]I have presented this problem at greater length in the article, *Religia i nauka (Religion and Science).*

[55]It is very significant that in the thinking of the tradition of Catholic theology, the divine Persons are understood as being constituted through an independent interpersonal relation. The being of a divine Person is being-for-another-person. A human person would be a participation in the divine Person.

CHAPTER XII

Notes and References

[1]The problematic of death appears more clearly in contemporary philosophical as well as theological literature than in that of the past. It is just this question that occupies some of the most prominent contemporary authors such as, for example, R. Guardini, K. Rahner, R. Trois-fontaines, V. Jankélewitch, L. Boros, J. Pieper, O. Cullmann, P.-L. Landsberg, N. Luyten, H. Urs von Balthasar, and others.

[2]Cf. *Tusculanae Disputationes* I, 75. Josef Pieper, in the work *Death and Immortality* (trans. Richard & Clara Winston, New York: Herder and Herder, 1969), writes on pp. 10–11: "Once formulated, this idea has fastened itself like a fishhook in Occidental thinking—not when his thought revolves upon death, but when it revolves upon the essence of philosophy or, to be more precise, when it revolves upon the meaning of philosophizing. Hence, when in twelfth-century Toledo the learned Spaniard Gonzales, one of the great mediators and translators in the history of European thought, collected the traditional definitions of philosophy, he mentioned among them the following: *cura et studium et sollicitudo mortis,* that is, philosophizing is not just meditative consideration of death, but nothing less than learning to die. Incidentally, six hundred years earlier Cassiodorus, the friend of Boethius, had noted that such a definition of philosophy was the one most appropriate for a Christian—although it originally sprang, as we know, from the soil of Platonism and the Stoa. Seneca praises the ancient philosophers for teaching how to die; and the *Discourses* of Epictetus states: 'Let others study cases at law, let others practise recitations and syllogisms. You learn to die.' "

[3]In a previously published article, "Człowiek w perspektywie śmierci" [The Human Being in the Perspective of Death] (*O Bogu* . . . , Vol. I, P. 124), I wrote that I would make use of a "somewhat different method of philosophizing, similar, although not identical, to the so-called transcendental method derived from Kant." To be quite honest, I must confess that neither then nor even more so here do I employ that method, since here there is admitted no *a priori* of the kind that appears in the transcendental method. Although these same questions were considered with the use of the transcendental method, e.g. by K. Rahner or L. Boros, yet it does not seem to me that anything could be really substantiated or proven with the use of such a method, because everything that would have to be demonstrated is already given in the very act of demonstration. Therefore, we will here employ the normal noncontradictable metaphysical method, which consists in this, that for indubitable facts we are seeking such objective factors of which the possible negation would simply be a contradiction, or would lead to a contradiction, or would necessarily be connected with the negation of the very fact previously admitted and given to us for explanation.

[4]Paul-Louis Landsberg, *The Experience of Death,* trans. Cynthia Rowland (New York: Philosophical Library, Inc., 1953), pp. 45–49.

[5]*The Confessions of St. Augustine,* trans. John K. Ryan (Garden City: Image Books, 1960), IV, 4, p. 98.

[6]Pieper, *op. cit.,* pp. 60–66.

[7]Marcus Aurelius Antoninus, *The Meditations,* trans. R. Graves (London: Methuen & Co., 1905), pp. 107–8.

426

[8]Pieper, *op. cit.,* pp. 50–51.

[9]As is evident from the previously conducted analyses, all intellectual-cognitive acts and especially acts of judgment refer to being. Being, however, in the proper sense, is constituted (real) through the act of existence. But that act of existence is not always in the object that is spoken about; for one can speak of nonexisting things. Although even then we make use of elements of content drawn from the real world, yet the fact remains that the act of existence does not then actualize the nonreal object. But even then our cognitive utterance is a real cognitive utterance, because it rests upon the act of existence of the speaking subject. On the other hand, the denial of the existence of a speaking subject renders a real cognitive act impossible. Of course, in no way does this mean that the truth of the utterance would be guaranteed when a real act of cognition is performed.

[10]Pieper, in the work here cited, devotes the whole of Chapter IV to the problem of the naturalness and unnaturalness of death, and he arrives at the conviction that this matter is insoluble: "Human death, we have said, represents a destruction, a shattering, something violent and catastrophic: something united by its nature and by virtue of its Creation is parted. This amounts to saying that, from the point of view of the man himself, dying is a senseless break, something strictly opposed to all natural impulse, and particularly to the natural impulse of human consciousness. To that extent, dying is not only not natural, but downright anti-natural. . . . Is death really against (man's) nature? . . . anyone who tried to answer this question with a flat Yes or No would find himself at odds with man's inner experience. On the contrary, we must be ready to encounter an extreme complication at this point. The complication arises out of the matter itself. For of course our understanding of what happens in death brings to a focus all the questions concerning man—not only the question of man's nature, moreover, but also of his history, of the *panthémata anthrópou,* as Plato says: all that has happened to man and all that he has undergone since the very beginning of his historical existence" (p. 47).

[11]Cf. Chapter IV.

[12]In the very work cited, Pieper declares himself in favor of the explanation of the fact of the death of a human being by the fact of an original transgression and punishment for it. St. Thomas, in *Quaestiones Disputatae De Malo,* formulates his thought on this topic in the following way: "*Sic ergo mors et corruptio naturalis est homini secundum necessitatem materiae; sed secundum rationem formae esset ei conveniens immortalitas; ad quam tamen praestandam naturae principia non sufficiunt; sed aptitudo quaedam naturalis ad eam convenit homini secundum animam; complementum autem eius est ex super-naturali virtute; sicut Philosophus dicit in II Eth., quod habemus aptitudinem ad virtutes morales ex natura; sed perficiuntur in nobis per consuetudinem. Et inquantum immortalitas est nobis naturalis, mors et corruptio est nobis contra naturam*" (q. 5, a. 5).

[13]This is seen particularly in Plato's dialogues, and especially in the *Phaedo.*

[14]*Diogenes Laertius,* trans. R. D. Hicks (Cambridge: Harvard University Press, 1958), Vol. II, Book X, p. 665.

[15]A. Krokiewicz, *Nauka Epikura,* Kraków, 1929, p. 321.

[16]*Ad Lucilium Epistulae Morales,* trans. Richard M. Gummere (New York: G. P. Putnam's Sons, 1916), Vol. I, IV, p. 15.

[17]Plato, *Phaedo,* trans. Hugh Tredennick, in *Plato: The Collected Dialogues,* ed. Edith Hamilton & Huntington Cairns (Princeton: Princeton University Press, 1961), 66b–67d, pp. 49–50.

[18]Cf. Chapter V.

[19]Cf. Chapter IV. Only the conception of soul as form can be the foundation of an explanation of the psycho-physical unity of the human being. Cf. ST, I, 75, as well as S. Swieżawski's commentary *(Traktat o człowieku,* pp. 57–83).

[20]ST, I, 75, 6.

[21]The question of the structure of the human being, the necessity of the acceptance of the immaterial, subsistent, and thereby immortal soul, is related necessarily to another question—the generation of the human soul. This problem is very broad and complicated, and, therefore, only in a most general way should it be observed that all traducianisms, whether materialistic or spiritualistic, explaining the generation of the soul by means of natural changes or the derivation of the soul from the parents, succumb before the thesis of the subsistence and immateriality of the human soul. Creationism alone explains the matter. This means that in searching for a noncontradictable ontical generation of the human soul, one cannot point to a factor explaining the generation of the subsisting immaterial soul other than the Absolute alone. Creationism means merely that all natural factors, so-called "secondary" ones, cannot be the reason of the generation of a subsistent, immaterial, and hence, essentially uncomposed being. The generation of the soul cannot be the result of either the organization of matter or the activity of any other factor whatsoever, except a creative factor—God. So far as the "time" of the generation of the soul in the embryonic life of the human being is concerned, it is not possible to say anything metaphysically substantiated on this topic. Various hypotheses are admissible. The admissibility, however, of hypotheses explaining the period of the generation of the human being, the possession by him of a soul, is not related to any practice and justification of action upon the foetus, since we are always dealing with a being who is a human either actually or potentially.

[22]*Ibid.*

[23]For if the human being alone among all the beings of nature asks a question about his own immortality, then there exist within the human being's very structure real foundations of the ever real questions. A real foundation, however, of the real question about one's own existence after biological death can be only the immaterial subsistence of the ontical foundation of our "Self," which, after all, is constantly manifested in the higher psychic (spiritual) acts of a human being.

[24]K. Rahner rightly drew attention to this already earlier in *Zur Theologie des Todes,* pp. 17–23.

[25]It seems to me that J. Pieper in the cited work (pp. 37 ff.) unduly radicalized the question of the death of a human being. Admittedly, none of his opinions taken separately is untrue, but the whole presents an overstated picture: "But it is forced upon us," he writes on pp. 45–46, "as soon as we accept the idea, with all its corollaries, that the man exists only in the union of body and soul and that, therefore, once these elements are separated the man no longer exists. Uncannily enough, there no longer exists something that in the strict sense of the word can be called 'human'. . . . Nevertheless, we might notice that traditional Christian theology and theories about man are somewhat wary about using the name 'man' in this context, so that Thomas Aquinas, for example, explicitly says that the *anima separata* cannot be called a 'person'. In no case at any rate—so much is clear at the present stage of our investigation—can we imagine that the soul is indestructible in the sense that after death this part of ourselves simply 'lives on', 'continues to exist'. By 'simply' I mean: as if 'death mercifully passed it by' and left it untouched. Nowadays we have little tolerance for such formulas by which the reality of death is exorcized away. We can no longer achieve a sham victory over death by such means, no longer hide from ourselves the metaphysical unity of the human person. Such conceits no longer fetch us; we can no longer bring them to our lips." The author, as I mentioned, assembling many one-sided opinions, overstated the picture. It is true that death affects the human being, that the whole human being dies, but the act of death can be understood passively or actively. Death in the passive sense is inflicted upon the whole human being, but understood in the active sense it is a personal act completing and, by an ultimate decision, definitively actualizing the personal potential be-ing. And although it is true that the subsisting soul cannot

in the strict sense be called a person, which is the subsisting "I" of a rational human nature actually embracing the whole of spirit and body, yet personal identity is not interrupted because self-cognition still remains! In addition, the soul does not lose its relation to the body, but at most only loses the actualization of this same necessary relation. Hence, the essential foundations of personal being are the same. The human soul, having an actual relation to matter, is expressed through the body organized for the soul. In losing the body it does not lose its inner richness, which it acquired through the body; it does not lose the relation to matter, thanks to which it is empowered in suitable conditions to organize for itself anew a body from matter, one that can continue to be regarded as the same body thanks to the identity of the relation (transcendental—necessary!) that it continues to maintain. After all, our body itself is in the constant "flux" of matter, and in spite of this it is identical thanks to the identity of the relation. Consequently, in the soul those functions that can be exercised without a body continue to be maintained, i.e., the whole acquired richness of the spiritual life. Futhermore, we do not know what sort of other functions will be added to the separated soul in the changed conditions. In any event, however, the act of existence constituting the human being as a person is not interrupted but changed. It is true that one cannot simply call the still subsisting being a human person, due to a lack there of a complete "nature," but nevertheless the being of the human does not perish. That which is the source and foundation of the being of the human survives. And for this reason perhaps Norwid's verse, composed under the inspiration of Fichte *(Die Anweisung zum seligen Leben, oder auch die Religionslehre,* 6. Vorlesung—cited by Pieper on p. 38), is closer to the truth than the analysis of Pieper himself. And here is an essential fragment of the verse to which Stefan Sawicki drew attention:

And yet she [i.e. death], wherever she touched,

The background—not the essence against the background having rent,

Except for the moment in which she took—took nothing:

—The human being—older than she!

[26]L. Boros presents some interesting thoughts on this topic *(Mysterium mortis. Der Mensch in der letzten Entscheidung,* Olten, 1964).

[27]I drew attention to the imperfection of human freedom in the article *"O wolność woli"* [On the Freedom of the Will], *Znak,* 1964, no. 5, pp. 597–609.

[28]*Le point de départ de la métaphysique,* Louvain, 1922–26. See especially V: *Le thomisme devant la philosophie critique.*

[29]Thomas repeatedly takes up this topic in his writings.

[30]*L'Action,* Paris, 1893.

[31]Paris, 1959.

[32]Already as early as the year 1933, in a lecture entitled "Outlines of a Phenomenology of Having," delivered to the Lyons Philosophical Society (published in *Being and Having,* trans. Katherine Farrer, Westminster, Dacre Press, 1949, pp. 154 ff.), Marcel reflects upon the later elaborated problem. I use the expression "ego-soul" here, wanting to emphasize that the soul constitutes the ontical subsisting foundation of the ego understood in the strict sense.

[33]Cf. *op. cit.,* pp. 17 ff.

[34]See, for example, *Contra Gent.* II c. 81.

APPENDIX

Notes

[1]Clarification of the complete vision of man is not keeping pace with the increasing number and tremendous development of the sciences about man. Man has proven to be a multi-faceted mystery, but one which, at the same time, is ontically identical. He is not captured completely by numerous cognitive formulations, but becomes more and more evasive in his own nature. See, E. Coreth, "Was ist die philosophische Anthropologie?," *Zeitschrift für katholische Theologie,* 1969, 252ff.

[2]A greater degree of anthropocentrism, however, can be discerned in the whole of Greek culture.

[3]This is the case with Socrates' motto, "Know thyself," for example. In this regard, one also touches important anthropological moments such as thinking (logic) or activity and competence (ethics). It is worth adding that the interest in human knowing was provoked by the variety of answers given to questions about the principium and nature of the world. The concentration of attention on human activity was caused, to a large extent, by the latter's relation with knowledge (Socrates) or with social questions (Plato). Only in the Hellenistic period were the problems of practical wisdom and the art of living strongly accented.

[4]For St. Thomas' philosophy of man, see, his *Treatise on Man, Summa Theologiae, I,* 75–89. See, also, A. C. Pegis, *At the Origins of the Thomistic Notion of Man,* New York, 1963; J. Stipičič, *Die Grenzsituation des Menschen und seine Existenz,* Fribourg, 1967; and K. Bernath, *Anima forma corporis,* Bonn, 1969.

[5]He considered man to be a microcosm. One can, thereby, understand man not only from the point of view of the world, but also the world from the point of view of man. Just as God creates real beings, so human thought dares create mental beings and artificial forms.

[6]Also worthy of note are L. Valli's attempts at treating the problems of human behavior from the point view of a changing life and of man's cognitive and volitive experiences. Religious influences of the philosophy of man did not cease playing a large role (Erasmus of Rotterdam, Malebranche, Leibniz). See, B. Suchodolski, *Narodziny nowożytnej filozofii człowieka (The Origin of the Modern Philosophy of Man),* Warszawa, 1963, and also his, *Rozwój nowożytnej filozofii człowieka (The Development of the Modern Philosophy of Man),* Warszawa, 1967.

[7]See, O. Cassman, *Psichologia anthropologica,* Hanau, 1594. In Francis Bacon, the term "anthropology," likewise, refers to studies about man from the point of view of the senses.

[8]In Christian Wolff, man is the subject of psychology only as *res cogitans.* The division introduced by Descartes that renders construction of a theory about one, complete man impossible was consolidated in many "regional" conceptions of man: for example, as a moral being— Shaftsbury, Mandeville, Hume (who emphasized more clearly than others the role of man in epistemology); or as an historical being—Vico, Montesquieu, Voltaire (the "universal man"), Herder.

[9]J. J. Rousseau adopted a characteristic position on this matter in accentuating the inconsistencies of human experience, and proclaiming the maxim of man's return to nature and the cult of feeling.

[10]Discourses devoted to philosophic-psychological anthropology that appeared around the mid-

nineteenth century convey these changes. C. L. Michelet *(Anthropologie und Psychologie,* Berlin, 1840) considers man to be a spirit, a product of the soul and its isolation and the highest level of opposites. J. H. Fichte *(Anthropologie* Leipzig, 1856) already accents the self-knowledge of the man-soul. On the other hand, H. Lotze *(Mikrokosmos,* 1856–64) concludes that the object of anthropology is the entire man: the corporeal, spiritual world and the soul.

[11]In Feuerbach, accenting man's activity led to anthropopathy (God did not create man, but man created God). According to Marx, man creates himself—he perfects or loses himself through his activity (work, production; work humanizes the ape, man is a productive beast). Essential, human characteristics are not stable, but relative to time, place, and socio-economic conditions. Hence, the nature of man becomes known in the light of history, sociology, and economics. Man is a product of the natural and social environment and, at the same time, he himself molds that environment.

[12]Linked with evolutionism, it treats man as an intermediate creature between beast and superman *(Also sprach Zarathustra).* The world tends towards the generation of a superman. The thread of his existence is biological life (spiritual life is only its offshoot) which possesses fundamental and absolute value. Superman is noble, a creator of authority who, in force of power and passion, is not restrained by any social shackles or any moral tradition. Like great works of art he stands above the sphere of the differentiation of good and evil *(Jenseits von Gut und Bose).*

[13]Bergson's conception of an *élan vital* and *évolution créatrice* and Dilthey's "science of the soul" *(Verstehen, Erlebnis, Hermeneutik)* as well as Klages' biologistic opposition of the spirit and the soul are evidence of this. See, O. F. Bollnow, *Lebensphilosophie,* Stuttgart, 1958 (Dilthey makes the same point in his work (of 1967) cited above).

[14]This type of anthropology took advantage of the phenomenologists' interest in the world of man's internal experience, the contents of his self-awareness, and the phenomenological method of grasping the subject with the help of intentionality. A person is experienced, but that experience is an appropriately protracted process. It emerges from contact with a concrete, human experience which subsequently prepares itself so that in the last phase of the experience *(Wesenschau)* we are in contact with essential moments of the grasped subject. See, M. Scheler, *Zur Idee des Menschen,* Bern, (1915) and *Die Stellung des Menschen in Kosmos,* Bern (1928); and F. Znaniecki, "Antropologia filozoficzna Maxa Schelera" ("The Philosophical Anthropology of Max Scheler"), *Studia Pelplińskie (Pelplin Studies),* 1969, pp. 143–179. One can say that the philosophy of man took the form of a distinct discipline during the years 1915–40.

[15]It most frequently conceives human existence as accidental (fragile), unrepeatable, not having support outside of itself ("man is cast into the world"), seldom opening itself to other beings, fluid, restless, and tragic. Peculiar to man, it is a subjective type of existence. Human existence is not an instance of reality, but a perspective in which the world of things is seen. See, M. Heidegger, *Sein und Zeit,* Tübingen, 1927; K. Jaspers, *Vernunft und Existenz,* Groningen, 1935, and also, *Von der Wahreit,* Munich, 1947; G. Marcel, *Homo viator,* Paris, 1944, and, *L'homme problématique,* Paris, 1955.

[16]See, for example J. P. Sartre, *L'existentialisme est un humanisme,* Paris, 1946, and M. Buber, *Das Problem des Menschen,* Heidelberg, 1948. Personalism takes on various hues as regards method and the results of studies about man. See, for example, E. Mounier, *Le personnalisme,* Paris, 1949; A. Vetter, *Personale Anthropologie,* Munich, 1966; H. Duesberg, *Person und Gemeinschaft,* Bonn, 1970; K. Wojtyła, *Osoba i czyn (The Acting Person),* Kraków, 1969. After Heidegger, human existence often is investigated in an existential-ontological hermeneutic of concrete being (the main emphasis being on language; one must understand the transcendental conditions of human existence that make possible man's self-under-

standing and self-perfection). See, for example, H. G. Gadamer, *Wahrheit .und Methode*, Tübingen, 1960; E. Coreth, *Grundfragen der Hermeneutik*, Freiburg, 1969.
[17]The following exemplify in order these three types of conceptions: M. Dufrenne, *Pour l'homme*, Paris, 1968; R. Chabal, *Vers une anthropologie philosophique*, Paris, 1964; J. F. Donceel, *Philosophical Anthropology*, New York, 1967; H. Hengstenberg, *Philosophische Anthropologie*, Stuttgart, 1957; J. Y. Jolif, *Comprendre l'homme*, Paris, 1967; J. B. Lotz, *Ich–Du—Wir. Fragen um den Menschen*, Frankfurt, 1968; J. Möller, *Zum Thema Mensch-sein*, Mainz, 1967; R. Verneaux, *Philosophie de l'homme*, Paris, 1956; E. Coreth, *op. cit.*; G. P. Klubertanz, *Philosophy of Human Nature*, New York, 1953; J. M. Ferrater, *The Idea of Man*, Kansas, 1961; S. Kaminski, "Anthropologia filozoficzna a inne dzia*ł*y poznania," *O Bogu i o człowieku* ("Philosophical Anthropology and Other Divisions of Knowledge" in *About God and Man)*, Vol. I, Warszawa, 1968, pp. 149–164.
[18]Following Scheler and Heidegger, he wants to maintain distance in relation to the particular sciences, and especially to psychology, but, at the same time, respect their findings which must be integrated in a more thorough understanding and conclusive consideration of human experience. See, *Die Stufen des Organischen und der Mensch*, Berlin, 1928.
[19]See, his *Der Mensch, seine Natur und Stellung im Weltall*, Frankfurt, Main, 1940, and *Die Seele im technischen Zeitalter*, Aachen, 1957.
[20]See, his *Von Ursprung des Menschen*, Basel, 1949; J. Huxley and J. von Uexküll, who accented the role of the environment in the determination of human life, present a philosophy of man with a biological bent.
[21]See, his *Le phénomène humain*, Paris 1955.
[22]See, for example, L. Binswanger, *Grundformen und Erkenntnis menschlichen Daseins*, Zürich, 1942, and E. Fromm's, *Das Menschenbild bei Marx*, Frankfurt 1963 and *The Heart of Man*, New York 1964.
[23]For example, O. F. Bollnow, *Neue Geborgenheit [. . .]*, Stuttgart, 1955, and Ph. Lersh, *Aufbau der Person*, München 1962.
[24]The first, the so-called historical-cultural variety, is a combination of Dilthey's historicism and the phenomenological method. Some examples are: E. Cassirer, *An Essay of Man*, New York, 1941; W. Sombart, *Vom Menschen*, Berlin, 1938; E. Rothacker, *Philosophische Anthropologie*, Bonn, 1964; M. Landmann, *Philosophische Anthropologie*, Berlin, 1955; and H. J. Schoeps, *Was ist der Mensch?*, Göttingen 1960. Marxist anthropology is interested in the economic, social, and political perspectives of an historically given man (it sees man's essence as consisting in: creating—in the course of overcoming alienation—his own existence in works; shaping his own environment; and assuming responsibility for created order). See, for example, R. Garaudy, *Perspectives de l'homme*, Paris (1959) 1969; A. Schaff, *Filozofia Człowieka (The Philosophy of Man)*, Warszawa, 1961; V. Eichron, H. Ley, R. Löther, *Das Menschenbild der marxistisch-leninistischen Philosophie*, Berlin 1969; I. Antonowicz, *Współczesna Filozoficzna Antropologia (Contemporary Philosophical Anthropology)*, Mińsk 1970; T. M. Jaroszewski, *Osobowość i wspólnota, (Individuality and Community)* Warszawa, 1970; J. Crosby, *Zur Kritik der marxistischen Anthropologie*, Salzburg 1970; Z. Kakabadze, *Człowiek jak filosofskaja problema (Man as a Philosophical Problem)*, Tbilisi 1970. The philosophy of the person explicated in the framework of structuralism has a naturalistic and a historical character. It is based on ethnology, linguistics, and sociology. See, C. Lévi-Strauss, *Anthropologie structurale*, Paris 1958; and, *La pensée sauvage*, Paris 1962; G. Schiwy, *Der französische Strukturalismus*, Reinbek 1970.
[25]For the last hundred years, there have been attempts to eradicate philosophy from modern divisions of science. Recently, neopositivism tried this by practicing metascience (in particular, a logic of knowledge or an analysis of scientific language) instead of philosophy. But in sol-

emnly throwing metaphysics out the front door, neopositivism had to let it back in via the kitchen. For one has to accept *implicitly* many fundamental ontological and epistemological assumptions to construct a complete theory of science. Moreover, even a person fascinated by the scientific-technical revolution, and tired by the pace of life does not cease being interested in the general existential aspect of reality, or cease seeking the ultimate bases of the world and an understanding of the deepest meaning of life. If it is not appropriate for him to engage in such tasks within the realm of academic philosophy, then they are carried over to the terrain of private mysticism or irrational reflections at the margin of scientific works.

26A. Carrel, in *Człowiek, istota nieznana (Man, the Unknown,)* Warszawa, 1930, shows that such knowledge does not suffice to know man as a whole.

27A particular science is abstract and fragmentary by nature. In studying reality it isolates a particular aspect while overlooking others, and adjusts its method of investigation to such an isolated fragment; whereas a philosophical grasp of man lays hold of him as a concrete, living whole. See, Coreth, *op. cit.,* p. 259 note.

28Experts in scientific methodology point out the difficulty of sharply distinguishing between observational and theoretical terms in the language of any science: the meaning of the observational terms also depends on the theories associated with them.

29An event given in self-awareness is, for example, fear, existential conflict, freedom, a questionable cognitive situation, the mind's activity, personal dialogue, etc. Existentialism undoubtedly contributed to the enrichment of this list, but, at the same time, it unjustifiably removed from the field of interest phenomena on the existential horizon that are grasped in a different way.

30There are various, very particular determinations of the method of classical metaphysics. According to the so-called "transcendental method," conceptions of the human phenomenon reveal the concrete existence of the entire person and the structure of his unity. Metaphysical reflection seeks the transcendental conditions of the possibility of human existence. Here, some speak of the ultimate reasons not contradicting human existence that is given not only in self-awareness, but also in prior understanding.

31Some speak of existential layers: corporeal, vegetal, sensual, and intellectual, but such terminology does not seem to be in harmony with the language of the theory of existence.

32Strictly speaking, psychology as a philosophical discipline is interested in the metaphysical explanation of psychic life. Only then does it assume a philosophy of man as a metaphysics of the entire human being. In addition to a metaphysics of the human psyche, philosophical anthropology as it was historically formed also included a very broad part of empirical psychology, and even many problems really belonging to philosophical anthropology.

33For an overview of contemporary discussions of the philosophy of man and issues related to it, see the list of papers delivered at Section X of the International Congress in Vienna in 1968. See *Akten des XIV Internationalen Kongresses für Philosophie,* Vol. V, Wien 1970, pp. 3–110.

CHAPTER I

Bibliography

Alquié, F. *La découverte métaphysique de l'homme chez Descartes.* Paris, 1955.
Anthropology and the Classics. New York, 1967.
Aristotle. *Aristotelis Opera.* Ed. Academia Regia Borussica. Vol. I–V. Berolini, 1831–70; Ed. altera quam curavit O. Gignon, Berlini, 1960–61.
_____. *The Works of Aristotle,* 11 vols. W. D. Ross, ed. Oxford, 1928–31.
Augustine, St. Sancti Aurelii Augustini *opera omnia.* Paris, 1841–77. Migne Latin Patrology, vols. 32–47.
_____. Sancti Augustini *opera.* Corpus Scriptorum Ecclesiasticorum Latinorum. Editio consilio et impensis Academia litterarum caesarae vindobonensis. Vindobonnae, 1866–1919.
_____. *Confessionum* Libri XIII. Recensuit P. Knell. Lipsiae, 1896. Vol. 33.
_____. *De Civitate Dei* Libri XXII. Recensuit R. Hoffman. Lipsiae, 1894. Vol. 26.
Avicenna. Avicenna Latinus. *Liber de Anima.* Ed. S. Van Riet, Louvain, 1968.
Bazán, B. C. "Pluralisme des formes ou dualisme des substances? La pensée préthomiste touchant la nature de l'âme." *Revue Philosophique de Louvain,* 67 (1969) 30–73.
Brentano, F. *Die Psychologie des Aristoteles insbesondere seine Lehre vom Nous poietikós.* Mainz, 1867.
Byrne, E. F., Maziarz, E. A. *Human Being and Being Human. Man's Philosophies of Man.* New York, 1969.
Cappelletti, A. J. *La teoria aristotelica de la visión.* Caracas, 1977.
Cartesian Essays. A Collection of Critical Studies. The Hague, 1969.
Changing Perspectives of Man. Chicago, 1968.
Chanteur, J. *Platon, le désir et la Cité.* Paris, 1980.
Chateau, J. *Les grandes de psychologie dans l'antiquité.* Paris, 1978.
Cicero. *Ciceronis Marci Tullii opera omnia.* C. F. Mueller ed. Leipzig, 1889–98.
Clark, S. R. L. *Aristotle's Man. Speculations upon Aristotelian Anthropology.* Oxford, 1975.
Cooper, L. *A Concordance of Boethius. The Five Theological Tractates and the Consolation of Philosophy.* Cambridge, 1928.
Cosenza, P. *Sensibilità, precezione, esperienza secondo Aristotele.* Napoli, 1968.
Courcelle, P. "Tradition platonicienne et traditions chrétiennes du corps-prison." *Revue des Etudes Latines,* 43 (1965) 406–43.
Cristofolini, P. "Sul problema cartesiano della memoria intelettuale." *Pensiero,* 7 (1962) 378–402.
Descartes, R. *Oeuvres et Correspondance,* publiés par Charles Adam et Paul Tannery. Vols. I–XIII. Paris, 1897–1913.

Dinkler, E. *Die Anthropologie Augustins.* Stuttgart, 1934.

Faggin, P. G. "L'anima nel pensiero classico antico." *L'Anima.* Brescia, 1954, 29–69.

Festugière, A. J. "La composition et l'esprit du *De Anima* de Tertullian." *Revue des sciences philosophiques et théologiques,* 33 (1949) 121–61.

Filipiak, M. *Biblia o człowieku* (The Bible about Man). Lublin, 1979.

Fortin, E. L. *Christianisme et culture philosophique au Ve siècle. La querelle de l'âme humaine en Occident.* Paris, 1958.

Francke, K. B. *Die Psychologie und Erkenntnislehre des Arnobius.* Leipzig, 1878.

Gangauf, T. *Metaphysische Psychologie des heiligen Augustinus.* Frankfurt, 1968.

Giacon, C. *I primi concetti metafisici. Platone, Aristotele, Plotino, Avicenna, Tommaso.* Bologna, 1968.

Giannini, G. "L'impostazione del problema antropologico nel presocratici." *Aquinus,* 6 (1963) 10–33.

_____. "L'involuzione del problema antropologico nelle scuole post-aristoteliche e nel neoplatismo." *Doctor Communis,* 16 (1963) 18–40.

_____. *Il problema antropologico. Linee di sviluppo storico speculativo dai Presocratici a S. Tommaso.* Roma, 1965.

Graeser, A. *Probleme der platonischen Seelenteilungslehre.* München, 1969.

Hare, M. M. *Microcosm and Macrocosm.* New York, 1966.

Jaeger, W. *Die theologie der frühen griechischen Denken.* Stuttgart, 1953.

_____. *Paideia. Die Formung des griechischen Menschen.* Berlin, 1959.

Jäger, G. *"Nous" in Platons Dialogen.* Göttingen, 1967.

Klebba, E. *Die Anthropologie des h. Ireneaus.* Münster, 1894.

Krokiewicz, A. *Studia orfickie* (Orphic Studies). Warszawa, 1947.

Krüger, G. *Eros und Mythos bei Plato.* Frankfurt a.M., 1978.

Kucharski, P. "L'affinité entre les idées et l'âme d'après le *Phédon.*" *Archivio di Filosofia,* 26 (1963) 483–515.

Kurdziałek, M. "Koncepja człowieka jako mikrokosmosu." *O Bogu i człowieku.* (Conception of Man as a Microcosm. *On God and Man,* T. II, Warszawa, 1969, 109–25.

Lefevre, C. " 'Quinta natura' et psychologie aristotélicienne." *Revue Philosophique de Louvain,* 69 (1971) 5–94.

Lloyd, G. E. R., Owen, G. E. L. *Aristotle on Mind and the Senses.* Cambridge, 1978.

Löwith, K. *Gott, Mensch und Welt in der Metaphysik von Descartes bis zu Nietzsche.* Göttingen, 1967.

Mathon, G. *L'anthropologie Chrétienne en Occident de saint Augustin à Jean Scot Erigene.* Lille, 1964.

Migne, J. P. *Patrologiae cursus completus. Series Latina.* T. 1–221. Paris, 1844–69.

Movia, G. *Anima e intelletto.* Padova, 1968.

Mueller, F. L. *Histoire de la psychologie de l'antiquité à nos jours.* Paris, 1968.

O'Connell, R. *St. Augustine's Early Theory of Man.* Cambridge, 1968.

Pastuszka, J. *Historia psychologii.* Lublin, 1971.

———. *Niematerialność duszy ludzkiej u św. Augustyna (The Immateriality of the Human Soul in St. Augustine),* Lublin, 1930.

Pfeil, H. *Das platonische Menschenbild.* Aschaffenburg, 1963.

Pieter, J. *Historia psychologii.* Warszawa, 1972.

Plato, *Platonis Opera.* Ed. J. Burnet in scriptorum classicorum Bibliotheca Oxoniensis. Vols. I–V. Oxford, 1955–57.

———. *The Dialogues of Plato,* trans. B. Jowett, 5 vols. Oxford, 1871.

Robinson, T. M. *Plato's Psychology.* Toronto, 1970.

Romano, F. *Logos e mythos nella psicologia di Platons.* Padova, 1974.

Schefer, J.-L. *L'invention du corps chrétien. Saint Augustin, le dictionnaire, la memoire.* Paris, 1975.

Siclari, A. *L'antropologia di Nemesio di Emesa.* Padova, 1974.

Stachowiak, L. "Biblijna koncepcja człowieka." *W nurcie zagadnień posoborowych.* (Biblical Conception of Man. *In the Wake of Post-conciliar Questions*). T. II, Warszawa, 1968, 209–26.

Swiezawski, S. "Nauka o duszy w *Metafizyce* Arystotelesa." (A Study on the Soul in Aristotle's *Metaphysics) Przegląd Filozoficzny,* 41 (1938) no. 4, 395–421.

Thomas, St. S. Thomae Aquinatis Doctoris Angelici *Opera Omnia,* jussu impensaque Leonis XIII P.M. rfita. T. I–XVI. Romae, 1882–1953.

———. S. Thomae Aquinatis. *Scriptum super Libros Sententiarum Magistri Petri Lombardi.* Ed. cura R. P. Mandonnet. T. I–IV. Parisiis, 1929–47.

———. Sancti Thomae de Aquino *Summa Theologiae.* Textus editionis Leoninae cum adnotationibus fontium . . . ex editione altera Canadiensi Ottawa, 1953. Romae: Alba Editiones Paulinae, 1962.

———. S. Thomae Aquinatis *Quaestiones disputatae et quaestiones quodlibetales* ad fidem optimarum editionum diligenter recusae. Romae, 1931.

———. S. Thomae Aquinatis *Opuscula omnia* . . . Parisiis, 1927.

———. Sancti Thomae Aquinatis *Quaestiones de Anima,* ed. J. Robb. Toronto, 1968.

———. S. Thomae Aquinatis *Sermo seu Tractatus de Ente et Essentia,* ed. L. Baur, editio altera emendata. *Opuscula et Textus. Series Scholastica.* I. Münster i Westf., 1933.

———. S. Thomae Aquinatis *Tractatus de Spiritualibus Creaturis,* editio critica, ed. L. Keeler. Roma, 1938.

———. S. Thomae Aquinatis *Tractatus de Unitate Intellectus,* ed. L. Keeler, Roma, 1936.

Tracy, T. J. *Physiological Theory and the Doctrine of the Mean in Plato and Aristotle.* New York, 1969.

Ushida, N. *Etude comparative de la psychologie d'Aristote, d'Avicenne et de St. Thomas d'Aquin.* Tokyo, 1968.

Verbeke, G. "Le *De Anima* d'Avicenne, une conception spiritualiste de l'homme." *Liber de Anima.* Louvain, 1968, 1–73.

———. "L'immortalité de l'âme dans le *De Anima* d'Avicenne. Une synthèse de l'aristotélisme et du neoplatonisme." *Pensamiento,* 25 (1969) 271–90.

CHAPTER II

Bibliography

Becker, E. *The Structure of Evil. An Essay on the Unification of the Science of Man.* New York, 1976.

Bocheński, I. *Philosophy.* Dordrecht, 1962.

Brennan, R. E. *Die menschliche Natur.* Bonn, 1961.

Bühler, W. *Der Mensch zwischen Uebernatur und Unternatur.* Nürnberg, 1966.

Chambliss, R. *Meaning for Man.* New York, 1966.

Comfort, A. *Natur und menschliche Natur.* Reinbek b. Hamburg, 1970.

Das Bild des Menschen in der Wissenschaft. Hildesheim, 1978.

Der Mensch und seine Symbole. Olten, 1968.

Der Mensch zwischen Natur und Technik. Stuttgart, 1967.

Durand, G. *Science de l'homme et tradition. Le nouvel esprit anthropologique.* Paris, 1980.

Etcheverry, A. *L'homme dans le monde.* Paris, 1964.

Flew, A. G. N. *A Rational Animal and Other Philosophical Essays on the Nature of Man.* Oxford, 1978.

Gehlen, A. *Antropologische Forschung.* Hamburg (1961) 1970.

————. *Der Mensch. Seine Natur und seine Stellung in der Welt.* Berlin, 1940; Frankfurt/M. 1971.

————. *Die Seele im technischen Zeitalter.* Hamburg, 1957.

————. *Urmensch und Spatkultur.* Bonn (1956), 1964.

————. "Zur Systematik der Anthropologie." *Systematische Philosophie,* ed. N. Hartmann. Berlin, 1942.

Gölz, W. *Dasein und Raum.* Tübingen, 1970.

Hoyle, F. *Man in the Universe.* New York, 1966.

Landgrebe, L. "Existenz und Autonomie des Menschen." *Philosophisches Jahrbuch,* 75 (1967–68) 239–49.

Landmann, M. *Fundamental-Anthropologie.* Bonn, 1979.

Litt, T. *Mensch und Welt.* München (1948), 1961.

Luyten, N. A. "Ordo Rerum." *Schriften zur Naturphilosophie, Philosophischen Anthropologie und Christlichen Weltanschauung.* Freiburg/Schweiz, 1969.

Marcie, R. *Mensch, Recht, Kosmos.* Wien, 1965.

Midgley, M. *Beast and Man.* Ithaca, 1978.

Mohr, H. *Wissenschaft und menschliche Existenz.* Freiburg (1967), 1970.

Nott, K. *Philosophy and Human Nature.* London, 1970.

Philosophy and the Future of Man. Washington, 1968.

Portmann, A. *Biologische Fragmente zu einer Lehre vom Menschen.* Basel (1951), 1969.

438

Rothaker, E. *Probleme der Kulturanthropologie*. Bonn, 1948.
———. *Zur Genealogie des menschlichen Bewusstseins*. Bonn, 1966.
Schmeisser, H. *Die Stellung des Menschen im Kosmos*. Linz, 1957.
Siegmund, G. *Tier und Mensch*. Frankfurt, 1968.
Stevenson, L. *Seven Theories of Human Nature*. London, 1974.
Szczepanski, J. *Sprawy ludzkie* (Human Affairs). Warszawa, 1978, 1980.
Thorpe, W. H. *Animal Nature and Human Nature*. New York, 1974.
  The Visage of Adam. Philosophical Readings on the Nature of Man. New York, 1970.
Vanni-Rovighi, S. *Elementi di filosofia*. Vol. III. *La natura e l'uomo*. Brescia, 1967.

CHAPTER III, PART I

Bibliography

Abélès, M. *Anthropologie et Marxisme*. Bruxelles, Paris, 1976.

Althauser, L. *Pour Marx*. Paris, 1966.

Amado, G. *L'être et la psychoanalyse*. Paris, 1978.

Anthropologie. (Cahiers de Philosophie) I, Janvier, 1966, Paris, 1966.

Antonowicz, I. *Sowriemiennaja filosofskaja antropolgoia*. Mińsk, 1968.

Baczko, B. *Weltanschauung, Metaphysik, Entfremdung*. Frankfurt, 1968.

Bartnik, C. *Problem historii uniwersalnej w teilhardyzmie (The Problem of Universal History in Teilhardism)*. Lublin, 1972.

————. *Teilhardowska wizja dziejów (The Teilhardian Vision of History)*, Lublin, 1975.

Bergeron, P. *L'action humaine dans l'oeuvre de Teilhard de Chardin*. Montréal, 1969.

Brodeur, C. *Du problème de l'inconscient à une philosophie de l'homme*. T. I. *Les théories freudiennes sur la structure de l'organisme psychique*. T. II. *La structure de la pensée humaine*. Montréal, 1969.

Brown, J. A. *Freud and the Post-Freudians*. London, 1963.

Cackowski, Z. *Człowiek jako podmiot działania praktycznego i poznawczego. (Man as the Subject of Practical and Cognitive Activity)*. Warszawa, 1979.

Czarnecki, Z. J., Dziemidok, B., ed. *Homo agens. Studia nad aktywnością i podmiotowością człowieka (Homo agens. Studies in the Activity and Subjectivity of Man)*. Lublin, 1981.

Evolution, Marxism and Christianity. Studies in Teilhardian Synthesis. London, 1966.

Folkierska, A. "Struktura mentalna—propozycja C. Lévi-Straussa dotycząca koncepcji człowieka." (Lévi-Strauss' Proposition of "Mental Structure" as It affects the Concept of Man). *Studia Filozoficzne,* 12 (1974) 75–87.

Frey-Rohn, L. *Von Freud zu Jung. Studie z. Psychologie d. Unbewussten*. Zürich, 1969.

Fritzhand, M. *Człowiek—humanizm—moralność* (Man, Humanism, Morality), Warszawa, 1961.

Fromm, E. *Marx's Concept of Man,* New York, 1961.

Garaudy, R. *Perspectives de l'homme*. Paris, 1961.

Hesnard, A. *L'oeuvre de Freud et son importance pour le monde moderne*. Paris, 1960.

Homans, P. "Transference and Transcendence: Freud and Tillich on the Nature of Personal Relatedness." *The Journal of Religion,* 46, (1966) 148–64.

440

Hook, S. ed., *Psychoanalysis: Scientific Method and Philosophy. A Symposium.* New York, 1960.

Huxley, J. *Evolution. The Modern Synthesis.* London, 1963.

———. *Man in the Modern World.* London, 1947.

Jacobi, J. *Psychologia Junga.* Warszawa. 1968.

Jaroszewski, T. M. *Osobowość i wspólnota (Personality and Community).* Warszawa, 1971.

Jung, C. G. *Psychologia a religia. Wybór pism (Psychology and Religion. Selected Writings).* Warszawa, 1970.

Kasia, A. "Leninowska koncepcja człowieka" (Lenin's Conception of Man). *Studia Filozoficzne,* 63 (1970) 138–50.

Kołakowski, L. *Der Mensch ohne Alternative,* München, 1967.

Koren, H. J. *Marx and the Authentic Man.* Pittsburg, 1967.

Korsch, K. *Marxismus und Philosophie.* Frankfurt, 1966.

Köhler, H. *Das Menschenbild des dialektischen Materialismus.* München, 1963.

Kuczyński, J. *Homo Creator. Wstęp do dialektyki człowieka (Homo Creator. Introduction to the Dialectic of Man).* Warszawa, 1966.

La conception marxiste de l'homme. Paris, 1965.

Landrière, J. *Anthropologie du Marxisme et le marxisme soviétique,* Paris, 1965.

Lauzan, G. *Sigmund Freud et la psychoanalyse.* Paris, 1962.

Lévi-Strauss, C. *Anthropologie structurale,* Paris, 1958.

———. *La pensée sauvage.* Paris, 1962.

———. "Philosophie et anthropologie." *Cahiers de Philosophie,* 1 (1966) 47–56.

Mader, J. *Zwischen Hegel und Marx.* Wien, 1975.

Marcuse, H. *Eros and Civilization.* New York, 1962.

———. *One-Dimensional Man.* Boston, 1964.

Mascall, E. L. *The Importance of Being Human. Some Aspects of the Christian Doctrine of Man.* London, 1959. *(Chrześcijańska koncepcja człowieka.* Warszawa, 1962.)

Milet, A. *Pour ou contre le structuralisme. Claude Lévi-Strauss et son oeuvre.* Tournai, 1968.

Moeller, C. "Renewal of the Doctrine of Man." *Theology of Renewal.* Montréal, 1968, 420–63.

Nowak, L. *U podstaw dialektyki marksistowskiej (At the Basis of Marxist Dialectic).* Warszawa, 1977.

Panasiuk, R. *Dziedzictwo heglowskie i marksizm (Hegelian Heritage and Marxism).* Warszawa, 1979.

Parinetto, L. *La nozione dei alienazione in Hegel, Feuerbach e Marx.* Milano, 1968.

Pigon, G. *Panorama mysli współczesnej (A Panorama of Contemporary Thought).* Paris (no date).

Plessner, H. *Die Stufen des Organischen und der Mensch Einleitung in die Philosophische Anthropologie.* Berlin, 1965.

———. *Macht und meschliche Natur.* Berlin, 1931.

———. *Philosophische Anthropologie.* Frankfurt/M, 1970.

Polkowski, A. *Świadectwo Teilharda* (The Witness of Teilhard). Warszawa, 1974.

Portmann, A. *Biologie und Geist*. Frankfurt/M, (1956) 1968.

———. *Vom Ursprung des Menschen*. Basel (1944) 1966.

———. *Zoologie und das neue Bild vom Menschen*. Hamburg (1956) 1960.

Rabit, O. A. *Dialogue avec Teilhard de Chardin*. Paris, 1958.

Ricoeur, P. *De l'interpretation. Essai sur Freud*. Paris, 1965.

Rothacker, E. *Mensch und Geschichte. Studien zur Anthropologie und Wissenschaftsgeschichte*. Berlin, 1944; Bonn, 1950.

———. *Philosophische Anthropologie*. Bonn (1964) 1970.

Schaff, A. *Filozofia człowieka (Philosophy of Man)*. Warszawa, 1962.

———. *Marksizm a jednostka ludzka (Marxism and Human Individuality)*. Warszawa, 1965

———. *Marx oder Sartre. Versuch einer Philosophie des Menschen*. Wien, 1964.

Schilling, O. *Geist und Materie in biblischer Sicht. Ein exeget. Beitr. z. Diskussion im Teilhard de Chardin*. Stuttgart, 1967.

Sève, L. *Marxisme et théorie de la personnalité*. Paris, 1969.

Stock. M. E. "Conscience and Superego." *Thomist*, 24 (1961) 544–79.

Stróżewski, W. "Na marginesi człowieka Teilharda de Chardin" *(On the Boundary of Teilhard de Chardin's Man)*. *Znak*, 15 (1967) 1314–38.

Ślipko, T. "Pojęcie człowieka w świetle współczesnej filozoficznej antropologii marksistowskiej w Polsce" (The Conception of Man in the Light of Contemporary Marxist Philosophical Anthropology in Poland). *Zeszyty Naukowe KUL*, 10 (1967) z. 2, 3–16.

Teilhard de Chardin, P. *Oeuvres*. T. I–X. Paris, 1955–69.

(Przekłady polskie: *Człowiek*, Warszawa, 1962, 1964; *Srodowisko Boże*, Warszawa, 1964.

Thompson, C. *Psychoanaliza, narodziny i rozwój (Psychoanalysis. Its Genesis and Development)*. Warszawa, 1964.

Tovar, S. A. "La vision humaine de Teilhard de Chardin." *Eidos*, 2 (1970) 86–105.

Walton, P., Gamble, A., Coulter, J. "Image of Man in Marx." *Social Theory and Practice*, 1 (1970–71) 69–84.

Watte, P. "L'ideologie structuraliste." *Bilan de la théologie du XXe siècle*. Paris, 1970, 339–45.

Wciorka, L. *Ewolucja i stworzenie. (Evolution and Creation)*. Poznań, 1976.

CHAPTER III PART II

Bibliography

Alpheus, K. "Was ist der Mensch? (Nach Kant und Heidegger)." *Kantstudien,* 59 (1968) 187–98.

Antropologias del siglo XX. Salamanca, 1976.

Bańka, j. *Problemy współczesnej filozofii człowieka (Problems of the Contemporary Philosophy of Man).* Katowice, 1978.

Barraud, J. *L'homme et son angoisse.* Paris, 1969.

Condette, J. R. *Søren Kierkegaard, penseur de l'existence.* Bordeaux, 1977.

Demske, J. M. *Being, Man and Death. A Key to Heidegger.* Lexington, 1970.

Derisi, O. N. *El ulhmo Heidegger. Approximaciónes y diferencias entre la fenomenologia existencial de M. Heidegger y la ontologia de Santo Tomas.* Buenos Aires, 1968.

Die Welt des Menschen—Die Welt der Philosophie. Den Haag, 1976.

Fazio-Allmayer, B. *L'uomo nella storia in Kant.* Bologna, 1968.

Gromczyński, W. *Człowiek, świat rzeczy, Bóg w filozofii Sartre'a (Man, the World of Things and God in the Philosophy of Sartre).* Warszawa, 1969.

Guéroult, M. "Nature humaine et état de nature chez Rousseau, Kant et Fichte." *Cahiers pour l'Analyse,* 6 (1967) 1–19.

Hegel, G. W. F. *Werke,* 18 vols. Berlin, 1832–45.

Heidegger, M. *Budować, mieszkać, myśleć (To Build, To Live, To Think).* Warszawa, 1977.

———. *Nietzsche.* Pfullingen, 196.

———. *Sein und Zeit.* Tübingen, 1927.

———. *Vorträge und Aufsätze.* Pfullingen, 1952.

Hopkins, J. "Theological Language and the Nature of Man in Jean-Paul Sartre's Philosophy." *The Harvard Theological Review,* 61 (1968) 27–38.

Izenberg, G. M. *The Existentialist Critique of Freud. The Crisis of Autonomy.* Princeton, 1976.

Jaspers, K. "Die Frage nach dem Menschen." *Universitas,* 20 (1965) 673–80.

———. *Psychologie der Weltanschauungen.* Berlin, 1966.

Juszezak, J. *L'anthropologie de Hegel à travers la pensée moderne: Marx, Nietzsche, A. Kojvé, E. Weil.* Paris, 1977.

Kierkegaard, S. *Samlede Veerker,* 2nd ed. by A. B. Drachmann, J. L. Heiberg, H. O. Lange. 15 vols. Copenhagen, 1930–1936.

Konigshausen, J. H. *Kant's Theorie des Denkens.* Amsterdam, 1977.

Kuderowicz, Z. "Klasyczna filozofia niemiecka jako źrodło wspołczesnej antropologii filozoficznej" (Classical German Philosophy as a Source of Contemporary Philosophical Anthropology). *Humanitas,* 1 (1978) 7–40.

Lacombe, O. *L'existence de l'homme*. Paris, 1951.

Laird, J. *Hume's Philosophy of Human Nature*. Hamden, 1967.

Lakebrink, B. *Klassische Metaphysik. Eine Auseinandersetzung mit der existentialen Anthropozentrik*. Freiburg, 1967.

Lepp, T. *L'existence authentique*. Paris, 1951.

Luijpen, W. A. *Existentiele Fenomenologie*, Utrecht, 1959. (Fenomenologia egzystencjalna. Warszawa, 1972)

Meyer, H. *Martin Heidegger und Thomas von Aquin*. München, 1964.

Michalski, K. *Heidegger i filozofia współczesna* (Heidegger and Contemporary Philosophy). Warszawa, 1978.

Norris, P. A. *Sartre's Concept of a Person*. Amherst, 1975.

Papone, A. *Existenza e corporeità in Sartre*. Firenze, 1969.

Pintor, Ramos A. *El humanismo de Max Scheler. Estudio de su antropologia filosofica*. Madrid, 1978.

Pflaumer, R. "Sein und Mensch in Denken Heideggers." *Philosophische Rundschau*, 13 (1966) 161–234.

Pruche, B. *L'homme de Sartre*. Paris, 1949.

Ramirez, N. *Filosofia de hombre en su realidad existencial*. Guadalajara, 1969.

Regina, U. *Heidegger. Dal nichilismo alla dignita dell'uomo*. Milano, 1970.

Rogalski, A. *Myśl i wyobrażenia (Thought and Images)*. Warszawa, 1977.

Rudziński, R. *Człowiek w obliczu nieskończoności. Metafizyka i egzystencja w filozofii Karla Jsspera. (Man in the Presence of Infinity. Metaphysics and Existence in the Philosophy of Karl Jaspers.)* Warszawa, 1980.

Salvucci, P. *L'uomo di Kant*. Urbino, 1963.

Sartre, J. P. *L'Être et le néant*. Paris, 1957.

———. *L'existentialisme est un humanisme*. Paris (1946) 1959.

———. *L'homme et les choses*. Paris, 1947.

Scheler, M. *Abhandlungen und Aufsätze*. Leipzig, 1915.

———. *Die Stellung des Menschen im Kosmos*. Darmstadt, 1928.

———. *Die Wissenformen und Gesellschaft*. Leipzig, 1926.

———. *Zur Idee des Menschen*. Leipzig, 1955.

———. *Zur Phänomenologie und Theorie der Sympatiegefühle*. Halle, 1913.

Schwartländer, J. *Der Mensch ist Person*. Stuttgart, 1968.

Siegmund, G. *Der Mensch in einem Dasein. Philosophische Anthropologie*. Bd. I. Freiburg, 1953.

Suchodolski, B. *Kim jest człowiek? (Who is Man?)*. Warszawa, 1974.

Trębicki, J. *Etyka Maxa Schelera. (Ethics of Max Scheler)*. Warszawa, 1973.

Wawrzyniak, A. "Filozofia Martina Heideggera w świetle nowszych opracowań." (The Philosophy of Martin Heidegger in the Light of More Recent Studies). *Roczniki Filozoficzne*, 13 (1965) 119–28.

———. "Metafizyka a człowiek." (Metaphysics and Man) *O Bogu i o człowieku*, 1968, 257–65.

Znaniecki, F. "Antropologia filozoficzna Maxa Schelera." (Philosophical Anthropology of Max Scheler) *Studia Pelplinskie*, 1969, 143–78.

CHAPTER IV

Bibliography

Abelson, R. *Persons. A Study in Philosophical Psychology.* London, 1977.

Adamczyk, S. "Pierwastki duchowe w człowieku w świetle nauki Sw. Tomasza z Akwinu" (Spiritual Elements in Man in the Light of St. Thomas Aquinas' Teaching). *Roczniki Filozoficzne,* 2–3 (1949–50) 60–84.

Bars, H. *L'homme et son âme.* Paris, 1958.

Bernath, K. *Anima forma corporis. Eine Untersuchung über die ontologischen Grundlagen der Anthropologie des Thomas von Aquin.* Bonn, 1969.

Bier, A. *Die Seele.* München, 1966.

Bejze, B. "W poszukiwaniu współczesnego pojęcia duszy ludzkiej" (In Search of a Contemporary Concept of the Human Soul). *W nurcie zagadnień posoborowych (In the Wake of Post-Conciliar Questions).* T. II. Warszawa. 1968, 51–78.

Bodamer, J. *Der Mensch ohne Ich.* Wien, 1960.

Brenton, G. "Le problème actuel de l'anthropologie thomiste." *Revue Philosophique de Louvain,* 61 (1963) 215–40.

Brod, M. *Von der Unsterblichkeit der Seele.* Stuttgart, 1969.

Bruaire, C. *Philosophie du corps.* Paris, 1968.

Carretero, L. A. *Presencia del animal en el hombre.* Mexico, 1962.

Chauchard, P. *Dès animaux à l'homme. Psychismes et cerveaux.* Paris, 1961.

Chirpaz, F. *Le corps.* Paris, 1969.

Collingwood, F. J. *Man's Physical and Spiritual Nature.* New York, 1963.

Conrad-Martius, H. *Die Geistseele des Menschen.* München, 1960.

Davy, M. M. *La connaissance de soi.* Paris, 1966.

Delay, J. *La psycho-physiologie humaine.* Paris, 1959.

Di Napoli, G. *L'immortalità dell'anima nel Rinascimento.* Torino, 1963.

Disertori, B. *De Anima.* Milano, 1959.

Donceel, J. F. *Philosophical Psychology.* New York, 1961.

Ehrenstein, W. *Probleme des höheren Seelenlebens.* München, 1965.

Etudes d'anthropologie philosophique. Par A. Waelhens, J. Ladrière, P. Marschal, R. Pirard, M. Renaud, J. Taminiaux, A. Vergote. Bibliothèque philosophique de Louvain, 28 26, Louvain-La-Neuve, 1980.

Eymann, F. *Die geistigen Grundlagedes menschlichen Lebens.* Bern, 1966.

Fromm, E. *The Heart of Man.* New York, 1964.

Garcia Fernandez, A. *El hombre y su encrucijada existencial.* Alcante, 1976.

Geist und Leib in der menschlichen Existenz. München, 1962.

Gogacz, M. *Istnieć i poznawać* (To Exist and To Know). Warszawa, 1969.

Grzegorczyk, A. *Refleksje o psychologicznej koncepcji człowieka (Reflections on the Psychological Conception of Man).* Teksty, no. 3, 9–36.

Hartman, E. *Substance, Body and Soul*. Princeton, 1977.

Hengstenberg, H. E. "Phenomenology and Metaphysics of the Human Body." *International Philosophical Quarterly*, 3 (1963) 165–200.

Henry, M. "Le concept d'âme a-t-il un sens?" *Revue Philosophique de Louvain*, 64 (1964) 5–33.

————. *Philosophie et phénoménologie du corps*. Paris, 1965.

Hirschberger, J. *Seele und Leib in der Spatantike*. Frankfurt/M, 1969.

Hirschmann, E. E. *On Human Unity*, London, 1961.

Hörz, H. *Materie und Bewusstsein*. Berlin, 1965.

Iwanicki, J. "Psychiczne i duchowe według materializmu dialektycznego i według tomizmu" (The Psychic and the Spiritual according to Dialectical Materialism and Thomism). *Studia Philosophiae Christianae*, 1 (1965) 17–44.

Javelet, R. "Le duo *corps et âme* en question? Anthropologie moderne et trichotomie." *Revue des Sciences Religieuses*, 44 (1970) 101–27.

Kłosak, K. "Dusza ludzka w perspektywie filozofii przyrody i metafizyki" (The Human Soul in the Perspective of the Philosophy of Nature and Metaphysics). *Analecta Cracoviensis*, IO (1978) 29–47.

Kostenbaum, P. *The New Image of the Person. The Theory and Practice of Clinical Philosophy*. Westport, 1978.

Kozielecki, J. *Koncepcje psychologiczne człowieka* (Psychological Conceptions of Man). Warszawa. 1976.

Krąpiec, M. A. "Die Theorie der Materie im physikalischer und philosophischer Sicht." *Philosophisches Jahrbuch*, 69 (1961) 134–76.

————. "O realizm metafizyki." *Zeszyty Naukowe KUL*, 4 (1969).

————. "Poznawalność Boga i duszy" (The Knowability of God and the Soul). *Znak*, 11 (1959) 745–63.

————. *Realizm ludzkiego poznania (Realism of Human Cognition)*. Poznań, 1959.

————. *Struktura bytu (Structure of Being)*. Lublin, 1963.

————. "Theoria materii ujęcia fizykalne i filozoficzne." (Theory of Matter: Physical and Philosophical Conceptions.) *Zeszyty Naukowe KUL*, 2 (1959) 3–48.

————. "Z filozoficznej problematyki badań nad koncepcja materii jako składnika realnego bytu" (On Philosophical Problematic Investigations on the Concept of Matter as a Constitutent of Real Being). *Studia Philosophiae Christianae*, 2 (1967) 17–48.

Kuksewicz, Z. *Filozofia człowieka. Teoria duszy./Dzieje filozofii średniowiecznej w Polsce (Philosophy of Man. Theory of the Soul. History of Mediaeval Philosophy in Poland)*. T. V. Wrocław, 1975.

Lakebrink, B. *Hegels dialektische Ontologie und die Thomistische Analektik*. Henn, 1968.

Langre de M. *Ame humaine et science moderne*. Paris, 1963.

Lanteri-Laura, G. *Phénoménologie de la subjectivité*. Paris, 1968.

L'Ecuyer, R. *La genèse du concept de soi*. Québec, 1975.

Lotz, J. *Der Mensch im Sein*. Wien, 1967.

Łukaszewski, W. *Osobowość: struktura i funkcje regulacyjne (Personality: Structure and Regulating Functions)*. Warszawa, 1974.

Manser, G. *Das Wesen des Thomismus*. Freiburg, 1948.

Marquette de J. *La créativisme, essai sur l'immortalisation de l'âme*. Genève, 1969.

Metz, J. *L'homme. L'anthropocentrique chrétienne. Pour une interprétation ouverte de la philosophie de saint Thomas*. Tours, 1968.

Montagné, P. *Manuel du connaître philosophique. T. I. La psychologie*. Paris, 1959.

Möller, J. *Von Bewusstsein zu Sein. Grundlegung einer Metaphysik*. Mainz, 1962.

Nancy, J.-L. *"Ego Sum."* Paris, 1979.

Nuttin, J. *Psychoanalyse et conception spiritualiste de l'homme*. Louvain, 1961.

Owens, J. "The Unity in a Thomistic Philosophy of Man." *Mediaeval Studies*, 25 (1963) 54–82.

Pegis, A. C. *At the Origins of the Thomistic Notion of Man*. New York, 1963.

Poirier, R. *Réflexions sur l'immortalité de l'âme*. Paris, 1970.

Psychologie et métaphysique. T. I–II. Paris, 1961.

Pucci, R. *La fenomenologia contemporanea e il problema dell'uomo*. Napoli, 1963.

Robb, J. H. *Man as Infinite Spirit*. Milwaukee, 1974.

Rocca, O. *Argamentazione scientifica sulla spiritualità ed immortalità*. Sorento, 1976.

Rossi, G. L. *L'uomo, animalità e spiritualità*. Torino, 1967.

Rodriguez, V. "Diferencia de las almas humanas a nivel substancial en la antropologia de Santo Tomaś." *Doctor Communis*, (1971) 25–39.

Roy, J. *La métaphysique de la vie*. Paris, 1964.

Royce, J. E. *Man and his Nature. A Philosophical Psychology*. New York, 1961.

Samona, A. *I misteri della psiche*. Palermo, 1966.

Scherer, G. *Strukturem des Menschen. Grundfragen philos. Anthropologie*. Essen, 1976.

Schwentek, H. *Mensch und Automat*. Stuttgart, 1965.

Schulze-Wegener, O. *Der Leib—Seele—Zusammenhang und die Wissenschaftliche Forschung*. Meisenheim am Glan, 1967.

Seifert, J. *Das Leib—Seele—Problem in der gegenwärtigen philosophischen Diskussion*. Darmstadt, 1979.

Siwek, P. *Psychologia metaphysica*. Roma, 1962.

Sombart, W. *Vom Menschen. Versuch einer geisteswissenschaftliche Anthropologie*. Berlin (1938) 1956.

Stępien, A. B. *"Zagadnienie genezy duszy ludzkiej z materii"* (The Question of the Genesis of the Human Soul from Matter). *Zeszyty Naukowe KUL*, 3 (1960) 108–17.

Stybe, S. E. *"Antinomies" in the Conception of Man. An Inquiry into the History of the Human Spirit*. Copenhagen, 1962.

Swieźawski, S. "Albertyńsko-tomistyczna a kartezjańska koncepcja człowieka· (The Albertinian-Thomistic and Cartesian Conception of Man). *Przegląd Filozoficzny*, 43 (1947) 87–104.

Thomas Aquinas, St. *Tommaso d'Aquino nel suo VII Centenario. Congresso Internazionale. Roma, Napoli: 17–24 aprile 1974*. Roma, 1974.

Ulrich, F. "Zur Ontologie des Menschen." *Salzburger Jahrbuch für Philosophie*, 7 (1963) 25–128.

Vanni-Rovighi, S. *L'antropologia filosofica di San Tommaso d'Aquino*. Milano, 1965.

Van Peursen, C. A. *Le corps—l'âme—l'esprit. Introduction à une anthropologie phenoménologique*. La Haye, 1979.

Verbeke, G. *Avicenna Latinus. Liber de Anima*. Louvain, 1968.

Vries de, J. *Materie und Geist*. München, 1970.

Weiler, R. *Die Frage des Menschen; wer bin ich?* Köln, 1968.

Węgiełek, J. *Mam ciało* (I Have a Body). Warszawa, 1978.

White, V. *Seele und Psyche*. Salzburg, 1964.

Witkiewicz, J. S. *Zagadnienia psychofizyczne (Psycho-physical Questions)*. Warszawa, 1978.

Wisser, R. "Homo vere humanus. Probleme und Aussagen der Philosophischen Anthropologie in Geistesgeschichtlicher Sicht." *Zeitschrift fur Religions und Geistesgeschichte*, 16 (1964) 223–50.

CHAPTER V

Bibliography

Adamczyk, S. *Obiektywizm poznania ludzkiego w nauce arystotelesowsko-tomaszowej (Objectivity of Human Cognition in Aristotelian-Thomistic Teaching)*. Lublin, 1967.

_____. "Ontyczno-psychologiczna struktura actu poznawczego w nauce Arystotelesa i św. Tomasza z Akwinu" (The Ontico-psychological Structure of the Cognitive Act in the Teaching of St. Thomas Aquinas). *Roczniki Filozoficzne*, 8 (1960) z. 4, 5–30.

Arendt, H. *The Life of the Mind*. Vol. *I*. *Thinking*. New York, 1977.

Aune, B. *Knowledge, Mind and Nature*. New York. 1967.

Ayer, A. J. *The Problem of Knowledge*. London, 1961.

Ayer, S. A. J., MacDonald, G. F. *Perception and Identity*. London, 1979.

Bateson, G. *Mind and Nature: A Necessary Unity*. New York, 1978.

Bertalanffy, L. *Robots, Men and Minds*. Wien, 1970.

Boden, M. A. *Artificial Intelligence and Natural Man*. New York, 1977.

Bogliolo, A. *De Homine*, Vol. I. *Structura gnoseologica et ontologica*. Roma, 1963.

Capaldi, N. *Human Knowledge*. New York, 1960.

Consciousness and the Brain. A Scientific and Philosophical Inquiry. New York, 1976.

Crossman, R. *The Structure of the Mind*. Madison, 1965.

David, A. *La cybernétique et l'humain*. Paris, 1965.

Denis, M. *Les images mentales*. Paris, 1979.

Feigenbaum, E. A., Feldman, J. *Computers and Thought*. New York, 1966 (*Maszyny matematyczne i myślenie*. Warszawa, 1972.)

Fink, D. G. *Computers and the Human Mind*. New York, 1966.

Flahault, F. *La parole intermédiaire*. Paris, 1978.

Glover, J. *The Philosophy of Mind*. London, 1977.

Gogacz, M. "Tomaszowa teoria intelektu i jej filozoficzne konsekwencje" (Thomistic Theory of the Intellect and its Philosophical Consequences). *Roczniki Filozoficzne*, 13 (1965) z. 1, 21–32.

_____. *Obrona intelektu (In Defense of the Intellect)*. Warszawa, 1969.

Hoffman, P. *Language, Minds and Knowledge*. London, 1970.

Juritsch, M. *Sinn und Geist. Ein Betrag zur Deutung der Sinne in Einheit des Menschen*. Freiburg/Schw., 1961.

Kainz, H. P. "The Multiplicity and Individuality of Intellects: A Re-examination of St. Thomas' Reaction to Averroes." *Divus Thomas*, 74 (1971) 155–79.

Kalinowski, J. *Teoria poznania praktycznego (Theory of Practical Cognition)*. Lublin, 1960.

Kamiński, S. *Pojęcie nauki i klasyfikacja nauki (The Concept of Science and Class-ification of the Sciences).* Lublin, 1970.

Kamiński, S., Krąpiec. M. A. *Z teorii metodologii metafizyki (On the Theory of the Methodology of Metaphysics).* Lublin, 1962.

Knittermeger, H. *Grundgegebenheiten des menschlichen Daseins.* München, 1963.

Krąpiec, M. A. *Realizm ludzkiego poznania (Realism of Human Cognition).* Poznań, 1959.

―――. *Teoria analogii bytu (Theory of the Analogy of Being).* Lublin, 1959.

―――. "The Problem of Cognition." *Modern Catholic Thinkers.* London, 1960, 548–62.

Levin. M. E. *Metaphysics and the Mind-Body Problem.* Oxford, 1979.

Margolis, J. *Persons and Minds.* Dordrecht, 1978.

May, W. E. "Knowledge of Causality in Hume and Aquinas." *The Thomist,* 34 (1970) 254–88.

Moreau, J. *De la connaissance selon S. Thomas d'Aquin.* Paris, 1976.

Neue Erkenntnisprobleme in Philosophie und Theologie. Wien, 1968.

Nicholas, J. M. *Images, Perception and Knowledge.* Dordrecht/Boston, 1977.

Ong, W. ed. *Knowledge and the Future of Man. An International Symposium.* New York, 1968.

Penfield, W. *The Mystery of the Mind. A Critical Study of Consciousness and the Human Brain.* Princeton, 1975.

Perception and Personal Identity. Proceedings of the 1967 Colloquium in Philosophy. Cleveland, 1969.

Rahner, K. *Geist in Welt. Zur Metaphysik der endlichen Erkenntnis bei Thomas von Aquin.* München (1957) 1964.

Rickman, H. P. "Philosophical Anthropology and the Problem of Meaning." *The Philosophical Quarterly* 10 (1960) 12–20.

Rossi, E. *Das menschliche Begreifen und seine Grenzen.* Bonn, 1968.

Ryle, G. *The Concept of Mind.* New York, 1959.

Schmidt, H. *Die Anthropologische Bedeutung der Kybernetik.* Quckborn, 1965.

Schneider, M. "The Dependence of St. Thomas' Psychology of Sensation upon his Physics." *Franciscan Studies,* 22 (1962) 2–31.

Stępién, A. B. "W związku z teoria poznania tomizmu egzystencjalnego" *Roczniki Filozoficzne,* 1 (1960) z. 1, 173–83.

The Philosophy of Perception. London, 1967.

Thinking in Perspective. Critical Essays in the Study of Thought Processes. Andover/Hampshire, England, 1978.

Thomas, S. N. *The Formal Mechanics of the Mind.* New York, 1978.

Toinet, P. *L'homme en sa verité. Essai d'anthropologie philosophique.* Paris, 1968.

Warnock, M. *Imagination.* London, 1976.

Werkmeister, W. H. *The Basis and Structure of Knowledge.* New York, 1968.

White, A. R. *The Philosophy of the Mind.* Westpost, 1978.

CHAPTER VI

Bibliography

Aquila, R. E. *Intentionality: A Study of Mental Acts*. Pennsylvania State University, 1977.

Augé, M. *Symbole, fonction, histoire. Les interrogations de l'anthropologie*. Paris, 1979.

Benoist, L. *Signes, symboles et mythes*. Paris, 1975.

Bosio, F. *Antropologia filosofica e occultamento ideologica*. Urbino, 1968.

Bril, J. *Symbolisme et civilisation. Essai sur l'efficacité anthropologique de l'imagination*. Lille, 1977.

Brun, J. *La main et l'esprit*. Paris, 1963.

Cassirer, E. *An Essay on Man*. New York, 1944.

Chauchard, P. *L'homme normale. Eléments de biologie humaniste et de culture humaine*. Paris, 1963.

Chiari, J. *Art and Knowledge*. London, 1977.

Court, R. *Le musical. Essai sur les fondements anthropologiques de l'art*. Paris, 1976.

Di Marco, D. *Scienza, arte e morale*. Roma, 1977.

Dirks, W., Hanssler, B. *Der neue Humanismus und das Christentum*. München, 1968.

Dumont, E. *Le lieu de l'homme. La culture comme distance et mémoire*. Montréal, 1968.

Flam, L. *L'homme et la conscience tragique. Problèmes du temps présent*. Paris, 1966.

Geneslay, E. H. *Un mal connu, l'homme*. Paris, 1968.

Godel, R. *De l'humanisme à l'humain*. Paris, 1963.

Hanke, J. W. *Maritain's Ontology of the Work of Art*. The Hague, 1973.

Heidegger, M. *Der Ursprung des Kunstwerkes*. Stuttgart, 1970.

Heimler, M. *Die Bedeutung der Intentionalität im Bereich des Seins nach Thomas v. Aquin*. Würzburg, 1962.

Helbling, H. *Der Mensch im Bild der Geschichte*. Berlin, 1969.

Hessen, G. *Studia z filozofii kultury (Studies in the Philosophy of Culture)*. Warszawa, 1968.

Huizinga, J. *Homo Ludens*. Warszawa, 1967.

Ingarden, R. *Spòr o istienie świata (Debate on the Existence of the World)*. Kraków, 1948.

Joyce, R. *The Esthetic Animal*. New York, 1975.

Kmity, J. ed. *Wartość, dzieło, sens. Szkice z filozofii kultury artystycznej (Value, Work, Meaning. Outlines of a Philosophy of Artistic Culture)*. Warszawa, 1975.

Krąpiec, M. A. "O filozofii kultury" (On the Philosophy of Culture). *Znak*, 16 (1964) 813–25.

————. "Próba ustalenia struktury bytu intencjonalnego" (An Attempt to Determine the Structure of Intentional Being). *Collectanea Theologica*, 28 (1957) 303–81.

La fonction symbolique: Essais d'anthropologie. Textes réunis par M. Izard et P. Smith. Paris, 1979.

Landmann, M. *Der Mensch als Schöpfer und Geschöpfer der Kultur*. München, 1961.

Langer, S. K. *Philosophical Sketches. A Study of the Human Mind in Relation to Feeling, Explored Through Art, Language and Symbol*. New York, 1964.

Löwith, K. *Natur und Humanität des Menschen*. Göttingen, 1957.

Marcel, G. *Les hommes contre l'humain*. Paris (1957) 1968.

Menschliche Existenz und moderne Welt. Berlin, 1967.

Pacholski, M., Znaniecki, F. *Społeczna dynamika kultury (The Social Dynamics of Culture)*. Warszawa, 1977.

Philippe, M. D. *L'activité artistique*. T.I. *L'homme dans son dialogue avec l'univers*. T.II. *Philosophie du faire*. Paris, 1968.

Reneville, R. J. "Signification anthropologie totalisatrice et intégrative des divers sciences de l'homme." *Laval théologique et philosophique.*, 26 (1970) 25–28; 147–66.

Rodziński, A. "Kultura i chrystianizm" (Culture and Christianity). *Roczniki Filozoficzne*, 17 (1969) z. 2, 107–18.

————. "Personalistyczna koncepsja kultury a prawo naturalne" (Personalistic Conception of Culture and Natural Law). *Roczniki Filozoficzne*, 18 (1970), z.2 (77–90).

Rotenstreich, N. *Theory and Practice. An Essay in Human Intentionalities*. The Hague, 1977.

Rösel, M. *Conditio Humana*. Meisenheim, 1975.

Rothacker, E. *Probleme der Kulturanthropologie*. Nonn (1948) 1965.

Sapir, E. *Anthropologie*. T.I. *Culture et personnalité*. T. II. *Culture*. Paris, 1967.

Stępień. A. B., *Nauki o kulturze (Studies about Culture)* Warszawa, 1971.

Znaniecki, F.

Stróżewski, W. *Studia z teorii poznania i filozofii wartośći (Studies in the Theory and Philosophy of Value)*. Warszawa, 1978.

Tatarkiewicz, W. *Dzieje sześciu pojęć (History of Six Concepts)*. Warszawa, 1975.

————. *Parerga*. Warszawa, 1978.

Zygulski, K. *Wstęp do zagadnień kultury. (Introduction to the Question of Culture)*. Warszawa, 1972.

CHAPTER VII

Bibliography

Amato, D. *Il problema della libertà*. Palermo, 1969.

Anderson, J. M. *The Truth of Freedom*. New York, 1979.

Aune, B. *Reason and Action*. Dordrecht/Boston, 1977.

Chauchard, P. *Biologie et morale*. Tours, 1959.

Choza, J. *Consciencia y afectividad/Aristoteles, Nietzsche, Freud*/Pamplona, 1978.

Cristaldi, M. *Libertà e metafisica*. Bologna, 1964.

Day, J. P. "On Liberty and the Real Will." *Philosophy*, 45 (1970) 177–92.

Dubouchet, J. *La condition de l'homme dans l'univers. Déterminismes naturels et liberté humaine*. Paris, 1977.

Edwards, R. B. *Freedom Responsibility and Obligation*. The Hague, 1969.

Foulquie, P. *La volonté*. Paris, 1968.

Frankfurt, H. G. "Freedom of the Will and the Concept of a Person." *The Journal of Philosophy*, 68 (1971) 5–20.

Freedom and Determinism. New York, 1966.

Gabaude, J. M. *Liberté et raison*. Toulouse, 1970.

Geiger, L. B. "On Freedom." *Philosophy Today*, 4 (1960) 184–95.

Gibbs, B. *Freedom and Liberation*. London, 1976.

Hartmann, O. J. *Freiheit: Wodurch? Wovon? Wozu?* Schaffhausen, 1977.

Gogacz, M. "Ontyczne wyznaczniki wolności ludzkiej według marksizmu" (Ontical Determinants of Human Freedom According to Marxism). *Studia Philosophiae Christianae*, 4 (1968) 5–20.

Guilead, R. *Etre et liberté*. Louvain, 1965.

Hampshire, S. N. *Freedom and the Individual*. London, 1965.

Jaffa, H. V. *The Conditions of Freedom*. Baltimore, 1975.

Kenny, A. J. P. *Free Will and Responsibility*. London, 1978.

Klubertanz, G. "The Root of Freedom in St. Thomas' Later Works." *Gregorianum*, 42 (1961) 701–24.

Körner, S. Experience and Conduct. Cambridge, 1976.

Krąpiec, M. A. "O wolności woli" (On the Freedom of the Will). *Znak* 16 (1964)0 597–602.

———. "Struktura aktu miłości u św. Tomasza" (Structure of the Act of Love in St. Thomas). *Roczniki Teologiczno-kanoniczne*, 6 (1950) z. 1–2, 135–54.

La liberté et l'homme du XXe siècle. Paris, 1966.

Lebacqz, J. *Libre arbitre et jugement*. Paris, 1960.

Lucas, J. R. *The Freedom of the Will*. Oxford, 1970.

Mazzantini, C. *Il problema filosofico del "libro arbitrio" in S. Tommaso e Duns Scoto*. Torino, 1966.

McCloskey, H. J. "Liberty of Expression. Its Grounds and Limits." *Inquiry,* 13 (1970) 219–37.

Montanari, G. *Determinazione e liberta in San Tommaso.* Roma, 1962.

Phenomenology of Will and Action. The Second Lexington Conference on Pure and Applied Phenomenology. Louvain, 1967.

Oakeshott, M. *On Human Conduct.* Oxford, 1975.

O'Sullivan, P. N. *Intentions, Motives and Human Action. An Argument for Free Will.* Brisbane, 1977.

Parsons, T. *Action Theory and the Human Condition.* New York, 1978.

Połtawski, A. "Czyn a swiadomość" (Act and Consciousness). *Logos i Ethos.* Kraków, 1971, 83–113.

Quilliot, R. *La liberté aux dimensions humaines.* Paris, 1967.

Reghaby, H. *Philosophy and Freedom.* New York, 1970.

Reitmeister, L. A. *A Philosophy of Freedom. An Attempt to Explain the Basis of Freedom.* New York, 1970.

Richardson, W. J. "Heidegger and the Quest of Freedom." *Theological Studies,* 28 (1967) 286–307.

Ricoeur, P. *Philosophie de la volonté.* Paris, 1963.

Rivier, W. *Deux exposés d'une philosophie de la liberté.* Neuchatel, 1975.

Sartre, J. P. *Of Human Freedom.* New York, 1967.

Scheler, M. "Rozważania dotyczące fenomenologii i metafizyki wolności." (Considerations Regarding Phenomenology and the Metaphysics of Freedom). *Znak,* 15 (1963) 1272–82.

Schrödinger, E. *Geist und Materie.* Braunschweig, 1956.

Simon, J. *Wahrheit als Freiheit.* Berlin/New York, 1978.

Siwek, P. *La conscience du libre arbitre.* Rome, 1976.

──────. *La psychophysique humaine d'après Aristote.* Paris, 1930.

Splett, J. *Der Mensch in seiner Freiheit.* Mainz, 1967.

Steenberghen, F. "Connaissance divine et liberté humaine." *Revue Théologique de Louvain,* 2 (1972) 46–68.

Thalberg, I. *Perception, Emotion and Action.* New Haven, 1977.

Tischner, J. "W poszukiwaniu istoty wolności" (In Search of the Essence of Freedom). *Znak,* 22 (1970) 821–38.

Vergez, A. *Faute et liberté.* Paris, 1969.

Welte, B. *Determination und Freiheit.* Frankfurt/M, 1969.

Wendt, D., Vlek, O. *Utility, Probability and Decision-Making.* Dordrecht, 1975.

Werner, C. *L'âme et la liberté.* Paris, 1960.

Woroniecki, J. *Katolicka etyka wychowawcza (Catholic Educational Ethics).* Krakow, 1948.

Wright, G. H. von *Freedom and Determination.* Amsterdam, 1980.

CHAPTER VIII

Bibliography

Amado, E. Levi-Valensi *Les niveaux de l'êtr et de la connaissance dans leur relation au problème du mal*. Paris, 1962.

Beehler, R. *Moral Life*. Oxford, 1978.

Bouillard, H. "Autonomia człowieka a obecność Boga" (Man's Autonomy and God's Presence). *Znak*, 19 (1967) 1096–112.

Brandt, R. B. *A Theory of the Good and the Right*. London, 1979.

Brennan, J. M. *The Open Texture of Moral Concepts*. London, 1977.

Brunner, E. *Der Mensch in Widerspruch*. Stuttgart, 1965.

Bujo, B. *Moralautonomie und Normenfindung bei Thomas von Aquin*. Paderborn, 1979.

Cua, A. *Dimensions of Moral Creativity. Paradigms, Principles and Ideals*. Pennsylvania State University Press, 1978.

Cultrera, F. *Mutabilità e immutabilità della legge naturale*. Napoli, 1977.

Donagan, A. *The Theory of Morality*. Chicago, 1977.

Etcheverry, A. *La morale en question*. Paris, 1977.

Gewirth, A. *Reason and Morality*. Chicago, 1978.

Gillet, M. *L'homme et sa structure. Essai sur les valeurs morales*. Paris, 1978.

Grenier, J. *Absolu et choix*. Paris, 1970.

Grygiel, S. "Ludzka twarz prawa natury" (The Human Face of Natural Law). *Znak*, 21 (1969) 1–30.

Hartmann, O. J. *Der Kampf um den Menschen in Natur. Mythos und Geschichte*. Freiburg/Br. 1969.

Hałowka, J. *Relatywizm etyczny (Ethical Relativism)*. Warszawa, 1981.

Krąpiec, M. A. *Człowiek i prawo naturalne. (Man and Natural Law)*. Lublin, 1975.
_____. *Dlaczego zło? (Why Evil?)*. Kraków, 1962.

Kozielecki, J. *O godnośći człowieka (On the Dignity of Man)*. Warszawa, 1977.

Lottin, O. *Psychologie et morale au XIIe et XIIIe siècles*. T. I–IV. Louvain, 1948–60.

Maguire, D. C. *The Moral Choice*. New York, 1978.

Manaranche, A. *L'esprit de la foi. Moral fondamentale*. Paris, 1977.

Olejnik, S. "Problem ostatecznego kryterium dobra w moralnośći" (The Problem of the Ultimate Criterion of Good in Christian Morality). *O Bogu i człowieku*. T. II. Warszawa, 1969, 175–91.

Patka, F. *Value and Existence. Studies in Philosophy and Anthropology*. New York, 1964.

Pinckaers, S. *Le renouveau de la morale*. Tournai, 1964.

455

Plessner, H. *Lachen und Weinen. Eine Untersuchung nach den Grenzen menschlichen Verhaltens*. München (1941) 1961.

Rodziński, A. "Egzystencjalny status moralnośći" (The Existential Status of Morality). *Logos i ethos*. Kraków, 1971, 357–69.

Rosik, S. "Formowanie sumienia praktycznego w etyce sytuacyjnej" (The Formation of a Practical Conscience in Situational Ethics). *Roczniki Teologiczno-kanoniczne*, 11 (1964) z. 3, 39–57.

Ślipko, T. "Etyka intencji czy etyka przedmiotu aktu. Zagadnienie wewnętrzej moralnośći aktu ludzkiego w filozofii św. Tomasza" (Ethics of Intention or Ethics of the Object of the Act. The Problem of Inner Morality of the Human Act in the Philosophy of St. Thomas). *Logos i ethos*, 1971, 281–326.

––––––. *Życie i płeć człowieka* (*The Life and Sex of Man*). Kraków, 1978.

Styczeń, T. "Doświadczenie moralnośći (Experience of Morality). *Logos i ethos*. Kraków, 1971, 327–55.

––––––. *Etyka niezależna?* (*An Independent Ethics?*) Lublin, 1980.

Szostek, A. *Normy i wyjątki* (*Norms and Exceptions*). Lublin, 1980.

Szyszkowska, M. *Człowiek wobec siebie i wobec innego* (*Man in the Presence of Himself and in the Presence of Another*). Warszawa, 197.

Taylor, C. T. *The Values*. New York, 1977.

Thomae, H. *Der Mensch in der Entscheidung*. München, 1960.

Ullmann-Margalit, E. *The Emergence of Norms*. Oxford, 1978.

Ulrich, R. *Weg und Weisung. Eine Philosophie des menschlichen Lebens*. Heidelberg, 1958.

Value and Man. New York, 1966.

Wallace, J. D. *Virtues and Vices*. New York, 1978.

Ward, R. *The Divine Image. The Foundation of Christian Morality*. London, 1976.

Wojtyła, K. *Miłość i odpowiedzialność* (*Love and Responsibility*). Kraków, 1962.

––––––. *Osoba i czyn* (*Man and Act*). Kraków, 1969.

CHAPTER IX

Bibliography

Addis, L. *The Logic of Society*. Minneapolis, 1975.

Aronson, E. *Człowiek istota społeczna (Man, a Social Being)*. Warszawa, 1978.

Bauman, Z. *Zarys marksistowskiej teorii społeczeństwa (An Outline of the Marxist Theory of Society)*. Warszawa, 1964.

Calvet, L. J. *Langue, corps, societé*. Paris, 1979.

_____. *Les jeux de la societé*. Paris, 1978.

Chantebout, B. *De l'Etat, une tentatative de démythification de l'univers politique*. Paris, 1975.

Fontanet, J. *Le social et le vivant*. Paris, 1977.

Fralin, R. *Rousseau and Representation. A Study of the Development of His Concept of Political Institutions*. Irvington, 1978.

Gehlen, A. *Studien zur Anthropologie und Soziologie*. Berlin, 1963.

Gilson, E. *La société de masse et sa culture*. Paris, 1967.

Harré, R., Secord, P. F. *The Explanation of Social Behavior*. Oxford, 1976.

Kampits, P. *Sartre und die Frage nach dem Anderen*. Wien, 1975.

Kaczmarek, E., ed. *W kręgu zagadnién antropologii społeczno-filozoficznej (In the Sphere of Socio-philosophical Anthropology)*. *Poznań*, 1978.

Kłys, J. "Powołanie do rozwoju." *W nurcie zagadnień posoborowych* (A Call for Development. *In the Wake of Post-Conciliar Questions*). T. II. Warszawa, 1968, 227–38.

Krąpiec, M. A. "Jednostka a społeczeństwo" (The Individual and Society) *Znak*, 21 (1969) 684–712.

Maccagnolo, E. *L'uomo e la società*. Brescia, 1967.

Majka, T. "Człowiek w społeczeństwie." *O Bogu i człowieku* (Man and Society. *On God and Man*). T. II. Warszawa, 227–38.

Man and Society. New York, 1966.

Maritain, J. *Principes d'une politique humaniste*. Paris, 1945.

Matson, F. W. *The Idea of Man*. New York, 1976.

Mordstein, F. "Die philosophische Anthropologie als Grundlage politischer Theorienbildung." *Philosophisches Jahrbuch*, 67 (1958) 115–29.

Morel, G. *Question d'homme*. Paris, 1976.

Northrop, S. *Philosophical Anthropology and Practical Politics*. New York, 1960.

Oraison, M. *Être avec la rélation à autrui*. Paris, 1968.

Otmann, H. *Individuum und Gesellschaft bei Hegel*. Berlin/New York, 1977.

Parsons. T. *The Evolution of Societies*. Garden City, 1977.

457

Plessner, H. *Diesseits der Utopie in Immer noch philosophische Anthropologie? Soziale Rolle und menschliche Natur.* Köln, 1966.

Pocock, D. F. *Social Anthropology.* New York, 1961.

Polin, C. *L'esprit totalitaire.* Paris, 1977.

Popper, K. R. *The Open Society and its Enemies.* London, 1948.

Riezler, K. *Man: Mutable and Immutable. The Fundamental Structure of Social Life.* Chicago, 1950.

Rouvier, J. *Les grandes idées politiques de J. J. Rousseau à nos jours.* Paris, 1978.

Rybicki, P. *Struktura społecznego świata (Structure of the Social World).* Warszawa, 1979.

Sarano, J. *Connaissance de soi, connaissance d'autrui.* Paris, 1967.

The Human Dialogue. Perspectives on Communication. New York, 1967.

Torowski, J. "Człowiek a społeczeństwo" (Man and Society). *Zeszyty Naukowe KUL,* 1 (1958), z.2, 3–28.

Walgrave, J. H. *Cosmos, personne et société.* Paris, 1968.

CHAPTER X

Bibliography

Abernathy, G. L., Langford, T. A., ed. *Philosophy of Religion*. London, 1968.

Berger, P. *La religion dans la conscience moderne*. Paris, 1971.

Brien, A. "L'homme religieux." *Seminarium*, 12 (1972) 203–19.

Burke, P. *The Fragile Universe*. London, 1979.

Cahn, S. M. *Philosophy of Religion*. New York, 1970.

Caracciolo, A. *Religione e eticità. Studi di filosofia della religione*. Napoli, 1971.

Collins, J. *The Emergence of Philosophy of Religion*. New Haven, 1967.

Comstock, R., Baird, R. D. *Religion and Man*. New York, 1971.

Donovan, P. *Interpreting Religious Experience*. New York, 1979.

Duméry, H. *Critique et religion. Récherches sur la méthode en philosophie de la religion*. Paris, 1957.

_____. *La problème de Dieu en philosophie de la religion*. Paris, 1957.

_____. *Philosophie de la religion*. Paris, 1957.

Durre, L. "Themes in Contemporary Philosophy of Religion." *New Scholasticism*, 43 (1969) 577–601.

Ferre, F. *Basic Modern Philosophy of Religion*. New York, 1967.

Filosofia e religione. Atti del XXV Convegno del Centro di Studi Filosofico fra Professori Universitari. Brescia, 1971.

Hessen, J. *Religionsphilosophie*. Bd. I–II. München, 1955.

Hick, J. H., ed. *Classical and Contemporary Readings in the Philosophy of Religion*. New York, 1970.

Hick, J. *Philosophy or Religion*. New York, 1963.

Hofmeister, H. *Wahrheit und Glaube. Interpretation und Kritik der sprachanalytischen Theorie der Religion*. Wien, 1978.

Jaworski, M. "Problem filozofii religii" (Problem of the Philosophy of Religion). *Studia Philosophiae Christianae*, 3 (1967), z. 2, 169–92.

Kaczmarek, L. "Człowiek—istota religijna." *W nurcie zagadnień posoborowych* (Man—a Religious Being. *In the Wake of Post-Conciliar Questions*. T. II, Warszawa, 1968, 171–210.

_____. *Istota i pochodzenie religii (The Essence and Origin of Religion)*. Poznań, 1958.

Kaufmann, W. *A Critique of Religion and Philosophy*. New York, 1958.

Kenny, A. *The God of the Philosophers*. Oxford, 1979.

Kowalczyk, S. *Bóg w myśli wspolczesnej (God in Contemporary Thought)*. Wrocław, 1979.

Ledure, Y. S. *Dieu s'efface: la corporéité comme lieu d'une affirmation de Dieu*. Paris, 1975.

460   *Chapter X Bibliography*

Leeuw, G. van der *Der Mensch und die Religion. Anthropologischer Versuch.* Basel, 1941.

Luypen, N. A. *Myth and Metaphysics.* The Hague, 1976.

Manzini, I. *Filosofia della religione.* Roma, 1968.

Majkowski, J. "Religia naturalnym wyposażeniem człowieka" (Religion as a Natural Endowment of Man). *Ateneum Kapłańskie,* 60 (1960) 31–44.

Mitchelle, B., ed. *The Philosophy of Religion.* New York, 1971.

Natanson, J. J. *La mort de Dieu. Essai sur l'athéisme moderne.* Paris, 1975.

Nédoncelle, M. "Les sources sensibles et axiologiques de l'affirmation religieuse." *Explorations personnalistes.* Paris, 1970.

Ortegat, P. *Philosophie de la religion.* T. I–II. Paris-Louvain, 1948.

Patterson, R. L. *A Philosophy of Religion.* Durham, 1971.

Penelhum, T. M. *Religion and Rationality.* New York, 1971.

Philippe, M. D. *De l'Être à Dieu.* Paris, 1977.

Plantinga, A. *God, Freedom and Evil.* London, 1975.

Proudoff, W. *God and the Self: Three Types of Philosophy of Religion.* Lewisburg, 1976.

Reardon, B. M. G. *Hegel's Philosophy of Religion.* London, 1977.

Rem, B. E. *Reason and Religion. An Introduction to the Philosophy of Religion.* New York, 1972.

Rideau, E. "Justification de la relation religieuse." *Nouvelle Revue Théologique,* 92 (1970) 56–75.

Roth, J. K. *Problems of the Philosophy of Religion.* Scranton, 1971.

Sarnowski, S. *"Zmierzch absolutu? Z problemòw filozofii Chrzescijańskiej i egzys-tencjalistycznej (The Twilight of the Absolute? Problems of Christian and Existentialist Philosophy).* Warszawa, 1974.

Smart, N. *Philosophy of Religion.* New York, 1970.

Szmyd, J. *Osobowość a religia (Personality and Religion).* Warszawa, 1979.

Tinello, F., ed. *Filosofia religioni.* Roma, 1966.

Trillhaas, W. *Religionsphilosophie.* Berlin, 1972.

Van Riet, G. *Philosophie et religion.* Louvain, 1970.

Vergote, A. "La philosophie de la religion." Revue Philosophique de Louvain, 68 (1970) 385–93.

Vries, J. de *Warum Religion?* Berlin, 1958.

Zdybicka, Z. J. *Człowiek i religia (Man and Religion).* Lublin, 1977, 1978.

CHAPTER XI

Bibliography

Ariotti, A. M. *L'homo viator en Gabriel Marcel*. Torino, 1965.

Arnitz, A. "Prawo naturalne i jego dzieje" (Natural Law and Its History). *Concilium,* 1 (1968) 363–74.

Arrese, D. de *La persona humana*. Madrid, 1962.

Beiträge zum Verständnis der Person. Düsseldorf, 1967.

Beni, G. *La persona umana*. Roma, 1967.

Benjamin, R. *Notion de personne et personnalisme chrétien*. La Haye-Paris, 1971.

Binder, H. *Die menschliche Person*. Stuttgart, 1964.

Boelen, B. J. M. *Personal Maturity. The Existential Dimension*. New York, 1978.

Chisholm, R. M. *Person and Object. A Metaphysical Study*. London, 1976.

Comfort, A. *Nature and Human Nature*. London, 1966.

Congar, Y. "L'historicité de l'homme selon Thomas d'Aquin." *Doctor Communis,* 2 (1969) 297–304.

Copleston, F. *Contemporary Philosophy: Studies of Logical Positivism and Existentialism*. London, 1963.

————. "Osoba ludzka w filozofii współczesnej" (The Human Person in Contemporary Philosophy). *Znak,* 15 (1963) 1283–1301.

Degl'Innocenti, U. *Il problema della persona nel pensiero di S. Tommaso*. Roma, 1967.

Domenach, J.-M. *Le sauvage et l'ordinateur*. Paris, 1976.

Fagone, V. "Dialogo e persona." *La Civiltà Cattolica,* 116 (1965), 1, 129–42.

Feldstein, L. C. "Reflections on the Ontology of the Person." *International Philosophical Quarterly,* 9 (1969) 313–41.

Frame, F. D. *Philosophy of the Human Image*. New York, 1968.

Frings, M. S. *Person und Dasein. Zur Frage der Ontologie Wertseins*. Der Haag, 1969.

Gebsattel, V. F. *Imago Hominis. Beiträge zur einer Personalen Anthropologie. (Das Bild des Menschen in der Wissenschaft.)* Schweinfurt, 1964.

Girardi, G. "Ente e persona in ontologia." *Salesianum,* 29 (1967) 368–408.

Gogacz, M. "Problem teorii osoby" (Problem of the Theory of Person). *Studia Philosophiae Christianae,* 7 (1971), z. 2, 46–67.

Gollwitzer, G. *Die Menschengestalt*. Stuttgart, 1967.

Granat, W. *Osoba ludzka (The Human Person)*. Sandomierz, 1961.

Guardini, R. *Welt und Person*. Würzburg (1937) 1962. *(Świat i osoba,* Kraków, 1969).

Häring, B. *Personalismus in Philosophie und Theologie*. München, 1968.

Horizons de la personne. Paris, 1965.

461

Ilien, A. *Wesen und Funktion der Liebe bei Thomas von Aquin*. Freiburg, Basel, Wien, 1975.

Jerphagnon, L. *Qu'est-ce que la personne humaine?* Toulouse, 1962.

Krąpiec, M. A. "O tomistyczną koncepcje prawa naturalnego." *W nurcie zagadnień posoborowych* (On the Thomistic Conception of Natural Law. *In the Wake of Post-conciliar Questions*). T. II. Warszawa, 1968, 11–37.

Lacroix, J. *Marxisme, existentialisme, personnalisme*. Paris, 1950.

Lichtenstein, H. *The Dilemma of Human Identity*. New York, 1977.

Litwin, J. *Horyzonty nieokreślenia i "Ja" (The Horizons of Indeterminateness and "I")*. Warszawa, 1980.

Lotz, J. B. *Der Mensch im Sein*. Wien, 1967.

Maaz, W. *Selbsschöpfung der Selbstintegration des Menschen*. Münster/Westf., 1967

Marcel, G. *Du refus à l'invocation*. Paris, 1940 (*Od sprzeciwu wezwania*. Warszawa, 1965.)

———. *Être et avoir*. Paris, 1968. (*Być i mieć*. Warszawa, 1962).

———. *Homo Viator*. Paris, 1944. (*Homo Viator*, Warszawa, 1959).

———. *Journal metaphysique*. Paris, 1927.

———. *La Dignité humaine*. Paris, 1964.

———. *L'homme problématique*. Paris, 1955.

Messner, J. *Naturrecht*. Wien, 1960.

Minkus, P. A. *Philosophy of the Person*. Oxford, 1960.

Moneta, G. C. *On Identity*. The Hague, 1976.

Montagu, A. *Anthropology and Human Nature*. New York, 1963.

Mounier, E. *Le personnalisme*. Paris, 1950.

———. *Qu'est-ce que le personnalisme?* Paris, 1947. (*Co to jest personalizm?* Warszawa, 1960).

Nasr, H. *The Encounter of Man and Nature. The Spiritual Crisis of Modern Man*. London, 1968.

Nédoncelle, M. *Personne humaine et nature*. Paris, 1963.

Pareyson, L. *Esistenza e persona*. Torino, 1966.

Perry, J. *A Dialogue on Personal Identity and Immortality*. Indianapolis, 1978.

Pinon, M. "The Metaphysics of Personality." *Philippiana Sacra*, 1 (1966) 396–451.

Pitteri, L. *La persona umana. Sua struttura, ontologica nella filosofia di Tommaso d'Aquino*. Pescara, 1969.

Plessner, H. *Conditio Humana*. Pfullingen, 1964.

Rothacker, E. *Die Schichten der Persönlichkeit*. Leipzig, 1938; Bonn, 1965.

Schwartländer, J. *Der Mensch ist Person*. Stuttgart, 1968.

Strauss, L. *Natural Right and History*. Chicago, 1953. (*Prawo naturalne w świetle historii*. Warszawa, 1969).

Szuba, J. *Tomistyczna teoria metafizycznej struktury osoby (Thomistic Theory of the Metaphysical Structure of Person)*. Lublin, 1953.

Szyszkowska, M. *Dociekania nad prawem natury czyli o potrzebach człowieka (Investigation of Natural Law or about Man's Needs)*. Warszawa, 1972.
The Nature of Man. New York, 1968.

Thomae, H. *Das Individuum und seine Welt. Eine Persönlichketistheorie.* Göttingen, 1968.

Tischner, J. *Świat ludzkiej nadziei (The World of Human Hope).Kraków, 1975.*

Vanni-Rovighi, S. *A proposito di uomo e natura nel secolo XII.* Torino, 1967.

Venable, V. *Human Nature.* Cleveland, 1966.

Verges, S. *Dimension transcendente et la persona.* Barcelona, 1977.

Vetter, A. *Personale Anthropologie.* Freiburg, 1966.

Warnach, V. "Satzereignis und personale Existenz." *Salzburger Jahrbuch für Philosophie,* 10–11 (1966–67) 81–104.

Waskiewicz, H. "Powszechność prawa naturalnego" (The Universality of Natural Law). *Studia Philosophiae Christianae,* 4 (1968), z. 2, 119–34.

Winckelmans de Cléty, C. *L'univers des personnes.* Paris, 1969.

Wojtyła, K. "Osoba: podmiot i wspólnota" (Person: Subject and Community). *Roczniki Filozoficzne,* 24 (1976), z. 2, 5–39.

Wright, von G. H. *What Is Humanism?* Lawrence, 1977.

Zdybicka, J. Z. "Osoba ludzka a filozofia jako problem współczesności." *Międzynarodowe Sympozjum Filozoficzne.* (The Human Person and Philosophy as a Contemporary Problem. International Philosophical Symposium). Kraków, 22–25 VIII, 1978 roku. *Znak,* 10 (1979) 1069–83.

CHAPTER XII

Bibliography

Alquié, F. *Le désir d'éternité*. Paris, 1968.

Boros, L. *Erlöstes Dasein*. Mainz, 1967 *(Istnienie wyzwolone*. Warszawa, 1971).

_____. *Mysterium mortis. Der Mensch in der letzten Entscheidung*. Olten, 1968.

Demsek, J. M. *Sein. Mensch und Tod. Das Todesprobleme bein Martin Heidegger*. München, 1963.

Durandeaux, J. *Wieczność w życiu codziennym (Eternity in Everyday Life)*. Warszawa, 1968.

Gargan, G. *L'amour et la mort*. Paris, 1959.

Guardini, R. *Freiheit, Gnade, Schicksal*. München, (1948) 1956. *(Wolność, łaska, los*. Krakow, 1969).

Hounder, Q. *Das Unsterblichkeitsproblem in der abendländischen Philosophie*. Stuttgart, 1970.

Huant, E. *Finalité temporalité . . . Une nouvelle analyse scientifique du problème de la survie*. Paris, 1975.

Jankélevitch, V. *La mort*. Paris, 1966.

Krąpiec, M. A. "Człowiek w perspektywie śmierci. *"O Bogu i człowieku* (Man in the Perspective of Death. *On God and Man)*. T. I. Warszawa, 1968, 124–48.

Lamont, C. *The Illusion of Immortality*. London, 1959.

Lamouche, A. *La destinée humaine*. Paris, 1959.

Landsberg, P. L. *O sprawach ostatecznych (On Ultimate Matters)* Warszawa, 1967.

Laporta, J. *La destinée de la nature humaine selon Thomas d'Aquin*. Paris, 1965.

Lavelle, L. *Le Moi et son destin*. Paris, 1936.

Marcel, G. *Présence et immortalité*. Paris, 1959.

Maritain, J. "Między czasem a wiecznością (Between Time and Eternity). *Więz*, 5 (1958) 8–10.

Martelet, G. *Victoire sur la mort. Eléments d'anthropologie Chrétienne*. Lyon, 1962.

Mayer, C. L. *L'homme face à son destin*. Paris, 1968.

Morin, E. *L'homme et la mort*. Paris, 1970.

Pieper, J. *Tod und Unsterblichkeit*. München, 1968. *(Smierć i nieśmiertelność*. Paris, 1970).

Rahner, K. *Zur Theologie des Todes*. Freiburg, 1938.

Scherer, G. *Das Problem des Todes in der Philosophie*. Darmstadt, 1979.

Sciacca, M. F. *Morte e immortalità*. Milano, 1968.

Sens choroby. Sens zycia. Sens śmierći. (The Meaning of Sickness. The Meaning of Life. The Meaning of Death). Kraków, 1980.

Sublon, R. *Le temps de la mort. Savoir, parole, désir*. Paris, 1980.

464

Thomas, L. V. *Anthropologie de la mort*. Paris, 1980.
Vanhengel, M. C. "Immortality, Experience and Symbol." *The Harvard Theological Review,* 60 (1967) 235–79.
Ziegler, J. *Les vivants et la mort*. Paris, 1975.
Zwolski, E. "U progu greckiej myśli eschatologicznej" (On the Threshold of Greek Eschatological Thought). *Zeszyty Naukowe KUL,* 11 (1968) z. 1, 44–57.

GENERAL BIBLIOGRAPHY

Ademar, G. *Zur medizinischen Psychologie und philosophischen Anthropologie.* Darmstadt, 1968.

Antonini, F. *Antropologia e filosofia.* Roma, 1966.

Atti del XII Congresso Internazionale di Filosofia (Venezia, 12–18 settembre 1958). Vol. II *L'uomo e la natura.* Firenze, 1960.

Brüning, W. *Philosophische Anthropologie.* Stuttgart, 1960.

Cantoni, R. *Scienze umane e antropologia filosofica.* Milano, 1966.

Caturelli, A. "Filosofia, metafisica, antropologia." *Eidos,* 2 (1970) 7–15.

Chabal, R. *Vers une anthropologie philosophique.* Paris, 1964.

Coreth, E. "Was ist philosophische Anthropologie?" *Zeitschrift für katolische Theologie,* 91 (1969) 252–73.

Cruz, J. "Sobre el metodo de antropologia filosofica." *Anuario Filosofico,* 1 (1969) 29–111.

Demolder, H. "Orientations de l'anthropologie nouvelle." *Revue des Sciences Religieuses,* 43 (1969) 147–73.

Diem, H. *Was ist der Mensch?* Tübingen, 1964.

Donceel, J. F. *Philosophical Anthropology.* New York, 1967.

Dufrenne, M. *Pour l'homme.* Paris, 1968.

Duroux, P. E. *La conception anthropologique.* Lyon, 1964.

Emonet, P. *Philosophie de l'homme.* Paris, 1967.

Ferrater, J. M. *The Idea of Man.* Kansas, 1961.

Giannini, G. "Rileri su alcuni aspetti dell'antropologia filosofica nella linea aristotelico-tomista." *Lateranum,* 29 (1963) 89–110.

Groethuysen, B. *Philosophische Anthropologie.* München, 1928.

Haecker, T. *Was ist der Mensch?* Frankfurt/M, 1959.

Hengstenberg, H. E. *Philosophische Anthropologie.* Stuttgart (1957) 1966.

Heschel, A. J. *Who Is Man?* London, 1966.

Ingarden, R. *Książeczka o człowieku (A Short Work on Man).* Kraków, 1972.

Jolif, J. Y. *Comprendre l'homme.* T. I. *Introduction à une anthropologie philosophique.* Paris, 1967.

Kamiński, S. "Antropologia filozoficzna a inne działy poznania." *O Bogu i człowieku* (Philosophical Anthropology and Other Divisions of Cognition. *On God and Man).* T. I. Warszawa, 1968, 149–64.

———. "O koncepcjach filozofii człowieka." (On the Conceptions of the Philosophy of Man). *Zeszyty Naukowe KUL,* 13 (1970) z.4, 9–17.

Keller, W. "Ueber philosophische Anthropologie." *Studia Philosophica,* 20 (1960) 37–57.

Kelly, W. J. Tallon, A. *Readings in the Philosophy of Man.* New York, 1967.

Knowledge and the Future of Man. An International Symposium. New York, 1968.

Krąpiec, M. A. "Idee przewodnie we współczesnej filozofii człowieka" (Principal Ideas in the Contemporary Philosophy of Man). *Zeszyty Naukowe KUL,* 13 (1970) z. 4, 21–33.

Landmann, M. *De Homine.* München, 1962.

———. *Philosophische Anthropologie.* Berlin (1955) 1969.

Landsberg, P. L. *Einführung in die philosophische Anthropologie.* Frankfurt/M (1934) 1960.

Le Trocquer, R. *Homme, qui suis-je?* Paris, 1957. *(Kim jestem ja—człowiek?* Paris, 1968).

Manners, R. A., Kaplan, D. ed. *Theory in Anthropology.* London, 1968.

Menschliche Existenz und moderne Welt. Bd. II. Ein internat. Symposion z. Selbstverständnis d. huetiger Menschen. Berlin, 1967.

Molear, G. F., ed. *Philosophy and Contemporary Man.* Washington, 1968.

Möller, J. *Zum Thema Menschsein.* Mainz, 1967. *(Człowiek w świecie.* Paris, 1969).

Pannenberg, W. *Was ist der Mensch?* Göttingen, 1962.

Peursen, C. A. van Lichaam—Ziel—Geest. Utrecht, 1956. *(Antropologia filozoficzna.* Warszawa, 1971).

Plessner, H. *Die Aufgabe der philosophischen Anthropologie.* Bern, 1953.

Readings in the Philosophy of Man. New York, 1967.

Ricoeur, P. "L'antinomie de la réalité humaine et le problème de l'anthropologie philosophique." *Pensiero,* 5 (1960) 273–90.

Ristrutturazione antropologica dell'insegnamento filosofico. Atti del II Convegno Nazionale dei Docenti nelle Facoltà, Seminari e Studentati d'Italia. Napoli, 1969.

Schoeps, H. J. *Was ist der Mensch?* Göttingen, 1960.

Tempo ed eternita nella condizione umana. Atti del XX Convegno del Centro di Studi Filosofici Universitari. Gallarte 1965. Brescia, 1966.

Was ist das, der Mensch? München, 1968.

Zimmerli, W. *Was ist der Mensch?* Göttingen, 1964.

INDEX

MARIEL PUBLICATIONS

Andrew N. Woznicki, A CHRISTIAN HUMANISM: KAROL WOJTYLA'S EXIS-
TENTIAL PERSONALISM
"There is no more useful introduction to the meaning and profundity of Pope John
Paul II's thought."—James V. Schall, S. J., Georgetown University.

. . . . . $2.95

Francis J. Lescoe, PHILOSOPHY SERVING CONTEMPORARY NEEDS OF THE
CHURCH: THE EXPERIENCE OF POLAND

. . . . . $1.50

Patricia J. Brewer, RAW JUDICIAL POWER: A CASE HISTORY

. . . . . $1.95

Francis J. Lescoe, David Q. Liptak, eds. POPE JOHN PAUL II LECTURE SERIES
IN BIOETHICS
Vol. I PERSPECTIVES IN BIOETHICS
I. Critical Reflections on Current Bioethical Thinking by Ronald D. Lawler
II. *"Begotten Not Made" : Reflections on Laboratory Production of Human Life* by
William E. May

. . . . . $3.75

ALSO AVAILABLE

Francis J. Lescoe, SANCTI THOMAE AQUINATIS TRACTATUS DE SUBSTAN-
TIIS SEPARATIS
"Unquestionably the best critical text available."—AUGUSTINIANUM (Rome)

. . . . . $8.95

Francis J. Lescoe, ST. THOMAS AQUINAS, TREATISE ON SEPARATE SUB-
STANCES
"The author has performed a valuable service for serious students of St.
Thomas."—PHILOSOPHICAL STUDIES (Maynooth)

. . . . . $9.95

Francis, J. Lescoe, GOD AS FIRST PRINCIPLE IN ULRICH OF STRASBOURG
"An excellent work, indispensable for every philosophical library."—REVUE
PHILOSOPHIQUE (Louvain)

. . . . . $11.95